The T. & T. Clark Story

The T. & T. Clark Story

A Victorian Publisher and the New Theology

with an epilogue covering the twentieth-century history of the firm

by

John A.H. Dempster

THE PENTLAND PRESS LTD.
EDINBURGH · CAMBRIDGE · DURHAM

First published in 1992 by
The Pentland Press Ltd
1 Hutton Close
South Church
Bishop Auckland
Durham

ISBN 1 872795 09 9

Typeset by Spire Origination, Norwich
Printed and bound by Antony Rowe Ltd., Chippenham

To
Mum and Dad
with love and gratitude
and
for Lorna
with anticipation

T & T Clark's premises in the late 1950s

Contents

Foreword		ix
Preface		xi
List of Tables		xiii
Abbreviations		xv
Clark family tree		xvi
Introduction		xvii
	Part I	
Chapter 1	Historical outline	3
Chapter 2	Aims and motives	15
Chapter 3	Relationships with other religious publishers	33
	Part II	
Chapter 4	Series of completely British origin and translations of Patristic works	43
Chapter 5	Translations	61
Chapter 6	Transatlantic publishing	85
Chapter 7	Periodicals and part-publications	147
Chapter 8	Standard reference works	175
Chapter 9	Miscellaneous theological works	191
	Part III	
Chapter 10	Advertising and promotion	213
Chapter 11	Distribution	225
	Part IV	
Chapter 12	Overall profitability	235
Epilogue		241
	Appendices	
Appendix A	Macniven and Wallace, Edinburgh	267
Appendix B	The profitability of each category of publication, 1896–97	269
Appendix C	Total annual overheads/Total prior outlay on stock in hand	280
Appendix D	Financial data from 1911–12 — 1989	286
Appendix E	Advertising platforms 1886–96	293
Notes		297
List of Sources		341
Index		347

Foreword

The House of T. &. T. Clark was under the direction of the one family for 166 years. As the last member of that family to have been actively engaged in the stewardship of the firm in which I spent much of my working life I feel honoured to have been asked to write this Foreword. Sad though I am that there is no longer a Clark at the helm I am delighted that after the traumas of the last few years the firm is now approaching the final quarter of its second century under the directorship of my friend and erstwhile colleague Dr Geoffrey Green.

I have read with enormous interest the results of John Dempster's painstaking research into the early history of the firm and its founders and have co-operated with him in the pleasant task of bringing that history up to date. I must admit to some relief that such an in-depth investigation has not, apparently, produced the inevitable skeleton in the cupboard!

The firm's records, many of which are held by the National Library of Scotland here in Edinburgh, include personal and business letters dating back to the turn of the century and earlier. These, both my cousin Sir Thomas and my father T.G. were prone to quote as surprisingly relevant to the problems and decisions of a hundred years on. Indeed, on reading the story of the firm's first century, I never ceased to be amazed at how similar our concept of successful and, I trust, ethical publishing in a specialist field was to that held with such determination by the founders.

In the latter days of my stewardship, the continuation of this *modus operandi* during our first excursion into the corporate world was made possible only by the understanding of the directors of John Bartholomew and Son. When a few years later we were swept willy-nilly into the world of international publishing groups both Reader's Digest and News International, whilst I suspect viewing our small input and operations with some amusement, continued this encouragement to retain our individuality in the vastly changed publishing world of today. The fact that titles published at the turn of the century could still be in print, selling and making a profit, never ceased to amaze these companies. I can only hope most sincerely that in this day of fads and fancies and the 'fast buck' that at least some of the many titles and series I have been involved with will still be selling at a profit half a century later.

T. & T. Clark as I knew it was always recognised as a small, specialist publishing house in the field of theology and to a lesser extent of law. Over the years it had become interdenominational to a degree that I suspect was never contemplated by the founders, and currently the firm's legal publishing is expanding rapidly.

I venture to think that, due to the acumen of my forebears, and to this increasingly interdenominational approach, the firm's impact on religious book publishing over the years has been out of all proportion to its size. Credit for this achievement must be attributed in large measure to the help, advice and commitment of many theologians, scholars, and friends, in particular the Hastings family to whom the firm owed so much and also to the dedication and commitment over these many years of an independent and loyal staff.

I sincerely wish T. & T. C. and the many friends I have made in the firm good luck and a successful and profitable future.

Ramsay Clark
Tyneford House
July 1991

Preface

This study, based on a PhD thesis, is a celebration of T. & T. Clark's theological publishing. The richness of the Clark archive at the National Library of Scotland ensures that it is a celebration backed up by hard data.

As I investigated T. & T. Clark's activities, I realised that while this George Street dynasty was no less competent, no less dynamic, no less socially involved than the other, much better known publishing dynasties of nineteenth-century Scotland – the Blacks, the Blackies, the Collinses – the significance of their activities as publishers had certainly been under-appreciated. Perhaps they limited their output to works of theology and law, but (to take the most outstanding example) the *Encyclopaedia of Religion and Ethics* is by any standards a major undertaking, perhaps ranking second only to the *Encyclopaedia Britannica* as the most significant sustained achievement in Scottish publishing history. It has been my aim therefore both to establish and to celebrate the significance of the firm, analysing its growth towards the point where the *Encyclopaedia* became possible, both financially possible, and possible in terms of the Clarks' sense of vision and confidence in their own abilities and in those of their editor.

I am deeply grateful to all those who, in various ways, have helped with this project. Special thanks are due to Mr T.G.R.D. Clark who granted me access to the firm's archives, was consistently interested in my researches, has arranged the publication of this volume by the Pentland Press and contributed a foreword to it. Thanks too to Dr Geoffrey Green of T. & T. Clark for sharing his vision of the firm's future, and to Mrs Jacqueline Milne for sharing her memories of its past.

I should like to thank the staff of the manuscript room of the National Library of Scotland for their help, and also to express gratitude to those who supplied specific pieces of information in response to my queries: Alice Langdaon of Edinburgh University Library, M.E. Townley, research assistant at the National Library of Scotland, and Joyce M. Barrie and Murray Simpson of New College Library.

I am very grateful also to the staff of the Department of Information Science, University of Strathclyde who were involved in the project: to Dr Graham Jones, who was my supervisor until his retirement; to Miss Antonia Bunch, who succeeded him (before herself moving on to head up the Scottish Science Reference Library) – her passion for semantic precision equals, if it does not exceed, my own; to the former Professor, W.E. Tyler, without whose encouragement I would never have begun.

I should like to thank Dr Lionel Madden, now Keeper of Printed Books at the National Library of Wales, who was external examiner on the thesis, for his helpful observations.

On a personal level, thanks are due to my parents as always, for their enthusiasm and support; to my 'vaguely designated' aunt, Marion Brown, who, together with her husband John until his death, accommodated me in Edinburgh while I was researching there; to Pam Rice and Mrs Dyson who typed the final text of the thesis; to all my friends, especially David and Karen Woodhouse, Liam and Christine Goligher, Tom and Elspeth Sargent, Norrie and Alison Mackay and (last but not least) Dr James Duthie, who have helped in so many ways.

Especial thanks are due to my fiancée Lorna Anderson who has encouraged me to spend time (which I would much rather have spent with her!) up to my ears in proof-reading and indexing.

John A.H. Dempster
Glenmavis
26 October 1991

Tables

Table 1	Unit cost of volumes in the *Ante-Nicene Library* reprinted 1895–96
Table 2	*Ante-Nicene Library*: Sales 1896–99
Table 3	Unit cost of volumes in the *St Augustine* Series reprinted 1896–97
Table 4	*St Augustine* Series: Sales 1895–99
Table 5	*Bible Class Handbooks*: Analysis of Profitability
Table 6	*Bible Class Primers*: Analysis of Profitability
Table 7	Unit cost of seven volumes in the *Foreign Theological Library* reprinted 1895–96
Table 8	Unit cost of two volumes in the Meyer commentary series reprinted 1898–99
Table 9	Lange's Commentaries: Stock and Sales 1895–99
Table 10	*History of the Christian Church*: Credit/Debit balances 1895–99
Table 11	*Eras of the Christian Church*: sales figures 1896–97 – 1898–99
Table 12	*Eras of the Christian Church*: Annual performance 1896–97 – 1898–99
Table 13	Sales to Scribner 1881–1900
Table 14	*International Theological Library*: Annual Credits/Deficits 1895–96 — 1898–99
Table 15	*International Critical Commentary*: Annual Credits/Deficits 1895–96 — 1898–99
Table 16	*Expository Times*: 1895–96 accounts
Table 17	*Critical Review*: 1895–96 accounts
Table 18	Moulton and Geden's *Concordance*: Costings of the first printing (800 copies)
Table 19	Moulton and Geden's *Concordance*: Costings of the second printing (540 copies)
Table 20	*Dictionary of the Bible*: Volume One accounts 1897–98
Table 21	Advertising expenditure on some 1895–96 titles
Table 22	Comparison of advertising costs with cost of printing a prospectus for some 1895–96 titles
Table 23	Cost of review copies distributed of some 1895–96 titles

Table 24 Promotional expenditure on certain titles issued 1895–96
Table 25 Sales to the London wholesalers, 1881–1900
Table 26 Profitability of T. & T. Clark's entire programme, excluding overheads 1895–96 — 1898–99
Table 27 Investment in new titles 1895–96 — 1898–99
Table 28 Overall profitability of T. & T. Clark
Table 29 *Dictionary of the Bible* — Sales to 1920
Table 30 Contribution of the *Expository Times* to total trading income
Table 31 *Expository Times*: Return on investment 1950–51 — 1954–55
Table 32 Estimated costings of three volumes of Barth's *Dogmatics*
Table 33 Cost of reprinting Thayer's *Greek-English Lexicon of the New Testament* (1958)
Table 34 Annual performance 1896–97
Table 35 Overheads 1896–97, 1897–98 and 1898–99
Table 36 Trading account data 1911–12 — 1989 with comparative data 1896–97 — 1898–99
Table 37 Allocation of total outlay in five sample years, 1930–31, 1940–41, 1950–51, 1960–61, 1970–71

Abbreviations

F.T.L.	*Foreign Theological Library*
Publishing House	*The Publishing House of T. & T. Clark, Edinburgh* (1882)
I.T.L.	*International Theological Library*
E.R.E.	*Encyclopaedia of Religion and Ethics*
I.C.C.	*International Critical Commentary*
W.E.M.	*World's Epoch Makers*
N.L.S.	National Library of Scotland

Partners in T. & T. Clark 1821-1987

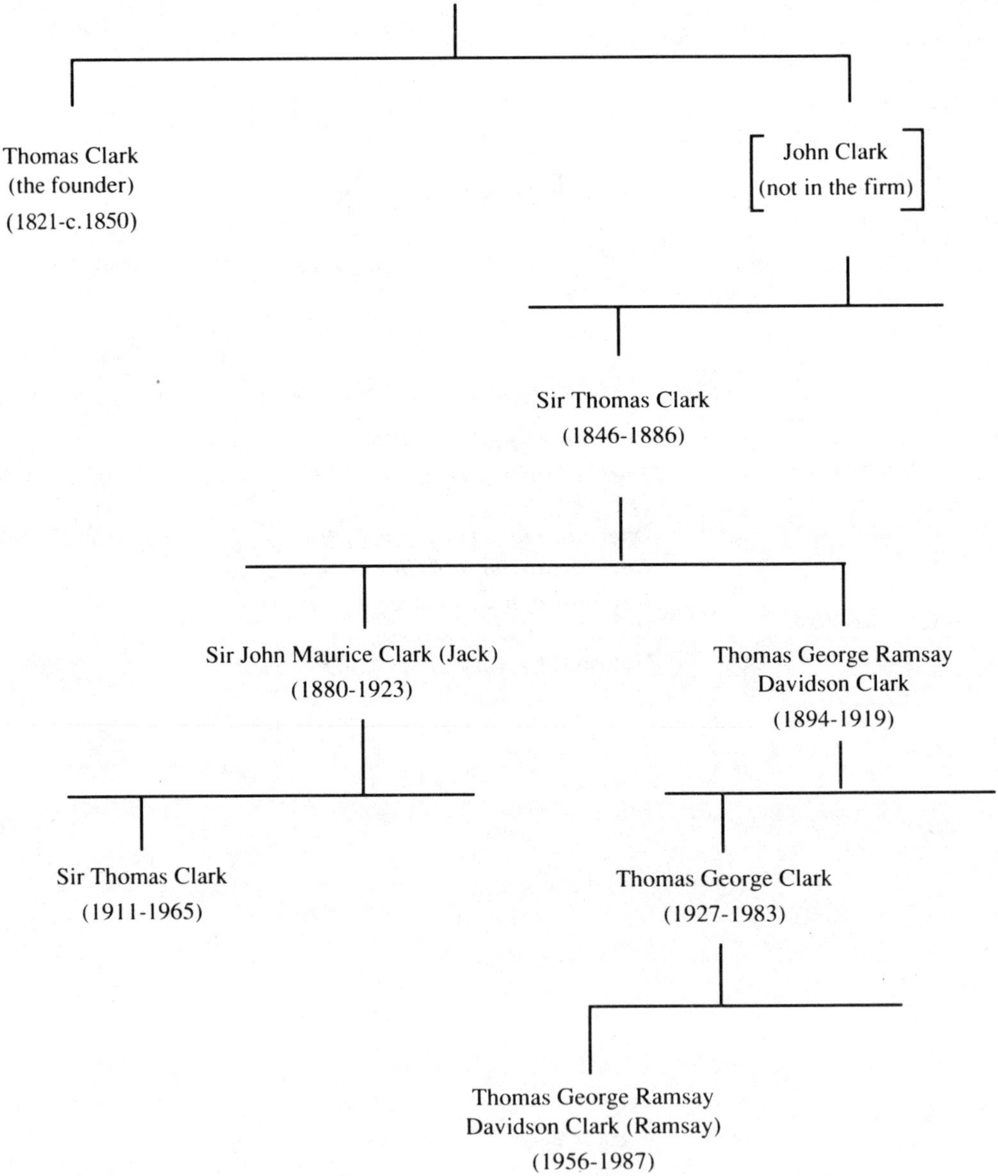

(The dates in brackets refer to the period of involvement with the firm)

Clark family tree (including only those members who were involved in the business)

Introduction

Introduction

A considerable proportion of the large number of books published in Scotland between 1801 and 1900 were on religious or theological subjects. The publishing houses responsible for these issues differed in aim, size, and specialisation; they can, however, be roughly categorised as follows. Some were businesses which entered the trade with the exclusive, or almost exclusive, aim of publishing religious works: such were the firms of Collins, Blackie, and Nelson. All of these, of course, later diversified into other areas of publishing. Others, such as Blackwood, were major general houses which established and maintained theological lists. Still others were predominantly local publishers, such as Alexander Gardner of Paisley, whose output included volumes of sermons and other religious material of local origin. Works were also issued by para-church organisations formed for the purpose of originating and distributing religious literature: such was the Religious Tract Society of Scotland and, later in the century, the Stirling Tract Enterprise. Finally, the Scottish denominations were all responsible for a limited amount of publishing: in the case of highly-centralised Churches such as the Church of Scotland, this was organised through Publications Committees answerable to the annual denominational Assembly: while in the case of decentralised groupings such as the Plymouth Brethren, the literary requirements of the denomination were met by privately established publishing businesses.[1] In a sense, the subject of the present study, T. & T. Clark does not fall into any of the above categories. The founder set up business as a bookseller and legal publisher, but he quickly diversified into theological publishing.

Unlike Blackie and Nelson, however, T. & T. Clark issued few works of a popular nature, concentrating instead on scholarly and academic theology. This single-minded commitment established the business over the years as the chief theological publishing firm in Scotland, which excelled the rest in the range and variety of material issued.

Two general observations can be made about this proliferation of publishing houses. In the first place, several of the most durable nineteenth-century firms were founded in the wake of the evangelical revival which had widespread effect at the start of the century. To the founders of these firms the desire to further this revival, and to meet adequately the literary requirements of those who had been spiritually awakened was, it seems, at least as important a motive as the accumulation of wealth.[2] An orthodox Christian faith, based on a traditional view of biblical authority, was a vital element in the lives of the founding fathers of the dynasties of Blackie, Nelson, and Collins, and other similar firms, and this faith clearly had important implications for the kind of material which would appear in these firms' lists. The second general observation is that, while some of the firms springing from the revival rose, flourished and fell within a generation, several, owing to visionary management and a readiness to diversify, proved to have a remarkable longevity, surviving into the twentieth century.

The religious publishers of 1900 were servicing a very different marketplace from that which their counterparts of a hundred years earlier had known. It therefore follows from the mere fact of its survival that a firm founded in the first two decades of the nineteenth century which survived until 1900 had successfully contended with, and adapted to, these changes in the market. Founded in 1821, T. & T. Clark was one of the survivors, its principals adapting to changes in market conditions and developments in theological attitudes while seeking not to compromise the commitment to truth which had characterised the founder. This study records and celebrates T. & T. Clark's development, paying particular attention to that blossoming of its lists in the 1880s and 1890s which established the firm as arguably the most significant theological publishing house in the United Kingdom.

Part I

Chapter 1
Historical outline

1821–1846

It would appear from the meagre sources which have bearing on this period of the firm's history that Thomas Clark founded his business in 1821.[1] He was then 22, and his previous experience included an apprenticeship served with David Brown of Edinburgh, and some years on the staff of Joseph Butterworth, a law bookseller of Fleet Street, London.[2] It is not surprising that the bookselling and publishing concern which he established in Parliament Square, Edinburgh, appears initially to have concentrated on issuing legal works.

Following the destruction by fire of these premises in 1823, Clark moved, first to 32 George Street and, a few years later, to 38 George Street[3] from where the business was to be conducted until the end of the century.[4] As well as his specialisation in legal works, Clark would appear to have cultivated an interest in foreign literature which led to his making several business visits to France, Holland and Germany[5] in the course of which he added to his knowledge of European literature and the European book market, and made the acquaintance of the leading booksellers in each country. This knowledge and these contacts he seems to have put to good use in importing foreign editions for sale in his Edinburgh shop, and issuing English translations of notable works, especially in the theological field.

The firm did not receive its present designation until 1846, when the founder's nephew, another Thomas Clark (1823–1900), was received into partnership, having completed his term of apprenticeship and having spent some time working for the wholesalers Hamilton, Adams and Co. in London.[6] The younger Thomas Clark immediately began to make his mark and show his competence, and some years later his uncle left him responsible for the practical management of the firm, and retired to Heath Park, Blairgowrie, where he lived until his death on 22 December 1865.[7]

Due to lack of evidence, it is difficult to build up a picture of the development of Thomas Clark's business in its early years. Two trends can, however, be noted. There was, firstly, an increasing specialisation: although it began as a bookselling and publishing firm, the publishing side of the business came to assume increasing importance. And secondly, there was a change of emphasis: initially the stress was on legal works, but gradually theology came to dominate the list, as it was to do in the latter part of the century. This change of emphasis was noted by James Thin who, writing of the 1830s, described the founder[8] as 'beginning to develop a theological as well as law business in the publication of a series called the "Biblical Cabinet" '.

The *Biblical Cabinet* began to appear in 1832 with a volume of J.A. Ernesti's *Principles of Biblical Interpretation of the New Testament* being issued, together with a volume of Dr John Brown's *Philological Tracts*. Between 1832 and 1844, thirty works were issued, completing the *Biblical Cabinet* in forty-five volumes. The Series consisted for the most part of translations of German commentaries and theological works. It is a tribute to the acumen of the founder that the majority of works in the *Cabinet* still featured in the firm's lists in 1889 (in some cases having been re-translated).

The 1830s saw the issue by Clark of two other, not exclusively religious, series, *The Cabinet Library of Scarce and Celebrated Tracts*, and *The Student's Cabinet Library of Useful Tracts*. His aim in issuing these, as stated in the 1838 *Catalogue*, was

> to publish a selection of the most useful, interesting and celebrated tracts . . . The publisher proposes to confine them to no particular class of literature, and to exclude nothing that can fairly come within the designation either of polite letters or useful knowledge; and hopes thus to present a series of cheap publications, which will interest the Antiquarian, the Theologian, the Philosopher and the Scholar.

By 1838 there had been eleven issues in the first of these series, and thirty in the second, these thirty also being available collected in bound volumes.

Clark also issued some miscellaneous titles: editions of the classics, philosophical works, and a *Greek and English Lexicon of the New Testament*,[9] a fore-runner of the great works of reference which the firm was to issue at the end of the century. There was also a collection of children's books translated from the German of Christophe von Schmidt. Schmidt (1768–1854) is perhaps best remembered for his *Das Blumenkörbohen* (*The Basket of Flowers*) which first appeared in 1823, and which Clark issued in translation. This work 'became the archetypal Sunday School book after its translation in 1833 . . . [and] was one of the most popular Reward Books throughout the 19th cent.'[10] Clark was not the only publisher to be issuing English translations of the Schmidt works. It is a matter of speculation how financially successful his editions were. But it is interesting that this departure into reward book publishing was not followed up. The reward book market, as many other publishers throughout the century found, was a growing, and increasingly lucrative, one. Had Clark opted for this line of development, the future story of the firm might have been very different. Another new departure which was not followed up was the issue of a novel. Little is known about this except that it was unsuccessful. Perhaps this failure is explanation enough why the experiment does not seem to have been repeated.

It is worth noting in conclusion, as indicative of the founder's enterprise, that through his firm the first law magazine ever to appear in Scotland, the monthly *Law Chronicle*, was issued from May 1829. This, however, did not find a market, and was discontinued within five years.[11]

In becoming a partner in 1846, the young Thomas Clark was joining a business which had been built up with considerable originality and enterprise. A firm foundation had been laid, on which the new partner was to build by further developing the publishing side of the business and increasingly majoring on the issue of theological works, especially those of German origin. There are no data on the profitability of the firm in 1846, but if one of the founder's obituarists is to be believed, it was more than merely financially sound. Clark, he felt, was able to retire to the country 'having won, what all booksellers long for and we fear so few obtain, a considerable fortune.'[12] And the first Thomas Clark's will confirms the accuracy of this statement. His total moveable estate was £23,748 16*s*. 10*d*., and he also owned property and land: Heath Park, Blairgowrie, a house at Rossness, Kinghorn, the office at 38 George Street, Edinburgh, and various other properties at Pettycur and Edinburgh.[13]

1846–1886

Over this forty-year period, the younger Thomas Clark was solely responsible for the consolidation and development of the firm which he joined in 1846. He would appear to have been cast in the same formidable mould as members of the other Scottish publishing dynasties — the Blacks, Blackies, Nelsons and Collinses. Like them he was able, despite heavy business commitments, to find time and energy for involvement in wide-ranging ecclesiastical and civic affairs.

Thomas Clark the younger was born in the burgh of Canongate, Edinburgh on 5 September 1823, and was educated at the High School.[14] It was said of his father, John Clark, that he was 'a man of great business capacity as well as of sincere Christian character'.[15] These were traits which would appear to have been reproduced in his son.

With regard to his business capacity, the strength of the Clark list in 1886 is, perhaps, sufficient testimony. Over four decades, 'he had to keep his eye on theology abroad, and on law at home, and anyone who wish[ed] to see how he succeeded [had] but to look in at 38 George Street, or study the firm's catalogues.'[16] His achievement was rooted in an alertness to the requirements of the market, and a discernment as to which new theological writings would endure. The *Publishers' Circular* attributed his success to the fact that 'he understood the tastes and appreciated the wants of his countrymen, who, almost without exception, [were] sticklers in theology.'[17]

Clark developed the links with the continent which his uncle had initiated. There are occasional references in the firm's letterbooks to his continental visits, and personal friendships with eminent European theologians. But as

English language writers both in Britain and in America to some extent seized the initiative from the Germans, so Clark was quick to cultivate relationships with the United States, in particular with the firm of Scribner and Welford, later Charles Scribner's Sons. This Edinburgh-New York axis was initiated to meet what Clark saw as an untapped transatlantic market,[18] but its development was both a response and a spur to the new British and American writers. Clark is said to have become the 'fast friend' of the first Charles Scribner.[19]

Not only Clark's church work, but also his civic duties were viewed by his contemporaries as being motivated primarily by Christian conviction. While James Harvey's *In Memoriam Sir Thomas Clark* is written in the fulsome style typical of such publications, it is valuable in charting the extent of Clark's involvement in church affairs, both at congregational and at denominational level. He was associated throughout his life with Lady Glenorchy's Church, Edinburgh, which his father had joined the year before his birth.[20] He superintended the Sunday School, was treasurer of the Sustentation Fund in the congregation, and was noted for his generosity and for the quality of his pastoral care. He was elected and ordained as deacon at the age of twenty (18 January 1844), and became an elder fourteen years later (28 March 1858). He was also active in the wider Free Church scene, serving on its committees and supporting it financially.[21] He was enthusiastically in favour of the Union of 1900, which he lived long enough to see: 'though in many respects holding by the old positions, he had broad and tolerant views on all questions, and kept an open mind to every new interest.'[22] Perhaps his most revealing comment on the quality of spiritual life which he felt became a committed Christian is found in a letter where he discusses apparently heterodox comments made by A.B. Bruce, and claims that these would cause him much more concern were he not convinced that 'there is with him a fast hold of a living Saviour'.[23] Clark himself sought to cultivate this inner dependence on God.

All the sources on Thomas Clark's public life are almost excessive in their praise for him. There would seem to have been virtually universal recognition that he was a good and just man. In entering public life Clark was following in the footsteps of his father, who had been a magistrate,[24] but James Harvey[25] discerns a religious motivation. Clark was involved in the Edinburgh Merchant Company, serving successively as Assistant, Treasurer and Master, to which position he was elected in 1883 or 1884[26] and re-elected the following year. He was a Fellow of the Royal Society of Edinburgh, a Curator of the University of Edinburgh, and one of the managers of the Royal Infirmary.[27] He first became officially connected with the Corporation as one of the City Auditors,[28] and in 1877 entered the Town Council representing St George's Ward. He filled this seat for eleven years, in the course of which he served as Convenor of the Public Health Committee (for four years from 1881), as a Magistrate (from 1883), and as Lord Provost (from 1885). He was associated with a wide range of civic projects, the most spectacular of which was the 1886 Edinburgh International Exhibition, at which he was given his Baronetcy by the Queen.[29]

Clark, it was said,[30] claimed to have 'entered upon his work having a high ideal to strive after.' There would seem to have been a general recognition that he had been a successful Lord Provost. The *Scottish Leader* was acknowledged[31] to have been 'expressing the public sentiment' in stating that 'Sir Thomas Clark [had] filled with dignity an office that he demits with most honourable credit', and the *Scotsman*'s obituarist held that 'his name was associated with much good civic work . . . as Lord Provost, he filled that high office with dignity, tact and forbearance, and generally managed the affairs of the city with no small amount of success.'

This, then, was the man who presided over the growth of T. & T. Clark. In 1880 he was joined in partnership by his eldest son, John Maurice Clark,[32] and six years later he retired,[33] although retaining an active advisory role in the firm for much of the remainder of his life. His was indeed an active retirement: we find him, for example, in 1897 as Honorary President of an Edinburgh association for Booksellers' Assistants.[34]

At the end of a year during which his health had steadily declined Sir Thomas Clark died on Christmas Eve, 1900, at his house at 11 Melville Crescent, Edinburgh.[35] He was survived by Lady Clark, and by two sons and two daughters.[36]

Sir Thomas, besides owning property at 38 George Street, 11 Melville Crescent, and various other locations in Edinburgh, left moveable estate totalling £202,183 16*s*. 6*d*. He had extensive investments in railways, banking and other concerns, and on the basis of the data we will be examining later, we can safely say that his income from these must have greatly exceeded his income from the firm's trading.[37]

A scrutiny of the list of works issued by the firm over the four decades between 1846 and 1886 reveals a pattern of almost continual growth.

The *Foreign Theological Library* (F.T.L.) appears to have been the first-fruits of the younger Thomas Clark's partnership. A 'new and enlarged' series of the *Biblical Cabinet* had, however, been announced as early as 1844[38] and the F.T.L. incorporated early volumes issued in that series. It was planned to publish four F.T.L. volumes annually at a subscription price and the Series was issued with great regularity until being wound up in the early 1890s. In this way many European theological writings were made available to an English-language audience.

The F.T.L. was soon joined by other series. The complete works of John Owen were issued in twenty-four volumes between 1850 and 1855; they must have sold well, for a re-issue was undertaken between 1862 and 1866. In 1859, Clark announced[39] that he had bought over the stock and copyrights of the series of works by Calvin, in fifty-one volumes, which had been issued by the Calvin Translation Society.[40] The imminent appearance of the first volumes in the *Ante-Nicene Library* was noted in the *Bookseller* for 30 September 1865.[41] This series was to be edited by Alexander Roberts and James Donaldson, with the object of presenting 'translations of all the Post-Apostolic Christian writings that appeared before the Council of Nicaea', with the exception of Origen's *Commentaries*. Twenty-four volumes were to be issued by subscription over six years. A series of translations of commentaries whose original appearance in German had been co-ordinated by J.P. Lange appeared in twenty-five volumes between 1868 and 1879. Later in the century at least, supplies of these volumes were imported by Clark from Scribner. In 1871, Clark began to issue a sixteen-volume series of the works of St Augustine, edited by Marcus Dods. Four volumes were to be published annually on a subscription basis, although volumes were also available separately. Clark claimed in a contemporary catalogue that 'the larger portion of those writings contained in this series [had] not been hitherto translated', and that the work contained in the first volumes, *The City of God*, had 'hitherto only been accessible to the English reader in a very old and feeble version'. In 1873, the issue began of a translation of H.A.W. Meyer's *Critical and Exegetical Commentary on the New Testament*. Four volumes were to be published per annum on subscription. In 1879, the more popular *Bible Class Handbook* series was launched and, five years later, the companion *Bible Class Primer* series was bought over from Macniven and Wallace, who were largely withdrawing from publishing. Another fruit of the American connection was the issue in this country of Philip Schaff's *History of the Christian Church*, the first part being *Apostolic Christianity A.D. 1–100* (Two volumes, 1883).[42] Further volumes were published intermittently until 1893.

What is notable is not only the fact that these series include such works, but also that, as a check against the 1901 catalogue readily shows, so many of them were still in print at the end of the century. It must be admitted however that in some cases, this was probably not so much due to Clark's judgement in selecting them for his list as to the fact that sales were very slow to come: he refused to remainder poor-selling titles. Even so, a considerable number of titles were reprinted; in 1879, for example, reprints were undertaken of thirty-four volumes, while in 1889 the number reprinted was forty-seven.[43] These figures indicate that the backlist was reasonably live.

Throughout this period, Clark continued to dabble in periodical publishing, without any marked success. The formerly prestigious *North British Review* was issued by him between 1860 and 1863. The *Monthly Interpreter*, shipwrecked by the disastrously lackadaisical editorship of J.S. Exell, survived only two years after its foundation in 1884. From 1885, an attempt which must be judged a failure was made to distribute the American *Presbyterian Review* in the United Kingdom. Thomas Clark was therefore unsuccessful in fulfilling his obvious desire to publish a theological journal which was at once highly respected and commercially viable, if not profitable. It was only when the firm made contact in 1889 with an editor of the calibre and industriousness of James Hastings, who was to edit several major works for the Clarks, that such a periodical became a possibility. Thomas Clark had a lasting success, however, with a legal serial, the *Journal of Jurisprudence*. This was founded in 1857 and, drawing contributions from many of the best-known men at the Bar, easily outshone the rival *Scottish Law Magazine*, which it absorbed in 1866. However, the *Journal*, which was originally marked by outspokenness, grew mellow in its maturity, 'for the good reason that contributors did not wish to imperil their chances of promotion at the bar by writing against the properly constituted authorities'. Mellowness limited its appeal: the new *Scottish Law Review* (founded in 1885) increased in popularity, and the *Journal*, then under the editorship of John Chisholm, was wound up in 1891.[44]

Over these years also, Clark issued a wide range of miscellaneous philosophical and theological works. Among the major Scottish ecclesiastical figures whose works feature in the Clark lists, Free Churchmen predominated. They included, from Free Church College, Glasgow, Professor A.B. Bruce, Professor J.S. Candlish, and Principal Patrick Fairbairn; from New College, Edinburgh, Principal William Cunningham, Professor A.B. Davidson, and Principal Robert Rainy; and from Free Church College, Aberdeen, Professor S.D.F. Salmond. The young William Robertson Nicoll also published a book with T. & T. Clark. That these authors all issued work through the Clark firm is indicative both of the important role played by Sir Thomas in disseminating Free Church theology, and of the confidence which the Church clearly placed in his firm.

In this period, Clark also published some major works, from the five-volume 1855 edition of J.A. Bengel's *Gnomon of the New Testament*, to C.L.W. Grimm's edition of C.G. Wilke's *Clavis Novi Testamenti* translated and revised by Joseph Thayer, and issued in 1886 as *A Greek-English Lexicon of the New Testament*.

It will be apparent that in the decades following 1846, Thomas Clark built solidly and consistently upon the foundation which he had inherited from his uncle. It was said in 1882 of the list which he had built up that it formed 'a most remarkable monument of well-directed energy.[45] During the thirty-eight years in which John Maurice Clark was senior partner in the firm, he in turn was to build with considerable flair and discrimination upon the foundation he inherited, and to lead T. & T. Clark into the third phase of its development, the most adventurous of all.

1886–1900

Discussing a publishing project in a letter to Philip Schaff in New York in 1882, Thomas Clark wrote 'my son would go in for it *con amore*.'[46] It is a phrase which characterises John Maurice Clark's approach to publishing throughout his life.

He was born on 7 March 1859 at 12 Forth Street, Edinburgh. After attending Mr Hunter's school for four years, he progressed to Edinburgh Academy in 1870, joining the class supervised by an outstanding master, Dr James Clyde. Clyde was a stimulating teacher, and several of Clark's classmates went on to illustrious careers. While at the Academy, Clark took prizes in writing, French, German, and book-keeping, before leaving earlier than might have been expected in 1874.[47] The following year, he matriculated in the Arts Faculty at Edinburgh University, where he appears to have attended classes only on a casual basis, for there is no record of his having graduated.[48] The late 1870s found him studying publishing in Leipzig.[49] The heir apparent was being groomed for his life's work in the family firm. At the age of 21, in 1880, he was taken into partnership.

Like Sir Thomas, John M. Clark, although deeply committed to publishing, was to devote considerable energy to matters military and civic. His obituary in

The Scotsman outlines these activities.[50] For many years (twenty-nine according to the *Glasgow Herald*)[51] he was associated with the Leith battalion of the Royal Scots, receiving his commission as Second Lieutenant in 1881, and becoming Colonel in 1905. As a subaltern he was present at a review by Queen Victoria of forty thousand Scottish volunteers in Edinburgh in 1881, and twenty-four years later he appeared as commanding officer at a review by Edward VI. He received the Volunteer Officers' Decoration, and contributed to the war effort in connection with the Territorial Force Association, being vice-chairman of the Midlothian Branch. He joined the Edinburgh Merchant Company in 1884, when his father was Master. In 1900 he was elected an Assistant, in which capacity he served for three years. In 1910 he was appointed Treasurer, and, the following year, Master. He fulfilled several responsible roles in connection with the Merchant Company, being, for example, a trustee of the Company's Widows' Fund. He was also chairman of the Scottish Life Assurance Company.

Like his father before him, John M. Clark was actively involved in church affairs.[52] In fact, he married the daughter of a Free Church minister, Henry Douglas of Kirkcaldy.[53] This was the man who, by his personal vision and dynamism, was to guide the firm into new areas of development well into the new century. He was, however, no radical. He had, according to an obituarist 'a distinct liking for the old courtly ways associated with Edinburgh publishing.'[54]

On Sir Thomas' retirement in 1886, John M. Clark became sole partner, a position he held for eight years until, in 1894, he received into partnership his brother, Thomas George Clark.[55] James Hastings testified that the brothers worked together 'with singular unanimity',[56] but there is no doubt that John was the dominant as well as the senior partner, shaping the evolution of the firm. Virtually until his death, however, Sir Thomas continued to exert an influence. He visited the office daily,[57] and Hastings claimed in 1901 that 'his advice was until quite recently an important factor in all the great decisions.'[58] John M. Clark himself was ready to acknowledge his debt to his father, both in private — 'our father . . . is still with us here, & gives us his valued advice';[59] and in public — 'his advice is invaluable to me, and I trust I may long have it.'[60] John Clark's high estimation of his father is evident from the following, written when he was about to embark in 1896 upon an American tour, in the course of which he was to meet many of those who were contributing to the two *International* series. To one of these American contacts he confided: 'I am getting quite alarmed at the thought that all those distinguished people should be invited to meet me. I, personally, accept the honour as being my father's son, & I assure you that he is exceedingly gratified & touched by all your kindness.'[61] The esteem in which Sir Thomas was held by his sons, and the consequent heed which was given to his advice meant that the important decisions of the late 1880s and 1890s — the launching of the *Dictionary of the Bible*, and the *International* series, decisions which ensured that the firm retained its position as a leading publisher of theology – were taken in full consultation with Sir Thomas.

John M. Clark's major contributions to the firm would appear to fall into three areas.

Firstly, while not neglecting T. & T. Clark's links with the continent of Europe, he worked hard to develop the transatlantic connection in which he considered the future lay. He visited both Germany, and the United States and Canada, making, for instance, the extensive transatlantic tour in the spring of 1896 principally to conclude negotiations with Scribners regarding American rights in the *Dictionary of the Bible*. His itinerary included New York (where he stayed with C.A. Briggs), Yale, Boston, Niagara, Toronto (where he stayed with W.R. Clark), Chicago, Washington and Philadelphia. In response to Clark's transatlantic forays, Charles Scribner II reciprocated by visiting Edinburgh, for example in the spring of 1887, to discuss the development of the *International* series.

Secondly, John M. Clark would appear to have been committed to the development of major theological works involving large investments and considerable risk. Because his judgements were mature, and because for the most part he was fortunate in his editors and contributors, these investments still further increased the size of the firm's live back-list. This policy of major investment is evident especially in the *Dictionary of the Bible* and the works which followed it, including the *Encyclopaedia of Religion and Ethics*.

Thirdly, and of major importance, Clark was successful in building a lasting relationship with James Hastings, whose editorial genius was to play such a considerable part in the firm's success.[62] John M. Clark was seven years younger than Hastings, but the two established a positive working relationship. On hearing of Hastings' death in 1922, Clark wrote to W.R. Nicoll 'I feel that I have lost a very dear friend with whom I have always had the happiest business relations',[63] and this view of the relationship is borne out by the letter books. For instance, in the course of smoothing out an area of contention in 1904, John M. Clark wrote to Hastings:

> My brother and I are most grateful to you for all the help and advice you so kindly give us. It is impossible, I suppose, that two, much less three, people can always see eye to eye, but I hope you will believe me that if I ever do write or speak in a way which surprises you, nothing personal is intended, that my sole desire is to act in the interests of all concerned, & that I am always grateful for your kind interest & advice. So far as I know there are only two instances in our personal intercourse where ever any *hesitation* on my part has occurred.[64]

For his part, grateful for the commitment with which the firm issued his works, Hastings dedicated the last volume of the *Encyclopaedia of Religion and Ethics* 'To Sir John Maurice Clark, Baronet, Publisher and Friend'. Commenting on this dedication, Clark wrote 'I knew nothing of his intention until he sent in his MS, and I feel touched by the way he puts it — "Publisher and Friend". Certainly our relations with him have always been most cordial.'[65] It is difficult to imagine how the Clark firm would have developed had it not been for the link with Hastings, for he not only brought major titles into its list, but also introduced to the firm a wide range of theological writers, and thereby greatly increased the prestige of the imprint.

The fourteen years from 1886 to 1900 were, as has been seen, a period of preparation and expansion. In the sense that John M. Clark's active involvement in the firm continued until his retirement in 1923, 1900 is an arbitrary cut-off point; but while it has been chosen largely because of the absence for the early years of the new century of such detailed source material as is available for the 1880s and 1890s, it is nevertheless true to say that by 1900 the major series had been initiated, and the important policy decisions made. Even the launch of the *Encyclopaedia of Religion and Ethics* can be seen as a natural outcome of the policy of dictionary publishing initiated when the Clarks agreed to issue the *Dictionary of the Bible*.

Works continued to be added to three of the earlier series over this period. More *Bible Class Primers* and *Handbooks* appeared, and, until around 1891, volumes were added to the *Foreign Theological Library*. Thereafter, although foreign translations continued to be issued, the regular publishing of four volumes per year in the F.T.L. was discontinued. This is symptomatic of the continuing development of the Edinburgh–New York axis, and it is perhaps not coincidental that, also in 1891, the first volume of the *International Theological Library* was published (S.R. Driver's *Introduction to the Literature of the Old Testament*). This series consisted of pioneering works by British and American theologians and, edited by S.D.F. Salmond of Aberdeen and C. A. Briggs of New York, was issued jointly by Clark and Scribner. A parallel venture was the *International Critical Commentary* series, also issued by Clark and Scribner. Edited by S.R. Driver of Oxford, A. Plummer of Durham, and C.A. Briggs of New York, the first volumes in this series appeared in 1895. Another American connection gave rise to the British publication by Clark of the *Eras of the Christian Church* series, which was produced by the Christian Literature Publishing Company of New York, the Clarks simply importing the works in sheets for binding in Scotland with the Clark colophon. A series initiated by the Edinburgh firm, and indicative perhaps of a broadening of the subject-spread of titles on their list, was the *World's Epoch Makers* series, edited by Oliphant Smeaton, the first volumes of which (including titles on *Muhammad and his Power* and *William Herschel and his Work*) appeared in 1900. Although not having a specific commitment to issue the material presented at any of the various endowed lecture series, the Clarks did intermittently publish the lectures given in a particular year in one or other of these series. For instance, the Cunningham Lectures appeared fairly consistently under the Clark imprint and the Gifford Lectures were published by the Clarks in 1890, the Hulsean Lectures in 1893, and the Kerr Lectures in 1900.

This period also saw the foundation of two periodicals which, whatever their success in financial terms (and this will be considered in depth in Chapter 7) contributed largely to the prestige of the Clark imprint. The earlier of these was the *Expository Times*, commenced in October 1889 by James Hastings, who published the first three issues through William Diack of Aberdeen before Clark, recognising the potential of the journal and of its editor, took it over from January 1890.[66] It has survived until the present day. Later in 1890, the first issue appeared of *The Critical Review of Theological and Philosophical*

Literature, edited by S. D. F. Salmond of Aberdeen. This quarterly, although it aimed at a catholicity of approach ('The Magazine will not be the organ of any particular section of the Evangelical Church, but will be conducted in the interests of all its branches',[67] and a non-specialisation of treatment, being directed both at clergy and intelligent laymen, was not a financial success, and passed out of the Clarks' hands in 1899.

Apart from the appearance of a wide range of miscellaneous theological works, this period also saw the issue of several major reference tools including Moulton and Geden's *Concordance to the Greek Testament* (1897), and the first three volumes of Hastings' *Dictionary of the Bible* (1898, 1899, 1900).

By the 1890s, therefore, T. & T. Clark was a moderately-sized enterprise, still operating from 38 George Street. In the three financial years ending in April 1889, profits of £2,208, £2,351 and £1,720 were generated.[68] Profits had risen slightly by the financial year 1896–97 (which ran from July–June); there were 674 titles in print, 352 of them belonging to the various series, and turnover amounted to £10,036 8*s*. 4*d*., yielding a profit before deduction of overheads of £2,890 18*s*. 0*d*.

The years during which Sir John M. Clark was principal of the firm were golden years of achievement, and it was in the 1890s that the foundations of that achievement were expertly laid. We turn now to examine the principles which guided Sir John and his predecessors as they sought the rock on which to lay those foundations among the sometimes perplexing quicksands of Victorian theological study.

Chapter 2
Aims and Motives

T. & T. Clark survived throughout the nineteenth century by successfully coming to terms with very significant changes in the theological marketplace. The altered conditions can be summed up in two propositions.

In the first place, the orthodox view of biblical authority was increasingly questioned by scholars, and this questioning led to a demand for material which had vastly different theological presuppositions from those which had obtained previously. At the start of the century, it would seem that apart from some scholars in Germany and elsewhere who were regarded as theological mavericks, the Bible was still held to be the inerrant and authoritative Word of God, the touchstone against which all theological constructs had to be tested. By the end of the century, the scholars were bringing the methods of what was known as the Higher Criticism to bear upon the biblical texts, emphasising the human-ness of their authors, and coming to regard the Bible as a vehicle through which God was pleased to speak, rather than a wholly inspired work. This new understanding of the status of the Bible had a considerable impact also on theology, encouraging a questioning of the old orthodoxy.

In the second place, in the more popular end of the market, there was a turning from the works of religious teaching and Puritan theology which were widely read at the beginning of the century towards the 'religious' novels which proliferated towards its close. This fact may well not be unrelated to the first proposition. It clearly takes time for scholarly attitudes to percolate downwards and influence the lay Christian, but there may be an element of cause and effect between on the one hand, the abandonment by many scholars of a full doctrine of biblical inspiration, and, on the other, this turning from popular theological reading towards the religious novel. Or again, it could simply be that both changes took place side by side in a general atmosphere of increasing scepticism.

These factors led throughout the century to a decline in the demand for theological works, and a decline also in the proportion of that demand which could be satisfied by works of a more orthodox nature.

Almost every British publishing house was affected to some extent by these developments. Firms heavily committed to theological publishing, such as T. &

T. Clark, were forced to examine their motives, assessing the relative importance to them of truth as they saw it and their commitment to furthering theological speculation on the one hand, and, on the other, the profitability of their firm, and the economic necessity of publishing material which fulfilled the expectations of their readership.

T. & T. Clark survived into the new century, and they survived triumphantly, serving an even wider section of the market than earlier. But they did this without in their eyes compromising their commitment to the truth of what they were publishing. It would seem that because they were open to the views of moderately progressive theologians, their perception of truth developed broadly in line with current theological perceptions.

There are a number of quotations which illuminate the Clarks' thinking at this time of theological change, highlighting their sense of mission, their commitment to truth, their awareness of responsibility to the Christian public, their concern over the profitability of the firm. (The Clarks were, of course, still issuing legal as well as theological works, but relatively few of these were appearing.)

Here, for example, is the inscription on the title page of a Clark letter book begun in June 1896:[69] *Nisi dominus frustra*, a quotation from Psalm 127:1 – 'Except the Lord build the house, they labour in vain that build it.' If this can be taken at all seriously as an unofficial motto of John M. Clark's, it would indicate that he ran his business in an attitude of conscious dependence on God, and with a corresponding sense of answerability to Him.[70]

Sir Thomas Clark stated his position clearly in a letter to Samuel Davidson, dated 25 June 1895.[71] He had, he observed 'always taken a higher view of the profession of a publisher', and continued

> You know the kind of book I have published. I have issued very few indeed in which I have not taken the whole risk and I can conscientiously say that I have looked more to the high character of the books than to the prospect of a pecuniary return.

And the delicate balance in which mission and profitability were held is perhaps nowhere better illustrated than by John M. Clark's somewhat enigmatic comment to A.J. Gossip:[72]

> 'I can't speak for Christ,' Sir John once said to me shyly, 'and I would like to do something for Him. Well, I can take this risk, seeking to help a little.' And then at once he added, 'But, with Hastings editing it, there is no great risk at all!'

Another revealing quotation on the theme of balancing mission and profitability dates from February 1900, when John M. Clark told S.D.F. Salmond of Aberdeen

> Repeatedly we have published books either for the sake of the Author, or in the interests of Theological Study, which we were quite sure could never repay us, & we have lost heavily by them. We merely mention this because we fear it is generally supposed that Publishers are not superior to those considerations.[73]

One final quotation: eighteen years earlier, when T. & T. Clark were considering issuing in the F.T.L. a translation of a *Life of Christ* by Bernhard Weiss of Berlin, Marcus Dods wrote perceptively to the firm as follows:[74]

> I sympathise with y. perplexity about Weiss. It is similar to my own perplexity about the publication of the truth about Genesis. To publish Weiss will be a new departure for you as a publisher & will be at once recognised as such. And I have little doubt there wd be a clamour agt. you & you wd lose subscriptions — At the same time I think you need have no fear of 'harming young minds' because young minds have already access to [illegible]. You will do no harm save to yourselves, but only good by publishing it — that is my decided opinion. But unless you yourself see that & are prepared for the condemnation of the fanatical, I think you shd leave it alone. Other publishers can take it up without producing the slightest shock to any one.

Here, commitment to theological advance had to be held in balance with the Clarks' sense of responsibility to the Christian public. The Weiss work was published by T. & T. Clark in 1883.

These quotations emphasise the importance to the Clarks of a number of key objectives.

Guarding their reputation for orthodoxy

Reviewing the final volume of Hastings' *Encyclopaedia of Religion and Ethics*, A.W. Fergusson commented:[75] 'A work like this is not so much a business proposition as a great public service — the greatest of all public services — the furtherance of truth.' This quotation could easily be applied to much of the Clarks' output in the nineteenth century. They were committed to the truth, which they defined largely in terms of evangelical orthodoxy, but they were also, as we shall see, committed to the 'furtherance' of truth, which involved them in encouraging reverent theological speculation.

Traditionally, the Clarks saw their role as being the defence of evangelical orthodoxy. Thus, for example, when they took over the *North British Review* in 1860, an advertisement in the *Bookseller*[76] commented that such theological articles as the *Review* might contain would maintain 'the cause of Evangelical Christianity in opposition to the various phases of infidelity and error'.

Twenty-two years later, it was the opinion of the anonymous Wesleyan Methodist minister who contributed to *The Publishing House* that 'Messrs. Clark have found it to their own advantage, as well as thought it their duty, to keep out all authors who would not be relished by the evangelical taste of Great Britain.'[77] The same author was happy to accept the even blunter comment that 'Clark have clung to their old evangelical tradition.'[78]

And around the same time, Marcus Dods clearly recognised the importance to the Clarks of ensuring that the commitment to theological advance did not endanger their reputation for orthodoxy. Thus, as we saw, he warned that to publish the work by Weiss might 'harm' the firm, and subject it to 'the condemnation of the fanatical'. The Clarks were made of sterner stuff, and issued the work. Nevertheless, guarding their reputation remained a vital issue.

This point is illustrated in an interesting letter written in December 1890 to Charles M. Mead of Berlin.[79] Mead had offered the firm a manuscript entitled *Romans Dissected*, a 'spoof' on the 'higher critics', to be published under the pseudonym of E.D. McRealsham. The Clarks were at first unenthusiastic about the work. The first point they made was this:

> We think, that were *we* to publish it, 'the point of the joke' might be lost as considering the reputation of our firm, it would at once be apparent to many that the essay is not seriously meant.

Presumably the point here is that were the work to appear under the Clark imprint, with its reputation for orthodoxy, it would be immediately obvious that a joke were intended, whereas if it appeared under an imprint with a less conservative reputation the reader might for a time be taken in by 'McRealsham' — a successful deception which would at once provide the author with more satisfaction, and prove his point.

The Clarks' second observation in the letter to Mead indicates their real fear of undermining the evangelical position through publishing his work, and thereby threatening the reputation for orthodoxy which the firm enjoyed:

> On the other hand, we naturally hesitate in case many *do* look upon it seriously. The book would get scattered round the world, and many readers might never hear that 'Mr McRealsham does not believe one atom of what he is ostensibly trying to prove!' In this way much harm could be done.[80]

But perhaps the most interesting example of the Clarks guarding their image as orthodox evangelical publishers is outlined in a series of letters regarding a work published in the I.T.L. in 1897, *A History of Christianity in the Apostolic Age* by an American scholar, Arthur C. McGiffert. Proofs of the book had not been seen by the British editor of the Series before publication, and John M. Clark wrote personally to Charles Scribner II complaining about McGiffert's position:

> The Introductory Chapter is highly offensive to good Christian people, perhaps as much from what it does *not* say as from what it does say . . . In the present case Dr Salmond finds his name subscribed as Editor to opinions diametrically opposed to those he himself holds, although he is by no means narrow in his views.[81]

Clark also wrote to C.A. Briggs, informing him of general, negative impressions of McGiffert and his work in Britain:

> A well-known London Editor wrote to me, privately, that he is amazed 'that the Presbyterian Church in America should have a man like McGiffert teaching their Students.' . . . He has given cause for offence even among Scholars.[82]

To both men, he emphasised the harm that publishing the book could do to the firm's reputation: McGiffert's work, he wrote, had 'awakened a general feeling of indignation'.[83] A fortnight later he commented 'I fear there is to be trouble about the book . . . People are saying hard things about us for publishing it.'[84] And even after the storm had passed, we find him writing to Scribner 'It is probably difficult for you to understand *our* position, as publishers, when new views are advanced in books issued by us.'[85]

It would seem that T. & T. Clark's broad adherence to evangelical principles continued to the end of the century and beyond. For example, in one of the regular letters to Scribners in New York in which the Clarks attempted to persuade the American firm to put more effort into the distribution of Clark titles on their side of the Atlantic, mention was made of William L. Walker's work *The Spirit and the Incarnation* (1899).[86] Commented the Clarks:

> there is special interest in this book because it is the result of a severe struggle through which the author passed some years ago, & shows (in the hope that service may be rendered to others who may have similar difficulties, & to the Church at large) the special course of study which led him back to the full evangelical faith.

Even given the facts, firstly that enthusiasm for the work was called for in what was essentially a sales letter, and secondly that John M. Clark's 1899 definition of 'the full evangelical faith' might have been somewhat different in essence if not in terminology from Thomas the younger's mid-century definition, the conclusion must be drawn that T. & T. Clark still saw their role as being the dissemination of evangelical works.

Facilitating the development of orthodoxy

Discussing the F.T.L. in a catalogue issued in the early 1890s, the Clarks claimed to 'trust and believe that the whole series [had] exercised, through the care with which the books [had] been selected, a healthful influence upon the progress of theological science in this country and in the United States'. This view was quoted and endorsed in the *Publishers' Circular*,[87] and it sums up the Clarks' commitment to the furtherance of truth through the issue of carefully-selected progressive works.

A Wesleyan Methodist minister writing in 1882[88] commended the firm's breadth of vision, its readiness to give place to different interpretations as long as these were consistent with reverent enquiry.[89] He implied that this attitude had been the hallmark of the Clarks' publishing from the earliest days. Depending on their viewpoint, he claimed 'some would say that Messrs Clark's publications have been among the most orthodox series of books in the language; others would say that they have introduced a great deal of original and liberal, not to say latitudinarian theology.'[90] Speaking particularly of the F.T.L., he drew attention to the importance of the firm's translation programme. It had, he commented, 'tended much to widen British sympathies, and counteract our insular narrowness';[91] it had played a major role in the development of biblical exegesis;[92] it had introduced to Britain 'what was almost a novelty–the scientific examination of the various types of doctrine in the Scriptures themselves';[93] it had given British theologians a broader point of view from which to consider church history.[94] It had, in short, 'been a very important factor in the formation of opinion and the direction of thought in religious matters'.[95]

It is obvious that this cautiously adventurous policy was continued in the 1880s and 1890s. There is the evidence, for example, of the Clarks' output: the contribution of the Weiss book to the development of theological understanding is one of the themes of Dods' letter. In publishing this work the Clarks were, by their commitment to theological progress, risking damage to their reputation, and any economic consequences of such damage. Other similarly audacious issues appeared, such as *Nature and the Bible* (1886), by a liberal Catholic Professor, Franz H. Reusch.[96] Then there is the evidence of the Clarks' statements of intent; it was said, for example, of the *Monthly Interpreter* (founded 1884) that in its pages, 'open discussion of topics [would] be permitted . . . within reverent and reasonable limitations.'[97] And there is the evidence of the firm's instructions to contributors to the I.T.L. which indicate the progressive nature of the series':[98]

> The library is international, interconfessional, and in the interests of Theology as a science. A catholic spirit should rule in all the work, and the authors should cultivate as far as possible an objective method, presenting a fair and complete statement of the results of theological science and the questions still at issue in these several departments.

The balanced approach to theological speculation taken in the *Dictionary of the Bible* was acknowledged by William Robertson Nicoll, the editor of the *British Weekly*, who commented that Hastings had 'shown great wisdom . . . observing an attitude of reasonable moderation.' This was, he felt, the attitude in which 'the Church must ultimately settle.'

Nicoll recognised the Clarks' boldness in issuing moderately progressive works, and understood from personal experience the problems which such a policy could give rise to. He sensed that John M. Clark was someone who had had 'to face constantly the same problems as I have to face which outsiders do not understand.' He was replying to a letter from Clark following the publication in 1901 of James Moffatt's *Historical New Testament*,[99] which was giving rise to some criticism, and felt 'a kind of impulse' to express himself to a kindred spirit. Moffatt's book was, he acknowledged, progressive in its approach. 'He goes as far as McGiffert.' Nevertheless, there was nothing 'really offensive' in the work. Moffatt wrote 'cautiously and temperately.' He was evidently a good scholar. His motives were genuine–'I am perfectly certain that Moffatt is not working with any desire for notoriety, but simply saying what he believes to be the truth.' In short 'it was inevitable that by & by in our Church someone should get up & claim the same rights of criticism in the New Testament as are granted in the Old, & Moffatt has been the man.' It grieved Nicoll that despite the cautious nature of Moffatt's work, he and the Clarks were facing criticism. And the approach of some of those who stood for a rigid orthodoxy irked him. He described an author, one Macintosh,[100] who would appear to have gone into print in criticism of Moffatt's book, as 'a conceited, bombastic, illiterate ass, & no more fit to deal with those delicate subjects than a ploughman.' (Small wonder his letter was headed 'Private!!') And he observed that such 'defenders of the faith do far more harm than those who attack it.'[101]

But the Clarks were widely viewed as being defenders of the faith of the best kind. Many twentieth-century observers have been quick to praise them for their balanced yet progressive attitude at the end of the nineteenth century. Writing immediately after Sir Thomas Clark's death, for example, at the very beginning of the new century, James Harvey praised the firm not only for giving the Free Church of Scotland 'a foremost place in the theological world of today',[102] but also for making a major contribution to the development of nineteenth-century Scottish theology 'in extending its horizon and shaping its course, and, to some extent, in moulding its character'.[103] Two of those who were most competent to assess the Clarks' achievements, Nicoll and Hastings, might even have regarded Harvey's view as an understatement. Nicoll felt able to refer to the E.R.E. and the other Dictionaries as the 'greatest achievement' of a firm which had always done 'immense service' for the cause of theology,[104] while Hastings commented of Sir Thomas that

> Scotland probably owes him more than can ever be acknowledged. For Scotland has passed through a great theological crisis with extraordinary ease and benefit, and the steady, evangelical, yet never intolerant hand that more than any other guided the theological reading of Scotland those trying years had not a little to do with it.[105]

Guarding against extremism

In all their activities, the Clarks carefully eschewed extremism, guarding against on the one hand narrowness of a denominational or sectarian nature, and on the other, against an irreverent radicalism. This desire for balance even led them to ensure that the scholarship on their lists was drawn from the widest spectrum of denominations.

Although the Clarks were Free Churchmen, and the majority of their British authors belonged to that Church, they nevertheless managed to avoid the extremism of being identified with the Free Church of Scotland so closely as to be regarded as being the mouthpiece of that particular denomination. They consciously pursued a policy of breadth in their publications: thus, the *Monthly Interpreter* was announced as being 'free from sectarian spirit';[106] thus, as we have seen, an objective catholicity was urged upon the contributors to the I.T.L.; and thus, too, it was said of the works in the I.C.C. series that they 'were entirely free from polemical and ecclesiastical bias.'[107]

It is interesting that, despite the preponderance of Free Church titles in the Clark list, the firm seems to have been eager to avoid over-emphasising the scholarship of any other denomination, however orthodox. Thus, when the possibility was being explored of appointing an American co-editor to assist J.H. Moulton in his preparation of a new edition of G.B. Winer's *Grammar of New Testament Greek*,[108] one likely candidate was passed over because he, like Moulton, was a Wesleyan Methodist and, Moulton was told, 'it *might* be wiser to have some one outside your own Denomination.'[109] Another factor which was influencing the Clarks in this was the impending publication of another work from the same denominational fold, W.F. Moulton and A.S. Geden's *Concordance to the Greek Testament*. 'Looking at the matter from a Publisher's point of view I am just afraid that if *both* of these important Works have Wesleyan names *only* (however much we should like it) little jealousies may be stirred up.' And then, anticipating criticism from Moulton over this attitude, the Clarks continued 'You may think it absurd, but in any case you must not be vexed with me for mentioning it.'[110] Rejections of authors or works on denominational grounds were usually made in order to preserve the non-sectarian balance of the list. Sometimes, this policy involved passing over men of indubitable scholarship, as in the example above. Usually those who were passed over were men who, although they might be well-known within their own denominations, did not have the stature, or perhaps the breadth of vision, to command an interdenominational audience. Thus the Clarks felt that two authors whose names Alfred Plummer had put forward as possible contributors to the I.C.C. series 'must [be] set aside simply for the reason that they are not sufficiently known outside their own Church, & a name carrying weight, and confidence, is imperative for this Series.'[111]

The other kind of extremism which the Clarks sought to avoid was an irreverent radicalism. The policy of avoiding 'destructive . . . theology', noted in 1882,[112] was continued until the end of the century.

As we have seen, the Clarks did publish progressive works, such as that by Weiss or, two years later in 1884, the book bought from Scribner despite the fact that the author's views were 'novel', so much so that the Clarks doubted 'how far they would receive acceptance'.[113] What was the nature of that progressive thinking which the firm eschewed?

There are some indications in the letters books. Some are vague, general comments. One work is rejected as being 'too advanced';[114] of another, bought from Scribner, the Clarks commented 'the rationalistic tone has damaged it'.[115] A more substantial indication lies in the fact that the firm were prepared eventually to publish 'McRealsham's' spoof on the higher critics, referred to earlier. John M. Clark clearly had little time for the more radical 'higher criticism': suggesting that some appropriate motto be included on the title page of McRealsham's book, he momentarily put forward for consideration Proverbs 26:5 — 'Answer a fool according to his folly, lest he be wise in his own conceit' — before deciding that 'perhaps that is too strong.'[116] We have also noted the Clarks' extreme disquiet over the work by McGiffert. The way in which this disquiet was to some extent mollified sheds further light on the issues involved from the Clarks' point of view. McGiffert had visited 38 George Street personally in the summer of 1898. As a result of this visit, John M. Clark was satisfied, not only that the author had been misunderstood in Britain — 'He courteously admits that he may himself be in some measure to blame for this by a not sufficiently emphatic statement of his non-agreement with certain other critics'[117] — but also that he gave full assent to the Christian fundamentals. Clark recounted that, during McGiffert's visit, Sir Thomas 'put the question straight to him upon the two most important points in the Gospel Story — viz. the Incarnation & the Resurrection & that he expressed in the fullest manner his hearty & unreserved belief in both.'[118] Given this position, it is understandable that the firm would be extremely doubtful about an author with known Unitarian connections (Crawford H. Toy of Harvard) being invited by the American editor of the I.C.C. to contribute a volume to that series.[119]

It would seem from this that T. & T. Clark were prepared to publish speculative work as long as it did not threaten or undermine what could be called the Christian fundamentals. This is precisely the point made in 1882 by the contributor to *The Publishing House*. Discussing the diversity of interpretative opinion to be found in the F.T.L., he felt able to comment[120] 'Not a page has ever been issued from this press which failed to pay its homage to the majesty of divine revelation, to the person of the Redeemer, and the acknowledged fundamentals of the Christian Faith.' At the end of the century, John M. Clark was aiming still to issue works to which this quotation could be applied, although his definition of some of the terms used in 1882 might have changed.

In steering this course between extremes, the Clarks were not merely responding to a market, or to economic imperatives, but acting out of a deep personal faith. If it was an act of faith to proceed with publication of the Weiss work when it seemed likely to prove damaging economically to the firm, it was not less an act of faith to hesitate over publishing the work (as it may be deduced from Dods' letter that the Clarks had done) in case it proved to be damaging, spiritually, to 'young minds'. It would seem that this element of faith influenced all the firm's publishing decisions. Thus James Harvey[121] claimed that 'No formal religiousness or sectarian prejudice but personal faith and devotion to the truth have influenced the firm in the selection of authors and publications', while it was James Hastings' opinion[122] that the Clarks conducted their business 'as "always in the great Taskmaster's eye" '.

Majoring on academic theology

The central principle which guided the Clarks in their assessment of manuscripts was therefore a desire to promote the cautious development of theology while preserving, through avoiding extremism of any kind, the firm's image as a custodian of orthodoxy. It follows that the titles they published were, in the main, works of academic theology, and that they actively sought out those authors whose scholarly reputation was highest.

Hence, unsolicited manuscripts outwith the Clarks' normal range of subject matter were summarily rejected. For example, the firm wrote to the author of a scientific work which it had been asked to consider that 'a Volume such as you describe is completely out of our line . . . Our publications are strictly confined to Theological & Philosophical works.'[123]

But works within the theological field might also find themselves rejected if they were not considered sufficiently academic to feature in the Clark list. Hence David Kerr of Greenock was told in 1887 regarding a manuscript which he had submitted: 'We fear . . . that it is hardly in our line of publication, being in fact too "popular" for our catalogue, which is mainly filled with German Theological & Philosophical Works'[124] while ten years later, the same view was held, as is evident from a letter to the firm's London advertising agent who was told that Clark books were 'not of a "popular" order'.[125] Another correspondent of the same period was informed: 'Our publications are mainly confined to such works as may be, & in many cases are, used as Theological Textbooks, Commentaries on the Bible, etc.'[126]

It is clear that from time to time that firm had experimented with the issue of more popular works, or at least of popular versions of academic works, and had discovered these to be uneconomic. Hence the firm wrote to an author who had proposed an abridged edition of an academic work 'we know from experience the difficulty of 'popularising' a scholarly work.'[127]

This reluctance to publish works which fell outwith the narrow category of academic theology which they claimed as their own field might be thought to expose the Clarks to the charge of unadventurousness: in fact, the firm did take risks, but they were the risks of going forward into unexplored tracts of the same countryside, rather than the risks of diversifying into completely new territories.

When it came to selecting authors, the Clarks sought to attract the most eminent scholars to their list, those who commanded attention and respect from their peers in all denominations. It helped if a prospective Clark author combined eminence with fluency and clarity of style, how he expressed himself mattering almost as much to the firm as what he said.

It was clearly important to the Clarks to be able to announce that the *Monthly Interpreter* would contain work contributed by 'the ablest scholars of Britain, America and the Continent.'[128] A similar quest for eminence lay behind the selection of the I.T.L. contributors who were assured that they and their fellow-authors had been 'chosen for their eminent ability in the department assigned to them.'[129]

On the other hand, we find individual authors being turned down by the firm because of their lack of experience, their circumscribed reputation, or their deficient or limited scholarship. For instance, C.A. Briggs was advised not to engage a particular writer[130] to contribute to the I.C.C. series on account of the deficiency of his previous performance. 'There is not the slightest doubt that his participation in the 1st vol. of the "Popular Commentary"[131] was detrimental to its success, at least in this Country. We are sure the general opinion here was that his work was unsatisfactory.' And again, Alfred Plummer was advised not to engage another writer for the work on *Hebrews* in the same series: 'While we have great regard for Mr Milligan, we feel that he would scarcely carry sufficient weight for this work'.[132] It helped, of course, if an author combined reasonable scholarship with real popularity. We find the Clarks writing somewhat breathlessly to the Revd James Stalker, whose *Life of Christ* (1879) and Life of *St. Paul* (1884) sold extremely well, to enquire whether there was any likelihood of his quickly completing a work on the *Mind of Christ*, which had been projected for some time. 'We hope you will allow us to have the pleasure of publishing it also for you.'[133]

It would appear that James Moffatt was the epitome of a Clark author. In trying to persuade Scribners to take an edition of his *Historical New Testament* John M. Clark presented the testimonies of others to Moffatt's qualities.[134] It was, for example, Professor A.B. Bruce's opinion that 'Mr Moffatt is a scholar of high-standing, the peer of such men as Professor Denney, & this book will be a great credit to him for scholarship & be a real contribution on the subject . . . Mr Moffatt is one of our coming men, likely to find his way into one of our Chairs.' And James Hastings had commented in the *Expository Times* that the work of translating and re-arranging the books of the New Testament 'had to be done. It had to be done cautiously. It had to be done fearlessly. Mr Moffatt was the man for it. Our readers know how conscientious & how reverent is his scholarship, how deep also is his interest in the Word of God.' This was the kind of scholar whose works it delighted T. & T. Clark to publish, even if, as we have seen, criticism resulted.

In assessing the competence of scholars and the merits of manuscripts the Clarks depended considerably on advice from among others James Hastings, Samuel Driver of Oxford, and Stewart Salmond of Aberdeen.

There is no indication in the letter books as to whether every unsolicited manuscript was read externally; the Clarks were clearly well-versed in theology, and it is most probable that only works in the case of which they felt a second opinion was necessary would have been sent out for reading. Thus, for example, the firm sought J.A. Selbie's advice on a work being considered for publication, F. Konig's *Deutero-Isaiah*:[135] 'we should be glad to have your opinion of it, & whether, in your opinion, it would be likely to attract attention.' Ten days later[136] we find that the firm prepared to go ahead with publication of the work in translation, even though the venture seemed to be economically dubious, because both Selbie and a Professor Skinner, who had also been consulted, believed that 'the proposed book would have to be taken account of by Old Testament Students.'

The firm was always open to suggestions from those whose opinions they trusted as to possible future publications. For example, although sales of the translated first volume of Bishop Hans Martensen's *Christian Ethics* (published by the firm in 1873) had not been high enough to induce the Clarks to proceed with the succeeding volumes, they nevertheless agreed to go ahead with these, having been urged to do so by the Bishop of Gloucester, 'in the hope that the completion of the work may call more attention to it'.[137] In another case, the firm was prepared to publish at great speed an uneconomically small volume, Thomas Adamson's *The Spirit of Power*, the manuscript of which had been forwarded to them, presumably with a recommendation, by James Hastings.[138] However, it must not be thought that the Clarks invariably accepted books which were recommended to the firm. In a letter declining two manuscripts by other authors which Hastings had sent to him, John M. Clark commented 'It is a mistake to publish too many books.'[139]

Occasionally, too, the Clarks would make the acceptance of a work conditional upon 'editorial support' being obtained in the form of an introduction or preface from some well-known theologian or churchman. Thus, for example, in showing cautious interest in a proposed translation of a work by August Nebe, the firm commented to the would-be translator: 'it would require some authoritative introduction such as you hint at from the Bishop of Bath and Wells.'[140] Similarly, when the widow of Professor James Candlish asked the Clarks to publish a posthumous collection of her husband's sermons, she was told that this would only be considered a viable proposition 'if Dr Denney could be persuaded to contribute a preface.'[141] Posthumous publications were unlikely to succeed, no matter how eminent the author had been in his lifetime. The Clarks commented tellingly that in several cases they had found that 'a living dog [was] better than a dead lion.'[142]

After all the letters had been written, all the consultations made, all the advice carefully evaluated, it was in that upstairs room overlooking George Street that the final decisions had to be made: the economic viability of a book estimated, its potential contribution to the advance of truth assessed.

Maintaining the overall profitability of the firm

While individual titles of dubious economic potential were issued as we will see, if T. & T. Clark was to continue in existence, its overall profitability had to be maintained. In the letter to Charles Scribner II in which John M. Clark complained of the apparent heterodoxy of McGiffert's *History of Christianity in the Apostolic Age*,[143] he made the following cryptic comment: 'It is certain that even from the lower point of success, this sort of thing will do great damage to the whole Series.' One possible reading of this sentence would suggest that, for Clark, there were two levels of success in publishing: a higher, the advancement of theological science, and a lower, the making of a profit. Such an interpretation would certainly be consistent with the letter of February 1900 from Clark to Salmond, in which he seems to indicate not only that he virtually had a settled policy of publishing some uneconomic works — and not only from time to time, but 'repeatedly', which implies greater frequency — but also that the Clarks were 'superior' to financial considerations. A man holding such an attitude would clearly speak of profit as being 'the lower point of success'.

This sounds like a recipe for economic suicide, but the mere fact that the firm continued to survive and expand is an indication that while the Clarks set their sights on the higher point of success, they in no way neglected the lower. Such decisions as were made to publish works of doubtful profitability must have been reached only after very careful consideration. 'Caution is necessary',[144] wrote John M. Clark, and, indeed, there are many examples in the letter books of works being rejected on economic grounds.

How are we to understand the thinking which lay behind the Clarks' decisions when there seemed to be a conflict between aiming at the higher and the lower points of success? How was it that some economically unviable books were published, while others were rejected?

The first point to be made is that John M. Clark indubitably knew his market. He himself claimed 'we know exactly the class who buy our books.'[145] And knowing his market, he knew the type of books which it could absorb. Thus what the *Publishers' Circular* was able to claim of his father was true also of him. 'He understood the tastes and appreciated the wants of his countrymen, who, almost without exception, are sticklers for theology.'[146] But Clark's vision of the market for the books he published was not limited to Scotland: he was consciously publishing for an international audience. Now this, clearly, is the way every successful publisher works: aiming at a particular audience, and setting up an effective distribution system to ensure that the product gets from warehouse to marketplace. If this process is effectively costed and efficiently operated, it should result in profitability. And indeed it was a fact that the Clarks 'found it to their own advantage' to produce evangelical works for the evangelical market.[147] We have already noted that the founder of the firm was said to have been reasonably wealthy at the time of his retirement.

But the second point to be made is that John M. Clark did not allow the taste of the audience to squeeze his publishing programme into its mould. He sought to lead, rather than to follow. In this he was perpetuating the policy established by his father. John M. Clark had published the work by Weiss because he believed in it, even although it was likely to prove a loss-maker both directly, through selling poorly itself, and indirectly, through undermining the Clarks' reputation for orthodoxy. It would appear then, that the firm was always prepared to publish a work which the principals considered would make an important contribution to theology. In certain cases, they realised that such works would never be profitable; in most cases where there was a risk, they hoped that, if the work's value were recognised, and if it had been efficiently costed, it would break even through time.

Thus, while the firm, in meeting the requirements of its market, sought to achieve success on both the higher and the lower levels, if there was a conflict between the two levels over a work of importance and merit, the Clarks were always prepared to sacrifice the lower level of success in setting their sights on the higher.

That this was the case is borne out by the letter books, where letters of rejection pleading the exigencies of the economic climate rub shoulders with enthusiastic letters of acceptance. We can contrast the case of certain books which were rejected on specified economic grounds with the case of others which were accepted despite the fact that similar economic objections applied.

The nature of the work

However worthy their subject matter, some manuscripts were rejected because the firm felt it would be economically unwise to publish them as similar works were already on the market, either on the Clarks' own list, or on the list of another publisher. Thus, for instance, Thomas Clark wrote to a correspondent who had sought a commission to translate a new work into English: 'With regard to [Rudolf] Koegel, from what you say of it, I would have liked very well to have asked you to undertake it, but we have so many commentaries on Romans . . .'[148] Thus, too, another author was told 'Although there can be no doubt of the ability of your work, I fear it is also not sufficiently popular in its form to supersede Hodge's and Cunningham's which have already a firm hold here.'[149] Such decisions are completely understandable. It is equally understandable that, on economic as well as on other grounds, the firm would decline to publish a work which specifically criticised another title on the Clark list. (The work in question was a critique by Professor W.P. Dickson of Glasgow, an old friend of Sir Thomas's, of the work by Arthur McGiffert alluded to above.[150]) But these decisions should be contrasted with, for example, the decision to proceed with a work which duplicated others in the Clark list, apparently not on the grounds of the book's high quality (which would have made the decision more understandable) but simply by reason of the close relationship the author had with the firm. The work in question was yet another commentary on Romans, by Friedrich Godet, which, wrote Thomas Clark, 'I was unwilling to undertake having Philippi, but, from personal friendship to Prof. Godet, I could not well help it.'[151]

Manuscripts were frequently rejected because, although the subject matter was relevant to the Clark list, and the treatment at a suitable level of scholarly eminence, nevertheless the format in which the material was presented made the work unlikely to be commercially viable. Just as surely as the Clarks could expect good sales of most (though by no means all) of the commentaries they published, so they could anticipate that volumes of collected sermons, articles, or lectures would, in general, sell poorly. With regard to books of sermons, the firm frequently declined such collections claiming that the time when books of sermons could be guaranteed to recoup their production costs had passed.[152] One particular work was rejected in these terms: 'It is very good, but we fear it is too much in the form of sermons to have much prospect of success.'[153] With regard to collections of articles and lectures, the following specific example is typical of the Clarks' general response:

> Without exception I think, we find that collected articles on such topics which have already either appeared in Reviews, or have formed the subject of Lectures or addresses, *never* pay the cost of production . . . we have published so much of recent years for which we have not been & probably never shall be, recouped.[154]

This is not to say that T. & T. Clark never published volumes of collected lectures or sermons. Such material did indeed feature in the firm's lists, but many of these volumes were published on commission. Thus, a commission arrangement was offered to two of the three writers mentioned above, one of whom accepted it.[155] The Clarks' commission publishing and its economics will be considered in depth in Chapter 9. It constituted a very small part of their total publishing programme, but enabled them to publish works which they believed had some merit at minimal risk to themselves.

The work's physical format

Clearly, the length of a manuscript had economic implications. Books were frequently rejected as being too short to be economically viable. Thus one translator was told that 'our experience of small books on abstruse subjects has not been very happy',[156] while an author was given the following bleak comment on the prospects of small books generally:

> We have looked over your MS . . . and, though it is very interesting, we do not see that it has any chance of a remunerative sale. The price would be small, and we very seldom can make a small book remunerative where there is not a large sale, as the cost of binding and advertising is out of all proportion.'[157]

And yet in other cases, we find the firm prepared to put small books into print even when there was no guarantee of a large sale. Thus, in writing to the author of a work recommended to the firm by James Hastings, while the Clarks outlined the difficulties — small books did not pay; the printers were busy; the booksellers' shops were 'quite full to overflowing' so that they 'rather shun[ned] "Theology"' (it was a fortnight before Christmas, and the author had wanted the work published 'to catch the New Year if possible') – nevertheless they accepted the manuscript for publication and sent it to the printers on the same day.[158] It would seem likely that in this, and in similar cases, sights were being set on the higher point of success.

Similarly, we find works being rejected on account of their inordinate length. Thus, for example, when a translation was proposed of a six-volume work by August Nebe, the Clarks commented that, without 'grave consideration' they would be inclined to 'shrink from it',[159] while they declined another proposed translation[160] being of the opinion that the volume was 'much too large to prove acceptable to English readers, and would require to be published at a price which would be practically prohibitive.'

And yet the firm undertook many works of great length and complexity. In many cases – such as the Moulton/Geden *Concordance to the Greek New Testament* or the Hastings *Dictionary of the Bible* – these works were fulfilling obvious needs, and therefore were likely to succeed if properly costed, but this in no way detracts from the very real economic risks involved in publishing them. John M. Clark commented before publication of the *Concordance*: 'it is undoubtedly an alarming undertaking for me.'[161] In issuing works such as these, the Clarks would seem to have been consistently living dangerously, to the extent that we may well conclude that, once again, the higher point of success was being aimed at.

The firm's commitment to other works

A reason frequently given for rejecting manuscripts was that the Clark programme for the season in question was already complete, and that if it were expanded by the acceptance of new works, the firm's energies would be so widely spread that they would be unable to do full justice to *any* of the new titles on the list. Thus one writer was told 'at present our hands are so full that we are unwilling to undertake more at least in the meantime.'[162] And there are at least two clear statements of the reasoning which lay behind such unwillingness. James Hastings was told 'It is a mistake to publish too many books. We are wiser to limit the list to such as we can give our whole attention to',[163] while Frank Ballard was informed

> If we undertake more than we can give our entire attention to, all books must suffer, & that is obviously unfair to Authors . . . As we usually take the entire risk & cost of production ourselves, owing to the class of books we publish, it is impossible for us – certainly it would be unwise of us – to accept all that are offered to us.[164]

Although the reason usually given by the Clarks for their reluctance to add to an already full list was that any additions to the publication programme would over-tax the resources of the firm's editorial, production, and distribution departments, we can probably assume – an assumption borne out by the letter to Ballard quoted above – that at the heart of their reluctance to expand the programme was concern over the additional financial commitment which the acceptance of further works would entail. In the letter to Hastings, there is perhaps also an indication that the Clarks were afraid of overloading the market.

And yet, almost side by side with letters rejecting manuscripts on the presumably genuine grounds of pressure of work, are others, accepting equally unsolicited manuscripts which the Clarks must have considered had spiritual or economic potential, or both. Once again, we see the firm, despite its heavy commitment of financial and manpower resources, being prepared to add to this commitment in the case of works the principals believed in.

The economic climate

A further reason occasionally given by the firm for the non-acceptance of manuscripts was that the economic climate generally was unfavourable, or the book trade specifically in a depressed state. If this was the case in 1885 – 'Everything is in such a depressed state that we are resting on our oars as much as possible'[165] – it was equally the case at the end of the century, particularly during the Boer War which seems to have had a deleterious effect on the book trade: 'Business is terribly depressed this year . . .'[166] 'Business is *very* quiet at present, & no one seems to be reading Theology. When the War is over – as I hope it will be soon – we trust things may improve.'[167]

And yet, even in these times of economic uncertainty, the firm's publishing programme continued to develop. Admittedly, some of the major works issued in the difficult years of 1900 and 1901 – two volumes of the *Dictionary of the Bible*, for example, and additions to the two *International* series – had been planned long before the trade was affected by the economic difficulties arising from the Boer War. But these years also saw the issue of several other important works, and the launch of the *World's Epoch Makers* series. This could well be seen as further evidence of John M. Clark's preparedness to live dangerously for the sake of what he was publishing, the same resoluteness which later brought the *Encyclopaedia of Religion and Ethics* to a conclusion despite the intervention of the Great War, whose economic consequences were more far-reaching than those of the Boer War.

Thus the Clarks in pursuing their objectives seem always to have been ready to sacrifice the lower level of success in setting their sights on the higher, provided the overall liquidity of the firm was not threatened.

In Part II we will examine in detail how the principles which we have outlined in this chapter were brought to bear by the Clarks on each of the main categories of theological publishing which they undertook. But before moving on this, it might be helpful to glance at T. & T. Clark's relationships with other religious book publishers. To this we will turn in Chapter 3. But in concluding this discussion of the firm's aims and motives, it is perhaps appropriate to quote Thomas the Younger's expression of the high ideal which motivated his publishing, together with his hopes, which were realised, that John Maurice would come to share fully in this sense of mission. Writing on 14 November 1877 to 'My Dearest Boy' (John was then studying in Leipzig), he commented[168]

I hope that my son may be spared to carry on the business in a bright and intelligent manner, and that he will endeavour always to have the fear of God before his eyes, and will remember that a publisher has a great responsibility, such as even few men in very responsible positions have, and that in his selection of publications he may do much for the advancement of God's cause in the world. . . .

Chapter 3
Relationships with other religious publishers

Where a small group of crusading publishers is engaged in issuing works within a limited subject field, tensions will almost certainly arise between, on the one hand, the desire to compete for authors and markets and, on the other, the desire to co-operate in furthering the common cause. We should not be surprised, therefore, to find such tensions evident in the Clarks' relationships with other British publishers of similar material.[169]

The Clarks' greatest competition obviously came from those houses which specialised in the issue of material aimed at a market similar or indeed identical to that at which the Clark list was targeted. Where a work was manifestly unsuited to that list, the firm was always glad to suggest alternative publishers which the author might approach more successfully. Thus, for example, Miss E. Wright of Musselburgh[170] was told that while the Clarks could not 'do justice' to the translation of a work by Otto Funke which she was offering them she might find the Religious Tract Society, Nelson, Gemmell, Hodder and Stoughton or Elliot Stock willing to undertake publication of the book. Or again, in rejecting a work as being 'too "popular" for our catalogue'[171] the firm suggested that it should be re-submitted either to Elliot or Macniven and Wallace of Edinburgh. In these cases, the Clarks would appear to have been gladly co-operating with fellow-publishers by putting suitable material in their way.[172] But with the exception of Hodder and Stoughton, none of these publishers were operating within their specific corner of the religious publishing field. Competition with houses working within that area was much greater, in terms of attracting authors to the list, of planning new titles and serials, and of marketing the products.

Attracting authors

As we have seen earlier, T. & T. Clark sought to publish works of the most eminent scholarship within their field: this high standard inevitably limited the number of potential contributors to the Clark list, and equally inevitably brought the firm into competition with houses publishing similar material as they attempted to attract and then to retain the services of these contributors.

Although theology publishing was, as we shall see, by no means highly profitable as a whole, the scholar who established a sufficiently eminent reputation found himself in a sellers' market. Thus, for example, the Clarks found it necessary to increase the rate of payment to certain contributors to the two *International* series.[173] The sum initially agreed had been £200 for each 500–page volume, but the Clarks were aware that some contributors found this figure rather small, especially in view of the fact that Longman were known to be paying £100 for each 200–page volume in their *Epochs of Church History* series. In the light of this, the firm considered it 'wise & just' to make additional payments to certain authors. Quite apart from the fact that the Clarks felt that 'the success of their books fully [justified] it', it was their opinion that these payments were necessary 'if such authors [were] to be retained as contributors to future Vols', and if potential contributors to the Series were not to be dissuaded from co-operating. This is a clear example of competition working to the financial benefit of the author.

From time to time, the Clarks had problems over attempts made by other publishers to issue works which, for one reason or another, the firm felt belonged on the Clark list. Hence, for example, when Hodder and Stoughton announced in the *Publishers' Circular* that they were about to issue a new translation, incorporating the author's latest corrections, of Franz Delitzsch's commentary on *Psalms*, the first edition of which had been published by the Clarks in three volumes in around 1871, the London publishers received an indignant letter from Edinburgh:[174]

> This is discourteous, and so different from the usual courtesy of trade, that we can hardly believe you are aware of our having published these works . . . you announce our books for which we paid Prof. Delitzsch; and you even have actually secured the services of translators whom we first sought out and employed.

In the end, the Clarks had to accept that the situation had arisen owing to misunderstandings and communication failures.[175] It would appear that Delitzsch had written to the firm in 1885 informing them that it had come to his notice that a certain committee in England intended to issue a new translation of the commentary, but that such an enterprise could not have his approval as he considered himself morally bound to stand by the Clark firm. At this point, Delitzsch, who had had a lasting and warm relationship with the Clarks, clearly hoped that the firm would negotiate with him and with the committee with a view to issuing the new edition under the Edinburgh imprint. But the Clarks made no response; Delitzsch assumed that their silence indicated lack of interest, and agreed to co-operate with the committee when they arranged to issue the work through Hodder and Stoughton. It is not clear how culpable Delitzsch was in all this — there was obviously a certain want of frankness on his side — but the whole episode is interesting for what it reveals of the Clarks' jealous custodianship of their rights, and indeed the need for such vigilance in the face of competition. In the event, the firm had to conclude 'it cannot now be helped',[176] but future work by Delitzsch appeared under their imprint. It may well have been that the Clarks' vigorous reaction in the case of *Psalms* made Delitzsch think twice about any future proposals from other houses; in any case an author might with some cause conclude that a publisher who vigorously defended his rights in a work would equally vigorously promote it in the market place.[177]

Problems could also arise where the Clarks felt that they had just claim to publish a lecture series in volume form because they had issued previous collections of lectures given under the same auspices. This happened, for example, in the case of the 1879 Cunningham Lecturers: again the culprit was Hodder and Stoughton.[178] The Clarks had published each series of Cunningham Lectures — a Free Church institution — except for the first, and considered it less than reasonable that Hodder should have intervened: 'had the position been reversed I would not on any consideration have gone to any Congregational Lecturer and made an offer for one of a series of which you published the others.'[179]

Although the Clarks suffered in this way at the hands of other publishers, there would seem to be no evidence that they themselves attempted to attract authors to their list in any way which would have contravened their high standards of courtesy. On the contrary, they would seem to have been remarkably scrupulous. Hence, for example, the letter to Hodder and Stoughton about lecture series quoted above continues

> A few months ago a personal friend for whom I had published several books delivered the Baird Lectures, all of which had formerly been published by Blackwood. I declined to do it till Blackwood had been communicated with and had expressed their willingness that I should publish it.[180]

And there would seem to have been few valid complaints from other publishers against the Clarks on these grounds. When W.R. Nicoll suggested that the firm had been attempting to persuade an *Expositor* contributor, a certain Dr Cox (very possibly Dr Samuel Cox, the previous editor of the *Expositor*) to write for the *Monthly Interpreter* by offering any terms Cox chose to name, the Clarks countered by saying that any approach to Cox had been made by the editor of the *Monthly Interpreter* on his own initiative, adding that they had 'no communication whatever with Dr Cox.'[181] And when C.A. Briggs, the American editor of the I.T.L. complained that the Clark firm was diverting the energies of *Library* contributors into producing copy for the *Dictionary of the Bible*, the Clarks countered with a firm and detailed refutation of this charge.[182]

The Clarks' actions, therefore, would seem to have been in accord with their stated view that frenzied competition to sign up other publishers' authors was beneficial to no-one — 'I think this system of beating up for books is not healthy either for authors or publishers'[183] — and that to act creditably was as important as, or more important than seizing opportunities to add to the profits: 'We might adopt reprisals [to Hodder's issue of the new edition of Delitzsch's *Psalms*] which would probably not be profitable to either party, but we should think any such course beneath us, and we trust you may yet see your way to abandon what cannot redound to your *credit*, and very likely not to your profit.'[184]

Issuing similar works

If there was a measure of competition between publishers over the attracting of authors to their lists, there was most certainly competition when it came to producing works which would fill gaps on the theological library shelves. Very often, more than one publisher would recognise that there was a need for, or a demand for, a work of a particular nature or on a particular subject: the publisher who could secure the best author and publish first would normally have the greatest success. The Clarks did not escape this kind of competition. For example, when Professor James Cooper of Glasgow suggested that the Clarks should issue a very specialist work in the *Ante-Nicene Library* — a translation of *Testamentum Domini Nostri Jesu Christi* — the firm suggested that the projected translation should be announced in the literary journals to alert other publishers to the Clarks' plans and thus, presumably, prevent them from launching their own translations which could hardly have proved to be profitable.[185] Very often also, where a publisher began issuing a manifestly successful series or type of publication, his competitors would quickly begin publishing similar material. Thus, from the beginning, the Clarks were said to have had 'imitators and rivals'.[186]

Here, too, among their chief competitors was the firm of Hodder and Stoughton. This partnership had been formed in 1868, out of the previous firm of Jackson, Walford and Hodder, official publishers to the Congregational Union.[187] Over the next decades, the new company built up a strong religious list, by no means limiting itself to Congregationalist authors. T. & T. Clark was not the only firm to feel the pressure of Hodder's competition. Dr Norman L. Walker, the editor of the *Free Church Monthly*, commented, for example, that the late Thomas Nelson had been anxious over 'the going away of our higher class books to Hodder and Stoughton', (when he used 'our' Walker was speaking on behalf of the Free Church) and had wanted to do something to 'stop the flow'.[188] In Walker's opinion, the issue of books of this nature had contributed greatly to the success of Hodder and Stoughton,[189] at the expense, it is implied, of Nelson. It is clear that if Hodder posed a threat to Nelson, in whose programme theology played only a small part, T. & T. Clark, with its major emphasis on theology publishing, might well have felt itself even more threatened by the London firm. And despite the fact that the Clarks could comment that 'we have always looked upon Mr Hodder as a personal friend'[190] there were occasional grounds for friction between the two firms.

The Clarks took justifiable exception to Hodder's *Foreign Biblical Library*: their criticism was based not only on the fact that Hodder and Stoughton were re-issuing works already on the Clark list, but also on the fact that the series title selected by the London firm bore such a striking resemblance to that of the Clarks' long-standing Series. They were also much aggrieved by the attitude of the Hodder editor, William Robertson Nicoll, to whom they reacted: 'We regret that you should have written to us in the manner you have done. You will allow us to say that it was unworthy of any one, much less a clergyman.'[191]

Besides discussion the *Foreign Biblical Library*, the letter of Nicoll's to which the Clarks were replying also touched on another area of friction between the two companies. Hodder's monthly periodical the *Expositor* had been founded in 1875 under the editorship of Dr Samuel Cox of Nottingham. He remained in the editorial chair until the end of 1884, when, because certain of his personal views were causing disquiet among the readership, he was replaced by W.R. Nicoll, who began a long-lasting and successful editorship with the January 1885 number.[192] This was a mere two months after the Clarks had begun publishing the short-lived *Monthly Interpreter* at the suggestion of J.S. Exell, its editor, and Nicoll appears to have felt that the *Monthly Interpreter* had been specifically launched to compete with the *Expositor* in general, and in particular with the *Expositor* as he shaped it during the early months of his editorship. In this case, it was the Clarks who were being accused of unfair competition, but their response was that the charge was preposterous. The idea for the *Monthly Interpreter* had originated with Exell, not with them (a somewhat weak point, one feels), and, moreover, it had been launched two months before Nicoll began to edit the *Expositor*.

> Besides, the two Magazines were not on the same lines, and you surely do not seriously mean to say that we are always to be excluded from the publication of a Magazine simply because yours happens to be in existence.[193]

It is difficult to understand why Nicoll made this charge in October 1886, by which time the last number of the *Monthly Interpreter* would have appeared. And, in any case, within a few years, Hastings' *Expository Times* was to prove that there was room in the market place for two similar (and similarly-titled!) periodicals, provided they were both of a sufficiently high quality.

But there was competition over particular works with other firms besides Hodder. For example, it became evident in the mid–1890s that a new Bible Dictionary was required, one which would incorporate the results of recent biblical scholarship. A revision of Dr William Smith's out-of-date work was abandoned after the first volume had been issued,[194] and thereafter two publishers attempted independently to fill the gap. One was T. & T. Clark, who published the first volume of James Hastings' *Dictionary of the Bible* in 1898; the other was A. & C. Black, whose *Encyclopaedia Biblica*, projected by William Robertson Smith, and edited by T.K. Cheyne and J. Sutherland Black, began to appear the following year. It is clear that these works, both of which represented major investment on the part of their publishers, would have been competing for an identical market. Both were initially intended to run to four volumes (in 1899, the Clarks complained to the editor of the *Daily News*, presumably in response to a review, that while Black's volumes were actually smaller than Clark's, they in fact appeared larger because the rival publisher had used thicker paper, and had numbered the columns rather than the pages to give the illusion of greater length).[195] Both were intended to represent modern scholarship although the Clarks did not see the aims of the two works as being identical: in 1896 they had written to Scribner:

As we are informed Black's one is not to include Biblical Theology at all, & the articles are to be written by a very limited number of scholars while our Dictionary will cover the whole range of Bible knowledge, including Biblical Theology.[196]

In the event, the reviewers and the bookbuyers preferred Hastings' work, at least in part, because although progressive, it did not share what was generally seen as the speculative radicalism of its rival. The *Dictionary of the Bible* enjoyed a long period in print both in the UK and in the United States, where Scribners agreed to distribute it in preference to the *Encyclopaedia Biblica*, even although they handled Black's other major reference work, the *Encyclopaedia Britannica*, in the USA.[197] There is no record of any correspondence with A. & C. Black over this issue. It would seem likely that each house discovered about the other's plans only when so many agreements with authors had been entered into that, for either, abandonment of their project would have been too costly to contemplate.

At one point, the Clarks would even seem to have been faced with the threat of competition from the Free Church itself. The Editorial Committee of the Church had received the impression that in issuing the *Bible Class Primer* series (for which the firm had been responsible since 1884), they had been profiteering at the expense of the Church: the Committee's response to this perception was to discuss making arrangements to publish a new series of primers through another publisher. The Clarks' initial response was pointed – 'we have our own opinion as to the expediency of any Church launching out into commercial undertakings'[198] – and in the end they agreed to publish the new primers themselves, on commission, the terms being that the Committee would meet all the literary expenses, and allow the publishers a 15% royalty on sales. The 1899 report of the Publication and Records Committee of the Free Church noted that

arrangements [had] been completed for the issue of a new series of Primers for the use of Bible-classes which [would] henceforth be published on behalf of the Church, and under the direction of her Committees.[199]

T. & T. Clark, therefore, seems to have faced considerable competition from other houses over specific works and series it issued; in turn, it received the occasional criticism over allegedly unfair competitive practices; but while it may have had to share the market place with imitators and rivals, there is no evidence whatsoever that the Clarks themselves ever followed a deliberate policy of imitation or destructive rivalry.

Competition in the market place

Works from rival religious publishing houses, once issued, would compete with one another in the market place,[200] and this competition would express itself in the areas of advertising, both to the Trade and to the potential audience, of representation and distribution, and of the attracting of support for a given work from influential figures within the various denominations. The Clarks' marketing operation will be considered in more detail in Part III: it is sufficient to note here that the major strategy adopted by the firm in order to compete in the market place was to ensure the excellence of their product.

There is the occasional hint that efforts were made to persuade professors and lecturers to adopt a particular text as a course book either within a given theological college, or within the educational programme of a denomination as a whole; obviously official endorsement from such a body could materially influence the success of a work. For example, we find the firm writing to the Revd Alexander Whyte[201] regretting that

> in the 'Welfare of Youth' Competition Syllabus 1887–88 . . . under Division I Professor Lindsay's 'St Luke's Gospel' in our Bible Class Handbook Series is not even mentioned, – Blackie's 4*d.* edition alone being prescribed as the Text Book. Do you not think this is rather unfair? . . .
>
> It certainly makes a material difference on the sales. I understand that one firm in town stocked 1000 copies of the small edition, whereas two dozen copies of our edition was considered quite sufficient because, as they said, it was '*not to be used as the Text book*'. Pray excuse me writing thus frankly on the matter, but I am anxious to push the Handbooks as much as possible and it requires a large circulation to make them pay at all.

There is the occasional hint also, that from time to time the Clarks were willing to increase their sales by selling direct at a discount to a specific client group, such as the students of a particular theological college, or the ministers of a given denomination. Although the main aim in this would appear to have been the altruistic one of assisting the somewhat impecunious ministers and students in question, there is no doubt that had such a policy been consistently followed, it would have boosted Clark's sales at the expense of its competitors' at no greater cost to the firm than selling through retail outlets. But, aware of the danger of antagonising the book trade, the Clarks made selling direct at discount the exception rather than the rule. This issue, too, will be considered in depth in Part III.

In the market place, therefore, as in the selecting of authors, and in the planning of works and series, the Clarks would not in general seem to have followed an aggressively competitive policy. In 1879, Hodder and Stoughton were told that, in the Clarks' view, mutual consideration by competing publishers would 'sweeten competition when it is unfortunately necessary.'[202]

They clearly held that the necessity of competition should never be seen as invalidating or obstructing the benefits of co-operation and harmonious relations. This position harmonises with their apparent commitment to the higher level of success, and there is no reason to doubt that the Clarks were voicing their genuine sentiments when they stated 'we . . . have ever been most scrupulous in avoiding any injury to our co-publishers.'[203]

Part II

The nineteenth century output of T. & T. Clark can be broken down into a number of distinct categories. There were works issued in series, excluding the F.T.L. (a category including 143 individual titles in the financial year 1896–97); there were translations, including works in the F.T.L. (310 titles); there were titles which had originated in the United States or which were produced in collaboration with American publishers (68 titles); there were periodicals (2 titles); standard reference works (1 title) and miscellaneous theological works (119 titles), plus 42 legal titles.

Publishing in each one of these categories presented the Clarks with different opportunities and challenges. Part II examines each of these categories in turn, with the exception of the legal titles, charting the development of each within the history of the firm, outlining the principals' commitment to each where possible, and assessing the profitability of each over the four financial years (beginning 1895–96) for which data are available.[1]

Chapter 4
Series of completely British origin, and translations of Patristic works

We have already noted in Chapter 1 the crucial role which the issue of series played in the development of the firm. Its reputation, established by the *Biblical Cabinet*, was reinforced by the *Foreign Theological Library*, and until the end of the century and beyond, the majority of the firm's publications were issued as part of one series or another.[2]

It is easy to see why the concept of issuing works in series appealed to the Clarks. Except in very unusual circumstances, a small work could only be published profitably as part of a series, where the cost of advertising could be divided among several works. The cost of independently advertising a small, cheap work which would yield a very modest sum per copy sold was just as much as that for independently advertising a large, expensive work which, yielding a considerably greater sum per copy sold would, it was hoped, quickly recover the advertising expenditure.

But series publishing was important in the case of larger works too, for the series, especially if it were issued on a subscription basis, would build up and maintain customer loyalty to the Clark imprint. The confirmed book-buyer has an instinctive desire to own all the volumes of a series which he has begun to collect, and will continue to acquire them as they appear as long as his economic circumstances remain constant, and as long as the quality of the succeeding volumes remains, in general, as high as it was in the case of the earlier ones. That this principle was very much to the fore in the Clarks' thinking, is demonstrated, for example, by their rejection of a manuscript on the grounds that 'An independent Commentary on Daniel (i.e. one not included in a Series) would, we are sure, have little chance of success at present. We fear the result would be disappointing.'[3] No doubt in making this comment the Clarks were motivated in part by a desire to sweeten a rejection letter somewhat, but the clear implication nevertheless is that a work which would on its own be unviable could be made to succeed as part of a series of repute. The problem arose, of course, when the reputation of a series was so badly undermined by one or more 'bad apples' — works of poor scholarship, or of a contentious nature — that sales of the series as a whole were affected. The Clarks feared that McGiffert's book, discussed earlier, would have this stultifying effect on customers' perceptions of the value of the I.T.L. In October 1897, the firm wrote to Scribners that 'this sort of thing will do great damage to the whole Series'.[4] Seven months later they were able to report a fulfilment of their prophecy: 'We regret to say that we find the sale of the Series is fast diminishing. Dr McGiffert's Vol. has done a world of harm to it, & is causing the whole Series to be looked upon with distrust.'[5] However, this problem proved to be of a temporary nature, and the reputation of the I.T.L. survived. Indeed, it seems to have been the case that almost all the series issued by the firm were held in high esteem, an esteem which genuinely, if unquantifiably, affected the sales of each of the works of which these series were comprised.

This Chapter deals with those series which were of completely British origin, or which featured translations of Patristic and other earlier writings. It seems appropriate that the *Foreign Theological Library*, and the series of commentaries by H.A.W. Meyer should be discussed in the section on translations; while consideration of the two *International* series, the *History of the Christian Church*, the *Eras of Church History* series, and the series of commentaries written or edited by J.P. Lange (which, although of European origin initially, were purchased by the Clarks from Scribners) belongs properly in the Chapter dealing with the firm's dealings and relationships with transatlantic publishers.

Works of John Calvin

In 1859, T. & T. Clark bought over the stock and copyrights of the works published by the Calvin Translation Society, which had been founded in Edinburgh in 1843. These works were kept in print at least until the turn of the century, all but five of the fifty-one volumes being still announced as available in the 1901 catalogue. We do not have figures for the performance of individual titles in this series between 1895 and 1899. However, a modest profit was shown by the Series as a whole over these years. This amounted to £1 2*s*. 4*d*. in 1895–96, rose to £1 11*s*. 7*d*. in the following year, before falling to £1 9*s*. 2*d*. in 1897–98 and 17*s*. 6*d*. in 1898–99. The Series may well have been successful in its day, but we are unable to reach any firm conclusions about its profitability on the basis of this limited evidence.

The Ante-Nicene Library

'From Presbyterian Scotland, of all places in the world the last from whence we should expect such a movement, we learn that an English translation of the Apostolic and other early Christian Fathers is in progress.'[6] Thus the *Bookseller* announced the imminent issue of the first volumes in the Clarks' *Ante-Nicene Library*, which aimed to present a 'collection of all the works of the Fathers of the Christian Church prior to the Council of Nicaea.'[7]

It was planned to issue the Series on subscription at the rate of four volumes per annum, under the editorship of the Revd Alexander Roberts, and James

Donaldson. Initially, it was intended that the Library would extend to sixteen volumes. In the event 'by the miscalculation of the Editors [accompanied, one supposes, by the supreme indulgence of the publishers], it actually turned out to be 24 volumes',[8] and an additional volume was later published.

The nineteenth century had seen a revival of interest in the writings of the early Church Fathers, spearheaded by the Tractarian movement. E.B. Pusey, one of the leading Tractarians, had, in 1836, initiated *The Oxford Library of Fathers* (the first volume was published in 1838); the last of the forty-eight volumes in this series did not appear until after Pusey's death (he lived until 1882[9]). The Clark Series was seen as 'supplementing' that of Pusey;[10] the *Bookseller*'s surprise in announcing the *Ante-Nicene Library* arose from the fact that T. & T. Clark, a Presbyterian, evangelical publishing house, should thus choose to associate itself with, or to follow in the footsteps of, an ultra High-Anglican movement. It was no doubt a similar sense of surprise which prompted a later writer in the *Bookseller* to describe the *Library* as 'Perhaps the most remarkable outcome of Patristic Theology'.[11] The fact that the Clarks were publishing for a Presbyterian and Nonconformist audience did to some extent restrict the scope of the Series: 'It was necessary, as much as possible, to exclude not only the Roman novelties, but the Episcopal element also; hence the greater limitation, as compared with [the Oxford series] "to the works of the Fathers of the Church prior to the Council of Nicaea." (AD 325)'[12] However, it could also be said of the Clark Series 'we have never heard a word against the faithfulness of their translations; apparently no attempt was made to tone down any of the Fathers, although some of their writings must have been found extremely unpalatable to many of the subscribers.'[13]

It would seem clear therefore, that not only were the Clarks taking a considerable financial risk in launching this Series, but also that they proceeded despite a full awareness of this fact. A letter written in 1884 commented of the *Ante-Nicene Library* 'we were the *first* to publish such a collected series, and we did so at a risk that no other Publisher has been found to undertake, at the outlay of many thousands of pounds and of very great thought and labour.'[14] There is no doubt that the market was limited, and indeed the same letter goes on to point out that penetration of the American market had been considered essential to the success of the project: 'undoubtedly we reckoned on a large sale in the United States: indeed without this the matter would have been hopeless.'[15] On the other hand, it was argued[16] that the fact that the Series bore a Presbyterian imprint made it acceptable to the widest possible audience within the United Kingdom. Episcopalians would have been interested in the works it contained as a matter of course, while Presbyterians and Independents would accept from T. & T. Clark what they would have been most unlikely to accept from Anglican publishers such as Rivington. Be that as may, however, the risk seems to have been considerable.

Regrettably, the only figures available for the years over which the Series was being issued are the trade and retail prices. We have no record of the Clarks' outlay (apart from the vague 'many thousands of pounds' mentioned above), and as the sales figures have not been preserved, we have no means of calculating the firm's income. The *Stock and Sales Book* from the late 1890s[17] lists the expenses and income against each title on an annual basis only, no running balance being kept. Thus we have no means of being certain that the total outlay on the Series had been recouped by the end of the century. The twenty-four volumes were available at a subscription price of £6 6*s*. 0*d*., averaging 5*s*. 3*d*. per volume (the trade price being £5 14*s*. 0*d*., averaging 4*s*. 9*d*. per volume). Individual volumes were available at the non-subscription retail price of 10*s*. 6*d*., to which the Clarks' normal trade discount applied.[18] These prices remained in force for the rest of the century,[19] with the additional offer of a selection of any four volumes at the subscription rate of 5*s*. 3*d*. per volume.

More detailed figures are available for the four financial years beginning 1895–96.[20] In that year, four volumes in the Series were reprinted, and it is possible to estimate the unit cost of these reprints.

Table 1

Unit cost of volumes in the Ante-Nicene Library reprinted 1895–96				
Volume	Tertullian Vol. I	Origen Vol. I	Tertullian Vol. III	Arnobius
Length of run	160	162	160	162
Printing	£10 11*s*. 6*d*.	£10 0*s*. 3*d*.	£11 0*s*. 6*d*.	£ 8 12*s*. 5*d*.
Paper	£ 2 15*s*. 5*d*.	£ 2 12*s*. 9*d*.	£ 3 0*s*. 0*d*.	£ 2 4*s*. 4*d*.
Binding*	£ 5 0*s*. 0*d*.	£ 5 1*s*. 2*d*.	£ 5 0*s*. 0*d*.	£ 5 1*s*. 2*d*.
Total cost	£18 6*s*. 11*d*.	£17 14*s*. 2*d*.	£19 0*s*. 6*d*.	£15 17*s*. 11*d*.
Unit cost	2*s*. 3½*d*.	2*s*. 2*d*.	2*s*. 4*d*.	1*s*. 11½*d*.

* The figures for binding costs are notional in that they assume that the whole edition was bound. In fact, only 270 volumes in the Series were bound during the year in question, and not all of these may have been copies of the reprinted works.

The average unit cost of reprinting these works was therefore 2*s*. 2¼*d*. (The work by Arnobius was cheaper because it was significantly shorter.) The Clarks' income from sales of these volumes was as follows: on works sold through retailers to subscriber — 4*s*. 9*d*., with no additional discount on this trade price; on individual volumes sold to the trade — 7*s*. 11*d*., on which a further 2½% discount would apply if the bookseller's account was settled promptly, reducing the firm's income to 7*s*. 9*d*.; on individual volumes sold to a wholesaler — 6*s*. 9*d*. Although it is not clear from the accounts, there is the possibility that a proportion of the subscription sales would be made direct to the customer at the full subscription price of 5*s*. 3*d*. per volume. Given a mean unit cost per reprinted volume of 2*s*. 2¼*d*., the firm's ultimate return on its investment in these reprints ignoring generalised overheads would have been:

on subscription through trade	— 2*s*. 6¾*d*.	= 117% return
on subscription direct	— 3*s*. 0¾*d*.	= 140% return
non-subscription through trade	— 5*s*. 6¾*d*.	= 254.28% return
non-subscription through wholesaler	— 4*s*. 6¾*d*.	= 208.57% return[21]

On the face of it, these figures seem reasonable. But a different picture emerges when we consider the annual sales of the Series. In 1895–96, for example, around 108 volumes were sold at subscription price (this figure would include both those sold direct, and those sold through the trade), and forty-six

were sold at non-subscription price. Thus only 154 volumes or an average of 6.4 per volume in the Series were sold. This was, in fact, a particularly poor year. Sales for the three succeeding financial years were as follows:
Table 2

Ante-Nicene library: Sales 1896–1899				
Year	Subscription Sales	Non-subscription Sales	Total Sales	Average Sales per Volume in the Series
1896–97	226	49	275	11.45
1897–98	194	63	257	10.7
1898–99	143	32	175	7.29

It is obvious that some titles would sell better than others, and that it would be those which were most likely to require reprinting. But it is clear nonetheless even on the basis of the best of the above figures, that the reprinting represented a long-term commitment by T. & T. Clark to the Series, that it would be some years before the firm saw even 160 copies sold, and that the *annual* rate of return on investment was unspectacular.

Over the financial year 1895–96, expenditure on the Series exceeded income by £25 17*s*. 4*d*. Over the next two financial years, income from the Series exceeded expenditure on it, by £51 4*s*. 3*d*. in 1896–97, and by £29 16*s*. 1*d*. in 1897–98. This reflects the fact both that sales were higher and that less expenditure on reprinting was required in the course of those years: the firm was gaining a small return on a great investment.

There would seem to be clear evidence here that the Clarks were proceeding with the Series because of its theological value, and almost in spite of financial considerations. That the *Ante-Nicene Library* was highly praised would no doubt have provided some consolation, but praise could not be guaranteed to ensure profitability.

The works of Saint Augustine

Closely related to the *Ante-Nicene Library* was the series, announced in 1871, which was to contain certain of the works of St Augustine. Here too, the Clarks were complementing the work of the Oxford translators; although the *Confessions* appear in both series, the Edinburgh firm consciously avoided the *Sermons* and *Commentaries on the Psalms* which had already been issued from Oxford, and concentrated for the most part on works 'of first-rate importance' which had not yet appeared in English translation.[22] It was intended that the Series, which was to appear under the editorship of Marcus Dods, would run to sixteen volumes. In the event only fifteen appeared, as Robert Rainy was unable to find time to complete a *Life* of St Augustine which was to have formed the final volume.[23]

Once again, the Series was issued on subscription, and once again also, the only figures available for the years during which it was appearing are the trade and retail prices. It was announced that the sixteen volumes would be available at a subscription price of £4 4*s*. 0*d*., averaging 5*s*. 3*d*. per volume (the trade price being £3 16*s*. 0*d*. averaging 4*s*. 9*d*. per volume). Individual volumes were available at the non-subscription retail price of 10*s*. 6*d*., to which the Clarks' normal trade discount applied.[24] In the event, the subscription price for the fifteen volumes was fixed at £3 19*s*. 0*d*.[25]

More detailed figures are available for the four financial years beginning 1895–96.[26] In 1896–97, two volumes in the Series were reprinted, and it is possible to estimate the unit cost of these reprints.

Table 3

Unit cost of volumes in the St Augustine Series reprinted 1896–97		
Volume	City of God Vol. I	City of God Vol. II
Length of run	270	270
Printing Paper Binding*	£12 11*s*. 1*d*. £ 4 18*s*. 2*d*. £ 7 17*s*. 6*d*.	£13 1*s*. 0*d*. £ 5 0*s*. 10*d*. £ 7 17*s*. 6*d*.
Total cost	£25 6*s*. 9*d*.	£25 19*s*. 4*d*.
Unit cost	1*s*. 10½*d*.	1*s*. 11*d*.
* The figures for binding costs are notional, in that they assume that the whole edition was bound. In fact, only 210 volumes in the Series were bound during the year in question, and not all of these may have been copies of the reprinted works.		

Taking the average unit cost of reprinting these works as being 1*s*. 11*d*., the Clarks' ultimate return on its investment in these reprints, ignoring generalised overheads, can be estimated. The firm's income on the sale of volumes in the Series was the same as on the sale of volumes in the *Ante-Nicene Library*. Hence the return on investment would have been:

on subscription through trade — 2*s*. 10*d*. = 148%
on subscription direct — 3*s*. 4*d*. = 174%
non-subscription through trade — 5*s*. 10*d*. = 304%
non-subscription through wholesaler — 4*s*. 10*d*. = 252%[27]

On the face of it, these figures appear extremely good. But once again, a less satisfactory picture emerges when we consider the annual sales of the series as laid out in the following Table.

Table 4

St Augustine Series: Sales 1895–1899				
Year	Subscription sales	Non-subscription sales	Total	Average sales per volume in the Series
1895–96	77	57	134	8.37
1896–97	46	30	76	4.75
1897–98	106	40	146	9.12
1898–99	45	14	59	3.68

It is obvious that some titles would sell better than others, and that it would be those which were most likely to require reprinting. Of all the works in the Series, the two *City of God* volumes sold better than the others when it came to the non-subscription market (subscribers, at least in the early days of the

Series, had to take it as a whole). But it is clear nonetheless, even on the basis of the best of the above figures, that as in the case of the *Ante-Nicene Library* the reprinting represented a long-term commitment by T. & T. Clark to the Series: it would be some years before the firm saw 270 copies sold, and the *annual* rate of return would be correspondingly reduced.

Over three of the financial years for which we have figures, income from the Series exceeded expenditure on it: by £28 19*s*. 0*d*. in 1895–96, by £29 16*s*. 1*d*. in 1897–98, and by £6 5*s*. 6*d*. in 1898–99. Expenditure exceeded income by £26 1*s*. 3*d*. in 1896–97, the year in which the *City of God* reprint was undertaken. Where no reprints were required, the Series could be relied upon to produce a modest profit, but once again we suspect that the Clarks were gaining a small return on a great investment. It may well have been, of course, that the Series was very much more profitable in its early days.

Bible Class Handbooks

The first volumes in the Clarks' series of *Bible Class Handbooks* were issued around 1879, under the editorship of Alexander Whyte and Marcus Dods. The Series included commentaries on biblical books, and works on doctrine and on the history of the Church. Its prospects seemed favourable from the first: thus Thomas Clark wrote to Whyte on 29 September 1879 'I think the series has done fairly well, and I have no doubt the sale will be largely increased as it proceeds.'[28] In 1879, the firm claimed that the first edition of each *Handbook* ran to 4,000 copies,[29] but by 1895–96 this had dropped, at least in the case of a work on *Ephesians* by J.S. Candlish, to 2,160 copies;[30] and this was a title which was likely to sell well.

Although the Series does not appear to have been in any way officially connected with the Free Church of Scotland, nevertheless the bulk of sales may well have been made to members of that Church and, as we have already noted in Chapter 3, the attitude taken towards a title by the Welfare of Youth Committee of the Free Church could either ensure or imperil its success.[31]

However, sales of the *Handbooks* were not confined to Scotland. Several were translated into Welsh,[32] and at least two titles, James Stalker's *Life of Christ* and *Life of St. Paul*, were given the accolade, a dubious one from the Clarks' point of view, of being 'pirated' on the other side of the Atlantic by the American firm of Fleming H. Revell.[33] There was very little that the Edinburgh firm could do about Revell's action, as they noted with some justified indignation:

> We understand that when Dr. Stalker was in New York, almost two years ago, he called at Revell's & got him to agree to pay the Author a small royalty, but the British Publishers have never been recognised, and as ... it is utterly impossible for us to undersell Revell ... we must just let the thing go. It is hardest of all for us.[34]

At least there was the consolation that Stalker's works continued to be the best-selling titles in the Series, and sold well also in the more expensive 3*s*. 6*d*. editions.[35]

Detailed financial data for the Series for the four financial years beginning 1895–96 are summarised in Table 5.

Table 5

Bible Class Handbooks: Analysis of Profitability				
	1895–96	1896–97	1897–98	1898–99
No. of titles in Series at the start of the year	40	41	43	44
No. requiring reprints in course of the year	7[2]	12	6	16
No. of new titles issued during year	1	2	1	0
Surplus				
Total showing profit	38	24	40	39
Total profit	£380 14*s.* 4*d.*[3]	£182 11*s.* 2*d.*	£449 8*s.* 5*d.*	£276 17*s.* 5½*d.*
Average profit	£10.02	£7.6	£11.24	£7.09
Deficit				
Total showing deficit	3[4]	19	4	5
Total deficit	£8 3*s.* 5*d.*	£118 17*s.* 0*d.*	£65 9*s.* 11*d.*	£13 4*s.* 1½*d.*
Average deficit	£2.72	£6.25	£16.37	£2.64
Net profit	£372 10*s.* 11*d.*	£63 14*s.* 2*d.*	£383 18*s.* 6*d.*	£263 13*s.* 4*d.*
Copies sold[1]				
Total – all titles	15,710[5]	14,205	14,360	12,396
Average	383[5]	330	326	281
Total – reprints/ new titles	10,175 (8 titles)	9,464 (14 titles)	5,035 (7 titles)	8,295 (16 titles)
Average	1,271	676	719	518
Total – works *not* reprinted	5,535 (33 titles)	4,741 (27 titles)	9,325 (37 titles)	4,101 (28 titles)
Average	168	176	252	146
% return on investment				
On reprints				
Example				
Size of printing	3,240[6]	540	540	1,080
% return on edition	90.04%	91.15%	104.35%	137.11%
No. of copies sold in the year	2,029	175	144	480
No. of years required to sell printing	1.6	3.08	3.75	2.29
% return per annum	56.27%	29.59%	27.82%	59.87%
On new books				
Example				
Size of printing	2,160[7]	2,160	1,080[8]	No new
% return on edition	34.19%	55.48%	−14.66%	titles
No. of copies sold in the year	1,687	1,087	358	issued
No. of years required to sell printing	1.28	1.98	3.01	1898–99
% return per annum	26.71%	28.02%	–	

Table 5 (*continued*)

Notes

(1) Excluding the '25th copy' which was given as a bonus to booksellers who ordered two dozen copies.

(2) When the Series was launched, Thomas Clark's opinion was that it was the commentaries which were likely to do best.[36] Significantly, perhaps, four of the seven titles which required reprinting in 1895–96 were commentaries.

(3) Two titles out of the 38, however – the works by Stalker – made between them a profit of £136 13*s*. 7*d*. When this is subtracted from the total profit realised by profit-making items in the Series, £244 0*s*. 9*d*. remains, an average of £6.78 having therefore been realised by the remaining 36 titles. Stalker's works made major contributions to the profits in the following years also.

(4) One of these three, Dods' book on Haggai, was reprinted during the year, and just failed to recover the cost of the reprint; another was the new title which did not break even within the financial year in which it was issued; the third was a work on the *Irish Presbyterian Church*: no copies of this were sold during the year, and credit was given on nineteen returns from booksellers. In two out of the three cases, therefore, the deficit was temporary, and did not reflect on the quality or marketability of the product.

(5) Once again, the average is distorted by Stalker's high-selling works, of which 6,729 copies were distributed. The remaining thirty-nine works in the Series sold 8,981 copies between them, an average of 230 copies per title. Only six titles sold fewer than ninety copies in the course of the year.

(6) The work in question is Stalker's *Life of St Paul*. As an example, the calculations on which the figures appearing in the Table are based appear below. It should be noted that the figures exclude any income from advertisements in the work which the Clarks might have received. It was apparently the firm's custom to sell advertising space in this series.[37] It should further be noted that the aim of the calculation is to arrive at the total cost of the edition: not all of this expenditure would be incurred at the time of reprinting. The editors' and author's royalties (Stalker received 1½*d*. per copy = 8.33% of the retail price), and the binding costs (the Clarks had copies bound as they were required) would be met as and when the edition sold out. It should be noted finally that advertising costs are excluded from the calculation. 7*s*. 2*d*. was set against the work for advertising over the year in question.

Stalker: *Life of St Paul* (Retail Price – 1*s*. 6*d*.)

Outlay		*Income*	
(Reprinting: 3,240 copies)		Sales of 3,240 copies at 1*s*. 0*d*.	
Printing	£ 7 19*s*. 6*d*.	per copy	£162 0*s*. 0*d*.
Paper	£14 5*s*. 4*d*.		
Binding	£28 7*s*. 0*d*.		
Maps	£ 2 5*s*. 0*d*.		
Royalty			
Editor	£12 3*s*. 0*d*.		
Author	£20 5*s*. 0*d*.		
	£85 4*s*. 10*d*.		
Profit	£76 15*s*. 2*d*.		
	£162 0*s*. 0*d*.		£162 0*s*. 0*d*.

Unit cost = 6.31*d*. % return on investment = $\frac{\text{£76 15s. 2d.}}{\text{£85 4s. 10d.}} \times 100 = 90.04\%$

Table 5 (*continued*)

(7) The work in question is *Ephesians* by J.S. Candlish. As an example, the calculations on which the figures appearing in the Table are based are given below. The points made in Note 6 apply in this case also, and in the case of the other titles whose performance is analysed in the Table.

Candlish: *Ephesians* (Retail Price — 1*s*. 6*d*.)

Outlay		*Income*	
(Printing 2,160 copies)		Sales of 2,160 copies at 1*s*. 0*d*. per copy	£108 0*s*. 0*d*.
Printing (casework and presswork)	£32 14*s*. 10*d*.		
Paper	£ 8 11*s*. 9*d*.		
Binding	£18 18*s*. 0*d*.		
Royalty			
Editor (estimate)	£ 6 7*s*. 0*d*.		
Author	£ 7 15*s*. 5*d*.		
Stereotyping	£ 5 13*s*. 1*d*.		
Back-stamp	9*s*. 6*d*.		
	£80 9*s*. 7*d*.		
Profit	£27 10*s*. 5*d*.		
	£108 0*s*. 0*d*.		£108 0*s*. 0*d*.

Unit cost = 8.94*d*. % return on investment $= \dfrac{\text{£27 10}s.\ 5d.}{\text{£80 9}s.\ 7d.} \times 100 = 34.19\%$

The work was issued in October 1895. Between then and June 1896, 1,266 copies had been sold, giving a rate of 1,687 copies per annum if the momentum were sustained.

(8) This work, J.P. Lilley's *Principles of Protestantism* was not costed to break even in its first edition. It had a retail price of 2*s*., and sold to the trade at 1*s*. 4*d*.

It will be clear that T. & T. Clark had no grounds for complaint over the profitability of the *Bible Class Handbook* Series. The majority of the *Handbooks* had a retail price of 1*s*. 6*d*., although some sold at 2*s*. 6*d*., and a few at higher prices.In the four financial years, a good proportion of the titles yielded a surplus, and in most cases where there was a deficit this was only temporary, as a reprint or a new title approached its breakeven point. As noted, the title by Lilley was not costed to break even in its first printing. It says much for the Clarks' commitment to the Series that they were prepared to face a loss on the first impression of a work. The average annual profit per title varied considerably, as did the percentage return figure for individual works. But although there were slow sellers in the Series, and the figure for average annual sales was rather low, nevertheless most of the titles which were reprinted were selling at a steady rate, and, if they continued to do so, would produce an encouraging annual return on investment. New titles were added to the Series virtually every year, and all titles were still in print in 1900. Even slow-selling works were, when they eventually sold out, reprinted by the firm, which thus showed itself to be committed to the maintenance of the Series as a whole. The *Handbooks* had, as a series, shown themselves to be both valuable to the Churches and profitable to the Clarks.

Bible Class Primers

In 1884 the Edinburgh bookselling firm of Macniven and Wallace, which had been founded in 1878 and had diversified into publishing the following year virtually abandoned the publishing side of the business. (See Appendix A for an outline history of Macniven and Wallace.) By 1884, the firm had some successful titles on their list, and attempts were made to sell these to other publishers. The Clarks, it is clear, expressed interest in the *Household Library of Exposition*, and the *Bible Class Primers*, two theological series published by Macniven and Wallace. They offered £300 for copyright, stock and plates of works in the first series, on condition that the series editor, William Robertson Nicoll, abandoned his right to a royalty of 1*d*. per copy sold. The Clarks were clearly aware that this was less than Macniven and Wallace had hoped for, but could not see the way to offer more because firstly, some of the works in the Series had been in print for a considerable time and were coming to the end of their marketable lives; secondly, one work at least would definitely never be reprinted, a fact which rendered the plates valueless; and thirdly, heavy royalties were payable to the authors of volumes in the Series.[38] In the event, Macniven and Wallace obviously declined the offer, and the *Household Library of Exposition* was taken over by Hodder and Stoughton in London. It is possible that they were more sanguine about the prospects of the Series than were the Clarks. But it is very likely that they took over the *Library* at the instigation of Nicoll, who began what was to be a life-long connection with them in the same year, 1884, and with his influence being brought to bear on their behalf, they may not have had to pay any more than the Clarks offered.[39] In contrast, the Clarks' offer for the *Bible Class Primer* series was clearly accepted, but there would appear to be no record of the terms involved. However the Clarks wrote to Macniven and Wallace on 24 March 1884, acknowledging receipt of 22,173 copies of the works in the Series.[40] It was fitting that the *Primers* should join the *Handbooks* on the Clark list. Both series were begun in 1879, and although it is not clear whether the similarity between their titles was as a result of competition or co-operation between the two firms, the second possibility seems more likely: the series were aimed at different markets, the *Primers* being briefer and more elementary than the *Handbooks*.

As in the case of the *Handbooks*, there would seem to have been no direct official link between the *Primers* and the Free Church of Scotland, although the editor of the Series was S.D.F. Salmond, Principal of the Free Church College in Aberdeen. The *Primers* were aimed at young people within the Churches in Scotland, however, and sales of a title could be greatly affected by the endorsement or lack of endorsement of the Youth Committees of the various Churches. The firm always was quick to point out that while the Free Church Welfare of Youth Scheme selected textbooks from the *Primer* series, and that this inevitably affected sales, the fruits of Welfare of Youth recommendations accounted for 'nothing like the *entire* sales'.[41] But such Committees were a useful scapegoat when sales flagged. On one occasion, Salmond was told that the 'real cause' of declining sales of *Primers* was to be found in 'the small support' which the Committees were giving. 'They certainly might give us more encouragement.'[42] It is perhaps ironic that, as we saw earlier, the Free Church had formed the opinion by 1898 that the Clarks were profiteering at its expense through the sale of the *Primers*, and wanted to come to an arrangement with another publisher for the issue, on its behalf, of a new series of primers.[43]

But sales of the *Primers* were by no means limited to Scotland. Charles Spurgeon's favourable notices of them in the *Sword and Trowel* would no doubt have influenced the market south of the border;[44] a work on the Reformation was adopted as a textbook by the Presbyterian Church of Canada[45] and 500 copies of the one-volume edition of F.H. Stead's *The Kingdom of God* were sold to America in 1895–96.[46]

Accounts for the Series are to be found in the *Stock and Sales Book*[47] but not as much detail is given as in the case of the *Handbooks*. Once again figures have survived only for the four financial years beginning 1895–96. These figures are summarised in the following Table.

Table 6

Bible Class Primers: Analysis of Profitability				
	1895–96	1896–97	1897–98	1898–99
No. of volumes in Series at the start of the year	30[2]	32	35	36
No. requiring reprints in course of the year	11[3]	7[9]	8	10[10]
No. of new titles issued during year	2[4]	3	1	1
Net profit	£148 7*s.* 4¾*d.*[5]	£208 8*s.* 4*d.*	£220 17*s.* 9*d.*	£223 5*s.* 8*d.*
Copies sold[1]	22,141[6]	29,112	23,119	24,089
% return on investment				
On reprints				
Example 1				
Size of printing	4,370[7]	3,200	2,160	3,240
% return	171.08%	161.37%	161.36%	145.6%
Example 2				
Size of printing	1,080	3,240	1,080	2,160
% return	156.76%	172.90%	123.34%	145.28%
On new books				
Example				
Size of printing	3,200[8]	4,320	5,400	3,240
% return	8.88%	60.94%	43.04%	−3.06%

Notes

(1) Excluding the '25th copy' which was given as a bonus to booksellers who ordered two dozen copies. A breakdown for individual titles is not available.

(2) Twenty-eight of these volumes were available at 6*d.* in papers, and 8*d.* in cloth. (Two works in the Series, each consisting of three 6*d.* volumes, were also available in one-volume format.) The Series was completed by two 'extra volumes', selling at 1*s.* 0*d.* each.

Table 6 (*continued*)

(3) Of these eleven, one work was reprinted twice. Hence there were twelve reprintings in all. In five cases, the print run was 1,080; in three, 2,160; in a further three it was 3,240; and 4,320 copies were reprinted of one title.

(4) In both cases, the print run was 3,200. Initially, the first printing of the *Primers* had run to 5,000 copies,[48] and it rose to this figure again in 1897–98.

(5) This net profit is calculated from the accounts, which may be summarised as follows:

Outlay		*Income*		
Printing	£95 10*s.* 0*d.*	Sales in paper covers		
Paper	£54 4*s.* 3*d.*	(excluding 768 '25th copies'):		
Cover paper	£12 6*s.* 9*d.*	1,542 doz. at 4*s.* 6*d.* per doz.		
Binding	£54 12*s.* 11*d.*		= £346 19*s.* 0 *d.*	
Advertising	£ 8 3*s.* 8*d.*	Less 7½%*	£26 1*s.* 11¼*d.*	
Proportion of lists	£15 0*s.* 0*d.*		£320 17*s.* 0¾*d.*	£320 17*s.* 0¾*d.*
Payments to authors/ editors	£30 0*s.* 0*d.*	Sales in cloth		
Samples	£2 8*s.* 2*d.*	(excluding 100 '25th copies'):		
Stereotyping	£7 11*s.* 4*d.*	207 doz. at 5*s.* 11*d.* per doz.		
Maps	£6 7*s.* 6*d.*		= £61 4*s.* 9*d.*	
Miscellaneous	£0 3*s.* 2*d.*	Less 7½%*	£4 11*s.* 9*d.*	
	£286 7*s.* 9*d.*		£56 13*s.* 0*d.*	£56 13*s.* 0*d.*
Profit	£148 7*s.* 4¾*d.*			
		Sales of more expensive vols.		£54 4*s.* 1 *d.*
	£434 15*s.* 1¾*d.*	Miscellaneous		£ 3 1*s.* 0 *d.*
				£434 15*s.* 1¾*d.*

* This further discount was obviously universally offered to retailers.

(6) This averages out at 692 copies per title, and is strikingly at variance with the Clarks' claim to Scribners that about 30,000 *Primers* were sold annually in Britain.[49] Only in 1896–97 did sales approach this figure.

(7) The work in question is C.A. Scott's *The Making of Israel*. As an example, the calculations on which the figures appearing in the Table are based appear below. It should be noted that not all the expenditure would be incurred at the time of reprinting, and that advertising costs, and the costs of '25th copies' have been excluded from the calculation. The binding costs is an estimate, as is the figure for the proportion of copies which would sell in cloth, as opposed to paper binding.

Scott: *The Making of Israel*

Outlay		*Income*		
(Reprinting 4,320 copies)				
Printing	£5 17*s.* 0*d.*	Sales in paper covers		
Printing paper		3,802 = 317 doz. @ 4*s.* 6*d.* per doz.		
covers	£2 10*s.* 0*d.*		= £71 6*s.* 6*d.*	
Paper	£7 0*s.* 1*d.*	−7½%	£5 7*s.* 0*d.*	
Binding	£9 0*s.* 0*d.*		£65 19*s.* 6*d.*	£65 19*s.* 6*d.*
(average ½*d.* per volume*)				
Author†	£4 6*s.* 6*d.*	Sales in cloth covers		
	£28 13*s.* 7*d.*	518 = 43 doz. @ 5*s.* 11*d.* per doz.		
			= £12 14*s.* 5*d.*	
Profit	£49 1*s.* 4*d.*	−7½%	£0 19*s.* 0*d.*	
			£11 15*s.* 5*d.*	£11 15*s.* 0*d.*
	£77 14*s.* 11*d.*			£77 14*s.* 11*d.*

Unit cost 1.59*d.* % return on investment $= \dfrac{\pounds 49\ 1s.\ 4d.}{\pounds 28\ 13s.\ 7d.} \times 100 = 171.08\%$

* This figure is an estimate

† Authors were paid £10 for the first edition of a work upon publication, and received £1 for each 1,000 copies sold thereafter. The editor received £5, payable upon publication.[50]

(8) The work in question is *Christian Character*, by T.B. Kilpatrick. As an example, the calculations on which the figures appearing in the Table are based appear below. The points made in Note 7 apply here also.

Table 6 (*continued*)

Kilpatrick: *Christian Character*

Outlay			*Income*	
(Reprinting 3,200 copies)				
Printing (including origination costs and cost of printing covers)	£21 11*s*. 2*d*.	Sales in paper covers 2,816 = 235 doz. @ 4*s*. 6*d*. per doz.	= £52 17*s*. 6*d*.	
		−7½%	£3 19*s*. 3*d*.	
Paper	£6 5*s*. 0*d*.		£48 18*s*. 3*d*.	£48 18*s*. 3*d*.
Binding (average ½*d*. per volume)	£6 13*s*. 2*d*.			
Royalty		Sales in cloth covers 384 = 32 doz. @ 5*s*. 11*d*. per doz.		
Author	£10 0*s*. 0*d*.		= £9 9*s*. 3*d*.	
Editor	£5 0*s*. 0*d*.	−7½%	£0 14*s*. 1*d*.	
Stereotyping*	£3 10*s*. 0*d*.		£ 8 15*s*. 2*d*.	£8 15*s*. 2*d*.
	£52 19*s*. 4*d*.			
Profit	£4 14*s*. 1*d*.			
	£57 13*s*. 5*d*.			£57 13*s*. 5*d*.

Unit cost 3.97*d*. % return on investment $= \frac{\text{£4 14}s.\ 1d.}{\text{£52 19}s.\ 4d.} \times 100 = 8.88\%$

* This is an estimate; figures are not given for the cost of stereotyping individual works.

(9) One of these required reprinting three times in the course of the year. (Gloag's *Life of St John*)

(10) Two of these works, *The Reformation* by T. Witherow and MacIntyre's *Elijah and Elisha* required to be reprinted twice in the course of the year.

It would seem that the Series of *Primers* was highly successful financially. The percentage return on reprints was in all cases excellent. If a large enough edition were printed, new titles too gave a good return. The return was marginal or non-existent in the case of those titles whose first printing it was felt prudent to limit to 3,200. Thus one work would have shown a loss of 3.06%. (Although it would have broken even had not the cost of stereos for the second printing been charged against the first.) We do not have figures for the annual sales of each individual title, and so we are unable to estimate the annual return on a title-by-title basis. But the frequency with which many of the works required reprinting — sometimes more than once in the course of a year — would indicate a very high annual rate of return. Over 1896–97 sales of the Series as a whole amounted to 71.92% of the stock in hand at the start of the year (40,478): at that rate the stock would turn over every seventeen months. The annual return on investment from the Series as a whole was also good, although these figures should be treated with some caution as the return was yielded by the Series as a whole and not only by works which had required investment in the course of the year. The *Primers* produced the following return:

1895–96 — 51.85%
1896–97 — 63.41%
1897–98 — 99.35%
1898–99 — 93.3%

The fact that returns of this magnitude were produced in years in which the firm had to lay out capital on reprints of around a quarter of the titles in the Series annually provides further evidence of the success of the *Primers*.

New titles were added to the Series virtually every year, and all the titles were still in print in 1900.

World's Epoch Makers

The forthcoming launch of the *World's Epoch Makers* series was announced by the Clarks to Scribner in a letter dated 13 May 1899.[51] The Edinburgh firm noted that 'many well-known Literary Men, in whose opinion and judgement we have every confidence, are agreed that there is a wide field for such a series, & they pronounce it excellently planned.' Oliphant Smeaton (who was already known as the editor of the *Famous Scots* series, which Oliphant, Anderson and Ferrier published), was to be in editorial control of the new project which was to feature biographical studies of key figures in world history, the major emphasis being on religious thinkers. Hence, for example, while Smeaton himself contributed a volume on *The Medici and the Italian Renaissance*, the majority of the early volumes in the Series dealt with individuals such as Cranmer, Buddha, Wesley, Luther, Anselm, Mohammed and Origen.

In each case, Smeaton clearly sought to enlist the services of the most capable writer available. This is made clear, for example, in the letter to Scribner cited above, the Clarks claiming that while the authors might not all be well-known in the US, they had nevertheless all been carefully chosen. In the few instances where the W.E.M. volume would be the first book by an author Smeaton was confident that excellent work would be produced.[52] It is made clear also by the Clarks' willingness to pay generously in order to secure the services of the most able contributors. Discussing with Smeaton the case of two scholars who had declined to contribute to the series, John M. Clark commented 'in the case of such good men I think we should perhaps stretch a point, & (if the terms have to do with their refusal) offer them say a 12½% royalty.'[53]

By June 1900, three volumes in the *World's Epoch Makers* series had been issued, and arrangements made with authors for a total of almost thirty,[54] while eleven volumes are mentioned in T. & T. Clark's 1902 *Colonial Catalogue*, which had appeared by mid-November 1901.

Regrettably, because no figures have survived from that period, we are unable to assess the profitability of the Series. Despite Smeaton's apparently judicious editorial methods, it clearly was not an unalloyed critical success — the volumes on Buddha and Wesley were severely criticised[55] and this criticism may have influenced the sales of the other titles, in the short term at least.

In some respects, the *World's Epoch Makers* series may be seen as a new departure for the Clarks, for it was aimed at a wider audience than that which they were attempting to serve with their main-line output. The appearance in the Series of works on the non-Christian religions is indicative of a growing contemporary interest in the study of comparative religion. One of the greatest manifestations of that interest, Hastings' *Encyclopaedia of Religion and Ethics* was also to appear on the Clark list.

Lecture Series

In the nineteenth century, there were, in Scotland as in England, several endowed lecturerships which provided for the organisation of regular series of lectures on various theological topics. In many instances, these series of lectures found their way into print.[56] Where a given publisher was in the habit of regularly issuing the lectures delivered under the auspices of a particular Trust some of the benefits of series publishing could be expected to come into play.

As we have seen, the Clarks were dubious about the economic potential of publishing lectures, but the fruits of these lecturerships generally made a much greater contribution to knowledge than did the sets of college lecture notes which they were frequently offered by academics, and just as frequently declined. Some collections of lectures from these endowed series did appear under the Clark imprint, therefore, But most of this lecture-publishing was done on a one-off basis, and not as part of an on-going commitment.

For instance, the Clarks issued the 1879 Baird Lectures, the 1890 Gifford Lectures, the 1892–93 Hulsean Lectures, the 1893–94 Kidd Lectures, and the 1897 and 1900 series of Kerr Lectures. The 1897 Kerr Lectures, David W. Forrests's *The Christ of History and Experience*, sold well: the first printing would have yielded a return on investment of 57.44%, and a second printing of 540 copies was required. Although there are no detailed figures for the other sets of lectures, it would seem that, in general, they sold very slowly, and that the Forrest work was an isolated exception to this rule.

The only lecturership with which the Clarks were connected with any degree of consistency was that bearing the name of the former New College Principal, William Cunningham.[57]

In 1879, Thomas Clark claimed that his firm had published all the sets of Cunningham Lectures with the exception of the first,[58] but thereafter the Clarks were less consistently involved. The reason for this sporadic involvement is to be found in a letter to W.G. Blaikie, dated 28 February 1888. Although they were prepared to publish Blaikie's Lectures, the Clarks pointed out: 'Unfortunately our experience of the "Cunningham Lectures" has been by no means encouraging, many of them not having yet paid — & we fear never likely to pay — the cost of production.'[59]

This somewhat pessimistic view is borne out by the only full set of figures we have for a series of Cunningham Lectures. The work in question is Somerville's *St Paul's Conception of Christ* which was published in 1897–98. The Clarks risked printing an edition of 1,080 copies which, once the whole edition had been bound, would have cost £122 2*s*. 8*d*. (no payment to the author appears to have been involved). The firm's average income per copy was 5*s*. 6*d*., the nominal retail price being 9*s*. 0*d*. Ignoring 100 presentation and '25th' copies, the edition would yield £269 10*s*. 0*d*. gross, the net profit therefore being £147

7*s*. 4*d*., and the return on investment 120.66%. The unit cost was 2*s*. 3*d*. These figures look encouraging, but in fact the work was only very modestly successful. Only 415 copies were sold in the financial year of issue, yielding a net profit of £8 0*s*. 1*d*. (only 540 had been bound: the outlay was therefore only £107 9*s*. 11*d*.). The work yielded a net profit of £10 5*s*. 7*d*. in 1898–99. At least however, it had covered its production costs, which would appear to have been more than some of the earlier volumes of Cunningham Lectures had done.

The Clarks clearly discovered that the benefits of series publishing did not apply in the case of these sets of Lectures, in which volumes dealing with discrete and highly-technical theological matters were published at lengthy intervals. When such works were issued, the principals were clearly setting their sights on the higher level of success.

But there is no doubt that these benefits — among them the self-promoting qualities of the Series, and the reductions in advertising costs which could be achieved by advertising them as a whole, made the *Primer* and *Handbook* series profitable ventures. It may well have been the case, although it is impossible to reach firm conclusions, that earlier series such as the *Ante-Nicene Library* were equally profitable in the years immediately following their issue, although in the 1890s the return they produced was certainly meagre to an extreme.

Chapter 5
Translations

The Clarks' Commitment to translations

The theological side of T. & T. Clark's publishing business owed its very existence to the founder's desire to make available in English important works by contemporary Continental theologians. From the earliest years of the firm's history until the 1890s, translations constituted a significant proportion of the Clarks' output. The majority of these appeared either in the early *Biblical Cabinet* series, or in the *Foreign Theological Library* which succeeded it.

In this area also, the Clarks aimed at achieving the higher point of success. Although some works were rejected because they were considered likely to be unprofitable — a new book by Weiss, for example,[60] or a major work by H.F.B. Jellinghaus[61] — where the firm was persuaded of a book's merit, publication of the translation went ahead, even if the Clarks could not be sanguine about its economic prospects. Hence, for example, they wrote to a correspondent in Leipzig offering to publish in translation a new work by Professor Christoph Ernst Luthardt even although his commentary on *St John* had been 'a very losing concern' to them.[62] Hence, too, they informed the potential translator of Lars Nielsen Dahle's *Life After Death* that although from a commercial point of view it might be better to let the matter rest — 'The present demand for English translations of even the most important Foreign Theological Works is so small that we have really no encouragement to undertake their publication. In fact, in several recent cases we have suffered serious loss by them' — nevertheless they would be glad to attempt to reach an agreement with him.[63] Perhaps the classic statement of the firm's readiness to undertake translations not justifiable on commercial grounds is to be found in a letter to Professor Friedrich Godet of Neuchâtel, presumably from John M. Clark 'My little disappointment about the sale of your "Epistles of St Paul" [1894] does not make me hesitate for one moment about the future Volumes [of the *Introduction to the New Testament* Series], as I consider it a pleasure & an honour to publish all your books in English whether they succeed or not.'[64]

It is clear, however, that the firm could not continue to finance an endless series of loss-making translations. And, by the 1890s, the demand for translated works had declined considerably. In 1882, the market had still, it would seem, been a large one:

> As the study of German has been extending of late years, it might be supposed that there is less need than there was for such an institution as the *Foreign Theological Library*. But it must be remembered that the number of theological readers and students is increasing in a larger ratio than the number of German scholars. We have no doubt that there are more young ministers who must read German theology through a translation, if at all, than there were when this *Library* was started. Besides that, it is the honest truth that fair scholars in German would prefer a thoroughly trustworthy translation to the original itself.[65]

Thereafter, however, a decline in demand gradually became noticeable. The *Foreign Theological Library* was wound up in the early 1890s; by 1895 the Clarks, in the letter regarding Dahle's work referred to above, were remarking on the infinitesimal nature of the market for translations; while in 1900, they observed that 'the demand for Translations of German Theological works [had] greatly fallen off during the past few years.'[66] This falling-off was due in part to the increasingly widespread knowledge of German: 'most students [were] now able to read the original'.[67] But there was a profounder reason. More pioneering work was being done by Anglo-Saxon theologians: the field of theological innovation, for so long the exclusive province of the Continental scholars, was now occupied by their English and American counterparts as well. Inevitably, 'students seem[ed] to prefer books by their own countrymen',[68] and there was less need to turn to works from Europe 'because there [was] more genuine scholarship in [the UK], as represented e.g. in the "International Theological Library", the "International Critical Commentary" & many other standard Works.'[69] This new progressiveness in English language theology was noted some years later in the great German rival of the *Encyclopaedia of Religion and Ethics, Die Religion in Geschichte und Gegenwart*.[70] Commenting specifically on the E.R.E., the German work remarked that 'in it the Anglo-Saxons, who up till now have leaned so much on German theology, have emancipated themselves; not only so, they have surpassed us in wealth of material and the fulness of individual contribution.'[71] T. & T. Clark, although not solely responsible for this process of emancipation, nevertheless played a part in it by encouraging the publication of progressive Anglo-Saxon theology. The translation side of their output may therefore be said to have fallen victim to the success of their policy of promoting works by English language scholars. This is symbolised by a letter written in 1897 regarding the commentary on *Job* by Delitzsch which was out of print. The Clarks had secured rights in the final German edition of this work with the intention of producing an updated English version. But since the death of Delitzsch, there had been very little demand for his books in general, and virtually no demand for *Job* in particular. Consequently, the Clarks had 'practically abandoned the idea' of a new edition of *Job*, and they noted that, in any case, they had the volume on *Job* in the *International Critical Commentary* series in active preparation. Thus, the new area of publishing was supplanting the old.[72]

Factors affecting the profitability of translations

Translation right

Whether a translation failed or succeeded financially very often depended on the size of fee payable to the author or to his original publisher for the *Obersetzungerecht*, as it was known in Germany, or translation right. According to Copyright Law in the 1880s, the original publisher had no legal claim to a fee for the right of translation unless an agreement were reached within one year of the initial publication; conversely, unless the Clarks had concluded an agreement with the original publisher, and issued a portion of the translation within a year of the initial publication, they could not expect to have the sole right of publishing an English translation, even if a fee had been paid *after* twelve months had elapsed since the initial publication.[73] And whereas the Clarks were usually quick to recognise the moral right of the initial publisher and the author to receive a fee, even after the twelve months had elapsed, there was always the danger that a less scrupulous publisher would rush into the market place with a competing translation. Thus, for example, the firm wrote to R.T. Cunningham, who was translating Professor Isaac A. Dorner's *Ethics*, to the effect that a rival translation of the work was being prepared:

> We certainly have the prior claim, having made arrangements with the Author & Publisher in Germany, but as there is no copyright . . . after *one year* in this country for translations the principal thing is to publish *first*.[74]

There are regular references in the letter books to the payment of sums to authors or publishers for translation right. Presumably, the author was paid if he held the copyright of the work, but payments to authors very often included an element to cover the revision and updating of the book prior to translation. Thus, F.E. König of Leipzig received £10 for rights in his *The Exiles' Book of Consolation*, which sold at 3*s*. 6*d*;[75] thus Bishop Hans Martensen was offered £25 for permission to publish translations of the second and third volumes of his *Ethics*,[76] the three volumes of which ultimately appeared in the *Foreign Theological Library* at £1 11*s*. 6*d*; thus Bernhardt Weiss received £60 for rights in his *Life of Jesus*, which appeared in three volumes in the same series, at £1 11*s*. 6*d*., and, owing to the size of payment made to the author, 'resulted in serious loss' to the Clarks.[77] They reported this loss on the Weiss work to Emil Schürer, who was asking a very high figure for the right of translating one of his works, presumably the first two volumes of his *History of the Jewish People in the Time of Christ*, which appeared in the F.T.L. in 1885. (The work was later completed in five volumes, selling at £1 6*s*. 3*d*., the volumes presumably being smaller than the others in the Series.) Schürer was apparently asking more than twice the highest figure which the firm had ever paid for translation rights — by implication the £60 which Weiss had received — and he was told that the most the Clarks could offer him was £70, which they considered to be a 'fair and liberal' sum in the circumstances.[78] Such was their desire to issue the work, however, that upon a further communication being received from Schürer, they made him the even more liberal offer of £100 — a truly massive sum — for rights in his work.[79] We do not have figures for individual works in the F.T.L., but it is very difficult to see how this one could have made a profit.

Occasionally, presumably in the case of less desirable works, or those even less likely to succeed financially, authors were asked whether they would agree to permit the Clarks to issue a translation on the understanding that they would receive an honorarium only if their work sold adequately. Thus G. Dalman of Leipzig, who approached the Clarks requesting that they publish a translation of his *De Morte Jesu*, had explained to him the economics of translation publishing, and was told that, should the work succeed, the firm would be happy to 'recognise the Rights of the Author to the fullest extent'.[80] A fuller statement of this position had been given, on a much earlier occasion, to the publishing firm of Hertz in Berlin by Thomas the Younger:

> As I have to defray the cost of translation and run the risk of want of success I cannot promise a sum for right of translation, but if the work is successful I will not be wanting in recognising the author and publisher.[81]

There are many references also to payment for the *Obersetzungerecht* being made to the publishers. In a letter written in 1893, the firm claimed 'we generally have to pay German Publishers at least £50 per Volume, often more' for the right of translation.[82] In fact, however, in the examples found in the letter books, the sum paid were significantly less than £50 per volume. (The Clarks can sometimes be caught out exaggerating, or quoting a 'best' figure as though it were a mean.) Isaac Dorner's publisher, Hertz of Berlin, received £35 for rights in his work *Christliche Gittenlehre*;[83] the same publisher persuaded the Edinburgh firm after some negotiation to pay £30 per volume for rights in the first two volumes of Dorner's *System of Christian Doctrine*, a work which eventually ran to four volumes, all of which were issued in the *Foreign Theological Library* at £2 2*s*. 0*d*. for the set;[84] while the publisher of a shorter work by Dr F. E. König (possibly his *Religious History of Israel*, which the Clarks published in 1885) was offered £5 for the translation rights.[85] And in one case at least, a work was refused because the Clarks felt that if they were to pay the £40 which the original publisher was seeking for English rights, the financial success of the translation would be jeopardised.[86] So it would appear that the sum paid for *Obersetzungerecht* could rarely have reached £50.

In fact, understandably, the firm was always keen to minimise the risk as much as possible. Where a work was out of copyright, its publishers might find themselves assured (as were Vandenhoeck and Ruprecht, who issued H.A.W. Meyer's works) that

> if it [the translation] is successful we will be most happy to pay you as you originally asked but it is a pure speculation and as you are aware that there is now from the lapse of time since publication no legal claim on your part for copyright of translation we must ask you to trust our honour in this matter.[87]

And in seeking to secure the rights for as low a figure as possible, the Clarks were always quick to point out the hidden benefits which the existence of an English translation would bring to the original publishers. Far from curtailing the sales of the original language edition, as the initial publishers feared, it was the Clarks' almost invariable experience, they claimed, that the issue of a translation increased the demand for the original edition as more people who were competent to read it learned of its existence. One of the clearest statements of this view was given in the course of a letter to Hertz of Berlin:

> the fact of a translation greatly increases the demand for the original. It gives it a publicity which it would not otherwise have and it impresses on the mind of the English public who can read German that a work worthy of translation must be worth buying in the original by those who can read it.[88]

But the Clarks were not always successful in persuading publishers to accept a low figure for translation right: one of the reasons given for the decline of their involvement in translation publishing was the fact that 'some publishers in Germany ... [were] putting an impossibly high tag on the *Obersetzungerecht*.'[89]

(It is interesting to note the Clarks' reaction when they received requests from foreign publishers for permission to issue translations of works on the Clark list, as happened increasingly frequently in the 1890s. For example, in response to a request from a European publisher for permission to issue S.R. Driver's *Introduction to the Literature of the New Testament*, the Clarks offered to sell the translation right for £35, commenting

> This we consider a very moderate sum when the great importance of the Book is considered. It has already reached a 4th edn. in this country, and is still selling steadily. It is admitted to be the most important work yet published on the subject.[90]

Writing to the author, John M. Clark claimed: 'I do not think we are asking too much in the case of so important a book', but he was grateful for a 'generous proposal' which Driver had made (presumably agreeing to waive or reduce his share of any payment), which would permit Clark to modify the £35 claim should the German publisher state 'that that sum is impossible'.[91] The Clarks responded differently in another case. When Professor König proposed issuing a German translation of Frank Ballard's *The Miracles of Unbelief* (1900), the firm, presumably because they did not want to burden the German publisher with too great a risk, the work being perhaps less certain of success than Driver's magisterial volume, proposed that a 10% royalty should be paid on the translation: 'we have no desire to put any obstacle in the way of this, especially as we think a German Edition might be of great service to the cause of Christianity.'[92]

The sums paid by the firm, either to author or publisher, therefore varied greatly. While the Clarks were quick to recognise the moral right of the original publisher and author to be recompensed, they were nevertheless always aware of the ruinous effect that a high payment for translation right could have upon the profitability of a work. In general they sought to minimise the risk to themselves as much as possible, and it is therefore surprising that they did not attempt to persuade original publishers to accept a royalty payment rather than a lump sum paid upon publication. As always, however, where a work had the genuinely innovative qualities so dear to the hearts of Sir Thomas and John M. Clark, we find them willing and ready to offer sums which must have made it extremely unlikely that the translations would ever break even.

Payment to translators

'Our rate of remuneration for translators is at the proportion of Fifty Pounds (£50) per 500 pages.' Thus T. & T. Clark set out their position in 1893.[93] This general principle had been in operation fourteen years previously,[94] but even at that stage it had not been universally applied. More might be paid if the translator were of an exceptionally high calibre. (One scholar was told, presumably in an attempt to persuade him to undertake a translation, that while the normal honorarium for those undertaking such work was £50 per 500 pages, in the event of his doing it the Clarks would increase the payment to £65.[95] On the other hand, less might be offered if a high fee to the translator were not considered economically practicable. Thus the firm explained to John A. Selbie that, on an edition of 1,000 copies, a translation of Dr F.E. König's *Exiles' Book of Consolation* would stand only £20 literary costs, and asked if Selbie would be prepared to accept half of this sum as his translator's honorarium, the other half going to König. König's work was a fairly short one, but even so, the fact that Selbie accepted just £10 was no doubt due in part to a gentle reminder from the Clarks that König was quite justified in expecting a share of the £20, especially as they believed he was 'miserably paid at Rostock.'[96] Thus too, Professor F. Crombie received only £55 for a translation of C.F. Keil's two-volume *Bible Archaeology*, which he had undertaken in collaboration with a Mr Christie who was to share the fee. 'I am quite aware', he was told, 'that that is not at all commensurate to your labour, but it is really as much as we can afford.'[97] The work appeared in the *Foreign Theological Library* at £1 1*s*. 0*d*. for the two volumes. So the standard rate was by no means universally applied. No doubt, as always, the Clarks acted pragmatically, feeling free to adjust the rate of payment to suit the particular case: the eminence of the translator, the complexity of the original text, and the economic soundness of the venture were all, no doubt, factors which influenced the firm's decision on the amount per page which the translator was to receive.

It is clear, however, that fairly large sums were paid to the firm's translators, and also obvious that the larger the fee paid, the longer it would be before the work broke even. Some works, doubtless, came into profit quickly: Beyschlag's *New Testament Theology*, for example, first issued in around 1894, showed a surplus of income over expenditure of £230 5*s*. 4*d*. for the financial year 1895–96, over which 415 copies were sold. The translator of that work was paid at the standard rate.[98] But in the case of many works, reaching breakeven point must have been long delayed by the size of the translators' fees. We have no figures for the unit cost of the first printings of volumes in the *Foreign Theological Library*, but we may make the assumption, based on the figures for the unit cost of reprinting F.T.L. volumes which will be discussed later, that the original unit cost would not be much less than three shillings per volume. The subscription price per volume to the trade was 4*s*. 9*d*., giving a profit of say 1*s*. 9*d*. per volume. In the case of a five hundred page work on which £50 had been paid, it would therefore take the not inconsiderable sale of 571 copies to recoup the cost of the translation alone. Small wonder, then, that in offering Professor Crombie £55 in respect of the work by Keil mentioned above, the Clarks commented that the sum was 'more than [they were] likely to see for many years'.[99] But it was no doubt necessary to pay as generously as possible in order to secure the services of translators of a suitable calibre, for an inferior translation would cause a work to fall dead from the press, resulting in financial loss to the firm, and, what was equally important, damaging its reputation. One translator, whose work had clearly failed to come up to the mark, received the following peremptory letter:

> We herewith enclose cheque for £9 sg for your translation of König's *Religious History of Israel*. It will be a dead loss to us & we heartily wish we had never undertaken it. All the reviewers are down upon the translation. Kindly acknowledge receipt.[100]

Given that it was necessary to pay well if the services of competent translators were to be secured, it is surprising that the firm does not appear to have considered paying a royalty to translators, thereby linking their reward to the financial success of the work. This would have reduced the degree of risk borne by the Clarks, and might have had the additional benefit of encouraging the translators to take as much care as possible over their work.

Alterations at proof stage

As with all works issued by the Clarks, the profitability of translations could be radically affected by printers' charges for substantive emendations made at proof stage. Although John M. Clark's advice to Neil Buchanan — that he should have his manuscript as much as possible finalised before it was placed in the printer's hands in order to keep down the charge for alterations on proofs[101] — was given to all the firm's translators, nevertheless most of them, either due to over-fastidiousness or to carelessness in the preparation of their copy, found it necessary to do some re-writing at proof stage, thereby incurring increased charges from the printer. The translator of R.H. Lotze's *Microcosmus* (1885) was clearly motivated by fastidiousness — 'The printing has been fabulously costly as the translator is particular in the extreme, and the corrections have been enormous'[102] — while in the case of work by the Revd J. Beveridge, alterations to the proofs were necessary because of the less than professional quality of the manuscript which he had submitted:

> A considerable number of alterations were no doubt made upon Sir Thomas Clark's suggestion, but such alterations were absolutely essential, & had the translation been published as you sent it for press, it would, you will excuse us saying, have been creditable neither to you nor to us.[103]

In view of the financial implications of heavy corrections at proof stage, it is most surprising that the Clarks did not scrutinise the manuscripts of translations more carefully *before* they were sent to the printer. The letter to Beveridge continues by commenting that 'Even beyond these alterations Sir Thomas Clark found many cases in which the translation was far from good English.' Such stylistic infelicities should surely have been picked up and corrected at a much earlier stage.

Sale to an American publisher

There was not in most cases a sufficiently large market for translations of foreign theological works in the United States to encourage an American publisher to negotiate terms with the Clarks for the production of an edition of one of their translations on American soil. The Clarks were, however, frequently able to sell a proportion of their edition of a work to a publisher on the other side of the Atlantic, thereby increasing the print run, lowering the unit cost, and guaranteeing the immediate sale of a substantial part of the edition, albeit at a price which would only produce the very minimum of profit. Thus, for example, the firm accepted Scribner's offer of eight shillings per volume for 250 bound copies of the translation of Lotze's two-volume *Microcosmus*.[104] The Clarks were willing, if Scribners wished, to add the American publisher's name to the title page and spine of these 250 copies. In the case of another work issued at that time, Reusch's *Nature and the Bible*, Scribners were offered an edition of 250 copies at eight shillings per *set* (not per volume, as was the case with Lotze's work).[105] In the UK, the Lotze work sold to the trade at £1 7*s*. 0*d*., and had a nominal retail price of £1 16*s*. 0*d*., while that by Reusch had a nominal retail price of £1 1*s*. 0*d*., selling to the trade at 15*s*. 10*d*.[106] The Americans were thus paying 59.25% of the UK trade price in the case of the Lotze work, and 50.52% of the UK trade price on that by Reusch, on which they clearly had a better bargain.

Case studies

The following series of case studies illustrates how some of these factors worked out in practice. The fullest information is clearly available in the case of projects which did not go according to plan, and hence provoked detailed correspondence. These studies are therefore not good *general* examples. They are however of value in showing the firm at work, in demonstrating how its principles stood up under test, in illustrating the practical difficulties which could threaten the profitability of potentially successful titles, and in illuminating the relationship which existed between the Clarks and the translators; a large degree of trust was involved, and in desiring to be graciously forbearing, the firm did not always find it possible to avoid gullibility.

Nöldeke's Syrische Grammatik[107]

The initial proposal to translate the *Syriac Grammar* by Professor Nöldeke of Strasburg was made by James MacDonald, who claimed to have secured the

English translation rights from the author in June 1884. Although the Clarks felt that the demand for a translation of this work, the merits of which they recognised, was likely to be infinitesimal, they nevertheless agreed to proceed owing, they claimed, to the intense pressure which MacDonald brought to bear upon them. This yielding to pressure seems uncharacteristic of the Clarks. Perhaps, in looking with hindsight upon a decision they wished they had never made, they sought to lessen their responsibility for it by emphasising MacDonald's attempts at coercion. In any case, an agreement with him was signed on 19 January 1885, and was made on the understanding that MacDonald held the translation right, that Nöldeke had agreed to supply corrections and amendments, and that no payment to Nöldeke or his publishers would be involved, for the book could quite simply stand no further cost. MacDonald was to receive £30 for his translation and, at his urgent request, quite contrary to the Clarks' normal practice, half of this sum was advanced to him.

In view of the terms of the agreement reached in January 1885, it came as a surprise to the Clarks that, in a letter dated 21 May 1886, MacDonald refused to proceed with the translation unless the firm paid an honorarium to Nöldeke. It can be deduced from later correspondence that MacDonald was conscious of the manifold deficiencies of his translation, and was hoping that Nöldeke might be persuaded to revise it for him upon the offer of a suitable sum from the Clarks. They were unaware of this on 24 May; they no doubt felt that MacDonald had deceived them with his claim to have secured the translation right, and held that the controversy was 'the most disagreeable [they had] ever had', but were anxious 'to end the matter amicably'.[108] Hence they offered to pay Nöldeke ten pounds on publication of MacDonald's translation, authorised, and corrected up to date, and a further fifteen pounds when 400 copies had been sold.[109]

The Clarks also wrote to Nöldeke, explaining the situation as it was seen from the Edinburgh end, and making an offer in the terms noted above. Nöldeke's reply opened up a new dimension to the controversy. Having inspected the manuscript of MacDonald's translation, he had been appalled by its ineptitude: it was clear to him that the translator did not sufficiently understand either German or Syriac, and he refused to have his name associated with such a production. Further, he told the firm that if MacDonald's translation were to appear, he, Nöldeke, would take immediate steps to make it known, both in the UK and in America, that it was issued completely without his authority. It was obvious that the Clarks could not proceed with the work; consequently they asked MacDonald for the immediate return of the fifteen pounds paid in advance.[110]

It would seem that the Clarks' graciousness and restraint knew no bounds. Their letter to MacDonald apparently produced a reply from the translator insinuating that Nöldeke was not in fact against the translation, but against its being issued by T. & T. Clark. This contention would seem to have been completely unfounded; had it been accurate, it would have been a simple matter for MacDonald to take his translation to another publisher. What he in fact did, in order to salvage his agreement with the Clarks and so retain the advance paid by them, was to propose that the firm should accept a Syriac Grammar *based* on Nöldeke's work, claiming that he could get a favourable recommendation of this work from Professors Driver, Wright, and Davidson. In retrospect, it is easy to see that MacDonald was little more than a confidence trickster, but the Clarks gave due consideration to his letter. They rejected absolutely the claim that Nöldeke was against the *firm* as opposed to the *translation*:

> As to our having *insulted* the author, he does not say a word about this, & his letter is perfectly friendly as regards our firm . . . You are mistaken in saying that Prof. N. refuses to allow us to publish his Grammar: it is *your* translation of it he refuses.[111]

Nonetheless, the Clarks stated their willingness to complete their agreement with MacDonald if he could produce a *Syriac Grammar* which eminent authorities felt able to recommend.

The crisis point had, however, been reached. Professor Davidson refused to have anything to do with a translation which Nöldeke had condemned, or with a Grammar based on the German's work. And the Clarks' reputation was dented by a paragraph which had appeared in the American journal *Hebraica* in which Nöldeke expressed the view that the firm was determined to publish the translation in spite of his objections, and disclaimed any responsibility for it. Explaining this to MacDonald, the Clarks concluded: 'The agreement must therefore be cancelled, & we leave it to your sense of honour to return us the Fifteen Pounds.'[112]

The Clarks emerge with great credit from this controversy. They may well have been more than a little gullible, but the fact remains that Nöldeke did authorise MacDonald to undertake the translation, as he admitted in the note in *Hebraica*.[113] He must bear at least some of the responsibility for the fracas for failing to gauge MacDonald's competence as a translator before giving that authorisation. But throughout, the Clarks behaved with restraint, showing a willingness to compromise even when it threatened the profitability of the project. In no way can the firm be accused of lacking backbone; but to their business affairs they brought graciousness as well as decisiveness.

MacDonald's 'sense of honour' was clearly not great. The fifteen pounds had not been repaid by 25 June 1886, and eventually it was written off. There is an interesting footnote to the controversy in a letter written eight years later.[114] Once again, a translation of Nöldeke's work had been proposed; the Clarks' correspondent was given an outline of the events of 1886, and told that MacDonald, who was not named

> not only turned out to be quite incompetent for the work, but acted most dishonourably towards us. We lent him, at his urgent request, an advance payment of £15 to account of his work. Almost immediately thereafter he left the country & we have not since heard of him!

The 1894 proposal to translate Nöldeke's work would seem, like its earlier counterpart, to have come to nothing.

Dillmann's Genesis

The difficulties which arose over the issue by T. & T. Clark of a translation of C.F.A. Dillmann's two-volume work *Genesis: Critically and Exegetically Expounded* (published around 1897) illustrate the problems which German theological prose could present to the translator. Also illustrated are the related difficulties faced by the firm in securing the services of competent translators, and in properly scrutinising the manuscripts of translations so that inaccuracies and solecisms could be detected before the work went to press.

Dillmann's German prose style must have been particularly convoluted: S.R. Driver of Oxford, hearing in the summer of 1894 of the Clarks' intention to publish the work sounded a note of caution regarding the complexities of Dillmann's writings. John M. Clark replied:

> I am very grateful to you for your opinion about Dillmann and I quite see the force of all your remarks and shall keep them in mind before deciding to translate the complete works. I fear however I am committed to go on with Genesis . . .[115]

It was, however, not until three weeks later that the Revd John MacPherson of Findhorn was finally authorised to proceed with the work and, in retrospect, Clark may well have wished that he had taken Driver's advice. MacPherson had done work for the firm previously, work which was presumably of an acceptable standard, for John M. Clark appears to have thought highly of his *general* competence. But the letter commissioning MacPherson acknowledges the complexity of Dillmann's style and it is difficult, with hindsight, to avoid detecting also some slight hesitancy on the firm's part as to the translator's ability with regard to the *particular* work in hand.

> With your kind assurance that no pains shall be spared on your part to do every possible justice to *Dillmann* I have pleasure in asking you to proceed with his *Genesis*. I say 'possible' justice, because I am aware of the difficulties of the work, and how *im*possible it must sometimes be to give an elegant rendering of Dillmann's style.[116]

MacPherson proceeded with the translation between September 1894 and March 1895. There are indications that, early on, Sir Thomas Clark saw a sample of his work and questioned the accuracy with which the German text was handled, but that John M. Clark was eager that the project should remain in MacPherson's hands. By March 1895, however, it was clear that MacPherson's work was seriously defective. From the reference to 'expense' in the following letter written by Sir Thomas to the translator in the absence of John M. Clark, it is obvious that part of the work was by then in type. 'It is impossible', wrote Sir Thomas

> that such a rendering can go out to the public; it would be at once condemned. . . . It is a great disappointment, & will involve a great expense. Indeed, I am not sure but that it would be better to abandon the whole thing. I fear your ear has not been able to get over Dillmann's curt style, & that thus you have been led to a far too literal rendering.[117]

It was decided by 4 April that MacPherson should be responsible only for the first volume of the work, responsibility for the second being assigned elsewhere.[118] It is not clear what amendments were made to MacPherson's translation in the spring of 1895, nor what supervision there was of his work thereafter. But a scrutiny of his text in August revealed further errors. He was told 'in many cases you have gone grievously wrong, not to speak of lesser inaccuracies.' A major mis-translation on the very first page would 'necessitate the cancelling of the whole impression (800 copies) of this sheet, for it is already printed off, & the loss of the plates'.[119] Presumably this stereotyping and printing off was done subsequent to MacPherson's revising the translation in the light of earlier criticisms; this July letter would lose much of its force if it were only elaborating on the cost to the firm of MacPherson's errors which Sir Thomas had dealt with so pointedly in March. The implication may well be that MacPherson revised his translation, that it was stereotyped, and then found to be still grievously defective.

It is open to question why, when the Clarks were fully aware of the complexities of Dillmann's style, and perhaps uncertain about MacPherson's competence as a translator, they did not ensure that the manuscript was more carefully scrutinised before it went to press. It would seem to have been particularly foolhardy to have had the work stereotyped before having been given such a critical reading.

That the Clarks went ahead in this way certainly indicates the degree of trust placed by them in their translators; perhaps it indicates too that, while they all knew the German language, their knowledge did not extend to unravelling the intricacies of German theological prose.

It is not surprising that in the financial year 1897–98 Dillmann's *Genesis*, eventually published in 1897, shows a debit balance of £256 5*s*. 1*d*.[120]

Diessmann's Bible Studies

In May 1899, the Revd Alexander Grieve of Forfar accepted the offer of a thirty pound honorarium for a translation of Professor Adolf Diessmann's works *Bibelstudien* and *Neue-Bibelstudien*.[121] The initial contact with Diessmann regarding the translation of the works had been made the previous year,[122] but *Bible Studies* was not published until 1901.[123] It would appear that the translation was undertaken at the suggestion of Professor W.M. Ramsay of Aberdeen, who was of the opinion that although the work was important, it could only succeed in the English language market place if accompanied by notes and an introduction, both of which he undertook to provide. With such notes, he estimated the work could sell 2,000 copies. This illustrates the extent to which the Clarks relied on the views of specialists in selecting material for publication and in deciding the form in which it would be presented. Great problems could arise when a given scholar was misinformed or frankly motivated by self-interest if the Clarks were not sufficiently prudent to seek the views of a range of experts rather than being guided by one personality.

The production of this translation was fraught with difficulties. There was the sheer administrative complexity of shuttling proofs between Grieve, Ramsay, Diessmann (who was to edit his two separate works into a discrete text), James Hastings (who had a watching brief) and 38 George Street. There was also Diessmann's attitude; at the end of 1899 he asked for additional remuneration for the work he had agreed to do. But Diessmann's irritability is perhaps hardly surprising in view of the interminable delays which beset the project.

The chief source of difficulty was W.M. Ramsay, who behaved in an incomprehensible and curmudgeonly manner. Certainly physical illness coloured his judgement over the crucial months, but it is likely that there was some psychological instability as well.

The first, minor, problem arose when he asked for a royalty on the translation. Initially it had been intended that, as well as providing an editorial apparatus, he would select the translator, and supervise his work. Involvement to this degree might have justified his expectations of receiving a royalty, but his chosen translator opted out, it was left to the Clarks to select Grieve, and they, uncertain how much work Ramsay intended doing on the project, felt that his avowed commitment to scholarship and friendship towards Diessmann would provide motivation enough for his work without payment being necessary. Ramsay thought otherwise, and insisted on a royalty, pointing out that his notes would be an important factor in the success of the English language edition. The Clarks, capitulating, offered him a royalty of 10% on the wholesale price.

Secondly, he insisted that the printing work should be done by Aberdeen University Press (A. King) rather than by the Clarks' normal printers Morrison and Gibb so that he could liaise closely with the printers. It later emerged that he had business links with that firm. He further insisted that he could not begin to write his notes until the work was in type. It had therefore to be set, and slip proofs produced before Ramsay could make any progress. The printers proved to be slow and less than satisfactory, and Ramsay took an unconscionable time to compile his notes. Since the type had to be kept standing until these notes were ready, his delay led to the printers' running out of Greek type (they were also at work on a Greek Lexicon for another publisher), and this resulted in ill-feeling between printer and publisher, and further delayed the setting of the work.

Thirdly, Ramsay suffered a debilitating accident in September 1899 which hindered the work and dulled his perceptions. The Clarks' patience was tried to the limit as Ramsay criticised Grieve's perfectly adequate translation. John M. Clark wrote to Grieve:

> in his [Ramsay's] present state of health, he says he finds it very difficult to explain to others even what he clearly understands himself, and doubtless he has, at present, similar difficulty in understanding other people, however clearly they may express themselves. We must just try to humour him, although I know it is not easy.[124]

Fourthly, with his thinking impaired in this way, Ramsay, who seems to have entered the project in a harmonious relationship with Diessmann, now began to question the German's editorial work in linking the two books and, it would seem, some of his views. 'It is most unlucky' wrote Ramsay, 'that [Diessmann] has such a firm belief in the absolute perfection of his work, and won't take the chance of improving it, and adapting it to a wider audience than 100 German Professors.'[125] The Clarks shared the view that much of the work that should have been being done by Diessmann was being left to Grieve. They were more concerned, however, that the final product might be a work which would appeal to only 100 *British* professors and, reminding Ramsay of his estimate of a potential market for 2,000 copies, they reminded him also of his responsibility to popularise the translation by means of his annotations. However, Ramsay remained at loggerheads with Diessmann. There seemed to be a real danger that this controversy between the author and the editor of the English translation would spill over into the pages of the book itself, for Diessmann was understandably reluctant to be slated in his own book without right of reply. The Clarks clearly felt that such a dualism of view would shipwreck the work's chances of success. They also, however, appear to have accepted that the success of the work would also be impaired if it appeared without notes for the English reader.

Fifthly, Ramsay delayed the project by lack of application, and apparent indecision as to exactly how much work he was to do. Was it to be notes only, or introduction, notes and appendix? If this was at issue in June 1899, it had still not been resolved by February 1900. In the end, following the tension with Diessmann (who clearly had seen *some* notes written by Ramsay), it was decided that notes would be sacrificed, and Ramsay would content himself with writing a short introduction.

In late June 1990, however, Ramsay's connection with the project was completely severed. The circumstances immediately preceding the taking of this decision were explained by John M. Clark to Grieve:

> I asked Prof. R. if he expected the royalty on every copy we may sell simply for the short *Introduction* he offers to write, and he replied 'certainly, it is a matter of business, and if I allow my name to go on the English edition it will enhance the value, and I am entitled to some recognition for it.' But he added that he would really prefer *not* to write an Introduction, and that if we think the book will not stand the expense, by all means to do without him. He is perfectly pleasant about this, and leaves it entirely to us to do as we think best. What do you think? He has behaved in such a strange way all along that I feel inclined to accept his proposal and let him off. I wonder, however, whether Diessmann would feel troubled about it. For all I know he might be immensely pleased![126]

The printing off of the work began on 21 July 1900, a year to the day after the first proofs had arrived. But that autumn saw further delay at the printers. In October, John M. Clark discovered that King had become a limited company with Ramsay as chairman, and remarked laconically 'Well, one is always learning!'[127] The work, initially scheduled for publication in the autumn of 1899, did not in fact appear until early spring 1901. On 23 March that year, Clark wrote to Grieve with jubilation and relief 'At last! We have got some copies from our binders this morning.'[128]

Throughout this extraordinary affair, Grieve worked uncomplainingly and expeditiously. We have no figures relating to the year in which this book was published, but it seems extremely unlikely to have proved a profitable speculation for the Clarks.

Having examined the Clarks' intrinsic commitment to the publishing of translations, and looked at the many factors, not all of them within their control, which could seriously affect the viability of such a publishing programme, we will now attempt to assess the profitability of the translations issued by the firm.

The economics of translation publishing

Individual works

Until the *Foreign Theological Library* was wound up in the early 1890s, most of the translations issued by T. & T. Clark appeared as part of a series, the firm not being sanguine about the prospects of such works issued on an individual basis. Hence the translator of *Nature and the Bible* by Reusch was told 'we do not think it would have any chance of success except in the series.'[129] This view that independent translations were unlikely to be profitable was still held after the firm no longer used the *Foreign Theological Library* as a vehicle for new translations. Hence the would-be translator of Dahle's *Life after Death* was told in 1895 that the likelihood of translations of foreign theological works making a profit was extremely remote, and that the Clarks had suffered serious loss through several recent publications.[130]

That this lack of enthusiasm for publishing individual translations was soundly based is borne out by examples of such works which made a considerable loss. 750 copies of Isaac A. Dorner's *History of Protestant Theology (particularly in Germany) from the Beginning of the Eighteenth Century* were issued in 1871. By 1879, the firm had 'not sold nearly that number', and were left with 'a considerable loss'.[131] The remaining 458 copies of H.W.J. Thiersch's *On Christian Commonwealth*, issued in 1877, were sold off cheaply to a Mr J. Bosworth in 1883. This work too resulted in 'a considerable loss'.[132] Sales of Ernest Naville's *The Christ* (1880) and Gustave Tophel's *The Work of the Holy Spirit in Man* (1882) were poor. In 1885 the translator of these works, the Revd Thomas Desprès of Malton, was told that neither was anywhere near covering its expenses, and that the firm had nearly 600 copies of the Naville work on hand 'besides what the booksellers [might] have'.[133] Over two years later, Desprès was told that there were still five hundred copies of *The Christ* left unsold, and that the firm had not yet recouped its outlay.[134]

Yet despite the lack of enthusiasm and the frequent losses, the firm persevered in the publication of translations outwith series. The only consecutive figures we have are from the *Stock and Sales Book, Individual Titles*,[135] which covers the four financial years beginning 1895–96. In this case as always, these figures have their limitations for they show whether or not a particular title made a profit or a loss within a given financial year, but not, except in the case of new works where we are given information about the origination costs, whether it had sold in sufficient quantities to approach, or pass, its breakeven point. By the mid–1890s, a fairly limited number of translations was being issued. For example, in 1895, 1,080 copies of Dahle's *Life after Death* were printed. The total cost of the edition, once it was bound in its entirety, would be £160 2*s*. 10*d*. The work had a nominal retail price of 10*s*. 6*d*. The Clarks' average income per copy sold was 5*s*. 10*d*., while the unit cost of production was 2*s*. 11½*d*. Around 100 presentation and '25th' copies were distributed. By the time the entire edition had sold out, the firm would therefore have received 5*s*. 10*d*. × 980 = £285 16*s*. 8*d*., a profit of £125 13*s*. 10*d*., or 78.48% on their investment. Only 239 copies were sold in the first year, however, and even at that rate of sales the work would have taken several years to realise its full profit. In fact, however, sales decreased in succeeding years, and the work had still not recovered its costs by the end of the century.

In 1897 810 copies of Christlieb's *Homiletic* were printed. The total cost of the edition, once it was bound in its entirety, would be £142 19*s*. 1*d*. The work had a nominal retail price of 7*s*. 6*d*., the Clarks' average income per copy sold was 4*s*. 4½*d*., while the unit cost of production was 3*s*. 6*d*. Around eighty presentation and '25th' copies were distributed. By the time the entire edition had sold out, the firm would therefore have received 4*s*. 4½*d*. × 730 = £159 13*s*. 9*d*., a profit of £16 14*s*. 8*d*., or 11.7% on their investment. Only 195 copies were sold in the first year, however, and very low sales over 1898–99 lead us to suspect that the work would have recovered its investment, if at all, only after many years.

We have already discussed the problems with the translation which increased the firm's outlay on Dillmann's *Genesis,* also published in 1897. 807 copies of this two-volume work were printed. The total cost of the edition, once it had been bound in its entirety, would have been £510 7*s*. 0*d*. The work had a nominal retail price of £1 1*s*. 0*d*; the Clarks' average income per copy sold was 11*s*. 11½*d*., while the unit cost of production was 12*s*. 8*d*. 71 presentation and '25th' copies were distributed. By the time the entire edition had sold out, the firm would therefore have received 11*s*. 11½*d*.× 736 = £440 1*s*. 4*d*., a loss of £70 6*s*. 4*d*., or 13.77% on their investment. 396 copies were sold in the first year, and over eighty in 1898–99. It would be several years before the edition sold out, and in this case, the work would not have recovered its costs even at that point. It is difficult to estimate the precise cost of the printing work which had to be written off owing to MacPherson's ineptitude. It seems likely that, but for this additional expense, the work would have been costed to break even and no more. Even without the problems with the translation *Genesis* was in no way a financially profitable venture.

It might be deduced from the letter books that, by the mid–1890s, the Clarks were publishing only those translations which they considered likely to succeed financially on account of the quality of their scholarship. If their judgement were sound, we would expect these works to show a reasonable profit. But in fact this did not happen in every case. Beyschlag's *New Testament Theology* (1894) sold well; 415 copies were disposed of in 1895–96, and a reprint ordered in 1896–97. Godet's *Epistles of St Paul* (1894) sold consistently if more slowly; 130 copies were disposed of in 1895–96. But the works by Dahle, Christlieb and Dillmann had not broken even by the turn of the century. We must conclude either that the Clarks' judgement failed them somewhat frequently, or else that, although conscious that little return could be expected, they nonetheless went ahead because of their desire to make available in English works which they considered valuable. The retail price of a book was to some extent dictated by its size, and the perceived value which it would have in the eye of the potential purchaser. But the fact that the Clarks proceeded knowing that the retail prices of these works would have to be set at a level which would at best produce only a very modest return on investment would indicate that, here again, they were motivated by a sense of mission.

Series

The Foreign Theological Library

> The *Foreign Theological Library* . . . became at once an institution. To hundreds and thousands of young ministers, and candidates for the ministry, of every denomination, in England and its colonies, and America, — in fact, wherever the English language is read, — it has brought its annual or half-yearly relay of instructive and stimulating works with unfailing regularity.

Thus an unidentified Wesleyan Methodist minister, writing in 1882,[136] described the Clark firm's longest-running series. As we noted in the historical introduction, the *Foreign Theological Library* was considered to be one of the first-fruits of the younger Thomas Clark's partnership. Four volumes were to be published annually at a subscription price of £1 0*s*. 0*d*.[137] The first issues appear to have taken place in 1846, and for the next forty-five years, 'with the utmost regularity',[138] four volumes were issued per annum, featuring English translations of major European theological works. 180 volumes were published in all: it is indicative of the firm's commitment to the Series that 171 of these were still in print at the end of the century.[139]

At least part of the motivation underlying this commitment is to be explained in terms of the Clarks' enthusiasm for progressive theology discussed earlier. But to have survived for well over half a century the Series must, one would expect, have been reasonably profitable. And one of the factors which surely affected the profitability of the *Library* was the quality and relevance of the works chosen for translation. If books were chosen with discernment, the Series would progressively establish its reputation, and sales would be self-perpetuating. Possibly this stage was reached; certainly, the Clarks considered that a book which though valuable was unlikely to break even if issued independently could be made to succeed if part of the F.T.L. However, every indication is that they were extremely discerning in selecting titles for translation. The Wesleyan Methodist minister commented that it was in his opinion 'a rare thing — so rare as to have no example — for a bad book to be translated',[140] and praised the range of authors represented, and the influence of the Series. Nor was he alone in his high estimation of the influence of the firm's translations. Professor W.R. Harper of Chicago University, for example, claimed that[141] 'The *Foreign Theological Library* has exercised a great influence upon the biblical studies in this country and in England.' But an influential series need not, *ipso facto*, be a profitable one. The works of C.F. Keil, for example, were held to be of great importance. Yet, as we have seen, in enclosing a fee to the translator of his *Handbook of Bible Archaeology* the firm commented that £55 was 'really as much as we can afford, and more than we are likely to see for many years'.[142] Volumes in the Series, it would seem, were long-term investments, even when their contents were of undisputed quality.

Another factor affecting the image of the Series, and hence its sales and profitability, was the quality of the translations. As we have seen, the language of the German theologians especially could often be far from easy to translate.

> The difficulties of putting into readable English the extraordinary composite of German theological style which some of the best authors in the series exhibit, can hardly be exaggerated.[143]

Apparently some of the earlier works in the Series were ineptly translated, 'indeed, in a few cases, the version had to be put into new hands and done over again',[144] but by 1882 it was the opinion of one commentator at least that 'Messrs. Clark's translators [had] greatly improved, and some of the later ones [left] hardly anything to be desired.'[145] Certainly, the firm was well aware of the supreme importance of accuracy. In the same year, they expressed the hope that a translator, albeit of a work not in the F.T.L., E.W.E. Reuss's *History of the Sacred Scriptures of the New Testament*[146] would 'execute the translation with as much accuracy & elegance as possible, as in such a work so much [depended] on the translation being an exact transcription of the author's opinions'.[147] The Clarks would have been gratified by a comment on the translation of a work by I.A. Dorner;[148] 'the author ought to be grateful to his translators for making him much more readable and comprehensible than he made himself.'[149]

There is no doubt that both the quality of the original works and the quality of the translations affected the success of the Series. But what conclusions about the profitability of the *Foreign Theological Library* can be drawn from the financial evidence?

Like the *Ante-Nicene Library* and the series of works by St Augustine, of which it was a forerunner, the *Foreign Theological Library* was issued on subscription. The benefits of this are obvious: subscribers paid in advance for the books, and there was a guaranteed market for a proportion of the initial print run. Subscription publishing ensured 'a large number of purchasers beforehand'.[150] The four annual volumes would appear to have been issued in two batches in the course of each year, and distributed to subscribers either direct, or through retailers who serviced subscribers for the firm. It is not clear whether the retailer, having received the subscription fee from the customer at the beginning of the year, had in turn to pay the firm in advance at the trade rate, or whether he was entitled to wait until the goods were delivered and invoiced before paying. If the latter were the case, the bookseller rather than the publisher would be benefiting the most and we may perhaps assume that the bookseller too had to pay in advance.

Regrettably, the only figures available for the years over which the Series was being issued are the trade and retail prices. We have no record of the

Clarks' outlay, and as the sales figures have not been preserved, no means of calculating the firm's income. And once again the figures which are available are limited in their value: we know from the *Stock and Sales Book, Individual Titles*[151] whether a given title or series made a profit or loss in a given financial year, but not whether that title or series had covered its origination costs. Thus we have no means of being certain that the total outlay on the Series had been recouped by the end of the century.

There were a number of different ways in which one could subscribe to the F.T.L.[152] In each case, the subscription price was at the rate of 5*s*. 3*d*. per volume, while the price to the trade was at the rate of 4*s*. 9*d*. per volume, a discount of 9.5%.[153] One could subscribe to the Series on an annual basis. The output of previous years could also be obtained at the subscription price, but one had to order a minimum of two years' issues. The Series as a whole could be bought at the subscription rate, there being no further discount in respect of the size of the order. Thus, for example, it was announced at one point that the 137 volumes in the Series could be had for £35 19*s*. 6*d*., at the rate, that is, of 5*s*. 3*d*. per volume. There were also a number of special offers. By the 1870s, a selection of any twenty titles was on offer at the subscription price, the only condition being that no duplicates could be supplied. By 1890, the minimum number of titles which one had to purchase in order to be supplied at subscription price was eight, and by 1901 it had been reduced to four. The point of these offers was, of course, that one was being supplied at the subscription rate without being committed to take the entire output of any given year.

It was also possible, of course, to purchase volumes from the Series individually. In that case, with one or two exceptions (such as *A System of Biblical Psychology*, by Delitzsch, which sold at 12*s*. 0*d*.) the nominal retail price was 10*s*. 6*d*., and the trade price 7*s*. 11*d*. (a discount of 24.6%, on which a further 2½% discount would apply if the bookseller's account were settled promptly, reducing the Clarks' income to 7*s*. 9*d*.). When individual works were supplied to wholesalers, the rate was 6*s*. 9*d*. (a discount of 35.71%).

More detailed figures are available for the four financial years beginning 1895–96.[154] In that year, fourteen volumes in the Series were reprinted, and it is possible to estimate the unit cost of these reprints. Table 7 presents the calculations for seven representative works.

The average unit cost of reprinting these works was 1*s*. 5*d*., considerably cheaper than the equivalent price in the case of the *Ante-Nicene Library*, although the retail price was the same in the case of both Series. Given the trade prices noted above, the Clarks' return on the investment in these reprints would therefore have been as follows:

on subscription through trade	−3*s*. 4*d*.	= 235.29% return
on subscription direct	−3*s*. 10*d*.	= 270.58% return
non-subscription through trade	−6*s*. 4*d*.	= 447.05% return
non-subscription through wholesaler	−5*s*. 4*d*.	= 376.47% return

On the face of it, these figures appear very healthy indeed. And over the financial year 1895–96 income from the Series exceeded expenditure on it by £846 13*s*. 4*d*. (The total income was £1,173 15*s*. 9*d*; the total expenditure

Table 7

Unit cost of seven volumes in the Foreign Theological Library reprinted 1895–96

Volume	Keil's *Pentateuch* Vol. 1	Martensen's *Individual Ethics*	Delitzsch's *Psalms* Vol. 1	Godet's *John* Vol. 2	Dorner's *Doctrine* Vol. 3	Schürer's *Jews* Div. I Vol. II	Godet's *John* Vol. 3
Size of printing	265	540	268	540	266	270	540
Printing	£11 1*s*. 11*d*.	£10 15*s*. 10*d*.	£10 0*s*. 0*d*.	£10 19*s*. 5*d*.	£ 9 11*s*. 9*d*.	£ 8 19*s*. 1*d*.	£ 9 14*s*. 0*d*.
Paper	£ 4 4*s*. 6*d*.	£ 8 11*s*. 0*d*.	£ 4 4*s*. 0*d*.	£ 7 4*s*. 5*d*.	£ 4 1*s*. 0*d*.	£ 4 4*s*. 6*d*.	£ 7 12*s*. 9*d*.
Binding*	£ 6 18*s*. 0*d*.	£14 1*s*. 1*d*.	£ 6 19*s*. 8*d*.	£14 1*s*. 1*d*.	£ 6 18*s*. 6*d*.	£ 7 0*s*. 8*d*.	£14 1*s*. 1*d*.
Total cost	£22 4*s*. 5*d*.	£33 7*s*. 11*d*.	£21 3*s*. 8*d*.	£32 4*s*. 11*d*.	£20 11*s*. 3*d*.	£20 4*s*. 3*d*.	£31 7*s*. 10*d*.
Unit cost	1*s*. 8*d*.	1*s*. 3*d*.	1*s*. 7*d*.	1*s*. 2*d*.	1*s*. 6½*d*.	1*s*. 6*d*.	1*s*. 2*d*.

* The figures for binding are notional ones, assuming the whole edition to have been bound. 4,177 volumes in the Series were bound during the year in question, but it was Clark's policy only to keep a very limited number of copies of each work in stock in bound form. When these were sold, a few more copies would be bound up.

£327 2*s*. 5*d*.) But this figure may well be deceptive, for it takes no account of the fact that several titles in the Series may not at that point have broken even. A different picture emerges when we consider the annual sales of the Series. In 1895–96, for example, around 1,570 volumes were sold at subscription price (this figure would include both any sold direct, and those sold through the trade), and 355 were sold at non-subscription price (apparently all of them to the wholesalers Hamilton, Adams and Co. or to Scribners in America.) Thus, 1,925 volumes were sold. It would appear that 173 volumes were in print at that time, so the average sale per volume was only eleven copies, a better figure than the corresponding one for the *Ante-Nicene Library*, but still very poor. It is obvious that some volumes would have sold better than others. In fact, in 1895–96, no copies at all were sold at the non-subscription price of ninety-four volumes (the subscription sales of individual volumes are not itemised). One would have expected that the volumes requiring to be reprinted would be those which sold best. While this was true in some cases — the first volume of Schürer's *History of the Jewish People in the Time of Christ* (Division I), which was reprinted, sold twelve copies over the year at non-subscription price alone — in others, sales of reprinted works were poor indeed. The first volume of Keil's *Commentary on the Pentateuch* sold only one copy over the financial year at non-subscription price (the reprinting was carried out at the beginning of the period, on 21 August 1895). It is clear that the reprinting represented a long-term commitment by the Clarks to the Series, for it would be many years before the reprinted copies would sell out, and consequently, the *annual* rate of return was modest. (It is also true, of course, that it would improve the chances of selling out of the slower-moving titles if the Series were kept 'live', and that to do this it was essential to reprint titles which had sold out. But the reprinting of slow-selling works such as that by Keil mentioned above can surely only be explained in terms either of the firm's over-optimism or of its single-minded commitment to theology.)

Over the next three financial years, income from the Series again exceeded expenditure on it, by £882 19*s*. 1*d*. in 1896–97, by £636 7*s*. 0*d*. in 1897–98 and by £622 12*s*. 3*d*. in 1898–99, when the total income was £875 12*s*. 11*d*., and the total expenditure £253 0*s*. 8*d*. The *Foreign Theological Library* was certainly contributing to the firm's cash-flow although its sales fell off over the period. But once again the fact that titles in the Series may not yet have broken even, and the fact that sales per volume were poor, would lead us to question whether the *Library* was as profitable as it appears to have been at first sight, or whether in fact the Clarks' prime motive in continuing it was a belief in the value of the works it contained.

Meyer's Commentary on the New Testament

It was apparently in around 1873, in the wake of the issue of the *Ante-Nicene Library*, and before the edition of the works of St Augustine had been completed, that the firm launched yet another subscription series, featuring the *Critical and Exegetical Commentary on the New Testament* by Dr H.A.W. Meyer of Hanover, an author 'who [had] been long and well known to scholars as one of the very ablest of the German expositors of the New Testament', and who was hailed as 'the ablest grammatical exegete of the age'.[155] The translation was to be prepared under the editorship of Drs William Purdie Dickson and Frederick Crombie, Professors in the Divinity Departments of, respectively, the University of Glasgow and St Mary's College, St Andrews. Although the firm did not commit itself in the initial advertising to issuing a specific number of volumes in the Series, such volumes as did appear were to be published at the same rate as those in the other subscription series, that is at the rate of four volumes per annum. The *Commentary* was eventually wound up after twenty volumes had appeared, but it would seem that there was a delay in their issue, for the final volumes were not published until 1882. Meyer had died in 1873, around the time at which the English translation began to appear. The work had been published in German in sixteen volumes between 1832 and 1852, Meyer himself contributing material on the Gospels, the Acts 'and most of the Pauline epistles'.[156] The Clark edition included all the commentaries written by Meyer himself; to these were added two volumes on the Epistles to the Thessalonians and Hebrews, and four volumes on the Pastoral and Catholic Epistles by other authors. At some point during the course of the Series' publication a third editor, Dr William Stewart of Glasgow University, joined the team which was superintending the translation of Meyer's part of the work.

In this case, we are particularly short of financial evidence with bearing on the Series. The volumes were issued at the firm's normal subscription price of £ 1 1*s*. 0*d*. per annum (5*s*. 3*d*. per volume; trade price 4*s*. 9*d*. per volume). Volumes could also be purchased individually at 10*s*. 6*d*. (trade price 7*s*. 11*d*., less 2½% = 7*s*. 9*d*. or 6*s*. 9*d*. to wholesalers). When the Series had been completed, it could be purchased as a whole at the subscription price of £5 5*s*. 0*d*., with no further discount. By the 1890s, a selection of any eight volumes in the Series could be had at the subscription price of £2 2*s*. 0*d*., the benefit being that one was supplied at the subscription rate without being committed to take the entire output of any given year.

No further figures are available for the years over which the Series was being issued. We have no record of the Clarks' outlay, and no indication of the level of sales which was achieved. There are suggestions, however, that the enterprise was far from profitable. In a letter to the German publishers of Meyer, Vandenhoeck and Ruprecht, the Clarks referred to 'the great outlay for translation and printing', spoke of 'realisation' (of the investment) as being a long way off, and in fact stated that they were proceeding with the Series only with extreme reluctance: 'We have most unwillingly found ourselves obliged to announce the continuation of Meyer for the sake of some of our subscribers.'[157] This letter is revealing on two counts. Firstly, as noted above, it indicates that the Series was not regarded as being potentially profitable, at least in the short term. (It should be pointed out however, that it was in the Clarks' best interests to take this line in the letter as they were hoping to persuade the German publisher to give them permission to proceed with the translation without any down-payment of a lump sum for translation right.) Secondly, the letter indicates that subscription publishing could sometimes work against the publisher's best interests. The acceptance of subscribers to a series of this nature virtually constituted an informal contract between publisher and customers. If the publisher had the right to expect an on-going demand for his series, the customer equally had the right to expect that volumes would become available as announced, and a publisher of moral vision would feel obliged to proceed with a series if it were at all possible, no matter how speculative it was proving. In fact the Series was *not* completed; once again the views of the subscribers were taken into account. 'So few . . . of the Subscribers have expressed a desire to have Dr [F.H.C.] Dusterdieck's *Commentary on Revelation* included, that it has been resolved in the meantime not to undertake it.'[158]

More detailed figures are available for the four financial years beginning 1895–96.[159] From the figures for the two volumes which were reprinted in 1898–99, it is possible to estimate the unit cost of these reprints. The calculations are presented in the following Table.

Table 8

Unit cost of two volumes in the Meyer commentary series reprinted 1898–99		
Volume	Matthew (Vol. 1)	Mark (it is uncertain which volume was reprinted)
Size of printing	162	270
Printing Paper Binding* (7*d.* per vol.)	£ 9 18*s.* 6*d.* £ 2 12*s.* 10*d.* £ 4 14*s.* 6*d.*	£ 8 2*s.* 6*d.* £ 3 16*s.* 4*d.* £ 7 17*s.* 6*d.*
Total cost	£17 5*s.* 10*d.*	£19 16*s.* 4*d.*
Unit cost	2*s.* 2*d.*	1*s.* 6*d.*
* Notional figures, assuming the whole edition to have been bound. 480 volumes in the Series as a whole were bound during the year in question.		

The average unit cost of reprinting these works was therefore 1*s.* 10*d.*, a similar figure to that for the *Ante-Nicene Library*. Given the trade prices noted above, the Clarks' return on the investment in these reprints would therefore have been as follows:

on subscription through trade	−2*s.* 11*d.*	= 159.09%
on subscription direct	−3*s.* 5*d.*	= 186.36%
non-subscription through trade	−5*s.* 11*d.*	= 322.72%
non-subscription through wholesaler	−4*s.* 11*d.*	= 268.18%

As in the case of the other series these figures seem, on the face of it, to be very healthy indeed. A different picture emerges when we consider the annual sales of the Series, although in fact it seems to have been selling better than the other subscription series. In 1895–96, around 308 volumes were sold at subscription price, and a further forty-six at the wholesalers' discount price of 6*s.* 9*d.* Thus, the average sale per volume in the Series was around eighteen over the year. In 1898–99, around 332 volumes were sold at subscription price, and a further twenty-seven at the wholesalers' discount price. Thus, the average sales per volume in the Series was again around eighteen over the year. It is obvious that some volumes would have sold better than others — over 1898–99 for example, nine volumes did not sell any copies at all at non-subscription price (subscription sales of individual volumes are not itemised.) It is clear once again that the reprinting represented a long-term commitment by the Clarks to the Series, for it would be at least a decade before the reprinted copies would sell out, and consequently, the *annual* rate of return was modest.

Over 1895–96 income from the Series exceeded expenditure on it (which was limited to outlay of £14 18*s*. 6*d*. on binding and advertising) by £73 14*s*. 2*d*. Over the next three financial years, income from the Series once again exceeded expenditure on it, by £63 12*s*. 11*d*. in 1896–97, by £48 13*s*. 11*d*. in 1897–98, and by £42 12*s*. 6*d*. in 1898–99, when total income was £86 18*s*. 1*d*. and total outlay £44 5*s*. 7*d*.

If we presume, and it is by no means certain that we are justified in so doing, that the Series had by then recovered the initial investment on it, then the Clarks were getting a satisfactory return on this investment, but given the sluggish rate of sale per volume it was a return which was very slow to materialise.

It is clear that the competence and stature of the work was without question, however many doubts remain as to its profitability. (The *Oxford Dictionary of the Christian Church* comments[160] that 'it was highly praised for its completeness and philological exactness, and has been constantly revised and rewritten by a long series of distinguished scholars down to the present time.') At one point, a rival firm was considering issuing its own translation[161] and the Clark translation was sufficiently sought after in the US to be pirated there by Funk and Wagnalls.[162]

While the occasional translated work, issued individually or as part of a series, could undoubtedly produce large returns, in general the firm's translation publishing was only modestly profitable, and in some cases, sizeable losses resulted. The dominant motive behind the Clarks' perseverance with translation publishing, certainly in the 1890s, was their commitment to the cause, their reaching towards the higher point of success.

Chapter 6
Transatlantic publishing

As the nineteenth century progressed, T. & T. Clark became increasingly involved in what might be termed 'transatlantic publishing'. Complex business relationships were evolved with several North American publishing houses, notably with Scribners and the Christian Literature Publishing Company. It would be possible for us to examine the Clarks' dealings with each of these firms in turn. In all of their transatlantic relationships however, there were three distinct, although inter-related dimensions, each with its own varied benefits and constraints. There was, firstly, the sale by the Clarks in the United Kingdom of works issued by US houses. Secondly, there was the sale by the Clarks to American houses of works and rights in works. Thirdly, there was the development of co-operative publishing between the Clarks and firms on the other side of the Atlantic, resulting in what would today be termed international co-editions. A company-by-company approach therefore, while it might have certain benefits, would fragment our understanding of the factors involved in these three discrete areas by denying us an overall picture of the Clarks' activities in each. In the light of this, it would seem most beneficial to deal with each of the three areas in turn. (It should be noted that the Clarks' income from transatlantic trading was not significantly affected by the dollar/pound exchange rate which, being controlled by the gold standard, was apparently subject only to minor fluctuations.)

Sales of works issued by US houses

The general impression received from the Clark letter books is that the Edinburgh firm rarely found it profitable to sell in the United Kingdom works originating with North American publishers. In 1880, for example, Thomas Clark wrote to an American author 'I have been so unfortunate in my purchases of several American books that I have little encouragement to bring forward more.'[163] Three years later, the position was much the same: writing to Scribners, who had been offering British rights in a work by G.T. Ladd of Yale University, the Clarks commented 'we have not been very fortunate with most of our American purchases',[164] and the same year Scribners' London agent was told 'we have been . . . unfortunate with almost every American book we have bought in quantities.'[165] All this brings forward at least two questions: precisely how unprofitable to the Clarks were these transatlantic works, and why, despite frequent protestations such as those noted above, did the firm persist in importing works issued by North American publishers?

Guiding Principles

There is in fact little concrete documentary evidence shedding light on the Clarks' motivation in accepting and rejecting offers of works of US and Canadian origin. One would have expected that the dominant criteria would have been the stature of the author and the competence of his work on the one hand, and, on the other, the related factor of its likely sales potential. These factors were undoubtedly taken into consideration, and, as always, where a work, though of major importance, was potentially only marginally profitable, the firm was prepared to take the risk in the interests of scholarship. Thus, for example, the Clarks agreed to take 200 copies of a second edition of Ernest De Witt Burton's *Syntax of the Moods and Tenses in New Testament Greek*, despite the fact that they had made only £5 on the copies they had sold of the first edition, which had been published four years previously. 'You will see that, commercially, it is scarcely worth our while, but we are greatly interested in the book. . . . It has a prominent place in our Catalogue.'[166] While these factors were never lost sight of, other pragmatic considerations frequently came into play when the firm was evaluating the offer of an American work. A book might be accepted simply because its author was on good terms with the Clarks and had done valuable work for them in the past. Dr Charles A. Briggs' *American Presbyterianism*, while no doubt a competent work, would be unlikely in the extreme to attract large sales in the United Kingdom because of the nature of its contents. Nevertheless, the Clarks expressed themselves willing to 'go a long way to oblige [their] friend Dr Briggs', and agreed to take 100 copies from Scribners 'if he [Briggs] cannot get or does not wish another Publisher to take it', promising to 'do all in [their] power for it'.[167] Presumably the motive here was not pure altruism, the Clarks no doubt hoping that this favour would lead to Briggs' being kindly disposed towards the firm when it came to future, more saleable works. And in fact many later works by Briggs of more general interest did appear in the Clark list.[168] But the major consideration governing the Clarks' acceptance of American titles was simply the fact that they hoped to sell editions of their works to American publishers, and indeed that the profitability of some of these works depended on the export of an edition to the US or Canada. If American houses were to be predisposed to purchase Clark titles — and Scribners were enthusiastically offered new works on a regular basis — then the Edinburgh firm had to show a willingness to reciprocate. This, it would seem, was the key factor. It was vital to the creation of goodwill in North America that T. & T. Clark should be prepared to buy regularly a certain number of titles originating there. It was in the selection of these titles that the other factors — stature of the author, competence of the work, potential profitability of the work, relationship of the author to the Clarks, potential future contributions of the author to the Clark list – came into play.

Financial considerations

T. & T. Clark does not appear to have had (or indeed to have sought) the exclusive British agency for the entire output of any one North American publisher, preferring rather to select and arrange terms for books on an individual basis. While, infrequently, works were supplied in bound volume form with a cancel title page bearing the Clark imprint, in most cases the Edinburgh firm bought the works in sheets and had them bound by Morrison and Gibb on their arrival in this country. On occasion, the Clarks were supplied with a set of plates by the American house from which to print an edition in Scotland.

There are few records of the sums paid for the British agency in individual works. One example dates from 1887, when the Clarks agreed to purchase from Scribners 250 copies of Professor Samuel Harris's *The Self-Revelation of God*[169] at a cost of 3*s*. 6*d*. per copy. For this sum Scribners would supply copies of the work in quires bearing the Clark imprint, and would assign the English market rights to the Edinburgh firm. The Clarks were to put a 12*s*. 0*d*. retail price on the book. The number of review copies which Scribners were to supply for distribution to British journals was not stipulated, the Clarks being content to ask for 'as many copies for Editors as possible'. No import duty was payable on books entering the UK,[170] but there were of course charges for shipping the goods across the Atlantic. These would be paid by the exporting publisher,[171] who would take them into consideration in arriving at the unit cost at which the books were supplied to the Clarks. In one case at least, however, that of the *Presbyterian Review*, the Clarks clearly had to meet the bill for carriage directly, for they wrote to Scribners on 1 March 1887 asking them to send the copies of the journal by the cheapest means possible. One batch had cost 16*s*. 6*d*. to ship from America, while another shipment cost £1 13*s*. 6*d*., more than double the lower charge.[172]

The Clarks' importation programme seems frequently to have been beset by problems, which led to additional expenses on titles whose potential profit margins were already very low. Damage could easily arise in transit. The problems which arose over the Clarks' import of Funk and Wagnalls' edition of Johan J. Herzog's three-volume *Religious Encyclopaedia*, while no doubt frustrating at the time, have about them a real touch of farce. On receiving copies of the first volume in sheets in December 1882, the Clarks wrote to complain that some copies had been damaged owning to poor packing.[173] 'A good many sheets have been destroyed by nails which were sticking up right through the sheets in numerous parts.' The problem was compounded by the fact that the sheets had not been gathered into copies before packing; had this been done, far fewer copies would have been damaged by the nails.

> We trust that when Vol II is ready you will send it gathered into *copies* — thus, if a nail damages, only one copy is destroyed, whereas if it goes through a *gathering*, fifty copies are rendered useless.

Funk and Wagnalls' response was to enquire, whether, in fact, the offending nails had been inserted by Scottish customs officials. Were the nails, they wondered, Scottish or American? The Clarks retorted 'we really cannot say.'[174] At least the Americans agreed to replace the damaged sheets, but the vexed question of the provenance of the nails continued to exercise their minds. The Clarks were obliged to agree that the nails originated on this side of the Atlantic (they were, however, English, and *not* Scottish nails), but refused to concede that they were inserted in the packing cases in Scotland.

> Although the nails may have been *Eng*lish in manufacture could they not have been imported [to America], or, could they not have been some which had been taken out of cases sent from this country.[175]

It is surely far more likely that English nails would have found their way into the hands of Scottish customs officials! Thereafter, thankfully, the matter of the nails is not raised again. In this case, no extra cost to the Clarks was involved as the American firm accepted the responsibility for making good the loss. When the third volume of Herzog's work arrived in Edinburgh in 1884, the consignment was once again found to be in an imperfect condition. The culprit on this occasion was not nails, but water. Once more the damage was compounded by the fact that, contrary to the Clarks' advice, the sheets had not been collated before packing, so that many more copies were affected than would otherwise have been the case.[176] This kind of problem could easily result in extra expense for the Clarks, and would certainly produce frustration, and a lack of enthusiasm for importing American works.

A further problem centred on differences in practice between American and British printers. Great difficulties arose in binding the first volume of the work by Herzog because the printers had not put signatures on each sheet. This no doubt resulted in the Clarks being faced with an increased binding charge.[177]

Where profit margins were narrow, it was clearly in the firm's interests to sell as many copies as possible, and to give away as few as possible. The legitimacy of the occasional demands from the Copyright Department of the British Museum for deposit copies of works originating in the US was firmly refuted by the Clarks in terms of the Copyright Act.

> . . . we quite understood that the former receiver admitted we were not liable for Lange [the series of commentaries by J.P. Lange] which it would be rather a serious matter for us to supply — the books, title page included are *entirely* printed in America *and we simply purchase so many copies*. The Act applies to books printed in Great Britain no doubt in whole or in part, but in this case there is no part. We cannot see that we are liable.[178]

In these ways, and no doubt in others, the Clarks could be threatened with additional expenses on top of those already agreed for the import of American works.

The sales level of works imported from the US was influenced by two main factors, the state of the UK market and the quality of the product.

It was in the context of low sales of American works that the following comments were made in the 1880s about the depressed state of the UK publishing industry, the Clarks explaining their lack of success with imported titles by referring to the diminished vitality of the home market. 'Business is so dull' (1889);[179] 'everything here is at a complete shambles at present, and it really seems little use publishing anything' (1885);[180] 'the fact is that the depression in trade has been so great that there has been no encouragement beyond what people really want, and we very much fear there is no prospect of any change for a considerable time' (1886).[181]

But if low sales of imports could sometimes be blamed on marketing problems in Britain, more often it was the quality of the product which was seen to be at fault. And here the blame must lie with the Clarks for allowing themselves to be persuaded to purchase works which could, with hindsight, be seen to have had little appeal to the UK audience. Very possibly, of course, the firm was once again promoting works it believed in, and hoping thereby to create a taste for books of American origin in the UK market and to make members of the British theological fraternity number American works among those they 'really wanted', to adapt a phrase from the letter quoted above.

But while this may have been the general aim, there is no doubt that the firm, prompted perhaps by their desire to accommodate transatlantic publishers, did make mistakes. The Clarks came to realise, for example, that the purchase of George T. Ladd's two-volume *The Doctrine of Sacred Scripture* (1883) had been 'very unfortunate'. His prolixity had made the work 'a dead weight' which the Clarks wished had been condensed; and his inconsistency had undermined the authority of what he had written.[182]

But if Ladd's work in common with some others failed because of literary obfuscation, its progress in the market place was also impeded by the theological position it took up: 'above all the rationalistic tone has greatly damaged it.'[183] On another occasion, the Clarks rejected a book which was offered to them by an American publisher because it was 'too advanced';[184] again, the theological audacity of another work and resultant uncertainty as to its marketability was used by the firm as a lever to obtain copies at a lower price than the American publisher had wanted. The work in question was Arnold H. Guyot's *Creation* of which the Clarks commented: 'Guyot's views are novel, and we doubt how far they would receive acceptance.'[185]

Problems arising from literary style and theological position could affect all Clark publications, and not simply those which were imported from America. But other problems unique to the transatlantic publications arose because the US and the UK, while sharing a common language, were culturally distinct. And even though the language was nominally shared, in fact differing semantic nuances on either side of the Atlantic could impede the transmission of the author's meaning, give rise to misunderstandings, and hence affect sales. In this area of language, difficulties arose, for example, in the case of Clinton Locke's volume on *The Great Western Schism* in the *Eras of the Christian Church* series. It was criticised for its style and vulgarity of expression: Locke had used the unfortunate phrase 'The Pope commenced dickering'.[186] Sales would, of course, be affected by such adverse criticisms. C.A. Briggs' *American Presbyterianism* failed to sell adequately because its content was of limited interest in the UK. And the cultural orientation of a work could also give rise to criticisms. For example the firm pointed out to Philip Schaff that a book they had handled was 'rather too American in tone e.g. in the article on "Divorce" which a High Church Bookseller in London pointed out at once.'[187] Faced with problems such as these, it is understandable that the Clarks would write of the *Eras of the Christian Church* series

> we wish the editor would kindly keep in view the advisability of suiting, as far as possible, the taste of readers on both sides of the Atlantic.[188]

Sales could be adversely influenced, then, by a variety of factors affecting the quality of the product. When mistakes were made, the Clarks seem to have been willing to accept responsibility. 'We are to blame ourselves for it', they said of the work by Ladd,[189] and their whole attitude towards the problems we have been discussing is probably best expressed by a phrase used in the context of that work: 'Publishers must just bear the fortunes of war.'[190]

Case studies

There is enough evidence in the case of certain individual titles, a periodical, and works in three series to allow an assessment of the profitability of importation.

Individual works

There follows financial data on some of the works of North American origin which were published by T. & T. Clark on this side of the Atlantic. The only detailed figures available relate to the four financial years beginning 1895–96.

In the case of one work published in the 1880s, C.A. Briggs' *American Presbyterianism*,[191] the Clarks offered Scribners 3*s*. 0*d*. per copy on an edition of 100 copies,[192] and sold the work to the trade at 5*s*. 8*d*., the nominal retail price being fixed at 7*s*. 6*d*. The difference between the Clarks' buying price and selling price would therefore have been 2*s*. 8*d*., but their profit would have been reduced by other expenses such as binding and advertising costs, and additional discounts to retailers who paid their accounts quickly. A realistic profit per copy sold would probably have been around 1*s*. 8*d*. For the edition of 100 copies, the Clarks would have paid £15; sales of the complete edition would have realised around £8 6*s*. 6*d*. profit for the firm, a percentage return on investment of 55.5%. Taking the Clarks' income per copy sold at around 5*s*. 6*d*. (5*s*. 8*d*. less additional 2½% discount), the breakeven point can be estimated as being 73% of the edition. These figures are interesting in that they are probably representative of those aimed at by the Clarks in arranging the import of American works. The Briggs title was not, however, a success. The firm recorded three years later that their experience with it had been 'by no means encouraging',[193] and while the work still appeared in the Clark catalogues until the end of the century, no figures are given for it over the four financial years beginning 1895–96, probably because no copies were sold over those years.

However, the most unambiguous figures relating to works imported by the Clarks from the US are those for Henry Clay Trumbull's *The Threshold Covenant* (published 1896), and *God the Creator and Lord of All*, by Samuel Harris, which was issued in two volumes in 1898. Neither of these titles was a success in economic terms.

The Threshold Covenant, indeed, was issued at a nominal retail price of 6*s*. 6*d*., and a trade price of 4*s*. 2*d*. At this level of remuneration, the edition could not cover its costs. The accounts for the edition as a whole would have been as follows:

Outlay		*Income*	
243 copies in folded sheets at 2*s*. 0*d*. per copy[1]	£24 6*s*. 0*d*.	240 copies at 4*s*. 2*d*.[4]	£50 0*s*. 0*d*.
Carriage and packing	£ 2 18*s*. 0*d*.		
Back Stamp	£ 2 2*s*. 0*d*.		
Binding 263 copies	£ 7 11*s*. 3*d*.		
Proportion of lists[2]	£ 0 10*s*. 0*d*.		
Advertising[3]	£11 5*s*. 3*d*.		
Prospectus	£ 1 0*s*. 6*d*.		
	£49 13*s*. 0*d*.		£50 0*s*. 0*d*.

(1) A further twenty copies for presentation were supplied gratis by Scribners
(2) A notional contribution to the cost of the firm's catalogues and 'lists'.
(3) £9 of this sum was expended on advertising in the *Critical Review* and the *Expository Times*. These were, of course, only paper transactions. This total is the amount spent on advertising the work in its first year.
(4) Twenty-three presentation copies were distributed.

A profit of some 7*s*. 0*d*. on the edition was therefore in theory possible, even given the high level of expenditure on advertising the title. The above accounts, however, do not include the costs of distributing the review copies and the prospectus. Further, certain booksellers clearly ordered a sufficient number of copies to earn extra discounts under the '25th copy' arrangement (which extended to supplying thirteen copies for the price of twelve and a half, and, apparently, seven copies for the price of six and three quarters). In the case of Trumbull's work, the Clarks' income was reduced by the extent of the value of 5¼ copies by this arrangement: they received 234¾ × 4*s*. 2*d*. = £48 18*s*. 1½*d*.

In fact, the work sold reasonably well, only eighteen copies being left at the end of 1896–97, one year after publication. At that stage, it showed a loss of £4 10*s*. 0*d*.[194] Over 1897–98 the remaining copies were disposed of; further outlay on advertising reduced the profit over the year to £2 7*s*. 8*d*. Very few Clark titles, imported or home-grown, sold out as quickly as this one did. Nevertheless, there was an overall loss on the undertaking of £2 2*s*. 4*d*. It could have been made profitable only if less had been expended on advertising, or if the retail (and hence the trade) price had been increased. Clearly the Clarks felt that either course of action would have jeopardised the sales of the work.

God the Creator and Lord of All was issued in two volumes at a nominal retail price of 16*s*. 0*d*., and sold to the trade at 10*s*. 3*d*. In this case the problem was not so much the costing of the work as its poor sales. Had the edition sold out, a modest profit would have been realised, but in fact by the end of the century sales were reduced to a mere trickle. The costing of the edition as a whole was as follows:

Outlay		*Income*	
250 copies in sheets at 6*s*. 0*d*.[1]	£ 75 0*s*. 0*d*.	242 copies at 10*s*. 3*d*.[3]	£124 0*s*. 6*d*.
Carriage and packing	£ 3 14*s*. 9*d*.		
Back Stamp	£ 0 12*s*. 6*d*.		
Printing 'Titles + Advts.'	£ 1 8*s*. 5*d*.		
Folding and collating	£ 0 18*s*. 0*d*.		
Binding 270 at 1*s*. 0½*d*. (6¼*d*. per volume)	£ 14 1*s*. 3*d*.		
Proportion of lists	£ 0 5*s*. 0*d*.		
Advertising[2]	£ 12 0*s*. 1*d*.		
Prospectus	£ 0 9*s*. 0*d*.		
	£108 9*s*. 0*d*.		£124 0*s*. 6*d*.

(1) A further twenty copies for presentation were supplied gratis by Scribners.
(2) £6 4*s*. 6*d*. of this sum was expended on advertising in the Clarks' own journals. The total figure given here is the actual outlay on advertising the work in the financial year in which it was issued. Further outlay would have been required in succeeding financial years.
(3) Twenty-eight presentation copies were distributed.

In this case, the estimate of the Clarks' income if the edition were to sell out is reasonably accurate: owing to the number of copies ordered by the booksellers being small, the '25th copy' arrangement came into play only once over the financial year of issue. The unit cost per copy available for sale was 9*s*. 0*d*. The Clarks' profit per copy sold was therefore 1*s*. 3*d*. A return on investment of 13.88% was therefore possible were the edition to sell out quickly without further promotional expenditure being required.

In fact, however, over 1896–97, only seventy-eight copies were sold. Clearly anticipating that orders would be low, the Clarks had only had 150 copies bound up. The loss on the year's trading on the title amount to £62 14*s*. 9*d*. Over 1897–98, an additional thirty-seven copies were disposed of. Thirty further copies were bound up, and the work showed a profit on the year of £15 14*s*. 11*d*. Over 1898–99, only eighteen copies were sold, and the profit on the year's trading was just £7 2*s*. 6*d*. Both 1897–98 and 1898–99, of course, saw additional advertising expenditure. By July 1899, 133 copies had been sold, 109 copies remained on hand, and the net loss was £39 17*s*. 4*d*.

A profit on the edition was still, therefore, a possibility: 109 copies could have yielded £55 17*s*. 3*d*., which would have cleared the loss and produced a profit of £15 19*s*. 11*d*. In fact, given that sales were so low and that further advertising would have been virtually essential, it seems unlikely that the work ever recovered its costs.

It would seem that very few of the imported individual titles proved to be profitable in the UK market. Even in those cases where the terms agreed seem to have been favourable, poor sales and additional promotional expenditure appear to have markedly eroded or indeed wiped out the Clarks' profits. It is small wonder that they felt, as we noted earlier, that most of their American purchases had proved to be unfortunate speculations.

A periodical: The Presbyterian Review

T. & T. Clark was granted the British agency of the American quarterly periodical *The Presbyterian Review* with effect from January 1885. Prior to that date, the periodical, which was issued by Scribners under the editorship of C.A. Briggs, had been supplied direct to British subscribers by the American publisher.[195]

It was recognised from the first that the prognosis for the magazine was not good, and its initial performance in the UK did little to encourage more sanguine expectations. 'We fear we cannot as yet give you a very favourable report,' wrote the Clarks to Briggs in February 1885;[196] only forty copies had been sold by then, and over a month later not more than a further nine or ten had been disposed of.[197] Nevertheless, although recognising that the British market was 'so flooded by magazines that a new one must have a hard struggle', the firm hoped that shortly they would be able to send Briggs 'a more encouraging report'.[198]

Despite this cautious optimism, the situation does not seem to have improved to any great extent. In December 1885 we find the Clarks reporting to Scribners that they had a considerable number of unsold copies of the October 1885 issue still in stock, and that consequently a supply of 200 copies of the January 1886 number would be 'quite sufficient'.[199] In point of fact however, owing in part to a general depression in the Trade, only eighty or ninety copies of that issue had been sold by late February.[200] The reports back across the Atlantic continued in much the same vein. 'We very much regret that circulation on this side is not increasing' was the assessment of the 1887 sales.[201] Earlier, writing to Professor Salmond, the Clarks had been blunter: '*The Presbyterian Review* has not been a success.'[202]

What reasons were given to account for this outcome? The quality of the product is never mentioned, and does not seem to have been open to question. Had there been any doubt as to Briggs' competence, the Clarks would have certainly given up the agency much sooner than they did. They considered that no fewer than five factors had contributed to the low level of sales, and of these only one is in any way connected with the journal's transatlantic origins. There was, firstly, the general lassitude of trade, referred to above. Secondly, also alluded to earlier, was the magazine boom, the proliferation of journals making it difficult for a newcomer to find a foothold in the market. Thirdly, there was the existence of a specific rival: 'The Free Church Students [were] starting a Magazine of their own'[200] (a reference, this, to the journal which later became the *Critical Review of Theological Literature*). Fourthly, there was the fact that most, if not all, of the College Libraries took copies, thereby obviating the need for students to take out personal subscriptions. And finally — this is the point where the journal's American origin is relevant — the *Review*, having to be shipped across the Atlantic, arrived in the bookshops, and, more importantly, on the review editors' desks, much later than did the home-grown quarterly reviews. Since the 'Quarterlies' were often reviewed together in one long article in reviewing journals, the *Presbyterian Review*, on account of its late arrival, was often overlooked altogether. 'We do wish it could be in our hands [?by] an earlier date.'[204] This lack of exposure in the reviewing journals undoubtedly cost the magazine sales.

The Clarks reacted to the poor prognosis for the *Presbyterian Review* by, in the first place, launching into an enthusiastic inaugural and on-going promotional campaign. When the January 1885 issue was received, seventy review copies and 3,000 prospectuses were distributed, and some judicious advertising was undertaken.[205] A year later, the firm reported that they had circulated between ten and fifteen thousand prospectuses (this, presumably, is the total for the twelve months) 'amongst Clergymen of all denominations'.[206] And in January 1888, the Clarks commented:

> Each number is regularly advertised, we have issued special circulars, & have in many cases asked present subscribers to try to induce their friends to take the Review but this apparently without [?result].[207]

The Clarks' second reaction to the journal's poor sale proposal was a dogged commitment to perseverance (albeit one which was reviewed on an annual basis). Thus they wrote in January 1887 'we have done all we can to work it up, and we are not without hope that we may yet be more successful.'[206] And a year later 'if you are still willing to leave the Agency for this country in our hands we shall continue to do all we can to push the sale.'[209]

It is uncertain when the commitment to perseverance was abandoned. Certainly, the journal still appears in the Trade Catalogue for 1889,[210] but there would seem to be no references in the letter books after 1888 to this venture which, even allowing for the fact that Scribners would have given credit on unsold copies, is unlikely to have been a profitable speculation.

Series

LANGE'S COMMENTARIES

The *Theological and Homiletical Commentary on the Old and New Testaments* had been produced by J.P. Lange with the assistance of several leading European theologians. There were twenty-five volumes in all: fourteen on the Old Testament books (of which Lange himself contributed three), one on the Apocrypha, and ten on the New Testament books (of which Lange bore the entire responsibility for three, and collaborated on a further two.) Scribners produced an edition of this work, 'translated, enlarged, and revised under the general editorship of [the] Revd Dr Philip Schaff, assisted by leading Divines of the various Evangelical Denominations',[211] and it was this edition which T. & T. Clark began to issue on this side of the Atlantic from around 1868 onwards.

Unfortunately, no figures have survived from the years in which the work was first published. It is just possible that, like many other Clark series, it was issued initially on a subscription basis. The retail price in the *c*.1894 *Catalogue* is given as a 'Subscription price', although according to the terms then prevailing, this seems rather inaccurate, for the price quoted held good whether one was purchasing the whole series, or merely one volume. In 1889[212] the trade price per volume was 12*s*. 9*d*., and the retail price 15*s*. 0*d*. By 1895–96,[213] the trade price had dropped to 12*s*. 0*d*. per volume, although the retail price remained the same. It is not clear whether Scribners had dropped their selling price to the Clarks between 1889 and 1895–96, when they charged 5*s*. 0*d*. per volume of the work in sheets. We cannot speculate on the profitability of the work as it was making its initial appearance, but by 1895–96, it would seem to have been proving moderately successful. The Series sold steadily, if modestly, and the Clarks had only to keep a small quantity of stock in hand.

For example, at the start of financial year 1895–96, the Clarks held in stock a total of 146 bound copies of the volumes in the Series, an average of 5.84 copies of each title. The largest number of bound copies held of any one title was eleven. More copies were ordered from America as they were required. Unless they were responding to a bulk order from a customer, the Clarks ordered no more than six copies of a given title at a time.

There is some mystery over the *Apocrypha* volume. It would appear that the Clarks held a sizable number of copies of this volume in sheets, and indeed periodically sold some of these sheets to Scribners. Possibly that particular title had been originated by the Clarks in collaboration with Scribners. Or again, the Clarks might have bought large quantities in sheets upon publication, discovered that there was no demand for that volume, and negotiated with Scribners to sell the stock back across the Atlantic as the American publisher required it. Certainly, in 1895–96, copies were sold to Scribners at 5*s*. 0*d*., the same price as the Clarks paid when purchasing copies of works in the Series from them. This would tend to support the second explanation for the *Apocrypha* aberration. Further copies were disposed of in 1898–99 at 2*s*. 6*d*., however. One assumes that Scribners were the recipients in this case also.

How profitable, then, was the Series? On the face of it, with volumes being bought at 5*s*. 0*d*. and sold at 12*s*. 0*d*., we would expect a reasonable profit. In fact, however, the margin was greatly reduced, firstly by the cost of binding copies at 8½*d*. per volume and, secondly and most significantly, by the outlay on such advertising and promotion of the Series as was considered to be necessary, which amounted to around £4 0*s*. 0*d*. per annum. It would take the sale of seven copies to cover this promotional outlay. On an annual basis, therefore, the Series would break even if the Clarks were successful in selling seven copies plus 47% of the total number of titles purchased from Scribners in the course of the year, 5*s*. 8½*d*. being around 47% of 12*s*. 0*d*. Table 9 shows how the Series in fact performed over the four financial years beginning 1895–96.

Taken as a whole, it was reasonably profitable. Certain individual titles were less successful: some volumes were extremely slow moving. Around 20% of the bound stock in hand was sold each year. The Series as a whole would therefore turn round once every five years. The profitability of the Series would have been severely affected, however, if the Clarks had been responsible for

Table 9

Lange's *Commentaries*: Stock and Sales 1895–1899[1]					
		1895–96	1896–97	1897–98	1899–99
Stock at start of year	Bound	146	146	169	172
	Unbound (*Apocrypha*)	204	154	154	154
Bought during year		30	56	57	12
No. of titles of which copies were bought		5	9	6	1
Sold during year	Bound	30	33	54	54
	Unbound (*Apocrypha*)	50	–	–	50
No. of titles of which copies were sold		15	12	13	25
Stock at end of year	Bound	146	169	172	130
	Unbound (*Apocrypha*)	154	154	154	104
Outlay		£12 1*s*. 9*d*.[2]	£20 17*s*. 4*d*.	£21 1*s*. 4*d*.	£ 6 4*s*. 9*d*.
Income		£30 10*s*. 0*d*.	£19 16*s*. 0*d*.	£32 8*s*. 0*d*.	£38 13*s*. 0*d*.
Profit/Loss		+£18 8*s*. 3*d*.	−£1 1*s*. 4*d*.	+£11 6*s*. 8*d*.	+£32 8*s*. 3*d*.

(1) Some stocktaking errors by the Clarks have been adjusted.
(2) The annual accounts for 1895–96 follow as an example. Some minor discrepancies in the Clarks' figures have been corrected.

Outlay		*Income*	
30 copies @ 5*s*. 0*d*.	£ 7 10*s*. 0*d*.	30 Bound copies @ 12*s*.0*d*.	£18 0*s*. 0*d*.
Binding 30 @ 8½*d*.	£ 1 1*s*. 3*d*.	50 *Apocrypha* sheets @ 5*s*.0*d*.	£12 10*s*. 0*d*.
Proportion of Lists/ Advertising	£ 3 10*s*. 6*d*.		
	£12 1*s*. 9*d*.		
Profit	£18 8*s*. 3*d*.		
	£30 10*s*. 0*d*.		£30 10*s*. 0*d*.

originating the *Apocrypha* volume, and if a reprint of that volume had been required.

We can estimate the annual percentage return on investment in the Series. At the start of 1895–96, the stock was valued at approximately £62 1*s*. 7*d*. (146 × 5*s*. 8½*d*. + 204 × 2*s*. 0*d*. The value of the sheet stock is estimated as being 2*s*. 0*d*.) Between August 1895 and July 1899, £60 5*s*. 2*d*. was invested in the Series. The total capital outlay on Lange over the years in question was therefore £122 6*s*. 9*d*. The profit on the Series over the same four-year period, ignoring general overheads, was £61 1*s*. 10*d*. The return on investment was therefore 49.93%, an average of 12.48% per annum. The Clarks would be reasonably satisfied with this level of return on such a venture.

HISTORY OF THE CHRISTIAN CHURCH

Although T. & T. Clark issued a three-volume *History of the Christian Church* by Philip Schaff in 1870, the same author's multi-volume series bearing that title did not begin to appear until 1883. The Series was issued in six 'Divisions', each containing two volumes:

1 – Apostolic Christianity, A.D. 1–100
2 – Ante-Nicene Christianity, A.D. 100–325
3 – Nicene and Post-Nicene Christianity, A.D. 325–600
4 – Medieval Christianity, A.D. 590–1073
5 – The German Reformation
6 – The Swiss Reformation

The *c*.1894 Clark *Catalogue*, although published after Schaff's death, carried a note to the effect that a work on the remainder of the Medieval period, covering the years 1073–1517 was 'in preparation', but this does not seem to have appeared.

Each Division had a retail price of £1 1*s*. 0*d*. and was sold to the retail trade at 15*s*. 10*d*. The Clarks' income on most of the copies sold was, however, 13*s*. 6*d*. Clearly, most of their trade in these works was done with the wholesalers. Bearing the recommendation of no less a figure than Robert Rainy – 'No feature of the book has struck us more than the way in which it combines learned accuracy with popular writing'[214] – it is not surprising that the work seems to have sold well and to have been reasonably profitable. Detailed figures for the financial years 1895–96 to 1898–99 are available in the *Stock and Sales Book, Individual Titles*.[215]

Copies of individual titles in the Series were bought from Scribners, usually in batches of fifty, at a cost of 4*s*. 6*d*. in the case of the works on *Apostolic Christianity* and *Ante-Nicene Christianity* and 5*s*. 0*d*. in the case of the others.[216] Further outlay was necessary to prepare books for sale and to promote the Series. Each work cost 1*s*. 0*d*. to bind (6*d*. × two volumes); the unit cost of miscellaneous expenditure on carriage, folding and printing new title pages amounted on average to approximately 6*d*; the contribution of each volume sold to the amount assigned to the firm's overall promotion strategy could be as high as 10*d*.[217] The Clarks' total outlay per unit could therefore reach 6*s*. 10*d*. in the case of the first two titles in the Series, and 7*s*. 4*d*. in the case of the others. The Clarks' profit was therefore 6*s*. 8*d*. in the case of the early titles, (a return on investment of 97.56%) and 6*s*. 2*d*. in the case of the rest (a return on investment of 84.09%). These are good figures, especially since the Series as a whole sold reasonably briskly. In the case of most titles, the Clarks could expect to sell a batch brought from Scribners in between two and three years. The annual return on investment would therefore have been good.

The *History of the Christian Church* series performed well as a whole. The following Table itemises the sums it realised over the four financial years beginning 1895–96.

Table 10

History of the Christian Church: Credit/debit balances 1895–1899				
Division No.	1895–96	1896–97	1897–98	1898–99
1	+£15 1*s*. 0*d*.	+£ 5 11*s*. 9*d*.	+£10 3*s*. 9*d*.	+£10 8*s*. 0*d*.
2	+£ 3 3*s*. 0*d*.	+£23 14*s*. 8*d*.	+£ 1 17*s*. 10*d*.	+£19 3*s*. 7*d*.
3	+£12 15*s*. 6*d*.	+£11 2*s*. 6*d*.	+£12 7*s*. 9*d*.	+£15 2*s*. 6*d*.
4	+£ 7 12*s*. 6*d*.	−£ 2 7*s*. 6*d*.	+£ 4 15*s*. 9*d*.	+£ 6 7*s*. 0*d*.
5	+£ 7 3*s*. 9*d*.	+£ 3 15*s*. 6*d*.	−£ 8 2*s*. 10*d*.	+£ 7 14*s*. 0*d*.
6	+£12 3*s*. 0*d*.	+£ 9 1*s*. 6*d*.	+£ 6 2*s*. 9*d*.	+£ 5 13*s*. 6*d*.
Total p.a.	+£57 18*s*. 9*d*.	+£50 8*s*. 5*d*.	+£27 5*s*. 0*d*.	+£64 8*s*. 7*d*.
Average per Division	+£ 9 13*s*. 1½*d*.	+£ 8 8*s*. 1*d*.	+£ 4 10*s*. 10*d*.	+£10 14*s*. 9*d*.

ERAS OF THE CHRISTIAN CHURCH

The series entitled *Ten Epochs of Church History* was issued under the editorship of John Fulton by the Christian Literature Publishing Company of New York. There were in all ten volumes, each focusing on a different period of Church history.

T. & T. Clark were approached in August 1896 regarding the possibility of their taking an edition of the work for sale in the United Kingdom. By then two volumes had been published in America,[218] probably *The Ecumenical Councils* by W.P. Du Bose, and *The Age of Hildebrand* by M.R. Vincent.[219] A copy of the Vincent work was sent as a sample to the Clarks.[220]

Their response was mildly enthusiastic, the enthusiasm tempered by the negative tone with which the *British Weekly*, to which a copy had been sent for review, dealt with the Du Bose work.[221] They agreed to take five hundred copies each of the as yet unpublished titles, but only three hundred each of those which had already appeared, as copies of these seemed to have been reaching Britain through some other channel. Their acceptance of the Du Bose work was conditional upon a revised edition being sent.[222] In the event, five hundred copies were purchased of all titles except that by Du Bose.[223]

All did not go smoothly in the implementation of this agreement; the history of this Series illustrates all the pitfalls of transatlantic publishing noted earlier. The problems which arose are detailed in a letter to the American firm dated 15 December 1896.[224] There were, first of all, problems occasioned by distance: the Clarks complained that the steamer had taken sixteen days. Secondly, a battery of miscellaneous production problems added to the Clarks' expense: a new title page had to be printed, changing the series name to *Eras of the Christian Church* to avoid clashing with a Longman series which used the work

'Epochs' in its title; inaccuracies in a list of translators had to be corrected; the sheets having arrived with no signatures had to be bound by the pagination, causing the binders additional work, with the result that their bill to the firm was correspondingly higher. The Clarks announced their intention of passing on the additional charges to the American firm. A third cause of difficulty was the apparent deviousness of the Christian Literature Publishing Company; possibly lack of communication was largely to blame. There was on-going debate about the number of copies of the Du Bose work which had reached Britain. The American firm claimed that none had been sent to the UK (except, presumably, the *British Weekly* review copy); the Clarks counter-claimed that a copy had been bought in Edinburgh and that a review copy had been sent to the *Expository Times*. Even more seriously, a letter sent by the Clarks on 26 September 1896 complaining that succeeding volumes in the Series were one hundred pages shorter than the sample volume which had been sent, and suggesting that a smaller sum should be charged for these shorter volumes, appears to have been completely ignored by the American firm. And on top of all this, the Christian Literature Company had made errors in rendering their statement. The American firm proved conciliatory on these points, eventually giving a reduction on the smaller volumes.[225] A fourth problem, which arose later, centred on the quality of the product. Clinton Locke's volume on *The Great Western Schism* was, as we noted earlier, criticised for its vulgarity of expression and infelicitous style. And a contributor to the *Critical Review* pointed out 'graver faults than these'. Such criticism was seen as undermining the reputation, and hence, of course, the profitability of the Series as a whole. 'It is a great pity that what might be a most valuable Series should be marred by blemishes.'[226]

An interesting attempt was made, at the instigation of the American publisher, to promote sales of the Series in the United Kingdom. The American author who had contracted to write the volume covering the earliest period, *The Apostolic Age*, had died, and the Christian Literature Publishing Company wrote thus to the Clarks: 'we have felt that if an English scholar could be secured for this first volume it would help the sale on your side.'[227] In consequence, the Clarks wrote on behalf of the American firm to the Revd Henry Gee of Highbury Training College, inviting him to undertake the volume while explaining that the Series was an American enterprise, and that financial arrangements would be concluded with him from the other side of the Atlantic.[228] In fact, Gee declined to accept the commission, but the volume was undertaken by J. Vernon Bartlet of Oxford.[229] Whether or not his participation increased the prestige of the Series in the British market is open to question.

All ten volumes had been published by the Clarks by 1901,[230] at a retail price of 6*s*. 0*d*. Detailed financial information is available for the three financial years beginning 1896–97, and it is possible to estimate the return which the Clarks could expect from their investment in the Series. There follows the costings of a representative title, assuming the sale of the whole edition.

The Age of Hildebrand (Published 1896–97)

Outlay		*Income*	
500 copies @ 50c	£51 13*s.* 3*d.*	500 copies @ 3*s.* 10*d.*	£95 16*s.* 7*d.*
Carriage	£ 3 0*s.* 0*d.*		
Collating and arranging	£ 1 10*s.* 6*d.*		
Contribution to cost of prospectus	£ 0 15*s.* 0*d.*		
Side stamp (contribution to cost)	£ 0 5*s.* 3*d.*		
Printing title pages etc.	£ 0 19*s.* 0*d.*		
Binding	£11 2*s.* 6*d.*		
Advertising and proportion of lists (the actual 1896–97 figure)	£ 4 4*s.* 5*d.*		
	£73 9*s.* 11*d.*		
Profit	£22 6*s.* 8*d.*		
	£95 16*s.* 7*d.*		£95 16*s.* 7*d.*

If this title had sold out, therefore, the Clarks would have received a return on their investment of 30.39%, the breakeven point being 76.6% of the edition. On the strength of this analysis we might assume that the Series was reasonably profitable. Unfortunately, however, the market for the works in the UK was simply not large enough to produce a profit for the Clarks. Table 11 lists the sales of titles in the Series in the year of publication and in the succeeding years.

Table 11

Eras of the Christian Church: Sales figures 1896–97 – 1898–99			
Title	1896–97	1897–98	1898–99
Age of Hildebrand	158	5	46
Great Western Schism	137	11	0
Age of the Crusades	150	30	17
Ecumenical Councils*	68	55	28
Age of the Renascence	—	138	34
Anglican Reformation	—	154	46
Age of Charlemagne	—	74	13
Post-Apostolic Age	—	—	76
* The Clarks bought an edition of only 300 copies of this work.			

Clearly, some titles sold better than others. But even the best-selling of these works, the Hildebrand volume, was still 174 copies short of its breakeven point by July 1899. It must be doubtful whether the Series as a whole ever showed a profit: if it did, the return averaged out per annum would be derisory. Table 12 shows the financial performance of the Series between 1896–97 and 1898–99.

Table 12

Eras of the Christian Church: Annual performance 1896–97 – 1898–99			
Title	1896–97	1897–98	1898–99
Age of Hildebrand	−£36 18*s*. 10*d*.	+£0 17*s*. 5*d*.	+£6 19*s*. 8*d*.
Great Western Schism	−£36 13*s*. 1*d*.	+£2 2*s*. 2*d*.	−£0 15*s*. 0*d*.
Age of Crusades	−£35 10*s*. 4*d*.	+£4 3*s*. 0*d*.	+£1 14*s*. 4*d*.
Ecumenical Councils	−£24 0*s*. 10*d*.	+£0 9*s*. 5*d*.	+£3 14*s*. 7*d*.
Age of the Renascence		−£40 7*s*. 2*d*.	+£3 15*s*. 7*d*.
Anglican Reformation		−£36 11*s*. 6½*d*.	+£5 7*s*. 9*d*.
Age of Charlemagne		−£52 17*s*. 8*d*.	−£1 1*s*. 2*d*.
Post-Apostolic Age			−£50 5*s*. 10*d*.
Total per annum	−£133 3*s*. 1*d*.	−£122 4*s*. 4½*d*.	−£30 0*s*. 1*d*.
Average per volume	−£33 5*s*. 9¼*d*.	−£17 9*s*. 2¾*d*.	−£3 15*s*. 0*d*.

Motives other than the hope of financial gain were clearly at work, otherwise the Clarks would have abandoned this manifestly unprofitable venture, rather than continuing to add new titles.

The Clarks' attempts to sell works of American origin on this side of the Atlantic were almost uniformly unsuccessful financially, whether they involved individual titles, a periodical, or series. Exceptions to this general principle, such as the *History of the Christian Church* series, by the very fact that they are so infrequent serve only to highlight the problems which the Clarks had with this area of publishing. The most that can be said is that these transatlantic agreements allowed them to develop and maintain the relationships with North American houses which would lead to the co-operative ventures which were so essential if some of their more ambitious projects were to succeed financially.

Sales of works and rights to North American houses

This section deals with the sale of editions of and rights in theological works and periodicals to publishers in North America. Excluded from consideration here are major theological works, such as the *Dictionary of the Bible*, which will be dealt with in Chapter 8.

In considering the Clarks' transatlantic dealings of this kind, we will be attempting to assess the profitability of these ventures; we will be investigating whether it was essential for the overall profitability of a given work that the print-run be increased by the number of copies required to fulfil the American publishers' order, thereby reducing the unit cost, or that the investment in the work be offset by the income from the sale of rights in that work to a transatlantic house; we will be considering whether the Clarks pursued the goal of appointing a single North American agency to handle their publications, or whether they felt it was equally profitable and desirable to let several American publishers distribute their output, the main emphasis remaining, nonetheless, on the Scribner firm.

It is extremely difficult to unravel the complexities of the Clarks' transatlantic exports.

There is, first of all, a geographical complexity. In the case of some works, blanket North American rights (that is, distribution rights in the US and Canada) would appear to have been sold by the Clarks. This was the case with many of the sales to Scribners, and the Christian Literature Publishing Company's agency in the *Ante-Nicene Library* and the *St Augustine* series, although most reluctantly granted by T. & T. Clark, as will be seen later, nevertheless was specifically stated to include the Canadian market.[231] On the other hand, separate Canadian franchises would seem to have been granted on occasion: the Willard Tract Depository, for example, was given the Canadian agency in the *Expository Times*.[232]

The major complexity however arises from the confusing nature of the Clarks' business relationships with the various transatlantic companies which were handling their works. The issue of a Clark title by an American publisher fell into one of three categories. Firstly, the issue might be the fruit of pure piracy, undertaken with no thought of obtaining permission from, and little if any thought of remunerating, the Edinburgh firm. Secondly, the work might be issued with the Clarks' reluctant blessing; this kind of situation arose where an American publisher had a sufficient sense of business morality to announce in advance his intention of proceeding with the issue of an edition with or without the Clarks' consent, and offered some (usually paltry) terms, which the original publisher felt compelled to accept, or at least to enter into negotiations over. A cheap American reprint was certain to undercut the exported product sold through the official US agent, thereby drying up demand through that channel, and hence reducing the Clarks' income from the book. The Clarks attempted to make the best of such situations by endeavouring to conclude as favourable terms as possible with the pirate. Thirdly, the work might be issued through the agent chosen and appointed by the Clarks. An edition bearing the agent's imprint might be shipped in sheets to the US or alternatively, and much less frequently, the American publisher might be sold a set of plates from which to produce his own edition. Bound copies were not usually exported.

All this would be relatively simple if a given American publisher had always stood in the same relationship to T. & T. Clark, consistently issuing Clark books as pirate, reluctantly-authorised agent, or selected franchise-holder. But there are further complexities.

In the first place, there would in some cases seem to have been a discernible growth in the Clarks' relationships. The out-and-out pirate, prepared to offer some kind of terms to the Edinburgh firm, would become the reluctantly-authorised agent, and, as time passed and the relationship developed, might eventually find himself offered rights in another Clark title. This progression is understandable.

In the second place, however, we find the Clarks willingly doing business with firms with regard to certain works while at the same time those firms were responsible for pirating other Clark titles, and giving an inconsequential remuneration. It is difficult to comprehend the Clarks' motivation in maintaining this dual level of relationship with the US firms.

There is no questioning the fact that the problem of piracy added greatly to the complexity of T. & T. Clark's transatlantic dealings in the decades under consideration. A convenient model could be constructed which would portray the Clarks in the 1880s as eager to have Scribners as their sole agent in the North American market over a decade which in fact saw the percentage of Clark titles handled by Scribners reduced as works were pirated by other houses with which the Edinburgh firm, however reluctantly, was forced to reach agreement. According to the model, however, this trend was offset by another – that of increasing co-operation between T. & T. Clark and Scribners on joint ventures, notably the *International* Series – so that the firms were very possibly closer in 1900 than they had been in 1880. Convenient though this model might be, however and worth bearing in mind as we proceed, it does not seem to tie in fully with the facts.

We will look first of all at the North American firms with which the Clarks were involved, and then consider the financial implications to the firm of piracy, reluctantly-authorised agencies, and grants of franchises to selected firms.

The companies

'We wish to be on good terms with every one' wrote the Clarks to Funk and Wagnalls.[233] In the field of nineteenth-century international publishing, this aim was virtually unattainable. In practice, the Clarks tended to favour Scribners wherever possible.

The major agency: Scribners

The American publishing house which was later to be known as Charles Scribner's Sons was a slightly younger firm than that of T. & T. Clark. Charles Scribner I (1821–1871) had established the business in partnership with Isaac D. Baker in 1846, interestingly the same year in which the future Sir Thomas Clark, two years Scribner's junior, joined his uncle's firm.[234]

It is uncertain when the first links were forged between T. & T. Clark and Scribner's firm (Baker died in 1850), but initial contacts were probably made through Charles Welford. An Englishman who ran a bookshop in New York, Welford joined Scribner's staff, and set up a London office from where he established relationships with all the leading British publishers and, with a fine intuitive tact, arranged the export of their books to America. At a time when the American market was inundated with such imports, Scribner wanted to keep his main list distinctively American, and so established a separate imprint, Scribner and Welford, to handle books from this side of the Atlantic. This imprint was used for almost four decades until Welford's death in 1885, by which time he represented the Scribner firm in all its affairs abroad.[235] Welford certainly knew Thomas Clark, and introduced him to the first Charles Scribner; although there were many differences between the two, there was also an identity of interest, for both majored on publishing philosophical and theological (mainly Presbyterian) books.

In the last years of the century, however, John M. Clark's dealings were with Charles Scribner II, and with the colourful Lemuel W. Bangs, Welford's assistant who succeeded him on his death. Born in 1854, Scribner was five years older than Clark. He had two brothers, John Blair (1850–1879), and Arthur Hawley Scribner (1859–1932). The first Charles Scribner died in 1871 before his middle son had completed his education at the College of New Jersey (later Princeton University), and John B. Scribner headed the business, then known as Scribner, Armstrong & Co., until he was joined by Charles II in 1878; it was presumably then that the firm became known as Charles Scribner's Sons. John Blair died in 1879, leaving the young Charles as head of the firm. He was to be its president until 1928, when he became chairman of the board, a position he retained until his death on 19 April 1930.[237]

According to the historian of American book publishing John Tebbel, the major contribution of the second Charles Scribner was

> to enlarge [the firm] from the narrow scope developed by his father, specialising in philosophy and theology, until its list was as comprehensive as any other publisher's, and then to make that list a symbol of high literary quality.[238]

A similar broadening of the list is discernible in many contemporary British theological publishing houses; John M. Clark's development of his firm's list, however innovative, was in contrast firmly rooted in his father's policies. But this did not stop a friendship from developing between the two men, and the relative mutual loyalty of the Clark and Scribner firms may be said to have been rooted in this relationship. The friendship was not without its problems. By all accounts Charles Scribner II was a forceful personality,[239] and his 'Stateside' ways of conducting business sometimes grated on John M. Clark who, for his part, could be equally forceful. But there would seem to have been enough good will on both sides to overcome these difficulties. John M. Clark has left on record his attitude towards Scribner, whom he met on several occasions. The relationship had been somewhat ruffled by a minor transatlantic misunderstanding in which James Hastings had been involved. Clark wrote to Hastings trying to restore calm, and encouraging him to see the matter from the American firm's point of view. While he said 'If Mr Scribner should ever say anything "strong" about *you*, you may rest assured that I shall not fail to let him know that I resent it', Clark's general attitude towards Scribner seems to have been positive and understanding:

> Well, as to Mr Scribner, you are quite right in saying that something must be set down to 'American ways of doing business'. They are certainly very different from our methods; & yet when one meets American friends personally, no people could be kinder or more courteous.

> I have known Mr Charles Scribner (the senior Partner) for many years, & altho' I recognise that his business ways are not always our ways, they are less estranged from British methods than those of any other American Publisher I know – & I have met a number of them. We cannot help those differences of nationality, & I have no doubt that the Americans think (in fact I know they do) that we 'Britishers' are just as peculiar.
>
> But as a friend, no one could be kinder than Mr Scribner. We were very happy together & I am anxious that the old family friendship should be maintained.[240]

Perhaps because of the strength of this relationship, and because they felt that Scribner's business methods were, of those of all other American houses, most akin to their own, the Clarks dealt extensively with the New York house. In 1884 they expressed the hope that the two firms might 'long continue [their] pleasant connections',[241] and, the following year, Scribners were assured: 'as you know, there is no house with whom we desire that our books should be placed compared with yours.'[242]

At no time however was Scribner's firm the sole American agent for Clark publications in either of the two meanings of that term. Scribners was never the only firm to handle Clark books in the US, and, except in the case of titles which they purchased in a sizable edition, bearing the Scribner imprint to which they were assigned sole rights, they did not have the exclusive franchise in individual works, the Clarks being free to supply copies to other firms in America. That Scribners was never the only firm to handle Clark books in the US is made quite clear, for example, in a letter to the Christian Literature Publishing Company dated 20 December 1884.[243] The Company, under the impression that Scribners was indeed the Edinburgh firm's sole agent, had asked if that agency could be transferred to them. This suggestion was, of course, declined, and it was pointed out that Scribners was only one of several firms handling Clark works in the US. There were good reasons for not giving the sole agency to one firm. There was the pragmatic reason that the Clarks had to be free to come to terms, however reluctantly, with firms which were pirating their works. But there were further sound business reasons. Other firms gave valuable support to Clark works, support which the Edinburgh firm was reluctant to lose. And again, however congenial the Scribners might find it to handle Clark titles, they would in all probability not have prosecuted their sale so zealously under a sole agency arrangement as under an agreement by which new titles would not come to them automatically, and could be withheld if the Clarks were less than satisfied with their conduct of the agency.[244] For instance, the American agency in the *Expository Times* was transferred by the Clarks from Scribners to the Christian Literature Publishing Company because the larger house was not, in the Clarks' view, devoting sufficient energy to promoting the periodical in the US.[245] That, except in the case of a few titles, Scribners did not have the exclusive franchise in individual works is made quite clear by a letter to an unknown American firm in which the Clarks stated that although their New York agents were Scribners, 'this [did] not (except in the case of a few books) prevent [their] having business relations with any other firm.'[246] And on one occasion at least, we find the Edinburgh firm selling direct to a retail customer in the US. The Clarks, on the evidence of the letter books, had a very highly developed sense of business ethics, and it was probably infrequently that they wrote as follows:

> Messrs Charles Scribner's Sons, of New York, are our agents for the States, but we think you would get these books much cheaper by ordering direct from us. You would have to pay carriage, of course . . .[247]

On at least one occasion the American firm sought to be appointed the Clarks' sole US agent, both in the sense of handling all titles and in the sense of being the sole US outlet for all the works it did handle. This elicited the following response, which sums up the Clarks' position:

> With regard to our giving you the exclusive sale in America, it is quite possible that this might result beneficially to both parties, as has no doubt been the case in [the *Ante-Nicene Library*] with you, and Lange's Commentaries with us. But this we fear must be confined to particular books, for we would otherwise lose powerful support from some houses for other books for which such an arrangement had not been made. So we prefer to allow things to remain as they are.[248]

And so Scribners remained only one of several houses handling Clark titles in the US.

In fact, however, the Clarks sought to channel most of their new output to the US market through Scribners. In a letter to another New York publisher, Putnam, they appear to assert that all new titles had to be offered to Scribners as a matter of course;[249] while in fact there was no obligation to do this it would seem to have been their normal practice. For instance, in seeking an American publisher for the *Monthly Interpreter*, T. & T. Clark invited the co-operation of Scribners. 'We make the first offer to you as our old friends.'[250]

In view of all these issues, how satisfied were the Clarks with the efforts of these 'old friends' on their behalf, and what volume of business was done? Apart from the doubts mentioned above over Scribners' commitment to the *Expository Times*, the Edinburgh firm seems to have been reasonably contented with their activities, although there were frequent suggestions that more extensive advertising could be undertaken. For example, a letter written in July 1894 wished Scribners well in their new premises, hoped 'that with the Autumn Season [they would] find an encouraging revival of business', gently remonstrated that their purchases for the period January to June 1894 were down on the total for the corresponding half of 1893, expressed understanding 'of the difficulties [they] must have had owing to the great depression of Trade in the States [that] season', reassured them of the Clarks' certainty that they had been doing all they could for Clark titles in the circumstances, and suggested more extensive US advertising of these titles, offering to pay half the cost of this and pointing out in passing how much advertising of Scribner-originated titles was undertaken by the Clarks in the UK.[251]

Scribners' increasing sales of Clark titles are shown in the following Table. These figures probably include sales of works produced on a co-edition basis, which are considered in a separate section.[252]

Table 13

Sales to Scribner 1881–1900	
1881	£ 172 2*s*. 9*d*.
1882	£ 212 5*s*. 0*d*.
1883	£ 282 9*s*. 6*d*.
1884	£ 198 2*s*. 11*d*.
1885	£ 611 7*s*. 7*d*.
1886	£ 489 7*s*. 1*d*.
1887	£ 570 13*s*. 4*d*.
1888	£ 299 0*s*. 0*d*.
1889	£ 584 16*s*. 5*d*.
1890	£ 656 3*s*. 10*d*.
1891	£1,099 5*s*. 4*d*.
1892	£ 951 1*s*. 1*d*.
1893	£ 647 15*s*. 9*d*.
1894	£ 800 17*s*. 5*d*.
1895	£1,233 7*s*. 9*d*.
1896	£1,109 10*s*. 1*d*.
1897	£1,454 0*s*. 7*d*.
1898	£1,291 16*s*. 0*d*.
1899	£1,374 6*s*. 7*d*.
1900	£1,493 8*s*. 1*d*.

The figures for 1891 and 1892 are corrected to exclude unpaid invoices carried over from the previous period. In most cases, the calculations were made in mid-December, an exception being the 1892 figure, which was calculated at the end of November that year.[253]

The Clarks' amicable relationships with the New York firm can therefore be seen to have produced concrete results in terms of steadily increasing sales. Over the financial year 1895–96, for example, the Edinburgh firm's total turnover amounted to £11,042 3*s*. 7*d*. Over those same months (July 1895–June 1896) total sales to Scribners reached £1,483 18*s*. 6*d*.,[254] a surprisingly high figure in the light of the annual totals in Table 13. Sales to Scribners therefore accounted for 13.43% of the Clarks' turnover. The Edinburgh-New York connection was clearly a successful one, at least as regards cash flow.

Other agencies and pirates

Apart from their business with Scribners, T. & T. Clark's American dealings were largely with three firms, the Fleming H. Revell Company, Funk and Wagnalls, and the Christian Literature Publishing Company.

FLEMING H. REVELL

Fleming H. Revell had been born in Chicago in 1849, and, according to John Tebbel,[255] combined the talent of salesmanship with that of managing money. It is not surprising therefore that he went into business: the firm which bore his name was founded in 1869, initially to publish the periodical *Everybody's Paper*. The character of Revell's rapidly-expanding publishing operation was shaped by the religious revival which swept the United States following the

Civil War. With this revival movement Revell was personally associated, and indeed his sister married one of its prime movers, the evangelist Dwight Moody. This link with Moody proved useful to Revell as he sought new markets. Although his firm, while specialising in evangelical works, was itself non-denominational, Revell nevertheless attempted to conclude co-publishing agreements with the denominational houses. The material he published was much more 'popular' in its approach than that issued by the Clarks, and his inventive exploitation of the mass religious market led to his firm's continued growth. Edinburgh and London branches were founded in association with the Edinburgh firm of Oliphant, Anderson and Ferrier. And in the financially difficult years of the 1890s, Revell was to discover that 'one of the virtues of religious publishing was its imperviousness to depression.'[256]

It is difficult to date Revell's first contacts with the Clarks, although a letter sent to him in April 1883 is couched in such terms as to indicate that the relationship was then only just beginning.[257] This relationship was a tempestuous one. Some of the storms arose over the American firm's unauthorised reprints of Clark titles. A further, intriguing problem arose in 1893, the year which saw the trade depression reach its lowest point. Revell, in that year, bought over a Canadian firm, the Presbyterian News Company of Toronto. John M. Clark owned fifty shares, worth $500, in that company. These shares he had accepted for whatever reason in lieu of payment for stocks of Clark publications supplied to Toronto in November 1892. The news of the takeover reached the Clarks via the Revell representative, and the Edinburgh firm wrote at once to the Presbyterian News Company, taking it to task for not informing its shareholders of the change in ownership, expressing the hope that the arrangement had been a satisfactory one, and that the interests of the shareholders had been fully taken into account, and pointing out that, as the stock of Clark publications had now presumably been sold to Revell, John M. Clark expected his money to be paid to him in full.[258] This, however, was not to be. The Clarks' summary of the outcome was that they had 'suffered financially to no small extent.'[259] It is easy to see how these problems would have caused tension in the Revell-Clark relationship, and yet, in other matters, the two companies continued to co-operate, the Clarks dealing both directly with Revell, and also with the Willard Tract Depository in Toronto, which became part of his organisation in 1893.

FUNK AND WAGNALLS

Funk and Wagnalls, another firm which co-operated with the Clarks on the one hand while issuing unauthorised reprints on the other, had been launched in 1877.[260] Isaac K. Funk provided the editorial direction, while his partner, Wagnalls, a lawyer, brought his administrative gifts to bear upon the firm's operations.

Funk had been born in Ohio in 1839. After graduating from Wittenberg College in Springfield, Ohio in 1860, he entered the Lutheran ministry the following year, and held several pastorates between then and 1872. That year saw his resignation from the pastoral ministry; a European and Middle East tour followed, and then, on his return to the United States, Funk became involved in periodical editing, first for others, and then on his own account. His periodical *The Metropolitan Pulpit* (later the *Homiletic Review*) was launched in October 1876.

Funk and Wagnalls began business 'on the smallest possible scale',[261] but Funk, with the dynamism characteristic of many nineteenth century publishers on both sides of the Atlantic, presided over a rapid expansion. Although it was later to develop a general list, the firm began as an almost exclusively religious house. Funk subscribed to the view (commonly held in the UK also) that what he saw as the negative effects of 'bad cheap literature' could be offset by 'good cheap literature', and, so much were his views in tune with contemporary perceptions, and so effective was his advocacy of those views, that large quantities of his firm's titles were sold, and Funk and Wagnalls prospered. A London office had been opened by the late 1880s.

Although some works of more academic theology did appear in the Funk and Wagnalls list, it is evident from the foregoing that the firm was aiming at a very different corner of the religious book market place from that in which the Clarks habitually traded. We may safely assume that in most cases the American firm would be interested only in the most 'popular' works on the Clark list, works which, by definition, would be most susceptible to piracy.

THE CHRISTIAN LITERATURE PUBLISHING COMPANY

John Tebbel[262] characterises the Christian Literature Publishing Company as 'a highly specialized religious house, but important in its own way.' The firm was founded in Buffalo in 1884 for the specific purpose of producing a perfectly legal, but in the Clarks' eyes most morally reprehensible, reprint of the *Ante-Nicene Library*. Although the reprint was issued under the nominal editorship of Bishop A.C. Coxe his editorial work, as we shall see, seems only to have been cosmetic. According to Tebbel, the new edition proved 'an immediate success.'[263] If this was so, it was presumably at the Clarks' expense.

In 1888, the firm moved to New York, and thereafter also reproduced the T. & T. Clark translation of the works of St Augustine, and issued other translations of patristic works, some in collaboration with James Parker and Company of Oxford and London.[264] The firm also published the series *Ten Epochs of Church History* which, as we have seen, was handled by the Clarks in the UK as *Eras of the Christian Church*. The Christian Literature Publishing Company was later bought over by the Scribner firm.

Unfortunately the *Trade Ledger 1895–1901*[265] does not include details of the extent of the Clarks' dealings with Fleming H. Revell, Funk and Wagnalls and the Christian Literature Publishing Company so we are unable to estimate the proportion of their total turnover which was contributed by this business.[266]

Financial implications

Having outlined the history of the principal firms which handled Clark works in the US, we turn now to look at the financial implications of the different arrangements under which these firms worked, varying from outright piracy to pre-authorised reprinting. As noted earlier, however, none of these categories is completely watertight. Owing to the volatile nature of this aspect of the Clarks' transatlantic publishing, a project which began as outright piracy could end up in a different category.

Piracy

For the purposes of the present study, the term 'piracy' is used in the very broad sense in which it was employed in the nineteenth century, defined thus by Simon Nowell-Smith: 'any appropriation by a publisher with no substantive right to it of a piece of writing to which its author or his assign claimed a title whether by statute, by natural law or in equity.'[267]

Nowell-Smith discusses[268] the complex procedures (constantly varying throughout the nineteenth century) which had to be implemented by the British and US publishers if a work were to be copyright in both countries. It is not always easy to be certain which of the many Clark works sold to US publishers were legally copyright in America through these procedures having been followed, but in general, at least until the 1890s, it would seem that few Clark titles had been copyrighted in this way. Consequently, in the cases where the Clarks refer to piracy, they use the word in the broad sense defined above, their moral indignation coupled with impotence at the realisation that legal redress was impossible.

Among works pirated in this sense were James Stalker's *Life of Christ* (1879) and *Life of St Paul* (1884), both issued in unauthorised editions by Revell, A.B. Bruce's *The Humiliation of Christ* (1876) and *The Training of the Twelve Apostles* (1871) both pirated by A.C. Armstrong, and the series of commentaries by H.A.W. Meyer, re-printed by Funk and Wagnalls.

There is no doubt that the unauthorised reprinting of works in the US had serious financial implications for T. & T. Clark.[269]

In the first place, it inevitably reduced the Clarks' US sales of their own editions of the works which had been reprinted without authorisation. Sales of the original edition did not always come to a complete halt, for some customers preferred the higher production standards of the imported edition, and were prepared to pay more for it than for a home-printed copy on cheaper paper. But there was bound to be a reduction in the demand for the Clark edition. Commenting to Philip Schaff on the Funk and Wagnalls piracy of several of their titles, the Clarks commented that it was a 'great nuisance', the sales being 'small enough' as it was.[270]

Secondly, when faced with the unauthorised reprinting of a work in the US, or with the possibility of such an unauthorised reprinting, the Clarks felt obliged to sell their edition to the official American agent at the lowest possible price, so that he could in turn sell the product very cheaply into the US market-place, thereby, it was hoped, either, as the case might be, effectively competing with extant piracies, or deflecting the attentions of would-be pirates. Such undercutting operations must have significantly reduced the profitability of Clark works, and the most that can be said for them is that they guaranteed that there would still be a demand in the US for Edinburgh-originated copies of the work in question. The initial print-run would have been determined with the likely requirements of the US market in mind. This lengthening of the run by the number of copies it was expected to sell in America would bring the unit cost lower than it would otherwise have been, and so produce a marginally larger profit on sales in the UK. If a pirated edition threatened to make the original edition unsaleable in America, however, the overall profitability of the work would be in danger. It therefore became an attractive option to sell copies to the US at little more than cost in order to undercut the pirates and ensure some return at least from the copies printed with the transatlantic market in mind.

A third factor to be taken into consideration in any discussion of the financial implications of unauthorised reprinting is that in the majority of cases, because of their specialised nature and complex type-setting, Clark works were proof against the pirates. As the firm commented to Scribners

> our publications are not usually of a 'popular' kind in the ordinary [illegible] of the word, and ... we have to a large extent, a guarantee against re-printing on account of the expense arising from the quantity of Greek and Hebrew.[271]

But if this were the case, then it follows that the works which were most susceptible to unauthorised reprinting were the more 'popular', and least 'academic' of those on the Clark list: precisely the works, in fact, which were likely to form the bulk of the firm's exports to the US. In other words, although only a minority of Clark titles may have been affected by piracy, it was a minority from which the bulk of the Clarks' profit on exports was likely to come. The economic impact of the piracies upon the firm, therefore, would be out of all proportion to the percentage of titles on the list which were affected.

It is clear from all this that unauthorised reprints had a large and serious, if unquantifiable, effect on the Clarks' profitability. The Edinburgh firm responded with a mixture of irritation and resignation, laced with a remarkable tolerance. At the same time as Revell was provoking irritation in George Street with his reprints of James Stalker's works, the Clarks were giving the Canadian franchise in the *Expository Times* to his subsidiary, the Willard Tract Depository.[272] And at the same time as Funk and Wagnalls were pirating the Meyer series and other works, the Clarks were acting as UK agents for one of their publications (J.J. Herzog's *Religious Encyclopaedia*), and considering their firm as a possible US distributor of the *Monthly Interpreter* if Scribners proved unwilling to handle it.[273] Given the character of the Clarks, this tolerance clearly sprang in part from Christian grace. But allied to this grace was a shrewd commercial pragmatism which sought to make the best — financially and theologically — of every situation which presented itself.

Unwilling accords

Having produced, or announced his intention of producing, an unauthorised reprint, the US publisher would very often attempt to persuade the Clarks to bow before the inevitable fact of its existence, and come to some kind of agreement. He was presumably eager to conclude terms so that his edition could be announced as appearing with the consent of the British publisher, and also, and more importantly, so that the flow of copies imported from Edinburgh could be staunched.[274] In some cases, the Clarks were forced to accede to this transatlantic arm-twisting, and reluctantly reached unwilling accords. Such agreements were concluded with A.C. Armstrong in respect of *The Humiliation of Christ* and *The Training of the Twelve Apostles* by A.B. Bruce, and with Funk and Wagnalls in respect of the series of commentaries by H.A.W. Meyer.

But the best documented 'reluctant accord' with a US publisher is that governing the Clarks' relationship with the Christian Literature Publishing Company (hereafter referred to in this section as 'the Company'). The first mentions in the Clark letter books of the Company's unauthorised edition of the *Ante-Nicene Library* date from the autumn of 1884. The American reprint was to be edited by the Bishop of New York, A.C. Coxe, and it was to him that the Clarks directed a strong letter of remonstrance on 25 September,[275] in which they attempted to persuade him that the proposed edition would not only be seriously disadvantageous to them, but also that it was morally indefensible.

The American edition would do 'serious injury' (presumably financial injury) to the Clarks. The Series was the fruit of considerable investment on the part of the Edinburgh firm, and it was considered that a large sale in the United States was essential if the work were to succeed. The appearance of a rival edition would reduce or obliterate the Clarks' transatlantic market for the Series, and hence jeopardise its profitability.

This moral case against the Company's reprint was strengthened by a number of related contentions. In the first place, it was argued, it could not be said that the reprint was justifiable in that it was making the work freely available in the US, for there had never been any problems of supply, the Series having been constantly available in America through Scribners. In the second place, the Company's edition was, although nominally a revision issued under the editorship of Coxe, in fact a reprint pure and simple.

> You purpose to deprive us of our reward, by quietly appropriating our labours, with some slight changes which are not worth speaking of, and which we could ourselves easily carry out as the work is stereotyped and a change in the arrangement is all that is required.

In the third place, the Company's action seemed all the more reprehensible in that they claimed to be motivated by a desire to further the interests of international copyright. In the absence of the other side of the correspondence, it is difficult to envisage how the Company imagined that their reprint would have this effect; their viewpoint seems to have been as incomprehensible to the Clarks at the time as it is to us now. The fact that the Company was aware of the need for an international copyright agreement made its flagrant denial of the Clarks' rights in the *Ante-Nicene Library* all the more indefensible in the Edinburgh firm's eyes.

> You do all this under the guise of a desire for an International Copyright. *We* are unable to see anything in this but the most obvious *non sequitur*.
>
> You are zealous for the protection of property and to prove this you seize our publications! We must say it is uncommonly like the Police force failing to protect private property, and, in order to remedy the matter making a raid upon it for their own benefit.

This firm letter concluded with a warning:

> We hope to hear that the matter is abandoned and that we shall not be forced to publish a correspondence which shows a state of matters altogether indefensible as between honourable men.

As was usual, therefore, when threatened with an unauthorised edition, the Clarks' initial response was to write in high moral dudgeon in an attempt to persuade the American publisher to abandon his plans. In fact, of course, the Clarks were powerless, and in this case too, their letter had little effect. The Company did not withdraw its edition, and its only concession was to offer an honorarium to the Edinburgh firm after one thousand copies of the reprint had been sold. The Clarks viewed this offer as being 'so small as to be altogether valueless',[276] but even in using that phrase they showed that they were accepting the inevitable: the reprint would go ahead, they were in a negotiating position, and all they could do was to put their case as forcibly as possible in order to secure the most advantageous terms. They expressed this position themselves in a letter to Scribners: 'finding we had no escape from anyone who chooses to pirate all we could do was to make the best bargain we could.'[277]

Once the Clarks had accepted the inevitability of the reprint, negotiations proceeded. On 22 November 1884, while still pointing out 'that it would be far more to our interest that you should not go on at all with this series', they expressed their willingness to accept a royalty of 5% on the selling price on *all* the Company's sales of the Series, and in return to offer the Company sole US rights in the work. A further condition was that the Company should purchase from Scribners (if that firm were in agreement) the copies of the Clark edition which they had in stock, sales of which were already drying up as potential American purchasers awaited the appearance of the Company's edition which had been announced. This clause was intended to prevent Scribners being financially embarrassed through being left with unsaleable stock on hand.[278] The Company accepted the Clarks' terms,[279] but the conclusion of an agreement was complicated by the reaction of Scribners. They wanted to continue on the old footing, and refused to sell their stock to the Company. In response the Clarks pointed out that they could not continue to supply Scribners after reaching an agreement with the Company, stressed that they had considered that they were acting in Scribners' best interests in inserting the clause which required the Company to buy over the stocks they held and agreed that it was ultimately entirely up to Scribners to decide whether or not to retain their stock of the Series.[280] In the event, Scribners did hold on to their fairly modest stock (amounting to some two hundred volumes),[281] and this fact weakened the Clarks' bargaining position with the Company, who argued that as its sales were being threatened by Scribners' sales from stock of the original edition, it was inappropriate for it to pay the full 5% royalty to Edinburgh. However, although these complications were to arise, the basic agreement had been reached by the end of 1884. But while the Clarks' letters to the Company were amicably businesslike, it was indeed a reluctant accord. For they could not understand as they said in a private letter to Philip Schaff, 'how *Christian* men — with Bishop Coxe at their head — could do such a thing. It is sheer *robbery*.'[282]

In May 1885 the Clarks wrote to the Company, expressing the hope that 'the royalty [would] amount to something considerable to make up for [their] loss of sale in the States.'[283] What were the financial implications of the agreement with the Company, and to what extent was the Edinburgh firm compensated by payments from the Company for loss of sales of its own edition in America? The Clarks originally expected to receive a 5% royalty on all the Company's sales of the American reprint. However, when Scribners insisted on holding on to their stock, the Company used this as an excuse to substitute a down-payment for a royalty agreement. This, to the Clarks, was patently ridiculous:

> To say that the small number of vols which Messrs. Scribner have on hand — equal to about nine sets — could have damaged you in any way is absurd.[284]

But the Clarks had little bargaining power. The down-payment on offer would total $800 for the set of twenty-four volumes. This, the Clarks pointed out, equalled £160, and as such was only at the rate of around £7 per volume. Had a 5% royalty agreement been in operation, the Clarks would have received £7 by the time 640 copies of a volume had been sold, and as sales were anticipated of far more copies than this, the down-payment proposed by the Company compared very unfavourably with the previously-agreed royalty arrangement. This unfavourable comparison prompted the Clarks' comment that they considered the Company's change in the terms of their offer to be 'exceedingly unfair.'[285]

In an attempt to persuade the Company to revert to the original terms the Clarks tacitly threatened to abandon *their* side of the agreement by continuing to supply copies of their edition to Scribners. They also held out the bait of the US rights in the *St Augustine* Library which they offered to assign to the Company if they would accept a 5% royalty agreement on both Series.[286]

The Company, however, refused to pay a royalty, and instead offered a much higher down-payment on each volume, apparently amounting to $125 per volume. To this the Clarks had to agree.[287] It was certainly a much healthier offer than had been previously made, for the earlier $800 for the twenty-four volumes would have amounted to only $33⅓ per volume. Although not a royalty agreement, this offer was therefore a substantial improvement on the previously offered terms, being the equivalent of a royalty of 5% on sales of 2,400 at the US selling price. In some ways, this may even have been a better arrangement than a straight royalty from the Clarks' point of view. The $125 was to be paid on publication (although the Company proved dilatory in sending payment: in the case of the first two volumes they were at least three months late),[288] and it must remain a matter of speculation whether the US market could have absorbed an edition as large as 2,400 copies.

This arrangement seems to have been continued. On 13 November 1885 $125 was received in respect of the Company's edition of Volume 3 of the *Library*,[289] and similar payments were made in respect of succeeding volumes. The Clarks also conceded to the Company the right to issue the *St Augustine* Library in the United States. While they would have preferred a 5% royalty agreement, they once again agreed to accept a one-off payment of $125 on each volume.[290]

This case study shows that, faced with the inevitability of an unauthorised reprint, the Clarks had no alternative but to come to terms with the American company, attempting to conclude the most advantageous agreement. And the figure finally agreed upon, $125 per volume, seems a not unreasonable sum; it was certainly far greater than that which the firm could have earned from sales to Scribners, at least in the short term. So while the Clarks' return per unit sold may not have been so high as from sales through Scribners, their overall income from US sales may not have been adversely affected by the agreement with the Company, and may even have been increased.

T. & T. Clark and the Company had an identity of interest, and it was no doubt because of this that a relationship which began so frigidly developed into a warmer and closer co-operation. In the very early stages of this relationship, the Company offered the Clarks the UK agency in a series they were producing of works by *Nicene and Post-Nicene Fathers*. Much of the material in the first seven volumes of this Series was in fact reproduced from T. & T. Clark publications, and the Clarks felt that 'their introduction into this country would greatly interfere with our Series.' But, nevertheless, they were prepared to take fifty sets of the Series as an experiment, on sale-or-return.[291] And in later years we find the Clarks willing to consider the Company as a possible distributor of the *Expository Times* in place of Scribners.[292] Towards the end of the century, T. & T. Clark, as we have noted, distributed the *Eras of the Christian Church* series, which had originated with the American firm. By then, the companies were functioning as partners rather than as competitors.

Unwilling though these accords with Armstrong, Funk and Wagnalls, the Christian Literature Publishing Company and others may have been, the Clarks sought to extract the maximum benefit for themselves in difficult situations, and it is hard to avoid the conclusion that, in the main, the agreements were reasonably favourable to the firm. While we do not have as many figures as would wish, the extant evidence suggests that the returns which the Clarks received as a result of these accords would have substantially offset, certainly in the short term, the loss to the firm of the profit on US sales which they would otherwise have made.

Willing liaisons

Although a considerable number of Clark works appearing in North America did so as a result of piracies or reluctant accords, it was clearly in the Edinburgh firm's best interests that as large a proportion as possible of their works should be issued there as the result of negotiations with a publisher who would accept terms favourable to them. The Clarks without doubt viewed the American market as vital to the profitability of individual titles. In the case of the *Ante-*

Nicene Library, for example, they commented not only that they had 'reckoned on a large sale in the United States', but also that 'without this [sale] the matter would have been hopeless.'[293]

When a Clark work was to be issued by an American firm, there were in theory three strategies which could be followed. The Edinburgh firm could export a set of stereoplates of the work from which the American company could print their own edition. The American firm would pay for the stereos, and remit a royalty on each copy sold. In practice, this was not normally done, except in the case of some of the major reference works which will be considered in Chapter 8. In most cases, the potential American market for the work was too small to make a US reprint from stereos a viable proposition. Secondly, the Clarks could authorise an American firm to issue a reprint of the work printed from type set in the US, a royalty on each copy sold being payable to Edinburgh. Although the firm claimed, as we noted earlier, that they were 'always ready to consider the question of republishing with a royalty',[294] in fact agreements of this kind seem to have been relatively infrequent and to have been prompted in most cases by the threat of piracy. As typesetting would be more expensive than printing from stereos in the US, the size of the potential American market would have to be considerable for this expedient to be justifiable financially under normal circumstances. The third and most common way of issuing a Clark work in the US involved the sale to the American firm of an edition printed in Edinburgh. The presses were simply run on after the number of copies the Clarks required for the UK and Colonial markets had been printed, the American publisher's imprint being substituted for that of T. & T. Clark in the additional copies.

There follows an examination of how these arrangements with US publishers were organised, and how terms were agreed upon; and an assessment of the Clarks' view that the US market was essential, presumably in guaranteeing a print run sufficiently long to make the unit cost acceptably low.

Although, as we noted, Scribners were not the Clarks' sole agents in the US, in fact most new Clark titles were offered to them. When new works for the spring and autumn publishing seasons each year were being prepared, a long and enthusiastic letter would inevitably be despatched to Scribners, extolling the virtues of the books in question, quoting favourable comments from James Hastings and others who had read the manuscripts, urging the American firm to agree to take editions, and pointing out the need for haste in placing an order before the works had to go to press. Similarly, new Clark periodicals were offered to Scribners. Thus, for example, they were told in September 1884 regarding the new *Monthly Interpreter*: 'we make the first offer to you as our old friends.'[295] Thus, too, they were offered the *Critical Review* in 1890.[296]

Considerable benefits were derived from a close working partnership of this kind. It was, as we noted previously, a double-sided relationship: if the Clarks were eager to sell works to Scribners, the Americans were equally eager to sell their works to Edinburgh. A judicious, regular purchase of the other's products made it more likely that one would, in return, receive regular orders for one's own productions. Seeing the benefits inherent in this kind of trade-off, the

Clarks, while not limiting their US sales exclusively to Scribners, nevertheless dealt for the most part with them.

A letter dated 24 February 1885 shows the subtlety with which the Clarks attempted to persuade Scribners to take on their works. The Americans had evidently expressed an interest in having exclusive rights in R.H. Lotze's *Microcosmus*, a work which had been 'fabulously costly'[297] to print. The Clarks responded by agreeing to offer the American firm the exclusive rights, and used three subtle arguments to ensure their continuing interest in the work. Firstly, in expressing the hope that *Microcosmus* would be a great success in the US, they added in parenthesis 'much greater, we trust than we regret to say Ladd has been on this side', thereby reminding the Americans that they, the Clarks, had been willing to take copies of a US work of dubious UK sales potential and had suffered accordingly. There is the implicit suggestion that Scribners should regard themselves as being under obligation to take a similar risk. Secondly, the Clarks pointed out that owing to the large quantity of Greek and Hebrew type used in the work, Scribners could rest assured that no pirate would touch it since an unauthorised reprint would be too expensive to produce at a competitive price. Thus the Clarks cushioned themselves against any complaints the American firm might make about the expense of the work, and pointed out that in fact its expense was a virtue, rendering it unlikely to fall prey to the pirates. Thirdly, the Clarks reminded Scribners of their willingness to consider assigning to the American firm the US rights in any Clark works for which they felt disposed to submit an offer. This was in a sense a bait to encourage in Scribners a favourable disposition towards the work currently on offer. The letter concluded with the sentence quoted earlier: 'As you know, there is no house with whom we desire that our works should be placed compared with yours.'[298] This letter illustrates the benefits of the close, co-operative relationship which existed between the two firms. It is not surprising that most of the Clark works which were legitimately issued in America appeared with the Scribner imprint.

PERIODICALS

The Clarks attempted to find American outlets for all their theological periodicals, the *Monthly Interpreter*, the *Critical Review*, and the *Expository Times*, and in fact offered all of these to Scribners. Most of the available documents relate to the *Expository Times* for which Scribners had the US rights from the time the Clarks assumed responsibility for it in January 1890.

Although the *Expository Times* did not make a profit in its early years, it was a prestigious periodical, and a valuable platform for Clark advertising, and it was clearly in the Edinburgh firm's best interests to see it circulated as widely as possible in the US as in this country. Over a number of years the Clarks were less than enthusiastic about Scribners' efforts on behalf of the periodical and, as early as August 1893, entered into negotiations with the Christian Literature Publishing Company to transfer the *Expository Times* franchise to them. These negotiations are of interest for what they reveal of the terms governing the export of Clark periodicals.

In the autumn of 1893, the Company clearly offered to be responsible for the *Expository Times* in the US. This offer was favourably received by the Clarks, who were concerned at Scribners' lack of dynamism in promoting a magazine for which they were certain there was a large potential Stateside market:

> if better known and properly pushed, the magazine would have a very large circulation in the States. You have no other Periodical on the same lines, & the Editor has received letters from many American Subscribers enthusiastic in their appreciation of it.[299]

In principle, then, the Clarks were in favour of giving the franchise to the Company. But the offer which it had made — 1*d*. per copy — was not viable from the Clarks' point of view. The *Expository Times* was expensive to produce, and the size of each issue had recently been doubled from twenty-four to forty-eight pages, the retail price having been increased accordingly from 3*d*. to 6*d*. The Clarks could not afford to supply the periodical to the States at less than 2*d*. per copy, although even that figure was 'much below the actual cost price'.[300] The Clarks therefore proposed to supply the Company with the periodical at 2*d*. per copy, on condition that they undertook to promote it vigorously in the US, and to take a minimum of two thousand copies per month.[301] They would be permitted to raise extra revenue by printing their own advertising pages, the rest of the magazine being supplied in sheets from Edinburgh. Three further conditions were laid down: the agreement would be subject to Scribners' acquiescence at the transfer of the agency; the Clarks would be entitled to one free page of advertising in each issue; and Scribners were to be permitted to retain any of the current subscribers who were their regular customers.[302] This offer was made on 17 August 1893. The Company clearly did not reach a decision immediately, for on 10 November 1893 we find the Clarks writing to them, urging them to make up their minds, and regretting that the Canadian market could not be included in the franchise on offer as this had recently been taken over by Revell's Willard Tract Depository where the staff were 'pushing [the *Expository Times*] all they [could] with great success.'[303] At that point, however, the Company must have decided against accepting the Clarks' terms, and the franchise remained with Scribners.

Negotiations were resumed four years later, however, when a representative of the Company, a Mr Bagley, visited the Clarks in Edinburgh, undertaking to 'make a great effort to establish the Magazine on a firm footing in the States'[304] if suitable terms could be decided. An agreement was concluded, in which both sides made some concessions on their 1893 position. It seems, however, that the Clarks conceded more than the American firm. They agreed to supply the Company with the periodical at the rate of 1*d*. per copy for the first six months, provided 2,500 copies of each issue were taken. Thereafter, the Company agreed to pay 1½*d*. per copy, but was to be free to reduce its order to no fewer than two thousand copies of each issue. Once again, the Clarks were to be entitled to one page of free advertising in each issue. The Company also attempted to influence the editorial content of the periodical, proposing that additional material with a US bearing should be inserted in America. James Hastings had strong objections to the magazine appearing with additions to it, promising only that it would in future be 'a little more representative of American scholarship.'[305] In the end, however, the Company won the right to make minor additions to the periodical: 'Provided its general character is not affected, & the Editor's writing is not tampered with, we do not think he will raise any serious objections to such slight additions.'[306] A major difference between the agreement proposed in 1893 and that finally concluded in 1897 lay in the attitude towards Scribners. The 1893 proposals had been conditional upon Scribners' consent; in 1897 the American firm was merely informed of what was happening, and that at very short notice. The new agents were to take over from the issue for October 1897. It was not until 27 August that the Clarks wrote to Scribners, notifying them that their *Expository Times* franchise was being withdrawn, and continuing as follows:

> We should of course have preferred that the E.T. remained in your hands if you had found it worth your while to make a special effort with it . . . but we quite understand that, amid the large number of your own important publications that is hardly to be expected.[307]

It is uncertain how many copies the Company actually sold in America. But clearly sales were not as high as had been anticipated, for, contrary to the terms of the agreement, it ordered 2,500 copies per issue for the first three months only, and thereafter two thousand copies. But the Clarks, although not compelled to by the terms of the agreement if the Company's order fell below 2,500, supplied the magazine for the first six months at 1*d*. per copy, thereafter raising the price to 1½*d*. per copy. The Company continued to take 2,000 copies of each issue.[308]

In 1897–98, the *Expository Times* was still trading at a loss, and the Clarks were heavily subsidising each issue exported to the US. (The total cost to the Clarks of each copy produced was now around 5.69*d*.)[309] This, then, is another example of the Edinburgh firm being willing to face financial loss in order to promote a product they believed in, although here the loss was offset by the value to the Clarks of the periodical as a prestigious shop window. The sequence of events also reminds us that, committed as the Clarks were to Scribners, theirs was not a mindless commitment; with their characteristically pragmatic approach they were willing to withdraw the franchise from Scribners when they felt that better distribution could be achieved elsewhere.

INDIVIDUAL TITLES

When selling copies of individual titles to American houses (usually, as we saw, to Scribners), it was the Clarks' normal practice to supply an edition on publication, usually shipped in sheets for binding in the US. If the American publisher sold the whole of his edition, further copies could be supplied from Edinburgh in smaller quantities. How profitable were these sales?

Unfortunately, in none of the cases where it is possible to ascertain the level of discount offered to Scribners is it also possible to calculate the unit production cost of the work in question; in consequence we are unable to estimate accurately the percentage of profit received by the Clarks on their American sales. On the face of it, their discounts were generous, but frequently they sold to America at a cut-throat price in order to deter would-be pirates. Scribners' normal rate of discount would appear to have been 50% on the (presumably trade) UK price. This is confirmed by the Clarks' comment to Professor Laidlaw of Edinburgh 'Owing to Duty, etc. we have to supply our American Agents at just about half price'.[310] It is confirmed also by comments made to Scribners themselves, in which the Clarks expressed regret that they were unable to give them a straight 50% discount on all their purchases, thereby implying that 50% was the norm.[311] Even larger discounts might be given in the case of works which the Clarks felt were particularly worth promoting, or where special distribution factors were involved. For example, Scribners were given special terms on some titles which they wanted to include in their Christian Literature Club.[312] Although these discounts were considerable, they were arrived at willingly by the Clarks in full recognition of the importance of the American market to the profitability of individual works. We may therefore assume that they would have given the firm an adequate return.

We can speculate about the percentage of profit which the Clarks would have made on their US sales. S.D.F. Salmond's work on *The Christian Doctrine of Immortality* was published in 1895 at a nominal retail price of 14*s*. 0*d*., the price to the trade being 10*s*. 6*d*. Excluding advertising and other incidentals, the total cost of the first impression of 1,078 copies was £269 18*s*. 1*d*.[313] The unit cost to the Clarks of bound copies was therefore around 5*s*. 0*d*. If copies of this work were sold to Scribners at a discount of 50% on the UK trade price, the American firm would have paid 5*s*. 3*d*. for each copy they purchased, yielding a very small return to the Clarks. Probably, however, the work would have been sold at this price in sheets: the unit cost to the Clarks of unbound copies was 4*s*. 4½*d*. Therefore, on these approximate figures, sales to Scribners would have produced a return of 20% on the investment: not a spectacular figure, certainly, but a useful source of income, particularly as it would be paid at the first settlement date after publication. We may assume that most sales of editions of works to US houses yielded a similar rate of return.

T. & T. Clarks' sales to Scribners were not limited to large editions at the time of publication. Once the American publisher's original stock had sold out, smaller quantities of the title could be purchased, no doubt at terms less advantageous to the importer. And it seems likely that, from time to time, Scribners ordered small quantities of works from the Clarks which they were unwilling, or never had had the opportunity, to purchase in large editions. For example, over the financial year 1896–97,[314] Scribners bought quantities of forty-eight Clark titles, including new works but excluding works in series. The total number of books purchased was 1,702, producing an average of 35.45 copies of each title. Of the forty-eight titles, only fifteen were purchased in bulk (that is, in quantities of fifty or over). Of those fifteen titles, a total of 1,306 copies were purchased, the average order per title being therefore eighty-seven. Of the remaining thirty-three titles, purchased in smaller quantities, a total of 396 copies were supplied by the Clarks, the average number of copies per title being twelve. While the bulk of the Clarks' trade with Scribners involved sizable editions, therefore, a not insignificant part of it consisted of smaller orders for a wide range of titles. Sales to Scribners of works in the series such as the *Foreign Theological Library* are difficult to quantify. They would, however, have contributed significantly to the Clarks' income.

It seems clear that the trade done with American publishers such as Scribners as a result of willing liaisons was reasonably profitable to the firm. Although the evidence falls short of proving that the US market was essential to the success of Clark titles, it indubitably provided a welcome source of return on investment. Although the profitability of these transactions was on occasion threatened by the irksome activities of the unauthorised reprinters, the reluctant accords which the firm pragmatically reached with these pirates were frequently not unfruitful. We have noted earlier that the Clarks were frequently willing to put theological considerations before financial ones, to risk loss in order to promote titles in which they believed. This was certainly the case, but had the furtherance of theology been their sole aim, they would perhaps have been content to acquiesce at the activities of the pirates in the interests of achieving the widest possible circulation for the works in question. But there was a limit to the firm's altruism; the twin concerns of theology and profit had to be held in tension, and the Clarks were not prepared to sit back and watch others reap where they had sown. In any case, if they were to continue furthering the interests of theology, an assured profit from previous ventures was essential. And so, as regards the American market, they sought to ensure that profit was forthcoming by extricating as large a royalty as they could from the pirates, and by entering into willing liaisons based on agreements which were as favourable to their interests as was possible.

Co-operative publishing

There was a third dimension to the Clarks' transatlantic publishing. Not only did they distribute in the UK books which had originated with American publishers, and arrange for the US distribution of certain of their own titles, but also, increasingly as the nineteenth century drew to a close, they moved into the area of co-operative publishing with North American houses, producing what would today be called co-editions.

Their entry into these ventures was prompted firstly, by the undoubted benefits of sharing the production and editorial costs of a work or a series with another publisher; such co-operation made possible more extensive and costly publications than could have been undertaken had either publisher been working on his own. Secondly, international products would presumably be more attractive to an international market than would works originating in one or other of the two countries. Thirdly, major co-operative ventures such as the *International Theological Library* were prompted by the increasing importance of English-language as opposed to German theological scholarship. It was natural that English-language scholarship, which was international in scope, should seek an international forum for the expression of its views. The standing which the two *International* series achieved, in turn stimulated the growth and prompted the recognition of English-language theology.

The success of these ventures in theological and financial terms is best evaluated through a series of analytical case studies of the firm's involvement with co-editions.

History of the Sacred Scripture of the New Testament

One of the Clarks' earliest co-operative ventures was the production, in co-operation with the American publishers Houghton, Mifflin and Company of Boston, of a translation of a *History of the Sacred Scriptures of the New Testament* by E.W.E. Reuss. The agreement was concluded in the summer of 1882, and the work had been published by 1884. The translation was undertaken by a Mr Houghton who was possibly a member of the US Company.[315] There is no record of the terms concluded by the two firms, or of the success of the title. Three copies were sold in the financial year 1896–97 and the work was still in print in 1901. It is clear that the American firm took the initiative in this venture.

Religious Encyclopaedia

In general, however, the Clarks' early experiences with co-operative publishing seem to have been anything but propitious. In 1879, the American theologian Philip Schaff proposed that T. & T. Clark should issue in collaboration with an apparently yet-to-be chosen US publisher a translation of J.J. Herzog's *Religious Encyclopaedia*. It was thought initially that the work, which was to include some new material, would run to four volumes. Thomas Clark was willing to agree to this proposal, subject to certain conditions. Firstly, the American publisher had to be one 'of substance'. Secondly, that publisher had to be prepared 'to run half the cost of literary production, of composition and a set of plates'. Thirdly, the sum expended on commissioning additional material must not exceed that mentioned by Schaff in his letter. Fourthly, a time limit of four years should be set on the project. Fifthly, and most importantly from Clark's point of view, all the work had to be done in Edinburgh where he could oversee it. He foresaw no difficulties in the arrangement, since proof sheets could be forwarded regularly across the Atlantic to Schaff.[316] In fact, Clark showed himself willing to compromise on the final point. Three weeks after his first letter he wrote to Schaff agreeing that, supposing the work were to run to four volumes, two could be set in Edinburgh, and two in America, the two publishers exchanging sets of plates. But in agreeing this, he insisted that a straight exchange should operate, the cost of plates received being set against the cost of those supplied; he envisaged that if it were done otherwise, disputes might arise due to the differing costs of typesetting and stereotyping on each side of the Atlantic.[317] In fact, the Herzog work ran to only three volumes: these appeared in 1882, 1883 and 1884, the US publishers being Funk and Wagnalls.[318] There is no record of the production costs of the Series, but its sales were clearly very poor, for in January 1885, the work was still showing a debit balance of £518.[319] However, it does not appear in the Clark catalogues in the 1890s, by which time it had presumably sold out. Given firstly that it had been properly costed, and secondly that it was not in any way remaindered (a course of action which the Clarks abhorred), it should have covered its costs, and yielded a fair return on the investment.

Commentary on the New Testament ('Illustrated Popular Commentary')

The issue of the *Commentary on the New Testament* prepared under the editorship of Philip Schaff would seem to have been the earliest significant co-operative venture between T. & T. Clark and Scribners. This work was issued in four volumes, published in, respectively, 1879, 1880, 1882 and 1883, and would seem, in the short term at least, to have been an unmitigated disaster from an economic point of view.[320]

It would appear from the letter books[321] that the initial plan was for an eight volume work, four volumes to be devoted to the Old Testament, and four to the New. The work was to be edited by Schaff, who would write some of the material himself, and commission the remainder from scholars on both sides of the Atlantic. The production arrangements were similar to those which Thomas Clark finally agreed for the Herzog work: each of the two publishers was to be responsible for an equal number of volumes, and would supply a set of stereoplates to the other. These were to be supplied on an exchange basis, with no money changing hands until the work was completed, when 'a final adjustment' would be made.[322] It would appear that each publisher was responsible for paying the authors on his side of the Atlantic, the British contributors receiving one pound per page from the Clarks.[323] Although contributions were commissioned for the Old and New Testament volumes, the New Testament section began to appear first.

The whole project was beset by difficulties, the most serious being the Scribners' sudden withdrawal from involvement in the Old Testament section of the work. This was due, apparently, to 'changes in the Scribner firm and other reasons on their side of the Atlantic';[324] the remote possibility remained that Scribners might be willing to proceed with the Old Testament section once the New Testament volumes had been issued. One reason for their reluctance to proceed was the impending appearance of the Revised Version of the Bible which it was considered would replace the King James Version. Scribners clearly felt that by waiting, they could base the *Commentary* on the new translation rather than on the old.[325] The Scribner decision left the Clarks in a difficult position: they could not afford to proceed with the Old Testament section on their own, and so were forced to extricate themselves from arrangements already made with British scholars who had been commissioned to contribute sections of the *Commentary*. Some of these scholars agreed to withdraw; Bishop Charles J. Ellicott was preparing a work on the Old Testament and could use their material. And Clark was able to use work prepared by George C.M. Douglas and J.G. Murphy in the *Bible Class Handbooks* series.[326] But, not surprisingly, he was aggrieved, commenting of the Old Testament section 'whilst it is a relief to have it off my mind, yet the blame is not mine, had Scribner gone on I would but it is now too late.'[327]

A further problem arose over alleged infringement by the Clarks in Volume One of the *Commentary* of the copyright of the Revised Version of the New Testament, which had at that point not yet been published,[328] but to which Philip Schaff appears to have been privy. In responding to the letter of complaint from the Secretaries of the University Presses, Messrs Price and Clay, the Clarks pointed out that they had frequently warned Schaff, both orally and in writing, to be 'exceedingly careful not to infringe upon any rights in [the UK]'; indicated that as the work had been stereotyped in America they had not seen it until it was complete; and reminded the Secretaries that, as they, the Clarks, were not privy to the deliberations of the A.V. Revision Committee, they could not possibly have known what alterations had been suggested by the Committee, or identified them in the text. They further pointed out that the alleged infringements could not in any way affect the sales of the Revision. All these arguments were employed in the hope that the Secretaries could be persuaded not to put an embargo on the first volume of the Commentary. The second volume, prepared by British scholars who would most certainly have avoided infringing the Revisers' copyright, was almost ready for publication, and an embargo on the first volume would seriously affect sales of the second also. The letter concluded:

> We have not the slightest doubt that the matter will be amicably arranged, and we are sure that . . . the . . . gentlemen of the Revision will not desire to injure a firm which has done so much to aid them in their labours through publications on similar subjects.[329]

Those pleas were contained in a letter dated 16 December 1879; they seem to have fallen on deaf ears, for the Secretaries wrote two days later to the Clarks requiring them to withdraw the volume from circulation. This was a major blow:

> not only is the annoyance and pain very great, both to Dr Schaff and myself, but the loss and damage caused by the paralysis which your letter has given rise to, is very serious to me . . .[330]

The Clarks never seriously doubted the integrity of Schaff, who sent a circular letter to the English Revisers, explicitly denying the charges they had made. He claimed that in dealing with the New Testament text he had been careful to eject from his mind what was peculiar to the Revision, but that nevertheless, evaluating the textual evidence, he had arrived at readings identical to those established by the Revisers.[331] It is difficult to see how Schaff could have achieved this mental compartmentalisation but Thomas Clark was convinced of his sincerity. More importantly, so too were the Revisers, who accordingly lifted their embargo, clearly agreeing with Clark's assessment of the situation:

> In no possible way can I see that those (what I must call) undesigned coincidences can damage your rights, but rather do them good by showing the unanimity of scholars in the changes.[332]

Of course, the Clarks took even greater care in the future to avoid a repetition of this problem. Accordingly some changes had to be made on the plates of Volume Two, and the firm contacted Price and Clay to ask on what terms the emendations and marginal references of the Revisers could be used by the Clarks and Scribners in the volumes of the *Commentary* which were still to be issued.[333]

All these problems irritated the Clarks:

> This Commentary has been a source of perpetual vexation to us, and we suppose to you and our friend Dr Schaff also, & we heartily wish we had never had anything to do with it.[334]

And the work was manifestly uneconomic, particularly in the short term. The fourth volume was published in 1883; by February 1884 only two hundred copies had been sold by the Clarks, who commented 'We still hope that the work may take a start, but it has been a very great failure as yet.'[335] Despite the lingering optimism, this position had changed little a year later, and the work was showing a massive deficit of £1,485.[336] The *Commentary* was still in print in 1901. Over the financial year 1896–97, seventeen copies were sold of Volume One, twenty-five copies of Volume Two, nineteen copies of Volume Three, and twenty-three copies of Volume Four. So sales did not dry up entirely, and, in the long term, the firm may have recouped its investment. But in the light of these experiences, it is small wonder that the possibility of proceeding with the Old Testament section was not alluded to again.

The production of this *Commentary* was a complicated exercise in co-operation. But more complicated by far, and also more successful by far, were the two major co-published series which began to come to fruition in the 1890s, the *International Theological Library*, and the *International Critical Commentary*. The same problems of co-ordinating production schedules, and balancing the interests of the two co-operating firms which had made the production of Schaff's *Commentary* exceptionally difficult, would inevitably be present in these larger and more complex schemes. In the light of the poor profitability of earlier ventures, the courage and vision of T. & T. Clark (and Scribners) in proceeding with the new series is truly remarkable.

The International Theological Library

It is not certain whether the *International Theological Library* was proposed by T. & T. Clark or by Scribners, but if, as seems most likely, the idea originated with the American firm, it met with an enthusiastic response in Edinburgh. One of the earliest references to the *Library* dates from February 1887 in a letter to S.D.F. Salmond, who had accepted an invitation to be British editor of the Series: 'we are delighted to hear that you heartily approve of the [illegible — ?plan] & are willing to co-operate.'[337] The Clarks felt that fourteen or fifteen volumes should be commissioned initially until it was seen how successful or otherwise the Series proved to be;[338] in fact only nine volumes had appeared by the turn of the century. The commercial and theological success or failure of the venture hung on a number of crucial issues, which we will now consider in turn.

Unity of purpose

If the Series were to succeed, the two collaborating publishers must share a substantial unity of vision, while at the same time preserving the security of their own financial interests by producing material which would be acceptable in their respective market places. And, by and large, the two companies did have an identical vision of the role of the Series, at least in general terms. In the autumn of 1887 a document was drawn up and approved by both T. & T. Clark and Scribners which aimed at advising potential contributors of the nature of the I.T.L.[339] The document dealt with the *range* to be covered by the *Library* – it was 'designed to cover the whole field of Christian Theology'; it mentioned the *target audience* – the *Library* would provide a series of text books for students of theology, and would also be aimed at 'scholars of every class who [wished] to have a systematic and thorough exposition of the several departments of theological science'; it discussed in detail the *approach* which the authors would be expected to follow

> The Library is international, interconfessional, & in the interests of Theology as a science. A catholic spirit should rule in all the work, and the authors should cultivate as far as possible an objective method, presenting a fair & complete statement of the results of theological science & the questions still at issue in these several departments;

and it gave guidelines as to the *depth of treatment* which was to characterise the Series – the treatment of each subject was to be 'exhaustive', and was to 'adequately represent the [current] stage of investigation in Great Britain and America'.

The fact that there was this general consensus on what the aims of the I.T.L. should be is not to say that the companies always saw eye-to-eye on every issue. In the 1890s, for example, Scribners complained, possibly with some justification, that the Clarks were delaying the appearance of certain volumes by enlisting *Library* contributors to write for the *Dictionary of the Bible*, and thereby diverting their energies away from their work on behalf of the Series.[340] Then again, there was some dispute between Scribners and the Clarks over the relative priority of the *International Theological Library* and the *International Critical Commentary*. The idea of the I.T.L. had probably originated with Scribners, whereas, as one of the Clarks wrote, 'the Commentaries were my suggestion'.[341] The Clarks, although totally committed to the *Library*, felt that the I.C.C. series was likely to prove the more successful financially, especially as it included less controversial matter, and considered that there was no question of the two series directly competing with one another.[342] Scribners saw things differently: they viewed the two series as being in competition, declined at least for the present to become involved with the I.C.C., and questioned the genuineness of the Clarks' commitment to the *Library*. A compromise was reached,[343] which involved the Clarks' affirming their commitment to the I.T.L., and agreeing to proceed with commissioning volumes for the I.C.C. on their own initiative, it being stipulated that no volume in that series should be published for two years. Before that time, Scribners would have the opportunity of opting either to co-publish the Series with the Clarks, or merely to distribute it in the US. Should Scribners decline both these options, the Clarks would be free to enter into negotiations with another US publisher. In the event, Scribners did join forces with the Clarks, and thus a potentially difficult situation[344] was defused, and an amicable settlement reached.

The fact that the two companies were essentially of one mind augured well for the success of the Series. It is interesting to notice that this unity was strengthened rather than weakened at a time of grave tension in Anglo-American political relations in the mid-1890s, which might have been expected to have implications for trading links. The tension had arisen in the latter part of 1895 over a boundary dispute between British Guiana and Venezuela. President Cleveland and Richard Olney, his Secretary of State, intervened on Venezuela's behalf; Britain resented this interference, but ultimately came to accept the American action, and submitted the boundary dispute to an arbitration panel which substantially accepted the British case.[345] Throughout these events feelings ran high on both sides, especially in America, but John M. Clark, who was planning a US trip, was able to write to the *Library*'s American editor, C.A. Briggs, expressing the hope that both governments would be 'guided to an amicable settlement':

> your President has hurled a thunderbolt which I fear will do much harm. Every one here is astonished at the bitter feelings which so many Americans seem to have against us, as we cherish nothing but friendship and affection for your nation.[346]

Despite this political storm, co-operation between the two companies on the *International Theological Library* continued apparently unabated.

Selection of authors

If the *Library* were to succeed, it was vital that the best possible authors — men whose scholarship was on both sides of the Atlantic held to be impeccable — should be enlisted as contributors. The editors of the Series were C.A. Briggs in America, and S.D.F. Salmond on this side of the Atlantic. In general, T. & T. Clark were prepared to accept their professional judgement on the wisdom of featuring a particular subject in the Series, or of inviting a specific scholar to contribute a volume: 'If a first class man can be got for a subject which commends itself to you both we shall not stand in the way.'[347] Initially, the Clarks had sought a veto for both parties upon both subjects and authors:[348] this veto may have been available, but it does not appear to have been used. The two editors did not always see eye-to-eye: a somewhat illegible letter from C.A. Briggs has been preserved in which he complains about a commission which Salmond has given of which he disapproves.[349] But while there were disagreements over both authors and subjects, all such problems seem to have been settled amicably, with give-and-take on both sides.

Four main criteria were involved in the selection of authors. Firstly, as has just been noted, the writer had to be a person of impeccable scholarship. Speaking of this series, the publishers claimed that authors had been 'chosen for their eminent ability in the department assigned to them.'[350]

But secondly, since it was important that the Series as a whole did not appear to be biased towards the scholarship of any particular denomination, the editors had to bear in mind the denominational affiliations of the scholars they were commissioning. There was, indeed, some apprehension that the Free Church was too strongly represented in the Series since both A.B. Bruce and A.B. Davidson had been invited to contribute volumes, but the Clarks felt that they were 'so popular and so highly esteemed in all denominations that [they did] not believe [their contributing would] prejudice the series. It [was] very important that they both take part'.[351] This leads neatly to the third criterion involved in selecting authors: they had to be popular within the target market as Bruce and Davidson certainly were. It is interesting to see an example of what amounts to putting popularity before scholarship. The firm was considering commissioning a volume from Dr John Watson, who, as 'Ian MacLaren', wrote popular fiction such as *Beside the Bonny Briar Bush*. Watson's name would 'popularise the Series', and in the interests of scholarship it was felt that he might be persuaded to undertake the volume in question, *The Christian Preacher*. 'There can be no doubt as to his popularity, & as regards his scholarship, I suppose this Volume would be the most suitable one for him.'[352] It is difficult to escape the conclusion that Watson's popularity counted for much more than his scholarship in the Clarks' eyes. Watson did not, in the end, contribute to the Series. The final criterion brought into play in the selection of authors was a practical one, involving an assessment of the competence of a scholar in preparing his work for the press. Authors were told that the manuscript of each volume had to be complete before printing was begun, to avoid expensive alterations to type,[353] and Salmond was advised that a potential contributor was not suitable because of his inability to abide by this condition:

> His method of preparing his work is ruinous. He seems to find it impossible to revise until it is in type, & those Volumes simply cannot stand that sort of thing.[354]

Having selected contributors, it was not always easy to get a completed manuscript from them. At least one, A.B. Davidson, threatened to withdraw from participation in the Series, while several in fact withdrew, among them Patrick Fairbairn, who provoked considerable consternation by reneguing on his agreement to contribute the volume on *Comparative Religion*.[355] Sometimes pressure of work was given as the reason for these withdrawals. Sometimes, too, men threatened to withdraw because of dissatisfaction with the level of remuneration. The Clarks realised that it was necessary to pay well in order to enlist the services of 'the best scholarship of the day', a goal which was of the greatest importance to them.[356]

It was agreed that the authors would be paid an honorarium, at the proportion of two hundred pounds ($1,000) for a volume of five hundred pages, this cost to be shared equally by the Clarks and Scribners. This two hundred pounds was to cover the cost of up to two minor revisions by the author for later printings. The Americans, while accepting this basic principle, held that prolixity would be encouraged if an author felt he had to stretch his subject matter to the full five hundred pages in order to gain the maximum remuneration, and proposed that each author should be paid two hundred pounds irrespective of the length of his work:

> indeed we would rather pay *more* to the author who kept well within the maximum number of pages it [sic] would be very unwise to encourage him to expand.[357]

In fact, the Clarks seem to have had their way, payment being made proportionately according to the length of the work. Scribners also had one other recommendation to make. They regarded it as vital, if squabbles over international copyright were to be avoided, that the initial payment should be clearly understood and stated to be for international rights in the work in question. 'Indeed', they wrote, 'we make this a necessary condition of procedure for the English author must understand that we do not steal their work.'[358]

This basic rate of payment seems to have been frequently increased by the Clarks at their own expense to secure key contributors, to retain their services, or simply to reward those whose works had sold especially well. For whereas two hundred pounds per volume had seemed a 'liberal' payment in 1887,[359] by 1898 it was felt to be rather low: a payment of 10*s*. 0*d*. per page (*i.e.* £250 per volume) being considered more realistic,[360] the Clarks felt obliged to increase the level of remuneration. When A.B. Davidson threatened to withdraw from his agreement to contribute a volume to the Series, he pleaded pressure of work, but made it clear that his main difficulty concerned the honorarium. He considered that it was hardly fair thus to put all the contributors on equal footing, irrespective of the subjects they were responsible for — some subjects, after all, would require far more time and effort to deal with than others — and suggested that he would prefer a royalty agreement. Being very eager to secure his co-operation, the Clarks were willing to make an exception in his case and accede to his wishes, and they wrote to America seeking the approval of Briggs and Scribners.[361] Again, once volumes in the Series had appeared, the Clarks occasionally gave additional remuneration to authors whose works were selling well. A letter written in 1898 speaks of

> subsequent payments which we have thought it wise and just to make . . . it is necessary, if such authors are to be retained as contributors to future Vols. Besides, we feel that the success of their books fully justifies it.[362]

Thus, the co-publishers aimed at making the Series as successful as possible by securing the services of the most gifted scholars, and by offering a level of remuneration which would provide them with the necessary incentive.[363] A 2½% royalty on all sales was paid to the editors. It is most likely that Briggs and Salmond each received this royalty on the basis of all sales of the Series on their own side of the Atlantic.

Selection of subjects

Although the *International Theological Library* comprised a series of independent volumes on different subjects by a variety of authors, it was intended that these volumes should form an organic whole which would present the totality of contemporary theological thinking.[364] It was therefore of vital importance for the commercial and theological success of the Series that the subjects should be wisely selected. Once again the Clarks seem to have been willing, in most cases, to rely on the judgement of the editors;[365] once again, disagreements were smoothed out by the exercise of give-and-take on each side; and once again some mistakes were made. It was necessary not only to select the most appropriate subjects, but also to ensure that, as far as possible, the manner of treatment which these subjects received was appropriate both to the British and to the American markets. An appropriate subject was one which belonged under the umbrella heading 'theological science'. Severe doubts were expressed, for example, over the inclusion of Washington Gladden's US-originated volume on *The Christian Pastor*, for not only was it a subject upon which much had been written but, more importantly, it did not seem 'to lie within the lines of such a series'.[366] Salmond supported this view, submitting that the volume and others like it had 'no claim to have a separate place at all in what professes to be a *Scientific* Series'.[367] The Gladden volume did appear, but the disquiet which it provoked only serves to illustrate the importance placed, on the UK side at least, on selecting subjects which lay within the field of strictly scientific theology. The dispute over the Gladden volume also points to a second criterion held to be vital in assessing the suitability of subjects for treatment in the Series: the topics dealt with must, if the *Library* were to be an international success, be those which were unaffected by cultural differences between the UK and North America. Doubt was expressed over the wisdom of including a volume on *Church and State*,[368] and Gladden's book, when it eventually appeared, was criticised because of the extent to which it was rooted in American culture:

> The whole tone of the book is so thoroughly *American* . . . methods of Pastoral work are so different in the two countries[369] — we feel now that the subject 'The Christian Pastor & the Working Church' should scarcely have been included in the Series.[370]

By December 1887, a draft list of the projected first twelve volumes in the Series had been prepared. It is interesting to compare this with the list of volumes which in fact appeared first: the comparison demonstrates how dependent the editors were on their contributors' continuing co-operation and health. The death of one commissioned author and the dilatoriness of another in delivering his manuscript could completely upset the planned structure of the Series. What had been envisaged as an organic whole could easily become a heterogeneous diversity, and consumer perceptions of the Series and its sales potential affected accordingly. The first twelve volumes, as initially proposed, were as follows:[371]

1.	Driver	*Literature of the Old Testament*
2.	Davidson	*Theology of the Old Testament*
3.	Sanday	*Literature of the New Testament*
4.	Brown	*Contemporary History of the Old Testament*
5.	Hatch	*Contemporary History of the New Testament*
6.	Fisher	*History of Christian Doctrine*
7.	Schaff	*Symbolics*
8.	Flint	*Religious Philosophy*
9.	Fairbairn	*Religion of the World*
10.	Bruce	*Apologetics*
11.	Brooks	*Homiletics*
12.	Broadus	*Pastoral Theology*

Only three of these twelve proposed volumes appeared among the first nine volumes in the Series which had been issued by 1901. These nine were:[372]

1.	Driver	*Literature of the Old Testament*
2.	Smyth	*Christian Ethics*
3.	Bruce	*Apologetics*
4.	Fisher	*History of Christian Doctrine*
5.	McGiffert	*History of Christianity in the Apostolic Age*
6.	Allen	*Christian Institutions*
7.	Gladden	*The Christian Pastor and the Working Church*
8.	Steven	*The Theology of the New Testament*
9.	Rainy	*The Ancient Catholic Church (AD 98–451)*

It is clear that this list is much less structured than that which had been originally planned. No matter how carefully subjects were selected, problems of one kind or another prevented treatments of those subjects appearing as planned in the order which had been intended.

Treatment and style

If a title were to sell well in its own right, and contribute positively to the image of the series of which it formed a part, the author's approach had to be acceptable both theologically and linguistically on both sides of the Atlantic.

Contributors were given guidance as to the style and treatment expected of them. The treatment had to be catholic and objective, yet orthodox, and the style 'concise', 'compact', 'clear', and 'pregnant'.[373] Yet in practice, what proved acceptable on one side of the Atlantic sometimes proved less so on the other; there was perhaps insufficient liaison between the British and American editors when works were in their early stages. With regard to *treatment*, the major problem, already discussed in an earlier section, arose over the supposed unorthodoxy of McGiffert's work. The Clarks felt that parts of the book were 'highly offensive to good Christian people'; it had been adversely reviewed in an influential newspaper, and this review had, as we saw, 'awakened a general feeling of indignation'. It was difficult to see, the Clarks held, how the work had been passed for press; we may conclude that Salmond, the British editor, was either not sufficiently involved in scrutinising the American contributions to the Series, or else was not adequately safeguarding the Clarks' interests.[374] It was inevitable that scholars would disagree with one another on some issues, but their virtual unanimity in dissenting from many of McGiffert's conclusions indicated that there was something suspect about his scholarship.[375] The visit by McGiffert to Edinburgh alluded to earlier mollified the Clarks as they were assured by him of his essential orthodoxy,[376] but undoubtedly damage was done to sales of the volume in the UK and to perceptions of the standing of Series on this side of the Atlantic. It was clearly vital that, if the *Library* were to be an international success, the boundaries of reverent speculation should not be overstepped. Problems arose too over the *style* and *language* of some of the American contributors. (There is no evidence that the literary style of the British contributors provoked any complaints on the American side of the Atlantic.) These problems arose with volumes in both the I.T.L. and the I.C.C. series, and specific examples were given by the Clarks in a letter to Scribners regarding Washington Gladden's volume on *The Christian Pastor*:

> at p.44 the expression 'on its own *hook*' is used. Such a word would be looked upon as a vulgarism here, & we do trust the Author will kindly seek to avoid such expressions as may give opportunity to critics. You will remember that no small indignation was aroused — & harm was certainly done to the sale of the book — by such expressions in Dr Gould's 'St Mark' as 'Jesus charged him sharply, "Shut up." ' We are sure that you will agree with us that such things are objectionable.[377]

Once again, the problem seems to have arisen through lack of proper supervision by the British editors as is made clear in a letter to one of the British editors of the I.C.C: 'The style of our American friends is occasionally so awkward that I do think there should be some supervision from this side.'[378] It is clear that the style in which a work was written, no less than the manner of treatment, could affect both its sales, and perceptions of the Series.

We may assume from all this that although the publishers and their editors endeavoured to select the most relevant subjects, and to ensure that they were given an acceptable stylistic and theological treatment, nevertheless problems did arise which to some extent hindered the success of the Series. One of the reasons for these problems was poor liaison between the British and American editors, and a lack of supervision at manuscript and proof stages of work produced on one side of the Atlantic by the appropriate editor on the other.

Technical arrangements

The technical arrangements involved in the production of a series on this scale were exceedingly complex, and it was obviously crucial to the financial success of the Series that they should proceed smoothly. Each publisher was to be responsible for commissioning and overseeing the typesetting of a stipulated number of volumes. The authors were instructed to supply their manuscripts ready for press, and accompanied by a concise and useful index.[379] Once the work had been set, the originating publisher would supply a set of stereoplates at cost to his partner, who would pay carriage on these. He would then be free to print his own edition, and would pay the originating publisher half the cost of the typesetting, and half the honorarium due to the author.[380] There is apparently no indication in the letter books that these arrangements went other than smoothly.

If the Series were to be a financial success on both sides of the Atlantic, it was obviously important that an equal number of works should be seen to be appearing from each of the two participating publishers. This was recognised from the first: 'We are glad you propose in the first instance to publish two volumes simultaneously, one by an author in each country', wrote the Clarks to Scribner in April 1887.[381] But problems arose with this programme, and of the nine volumes which had been produced by 1901, only three were of British origin.[382] This is all the more surprising in that initially it would seem to have been Scribners who were lagging behind in the production of their tally of works; of the first three volumes to appear, two were British in origin. Driver's *Introduction* was published in 1891, and Bruce's *Apologetics* in 1892. The first work of US origin, Smyth's *Christian Ethics* appeared in the same year. No volumes in the Series were published between 1893 and 1896, when the second American volume, Fisher's *History of Christian Doctrine*, was issued. In April 1895 C.A. Briggs wrote to the Clarks explaining the delay in the appearance of volumes of American origin. He himself had been asked to undertake a different title from that which he had initially agreed to write; two of the commissioned contributors had died; and yet another had been beset by serious health and family problems.[383] But soon, far more volumes had appeared from the American side than from the British, and this was causing consternation in Edinburgh in that it inevitably affected the impact and standing of the Series in Britain. Thus the Clarks wrote to Salmond 'It is of *very* great importance that the British contributors should be pressed on',[384] and two years later, the problem not having been resolved, to Scribners, requesting that they delay the publication of further volumes until the Edinburgh firm could catch up. The implication of the letter is that the success of the Series in the UK was being affected both by the very fact that US-originated titles proliferated, and by the closely-related fact that some of these US titles had in themselves provoked adverse criticism of the *Library* in the UK, criticism which would have been less damaging to the Series had it contained more books of British origin to which UK critics would have been more favourably disposed.[385] The Series was thus less successful than it might have been in the UK in the 1890s owing to the failure of the Clarks to spur on their dilatory contributors and so match the Scribners' rate of output. The third British volume, Robert Rainy's *Ancient Catholic Church* did not appear until 1901.[386]

Financial considerations

That the *International Theological Library* was a financially risky venture was recognised from the outset. Prospective contributors to the Series were reminded that 'the moderate price at which the volumes [were] to be sold [made] it necessary to spare the Publishers all avoidable expense of production'[387] and there is no doubt that the Clarks' comments regarding the

International Critical Commentary could equally well have been applied to its sister Series: 'The whole undertaking is a very considerable speculation for us, & it will take a *very large sale* to reimburse us.'[388] Indeed, in their early negotiations over the *Library*, the Clarks wished to stipulate that, if the Series were clearly not a success after the publication of, say, eight volumes, either party should be completely free to withdraw from their agreement.[389]

How successful did the Series in fact prove to be? Unfortunately, because of the problems discussed earlier, all the works published during the four financial years for which we have figures were of US origin. We do not therefore have detailed costings for a UK-originated title. One of the works for which figures are available is G.P. Fisher's *History of Christian Doctrine*, which was commissioned and typeset in America, and published in the spring of 1896.[390] An impression of 802 copies was printed by the Clarks from plates supplied by Scribners. The total cost of this can be calculated as follows:

½ cost of composition; cost of plates etc. (Paid to Scribner)	£141 3*s*. 4*d*.
Printing	£18 12*s*. 7*d*.
Prospectus	£1 14*s*. 9*d*.
Carriage from USA (of plates)	£3 15*s*. 0*d*.
Stamp for spine	12*s*. 6*d*.
Paper	£17 5*s*. 0*d*.
Binding[1]	£20 15*s*. 7*d*.
Proportion of Lists	£3 0*s*. 0*d*.
Advertising (Expenditure in first year)	£4 2*s*. 4*d*.
½ fee to author[2]	£103 7*s*. 8*d*.
	£314 8*s*. 9*d*.

(1) This figure is calculated pro rata. Only 702 volumes were bound up when the work was first printed.
(2) Surprisingly, the figures for the first edition do not include this sum. In fact payment was not remitted to Scribners in respect of the author's fee until the financial year 1898–99. (Presumably the author would have been paid upon publication by Scribners.) The editor's royalty is excluded from these figures. It was paid as the work sold out. For example, the editor received £10 6*s*. 0*d*. over 1896–97 in respect of a 2½% royalty on sales of 687 copies.

The unit cost of each copy of the book was consequently 7*s*. 11*d*. The nominal retail price of the work was 12*s*. 0*d*., and the Clarks' income per copy sold 7*s*. 8*d*. It therefore follows that the work would not have shown a profit had the author's fee been included in the costing of the first impression. Excluding that fee, the unit cost would have become 5*s*. 3*d*. and on that figure a profit of 2*s*. 5*d*. per copy would be shown, representing a not inconsiderable 46% return on investment. But it would seem that the work was not costed to break even on the first impression. A subsequent reprint would be much cheaper to produce, as plates and typesetting costs, and other one-off expenses such as the cost of carriage of plates and the cost of the spine block had been set against the first printing. Given a print run of the same length, the unit cost of reprinted volumes would have been 1*s*. 7*d*., and on that figure a profit per copy sold of 6*s*. 1*d*. would have been shown, representing a sizable return on investment of 384.2%. How did the work perform in practice? Sales were good, only 192 copies remaining at the end of financial year 1895–96. Over that year, the work showed a loss of £5 16*s*. 9*d*., but of course, the Clarks had not yet made their contribution to the author's remuneration. A second impression of 810 copies was ordered in financial year 1896–97, at the end of which there were 685 copies in hand. Despite the cost of the reprint, sales of over three hundred copies had produced a profit of £46 7*s*. 4*d*. Over 1897–98, sales of a further 150 copies produced a profit of £42 18*s*. 10*d*. Ninety-eight copies were sold over 1898–99, but that year saw the payment of £103 7*s*. 8*d*. to Scribners in respect of the author's fee, and the work in consequence showed a loss of £78 4*s*. 11*d*. over that year. Fisher's *Doctrine* therefore yielded a net profit over the four years of just £5 4*s*. 6*d*. More than 430 copies remained in stock, however, and if these continued to sell, there would be a satisfactory return of at least a further £164. The work was announced as being in its second edition in the 1901 catalogue; this probably refers simply to the second impression. Clearly, the remaining copies were selling slowly. But although in the short term the book was a dubious speculation, in the end it almost certainly produced a satisfactory return.

Another representative title for which we have figures is Washington Gladden's *The Christian Pastor*, which was also originated in America and appeared in 1897.[391] An edition of 810 copies was printed by the Clarks from plates supplied by Scribners. The total cost of this can be calculated as follows:

½ cost of composition; cost of plates etc. (Paid to Scribner)	£80 1*s*. 10*d*.
Printing	£14 16*s*. 7*d*.
Carriage from USA (of plates)	£ 2 4*s*. 6*d*.
Stamp for spine	10*s*. 6*d*.
Paper	£14 12*s*. 5*d*.
Binding[1]	£18 4*s*. 6*d*.
Proportion of Lists	£3 0*s*. 0*d*.
Advertising (expenditure in first year)	£4 19*s*. 6*d*.
½ fee to author[2]	£103 7*s*. 8*d*.
	£241 17*s*. 6*d*.

(1) This figure is calculated pro rata. Only 500 copies were bound at the time of publication.
(2) This sum was remitted to Scribners at the end of the financial year 1898–99, probably around two years after publication.

The unit cost of each copy of the book was consequently 6*s*. 0*d*. This was one of the minority of works in the Series (three out of the first nine) which had a nominal retail price of 10*s*. 6*d*. The Clarks' income per copy sold was 6*s*. 9*d*., which yielded a profit of 9*d*. per copy. The return on investment would therefore have been 12.5% Breakeven point would have been reached when 717 copies, or 88.51% of the print run had been sold.

A subsequent reprint would have been even more profitable. Given a print run of the same length, the unit cost of reprinted volumes would have been approximately 1*s*. 4½*d*., and on that figure a profit per copy sold of 5*s*. 4½*d*. would have been shown, representing a sizable return on investment of 391%.

The Clarks were not sanguine about the prospects of Gladden's work, but in fact it seems to have sold steadily if unspectacularly, 226 copies being disposed of over 1897–98, and a further 297 copies over 1898–99. By the summer of 1899, therefore, sales of the edition were within 154 copies of the breakeven point, and the Clarks were on target to reap a modest return.

We will consider a third example, as the evidence relating to the works by Fisher and Gladden has been somewhat in conflict. Arthur C. McGiffert's *History of Christianity in the Apostolic Age* was originated in America and published in the UK in 1897.[392] In the case of this work, 1,080 copies were printed by the Clarks from plates supplied by Scribners. The total cost of this edition can be calculated as follows:

½ cost of composition; cost of plates etc. (Paid to Scribner)[1]	£154 5*s*. 3*d*.
Printing	£23 18*s*. 2*d*.
Stamp for spine	16*s*. 6*d*.
Paper	£23 7*s*. 9*d*.
Binding[2]	£23 16*s*. 6*d*.
Proportion of Lists	£3 0*s*. 0*d*.
Advertising (expenditure in first year)[3]	£15 3*s*. 6*d*.
½ fee to author[4]	£103 7*s*. 8*d*.
	£347 15*s*. 4*d*.

(1)Cost of the carriage of plates is included in this figure.
(2)This figure is calculated pro rata. Only 850 copies were bound at the time of publication.
(3)More was spent on advertising this work than on the other works we have examined. The edition would, as well, have to cover the cost of advertising in subsequent years, which seems to have been high also. £10 8*s*. 5*d*. was spent on advertising the work over 1898–99.
(4)Remitted to Scribners at the end of the financial year 1898–99.

The unit cost of each copy of the book was consequently 6*s*. 5*d*. The nominal retail price of the work was 12*s*. 0*d*., and the Clarks' income per copy sold 7*s*. 8*d*. This would have yielded a profit of 1*s*. 3*d*. per copy, the return on investment being 19.48%. Breakeven point would have been reached when 907 copies, or 83.98% of the print run had been sold.

A subsequent reprint would have been more profitable. Given a print run of the same length, the unit cost of reprinted volumes would have been approximately 1*s*. 7*d*., and on that figure a profit per copy sold of 6*s*. 1*d*. would have been shown, representing a sizable return on investment of 384.21%

If the Clarks were doubtful about the prospects of the Gladden work, they were even more doubtful about the reception which would be given to that by McGiffert. Sales in the first year totalled 560, but only 124 copies were sold over 1898–99, and it would clearly be several years before the work broke even. If the Clarks continued to spend extensively on advertising over those years, the first impression of the work may in the end have done little more than cover its costs.

On this evidence, it would seem that while a shorter, 10*s*. 6*d*. title in the Series could be made to show a profit in an edition of around eight hundred copies, if a 12*s*. 0*d*. title were to break even, a print run of over one thousand copies was required. It was probably because they realised this that the Clarks printed 1,080 copies of both the 12*s*. 0*d*. titles published in 1897–98. (Allen's and McGiffert's) The fact that a shorter work would show a profit on a smaller edition demonstrates the wisdom of the Americans' contention that authors who kept well within the maximum number of pages should be given greater reward. However, given the sales figures of these books it is difficult to see how profit on the first printings could have been other than modest. If second printings were required of course, the return on investment would have been considerable. By 1901,[393] of the nine works issued, four had gone beyond the first printing: Driver's work was in its seventh, Fisher's in its second, and Smyth's and Bruce's in their third. In the medium term, therefore, the Series as a whole may have been successful despite the poor performance of individual titles.

Indeed, according to the *Stock and Sales Book — Individual Titles*,[394] the firm's annual return on the *Library* was not inconsiderable. (See Table 14) The figures, of course, merely give the profit or loss on the year's trading, and do not indicate whether the work in question had broken even.

From a commercial point of view the Series was therefore a finely-balanced venture in the mid 1890s. At first, owing to the quality of the work produced, it was reasonably successful: thereafter, owing to errors made in the selection of subjects and contributors, to a lack of supervision by both the editors, and to other factors, that financial success was temporarily jeopardised.

There would seem to be little doubt, however, that the *International Theological Library* was widely regarded as a solid success from a theological point of view, and that it contributed to the international esteem not only of Scribners and T. & T. Clark, but also of English language theology as a whole. We saw earlier that in a neat turning of the tables, a German publishing firm applied to the Clarks for permission to translate Driver's work into that language. The *Library* was not only made possible by the increase of 'genuine scholarship' in the US and Great Britain,[395] but also contributed to the growth of that scholarship by providing an international forum for first-rank scholars.

The International Critical Commentary

The *International Critical Commentary* was a sister series to the *International Theological Library*, and there were considerable similarities in the planning and execution of both series. The I.C.C. was issued under an editorial triumvirate. C.A. Briggs was responsible for commissioning and overseeing the publication of all works in the Series, on both Old and New Testament books, which originated in the US. S.R. Driver of Oxford had editorial responsibility for works on the Old Testament books originating in the UK; he was initially to be assisted by William Sanday, who was to be British New Testament editor. Sanday, however, declined the offer, and was replaced by Alfred Plummer of University College, Durham.[396]

Table 14

International Theological Library: Annual Credits/Deficits 1895–96 — 1898–99

Author	Date published	1895–96	1896–97	1897–98	1898–99
Driver	1891	+£ 74 4*s.* 6*d.*	+£ 86 11*s.* 6*d.*	−£ 32 7*s.* 1*d.*[1]	+£281 3*s.* 10*d.*
Smyth	1892	+£ 48 3*s.* 4*d.*	+£ 54 5*s.* 7*d.*	+£ 43 4*s.* 8*d.*	−£ 40 2*s.* 0*d.*
Bruce	1892	+£ 97 5*s.* 8*d.*	+£101 11*s.* 10*d.*	+£ 24 19*s.* 7*d.*	+£132 13*s.* 2*d.*
Fisher	1896	−£ 5 16*s.* 9*d.*	+£ 46 7*s.* 4*d.*[2]	+£ 42 18*s.* 10*d.*[2]	−£ 78 4*s.* 11*d.*
McGiffert	1897			−£ 26 14*s.* 6*d.*	−£ 66 15*s.* 5*d.*
Gladden	1897			−£ 41 18*s.* 3*d.*	−£ 33 2*s.* 1*d.*
Allen	1898			−£ 63 14*s.* 3*d.*	−£ 66 14*s.* 5*d.*
Stevens	1899				−£142 19*s.* 0*d.*
		+£213 16*s.* 9*d.*	+£288 16*s.* 3*d.*	−£ 53 11*s.* 0*d.*	−£ 14 0*s.* 10*d.*

(1) Clearly, a reprint was undertaken this year.

(2) These figures show profit where our earlier analysis would have led us to expect a loss because, for some reason, the author's fee had not been remitted to Scribners.

Unity of purpose

As we noted earlier, the *International Critical Commentary* was begun at the suggestion of Sir Thomas Clark. It would appear that he had approached C.A. Briggs, inviting him to participate as American editor of the Series, confident that the scheme would meet with Scribner's enthusiastic approval.[397] Clark, in fact, viewed the I.C.C. as a potentially more successful venture than the I.T.L.: for him to launch out into a commentary series in no way involved a commitment to publish a work on every book of the Bible

> As each volume would be sold separately . . . we do not think the selection of 10 vols on the more important books of the Old Testament and a few on the New Testament would be a very great risk even if it were resolved to go no further.[398]

In fact, however, as we saw, Scribner's greatest enthusiasm was directed towards the I.T.L., and he was initially reluctant to commit his firm to participation in the *Commentary* series.[399] However, the situation was resolved, the Clarks agreeing to continue on their own initiative with the commissioning of works for the Series; nothing, however, was to be published for two years, by which time Scribner would have had the opportunity to assess his position. If he wished, he could join the Clarks either as co-publisher or as agent.[400] Because of the possibility that the Clarks might have to bear the entire risk of the I.C.C., they initially commissioned only twelve volumes in order to test the market.[401] It was no doubt with considerable relief, especially as the copyright protection of the works in North America was at issue,[402] that the Clarks learned of Scribner's willingness to co-operate with the I.C.C. series on roughly similar terms and conditions as applied in the case of the I.T.L. From the moment that decision was made, the two firms seem to have shared a unity of purpose which could only have contributed to the success of the Series.

Selection of authors

As was the case with the I.T.L., it was crucial to the commercial and theological success of the Series that the co-operation of the most competent scholars should be sought and won. It might have seemed most practical to decide first which scholars in Britain or America were best equipped to deal with which books, and then to commission accordingly, but the Clarks and Briggs appear to have decided to apportion biblical books between the two countries, and only then to look for suitable contributors,[403] Briggs commissioning in America, and Driver and Plummer in the UK.

As in the case of the other Series, the Clarks seem to have put considerable trust in the judgement of their editors, whom they anticipated would act as a panel — 'it is expected that the British and American Editors confer with each other as to the selection of contributors'[404] — but they occasionally made suggestions of their own. For instance, when Briggs proposed a certain Henry P. Smith as author of one of the volumes, the Clarks, ever mindful that an international series had to have international sales potential, commented that Smith was 'almost quite unknown in this country', conceded that Briggs had a 'high opinion of his scholarship', but posed the question 'Do you really think he is the best man you can get for this subject[?]'[405] (In the event a work was commissioned from Smith.) Again, the Clarks warned Briggs against commissioning an author whose participation in an earlier co-publishing venture, Schaff's *Popular Commentary*, had undoubtedly been detrimental to its success, at least in Britain. 'We are sure the general opinion here was that his work was unsatisfactory.'[406] Yet again, as we noted earlier, Driver and Briggs were warned to consider carefully before commissioning a work from an American scholar who, if not a Unitarian himself, certainly had Unitarian connections, and whose participation, even although his work was to be on the book of *Proverbs* where there would be little conflict between Unitarian and orthodox Christian views, might be detrimental to the standing of the Series as a whole. The Clarks, writing to Driver, diplomatically suggested that he might care to take no notice of their advice, or else to discuss the matter with Briggs; clearly they hoped he would take the latter course.[407] So while for the most part relying on the judgement of their editors, the Clarks who, over the years, had built up a formidable acquaintance with biblical scholars and scholarship and who, moreover, were more aware than their editors could ever be of the commercial implications in the international market place of the selection of one author as opposed to another, were not slow to make their opinion known. And such was the esteem in which they were held by their editorial panel (who, besides, would not forget who held the purse-strings) that their comments were always carefully evaluated, if not inevitably followed.

As with the *International Theological Library*, publishers and editors alike agreed that what was wanted was the best scholarship. It was agreed that the earlier volumes in the Series should be contributed by authors other than those who were working on the early I.T.L. volumes,[408] but apart from that the field was open. They were looking for 'the best man' for each subject;[409] it was their aim to secure the services of 'the best scholars of the day',[410] for they felt that 'a name carrying weight, and confidence, [was] imperative for this Series'.[411]

The Clarks seems to have been reasonably satisfied with those who were enlisted. Once again, scholars of weight would expect adequate remuneration, and in fact they were paid on the same terms as were contributors to the sister Series, at the rate of £200 for a 500-page volume. For that sum, they were selling the copyright in their work, and agreeing to undertake two minor revisions (merely emendations on the existing stereoplates)[412] for no additional fee.[413] No doubt an additional sum would be paid if a major revision became necessary; and if a work were especially successful, the Clarks would not be found wanting in their generosity to the author, as they showed in the case of some of the I.T.L. volumes. The editors were remunerated by means of a royalty on sales. Briggs received 2½% on all US sales; Driver received the same amount on all UK sales of the OT volumes, and Plummer earned a similar royalty on sales of the NT volumes in the same market place. It would seem that in their commitment to locating, commissioning and adequately reimbursing the best possible scholars within their theological tradition, the Clarks did all they could to ensure the success of the Series.

Selection of subjects: treatment and style

In the case of the *International Critical Commentary*, the selection of subject posed no problems. It was simply a matter of dealing first of all with the major books of the Bible. By 1901, ten volumes had been published, covering the following books:[414]

1. Deuteronomy (Driver)
2. Judges (Moore)
3. The Books of Samuel (Smith)
4. Proverbs (Toy)
5. Romans (Sanday and Headlam)
6. St Mark (Gould)
7. St Luke (Plummer)
8. Philippians and Philemon (Vincent)
9. Ephesians and Colossians (Abbot)
10. Peter and Jude (Bigg)

As with the I.T.L., however, the financial success of the Series was to some extent (probably less than in the case of the *Library*) jeopardised by difficulties regarding treatment and style. With regard to *treatment*, for example, the volume on Judges by G.F. Moore was criticised by an influential reviewer (Professor Herbert E. Ryle, writing, embarrassingly enough, in the Clarks' own *Critical Review*) for practically omitting any discussion of the religious element of the book in question. The Clarks agreed with his criticism. If sales of volumes in the Series to a wider public than the academic coterie pure and simple were to be encouraged, it was vital, they felt, that the religious value of the book being commented on should not be ignored. Moore's volume had sold a paltry four hundred copies. It was clearly important that the scholars should keep the commercial imperatives in mind.[415] But sales of individual volumes and perceptions of the Series as a whole could also be affected by the usual problems of *style* arising from the differences between what was acceptable on each side of the Atlantic. We have already seen that some expressions used by the author of the volume on *St Mark* – notably his 'Shut up', put into the mouth of Jesus in the context of his addressing the unclean spirit – caused offence.[416] The Clarks recognised that such offence was justified – 'Our American friends put a different construction upon many expressions which are to our minds offensive'[417] – and attempted to ensure that the Series was not jeopardised by transatlantic language differences. And in the main they seem to have succeeded, for there is no evidence to indicate that sales of the I.C.C. were adversely affected by disquiet on stylistic and linguistic grounds.

Technical arrangements

The procedures agreed by T. & T. Clark and Scribners for the production of the I.C.C. were similar or identical to those covering the issue of the I.T.L. Once again, these arrangements proceeded relatively smoothly. The only technical difficulty referred to in the letter books concerns complaints made by the

American printers over the quality of plates shipped from this country. These plates had been made by the Oxford University Press, who had been entrusted with the typesetting of the volume in question, perhaps so that Driver or Plummer could personally supervise their work. The Press prepared a defence of the quality of their platemaking, and the Clarks sent a copy of this statement to Scribners. It was not the plates which were at fault, they contended, but the American pressmanship. There were differences between British and American ways of 'making ready'; the Americans had been lax by British standards, and this had resulted in the inferior product of which Scribners had complained. This incident, relatively minor in itself, highlights another area — that of technical compatibility between the two countries — which increased the hazards of co-operative international publishing.[418]

The issue of the *International Critical Commentary* proceeded, in marked contrast to that of its sister Series, at the same rate on both sides of the Atlantic: of the ten volumes which had appeared by 1901,[419] five were American in origin, and five British. The fact that this harmonious balance was maintained no doubt encouraged positive perceptions of the Series on the part of potential purchasers and thereby increased its sales.

Financial considerations

The Clarks clearly felt that the *International Critical Commentary* Series was less of a financial risk than was the *International Theological Library*. How successful, in fact, was the I.C.C.? Detailed figures are available in the cases of several works. S.R. Driver's volume on *Deuteronomy* for example, published in 1895, was originated in the UK, and had a nominal retail price of 12*s*. 0*d*., being sold to the British trade at 7*s*. 8*d*. The first edition of 1,612 copies (significantly larger than the first editions of I.T.L. volumes) cost as follows:[420]

Typesetting etc.[1]	£73 8*s*. 3*d*.
Stereoplates for British edition	£23 17*s*. 7*d*.
Printing	£28 7*s*. 0*d*.
Binding (whole edition bound on publication)	£36 11*s*. 6*d*.
Stamp for spine	£1 6*s*. 0*d*.
Paper	£39 5*s*. 2*d*.
Promotional material	£ 6 5*s*. 11*d*.
Advertising	£25 2*s*. 1*d*.
Proportion of lists	£3 0*s*. 0*d*.
Author[2]	£200 0*s*. 0*d*.
Editor[3]	£24 3*s*. 7*d*.
	£461 7*s*. 1*d*.

(1) The total cost of typesetting, etc. was £165 3*s*. 6*d*., of which Scribners paid £91 15*s*. 3*d*. They also bought an additional set of plates for the US edition.

(2) This sum was the author's total fee. Clearly each publisher paid the total fee to the author of books appearing on his side of the Atlantic, rather than paying half the fee of every contributor to the Series.

(3) This figure is an estimate — the editor received a royalty of 2½% on, presumably, the retail price of each copy sold.

The unit cost of volumes in the first edition was consequently 5*s*. 9*d*., giving 1*s*. 11*d*. profit on each copy sold at the normal trade price. The return on investment was therefore a reasonable 33.33%. Breakeven point would be reached when 1,203 copies (74.62% of the run) had been sold. Were a second edition to be required, the percentage return on it would be much higher. The total cost of a second printing of the same size as the first, including advertising, would be £162 5*s*. 3*d*. The unit cost of volumes in that impression would therefore be 2*s*. 0*d*., giving 5*s*. 8*d*. profit on each copy sold at the normal trade price. The return on investment would be very high, at around 283.33%. And in fact the work did sell well, to the extent of having reached its second printing by 1901.

G.F. Moore's volume on *Judges* (also published in 1895) was originated in the US, and had a nominal retail price of 12*s*. 0*d*., being sold to the British trade at 7*s*. 8*d*. The first edition of 1,000 copies cost the Clarks as follows:[421]

½ cost composition; plates, packing	£195 13*s*. 5*d*.
Carriage of plates from US	£3 12*s*. 11*d*.
Printing	£20 2*s*. 4*d*.
Paper	£25 4*s*. 8*d*.
Stamp for spine	3*s*. 6*d*.
Binding (whole edition bound on publication)	£22 15*s*. 0*d*.
Proportion of lists	£3 0*s*. 0*d*.
Advertising	£24 14*s*. 11*d*.
Editor	£15 0*s*. 0*d*.
	£310 6*s*. 9*d*.

The unit cost of volumes in the first edition was consequently 6*s*. 2½*d*., giving 1*s*. 5½*d*. profit on each copy sold at the normal trade price. The return on investment was therefore a reasonable 23.48%. Breakeven point would be reached when 810 copies (81% of the run) had been sold. Were a second printing to be required, the percentage return on it would be much higher. The total cost of a second printing of the same size as the first, including advertising, would be £110 16*s*. 11*d*. The unit cost of volumes in that impression would therefore be 2*s*. 3*d*. giving 5*s*. 5*d*. profit on each copy sold at the normal trade price. The return on investment would be very high, at around 240%. And like Driver's work, Moore's was into its second printing by 1901.

E.P. Gould's volume on *St Mark*, published in 1896, was originated in the US, and in contrast to the other works we have considered had a nominal retail price of 10*s*. 6*d*., being sold to the British trade at 6*s*. 9*d*. The first printing of 1,080 copies cost as follows:[422]

½ cost composition; plates, packing	£108 14*s*. 8*d*.
Carriage of plates from US	£1 19*s*. 7*d*.
Printing	£13 9*s*. 3*d*.
Paper	£19 17*s*. 6*d*.
Binding (Pro rata. Only 750 were bound on publication.)	£24 9*s*. 7*d*.
Stamp for spine	£1 9*s*. 6*d*.
Proportion of lists	£3 0*s*. 0*d*.
Advertising	£24 14*s*. 11*d*.
Editor	£14 3*s*. 5*d*.
	£211 18*s*. 5*d*.

The unit cost of volumes in the first impression was consequently 3*s*. 11*d*., giving 2*s*. 10*d*. profit on each copy sold at the normal trade price. The return on investment was therefore 72.34%, much higher than on the first printings of the volumes priced at 12*s*. 0*d*. Breakeven point would be reached when 628 copies (58.14% of the run) had been sold. The percentage return figure would be even greater were a second impression required. The total cost of a second printing of the same size, including advertising, would be £99 14*s*. 8*d*. The unit cost of volumes in that impression would therefore be 1*s*. 10*d*., giving 4*s*. 11*d*. profit on each copy sold at the normal trade price. The return on investment would accordingly reach the excellent level of 268.18%. But, as we saw, the Clarks had doubts about the saleability of this work, doubts reflected in the fact that initially they had only 750 copies bound up. In fact, their caution proved justified: a second printing had not been required by 1901. While a percentage return of 72% on the first impression looks favourable, it appears much less so when spread over five or more years.

All the preceding calculations, of course, assume the sale of the whole of each impression, and ignore factors such as the distribution of review and presentation copies, and the practice of giving retailers twenty-five copies when twenty-four were ordered, and allowing an additional discount of 2½% for prompt payment. But it would seem that the Clarks were correct in assuming that the Series would be successful. Of the ten volumes in print by 1901, four had gone beyond a first impression by then, and the firm's annual return on the Series, according to the *Stock and Sales Book, Individual Titles*[423] was considerable. Six of the first ten volumes were priced at 12*s*. 0*d*., three at 10*s*. 6*d*., and one at 8*s*. 6*d*. On the basis of the evidence we have examined, it would seem that, as was the case with I.T.L. titles, smaller volumes, though selling more cheaply than full-length ones, could nevertheless be costed to yield a larger return. Table 15 presents the figures from the *Stock and Sales Book*. These figures, of course, merely give the profit or loss on the year's trading, and do not indicate whether the work in question had broken even.

According to all this evidence, therefore, the *International Critical Commentary* would seem to have been a highly profitable venture, much more so, as the Clarks had anticipated, than its sister series.

T. & T. Clark's early experiences in the publication of transatlantic co-editions were not encouraging; nevertheless, they persevered, and their ventures in this field at the end of the century, particularly the *International*

Critical Commentary, were successful and profitable. This success was due to the wisdom of the editorial panel, to the competence in most cases of the scholars selected to contribute, to the relatively harmonious working relationship which existed between the two publishers, and perhaps above all to the theological awareness and commercial astuteness of T. & T. Clark, to say nothing of that firm's patience and tact, laced, when necessary, with firmness.

The Clarks' transatlantic publishing ventures thus made a significant contribution to the late nineteenth-century development of the firm. The name of T. & T. Clark became more widely known, and its international standing was increased. The firm played a significant role in furthering the cause of English-language theology, and the principals came into contact with many leading scholars of international repute. This reputation and these contacts helped to give the Clarks the necessary pulling-power to draw together the contributors who were to make James Hastings' *Dictionary of the Bible* and *Encyclopaedia of Religion and Ethics* the international successes they were. In purely commercial terms, the transatlantic publishing operation was perhaps less successful; only modest sums were to be realised by selling in this country works originating in the US; and the sales of works to the US, sometimes at very low cost to deter unauthorised reprinters, brought in equally small amounts. After difficult beginnings, it was the programme of co-publishing with Scribners which proved, speaking both commercially and theologically, to be the most fruitful part of the firm's transatlantic dealings.

Table 15

International Critical Commentary: Annual Credits/Deficits 1895–96 – 1898–99					
Title	Date published (approx)	1895–96	1896–97	1897–98	1898–99
Deuteronomy	1895	+£355 8*s.* 8*d.*	+£ 28 9*s.* 7*d.*	+£ 82 7*s.* 8*d.*	+£168 8*s.* 0*d.*
Judges	1895	−£ 36 17*s.* 9*d.*	+£ 64 4*s.* 4*d.*	+£ 21 9*s.* 7*d.*	−£ 79 17*s.* 11*d.*
Romans	1895	+£ 47 3*s.* 5*d.*	+£207 1*s.* 8*d.*	+£ 43 12*s.* 10*d.*	+£263 15*s.* 7*d.*
Mark	1896	+£ 10 16*s.* 1*d.*	+£ 79 4*s.* 6*d.*	+£ 30 3*s.* 6*d.*	−£ 43 18*s.* 8*d.*
Luke	1896		−£ 88 9*s.* 6*d.*	+£108 3*s.* 9*d.*	+£159 6*s.* 5*d.*
Philippians	1897			+£ 66 9*s.* 3*d.*	−£ 41 15*s.* 4*d.*
Ephesians	1897			+£ 44 11*s.* 11*d.*	+£128 2*s.* 3*d.*
Samuel	1899				−£115 15*s.* 2*d.*
		+£376 10*s.* 5*d.*	+£290 10*s.* 7*d.*	+£396 18*s.* 6*d.*	+£438 5*s.* 2*d.*

Chapter 7
Periodicals and part-publications

'Our experience has been very far from encouraging', commented the Clarks in 1886 on the subject of periodical publishing.[424] In the nineteenth century, many book publishers also issued periodicals. A popular periodical could contribute significantly to the profitability of a firm, but a more esoteric, scholarly title might fail to break even, depending for its continued existence on the general prosperity of the business, and on the publisher's awareness of the intangible benefits which might accrue to him through being associated with a prestigious journal. The periodicals issued by the Clarks fell into this second category, yet they were always ready to respond positively to proposals that they should initiate, or take over control of, significant titles where there was a reasonable chance of their outlay being recovered.

Legal works were one of the firm's earliest preoccupations; it is not surprising then, that the Clarks' earliest ventures in periodical publishing were in the field of Scots Law. It was through the first Thomas Clark that Scotland's first law magazine, the *Law Chronicle*, made its appearance in May 1829, at the instigation of some 'professional gentlemen'. This monthly *Chronicle* survived, in one form or another, for around five years. There were a number of other short-lived Scottish legal serials before, in January 1857, the Clarks initiated the *Journal of Jurisprudence*. This *Journal* impressed the profession both by the breadth of its coverage, and by the dynamism and outspoken nature of its contents. Absorbing the rival *Scottish Law Magazine* in 1866, it survived until 1891. By then, despite a change of editor in 1888, its columns had become permeated by a conservatism which affected its circulation and made it easy for another rival, the *Scottish Law Review* (founded in 1885) to find a footing.[425]

A prospectus was issued, probably in 1841, announcing a theological quarterly which was to be titled *Clark's Biblical Magazine and Review*. The first Thomas Clark felt that there was need for a British periodical to chronicle and present a critical assessment of current theological developments, especially those in Germany, and to encourage British theological writing. He hoped that, by countering the rationalistic tendencies of many works of continental origin, the publication would 'prevent the influx of foreign works from enervating the spirit, and deteriorating the character of our native literature' and also that it would 'promote the cultivation of Biblical Studies, and render them subservient to the establishment of Scriptural views of Divine truth.' The journal was to include original papers, reviews, and translations of articles from foreign journals. The project was endorsed by W. Lindsay Alexander, John Brown, Professor of Exegetical Theology in the United Secession Church, William Cunningham, Robert Lee, Regius Professor of Biblical Criticism at Edinburgh University, and Bishop C.H. Terrot. However, this project failed to come to fruition. Very similar in intent was the *Foreign Evangelical Review*, launched in May 1852 under the editorship of Andrew Cameron (1823–77) and published by Johnstone and Hunter of Edinburgh. (From March 1853 it became the *British and Foreign Evangelical Review*).

In the early 1860s, T. & T. Clark assumed a short-lived responsibility for the famous *North British Review*, while the 1880s saw an unsuccessful attempt to sustain a theological monthly. And in the last decade of the century, the Clarks, with the *Expository Times* and the *Critical Review of Theological Literature* were issuing works which, if not financially profitable, were *succès d'estime* in theological circles in Scotland and beyond.

But enthusiastic as the Clarks were about periodical publishing if the format and the editor were 'right', they had little time for what would today be termed 'part-publication', the issue of major works in parts prior to, or concurrently with, their appearance in volume form. This method of publishing, the firm felt, caused

> a great deal of trouble and annoyance, especially with the Trade. The Parts lie about the Booksellers' shops, get soiled and torn, & are frequently returned to the Publisher quite unsaleable. We do not think it materially helps the sale . . . .[426]

We do not know what unfortunate, early experiences with part-publications the Clarks may have had. Certainly, in the last two decades of the century, the only work issued by them in parts as well as in volume form was their edition, co-published with Reuther and Reichard of Berlin, of Carolo Brockelmann's *Lexicon Syriacum*, which was available in seven parts.[427] In this case the Clarks' scepticism seems to have been borne out by the sales figures: while twenty-one copies were sold in volume form over 1895–96, only twenty-eight individual parts were disposed of, and set against these were fifteen parts returned from booksellers, making a net sale of only thirteen parts.[428] And this was not an isolated figure: over 1896–97 there were no sales in parts while eight volumes were disposed of.[429] There was obviously very little additional expenditure involved in issuing a work in parts as well as in volume form — only, perhaps the cost of printing separate covers for the individual parts — but the Clarks' chief objection seems to have been that while the increase in sales was minimal, the booksellers felt free to treat part-publications as taken on a see-safe basis.

Motives for periodical publishing

The Clark's commitment to the higher point of success, their willingness to put the advance of truth before financial considerations is evident in their periodical publishing as elsewhere.

They were always ready to proceed with uneconomic ventures if they considered these would help push back the frontiers of theological enquiry. The modest loss made by the *Expository Times* through most of the 1890s, for example, was clearly acceptable to them as long as the journal was valued by the church and by the scholarly community. They commented, no doubt with some pride, that 'nearly all the well-known scholars [saw] and read the E.T. *regularly*', and that when issues were raised in its columns, the editor frequently received unsolicited copy from leading authorities who wanted to join in the discussion.[430] The *Critical Review* also was scarcely a profitable venture, but the Clarks continued with it for several years, heartened, no doubt, by the comments of one American expert who considered that 'in many respects it [was] the most useful specialist Magazine [then] published', and by the confession of another that the *Review* was 'his *vade mecum*' for theological and philosophical literature.[431] Journals which served the academic community to this degree the Clarks were pleased to subsidise.

Nevertheless, while not in themselves generating profits, prestigious periodicals such as these could contribute significantly to the general profitability of the firm, to the extent that losses on the periodical account could be regarded as an investment. In the first place, these journals promoted the status of the Clark imprint among the very people most likely to purchase Clark publications. Thus John M. Clark commented of the *Critical Review* that, though its success could not be expressed in the balance sheet, it was nevertheless valuable to his firm 'in many other ways', and that he would be '*exceedingly* sorry' to be without it.[432] These 'other ways' must have included the association of the Clark imprint with high-level theological writing. In the second place, and much more specifically, these journals could be (and frequently were) used to promote individual titles published by the firm, by advertising, by editorial endorsement, or by sympathetic reviewing. Thus, for example, an estimated thirty pounds worth of advertising space was used by the Clarks in the four 1896 issues of the *Critical Review* to promote their own publications.[433] Thus too, John M. Clark wrote to James Hastings twelve months after the firm had taken over the *Expository Times:* 'I am hopeful that even already some good has resulted from your kind reference to our books in the E.T.'[434] However, Clark titles in no way monopolised the review space in the *Expository Times*. In Volume Four, for example, out of 283 works reviewed, only seventeen (six percent) were Clark titles, and the reviews of these publications occupied just seven percent of the 961 column inches given over to reviews.

Relationships with the editors

Since these periodicals had a significant power to influence the firm's reputation, it might have been expected that the editors would have been fairly tightly controlled by the Clarks to ensure that the identity of the firm as a whole was suitably presented, that individual titles were favourably reviewed, and that the theological line taken was not more liberal, or, indeed, more conservative than that with which they were prepared to be associated. In fact, however, they were by and large very fortunate in their editors who shared their broad aims and their theological perspectives. In consequence, there was little need for them heavy-handedly to prescribe the editorial line they wanted taken, and little discord between editor and proprietors. The editor with whom the firm had the least cordial relationship was undoubtedly J.S. Exell of the short-lived *Monthly Interpreter* who, if not downright incompetent, certainly did not apply himself fully to his duties. We find the Clarks commenting on the disappointing mundaneness of much of the journal's contents, and urging its editor: 'Try to get some stirring articles.'[435] But we also find them taking into account Exell's susceptibilities. He had suggested soliciting articles from C.A. Briggs, the important American scholar whose works were just starting to appear under the Clark imprint. Clearly the Clarks could have had no objection to work by him featuring in one of their journals, but they wrote to Exell thus:

> we think Professor Briggs would be quite willing to write, but you know he is *broad*, and he would not allow his Articles to be altered.[436]

The implication of this is firstly that Exell was not enamoured with 'broad', more liberal theology, secondly that he was in the habit of editing contributions so that they accorded with his own views, and thirdly (and from our point of view most importantly) that the Clarks, on account of their editor's predilections, were prepared to forego the possibility of a contribution from a scholar whose work they would otherwise have been pleased to publish. There is no evidence here of heavy-handed control of the editor.

The Clarks had discussions with Exell also over the content of certain reviews of their publications which he was proposing to print. Here again, their policy was balanced and reasonable; while they were not averse to the publication of reviews which fairly and moderately criticised aspects of any of their titles, they felt it was inconsistent with their proprietorial interests that completely negative reviews should appear. This position was set out, for example, in a letter to Exell regarding G.T. Ladd's *Doctrine of Sacred Scripture*.

> We should like to send you a copy but we are not sure whether it is a book you might like to speak favourably of, & we should rather not have it reviewed at all than have a very severe one, & we may say the same about Weiss's *Life of Christ*.[437]

Exell clearly asked for a copy of the Ladd work, thereby tacitly accepting these conditions. On sending a damning review for publication, he could not have been surprised at the Clarks' response, in which they restated their position, and asked for the article to be omitted:

> We must make a mild protest against the article on *Ladd*; we do not ask it to be noticed at all, but, to insert such a notice is to break our own head. Kindly leave it out altogether.[438]

A similar policy towards reviews of Clark titles seems to have applied in the case of their other journals also. Hence, for example, Salmond was told that it was best not to include in the *Critical Review* a critique of Dr W.N. Clarke's

Outline of Christian Theology which, while admitting the readability of the work, was severely critical of it. True, there were special circumstances in this case: no other unfavourable reviews had appeared, and the Clarks felt it would be 'unseemly' to publish in their own magazine the one critical review which they had seen; further, the reviewer in question, one MacPherson, seems to have been less than competent, and to have been attempting to urge on Clarke a method of treatment used in his own books which were virtually unsaleable.[439] The Clarks therefore were prepared to publish mildly critical reviews of their own works, but not notices shot through with antagonism, which, to use their phrase, would break their own heads. To publish such a notice would also, in the case of the Clarke book 'lead to unpleasantness' with Scribners, with whom the work had originated, and in addition, 'vex Dr Clarke' for whom the Clarks had 'very great respect'.[440]

In general, therefore, editors and proprietors worked cordially together, sharing a common vision and aiming to issue periodicals which would serve a useful function in the scholarly community, and enhance the reputation of T. & T. Clark as a theological publisher. But the Clarks, while they were aiming at this higher point of success, and while they recognised the value of the periodicals to them in intangible ways, could not afford to ignore financial considerations. There was a level of risk beyond which they would not venture, and before launching a new periodical its potential profitability had to be carefully assessed.

The profitability of periodical publishing

The factors influencing the profitability of a periodical fell into three categories: the nature of the journal; the costs involved in, and the extent of, its promotion and distribution; and the success of the publisher in attracting advertisers.

The nature of the periodical

Its success in finding a gap in the market

A crucial factor affecting the profitability of a periodical lay in the extent to which its editor and publisher had been successful in locating and adequately plugging a gap in the already-crowded market-place. The more distinctive a new periodical was in comparison with existing journals, the greater was its chance of success, given wise editorial management. This factor was taken into consideration even when the physical appearance of a projected magazine was being discussed. Thus, for example, when a dummy cover of the forthcoming *Monthly Interpreter* was produced, it was with satisfaction that the Clarks were able to tell the editor 'we think it looks very well and it does not bear a resemblence [sic] to any existing periodical we know of.'[441] But if distinctiveness of physical appearance was important, distinctiveness of content was even more vital. Thus the Clarks, with considerable gratification, reported to Scribners that the 'unanimous opinion' of the *Critical Review* held by British scholars was that it supplied 'a long standing want in . . . Theological Literature.'[442]

On the other hand, where there was direct competition, where a projected publication was unlikely to have a field, however small, to itself, the Clarks were reluctant to proceed. One of their reasons, for example, for viewing with some scepticism the proposal that they should take over the *Theological Review* was the fact that it faced direct competition from the *Expositor*, the *Theological Monthly* 'and other periodicals of the same class.'[443] Again, Exell's initial proposal for what eventually became the *Monthly Interpreter* was met with a similarly-based scepticism, the Clarks wondering what the new magazine would have that was not already provided by others such as *Clerical World*, and *Preachers' Monthly*.[444] That such scepticism was well-founded is borne out by subsequent events. The Clarks did proceed with the *Monthly Interpreter*, and thus generated tension between themselves and Hodder and Stoughton, who regarded it as competing with their *Expositor*. There would seem to be no doubt that the two periodicals did appeal to the same audience: it was because of the intensity of competition between them that the Clarks wrote thus to Exell 'The Expositor for January [1885] is very "strong", it is rather a pity we had not some more striking articles.'[445] In a situation such as this, it is clear that the least competently-edited of the competing periodicals would suffer, a fact which goes at least part of the way towards explaining the rapid demise of the *Monthly Interpreter*.

If a periodical were to succeed, therefore, it had to find a gap in the market, and plug it distinctively.

Frequency of issue

It would appear from the Clark letter books that the frequency with which issues of a periodical appeared had some bearing on its success, financial and otherwise. In 1886, S.D.F. Salmond suggested that the firm should launch a quarterly theological journal. The Clarks responded tepidly — 'We cannot say we are sanguine about it' — their tepidness due to a perception that the days of successful quarterlies were past. The *British Quarterly Review* and Dickinson's *Quarterly* had recently ceased publication, and the *Presbyterian Review*, the US journal distributed by the Clarks, had been anything but a success. Further, they considered that the heavy constraints placed upon the editor of a quarterly proved an obstacle to its success: series of articles on any particular subject had, for example, to be avoided because of the long gap between issues. 'All this seems to warn us against a "Quarterly".'[446] The pace of life had quickened; quarterly publication, even in the field of theology, no longer seemed appropriate to potential readers, and hence could no longer be justified on economic grounds. Nevertheless, the firm did undertake the *Critical Review* some years later, only to find all their misgivings about quarterly publication borne out by experience. With regard to that journal, John M. Clark commented sadly to Salmond:

> I see that in the current *British Weekly* Dr. Nicoll says that a theological quarterly 'can probably never be remunerative' & I fear that is only too true.[447]

The firm regarded a periodical issued monthly as having much better prospects. Faced with Salmond's initial suggestion that a quarterly should be undertaken, the Clarks responded 'If a *Monthly* could be faced we almost think it would have a better chance', although they were still very doubtful about the economic prognosis for such a serial.[448] They were, however, willing to launch Exell's *Monthly Interpreter*, and to take over Hastings' *Expository Times*: clearly monthlies were seen as having the best chance of success.

Exell's initial suggestion, indeed, had been for a weekly magazine. This idea was rejected by the Clarks not, apparently, because they considered such a periodical unlikely to be profitable in principle, but because they did not have 'the machinery' for such a venture.[449] A small firm such as T. & T. Clark lacked the staff, and possibly the experience with distribution and the economic resources necessary for embarking on such a major, intensive project.

For the Clarks, therefore, a journal's financial success or failure could be directly affected by the frequency with which it appeared.

Size of each issue

If a periodical were to sell adequately, potential customers had to be made to feel that they were receiving value for money. Presumably, if this impression were to be given, type-size was an issue as well as the number of pages. It is however this second factor which is always referred to in the letter books: the physical bulk of a publication is what the potential customer first assesses. It might seem strange that such a mundane factor should come into play when the merchandise in question dealt with the higher levels of theological and philosophical thought, but nevertheless it was considered by the Clarks to be of great importance. Thus, Exell was told that eighty pages would be necessary for a one shilling magazine.[450] Thus also, from its third volume, the *Expository Times* was doubled in size (although admittedly the price was doubled also) and, in a desperate attempt to boost flagging sales, each issue of the *Critical Review* was increased in size by one sheet.[451] It was clearly the firm's view that to meet customer expectations, a publication appearing with a given frequency (be it quarterly or monthly) must have a certain number of pages, and also that a journal with a given cover price would be regarded as poor value for money if each issue were not of a certain length.

Marketability in the US

The likelihood of a Clark periodical showing a profit would be greatly increased if a regular, substantial market could be won for it on the other side of the Atlantic. A recognition of this factor had a certain influence upon the content of the firm's periodicals: if it helped to win sales in America that, for example, Exell was 'well known on [Scribners'] side',[452] it also helped if the contributors were held in esteem in the US, and it was better still if a satisfactory proportion of them were Americans. Thus, to take an example, C.A. Briggs advised the Clarks with regard to the *Monthly Interpreter* that they should 'make American contributions a feature so as to get up a demand for it in the States.'[453] Efforts were also made to increase the appeal in the US of the *Critical Review*. As early as 1891, Salmond was said to have made arrangements with several of the American colleges to ensure adequate coverage of the different branches of American theological literature.[454] But for all that, John M. Clark could write of the *Review* to Salmond in 1896 'it hasn't much hold in the States, & doesn't cover as many U.S. books as it might do.'[455] An American theologian, R.M. Wenley, had offered to act as US co-editor in an attempt to improve the *Review*'s American coverage;[456] his theological credentials seem to have been impeccable, and he had specialised in the subject area with which the *Review* dealt, the border-line between philosophy and theology. Perhaps impelled by economic as much as by theological motives, the Clarks seem to have considered the appointment of Wenley a sensible move. Salmond, however, was of a different opinion, and the matter was allowed to drop. It is in any case doubtful whether anything could have been done at that stage to remedy the *Critical Review*'s unprofitable position, but the incident emphasises the importance of the American market to the Clarks.

The calibre of the editor and contributors

The most crucial factor, however, was the perceived calibre of the editor and his team of contributors. If they were suitably influential, the other factors might possibly be over-ridden: the periodical would be preferred before any competitors; its frequency of issue would become relatively inconsequential, as would the size of each issue; and an extensive American sale would become more readily attainable.

That the editor should be influential, competent and committed was clearly vital. The *Monthly Interpreter* failed, as we will see, because Exell, while being influential and possibly competent, was totally lacking in commitment. Hastings, enlisted with great foresight by the firm at a time when he was competent and committed but hardly influential, grew in influence through the impact of the *Expository Times*, but he could not make it break even until the last years of the century. Salmond, greatly respected by the Clarks, had all three qualities, influence, competence, and commitment, but even this combination was not enough to ensure the prosperity of the *Critical Review*.

There was a link also between the standing of the contributors and the level of sales. If W.G. Blaikie in editing the *North British Review* for the Clarks had sought to gain the co-operation of the most illustrious writers,[457] so too did the later Clark editors, although they were working within a narrower subject field. At least one of the reasons why the Clarks agreed to publish the *Monthly Interpreter* was the fact that they were impressed by the range of contributors whose help Exell was proposing to enlist.[458] And John M. Clark, having sent W.E. Gladstone a copy of S.D.F. Salmond's work on *The Christian Doctrine of Immortality*, was not above trying to solicit a notice of it for the *Critical Review* from the great man.[459] This plan seems to have come to nothing. But if men of influence were wanted, it was also necessary that contributors should come from as wide a range of denominational backgrounds as possible in order to win support for the periodical in question from all sections of the Christian Church.

Thus, for example, when Salmond proposed that the Clarks should launch a quarterly, he was told that

> If articles could be got from such men as Prof Cave & Principals Simon, Fairbairn etc. (& we think they would gladly contribute) we might gain the interest of the Congregationalists, now that the Brit. Quarterly is defunct.[460]

However, if on the one hand, influential contributors could win a wider audience for a periodical, and thereby increase the publisher's income, on the other hand the more influential a contributor was, the more, in general, he would expect to be paid. In discussing with Salmond the possible takeover of the *Theological Review* the Clarks, while anticipating that the contributors would expect to be paid, did enquire in passing about the possibility of obtaining 'Critical Notices' without payment.[461] But their customary attitude towards those who would contribute without expecting remuneration was expressed in a letter to Exell: 'Some may be inclined to write for nothing, though such are not usually worth much.'[462] In the Clarks' eyes, a good contributor was worthy of his hire. In the short term the firm might be more out of pocket than would have been the case had they enlisted the services of an inferior contributor. But they regarded this as an investment to be recouped in the longer term as the stock of their periodical rose as influential contributors were increasingly and repeatedly attracted to its columns in part by the level of remuneration, and in part by the growing stature of the journal, a stature which their participation would further augment. This at least was the theory.

In practice, too, the firm was concerned that its contributors be adequately remunerated. In discussing the suggestion that they should take over the *Theological Review*, for example, they proposed that contributions should be paid for at the rate of £4 per sixteen-page sheet;[463] and they had to take Exell (who was remitted a monthly sum which covered his editorial expenses and his own fee) to task for inadequately remunerating his contributors. One author, a Dr Mair, had received only £4 4*s*. 0*d*. for a twenty-nine page contribution. The importance to the Clarks of adequate remuneration both for the sake of fairness and for the sake of increasing the journal's stock among potential contributors is evident from the following comments made to Exell:

> [Mair] is one of the best men we have and cannot be expected to contribute for that. The tidings of such miserable remuneration spread round will paralyse the whole affair . . . whilst we do not expect you to lose money the Editor as well as the publisher must make some sacrifice if the periodical is to be established . . . we certainly never anticipated . . . that anyone would be put off with 3s/- (& less) per page . . . to make a payment as the above is looked upon as an insult.[464]

In general, therefore, in a move to attract the best contributors, the Clarks paid adequately, even generously. It is curious that in the case of all Clark periodicals for which we have relevant data, the contributors were not paid directly by the publishers, but by the editor, out of a lump sum entrusted to him to cover all editorial expenditure. Direct payment would have enabled the Clarks to assess themselves how much remuneration each contributor should receive.

If the editor and contributors were of a sufficiently high calibre, and the other factors discussed above were operating in its favour, then there was at least some chance that a periodical might make a profit. Other factors, however, have also to be taken into consideration.

The cost and effectiveness of promotion and distribution

Considerable sums were expended in promoting the Clarks' periodicals through advertising, the distribution of free copies and review copies, and the circulation of prospectuses. The success or failure of a journal could depend on the cost-effectiveness of this strategy.

The *Monthly Interpreter*, for example, was heavily promoted. Upon its launch, several hundred review copies were sent out (the reviews, however, were 'few and rather indifferent'), and Exell was asked if he had 'any influence with some of the leading papers';[465] the firm also distributed 'many thousand' copies of a prospectus and a large number of gratis copies of the magazine; and Exell, who had clearly urged the Clarks to embark on a more energetic advertising campaign was told 'we think you cannot be aware of the extent we have already been advertising.'[466]

The *Expository Times* was promoted similarly; five hundred copies, for example, being freely supplied to a representative of The Church of England Association for distribution among its membership in the hope of attracting new subscribers.[467] So, too, was the *Critical Review*. Salmond, who had clearly wanted the Clarks to advertise the journal more extensively, was told that it was out of the question for them to spend more money on it.

> I am sure you can have no idea of the sum we have already expended in advertising — in addition to the free distribution of several thousand copies.[468]

John M. Clark felt that the distribution of free copies was 'the most effectual way' of promoting a periodical.[469] He may well have been right, for it was certainly relatively cheap compared with the expense of advertising; many new subscriptions had to be attracted to recover the cost of each advertisement. The distribution of free copies had the further benefit of being specifically targeted at those who were most likely to be interested in the journal. But in the case of all the Clark serial publications the promotional spending would seem to have been fairly limited in its impact, certainly in terms of attracting new subscribers. It may well have attracted new *readers* who would consult copies at their College Library, but that was of no financial benefit to the Clarks. What was true of the *Journal of Jurisprudence* — 'the majority [of lawyers] appeared to be satisfied with reading it in the Libraries'[470] — seems to have been true also of the Clark theological publications. For instance, of the American response to the *Critical Review*, John M. Clark commented that 'individuals, however enthusiastic they might be about the Review, tended to be content with the library copy.'[471] The *Monthly Interpreter* failed despite heavy promotional spending; and similar expenditure appears to have had very little impact on the sales figures of the *Critical Review* and *Expository Times*. It must remain very doubtful whether income from the new subscriptions gained in fact covered the cost of attracting them.

Another promotional strategy was the supplying of copies of the *Critical Review* at a reduced rate (one shilling per issue instead of one shilling and sixpence) to *bona fide* students, who had to pay a year's subscription in advance. This scheme was launched because the Clarks were 'particularly anxious to interest the Students of the various Universities & Colleges in [the journal]',[472] but it does not appear to have been particularly successful, at least in the long term; John M. Clark reported in 1897 that while Salmond's own students at Aberdeen loyally supported his periodical, subscribing at the student rate, it had been similarly offered to Glasgow and Edinburgh students without success.[473] If Scottish students showed little interest in the *Review*, those south of the Border are even less likely to have responded to the offer.

The Clarks' return on those copies which *were* sold to students at the special rate would, of course, have been drastically reduced. The firm's motivation in launching the scheme appears, at least in part, to have been a desire to further the theological awareness of the students, but they were no doubt hoping that those who began to subscribe at the student rate would keep up their subscriptions at full price once their student days were behind them. On the limited evidence available, it would seem unlikely that this happened in other than a few cases.

The Clarks' promotional expenditure, therefore, seems to have done little to further the financial prospects of their periodicals.

Attracting advertisers

The regular sale of advertising space in periodicals (usually, in the Clarks' case, to other theological publishers) could be a fruitful source of income. Obviously, the easiest way to achieve this was to present potential advertisers with a product which had the highest possible circulation. The Clarks could be guilty of hyperbole over this issue, for example in telling a potential advertiser in May 1893 that

> The *Critical Review* has a very large circulation both in Great Britain and America. Many Students at the various Universities and Colleges subscribe to it individually.[474]

In general, Clark periodicals do not seem to have sold as extensively as the publishers hoped. Therefore, if they were to sell advertising space successfully, without resorting to exaggeration, the Clarks had to persuade potential advertisers that it was more economic for them to take space in a lower circulation periodical, each of the readers of which, because of his specialist interests, was genuinely a potential customer, than in a high-circulation journal, many of whose subscribers would be most unlikely to be interested in what was being advertised. This principle was stated very clearly by the Clarks:

> I do wish London Publishers could be brought to realise the importance of [the *Expository Times*], & not be carried away [by] 'enormous circulations' of Papers which really are not nearly so valuable for their Publications. If they would only believe, too, the *fact* that nearly all the well-known Scholars see and read the E.T. *regularly*.[475]

A further problem faced by the firm in attempting to sell advertising space was hinted at in the letter just quoted, and spelled out unequivocally in another:

> London Publishers have no conception (because they happen to be published in Scotland!) of the value of those two Magazines [the *Expository Times* and the *Critical Review*] for Advertising purposes. They circulate all the world over.[476]

It was clearly difficult for an Edinburgh publisher, distanced from Paternoster Row, to persuade the London houses of the importance of his product as a platform for advertising. In an attempt at overcoming this difficulty, the Clarks used the services of an advertising agent in the English capital, William Cruickshank. Cruickshank's activities were not uniformly successful. If the *Critical Review* was at first regarded as a valuable advertising forum – 'British Publishers are showing their high opinion of it by their readiness in sending us their advertisements. In both the 1st & the 2nd Numbers most of the leading Publishers lists appear'[477] – the *Monthly Interpreter* never was: 'We find also the greatest difficulty in procuring advertisements. We have had one of the best London canvassers but he has utterly failed. It is very disheartening.'[478] For all their praise of Cruickshank in this letter, the general impression one receives from the letter books is that the Clarks suspected that he was not sufficiently exerting himself on their behalf. Matters came to a head in 1897 when, Cruickshank having featured in *Police News*, they withdrew the agency from him, fearful that the reputation of their firm and its publications would in any way be tarnished by his nefarious pursuits. 'We greatly regret that this decision is obviously necessary and *final*.'[479] Cruickshank was succeeded as the Clarks' advertising agent by one Spriggs.[480]

Whether because of lack of effort on the part of the advertising agent or not, it would seem that there was a dearth of advertising income. There certainly was insufficient revenue from this source to bring the loss-making periodicals into profit. Clark publications were, of course, profusely advertised in the firm's own journals, and the loss on a periodical could be notionally reduced by crediting its account with the cost of the firm's own advertising. Hence, for example, when the *Critical Review* showed a deficit of £55 over 1896, this figure was reduced to £25 by crediting £30–worth of Clark advertisements which had appeared in the course of the year.[481]

In persevering with these highly speculative ventures which, though they might conceivably cover their costs, were extremely unlikely to make a profit, the Clarks clearly had the higher point of success in their sights.

The history and profitability of individual titles

The North British Review

The *North British* was by no means a specifically theological journal. It was founded following the Disruption by a group of Free Churchmen who were dissatisfied with the *Edinburgh* and *Quarterly* Reviews, considering the first to be too secular, and the second, too conservative, and who

> desired to give their due place as within the Kingdom of God to interests that had too often been left out in the cold – art, science, philosophy, literature, and culture in general; and without being professedly theological, to look out as from the Christian standpoint on the interests of humanity, and try to preserve a wholesome balance between progress on the one hand, and conservative order on the other.[482]

The founders' aim, therefore, was to consider every department of human life within the framework of a theological perspective; but the *North British* remained a literary, rather than a theological journal, as was made clear in the notice in *The Bookseller* which announced the Clarks' takeover.[483] The history of the *Review* is well covered in primary and secondary sources.[484] In two papers,[485] Joanne Shattock attempts to chart its complex development, and discerns a protracted and ultimately unsuccessful attempt to free the *North British* from the initial dominance of the Free Church of Scotland. Founded as it was in the wake of the Disruption, it was inevitable that the *North British* would be seen as a Free Church journal, although, according to Shattock, it was never designed to be an official organ of that Church. But undeniably, its links with the Church were many, for its proprietor and publisher were drawn from the ranks of the committed, and it stood with Free Church sentiments both politically (supporting the Whigs) and socially (committing itself to current matters of social concern.) As a result of this the editor was urged by its subscribers (the continuance of whose support was obviously vital) to take a clear Free Church line.

Although the North British initially sold well (4000 copies of the first issue, that for May 1844, being sold),[486] its financial position became precarious, and, according to Shattock, successive editors realised that, if it were to succeed, it had to be freed both from its provincialism and from its flavouring of Scottish theology. But it was essential that this independence of thought be achieved without giving offence to the Church. The liberation of the *North British* was made difficult because of the complex web of relationships which existed between successive editors and proprietors and the Church, which Shattock describes as being the *de facto* proprietor.[487] Matters came to a head during the seven-year editorship of Alexander Campbell Fraser, who took up office in 1850. On his assuming the post, the Free Church apparently made a bid for control of the journal, offering to promote the *North British* if it would announce itself as being a Free Church publication. Fraser held out against this, and Shattock seems to regard the period of his editorship as being the journal's high point, the time during which its reputation, especially south of the Border, reached its zenith.

Fraser relied heavily on the services of reviewers from the south, and so much did he submit to their wishes in his eagerness to secure copy from them that at times his editorial policy would seem to have been haphazard and even inept. He freed the *North British* from provincialism, but did not succeed in liberating it from Free Church influence. His acceptance of 'liberal' material antagonised the Free Church element in his readership, and when he published a review critical of Thomas Chalmers' standing as a writer, he was openly condemned by the Church. The proprietor, W.P. Kennedy, joined in this condemnation, and Fraser resigned, to be succeeded by John Duns, a Free Churchman who, according to Shattock, was very much under Kennedy's influence. Thereafter, she sees the *North British* as declining in reputation and influence, the Free Church remaining 'an albatross around the necks of successive editors.'[488]

It was into this situation that the Clarks stepped in 1860, buying the journal from Kennedy, and replacing Duns with William Garden Blaikie. In his autobiography Blaikie[489] describes his perception of the reasons for this takeover. Clearly, circulation had been affected by the débâcle over the Chalmers article, and it was hoped that, with a new proprietor and a new editor, the journal might win back the support of its former coterie of subscribers 'if [it] were conducted with tact, and care were taken not to tread on tender toes.'[490] Clearly, Blaikie was hoping that the Free Church readers in particular might be won back. He also describes his reluctance to take over the editorship, a reluctance fuelled by an awareness of the extensiveness of his other commitments, and by doubt as to his competence for the task. He describes his uniformly amicable relationship with Thomas Clark, and his attempts to enlist the services of as wide a range of contributors as possible. There were for example, abortive attempts to persuade John Ruskin and W.E. Gladstone to contribute. Blaikie also describes his editorial strategy. He sought to avoid giving offence by ensuring that each issue of the journal had what he calls 'a manifest unity',[491] which appears to mean that all contributors had to conform to a predetermined editorial line.

The task was obviously a difficult one, and, after three years in the editorial chair, Blaikie resigned owing to ill health. At around the same time, Clark sold the *North British* to the Edinburgh firm of Edmonston and Douglas, who took it over from mid–1863. From 1869, it was issued from London on behalf of Edmonston and Douglas by Williams and Norgate, and in 1871 it was sold by Douglas to Lord Acton, becoming a liberal Catholic journal under the editorship of Acton and a Mr Wetheral. It finally ceased publication in 1875.

We have no financial data from the 1860s, but the fact that Clark so quickly disposed of the *North British* would seem to indicate that the six shilling review was making a serious loss. Blaikie certainly implies that it was of questionable profitability in his comment: 'considering the circumstances of the *Review*, payments were made on a generous scale.'[492] But it was clearly a marketable property; if Edmonston and Douglas considered it worth purchasing it is surprising that the Clark firm did not consider it worth retaining, especially since, although Shattock holds that its heyday was before the Clark period, there is some evidence to the contrary. Alvar Ellegård notes of the *Review* 'the contemporary press attested the rise in importance and circulation of this periodical during the 1860s.'[493] If this is true it makes it hard to determine the reason for the Clarks' disposal of the journal.

The Monthly Interpreter

> The ablest scholars of Britain, America and the Continent will contribute to its pages. Open discussion of topics will be permitted, free from sectarian spirit, within reverent and reasonable limitations. Its articles will be practical as well as learned; not hyper-scholastic, or unduly technical; adapted to the Lay reader as well as to the professional Student.[494]

With these positive words a new Clark periodical, the *Monthly Interpreter* was announced in October 1884. The first issue appeared in the November of that year, less than three months after the Clarks had agreed to publish the journal. The proposal had come from the *Monthly Interpreter*'s editor, J.S. Exell, whose initial plan had been for a weekly magazine for preachers. Such a project would have over-stretched the Clarks' capacity; the firm, however, impressed by Exell's list of would-be contributors, announced their willingness to consider publishing a monthly magazine along the lines he had in mind. They did wonder, however, whether in fact Exell would be better advised to arrange its issue through a London publisher, since he seemed to envisage that a substantial proportion of the *Interpreter*'s purchasers would be Church of England clergy, a perception which would inevitably influence his editorial policy.[495] By the end of August 1884, however, the Clarks had firmly agreed to take responsibility for the new monthly.[496] Thereafter, the project moved ahead with remarkable speed. Scribners were contacted on 8 September to enlist their services in organising the American distribution of the *Monthly Interpreter*, Exell being well-known in the US.[497] By 23 September, a prospectus for the magazine was in proof, and plans to circulate sample pages of the first issue well advanced.[498] By 24 September, a specimen cover was in print, and review copies of books had been sent to Exell.[499] The first issue of the one-shilling monthly was produced in time for November publication.

Almost from the very start, sales were poor and losses began to mount up. There is no record of the sales of the first issue, which presumably were high, but out of one thousand copies of the second issue supplied to the London agent, only two hundred had been sold by 19 December. This augured ill for the success of the venture, as did the lack of interest on the part of publishers in the *Monthly Interpreter* as an advertising medium.[500] There is no detailed financial data, but the letter books note that £360 had been lost up to 9 October 1885;[501] by 12 May 1886 the firm had lost 'about £700';[502] and by the time the *Monthly Interpreter* was finally wound up after two years and four volumes in October 1886, the very large loss of 'about £1000' had been sustained, a staggering average of around £41 per issue.[503]

What were the reasons for the *Monthly Interpreter*'s rapidly spiralling losses? Undoubtedly, the distribution system left something to be desired.

Kegan Paul were appointed to distribute the magazine in England. Clark normally dealt with Hamilton Adams, and it would appear that the agreement with Kegan Paul was made at Exell's request — the following sentence from a letter to him would certainly bear that interpretation — 'We have arranged everything with Kegan Paul, but their terms allow very little to the publisher. Their name may be of service . . . .'[504] That the arrangement was made at Exell's suggestion is possibly also implied by the following, which was inspired by the poor sales of the second issue: 'If you have any interest with [Kegan Paul] will you try to poke them up?'[505] The terms agreed with the distributors were that they would pay 8½*d*. for each copy of the journal sold by them. There was an additional 10% discount, presumably for prompt payment.[506] As we have no idea of the production costs, we cannot calculate the Clarks' return on each copy sold, but clearly the margin was minimal. And one receives the distinct impression that the Clarks were less than satisfied with Kegan Paul's efforts on behalf of the *Monthly Interpreter*. Other than the disastrous figure for issue two, there is no record of the distributor's success or otherwise. They did remit a cheque for £27 to the firm in July 1885[507] — under the terms of the agreement, this would represent sales of 847 copies[508] — but there is no indication of how many month's sales were covered by this remittance. The Clarks clearly felt that the unfavourable terms demanded by the distributors and their lack of effort in promoting the journal contributed significantly to the losses it made.

Undoubtedly also, the rate of payment to Exell, and through him to the contributors, added to these losses. The initial arrangement proposed by the Clarks was that they would pay him £275 annually to cover his fee and expenses, and his payments for contributions to the magazine. If the British sales topped 3000 copies, they were prepared to increase that sum to £300 per annum, the figure which Exell had requested.[509] He, however, seems to have held out successfully for £300 per year irrespective of sales, for his first monthly cheque was for £25.[510] Although it was necessary to pay adequately if contributors of a suitable calibre were to be attracted, there is no doubt that given the low sales figures the periodical could simply not support an annual payment of £300.

The major, and root cause of the *Monthly Interpreter*'s losses, however, seems to have been Exell's own lack of commitment, if not downright incompetence. It is surprising that, before agreeing to his proposal in the first place, the Clarks did not make more of an effort to ascertain his suitability for such an editorial role. There is no indication in the letter books that they made any attempt to investigate his credentials. Very possibly, he was a well-known figure in theological circles with an impeccable pedigree, so that they felt safe in signing an agreement with him. The indications are, in fact, that it was not that Exell could not effectively sustain the editorship of a monthly, but that, perhaps because of indifference, or of the weight of other responsibilities, he did not devote sufficient time and care to the task. There are also, regrettably, indications that he was driven by a self-centred rapacity, so that one is forced to ask whether he put up the proposal merely to secure a source of regular income with little intention of committing himself wholeheartedly to the journal. Much as the Clarks regretted having undertaken the *Monthly Interpreter*, they must have been glad that they did not agree to Exell's initial proposal that they should launch a weekly.

Exell's work was marked by general lack of professionalism. For example, he did not return proofs of the November 1885 issue until 23 October, despite the fact that finished copies were due in London by 25 October.[511] And he was later to receive this rebuke, apropos of the firm's £1000 loss:

> we must say that we think a good deal of this has been caused by the loose way in which articles have been inserted. Beyond sending us a supply of Papers, many of which had been obtained for a quite different purpose the Editor did nothing; few if any of the articles receiving any editorial care of revision. This contrasted so strikingly with the care shown by the Editor of the 'Expositor' that it is no wonder the 'Monthly Interpreter' did not succeed.[512]

The limited extent of Exell's commitment to the journal is demonstrated not only by his lack of care, and unresponsiveness to communications from Edinburgh, but also by his financial dealings. The £25 he received each month was intended both to remunerate him for his efforts, and to enable him to make adequate payments to his contributors in order, as was noted earlier, to attract material from the most competent scholars, and to build the journal's reputation as one which paid well for good work. In one case at least, as we saw, he was guilty of making what the Clarks considered a grossly inadequate payment, £4 4*s*. 0*d*. for twenty-nine pages of text.[513] His motive must simply have been to retain as much as possible for himself and he was told bluntly by the Clarks that some sacrifices were called for from the editor, as well as from the publishers of an unsuccessful magazine. Whether Exell underpaid all his contributors is a matter for conjecture; certainly an author whose work had appeared in another periodical edited by him — the *Homiletical Quarterly*, a US journal — is known not to have received payment for his article, although it is unclear whether this was the fault of Exell, or of the American publishers, Randolph.[514]

Exell's attitude and approach, therefore, contributed significantly to the loss made by the *Monthly Interpreter*. One's suspicion that his main aim was to enrich himself is deepened when one considers his attempts to involve the Clarks in other projects. For instance, before the magazine was launched, he proposed that the firm should distribute a work of his own, *Thirty Thousand Thoughts*. This they declined to do, although they did grant him free advertising space in the first issue of the new periodical to promote it.[515] Again, in the *Monthly Interpreter*'s dying months, he invited the Clarks to publish one of his own works: they declined, pleading the state of the market. But in the face of Exell's audacity in making the proposal in the circumstances, is there a touch of sarcasm in their response, or were they simply showing their customary Christian graciousness?

> We have no doubt that you will easily find another Publisher, as the collection must be a valuable one: we wish you great success with it.[516]

The decision to wind up the periodical at the end of Volume Four had been taken in May 1886, no doubt on the grounds both of the extent of the losses and of the poor quality of the editing. It would seem that Exell demanded a severance payment of £100. Amazingly, the Clarks agreed to pay him three-quarters of this amount on his resignation, an act which, in the light of his behaviour, would seem to have been one of incomprehensible charity.[517] The £75 was duly paid on 1 October 1886, together with the £25 due for the last issue of the journal. The firm pointed out to Exell that the £1000 loss had been largely due to his carelessness, and suggested that 'in common justice' he should return the cheque for £75.[518] It says much for the Clarks that the cheque was sent. There is no evidence that Exell returned it, and it seems unlikely that he would have done so.

On hearing that Exell had secured the editorship of the *British and Foreign Evangelical Review*, Thomas Clark expressed his surprise, and put on paper his last word on the *Monthly Interpreter*'s editor: 'I . . . certainly very much regret having had anything to do with him.'[519]

The Expository Times

'I am hopeful it will succeed ere long.' wrote one of the Clarks in January 1890 about the *Expository Times*, which was just beginning to be issued under the Clark imprint.[520] If he was thinking of financial success then he was sadly mistaken, for the new magazine did not show a profit until the late 1890s. If, however, he was thinking of its influence and standing among theological scholars, then his hopes were to be fully justified, for in those terms the *Expository Times* was a success almost from the first.

On the face of it, the Clarks showed considerable acumen in agreeing to publish another theological monthly, similar in intent to the *Monthly Interpreter*, just over three years after that periodical's disastrous failure. But they were helped in reaching a decision by significant differences between the two undertakings.

For a start, James Hastings, the founder of the new magazine, was clearly no careless opportunist such as Exell had been. The first three issues of the *Expository Times* (October-December 1889) had been published at Hastings' own risk by an Aberdeen bookseller, William Diack of Schoolhill. The editor's commitment to the journal was unquestionable: an often-repeated story has it that Hastings,

> when he had the second number ready, found, on going to Aberdeen, that his publisher had been ill and away from business for more than a week. Dr. Hastings, equal to the occasion, went behind the counter in the little shop, and for more than a fortnight remained there and sold 'The Expository Times', and also any books that anybody wanted to buy.[521]

But if the enthusiasm of the editor was indubitable, so too was the quality of his product. The first three issues of the journal, largely written by Hastings himself, would have been before the Clarks as they were discussing their takeover plans. Moreover, it was already attracting attention in theological circles. If the brief note announcing the launch of the *Expository Times* in the *Bookseller* was encouraging — 'It is intended for popular reading, its object being to encourage an intelligent interest in the study of the Bible, and it will doubtless do so.'[522] – of much greater significance and importance was the fact that the new journal was commended by William Robertson Nicoll in the *British Weekly*.[523]

In deciding to undertake the *Monthly Interpreter*, all the Clarks had to base their judgement on was the reputation of the editor and his list of potential contributors; in the case of the *Expository Times*, although the editor was relatively unknown beyond his own circle, the quality of the product was clear. The risk to the Clarks may therefore have been less. The *Monthly Interpreter* episode both demonstrated that the firm was eager to issue a monthly magazine, and showed how important it was that the editor be a man of commitment and calibre. In Hastings, the Clarks found such a man. Their decision to publish the *Expository Times* was to have far-reaching consequences both for Hastings and for the firm. His reputation as an incomparable theological editor grew, and he launched into the ambitious publishing programme which was to occupy him for the rest of his life, and which produced the *Dictionary of the Bible*, the *Encyclopaedia of Religion and Ethics*, and many other works, the majority of which were issued by T. & T. Clark. If it is difficult to imagine how his work could have been effectively issued other than by the Clarks, who gave it unswerving commitment backed by capital, it is equally difficult to imagine how T. & T. Clark would have developed had it not been for the works by Hastings which for many years were one of their chief pre-occupations. More was involved in the decision taken in late 1889 than either party could ever have imagined.

The tumultuous course of the *Monthly Interpreter* is well-documented in the letter-books; the issue of the *Expository Times* proceeded much more smoothly, and hence generated less correspondence, which makes it more difficult to chart its development. It would appear that the immediate cause of the Clarks' takeover of the journal was some crisis which affected William Diack's business, possibly related to his ill-health. A letter to Hastings dated 20 January 1890 goes so far as to speak of Diack's 'failure'[524] but the Aberdeen bookseller was clearly still in business, for he was reluctant to give up the Aberdeen franchise for the *Expository Times*.[525] It is not clear whether the Clarks approached Hastings with a view to taking over the periodical, or whether the initial contact had been from him.[526] In any case, as from January 1890, the *Expository Times* bore the Clark imprint.[527] The aims of the periodical at the start of the Clarks' proprietorship were stated in a note in the editorial columns of the *Bookseller* for January 1890,[528] copy for which was presumably provided by the firm. The periodical aimed to present 'exegesis and commentary of the higher class' to the widest possible readership, both lay and clerical, from as many theological camps as possible. It intended keeping abreast of contemporary thought: the editor's competence for this work had already been attested by his readership. The *Expository Times* was praised for the commendable clarity and incisiveness of style with which the articles it contained were written.

The following financial arrangements appear to have been agreed at the time of the takeover. Hastings was to be paid a monthly sum of £17 on the day of publication to cover all the literary expenses of the magazine. This was much less than the £25 per month which Exell had been receiving for the *Monthly Interpreter*, but at this point the *Expository Times* contained only twenty-four pages per issue, whereas the *Interpreter* had been much longer, containing eighty pages per issue.[529] The Clarks agreed to pay an outstanding printers' account for the first three issues, which amounted to £45; they also agreed to pay Hastings £35 for the literary expenses of those early issues,

> this sum being fixed upon in consideration of the loss of the majority of the subscriptions for the first year secured by Mr. W. Diack and consequent upon his failure.[530]

Thus Hastings' personal losses on the early numbers of the *Expository Times* were refunded to him by his new publishers who, in effect, retrospectively took financial responsibility for the journal from its commencement.

The *Expository Times* quickly gained in critical esteem and (to a lesser extent) in circulation. We have noted that, by 1896, the firm were claiming that it was read regularly by 'nearly all the well-known Scholars',[531] and in 1897 the comment was made that it, together with the *Critical Review*, circulated 'all the world over.'[532] From the beginning of Volume Three, with the issue for October 1891, the number of pages in each issue was increased from twenty-four to forty-eight. Hastings had wanted this increase to take place in the middle of the second year of issue, but was advised by the manager of John Menzies, whose guidance had been sought by the Clarks, that a mid-volume increase in size (and in price, from 3*d*. to 6*d*. per issue) would be a sure way to 'kill the magazine'.[533] As we have noted, the periodical was circulated in America first by Scribners, and then by the Christian Literature Publishing Company.

The picture, then, is of a journal with a firm commitment to the dissemination of contemporary theological thought, steadily gaining an influential, international readership under Hastings' positive editorship. All this was very much in line with the aims of the Clark firm. On the face of it, the *Expository Times* was a success story. But how profitable was it? Detailed financial data are available for the four financial years beginning with 1895–96, and they clearly demonstrate that until 1898–99 the magazine lost money each year.[534] Table 15 itemises the firm's outlay on and income from the *Expository Times* over 1895–96.

One or two general observations should be made. Monthly sales figures are given for 1895–96, and these show a marked, if not steady, upward trend. 3,227 copies of the July 1895 issue were sold; the February 1896 issue sold 3,573 copies; and the issue for the June of that year sold 3,605 copies. The total number of copies sold over the year, after adjustments to take into account stock on hand at the agents, was 38,734. After the deduction of 2,980 '13th copies', for which the Clarks were not paid, this figure was reduced to 35,754, the 2,980 dozen mentioned in the Table.

Over 1896–97 the total sales were 3,227 dozen, and the following year, the figure dropped only slightly to 3,183 dozen. In 1898–99, the year in which the

Table 16

Expository Times: 1895–96 accounts			
Outlay		*Income*	
Printing[1]	£385 15*s*. 7*d*.	Sales: 2980 dozen[5]	£558 15*s*. 0*d*.
Paper[2]	£142 6*s*. 11*d*.	Volume sales[6]	£46 9*s*. 1*d*.
Binding	£11 14*s*. 3*d*.	Sales of binding cases	£7 12*s*. 9*d*.
Editor[3]	£360 0*s*. 0*d*.	Advertising income	£136 0*s*. 11*d*.
Carriage	£20 0*s*. 0*d*.	Credited for T. & T. Clark's advertising	£69 7*s*. 10*d*.
Advertising	£30 5*s*. 1*d*.		
Proportion of Lists	£5 0*s*. 0*d*.		
Miscellaneous[4]	£22 2*s*. 10*d*.		
			£818 5*s*. 7*d*.
		Less stock at agents	£1 17*s*. 6*d*.
			£816 8*s*. 1*d*.
		Loss	£160 16*s*. 7*d*.
	£977 4*s*. 8*d*.		£977 4*s*. 8*d*.

(1) This sum included the printing costs of the magazine itself, and of the sundry items related to its publication.
(2) This sum includes the cost of paper for the magazine itself, and for its cover.
(3) With the increase in size of each issue of the journal, the literary expenses had, of necessity, increased also. Hastings was by now receiving £30 per month to cover his literary costs, and to remunerate him for his activities.
(4) This sum includes the cost of such items as the distribution of presentation copies of the magazine, and the reproduction of a portrait of Professor Sanday.
(5) The *Expository Times* was sold to the trade at 4*s*. 2*d*. per dozen copies, on the top of which there was an additional discount of 10%. 2980 dozen at 4*s*. 2*d*. = £620 16*s*. 8*d*. — £62 1*s*. 8*d*. = £558 15*s*. 0*d*. The trade price per copy was therefore in effect 3.75*d*.
(6) All the previous issues of the *Expository Times*, with the exception of the first year's, were available in bound volume form. These volumes, from Volume 3 onwards, retailed at 7*s*. 6*d*., and were sold to the trade at 4*s*. 9*d*., a discount of 36.66%. Volume 2 sold to the trade at 2*s*. 6*d*. The majority of sales over 1895–96 were of the previous year's volume, of which 144 copies were disposed.

journal broke into profit, sales totalled 3,246 dozen. The *Expository Times* sales figures were therefore growing reasonably consistently.

But the Clarks had difficulty in making the journal turn in a profit. We have insufficient data to calculate the unit production cost of each copy printed, but a very rough figure may be reached for 1895–96 by dividing the total outlay by the total sales, including '13th copies'. This gives the Clarks' cost per issue sold at 6.05*d*. — .05*d*. above the retail price. And the deficit of £160 16*s*. 7*d*. takes into account the sum legitimately credited for the firm's advertising, without which the loss would have been even greater.

Deficits over the two succeeding years were slightly reduced. In 1896–97, there was a loss of £45 13*s*. 11*d*., but a much larger sum, £131 1*s*. 0*d*., a rough estimate it would seem, was credited on account of Clark advertising. And over 1897–98, there was a loss of £50 1*s*. 9*d*. That is the year in which the Christian Literature Publishing Company took over from Scribners as American distributors, and for the first time separate figures are given for American sales. These totalled 19,500 over nine months, but as each copy was sold at 1*d.* until February 1898 and thereafter at 1½*d.*, it is clear that the Clarks were making a massive loss on these sales. This they must have considered a worthwhile investment if it gained for them a platform in the US.[535] Over 1898–99, the *Expository Times* showed a profit for the first time. It amounted to £92 17*s.* 10*d.* A comparison of the figures for 1895–96 with the corresponding ones for 1898–99 reveals that there were three reasons why the latter year's trading showed a profit. In the first place, outlay fell, from £977 4*s.* 8*d.* to £956 1*s.* 10*d.*: a fall totally accounted for by the decrease in promotional advertising. Whereas in 1895–96, £30 5*s.* 1*d.* was spent on advertising, only £5 13*s.* 4*d.* was expended in this way over 1898–99. In the second place, sales increased. Over 1895–96, total income from sales (including sales of binding cases) amounted to £612 16*s.* 10*d.* Over 1898–99, total income from sales (including sales of binding cases and US sales) amounted to £762 16*s.* 6*d.* In the third place, advertising revenue increased, from £205 8*s.* 9*d.* over 1895–96 to £286 3*s.* 2*d.* over 1898–99. All of this increase is accounted for, however, by a corresponding increase in the sum credited for the firm's own advertising, from £69 7*s.* 10*d.* in 1895–96 to £147 6*s.* 3*d.* in 1898–99. Although there had been a significant increase in income from sales, therefore, the journal would still not have shown a profit had it not been for the large sum notionally credited in respect of the Clarks' own advertising. In real terms, the *Expository Times* was still not making a profit at the end of the century.

As the *Expository Times* gained in critical esteem, so it made slow progress towards profitability in real terms. If the trend continued, this goal would have been reached by the early 1900s. It is clear, however, that the losses on the *Expository Times* were slight compared with those on the *Monthly Interpreter*. Moreover, unlike Exell, Hastings was proving himself to be a dedicated and fastidious editor. The reputation of the periodical, and hence the Clarks' reputation as its publisher, was being enhanced. At the very least, the *Expository Times* was bringing T. & T. Clark's name before that public which was most likely to buy their books, and providing a platform where they could be advertised and (if they met with Hastings' approval) sympathetically reviewed.

The Critical Review of Theological and Philosophical Literature

This journal, featuring as it did reviews by specialists of theological and philosophical works, was very much within the field which T. & T. Clark had made their own. The firm, however, was far from eager to embark upon the project; responding to one of the earlier manifestations of the plan which eventually resulted in the *Critical Review*, John M. Clark commented that there was 'great risk in the undertaking.'[536]

S.D.F. Salmond's first approach to the firm on the subject of a quarterly review had come in the summer of 1886; as we have seen, the Clarks did not hold high hopes for the success of such an undertaking, feeling that the days of the Quarterlies were past. They did entertain the proposal to the extent of asking Salmond to 'consult with a few friends, & get their candid opinion',[537] but beyond that, whether or not because of the candid opinion of the few friends is uncertain, they did not go. Another Edinburgh house, Macniven and Wallace, was, however, prepared to accept Salmond's proposal, and, under the editorship of a committee, the *Theological Review and Free Church Quarterly* was issued by them, in collaboration with Hodder and Stoughton of London with whom they had close links. The editorial policy of the journal was set out in a note in the first issue (November 1886). It aimed to provide a forum where the results of study into scientific theology within Scotland in general and within the Free Church in particular could be aired, and where also reviews of work published elsewhere would appear. 'One of the principal objects of the *Theological Review* will be to maintain a watchful observation on the periodical literature of France, Germany, and Italy.' While hoping that the *Review* would have the support of many outwith the Free Church, Salmond and his fellow-promoters clearly regarded it as a Free Church journal as its title proclaimed: its policy would be to rely mainly on contributions from within that Church. Fifteen issues were published by Macniven and Wallace between 1886 and 1890, with a cover price of 1*s*. 0*d*. per issue.

It would appear that by 1889 that firm were considering divesting themselves of the journal, presumably because, as the Clarks had expected all along, it was proving unprofitable. Nothing daunted, Salmond wrote once again to T. & T. Clark, suggesting that they should take over the periodical, which by now seems to have been known as the *Theological Review and New College Quarterly*, perhaps in order not to deter potential non-Free Church purchasers. Once again the project was considered, and once again John M. Clark was far from sanguine. 'There is considerable difficulty, as I have so little to guide me.' He estimated that, given that contributors were to be paid at the rate of say £4 per sixteen page sheet, and the editor at the rate of £10 per number, it would take sales of at least two thousand copies, far more than could be realistically expected, before the journal would break even. In consequence, he saw little hope of his firm taking over the *Review*.[538]

Discussions with Salmond continued, however, and a new idea emerged, probably suggested by the Clarks. This involved not a mere continuation of the old periodical, but its transformation into something new and different. The new periodical would be a theological and literary review, with a much broader denominational base than had the existing one. This idea was discussed throughout December 1889 and January 1890. Salmond and his committee clearly favoured the continuation of the journal in its existing form; the Clarks insisted that this was impossible. They did, however, allow themselves to be persuaded to increase an initial offer which they had made of £15 per number for all literary expenses to £20 per number. Even this was significantly less than the rate of payment for editor and contributors (£10 per number for the editor and £4 per sheet for contributors) which John M. Clark had, a few weeks earlier, clearly regarded as the appropriate rate for the job. However, it was obviously the maximum figure which the Clarks were prepared to risk, even given the more catholic basis of the new journal.[539] Agreement was reached, and a preliminary notice announcing the Clarks' forthcoming launch of the *Critical Review* was issued in April 1890.[540] This coincided with the publication of the last issue of the *Theological Review* which carried an editorial note claiming that the journal had largely fulfilled the expectations with which it was founded, and that its success had encouraged its conductors to aim at an extension of its usefulness. (In fact, it would appear that the *Review*'s change of emphasis resulted more from the insistence of the new publishers than from the desire of the editorial committee.) In future, S.D.F. Salmond would be the editor, and T. & T. Clark the publishers. The contents of the journal would be significantly different, being in future restricted to reviews of literature rather than featuring a combination of such reviews with original pieces of work as had happened before. In every other way, however, the contents would be broadened. The *Review* would no longer be the mouthpiece of one denomination, but would provide a forum for scholars of all branches of the Evangelical Church; it would no longer limit itself to reviews of theological writing, but would feature philosophical works as well. There would be a truly international dimension.

The first issue of the *Critical Review* was published in October 1890, and between then and 1899 it appeared under the Clark imprint. An editorial note in the first number listed the journal's aims in terms similar to those which had been used in the last issue of the *Theological Review*. It was to be an English-language equivalent of such Continental organs as Harnack and Schürer's *Theologische Literaturzeitung* and Lipsius's *Theologischer Jahresbericht*. Initial responses to the new journal seem to have been largely favourable. 'It has met with quite a hearty welcome in this country', the Clarks commented to Scribners, or again, 'It is doing remarkably well here, & the unanimous opinion is that it supplies a long-standing want in our Theological Literature.'[541] But there was some criticism too. A review in the *Publishers' Circular*, for example, while generally commendatory in tone, felt that the journal was 'written too exclusively by specialists for specialists ever to find favour with the public at large.'[542] But this was a criticism which the Clarks could accept: the journal was addressing a small audience. Attempts were made, of course, to promote its sales as extensively as possible. It was circulated in America and, as we have noted, was offered to students at a special rate. Still, however, it did not make a profit in its early years. The firm commented in 1896 they were carrying on the *Review* 'at considerable loss' to themselves,[543] and in January 1897 they noted that it had made a loss of £55 over the previous year:[544] this would refer to the 1896 calendar year, rather than the 1895–96 financial year, the figures for which we will be examining shortly. At one point the *Review* was increased in size by one sheet per issue in an attempt to promote sales.

From the letter books, one gets the impression that the *Critical Review* was hopelessly unprofitable. In fact, as the financial data show things were less gloomy. We have detailed figures for the four financial years beginning 1895–96,[545] and those for 1895–96 are presented in abbreviated form below.

Over 1895–96, the loss was considerable. The journal sold an average of 959 copies per issue, or 71.03% of the print run. But the unit production cost per copy printed (excluding the American promotional expenses) was 12.53*d*. – .53*d*. above the trade price. Increased advertising revenue or a decrease in expenses were therefore vital if there was to be a profit, for without the help of advertising revenue, a surplus was impossible, even on 100% sales. There were, of course, notional figures on both sides of the accounts in 1895–96. £18 15*s*. 6*d*. was debited in respect of copies shipped to America for promotional purposes. These were no doubt copies which would otherwise have remained unsold: hence no actual outlay was involved. £27 12*s*. 0*d*. was credited in Table 17.

Table 17

Critical Review: 1895–96 accounts

Outlay		*Income*	
Printing[1]	£128 6*s*. 2*d*.	3835 @ 1/-[5]	£191 15*s*. 0*d*.
Paper[2]	£23 11*s*. 0*d*.	Back nos[6]	£6 18*s*. 6*d*.
Honoraria[3]	£105 0*s*. 0*d*.	Advertising	£48 3*s*. 1*d*.
Binding	£1 16*s*. 6*d*.	T. & T. Clark's	
Proportion of Lists	£6 0*s*. 0*d*.	Advertising	£27 12*s*. 0*d*.
Advertising	£11 4*s*. 1*d*.	Sale of cases	£ 1 4*s*. 8*d*.
US Promotional			
Copies[4]	£18 15*s*. 0*d*.		
Miscellaneous	£6 3*s*. 6*d*.		
			£275 13*s*. 3*d*.
		Loss	£25 3*s*. 0*d*.
	£300 16*s*. 3*d*.		£300 16*s*. 3*d*.

(1) Printing 1,350 copies each of four numbers, plus miscellaneous printing.
(2) Paper for the journal, and for miscellaneous related printing.
(3) At the rate of £26 5*s*. 0*d*. per issue.
(4) 500 assorted copies supplied free to Scribners.
(5) The retail price was 1*s*. 6*d*. The sales figures here are adjusted to take into account stock in hand at the distributors. There is no data for US sales.
(6) Previous years' volumes were available at a trade price of 4*s*. 6*d*. The majority of those sold were of the most recent volume, Volume 5.

respect of advertising space used by the Clarks. This too, was a notional figure.

By 1896–97, however, things had improved somewhat, and a profit of £4 10*s*. 5*d*. shown. The print run and costs remained similar, and the sales figure actually dropped to 3,688 — 68.29% of the print run. That the accounts showed a profit was the result of the facts firstly, that there was no notional expenditure on sending promotional copies to the US as there had been in 1895–96, and secondly, that advertising revenue was greatly increased, reaching £103 12*s*. 9*d*., of which £60 16*s*. 9*d*. came from outside firms, and £42 16*s*. 0*d*. from Clarks' own advertising. It will at once be realised, of course, that the *Review* did not show a profit in real terms. The loss would have been considerable had it not been for the notional sum credited to the account of the journal in respect of Clark advertising.

The position was the same over 1897–98, when a notional profit of £5 12*s*. 10*d*. was shown. Again, the print run and costs remained similar; the sales rose to 3,985 — 73.79% of the print run. That a profit was shown was due to a combination of increased sales, and the continuing level of income from advertising: that year it reached £102 2*s*. 6*d*., of which £49 2*s*. 6*d*. came from outside firms, and £53 0*s*. 0*d*. from the Clarks' own advertising.

Over 1898–99, although once again a considerable sum was credited to the account of the *Review* in respect of Clark advertising, it showed a loss of £33 16*s*. 2*d*. Again, the print run and costs remained similar, but the sales fell to 3285 — 60.83% of the print run. There were two reasons for the loss: firstly, decline in sales reduced the Clarks' income by £35 on the previous year's figure; secondly, decline in income from advertising reduced their takings by £19 6*s*. 10*d*. (Over 1898–99, advertising income totalled £82 15*s*. 8*d*., of which £40 13*s*. 8*d*. came from outside firms, and £42 2*s*. 0*d*. from the Clarks' own advertising.) Losses would have been even greater had not the outlay on the *Review* been somewhat reduced that year, printing costs and promotional expenditure being less than over 1897–98.

That such a specialist journal should have come as close as it did to making a profit in real terms would have been a great encouragement to the Clarks. Given that sales appear to have been reasonably buoyant in the late 1890s, it seems uncharacteristic that, at the end of 1899, they sold the *Critical Review* to William and Norgate of London. This change of proprietorship may in fact have come about at the instigation of Salmond, who seems to have had some doubts as to whether T. & T. Clark could promote the *Review* effectively to the whole of the English language market. In 1896, for example, he had proposed that the Clarks should issue the journal jointly with an English firm, an idea which his publishers swiftly turned down, implying that it would be difficult to find another publisher willing to take the risk:

> I question if more than one or two of the high class English Reviews are financed by their *Publishers*. In most cases they are *subsidised*, & the Publishers run no risk.[546]

It may, however, have been the persistent renewal of this kind of request from Salmond which led to the sale to the English firm of a prestigious property which otherwise one would have expected the Clarks to continue handling.[547]

The Clarks' periodical publishing programme illustrates further their aim to keep in their sights both the lower and the higher points of success with a definite bias towards the latter. The examples of the *Expository Times* and the *Critical Review* demonstrate that they were willing to persevere with loss-making projects provided the losses were modest, and provided the quality of the product was unquestionable. The *Monthly Interpreter* was wound up because it was of poor quality editorially, and because the poverty of its contents led to low sales and unacceptably high losses. The Clarks commented that most 'high class' English reviews were subsidised by individuals or by bodies other than the publisher. It was no doubt with a certain justifiable pride that they could thus highlight the fact that, unlike many other publishers, they were prepared to subsidise, sometimes fairly substantially, and for many years, periodicals which they believed deserved their support.

Chapter 8
Standard reference works

The issue of major works of reference was always part of the Clark tradition. In the earlier days, works of German scholarship in this category were issued in translation (Hermann Cremer's *Biblico-Theological Lexicon of New Testament Greek*, for example, appeared in English in 1872 under the Clark imprint.) But by the 1880s and 1890s the firm, as in other areas of their activities, were able to rely more on the output of English-language scholarship. Such works, although in some cases they may have originated in proposals made by their editors to the Clarks, were for the most part commissioned by the firm to fill recognised gaps on the theological library shelves. They involved a large outlay spread over several years as a project gradually came to fruition, and consequently they were published at considerable risk to the firm. If they were to be successful, they had to establish a toe-hold in the market-place, win a reputation, and outsell the works of competitors and imitators for a considerable period of time.

Several major works were issued in the last two decades of the nineteenth century: this chapter examines two of them, W.F. Moulton and A.S. Geden's *Concordance to the Greek New Testament* (1897) and James Hastings' *Dictionary of the Bible* (1898+). These were both completely new works for which reasonably detailed financial information has been preserved.

A further standard reference work issued by the Clarks was a translation and revision of C.L.W. Grimm's version of C.G. Wilke's *Clavis Novi Testamenti*, produced by an American scholar, Joseph Henry Thayer of Harvard, and published in 1886. The Clarks were not, however, involved in the editorial stages of this project, nor did they bear any appreciable risk, merely undertaking, it would seem, to buy a set of plates from Scribners, and to pay a royalty of three per cent on sales up to 600 copies, and seven and a half per cent thereafter, these percentages to be reckoned on the British selling price.[548] The work was published as *Greek-English Lexicon of the New Testament* with a nominal retail price of £1 16*s*. 0*d*. and a trade price of £1 7*s*. 0*d*. From the first, it seems to have sold steadily, if not particularly rapidly,[549] and in the 1890s it was still producing a high annual return for the Clarks. In the financial year 1895–96, on sales of 230 copies, it showed a profit of £152 2*s*. 6*d*; over 1895–97 on sales of 238 there was a profit of £212 1*s*. 11*d*. A reprint of 810 copies was produced in the financial year 1897–98, but even so, on sales of 184, there was a net profit of £62 7*s*. 9*d*. Sales over 1898–99 totalled 276 copies, yielding a profit of £235 1*s*. 10*d*. These figures were achieved despite the fact that a sizable royalty was due to Thayer each year. For example, he received £43 11*s*. 1*d*. in 1896–97, £37 12*s*. 4*d*. in 1897–98, and £61 18*s*. 4*d*. in 1898–99.[550] Grimm/Thayer was clearly an ongoing success.

Moulton and Geden's 'Concordance'

It is undoubtedly an alarming undertaking for me,' wrote John M. Clark of Moulton and Geden's *Concordance to the Greek New Testament*.[551] It was, however, the kind of venture upon which the firm thrived, and it was no doubt with some pride that the Clarks emphasised their belief that no other publisher 'would face the cost of production of such an undertaking', especially once the Clark edition was in the market place, when it would be unlikely to be threatened by rival works.

What motives led the firm to commit themselves to its publication? The clearest statements of intent focus, as they did in the case of so many Clark works, upon the uniqueness of the *Concordance*, and upon the gap on the theological library shelves which it was felt to be filling. For example, in a letter to Scribners, the Clarks commented: 'as for the *need* of the Work, that is universally admitted.'[553] The announcement in the *Bookseller* immediately following publication of the *Concordance* developed this theme.[554] The standard concordance to the Greek Testament was that by C.H. Bruder, which in its original form rested entirely upon the Textus Receptus. Attempts in an edition published in 1888 to bring it abreast of contemporary textual scholarship were held by the Clarks to have been 'unsatisfying and incomplete'. The only rivals to Bruder's work were small volumes 'of totally insufficient compass', based entirely on the Textus Receptus. This was the gap which Moulton and Geden intended to fill. Their work, it was claimed, 'adopts a new principle, and aims at providing a full and complete Concordance to the text of the Greek Testament as it is set forth in the editions of Westcott and Hort, Tischendorf . . . and the English Revisers.' It is not surprising that, when initially offered the *Concordance* by A.S. Geden in April 1895 the Clarks replied 'the work would be quite within our line of publication.'[555]

Initially, another firm, George Bell and Sons, had contracted to issue Moulton and Geden's work. Bell had laid down a number of conditions, the chief among them being that the editors had to undertake that they would secure five hundred advance subscriptions for the *Concordance*. It is not clear by which party the agreement between Bell and the editors was severed. Certainly, the terms concluded with T. & T. Clark were more favourable to Moulton and Geden than those agreed with Bell had been: the clause stipulating that advance subscribers had to be found by the editors was withdrawn.[556] The fact that they were taking over a project which was already under way caused the Clarks certain difficulties when the work came to be published. A number of subscribers had been enlisted under the terms of the Bell contract prior to the Clarks' assuming responsibility for the work. They had been promised copies at a price of one guinea which they had paid in advance. When the *Concordance* eventually appeared in 1897 it had a selling price of £1 6*s*. 0*d*., but although it was published as a net book, the Clarks felt obliged to supply copies to these original subscribers at one guinea. Similarly, booksellers who had committed themselves during the Bell period to order a certain number of copies at a trade price guaranteed then were supplied with those copies at the price quoted. This led to slight disharmony between the Clarks and other booksellers and customers.[557]

Agreement with Moulton and Geden was reached in late April 1895, but owing to editorial fastidiousness and production difficulties, the *Concordance* was not published until 3 April 1897. Throughout those years, a constant theme in the letter books is the extent of the risk being borne by the Clarks: even if the work did prove successful, they envisaged being 'out of pocket for years.'[558] The size of the risk seems in part to have been due to the sheer scale of the *Concordance*. Initially, it was agreed that it should run to seven or eight hundred pages; by October 1895, it was calculated on the basis of manuscript submitted by Geden that it would run to over 1,028 pages, bringing the estimated cost to £1,030.[559] In the event, it was claimed that printing costs alone, excluding the cost of paper, reached £1,054 15*s*. 6*d*., a massive investment for a firm of T. & T. Clark's size.[560] This figure, however does not take into account the fairly substantial discounts offered by the printers, which reduced the sum payable by the Clarks to £793 18*s*. 3*d*. The extent of this reduction was possibly due to technical problems which arose in the course of production.[561]

As usual, the Clarks were aiming at the highest production standards possible, using very fine quality, highly super-calendered paper,[562] and having a new fount of type specially cut for the work.[563] In the end it was their view that 'a more beautiful book of the kind [had] never been produced.'[564] But these design factors no doubt contributed to the scale of the investment.

This was affected also by the fastidiousness of the editors. In autumn 1895, Geden was taken to task on account of the number of corrections he was making on the proofs,[565] while a year later Moulton and his son were laboriously re-checking the proofs after the Clarks thought the work had been finally passed for press.[566] All this was completely understandable in view of the facts that the two editors were jointly responsible for the work, and that the reputation of their scholarship was at stake. But it was frustrating for the Clarks to see time elapsing and costs increasing as the proofs passed through these numerous revisions.

Although the Clarks contemplated making substantial payments to the editors in recompense for the 'enormous labour' they had expended on the *Concordance*[567] they do not in fact seem to have received anything. On the contrary, the amount of capital invested in the project by the firm was somewhat lessened by a contribution of £200 towards the outlay from A.S. Geden. In October 1895, when it became clear that the work was going to be substantially longer than first planned, he offered to contribute a further £50.

This second offer was not immediately taken up by the firm; however, they asked to reserve the right to claim the additional £50 one year after publication if the work showed serious financial loss.[568] And in fact Geden did remit an additional £50 on 26 November 1897. In spite of these contributions from Geden, however, the firm's investment was very sizable.

But on publication, the Clarks were sanguine about the work's prospects. There had been pre-publication orders for 400 copies in the UK,[569] and the firm anticipated a steady demand for it owing to its importance, and to the fact that it would be several years before it could possibly be superseded.[570] Financial data relating to the *Concordance* has been preserved for the three financial years beginning with 1896–97 in the course of which the work was published.[571] This information enables us to estimate with reasonable accuracy the costings of the first two printings of the work (800 copies in 1897, and a further 540 copies in 1899) and the levels of return which these produced. Although only 750 copies of the first printing were ordered and paid for, the printers appear to have supplied an extra fifty copies gratis.

Table 18

Moulton and Geden's 'Concordance': Costings of the first printing (800 copies)

Outlay		*Income*	
Composition and Printing[1]	£793 18*s*. 0*d*.	Sales[5]	£837 11*s*. 8*d*.
Paper	£50 1*s*. 0*d*.	Paid by A.S. Geden	£250 0*s*. 0*d*.
Stereoplates	£105 5*s*. 0*d*.	Profit of sale of of plates to Scribners[6]	£89 19*s*. 3*d*.
Binding[2]	£39 7*s*. 9*d*.	Royalty on Scribners' sales[7]	£26 19*s*. 11*d*.
Back Stamp	£1 1*s*. 0*d*.		
Promotion[3]	£5 3*s*. 9*d*.		
Advertising[4]	£36 12*s*. 1*d*.		
Proportion of Lists	£4 0*s*. 0*d*.		
Miscellaneous	£1 0*s*. 11*d*.		
	£1,036 9*s*. 6*d*.		
Profit	£168 1*s*. 4*d*.		
	£1,204 10*s*. 10*d*.		£1,204 10*s*. 10*d*.

(1) This was the sum which was payable after the deduction of various discounts and reductions allowed by the printers.
(2) This figure is an estimate: only 600 copies were bound up in the year of publication. The binding cost of £39 7*s*. 9*d*. for the entire edition is arrived at as follows:
An estimated 730 copies bound in cloth at 8.83*d*. per copy = £26 17*s*. 0*d*.
An estimated 70 copies bound in leather at 43*d*. per copy = £12 10*s*. 9*d*.
(3) The cost of printing 7,500 prospectuses, and 2,810 other promotional items.
(4) This figure is made up as follows:
Credited in respect of the Clarks' advertising —
£15 12*s*. 0*d*. (*Critical Review* £2 8*s*. 0*d*., *Expository Times* £13 4*s*. 0*d*.)
Payments made for outside advertising — £21 0*s*. 1*d*.

Table 18 (*continued*)

(5) The pricing of the *Concordance* was extremely complicated. In the first place, copies were available both in cloth and in leather. But in the second place, a wide range of trade prices obtained in each of these categories. Some of these discounted prices were 'net' — a fixed price without further discount, be it 21*s*. 0*d*., 19*s*. 6*d*., 19*s*. 0*d*. or one of a number of other prices; others were non-net — the basic trade price was subject to further discount, as for example in the case of 115 copies in cloth which were sold at £1 1*s*. 8*d*. less 2½% = £1 1*s*. 2*d*. (These 'net' and 'non-net' descriptions refer, it is important to notice, to the trade, and not the retail prices, for the Clarks had decided that the *Concordance* should be a net book. Hence all copies sold through the trade would be retailed at £1 6*s*. 0*d*. Some at least of the net discounted prices referred to above would be accounted for by the fact that the Clarks had to supply copies of the work to the original subscribers at the price quoted when they subscribed.) Despite these complexities, however, the firm's average income per copy sold can be calculated as follows:

In cases where the discounted price was 'net'	— Cloth	£1 0*s*. 11*d*.
	— Leather	£1 6*s*. 2*d*.
In cases where the discounted price was subject to further discounts	— Cloth	19*s*. 10*d*.
	— Leather	£1 5*s*. 6*d*.

On the basis of the 1897–98 sales, it can be estimated that the 800 copies in the first impression sold as follows:

230 — Cloth binding (discounted price 'net')	—	£240 10*s*. 10*d*.
464 — Cloth binding (discounted price non-net)	—	£460 2*s*. 7*d*.
53 — Leather binding (discounted price 'net')	—	£69 6*s*. 10*d*.
53 — Leather binding (discounted price non-net)	—	£67 11*s*. 5*d*.
		£837 11*s*. 8*d*.

(6) A set of stereoplates was produced and shipped to Scribners at a total cost of £114 8*s*. 11*d*. The American firm remitted £200 for the plates, and £4 8*s*. 2*d*. in respect of additional expenses. The Clarks' profit on this transaction was therefore £89 19*s*. 3*d*.

(7) Scribners paid a royalty of 60c on each copy sold of the American edition. During the lifetime of the first British printing, the Clarks received £26 19*s*. 11*d*. from Scribners in respect of sales of 219 copies of their edition.

On the basis of these figures, the first impression would have yielded a profit of £168 1*s*. 4*d*., a return of 16.21% on the total investment. The Clarks would probably have seen this as a reasonably satisfactory performance. In fact, as Geden bore almost a quarter of the risk, the Clarks' own investment in the work totalled only £781 16*s*. 1*d*.: on this figure, the profit represented a return of 21.49%. There is no evidence in the accounts up to 1899 that Geden received any return on his investment. The percentage return figures for the first printing were significantly improved due to the fifty extra copies supplied by the printers; had it not been for these the impression would have yielded a profit of only £120 11*s*. 10*d*., a return of 11.68% on the total investment, and 15.42% on the Clarks' own outlay.

A second impression was required early in 1899. In Table 19, we estimate the costings of this impression, which was significantly more profitable than the first one.

On the basis of these figures, the second impression would have yielded a profit of £427 4*s*. 4*d*., a return of 286.09% on the investment. From this profit, Geden's initial contribution of £250 could have been refunded. Only 96 copies of the work were sold over 1898–99 however; at that rate of sale, it would have been over five years before the second impression produced its full return. The annual rate of return would therefore have been a more modest, but still highly satisfactory 57.218%.

The annual accounts give a confusing impression of its performance. The 1896–97 figures show a profit of £175 16*s*. 6*d*. In fact, however, £325 8*s*. 6*d*., expended in having the work set up in type, had been charged against the firm's

Table 19

Moulton and Geden's 'Concordance'.: Costings of the second printing (540 copies)

Outlay		*Income*	
Printing	£ 76 17*s*. 2*d*.	Sales[2]	£556 10*s*. 10*d*.
Paper	£33 14*s*. 6*d*.	Royalty on Scribners' sales[3]	£ 20 0*s*. 0*d*.
Binding[1]	£ 25 11*s*. 3*d*.		
Advertising	£ 8 17*s*. 9*d*.		
Promotion	£ 1 5*s*. 10*d*.		
Proportion of Lists	£ 3 0*s*. 0*d*.		
	£149 6*s*. 6*d*.		
Profit	£427 4*s*. 4*d*.		
	£576 10*s*. 10*d*.		£576 10*s*. 10*d*.

(1) Pro rata. (500 Cloth — £18 8*s*. 0*d*. 40 Leather — £7 3*s*. 3*d*.)

(2) On the basis of actual sales, it can be estimated that the 540 copies in the second impression would sell as follows:

167 — Cloth binding (discounted price 'net')	—	£174 13*s*. 0*d*.
333 — Cloth binding (discounted price non-net)	—	£330 4*s*. 6*d*.
20 — Leather binding (discounted price 'net')	—	£ 26 3*s*. 4*d*.
20 — Leather binding (discounted price non-net)	—	£ 25 10*s*. 0*d*.
		£556 10*s*. 10*d*.

(3) This figure is a conservative estimate. £9 7*s*. 2*d*. was paid by Scribners in 1898–99 in respect of sales of 76 copies of their edition. Given that the British second impression would be likely to last for at least five years, it seems probable that the Clarks would receive more than £20 in royalty payments from Scribners while it was still in print.

overheads in the previous year, 1895–96. Therefore at the end of 1896–97, the *Concordance* was still £149 12*s*. 0*d*. short of covering its costs. Over 1897–98, the work showed a profit of £165 9*s*. 1*d*. on the year's trading: the overall profit was therefore £15 17*s*. 1*d*. Owing to the printing of the second impression in 1898–99, that year's trading showed a loss of £27 1*s*. 5*d*.: by mid–1899, the work was therefore £11 4*s*. 4*d*. in deficit. Over 1899–1900, it is to be expected that the *Concordance* broke even and began to show a solid profit. The work was to remain in print for many decades, the long-term return must have been considerable, even allowing for the fact that Geden's loan had to be repaid and some remuneration for the work given to him and Moulton.

The Dictionary of the Bible

One of the earliest mentions of the five-volume *Dictionary of the Bible* in the letter books occurs in September 1893, when John M. Clark informed a correspondent that he had 'almost' made up his mind to undertake the project.[572] It is uncertain whether the initial proposal had come from the editor, Dr James Hastings or from the Clarks, but is would seem that Hastings was the prime mover, for Clark confessed that he had been 'pressing [him] about it.'[573]

The bulk of the editorial work on the *Dictionary* was done by Hastings, but he had a number of assistants, chief of whom was an old school-friend, John A. Selbie. Selbie was, when the *Dictionary* was first discussed, minister of the Free Church at Birsay on Orkney.[574] When, in 1896, he succeeded his father as pastor of the Free Church at Maryculter near Aberdeen, he and Hastings were able to work very closely together.[575] Also on the editorial team were A.B. Davidson, Professor of Hebrew at New College, Edinburgh; S.R. Driver, Regius Professor of Hebrew at Oxford: and H.B. Swete, Regius Professor of Divinity at Cambridge. Apparently, W. Sanday, Lady Margaret Professor of Divinity at Oxford was also closely involved in the work, but he did not wish his name to be on the title page as illness had prevented him from contributing as much as he would have liked to the project. It is clear that Hastings was captaining a strong team.

Work on the *Dictionary* was under way certainly from early 1894, but its forthcoming appearance was not publicly announced until January 1896. At that point, although a large part of the first volume was in type, the firm did not envisage its being published until autumn 1897, as they intended having the whole work in type before any part of it was issued.[576] Such a policy would have necessitated a very large investment before there was any return whatsoever; in fact the plan was changed and when the first two volumes were issued much work remained to be done on the third and fourth. The news that the *Dictionary* was about to be published seems to have been greeted with enthusiasm. The *British Weekly*, for example, gave it prominent advance publicity,[577] and on the eventual appearance of the first volume (delayed until the spring of 1898 owing to the dilatoriness of some of the contributors),[578] sales were satisfactory. Two thousand copies were disposed of in the first few months after publication,[579] and Hastings was pleased with early reactions to the work, commenting that in Germany and America, as well as in the UK, it had had 'a great reception — the reception for which [the team had] all worked hard, but which [they] scarcely dared anticipate', and moreover, that it was proving itself to be an indispensable tool in the sermon-preparation of many ministers.[580] The response to the remaining volumes was equally warm. These were published in, respectively, 1899, 1900 and 1902, and 1904 saw the issue of a supplementary volume.[581]

When we examine the reasons leading the Clarks to undertake the project, it seems clear that although financial factors were very carefully taken into consideration, the prime motive lying behind the decision to proceed was their desire to further theological understanding and enlightenment. Once again, they were aiming at the higher point of success. There was, they recognised, an indubitable need for a Bible dictionary which would reflect contemporary theological thinking. The earlier nineteenth century dictionaries, such as Fairbairn's *Imperial Bible Dictionary* were considered to be out-dated in presupposition, technique, and style of presentation.[582] True, there had been an attempt to update one of the earlier works, that by Dr William Smith which had initially appeared in three volumes between 1860 and 1863. The first volume was revised, and issued in two parts in 1893, but although there were plans for similar re-issues of the other two volumes, these never appeared, possibly because of the negative response accorded to the Volume One re-issue. Of that work, the Clarks commented: 'Great disappointment is felt here [in the UK] regarding the new edition of Smith's *Bible Dictionary*.' This disappointment they felt augured well for their forthcoming work: a potential rival had been pronounced wanting.[583] Their *Dictionary* aimed adequately to reflect the advances which scholarship had made over the previous three decades. And simply because it was meeting such a widely recognised need, the firm felt that the market for it would be considerable.

> There is no rival Dictionary of the same scope; it is a book which is being eagerly looked for, & one which all scholars, clergymen & students must have.[584]

It is clear that in producing the *Dictionary*, the Clarks, from sound financial as well as spiritual motives, were aiming at the widest possible audience. The work was not targeted simply at the academic theologian, but at the ordinary pastor in his study. As Hastings pointed out in the foreword to the first volume, the *Dictionary* was being published to equip the Church for its teaching ministry. The fact that it was aimed at a wide audience affected the editorial strategy governing the *Dictionary*'s production. Acting very much in line with the Clarks' basic principles, Hastings excluded unsubstantiated speculation from its pages, admitting only what he accepted as proven facts. His success in following this policy was recognised: one reviewer pointed out:

> The true aim of a Bible Dictionary is always kept in view, the reporting of those results which have been certified by the general verdict of scholarship rather than the actual discussion of problems which are only now in the course of solution.[585]

Once the basic formula for the work had been agreed, decisions had to be reached on several other matters which also had bearing on its potential profitability. If the *Dictionary* were to be successful, its contents had to be of a consistently high quality. Hastings unwaveringly aimed at the highest standards of scholarship and accuracy: thus he commented: 'for all our sakes, & for the sake of truth, we must make the Work as accurate as possible.'[586] Such accuracy was all the more important in the light of the competition which the *Dictionary* was to face from A. & C. Black's *Encyclopaedia Biblica*. If it were to outsell this rival, it was not enough that the *Dictionary* appear on the scene first (vital though this was): it must also outshine the *Encyclopaedia* in breadth of appeal and quality of content. It was successful on both counts, for the first volume of the Black work did not appear until 1899, the year which saw the publication of Hastings' second volume, and the editorial policies on which the *Dictionary* was based made it the more appealing of the two works. It seems unlikely that the Clarks knew of the *Encyclopaedia Biblica* project when their work was in the early stages of planning, but they were certainly aware of Black's activities by January 1896. Even at that point, they seem to have considered that their work, by virtue of its breadth of coverage, and its tapping of a larger reservoir of scholarship, was the more likely to succeed,[587] and Hastings' awareness of the nature of the *Encyclopaedia* no doubt led him in the course of preparing his work to heighten further those features which it was felt gave it the edge over its rival. The *Dictionary*'s greater success seems to have resulted not only from its wider range of subject coverage, but also from the more moderate theological stance of the editor. Hastings' 'sympathies were with "moderate" as distinguished from "advanced" criticism, and the preacher [and preachers were likely to form the largest proportion of the market for the *Dictionary* or the *Encyclopaedia*] tends to favour "moderate" criticism unless he be under some compelling conviction.'[588]

As befitted a firm which consistently put theological considerations before financial ones, the Clarks seem to have left the matter of the length of the *Dictionary* entirely in Hastings' hands. Initially, it was planned to issue four volumes; at one stage, it seemed likely that only three would be required ('the Editor believes the entire work is contracting rather than expanding');[589] in the event, the work stretched to the initially anticipated four volumes, and then extended to a supplementary volume.

There was some discussion as to which form of issue would be most appropriate if the circulation of the work were to be maximised. At one stage, the Clarks contemplated publishing it in parts or divisions, presumably prior to, or concurrently with, its publication in volume form,[590] but in the event it was decided not to issue any parts or divisions until after the first volume had appeared.[591] In Chapter 7 we noted the Clarks' aversion to part-publication; there is in fact no evidence that the *Dictionary* ever appeared other than in volume form.

In considering presentation and production standards, the firm, as was their wont, aimed high. Attractive layout and sheer bulk were clearly held to be important factors in winning sales. Indeed the Clarks seem to have felt that sales of the *Dictionary* were affected by the apparently mildly devious practices of A. & C. Black: as we have seen, although the *Encyclopaedia* volumes contained less material than those of the *Dictionary*, Black had made their volumes appear to be larger by using thicker paper than the Clarks and by numbering columns rather than pages.[592]

Presentation and form of issue clearly influenced sales; the Clarks prided themselves on the quality of their products:

> We always use the very best workmanship & material, & the result is that our books are greatly superior in those respects to the mass of books produced in London.[593]

It is of no small interest that the Clarks were fixing the price of the *Dictionary of the Bible* in late 1897, in the middle of the long series of negotiations, described by Frederick Macmillan,[594] which led to the acceptance of the Net Book

Agreement. In the three decades which followed the collapse of the Booksellers' Association in 1852, purchasers of new books came to expect a habitual discount of twenty-five percent on the nominal published price. The granting of this discount had extremely deleterious effects on the profitability of serious bookselling firms for, according to Macmillan,[595] the profit to be made on the sale of new books was 'so exiguous that it became more and more difficult for booksellers to make a living'. To resolve this problem, Macmillan suggested that certain new books should be designated 'net' books and that these should be sold at a fixed price, lower than the nominal published price would have been under the old system. The bookseller would be assured that his profit on each transaction would remain intact, and would therefore be encouraged to stock larger quantities of new titles. Opposition to this scheme was to be expected from some authors who might feel that it would affect the sales of their works and the level of their royalties, if these were calculated on the published price, and from some booksellers who might resent this interference in the way they conducted their business. And indeed, when Macmillan first outlined his plan in the *Bookseller* for 6 March 1890, it met with considerable opposition, many holding it to be impracticable. Macmillan's firm however began to issue a limited number of books under the net system with the full consent of the authors, and refused to supply any Macmillan titles to booksellers who did not sell the net books at their published price. Soon, other publishers joined Macmillan in issuing some net books, and certain leading booksellers were sufficiently persuaded of the merits of the system by 1895 to form a society – The Associated Booksellers of Great Britain and Ireland – with the intention of supporting the issue of net books, and persuading fellow-booksellers to lend similar support to the net system. In the same year, 1895, the Publishers' Association was founded with the initial aim of negotiating with the booksellers. Two proposals put forward by the booksellers over the next few years were rejected by the publishers, one, dating from 1897, because it sought to limit discount on non-net, or 'subject' books also, and was opposed by the Society of Authors, the second, dating from March 1898, because although it had the support of the authors, it was, in Macmillan's view, so complex as to be unworkable. Finally, in November 1898, the publishers agreed on a proposal which was put to the booksellers in early 1899, and accepted by them on 24 February. The key principle was that new books should be issued as far as possible at net prices, and existing books should, where practicable, be converted into net books by taking off one-sixth of the current price.[596] Following the acceptance by the Associated Booksellers of the Net Book scheme, that body successfully canvassed their colleagues across the country, persuading them (not without difficulty in some cases) to append their signatures to the Net Book Agreement.

Was the new *Dictionary* to be net or non-net? Clearly, the Clarks made their decision not on the basis of any strong views on the rights or wrongs of the net system, but on grounds of pragmatic expediency. They sought to ascertain which method of pricing the book would maximise its circulation by making it acceptable to the majority of booksellers. The Moulton/Geden *Concordance* was, as we noted, issued as a net book, but the Clarks' initial decision was that the *Dictionary* should be non-net; this was agreed owing to the poor performance of net books issued by the firm (although in fact there are only eight such books in the 1902 Catalogue). 'We and other Publishers too, I know, have been so much disappointed with *nett* books', they claimed,[597] and elsewhere expressed the same sentiment even more strongly, complaining that it was their 'invariable experience' that the trade would not stock net books.[598] If a work like a Bible dictionary were to achieve its maximum sales potential, it had to be prominently displayed in the bookshops, and this, the Clarks felt, would not happen if it were issued with a net retail price.[599] Their decision that the work should be non-net was conveyed to Hastings in July 1897; given their strength of feeling, it is surprising that, following pressure from the Edinburgh booksellers who urged in line with Macmillan's views that they had 'far more encouragement & pleasure in pushing [net books]', the Clarks seriously considered reversing their decision later in the year. They seem to have come close to agreeing to the Edinburgh trade's request, feeling that the work was of such importance — 'there is no rival Dictionary of the same scope' — that booksellers everywhere, regardless of their attitude to the net book scheme, would have to stock it in order to satisfy the demands of their customers.[600] However, before the end of 1897 they had reverted to their initial position: the work would be non-net.[601] The pressure of the Edinburgh booksellers had been outweighed by the pressure of others in the trade who had 'appealed earnestly' to the Clarks against the net system. One Scottish bookseller had gone so far as to say that a net price would 'kill' the *Dictionary*, and while the publishers, believing that the work would sell whatever price system was used, did not wholly agree with him, they were clearly afraid that its sales would be reduced if it were issued with a net price. This fear over-rode any commitment they may have felt to the net system.[602] And so the *Bible Dictionary*'s first retail purchasers received the customary twenty-five percent discount on a nominal price of £1 8*s*. 0*d*. per volume. There is, of course, no means of calculating the extent to which sales of the work were affected by its being issued non-net; what is significant is that the Clarks made the decision to issue it outwith the net system in a conscious effort to maximise sales.

From the enthusiasm with which the Clarks committed themselves to the task of marketing the *Dictionary* in the US, it is clear that they considered an agreement with a US publisher vital to the success of the work. Scribners were notified in March 1894 that the *Dictionary* was forthcoming,[603] and were urged to negotiate for the American agency, it being pointed out to them firstly that several other American houses were showing an interest ('but we certainly prefer to arrange with you if possible, & we hope there will be no difficulty about it'),[604] and secondly that, as it would be impracticable for the one US firm to hold the agency for both the *Dictionary of the Bible* and the *Encyclopaedia Biblica* due to the clash of loyalties which would result, it was important that they reach a decision quickly, preferably in favour of the Clark work. The Clarks would grant the agency to another house if Scribners agreed to handle the *Encyclopaedia Biblica*.[605] The main reason for John M. Clark's US visit in the Spring of 1896 seems to have been to negotiate the terms under which Scribners would handle the *Dictionary*,[606] and an agreement had been reached by May of that year. It was not, apparently, as favourable to the Edinburgh firm's interests as John M. Clark had hoped for: 'The copyright question has proved a most serious difficulty, and our American friends are not slow to profit by it.'[607]

The full significance of this comment is unclear. Certainly, in order to secure the US copyright, a certain proportion of each volume had to be printed in America from type set on American soil. In order to get round this difficulty, the Clarks supplied Scribners with plates for most of the work, and also with loose type so that certain of the articles amounting, it would seem, to some thirty pages *in toto* per volume, could be set and printed in the US.[608] But this procedure, although irksome, was surely a fairly minor problem, unlikely to have significantly affected the terms concluded with the American firm.

And indeed, these terms would seem to have been reasonably satisfactory from the Clarks' point of view, although there is no formal record of them. It would appear from the account books, however, that Scribners were to pay a total of £1,250 for the plates of the four volumes. This figure was payable in four instalments as the volumes appeared. Scribners also paid for incidentals such as the Consul's certificate and packing charges, and possibly also for the carriage of the plates across the Atlantic although this is unclear.[609] It would also seem that they paid the Edinburgh firm a royalty on copies sold in the US (perhaps this royalty only became payable after a certain number of copies had been disposed of). In 1899, for example, the Clarks received £128 14*s*. 7*d*. from Scribners, a royalty on 1391 volumes sold, 45c. being payable on each volume. (The royalty was at the rate of 7½% in most instances, but sometimes rose to 10%, presumably in the case of leather-bound volumes.[610]) When one considers that the actual cost of a set of plates produced for Scribners was £66 16*s*. 6*d*.,[611] it becomes obvious that the American firm was making a not inconsiderable contribution to the editorial costs of the work. The part which income from America played in the overall profit-and-loss accounts of the *Dictionary* will be considered shortly. Certainly, despite their private complaints about the difficulties they had faced in reaching agreement with Scribners, the Clarks were publicly delighted that terms had been concluded with that firm. 'We rejoice that our two houses are again to be united in the publication of so important an enterprise.'[612]

Effective promotion and efficient distribution were considered vital to the success of the *Dictionary*. To promote the work, between twenty and thirty thousand copies of a prospectus were printed,[613] and review copies (it is uncertain how many) distributed. The results of this strategy are, of course, difficult to quantify. The work seems, in general, to have been favourably reviewed, but this did not always affect the sales. A positive review (in the *Guardian*) which the firm expected would result in the sale of several hundred copies seemed, at least at first, 'to have done no good.'[614] But the very fact that such a comment was made indicates that it was normal for a good review to generate sales. And even if it did not, the benefits of the favourable climate of opinion towards a work which would be engendered by such a review were not to be minimised.

When it came to distributing the work, although the firm never employed door-to-door canvassers,[615] there was always the possibility of selling direct to the customer, thereby cutting out the booksellers. Jealous of their good relationship with the trade, the Clarks clearly attempted to avoid direct selling as much as possible, but it always remained a temptation, especially as the firm was aiming at such a clearly definable target audience. Moreover, in selling direct, the firm could supply the work more cheaply than it could be obtained through the trade; while this inevitably antagonised booksellers, it might well, if the customer were an impecunious student or pastor, have secured sales which would otherwise have been lost. Thus, occasionally, the firm sold direct. For example, when one W.E. Adam of Manchester requested that he be supplied with a copy of the *Dictionary* at a reduced rate, presumably stressing in doing so his financial stringency, he was told that the retail price of £1 1*s*. 0*d*. after discount of 25% was the lowest possible one, given the production costs, and then informed that if he would 'kindly consider [it] a private matter, [the Clarks would] be glad to send [him] a copy at the rate of 15s/- per Volume':[616] that is, 3*s*. 0*d*. less than the normal trade price. Sometimes, discounts were given to members of a particular institution, or pastors of a given denomination. In the case of the *Dictionary*, for example, the Primitive Methodist Book Room in London was supplied with copies cheaply on the understanding that they were to be offered at a reduced price to impoverished Primitive Methodist ministers. No doubt the firm's motive here was as much to further the beneficial influence of their work as it was to maximise sales. But the arrangement provoked considerable antagonism from the trade, largely due, however, to the fact that the Book Room broke the conditions of the agreement by circulating an advertisement to some Congregational and Baptist ministers offering the book at 19*s*. 6*d*., a reduction of 1*s*. 6*d*. on the price for which the booksellers would have supplied it after discount.[617] But the bulk of the work's sales were through normal retail outlets.

There are no specific data available on the rate of payment to *Dictionary* contributors; such general figures relating to the editorial costs of the work as have been preserved are considered below.

The Clarks sought to fill a significant gap in the market with a work which had the maximum possible sales potential; having created that work, they endeavoured to secure its widest possible distribution. How successful in financial terms did the whole enterprise prove to be?

Although sales of the first volume of the *Dictionary* were not as steady as the Clarks had hoped for (expecting a good sale during the Assembly season in Spring 1898, they were disappointed that only two copies were disposed of)[618] nevertheless they were sufficiently high for a second impression to be required before the end of the financial year 1897–98. It is impossible to isolate the cost of either of these impressions, but the data we have available[619], presented in Table 20, give a full picture of the income and expenditure relating to the work over 1897–98.

At first sight, the loss over 1897–98 seems sizable.[620] One notices that the largest single item of expenditure was the editorial work, which cost £1,325 18*s*. 3*d*., 38.13% of the total outlay. One notices also that the income from

Table 20

Dictionary of the Bible: Volume One accounts 1897–98

Outlay		*Income*	
Composition[1]	£1,040 11*s*. 0*d*.	Sales	
Blockmaking[2]	£19 17*s*. 6*d*.	Cloth — 1692¾ copies[11]	£1,551 4*s*. 6*d*.
1st set stereos	£96 16*s*. 6*d*.	Morocco — 339 copies[12]	£374 11*s*. 0*d*.
2nd set stereos[3]	£66 16*s*. 6*d*.		
Printing — 1st imp.[4]	£75 9*s*. 9*d*.		
Printing — 2nd imp.[4]	£68 15*s*. 0*d*.	Income from Scribners[13]	£377 9*s*. 6*d*.
Paper — 1st imp.	£121 9*s*. 8*d*.		
Paper — 2nd imp.	£120 16*s*. 5*d*.		
Maps[5]	£92 10*s*. 0*d*.		
Binding[6]	£156 13*s*. 9*d*.		
Promotion	£90 0*s*. 5*d*.		
Advertising[7]	£105 10*s*. 4*d*.		
Contributors' fees[8]	£1,325 18*s*. 3*d*.		
Insurance on Hastings	£77 0*s*. 0*d*.		
Proportion of Lists	£10 0*s*. 0*d*.		
Miscellaneous[9]	£8 6*s*. 0*d*.		
	£3,476 11*s*. 1*d*.		£2,303 5*s*. 0*d*.
Discounts on printing	£127 10*s*. 3*d*.	Loss	£1,045 15*s*. 10*d*.
	£3,349 0*s*. 10*d*.[10]		£3,349 0*s*. 10*d*.

(1) Includes miscellaneous costs such as that for the purchase of Hebrew and Coptic type, and £27 10*s*. 0*d*. for proofs. (110 formes at 5/-).
(2) The cost of 84 blocks, of which 53 were used in the first volume.
(3) This second set of stereos would be for Scribners.
(4) The size of these impressions was 2,160 each.
(5) 6,100 copies of seven maps.
(6) Cloth — 1,950 copies at 10*d*.
Morocco — 359 copies at 3*s*. 9*d*.
— 50 copies at 3*s*. 3*d*.
(7) Includes £79 8*s*. 4*d*. in outside publications, and £26 2*s*. 0*d*. in the *Expository Times* and the *Critical Review*.
(8) Includes £169 2*s*. 3*d*. paid to Hastings on account of royalties. He must have had a royalty agreement with the firm. Selbie received £150, and R.M. Boyd, who had presumably undertaken some editorial duties, received £10 14*s*. 6*d*. The rate of payment to contributors is not specified. Presumably this total includes payment for contributions which were still to appear in future volumes, unless payment was only made on publication.
(9) Includes the cost of packing cases for sending stereos to Scribners; the cost of type sent to them so that they could print certain articles from the *Dictionary* from type set in the US in order to conform to US copyright law; the cost (£1 11*s*. 0*d*.) of a Consular Certificate; and the cost of a stamp for the lettering on the spine of the work (£3 2*s*. 0*d*.).
(10) The account book erroneously totals this £3,349 10*s*. 10*d*.

Table 20 (*continued*)

(11) These sales were at a variety of rates —

Terms	Quantity & Price	Total
10% + 13/12	799¼ @ 18*s*. 0*d*.	£719 6*s*. 6*d*.
10% ordinary	240 @ 18*s*. 0*d*.	£216 0*s*. 0*d*.
71/2%	294¼ @ 18*s*. 6*d*.	£272 3*s*. 8*d*.
5%	310¼ @ 19*s*. 0*d*.	£294 14*s*. 9*d*.
Net	48 @ 20*s*. 0*d*.	£48 0*s*. 0*d*.
28*s*. 0*d*. – 30%	1 @ 19*s*. 7*d*.	19*s*. 7*d*.

It will be seen that the percentages were calculated on a base price of £1 0*s*. 0*d*.

(12) These sales, too, were at a variety of rates —

Terms	Quantity & Price	Total
10% + 13/12	144 @ 21*s*. 9*d*.	£156 12*s*. 0*d*.
10% ordinary	83½ @ 21*s*. 9*d*.	£90 16*s*. 1*d*.
7½%	43 @ 22*s*. 5*d*.	£48 3*s*. 11*d*.
5%	65½ @ 23*s*. 0*d*.	£75 6*s*. 6*d*.
Net	3 @ 24*s*. 2*d*.	£3 12*s*. 6*d*.

It will be seen that the percentages were calculated on a base price of £1 4*s*. 2*d*.

(13) This income includes £3 19*s*. 2*d*. paid for miscellaneous items, such as packing cases; £61 0*s*. 4*d*. paid for maps; and £312 10*s*. 0*d*. paid in accordance with the agreement reached with the Clarks for a set of plates.

Scribners, although not inconsiderable, went a comparatively small way towards offsetting the loss.

The crucial factor, however, is that although a second impression of 2,160 copies had been printed and the printing paid for by the end of the financial year, only 84 copies had been disposed of. Over 1897–98, 2,031¾ copies were sold, and 212½ distributed free. (The reason for the curious fraction is that where the rate of twenty-five for the price of twenty-four, or thirteen for the price of twelve applied, booksellers were invoiced at that rate for any number of volumes over the basic twenty-four or twelve. Hence, a bookseller purchasing 19 copies where a thirteen for twelve agreement applied would be charged for 17½ copies. The total of copies freely distributed includes review copies, but also copies 'given' to booksellers under such arrangements.)

Out of the 4,320 printed, therefore, 2,076 remained. So, at a total cost of £3,349 0*s*. 10*d*., 4,320 copies were produced: the unit cost to the firm was 15*s*. 6*d*. per copy, and each sale would yield a profit of at least 2*s*. 6*d*. per copy, a return on investment of 16.13%. The loss of £1,045 15*s*. 10*d*. would be wiped out by the time a further 1,218 copies of the second impression were sold.[621] On the remaining 858 copies of the second impression[622] a profit of £736 9*s*. 0*d*.[623] would be realised, leaving out of the reckoning copies sold in morocco bindings. Thus, the two impressions would yield a return on the initial investment (£3,349 0*s*. 10*d*.) of 21.98%.[624] These calculations ignore on the one hand the income from Scribners, and on the other the royalty payable to Hastings, but this figure of 21.98% is a remarkable one especially as the object of some of the initial expenditure — such as the promotion and advertising budget — should be seen as building up an awareness of the work as a whole, and as such should not in total be charged against the first volume. 709 copies of the second impression were in fact sold over 1898–99. A third impression, if required, would produce even better results: its costs would amount to £373 3*s*. 5*d*. (again excluding whatever royalty Hastings received).[625] The unit cost would be 3*s*. 5*d*, and the profit per copy sold 14*s*. 7*d*. The return on investment would be 426.82%, and the breakeven point 19.21% of the print run.

The costings of the second volume, produced in 1898–99 in an impression of 4,320 copies are similar to those of the first. Its sales were at a corresponding level, and it would yield a similar return.

Obviously, substantial overall profits would not be shown in the annual accounts until the whole work had appeared, and the origination costs of the five volumes had been recovered. But if the quality of the work were maintained, and if sufficient copies were sold, the *Dictionary* would prove extremely profitable. These, of course, are major qualifications. It was to the credit of Hastings and the Clarks that the work met the needs of a sufficiently large number of people to guarantee the sales figures which were essential if it were to break even. Had further impressions of each volume not been required, the firm's position would have been very different.

While very real risk was involved in the firm's issue of major reference works calling for a large investment, in fact, due to the Clarks' shrewd assessment of the market, and due to the scholarship and literary competence of the editorial teams, large profits accrued.

Chapter 9
Miscellaneous theological works

The remaining theological titles on the Clark list fit in to none of the preceding categories. Many of these monographs and miscellaneous works were initially sent unsolicited to the firm who, like any established publishers, regularly received manuscripts from authors seeking publication. While some of the miscellaneous titles issued by the Clarks were important works by well-known figures, a good proportion of them were therefore by authors unknown outwith their immediate circles.[626]

The letter books suggest that the publishing of miscellaneous works was, financially speaking, more of a hit-or-miss affair than the issue of titles in the other categories handled by the firm, where the potential market could, it seems, be more accurately estimated.

Although the average miscellaneous work called for only a modest investment, so that losses when they occurred were not substantial, nevertheless losses on a range of titles did mount up, causing some alarm to the firm. Towards the end of the century, the Clarks grew more reluctant to commit themselves to the issue of this kind of work, feeling that publishers were flooding the market with more titles than it could absorb, and that losses were therefore all the more likely. Thus they averred 'it is a mistake to publish too many books',[627] being of the opinion that 'considering the enormous mass of books [then] being issued from the Press, far greater caution [was] necessary than [had formerly been] the case.'[628] These comments date from 1899: in fact, we find very similar views being expressed in the previous decade. In September 1887, John M. Clark, doubtful about the sales potential of a manuscript which he had received, commented 'we have published so much of recent years for which we have not been, & probably never shall be, recouped.'[629]

In accepting miscellaneous theological works for publication, there were two courses open to the Clarks: either they could take the entire risk themselves, or else they could reach some kind of risk-sharing agreement with the author. In certain cases they went so far as to publish on commission, the author bearing the entire risk. This chapter discusses the factors which influenced the Clarks' decision to publish or not to publish a given work, investigates how they calculated the degree of risk they were prepared to bear, and assesses the profitability of their miscellaneous publications.

Publication at the firm's risk

There is no doubt that, wherever possible, the Clarks preferred to take the entire risk. It was, they felt, 'the simpler plan. . .more pleasant for both Author & Publisher'.[630] More pleasant it might be, but only if the work had a reasonable chance of success. Several factors had carefully to be evaluated, therefore, before the Clarks agreed to publish at their risk.

Selection Policy

If a theological work were to be issued at their expense, it had to pass a number of tests. In the first place, the work's content and style had to be of unquestionable merit. As always, the Clarks were prepared to look favourably on a work whose scholarship was demonstrably competent. There was no question, for example, of James Moffatt's *The Historical New Testament* being rejected: he was, the firm felt, 'a scholar of high standing, the peer of such men as Professor Denney, & [the] book [would] be a credit to him for scholarship.'[631] Or again, the quality of another work which, it was felt, would be 'useful to . . . students' led to its acceptance at the firm's risk, despite the fact that the market was in such a depressed state that Thomas Clark could not envisage the demand for it being large.[632] Equally, a work whose scholarship was clearly defective would face certain rejection. For instance, a manuscript from one E.J. Nurse of Edgbaston was turned down because it was deemed to be 'full of inaccuracies', 'totally uncritical', and 'inconsistent'.[633]

But even a work of proven ability and accuracy was not guaranteed publication, for the firm had discovered that scholarship did not 'unfortunately . . . always ensure a large sale for a book'.[634] It was difficult to predict how successful a title would prove to be from a commercial point of view; the Clarks had been surprised to observe that 'some books of marked ability [fell] dead from the press, while others, undoubtedly inferior, [took] the public fancy'.[635] The author to whom this remark was addressed had his work *Words to Young Christians* (1893) published by the firm at their risk, but it was by no means their invariable practice to issue every miscellaneous work of proven quality which was offered to them. In the case of several other categories of publication, we have seen that the Clarks were ready to proceed with works of quality even when it was extremely doubtful that they would break even. When it came to the miscellaneous works, however, although they did take the risk in the case of certain titles whose profitability was by no means guaranteed, in most cases where the quality was high but the sales potential dubious they suggested sharing the risk with the author.

If he were to have some prospect of having his work accepted by the Clarks, an author had to demonstrate not only the competence of his scholarship, but also the effectiveness of his literary style. The firm was inclined to be favourably-disposed towards one work because 'there was a freshness about it'.[636] Three months earlier they had gently pointed out to another author that his style, which reviewers had found 'tough', 'difficult', 'knotted' and 'gnarled', had adversely affected the sales of an otherwise excellent monograph; by way of illustration the Clarks had contrasted its performance with that of a title by an unknown American, the *Outline of Christian Theology* by W. Clarke, which had sold 1,700 copies in a few months, with little advertising. Its sales were due largely, the Clarks felt, to the simplicity of the author's style.[637] If quality of style were important, so too was the title, which could of course be readily changed with the author's agreement. 'The *Title* is of great importance [to the sales potential of the book], & would require to be very carefully considered',[638] one author was told; another had it pointed out to him that his working title *A Bishop's Anathema* would 'never do',[639] while a third changed the title of his book from *The Problem of Philosophy* to *What* is *Thought*?, only to discover that the Clarks were concerned over the italicised *is* which they felt did not 'look well.'[640]

These factors, quality of content and of style, were taken into account when the Clarks were considering a work. A well-written work of indubitable value would be seriously considered, but quality alone was not enough to guarantee its acceptance, certainly at the firm's own risk.

Secondly, if a miscellaneous title were to be published by the Clarks, it had to belong to a category which, in their experience, was likely to perform well. As a general principle, it can be said as we noted earlier that the Clarks considered collections of lectures, sermons, and previously-published or posthumous material most unlikely to be profitable, and avoided them almost irrespective of their quality in theological terms.

This principle is clearly illustrated in the letter books. Hence, for example:

> Without exception I think, we find that collected articles on such topics [It is not clear what the subject of the manuscript in question was.] which have already either appeared in Reviews, or have formed the subject of Lectures or addresses, *never* pay the cost of production.[641]

Admittedly, that letter refers to collections on particularly abstruse themes rather than to collections in general, but the impression given by the letter books is that it in fact expresses the firm's general attitude. Again, the Clarks refused to bear the entire risk of publishing a particular manuscript because, although they considered it 'very good', they feared that it was 'too much in the form of sermons to have much prospect of success':[642] their experience had led them to the view that 'nowadays [sermons] very rarely pay the cost of production.'[643] Unless they had the support of some kind of editorial apparatus, posthumously-published collections of material were also 'impossible' to market.[644] Finally, works which, though of good quality, were presented in a form which was unlikely to be acceptable to the audience at which the book was aimed did not have much prospect of being published at the Clarks' risk. Hence James Aitchison of Falkirk was told that while the firm saw much in a manuscript which he had submitted which was 'good & deeply interesting', nevertheless they could not accept it as it seemed to 'fall between two stools', appearing to be aimed more at a popular readership than at critics and scholars, and yet, running as it did to six hundred pages, being 'scarcely likely to take with the ordinary public'.[645]

All this is not to deny that, on occasion, the Clarks did publish collections of lectures, sermons, and posthumous material at their own risk. But it was their normal practice, when publishing manuscripts of this type, to share the risk with the author, and the salutary experience gained in these undertakings only served to strengthen their resolve to avoid taking the full risk of such collections except in special cases. What is significant is that, once again, these decisions were being made on purely commercial rather than theological grounds. No matter how good the Clarks considered the manuscript of a miscellaneous work to be they were most unlikely to publish it at their risk if it were not presented in a form which they felt would produce an acceptable level of sales.

The third test was that of physical extensiveness. The Clarks' frequently-re-iterated view was that small works, especially if they were on recondite subjects, were unlikely to make a profit, except if part of a series. For example: 'Our experience is that small books on abstruse subjects never pay'[646] Or again: 'we very seldom can make a small book remunerative where there is not a large sale.'[647] Whereas small books had to be sold more cheaply than larger titles, and hence brought in a smaller return per copy sold, they nevertheless had to be advertised as widely as larger books if they were to become known. And the advertising expenditure was the same whether a book were large or small. Whereas larger books could therefore support reasonable outlay on advertising, small books, unless their sales were, in the Clarks' terms, spectacular, could not. Another problem was that it cost almost as much to bind a small volume as it did a large one: once again, the large volume, producing more per copy sold, was better able to cover its binding costs than the small one, with its low return per copy sold. In general therefore, small books regardless of their quality were not published by the Clarks at their risk.

There were, of course, exceptions to this rule. Thomas Adamson's *The Spirit of Power*, submitted to the firm via James Hastings, was as we saw published with great speed at the firm's risk, although the Clarks made the general point to Adamson that small books were unlikely to pay, and then itemised particular reasons why the work in question would be unlikely to succeed.[648] It is uncertain why the firm were prepared to bear the risk in that instance: perhaps they were swayed by Hastings' enthusiastic advocacy of the work.

But the general principle was that, regardless of the merit and quality of a work, if it appeared likely to be a commercial failure on account of its size it was not undertaken by the firm.

Fourthly, there were a number of general factors which, while they were not crucial, could nevertheless influence the Clarks' evaluation of a manuscript. It helped, for example, if a work were not too closely linked with any one denomination, for such a denominational stamp would curtail the circulation of the book. If the work were identified closely with a Presbyterian denomination sales in England would inevitably be restricted.[649] To take this factor into account was, once again, to be influenced by purely commercial judgements. It helped also if a work came to the Clarks with the recommendation of some churchman or academic such as Hastings. For example, as we have seen, it was at Hastings' suggestion that the Adamson work on *The Spirit of Power* was published. Thus, too, V.H. Stanton's *The Jewish and the Christian Messiah* was published at the Clarks' risk because it came to them with the recommendation of Canon Brooke Foss Westcott, later Bishop of Durham.[650] If such recommendations guaranteed the quality of the work in question, they would also, if they were publicly announced, help to generate sales following publication. Thus, for example, the Clarks conceded that if A.B. Bruce could be persuaded to write an introduction to A.H. Moncur Sime's *The Epic of God* it would very possibly help the commercial prospects of the work.[651]

This analysis confirms that, in considering miscellaneous works for publication at the firm's risk, the Clarks based their decisions wholly on the commercial prospects of the manuscript in question; for once, it would seem, aiming at the lower level of success. Perhaps it was simply that it was practical in the case of smaller works to expect the author to share in the comparatively small investment, whereas it would have been unrealistic to expect, say, Hastings to share the risk of the *Dictionary* or Exell of the *Monthly Interpreter*.

If a work were judged to be of merit, and likely to yield a profit, the Clarks were usually prepared to publish it at their risk. The next factor to be considered was the method of remunerating the author. A number of different systems were used; the level and method of payment to the author seems to have been decided on in the light of the potential profitability of his work. This once again served to safeguard the Clarks' profits.

Payment to authors

Very few of the firm's contracts with their authors have been preserved, so for details of terms we are dependent upon references in the letter books. It would seem that, regardless of the terms agreed, the copyright remained with the author in most cases.[652] The Clarks employed two main methods of remuneration — profit-sharing, and royalty payments — but there were variations in practice within each of these categories. It is never clearly stated what principle guided the firm in deciding which method of remuneration should be used in the case of a given book. We may assume, however, that in concluding terms with an author, the firm were seeking to minimise their own risk.

There are in the letter books at least fourteen clear statements of terms agreed with authors. Of these fourteen two are profit-sharing agreements of one kind or another, and the other twelve royalty agreements.

In the case of one work, A. Cave's *Introduction to Theology*, the author was promised payment of £25 on the first impression, but only if it were entirely sold out.[653] This was a form of profit-sharing which minimised the risk to the firm, for they would have in their hands the profit on the entire impression before having to give any remuneration to the author. Perhaps these terms were stipulated because the Clarks regarded the book as being an especial risk — an earlier letter to Cave mentioned the depressed state of the market — but it is surprising that they were not prepared to do as they did in other cases and share the profits of the book in a more equitable way with the author once it had broken even. It was agreed for example that Paton J. Gloag would receive half of any profits accruing from the publication of his *Introduction to the Catholic Epistles* (1887).[655]

One would assume that such profit-sharing agreements were concluded in cases where the risk to the firm was considerable, and that the signing of a royalty agreement indicated that in the Clarks' estimation, the risk was less. In fact, however, seven of the twelve royalty agreements noted were profit-sharing agreements in disguise.

In these cases, the authors were promised a royalty of 10% of the nominal retail selling price on sales of their works above a certain number of copies. The number of copies on which the royalty was *not* payable varied between 300 and 450; what the firm were doing in most of these cases was recovering their costs before beginning to pay a royalty. This was clearly stated in at least one case. J. Hamlyn Hill was promised a royalty on sales of his edition of Tatian's *Diatessaron* from the 401st copy, it being pointed out to him that it would certainly take sales of four hundred copies to reimburse the firm for their outlay.[656] On the other hand, when R. Johnstone was offered a royalty of 10% of the selling price of his commentary on *1st Peter* on sales over 350 copies, he was informed that it would take sales of considerably more than 350 copies to reimburse the firm.[657] In general, however, under these arrangements, the Clarks hoped to recover their costs before paying the royalty and were, in effect, sharing their profits with the author: it could be argued none too generously. The trade discount on the nominal retail price could reach 42%.[658] Once the work had covered its costs, the firm were therefore left with a minimum of 58% of the total retail price of each copy sold, yet only 10% of this price was shared with the author. Considering that he had received nothing while the work recovered the publisher's outlay, he might well have felt somewhat aggrieved that a larger percentage of the income did not come his way once the book had broken even. By concluding agreements such as these, the Clarks were certainly protecting their own interests.

Five instances were noted where the royalty was payable on sales of the entire edition. In the case of three of them, 10% was paid, and at least one of these three books, a work by George Matheson, made a loss. The author received a cheque for £33 14*s*. 0*d*., 10% of the selling price of the 321 copies which had been disposed of, and it was pointed out to him by Thomas Clark that the firm was far from making a profit on the work.[659] In one case, that of A.B. Bruce's *Pauline Conception of Christianity*, where the author was a prestigious scholar with a good sales record, the firm offered a 12½% royalty.[660] In another case, the royalty was calculated differently. For his work on *The Ritschlian Theology* (1899) A.E. Garvie was to receive a royalty of 10% on the net wholesale price of the first four hundred copies sold (that is, until the work had reached its estimated break-even point), and thereafter a royalty of 15% on the net wholesale price.[661] It is difficult to pinpoint the distinctive factor which led the Clarks to pay a royalty from the first copy in these particular cases. With the exception of Bruce's book, these works could not have been expected to sell better than many of those whose authors were not remunerated until their work had recovered its costs.

When a work had begun to yield royalties to its author according to the particular terms of his agreement with the Clarks, he received a payment in respect of copies sold in Britain and the Colonies, and also in respect of sales in the United States, although because books were exported to America at a low cost to undercut pirates or to deter would-be pirates, he received a lower royalty on copies destined for the US. The normal Clark rate in such cases was 5% on the *British* trade price; again Garvie's *Ritschlian Theology* proves an exception to the rule. On both American and Colonial sales, Garvie was to be paid 10% of the price the Clarks received from their agents, which usually was half of the British trade price.[662] This was only a difference in the method by which the royalty was calculated; what Garvie would receive would be the equivalent of the normal 5% of the British trade price.

In calculating the extent of their payment to authors, the Clarks seem to have had in mind the same governing principle which directed their evaluation of manuscripts: they sought to publish competent works while minimising the risks to themselves.

Profitability

Factors affecting profitability

In fact, the profitability of a given title was influenced by a number of factors besides the quality of the manuscript, and the rate and system of payment to the author. A book's financial success could be influenced by the selling price, by the level of the production costs, and even by the political and economic conditions pertaining at the time it was published.

THE SELLING PRICE

Based on the production costs of a given work, a selling-price could be calculated which, if the whole impression sold out, would guarantee the firm an adequate return on their investment. If however, this 'ideal' selling price was above what the Clarks felt would be the buying public's perception of the value of the work, the price would militate against sales. In such cases, the firm were prepared to reduce the nominal selling-price of the work in question in the hope that, although their return on each unit sold would be correspondingly lower, a sufficient number of buyers would be attracted to ensure that the edition would at least break even. Thus, for example, the retail price of G. Elmslie Troup's *Words to Young Christians* (1893) was fixed at 4*s*. 6*d*., even although the production costs had been so high that it would take the sale of almost the whole edition at that price to cover costs and Troup's royalty. (He was to received 10% on the retail price of the entire edition.) Of this selling price one of the Clarks commented 'It certainly cannot be less, but I fear it might injure the sales were we to make it more.'[663]

The case of G.C. Workman's monograph on *The Text of Jeremiah* (1889) provides another example of a book with high origination costs being sold at as low a price as possible (9*s*. 0*d*. retail); on this occasion the reason was the Clarks' expectation that it would be recommended to students of Hebrew who could afford to buy it only if the price did not exceed a certain level.[664] And a reprint of Peter Bayne's *The Free Church of Scotland* (1893) was issued 'at a mere fraction over the actual cost price'; the motive for this was a desire to ensure the popularisation of the work, the firm claiming to be 'very anxious for Dr Bayne's sake that it should be largely circulated'.[665]

THE PRODUCTION COSTS

The normal print run for a Clark theological work was either 750 or 1,000 copies; editions of both lengths were priced to break even when sales reached around 400 copies.[666] The profitability of a work would be threatened if there were any unanticipated increases in the production costs, and there was one factor which could not be accurately assessed when a work was being costed prior to typesetting: the charge for alterations which the author might wish to make at proof stage. Making extensive corrections to type was extremely time-consuming, and the printers charged accordingly, except where they were merely correcting their own errors. Several Clark titles made a loss simply because the author had insisted on virtually rewriting his work when it was in proof. Thus J.E.H. Thomson, whose *Books which Influenced our Lord* (1891) was in any case selling badly, had it drawn to his attention that there had been an 'unfortunate charge of £25 for "Authors [sic] Alterations" on proofs'.[667] In order to prevent their careful costings being unbalanced by such charges, it became customary for the Clarks to charge authors for the cost of alterations to proofs above a certain sum. Thus, W.F. Skene agreed to pay the cost of all alterations on proofs (excluding printers' errors) over 5*s*. 0*d*. per sixteen-page sheet.[668] J. Hamlyn Hill agreed to similar conditions in the case of his translation of Tatian's *Diatessaron* (1894).[669] And later still, it seems to have been the Clarks' custom, where they were taking the entire risk, to ask the author to pay the cost of *all* alterations, as opposed to corrections, made at the proof stage.[670] By this means, the firm protected themselves from losses arising from this unpredictable element in the costing of a book.

THE DATE OF PUBLICATION

The success of a work could, in the short term at least, be affected both by the time of year at which it was published and by any special conditions pertaining at the time of publication. If the Clarks had some control over the first of these factors, they had absolutely none over the second. We find them expressing disquiet, for example, over delays in producing Hamlyn Hill's edition of the *Diatessaron*: 'we are losing the best of the publishing season', they wrote in November 1893, 'and the Booksellers will immediately be so occupied with Xmas Books that it may not have a fair chance.'[671] But at least in that case they could do something in an attempt to have the book ready at a propitious time. Among the many factors over which the firm had no control was the Boer War, which significantly affected the book trade. Publication of J. Hutchison Stirling's *What is Thought?* was delayed in the hope that hostilities would cease and business improve. The work was eventually published on 5 February 1900; a letter dated 18 January reveals the Clarks' concern at the influence of the war on its prospects:

> Surely Ladysmith will have been relieved by that time! [Publication day. In fact Ladysmith was not relieved until 28 February 1900.[672]] And although that event will not probably mean the end of the War, still . . . this waiting gets wearisome, & it may be wiser after all to publish your book soon than to wait for the *rush* of books which is sure to come when things get more settled.[673]

There are sufficient financial data in the case of a number of the miscellaneous works to enable an assessment to be made of how these factors worked out in practice.

Case Studies

Having noted the concern which the Clarks took to ensure that they bore the risk only in the case of works which were likely to make a profit, it comes as something of a surprise to discover that many works, especially those published in the 1880s and earlier, seem to have failed to break even. The only source of information from that decade, of course, is the letter books, and the firm was perhaps more likely to have occasion to write to authors about loss-making titles than about those which presented no cause for concern. A poem by John Cole on the *Life of St Augustine* proved 'a complete failure'.[674] A sale of 321 copies of George Matheson's *The Growth of the Spirit of Christianity* (1877) did not, Thomas Clark noted, come near to reimbursing the firm.[675]

Given the Clarks' care in the evaluation of manuscripts, one would expect to find that the miscellaneous theological works published by the firm in the 1890s were profitable. But some works published in the last decade of the century seem to have made a loss also. James MacGregor's *Apology of the Christian Religion* (1891) was still showing a debit balance of £70 by 1893, when it was said 'there seems very little hope now of this heavy loss being reduced as there is no demand for the book.'[676] W.S. Bruce's *Ethics of the Old Testament* (1894) was euphemistically said to have been 'disappointing financially'.[677]

Clearly, as the following three case studies show, no matter how carefully a manuscript had been evaluated, the market could prove fickle.[678]

PATON J. GLOAG'S INTRODUCTION TO THE SYNOPTIC GOSPELS

Gloag's work on the Synoptic Gospels was published in the autumn of 1895 at a retail price of 7*s*. 6*d*. Production costs of the edition were as follows:

Printing (806 copies) (Includes typesetting)	£62 12*s*. 10*d*.
Paper	£9 9*s*. 7*d*.
Binding (6½*d*. per copy)	£21 16*s*. 6*d*.
Back stamp	15*s*. 6*d*.
Proportion of Lists	10*s*. 0*d*.
Advertising	£8 4*s*. 4*d*.
Prospectus	8*s*. 7*d*.
	£103 17*s*. 4*d*.

The unit production cost on the whole run was therefore 2*s*. 7*d*.; the unit cost of the copies available for sale after the distribution of eighty presentation copies was 2*s*. 10*d*, while the average income per copy sold was 4*s*. 8½*d*.[679] If the entire impression were sold, the return on investment per unit would be 1*s*. 10½*d*. or 66.17%. The work would break even when 441 copies were sold. That is, breakeven point was 54.71% of the print run, or 60.74% of the copies available for sale.

The work was therefore potentially successful. Over 1895–96, actual expenditure was £93 8*s*. 4*d*. (only 420 copies being bound up), and the income on sales of 283 copies was £66 12*s*. 4*d*. There was therefore a deficit of £26 16*s*. 0*d*. But only 38.98% of the copies available for sale were disposed of in the financial year of issue. If this rate of sales were continued, the work would break even in the following financial year. In fact, over 1896–97, a profit of £42 12*s*. 10*d*. was realised: the work was thus £15 16*s*. 10*d*. into profit overall. But its performance was not as healthy as these figures would lead one to expect. Curiously, although in 1896–97 £18 6*s*. 1*d*. was paid to the author in respect of sales of his work (probably a royalty of 12½%), he himself paid £50 0*s*. 0*d*. to the book's account in April 1897. Sales of the title were slow, only sixty-two copies being disposed of over 1896–97, and possibly Gloag had guaranteed to underwrite any loss. But it seems strange that he should have paid as much as £50 0*s*. 0*d*. as the book was slowly approaching its breakeven point. A profit of £6 15*s*. 0*d*. was shown on the following financial year's trading. (1897–98)

It is of some interest that four '25th copies' were distributed over 1895–96, indicating that, out of sales of only 283 copies, 96 had gone to a maximum of four booksellers. These would, of course, include the Clarks' London agents.

S.D.F. SALMOND'S THE CHRISTIAN DOCTRINE OF IMMORTALITY

Salmond's work was clearly more successful than the Clarks had anticipated. Two impressions were required within the financial year of its first publication (in December 1895 and May 1896), yet no moulds or stereos had been made of the original typesetting; this omission necessitated the complete re-setting of the book. It is not easy to disentangle the costs of the two impressions; what follows is an estimate. The retail price was 14*s*. 0*d*.

Costs of the first impression (1,078 copies)

Printing and typesetting	£132 13*s*. 3*d*.
Paper	£28 10*s*. 2*d*.
Binding (7½*d*. per copy)	£33 13*s*. 9*d*.
Back Stamp	15*s*. 6*d*.
Proportion of Lists (½ of the 1895–96 figure)	£1 10*s*. 0*d*.
Advertising (⅔ of the 1895–96 figure)	£9 15*s*. 5*d*.
Prospectus	£1 8*s*. 4*d*.
Miscellaneous	10*s*. 10*d*.
Royalty*	£75 1*s*. 1*d*.
	£283 18*s*. 4*d*.

*Salmond received a royalty of 12½% = 1*s*. 9*d*. But it was only paid on 858 copies of the first impression. True, 111 presentation copies were distributed, but this still leaves 109 copies on which no royalty was paid. Perhaps this shortfall was Salmond's contribution to the costs of alterations at the proof stage, which amounted to £43 10*s*. 0*d*.

The unit production cost on the whole run was therefore 5*s*. 3*d*.; the unit cost of the copies available for sale after the distribution of 111 presentation copies was 5*s*. 10½*d*, while the average income per copy sold was 8*s*. 10*d*.[680] If the entire printing were sold, the return on investment per unit would be 2*s*. 11½*d*, or 50.35%. The work would break even when 643 copies were sold. That is, breakeven point was 59.64% of the print run, or 66.49% of copies available for sale.

Costs of the second impression (1,080 copies)

Printing and typesetting*	£85 19*s*. 5*d*.
Paper	£29 7*s*. 0*d*.
Binding (7½*d*. per copy)	£33 15*s*. 0*d*.
Proportion of Lists (½ of the 1895–96 figure)	£1 10*s*. 0*d*.
Advertising (⅓ of the 1895–96 figure)	£4 15*s*. 9*d*.
Royalty (on the whole run at 12½%)	£94 10*s*. 0*d*.
	£249 17*s*. 2*d*.

*The printing and typesetting figure is smaller than that charged for the first impression largely because there were fewer corrections at proof stage. The charge for these in the case of the first impression was £43 10*s*. 0*d*.: in the case of the second edition, it was only £9 12*s*. 6*d*.

The unit production cost on the run was therefore 4*s*. 7½*d*. The average income per copy sold was, as before, 8*s*. 10*d*. If the entire edition were sold, the return on investment per unit would be 4*s*. 2½*d*. or 90.99%. The impression would break even when 566 copies were sold. That is, breakeven point was 52.4% of the print run.

These figures are extremely good. And, as moulds were made of the second typesetting, profit from the third printing, if and when it was required, would be even greater. In fact, the work was in its fourth impression, entirely reset, by 1901.

Estimated costs of the third impression (if 1,080 were printed)

Making stereos from moulds (Estimate)	£10	0*s*.	0*d*.
Moulds*	£14	10*s*.	1*d*.
Presswork (Estimate)	£25	0*s*.	0*d*.
Paper	£29	0*s*.	0*d*.
Binding (7½*d*. per copy)	£33	15*s*.	0*d*.
Advertising (Estimate)	£5	0*s*.	0*d*.
Proportion of Lists (Estimate)	£1	10*s*.	0*d*.
Royalty (on the whole run at 12½%)	£94	10*s*.	0*d*.
	£213	5*s*.	1*d*.

*In fact, the moulds were charged against the second edition.

The unit production cost on the run was therefore 3*s*. 11½*d*. The average income per copy was, as before, 8*s*. 10*d*. If the entire impression were sold, the return on investment per unit would be 4*s*. 10½*d*. or 123.15%. The printing would break even when 483 copies were sold. That is, breakeven point was 44.72% of the print run.

As long as the demand did not suddenly dry up once a new impression had been printed, therefore, the work would have been extremely profitable.

Over 1895–96, it showed a profit of £109 11*s*. 9*d*. 2,158 copies were printed at a cost of £432 15*s*. 0*d*. (only 1,485 were bound). Sales of 1,227 copies had realised £542 6*s*. 9*d*. Over 1896–97, the work realised £238 11*s*. 11*d*., and, over 1897–98, £71 10*s*. 11*d*.

It is interesting that over the financial year 1985–96, twenty-eight '25th' copies were distributed, indicating that twenty-eight booksellers had purchased two dozen copies of the work.[681] The first two impressions yielded a royalty of £169 11*s*. 1*d*. to the author, while the Clarks reaped a profit of £370 2*s*. 0*d*.

T. ADAMSON'S THE SPIRIT OF POWER

Early in December 1896, James Hastings forwarded to the Clarks the manuscript of a very short work (around eighty pages in length) by T. Adamson of Glasgow on *The Spirit of Power*. Adamson was eager to see it in print 'to catch the New Year if possible', and his work clearly had won Hastings' approbation. The Clarks, as we have seen, outlined the problems which would face such a work, especially at that particular time of year — small books did not pay outwith a series, the printers were 'simply blocked with work', booksellers shops were quite full to overflowing so that they had little time for theological titles — but they agreed to issue the book at their risk, and there and then despatched Adamson's text to the printers.[682] Its costs were as follows:

Costs of the first edition (1,086 copies)

Printing and typesetting	£7	2*s.*	3*d.*
Paper	£3	4*s.*	2*d.*
Binding (1.34*d.* per copy)	£6	1*s.*	3*d.*
Back Stamp		8*s.*	0*d.*
Advertising	£6	17*s.*	6*d.*
Proportion of Lists		10*s.*	0*d.*
	£24	3*s.*	2*d.*

The unit production cost on the whole run was therefore 5.33*d.*; the unit cost of copies available for sale after the distribution of 102 presentation copies was 5.89*d*, while the average income per copy sold was 7.85*d.*[683] If the entire impression were sold, the return on investment per unit would be 1.96*d*, or 33.27%. The work would break even when 739 copies were sold. That is, breakeven point was 68.42% of the print run, or 75.1% of the copies available for sale.

This impression sold well, and by the end of the financial year the work was showing a profit of £2 3*s.* 11*d.* The Clarks, ill-advisedly as it transpired, ordered a second printing of 1,080 copies in December 1897. As the work had to be reset, this second impression cost almost as much as the first to produce, but sales were slow, and at the end of the financial year 1897–98, 920 copies of the new impression were still in stock, and it was showing a loss of £5 2*s.* 8*d.* By the end of the following financial year only a further fifty-six copies had been disposed of. Due to the extent of advertising undertaken that year, the work showed a loss of 15*s.* 9*d.* The Clarks had, therefore, misjudged the demand for this title. The profits realised by the first impression were more than cancelled out by the losses incurred by the second.

It is interesting to note that over the financial year 1896–97, forty-one '25th copies' were distributed, indicating that of the total sales of the two impressions over that year, 984 copies were sold in batches of two dozen. This would almost suggest that the Clarks did not accept orders for smaller quantities. This in turn might provide an explanation for the failure of the second impression: although the first had sold quickly to the booksellers, thereby encouraging the Clarks to imagine that the demand was large, the interest shown in the work by the public may have been less. The booksellers would therefore have been left with unsold copies, and would have had no need to order further stock from Edinburgh. It was clearly difficult to estimate the demand for a book. If the Clarks underestimated in the case of the work by Salmond, they clearly overestimated in the case of Adamson's title, with financially damaging results.

Despite the care with which the Clarks evaluated works before accepting them for publication, and the careful consideration which was clearly given to the means by which the authors should be remunerated, the profitability of a work could not be guaranteed.

Risk-sharing and commission publishing

A significant proportion of the miscellaneous theological works issued by T. & T. Clark appeared under risk-sharing or commission agreements, means by which the risk to the firm could be minimised.

The letter books give the distinct impression, however, that in many cases, the Clarks were *not* in favour of such agreements. Thus one author was told (and this would seem to have been hardly true), 'we very rarely publish otherwise than at our own risk.'[684] Other letters state clearly that the firm was not in favour of either risk-sharing or commission publishing. A risk-sharing agreement was under discussion when J. Hamlyn Hill was told 'we always shrink from undertaking the publication of a Work which we feel confidently will be unremunerative to the Author.'[685] As for commission publishing, J. Hutchison Stirling was informed 'We are always unwilling except in very special circumstances to allow the *Author* to take the entire risk of publication.'[686] There were two reasons for the Clarks' apparently strong antipathy towards publishing other than at their own risk. In the first place, the works likely to be issued under such agreements would almost certainly make a loss, and they found it distasteful to see an author suffer financially. Secondly their reputation was likely to suffer as a result of such losses, since the author would be tempted to conclude that they were not promoting his work adequately. Concern for the author's financial position was given as the reason for declining a risk-sharing proposal from the Revd Dr Stock of Huddersfield, who was told 'we do not like to undertake where we feel quite satisfied a friend would lose, not only his trouble, but his money besides.'[687] Similarly, H.E. Ryle was told seventeen years later in 1896 that it was 'always unsatisfactory to publish work which [was] unremunerative.'[688] Concern over the reputation of the firm in the eyes of the author is mentioned, for example, in a letter to A.H. Moncur Sime, who was told that the Clarks did not usually publish on commission because where there was a commission agreement the author tended to blame the publisher if the book failed.[689] And in agreeing to issue a work by J. Hutchison Stirling on commission, they pointed out that, should the book not sell adequately, he would have to accept that it would not be for lack of effort on the part of the publisher.[690]

But the fact remains that a significant proportion of the Clarks' books were issued under such agreements.[691] What is the reason for this apparent discrepancy between their attitude and their actions?

It would seem that they were quick to suggest risk-sharing or commission publishing agreements in the case of works which, though not certain to break even, were considered to be eminently worthy of publication because of the quality of their contents. Such works the firm wished to have on their list, but they wished too to minimise the risk to themselves, and thus sought to share it with the author. Thus, when Richard Chandler submitted a manuscript, the firm was quick to point out its quality — 'There are many Commentaries on the Epistle to the Hebrews, but perhaps none exactly on your lines'; they went on to discuss the work's chances of commercial success — 'you must be prepared for some loss'; and finally agreed to publish it on commission — 'we shall do our very best for the sales.'[692] Where a work was of demonstrable quality, then the firm showed themselves willing to proceed under a risk-sharing or commission agreement.[693]

They did not wish, however, to be regarded as being a 'commission publisher' — what would today be termed a 'vanity publisher', a firm prepared to issue any manuscript submitted regardless of its quality, provided the author would bear the risk. To deviate into this kind of publishing would have harmed the firm's reputation and standing as a seriously-intentioned house. Hence manuscripts of poor quality were summarily rejected, and the firm made it clear that, while they might on occasion publish on commission, they were not to be regarded as a commission house. Herein lies the explanation for the many anti-commission statements in the letter books.

An interesting commentary on the Clarks' attitude to commission publishing appears in a letter to Frank Ballard, whose work on *The Miracles of Unbelief* was published in 1900:

> If we undertake more than we can give our entire attention to, all books must suffer, & that is obviously unfair to Authors. There are plenty of Publishers in London who will accept an unlimited number of books provided the Authors pay cost of production — & there is no doubt that *far* too many books are published now-a-days; only a comparatively small number of them ever succeed. As we usually take the entire risk & cost of production ourselves, owing to the class of books we publish, it is impossible for us — certainly it would be unwise of us — to accept all that are offered to us.[694]

Having decided to publish a work without taking the entire risk themselves, the Clarks had next to make up their minds what was the best kind of agreement to conclude with the author. The choice lay between one whereby the risk was in some way shared between author and publisher, or one in which it was stipulated that the author should take the entire risk. In making this decision, the Clarks would seem, once again, to have been motivated by their own financial interests: the greater the likelihood of loss, the less prepared the firm was to share the risk.

The general principle governing the Clarks' risk-sharing agreements was that the authors contracted to pay a stated proportion (usually half) of the cost of printing, paper and binding, advertising costs being in most cases borne by the firm. Thus, for example, when Robert Watts' work on *The Reign of Causality* (1887) was accepted, he was asked to pay £35 towards the production costs, which would amount to over £70.[695] Again, W.F. Skene contributed £25 towards the £50 production costs of his work on *The Lord's Supper* (1891)[696] This down-payment by the author, usually paid, it would seem, upon publication, was sometimes referred to as a 'guarantee'.

The sum was returned to the author after a stated number of copies of the work had been sold, usually when it reached its breakeven point. Occasionally, the 'guarantee' seems to have been repaid in stages as the work gradually recovered its costs: thus J.E.H. Thomson, having paid £55 towards the production of his *Books which Influenced Our Lord* (1891), received that sum back in two instalments: £35 was repaid on 1 February 1892, and the remaining £20 on 12 May 1893.[697]

After a work which had been published under a risk-sharing agreement had recovered its costs, and the 'guarantee' had been returned to the author, he either received a royalty from the Clarks on the remaining copies of the impression, or shared an agreed proportion of their profits. When the firm was considering publishing A.H. Moncur Sime's work on *The Epic of God*, they proposed that Sime should pay half the production costs. After the book had broken even, he would receive a 15% royalty on the net wholesale price, and 10% on overseas sales. This might seem to be less than generous in the light of the author's financial commitment to the project.[698] The more common arrangement, profit-sharing, would seem to have been more equitable — W.F. Skene was to received half of any profits realised by his work.[699] And, in discussing terms with J. McDonald Inglis for a work which does not in the event seem to have been published by them, the firm offered him also 50% of the profits after the work had recovered its costs: that at least would seem to be the implication of their comment 'we will divide the profits with you'.[700]

These then were the normal terms included in the firm's risk-sharing agreements. Certain of these, however, included different terms: in the case of W.D. Killen's work *The Ignatian Epistles Entirely Spurious* (1886), for example, the Clarks bore the main cost of production, but asked the author to be responsible for the advertising costs, and for the cost of any Greek type required in the book.[701] When Robert Watts submitted an unidentified work, the firm carefully considered the financial implications of publishing it at their own risk, and decided not to proceed. But having notified Watts of their decision, they added 'Do you see any possibility of guaranteeing the sale of a number of copies?'[702] This implies that the Clarks might have been prepared to take the risk if Watts had undertaken to dispose of a certain number of copies, perhaps by having the work adopted as a college text. This was a form of risk-sharing. In the case of the work by C.M. Mead discussed earlier, *Romans Dissected* (1891) which was published under the pseudonym of E.D. McRealsham, it was agreed that the author, who lived in Berlin, should pay for the printing of the work in that city. The Clarks would meet the cost of binding and advertising. Once the work had broken even, Mead was to receive 40% on the nominal retail price of each copy sold.[703]

Almost every risk-sharing agreement made by the firm therefore, was unique in some particular. Having assessed the likely cost of production, and the potential sales of a work, the Clarks appear to have drawn up a contract in such terms as to give the book the best chance of success, while minimising the risk to themselves.

In the case of works which, though valuable theologically, seemed extremely unlikely to make a profit, the Clarks were willing to sign a commission agreement with the author, thus guaranteeing the book's publication while ensuring that the firm made no loss. When the possibility of publishing Richard Chandler's work on *Hebrews* was under discussion, it was proposed that the author bear the entire cost of production and advertising. The firm would pay him 50% of the nominal retail price on all copies sold, making payment on the August or February after publication, and thereafter on an annual basis. The costings of this work are not available, but such an agreement would, given a trade discount of 40%, yield the firm 10% of the retail price of each copy sold.[704] The terms agreed with Professor John Laidlaw of Edinburgh in respect of the publication of the recently-deceased E.A. Thomson's sermons (*Memorials of a Ministry* (1892)) seem to have been more typical of the firm's normal practice and less profitable to them. Thomson's family were to bear the cost of production (and presumably advertising), and the Clarks' return was to be a commission of 10% on the net *wholesale* price of copies sold in the UK and the Colonies, and a commission of 5% on copies sold to America.[705] Once again we have no costings for this work. An agreement containing yet another mix of terms was concluded with C. Salmond in respect of James McGregor's book of *Studies in the History of New Testament Apologetics* (1894). McGregor (who lived in New Zealand) was to cover all costs; the Clarks would retain the 'usual Publisher's Commission' of 10% on the net wholesale price on UK and Colonial sales (excluding those to Canada), with an additional 10% on US and Canadian sales.[706] The income from transatlantic sales being less than that from British and Colonial sales, it is understandable that the Clarks should wish to secure a larger proportion of that income. (It is not clear whether they were to receive a straight 20% of the income from the US sales, or 10% + 10% of the remaining 90%). It is surprising that, in the case of the work by Thomson referred to above, the firm sought a *smaller* commission in the case of transatlantic sales.

The absence of detailed costings prevents us from assessing the firm's income in these cases. It was no doubt small, and very possibly did not cover the Clarks' incidental expenses in preparing the works for publication, seeing them through the press, and organising advertising and distribution. But, if a small loss were made, the Clarks had the satisfaction of knowing that they were aiding in the circulation of works which they believed to be of some value at no substantial risk to themselves.

Another kind of commission publishing was the distribution of a work which its author had already had printed at his own expense through another agency. On the face of it, this kind of agreement might seem appealing to the publishers: in return for his commission, all he has to do is to superintend the advertising and distribution of a work which has already been seen through the press. There is no evidence that the Clarks ever concluded an agreement of this nature. There is, however, an example of their rejecting a proposal that they should thus distribute a book. The rejection was made not on the grounds that they would never contemplate such an arrangement, but because the quality of production of the work in question was poor, and it might have prejudiced the good name the Clarks had for 'high class work'.[707]

The *Stock and Sales Book, Individual Titles*[708] gives detailed information on the costings of some of the titles published under risk-sharing, if not commission agreements. Two case-studies follow.

The Brotherhood of Man by J.H. Crawford was published in September 1895 at a retail price of 5*s*. 0*d*. Production costs of the impression were as follows:

Typesetting/Printing (808 copies)	£49 8*s*. 8*d*.
Paper	£11 9*s*. 0*d*.
Binding (6¼*d*. per copy)	£21 0*s*. 10*d*.
Back Stamp	11*s*. 0*d*.
Proportion of Lists	10*s*. 0*d*.
Advertising	£9 2*s*. 6*d*.
Prospectus	15*s*. 5*d*.
Miscellaneous	10*s*. 10*d*.
	£93 8*s*. 3*d*.

The unit production cost on the whole run was therefore 2*s*. 4*d*.; the unit cost on the copies available for sale after the distribution of 83 presentation copies was 2*s*. 7*d*, while the average income per copy sold was 3*s*. 2*d*.[709] If the entire impression were sold, the return on investment per unit would be 7*d*., or 22.58%. The work would break even when 590 copies were sold. That is, breakeven point was 73% of the print run, or 81.37% of the copies available for sale.

The work, therefore, had the potential to realise a modest profit. Over 1895–96, actual expenditure was £81 14*s*. 11*d*. (only 360 copies being bound up), and the income totalled £81 3*s*. 0*d*., of which £41 3*s*. 0*d*. was yielded by sales of 259 copies, the remainder coming from Crawford, who contributed £40 0*s*. 0*d*., just under half of the production costs. The Clarks' deficit on the work within the financial year in which it was issued was only 11*s*. 11*d*.: this would have been recovered by the time four more copies had been sold. Crawford's contribution had therefore effectively protected the firm from immediate loss; their investment was virtually recovered within the financial year of issue, and there would be presumably no need to repay Crawford until sales had realised a further £40. (He received £20 10*s*. 0*d*. in the financial year 1897–98). Over 1895–96, just 35% of the copies available for sale were disposed of. Considering that a work's largest sales will in normal circumstances come within the first few months after publication, this percentage did not augur well for the success of Crawford's book. Even if, as was most unlikely, sales continued at the same pace, it would be at least a year before *The Brotherhood of Man* broke even. This being the case, it was clearly prudent of the Clarks to issue the book under a risk-sharing agreement.

Over 1896–97, a profit of £6 15*s*. 7*d*. was shown, while the following financial year saw a deficit of £19 18*s*. 3½*d*.; this was due to the fact that repayment of just over half his investment was made to Crawford. Once this payment was made, the loss on the work was shared equally by the authors and the publishers. The work showed a profit of £1 11*s*. 9*d*. on the year's trading over 1898–99. It is of some interest that, over 1895–96 three '25th copies' were distributed, indicating that out of sales of only 259 copies, seventy-two had gone to a maximum of three booksellers, including, no doubt, the wholesalers.

A Dissertation on the Gospel Commentary of St Ephraem the Syrian by J. Hamlyn Hill was published in May or June 1896 at a retail price of 7*s*. 6*d*. Although it was issued under a risk-sharing rather than a commission agreement, Hill in fact paid the largest part of the production costs of the impression, which were as follows:

Typesetting/Printing (538 copies)	£31 5*s*. 0*d*.
Paper	£3 17*s*. 0*d*.
Binding (6¾*d*. per copy)	£15 2*s*. 7*d*.
Back Stamp	12*s*. 6*d*.
Proportion of Lists	£1 0*s*. 0*d*.
Advertising	£2 6*s*. 2*d*.
	£54 3*s*. 3*d*.

An additional charge of £4 0*s*. 6*d*., for the production of stereos from moulds, is noted in the accounts for the book, but is not actually included in the charge against it. Just over a quarter of the work — 3¼ sheets — was involved. The most likely explanation is that additional copies of a section of the work were required by the author for separate distribution: this is substantiated by the fact that the charge includes £1 18*s*. 8*d*. levied for 'altering headlines.' If this were the case, it would explain why the additional charge was not set against the book.

The accounts also note that a prospectus was produced, but no charge is listed against this. Possibly, the work being published so near the end of the financial year, the printer's account for the prospectus had not been received by the time the Clarks' accounts were made up.

The unit production cost on the whole run was therefore 2*s*. 0*d*.; the unit cost of those available for sale after the distribution of 65 presentation copies was 2*s*. 3½*d*., while the average income per copy sold was 4*s*. 10*d*.[710] If the entire edition was sold, the return on investment per unit would be 2*s*. 6½*d*., or 111%. The work would break even when 224 copies were sold. That is, breakeven point was 41.63% of the print run, or 47.35% of the copies available for sale. The work was therefore potentially highly profitable since the selling price was high given the level of production costs. Whether it fulfilled this potential depended, of course, on how well it sold. Only 50 copies — 10.57% of those available for sale — had been disposed of by the end of the financial year in which the book was published, but those copies had been sold in the few weeks remaining between the date of publication and the end of the financial year. Moreover, the work had appeared in early summer, when business was slack. The real test would come in the first full financial year after publication.

Over 1895–96, actual expenditure was £43 5*s*. 0*d*. (only 150 copies being bound up), and income totalled £42 3*s*. 8*d*., of which £12 3*s*. 8*d*. was yielded by sales of fifty copies. The remainder came from Hill, who contributed £30, which almost covered the typesetting and printing costs. The Clarks' deficit on the work within the financial year in which it was issued was therefore only £1 1*s*. 4*d*.; this would be recovered by the time four more copies had been sold. Once again, the author's contribution had effectively protected the firm from immediate loss, their investment being virtually recovered within the financial year of issue. If the book failed to make a profit in the longer term, however, £15 would no doubt be returned to Hill, the loss being thus divided equally between the two parties.

Over 1896–97, a profit of 4*s*. 5*d*. was shown. (Income from sales totalled only £8 16*s*. 1*d*., while the major charge against the work was £6 17*s*. 11*d*. spent on advertising.) Over 1897–98 there was a deficit of 12*s*. 7*d*. Over 1898–99, there was no outlay: one copy of the book was sold, bringing in 4*s*. 10*d*. It is of some interest to note that, over 1895–96, one '25th copy' was distributed, indicating that out of sales of only fifty copies, two dozen had gone to one bookseller, probably the wholesaler.

It is clear, from the foregoing analysis and from these case studies, that risk-sharing agreements, while not guaranteeing that there would be no losses, at least reduced their extent. Commission agreements would, in theory, remove them altogether.

In developing their programme of miscellaneous theological publishing, the Clarks sought to minimise the risk to themselves by ensuring that the works they issued were not only of demonstrable merit, but also had a reasonable expectation of breaking even. This is, of course, simply sound publishing sense, yet it is more evident in their approach to the miscellaneous works than in their attitude towards some of the other titles on their list, in the case of which even though a much larger investment was involved, they seem to have been more ready to put theological importance before profitability.

Part III

The profitability of a publishing house depends not merely on the quality or popular appeal of its publications, or on the efficiency of its production and costing, crucial though these factors are, but also on the success and effectiveness of its promotion and distribution. Part III assesses the effectiveness — and the cost-effectiveness — of T. & T. Clark's advertising and promotional strategy, and their system of distribution.

Chapter 10
Advertising and promotion

Advertising

It would be a relatively simple matter to assess the total sum spent by T. & T. Clark on advertising over the years for which we have figures: it is much more difficult to evaluate the fruitfulness of that expenditure in terms of generating sales, let alone its cost-effectiveness. For it is impossible in this case to quantify the relationship between advertising and sales with any degree of exactness; the Clarks themselves seem to have proceeded largely by instinct. The letter books, however, give some insights into their assessment of the value of advertising.[1]

In a letter to their new advertising agent J.F. Spriggs, for example, the Clarks explained why press advertisements were not in their experience the most effective weapons in their arsenal of promotional strategies:

> You may possibly wonder that we do not advertise more extensively, but the fact is that we know exactly the class who buy our Books — which, as you know are not of a 'popular' order — & can reach them far more effectively by our catalogues and circulars.[2]

In other words, the firm considered that while advertising was useful in certain cases, the audience at which Clark publications were targeted could be most efficiently reached through direct-mail promotion.

In fact, however, the Clarks employed press advertising more widely than this quotation would lead one to expect; the costings for each publication include a sizable outlay on this kind of promotion. The major advertising campaign on behalf of a work usually took place immediately after its initial launch, or the launch of a new edition. But the firm, where they considered it appropriate, also advertised certain titles on an on-going basis and urged Scribners to do likewise.[3] Advertising for S.R. Driver's *Introduction to the Literature of the Old Testament,* first published in 1891, was continued, for example, even when the book was temporarily out of print in 1897. Such advertising the Clarks considered 'judicious' as it would keep the work 'constantly before the public'.[4] They used advertising, therefore, to inform the wider public of new titles, and to give continuing prominence to successful works from the back list.

But in many cases they discovered that advertising was relatively ineffective. W.S. Bruce's *Ethics of the Old Testament* (1895) was advertised in 1899 in a new, widely-circulated Church of Scotland serial, *St Andrew*, without a single enquiry being generated.[5] The *Monthly Interpreter* and the *Critical Review* likewise were both advertised extensively with no appreciable results[6] while advertisements for the *Presbyterian Review* were placed both 'judiciously'[7] and 'regularly'[8] without the circulation being significantly increased. And the firm wrote to G.T. Ladd about their promotional activities on behalf of his *Doctrine of Sacred Scripture* (1883):

> We are keeping up a run of advertising in the direction you indicate, but the book is not going off. When better known it may succeed better.[9]

All these examples are of works which, for one reason or another failed to win the kind of reputation among potential purchasers which would have resulted in larger sales. Of Ladd's book, the firm commented: 'When better known it [might] succeed better.' Clearly it was not becoming 'better known' despite extensive advertising; the Clarks were discovering what Stanley Unwin, four decades later, knew well, that 'it pays to advertise a book if it shows signs of being successful without advertising, but . . . it does not pay to advertise at all extensively a book that shows no signs of catching on.'[10] Thus, a book which had won favour in the eyes of its reviewers and hence of its potential audience, W.N. Clarke's *Outline of Christian Theology* (1898), sold satisfactorily with very little advertising, while another work which did not share its high repute, D.W. Simon's *Reconciliation by Incarnation* (1898) sold poorly despite extensive advertising.[11]

The Clarks, therefore, aimed to reach the core of the potential market through direct mail; they recognised, however, that advertising was essential in the case of new titles, which had to be drawn to the attention of the widest possible market, and particularly effective in the case of back-list titles with a proven record of success. Even the most extensive advertising could, however, do little to improve the sales of titles which were performing badly. It is difficult to avoid the conclusion that the firm, while accepting that some advertising was necessary, regarded it, except in the case of a very few titles, as being far less cost-effective than the other methods of publicity and promotion.

The Clarks made use, for advertising purposes, of the trade press, denominational publications, and general theological serials, both scholarly and popular. Appendix E lists those periodicals in which the Clarks regularly inserted advertisements between 1886 and 1896. Advertisements for a particular title were inserted in the publications whose subscribers were those to whom the work in question was most likely to appeal. In this respect, the *British Weekly*, for example, proved highly effective: 'we well know its value as an Advtg. medium for our publications.'[12] There was, on the other hand, little point in advertising in journals whose theological position was antipathetic to that taken by the Clarks' authors; Scribners were taken to task for advertising works by Robert Watts ('the orthodox of the orthodox!') using commendatory quotations from the equally orthodox C.H. Spurgeon in the 'advanced' liberal journal *New World,* whose readers were most unlikely to be potential customers for Clark publications.[13]

Having selected a suitable list of periodicals in which to advertise a given title, the Clarks found it expedient to concentrate their advertising at certain times of the year. The Christmas numbers were always avoided: 'They are naturally filled up with Xmas Gift Books — of which we have really none — & it is practically useless for us to advertise in them.'[14] The bulk of advertising for a new work was concentrated around the time of publication, and thereafter it would be advertised at the start of the spring and autumn publishing 'seasons'. Special advertisements would appear in the Scottish denominational publications around the time of the Churches' annual General Assemblies, when many ministers from outlying parts would be within reach of an Edinburgh bookshop.

Not only was it important to select the most appropriate periodicals in which to advertise, and the time of year at which advertisements proved to be most effective, but it was also vital to phrase the text of the advertisements as tellingly as possible. In fact, the Clarks' normal procedure was simply to give full details of the work in question and then to quote from favourable reviews. They sought to be guided in their advertising as in everything else by standards of honesty and honour.[15]

The Clarks seem to have considered that, even in the case of the smallest book, it was necessary to spend between £10 and £15 on advertising. Thus, when they were discussing the publication under a commission agreement of J.M. Hodgson's *Theologia Pectoris,* they commented regarding advertising outlay that 'if worked judiciously £10 to £15 should suffice.'[16] In practice, however, their advertising expenditure on a given title sometimes fell short of the lower figure.

On comparatively few occasions, the Clarks exchanged advertisements with another publisher: in such cases, for the most part, no money changed hands. For instance, in 1879, the Clarks inserted a one-page advertisement for James Nisbet's publications in one of the *Bible Class Handbooks;* Nisbet for his part carried a page of Clark advertising in the *Catholic Presbyterian.*[17] Such exchanged advertisements were not necessarily 'free', very possibly, had the page in question not been assigned to Nisbet, it would have been sold to another publisher. But exchanges of this nature permitted both houses to experiment with a new advertising medium for a minimum of outlay. In some cases, an exchange agreement could include a financial element. For example, when Elliot Stock solicited a page of advertising from the Clarks for the *Churchman* at £2 15*s.* 0*d.*, the Edinburgh firm agreed to comply only on the express condition that Stock would advertise in an issue of the *Monthly Interpreter.*[18]

To allow a comparison of the firm's advertising expenditure on different titles, Table 21[19] analyses the figures for some of the 1895–96 titles, and expresses the expenditure on advertising (including that credited to the accounts of the *Critical Review* and the *Expository Times*) as a proportion of

Table 21

Advertising outlay on some 1895–96 titles						
Title	Date of publication	Total outlay borne by the Clarks 1895–96	Advertising expenditure	Turnover 1895–96	Advertising expenditure as a proptn. of the Clarks' outlay	Advertising expenditure as a proptn. of turnover
S. R. Driver *Deuteronomy*	?	£436 7*s.* 3*d.*	£25 2*s.* 1*d.*	£523 8*s.* 0*d.*	5.75%	4.79%
G. F. Moore *Judges*	Sept. 1895	£295 6*s.* 9*d.*	£24 14*s.* 11*d.*	£258 9*s.* 0*d.*	8.37%	9.57%
E. P. Gould *St. Mark*	Feb. 1896	£190 5*s.* 5*d.*	£24 14*s.* 11*d.*	£201 1*s.* 6*d.*	13.00%	12.30%
W. Sanday *Romans*	July 1895	£574 3*s.* 3*d.*	£27 14*s.* 11*d.*	£621 6*s.* 8*d.*	4.83%	4.46%
G. P. Fisher *History of Christian Doctrine*	March 1896	£208 9*s.* 5*d.*	£4 2*s.* 4*d.*	£202 12*s.* 8*d.*	1.97%	2.03%
P. J. Gloag *Synoptic Gospels*	Oct. 1895	£93 8*s.* 4*d.*	£8 4*s.* 4*d.*	£66 12*s.* 4*d.*	8.79%	12.33%
J. Crawford *Brotherhood of Mankind*	Sept. 1895	£81 14*s.* 11*d.* (shared by the author)	£9 2*s.* 6*d.*	£41 3*s.* 0*d.*	11.16%	22.17%
S. D. Salmond *Immortality*	Dec. 1895	£432 5*s.* 0*d.*	£14 11*s.* 2*d.*	£542 6*s.* 9*d.*	3.36%	2.68%
C. J. Hefele *Councils of the Church (Vol 5)*	?	£168 19*s.* 6*d.*	£1 17*s.* 6*d.*	£64 8*s.* 3*d.*	1.1%	2.91%
J. S. Candlish *Ephesians (Bible Class Handbook)*	Oct. 1895	£68 2*s.* 7*d.*	3*s.* 7*d.**	£63 6*s.* 0*d.*	0.25%	0.26%

* No doubt this work was also advertised in general announcements of the Series.

the expenditure on all aspects of the work's production, and as a proportion of its turnover. All these figures relate to the financial year in which the titles were issued, and exclude the 'Proportion of Lists', a sum charged to the account of each book as its contribution to the firm's general promotional expenses.

No particularly clear pattern emerges from this Table. It is obvious that, although greater sums were spent on promoting books which were larger and cost more to produce, and smaller sums on lower-budget productions, the firm did not allocate a regular percentage of the outlay for advertising purposes. Clearly, some other factor (possibly instinct or pragmatism) guided them in ascertaining how extensively a particular work should be advertised.

In the case of most of the items in the Table, the figure expressing expenditure as a proportion of the total outlay marches in tandem with that expressing expenditure as a proportion of turnover. This would suggest that, however successful the advertisements may have been in generating sales, they could hardly, on the face of it, have been cost-effective; had they been so, one would have expected the proportion of turnover figure to decrease as the proportion of outlay figure increased. (The advertising in the case of the *Brotherhood of Mankind* would seem to have been especially lacking in cost-effectiveness.) But many other factors besides advertising affected the turnover of Clark titles, and it is therefore impossible accurately to assess the cost-effectiveness of their advertising.

Catalogues and brochures

> We confess, however, that we have more faith, for our class of books in direct 'circularising' than in Press advertising.[20]
>
> We know from experience that we get far greater returns from the circulation of our Catalogues than from Advertisements.[21]

Although the success and cost-effectiveness of direct mail promotion is as impossible to quantify as it was in the case of advertising, the very clear impression given by the letter books is that this kind of promotion was much cheaper, more successful in terms of generating orders, and hence far more successful and cost-effective than press advertising. Two categories of promotional material were regularly circulated to booksellers and potential customers: catalogues itemising all or most of the firm's list, and brochures highlighting particular, usually new, titles.

Four different catalogues were produced, usually at least once a year. There was a UK retail catalogue, a UK trade catalogue (the latter giving trade prices), a catalogue for the Colonial market, and one produced for Scribners to distribute in the US, listing the US retail prices and excluding titles for which Scribners did not hold the American franchise. These catalogues were widely distributed: Philip Schaff was informed in 1885 that thirteen thousand copies of a new catalogue were being set out,[22] while, two years later S.D.F. Salmond was told that between twenty and thirty thousand copies of the general catalogue were distributed each year.[23] These catalogues were sent to clergymen (ten thousand copies of the new catalogue were dispatched in

January 1896 to 'Clergymen of all Denominations'[24]) and to booksellers, who could be supplied with substantial quantities overprinted with their name and address for distribution to customers. (Macmillan and Bowes in Cambridge were sent five hundred copies of a new catalogue, overprinted in this way, in 1883.[25]) It is not unreasonable to suppose that the bulk of the Clarks' business was generated by these catalogues which, compared with advertising, were relatively inexpensive: the cost of printing catalogues over 1895–96 seems to have totalled less than one hundred pounds.[26] To this should be added the postal charges involved in their distribution, which are unspecified, but must have been considerable.

Brochures, leaflets or postcards were frequently produced to advertise new titles, periodicals and 'live' series, and were distributed to bookseller and potential customer alike. The Clarks were aiming at a clearly-defined target audience (the theological fraternity) and, as we have seen, they considered that such direct-mail 'circularising' was the most effective way of hitting the target. Moreover, a campaign could be targeted at a specific sub-group within the theological fraternity; thus when Samuel Green's book *The Ancient Faith* was published in 1897, postcards were sent to two thousand Congregational and Baptist ministers, the Clarks claiming 'we think this is the most direct way of reaching them.'[27] Authors were frequently consulted when the list of those who were to receive promotional material was being drawn up. When, for example, the booksellers were showing a singular lack of interest in and enthusiasm for C. Newman Hall's new work on *The Lord's Prayer* (1883), the firm told him that it was 'very necessary' to 'make an effort in the direction of [his] congregation and friends', and asked him to send to George Street 'a list of individuals (ladies as well as gentlemen) to whom [they] could send circulars.'[28]

Promotional items were sent out in very large quantities indeed. 'Many thousand' copies of a prospectus advertising the *Monthly Interpreter* were circulated;[29] by February 1885 the *Presbyterian Review* had been promoted by means of three thousand copies of a prospectus,[30] and over the next year a further seven to twelve thousand copies were distributed.[31] 'An immense number' of copies of a prospectus advertising Thayer's edition of Grimm's *Lexicon* was circulated,[32] while between twenty and thirty thousand copies of yet another prospectus advertising the *Dictionary of the Bible* were printed.[33] All this 'circularising' was not invariably successful, failing miserably, for instance, in the case of the *Presbyterian Review* which sold only ninety copies despite extensive promotion in this way.[34] But where the product met a genuine need, and where the target audience was clearly defined and easily accessible by direct-mail solicitation, it was without doubt the best means of promotion. Table 22 compares the cost of advertising with the cost of printing a prospectus in the case of some of the titles published in the financial year 1895–96.[35] No record has been kept of the cost of distributing copies of the prospectus once it had been printed.

There was probably some cross-fertilisation between direct mail promotion and press advertising. Receipt of a prospectus might persuade a potential customer to purchase a work which he had previously seen advertised; conversely, an advertisement might propel into the bookshop someone whose

Table 22

Comparison of advertising with cost of printing a prospectus for some 1895–96 titles		
Title	Advertising Expenditure	Cost of printing Prospectus
S. R. Driver – *Deuteronomy*	£25 2*s*. 1*d*.	£6 0*s*. 5*d*.
G. F. Moore – *Judges*	£24 14*s*. 11*d*.	None
E. P. Gould – *St Mark*	£24 14*s*. 11*d*.	None
W. Sanday – *Romans*	£27 14*s*. 11*d*.	None
G. P. Fisher – *History of Christian Doctrine*	£4 2*s*. 4*d*.	£1 14*s*. 9*d*.
P. J. Gloag – *Synoptic Gospels*	£8 4*s*. 4*d*.	8*s*. 7*d*.
J. Crawford – *Brotherhood of Man*	£9 2*s*. 6*d*.	15*s*. 5*d*. (3000 copies)
S. D. F. Salmond – *Immortality*	£14 11*s*. 2*d*.	£1 19*s*. 2*d*. (4000 copies)
C. J. Hefele – *Councils of the Church* (*Vol. 5*)	£1 17*s*. 6*d*.	£1 11*s*. 3*d*. (4000 copies)
J. S. Candlish *Ephesians* (*B.C.H.*)	3*s*. 7*d*.	None

One might have expected that prospectus advertising would have been used in every case. Possibly the works by Moore, Gould and Sanday were promoted in general leaflets advertising the *International Critical Commentary* series, to which they belong.

interest in a work had previously been awakened by a review or a prospectus. No one strand of the firm's promotion strategy can therefore be considered in isolation. But catalogues and brochures were undoubtedly the most successful element of that strategy.

Review copies

It was the Clarks' considered opinion that there was a direct relationship between good reviews and sales, and in consequence their promotional programme included the distribution of sizable numbers of review copies to editors. Their faith in the power of the reviewer is illustrated by quotations from the letter books. Of the slow-selling *Doctrine of Sacred Scripture* by G.T. Ladd (1883), for example the firm wrote to Scribners 'when we get reviews it may move'[36] ; again, when buying the *Eras of the Christian Church* series from the Christian Literature Publishing Company, the Clarks asked for as many gratis copies of each volume as possible for distribution to editors, saying as an inducement: 'The larger the number you can send, the greater the probability of repeat orders.'[37] But if good reviews helped to increase sales, poor reviews inevitably diminished them. The firm anticipated that their edition of F.E. König's *Religious History of Israel* (1885) would be 'a dead loss' to them, at least part of the explanation for this being that 'all the reviewers [were] down upon the translation.'[38] However if there was a risk involved in distributing review copies, it was far offset by the potential benefits that could accrue from positive reviewing.

Statistics, where available, confirm that large numbers of review copies were sent out.[39] In purchasing works from American houses, the Clarks, as they did in the case of the Series referred to above, usually asked for as many review copies as could be spared.[40] Twenty-nine copies of E. de W. Burton's *Syntax of the Moods and Tenses in New Testament Greek* (1894), a work of American origin, were distributed in this way.[41] In the case of works which they had themselves originated, larger numbers of editors' copies were sent out by the Clarks. Thus, for example, at least sixty editors received C.H.H. Wright's *Biblical Essays* (1886).[42] At the request of J. Vernon Bartlet, an author who wanted more review copies of his work on the *Apostolic Age* distributed than the sixty which was at that time the Clarks' normal figure, and who agreed to bear half the cost of the additional copies, eighty review copies of that work were sent out.[43]

Considerable wisdom had to be exercised in the distribution of review copies if they were to bear the maximum fruit. 'We know something of the ways of Editors!', the Clarks commented.[44] At least three principles were involved. In the first place, it was essential to select as recipients of review copies the periodicals whose editors were most likely to be interested in and sympathetic to the work in question. Given that Victorian religious periodicals represented a wide spectrum of attitudes and emphases, this was very far from easy. One obviously avoided periodicals which were theologically more advanced or more conservative than the theological position of one's own publications. One editor in fact wrote to the Clarks notifying them that their publications were not sufficiently liberal to be noticed in his journal (the *New World*) and asked that no further review copies be sent except at his specific request.[45] In some cases however, although one would rather not have sent a particular book for review to a given journal, it was politic to let the editor have one, since failure to send a review copy might result in the appearance of an even more damaging notice than would have been printed had a copy been sent. Hence, for example, when D.W. Simon requested that review copies of his *Reconciliation by Incarnation* (1898) should, for some reason, personal or theological, not be sent to the editors of the *British Weekly* and the *Christian World* he was told, no doubt on the basis of the Clarks' past experience,

> If we purposely omit papers . . . it tells against us in other ways & may do us serious injury, for the Editors take offence & the almost certain result is a slashing review not only of the book withheld but of other of our publications also . . . You will be far wiser to face those two papers boldly.[46]

One's list of periodicals whose editors were to receive copies of a given work had always to contain fewer titles than the number of books available for free distribution, for inevitably, after publication, requests for review copies would be received from editors omitted from the list.[47] These it would have been foolish to ignore.

The second principle was that, contrary to the opinion of many authors, review copies bore the most luxuriant fruit if sent to editors rather than direct to those who contributed reviews to the theological press. In writing to J. Beveridge of Wolverhampton, the Clarks made their views on this clear:

> Experience has proved to us that it is not wise to send to private individuals for review in particular Magazines. Editors generally resent this, & prefer that the Review copy should be sent to their office direct.[48]

The third and final principle was that if the distribution of review copies were to prove fruitful, editors who did not print reviews quickly, or who made do with brief notices, should not be constantly harried either by the author or by the publisher, great though the temptation to do this might be. Such harrying would only prove counter-productive. There were times, however, when the Clarks felt that some polite communication with an editor was essential. Thus, after the *Guardian* had reviewed only one Clark title in a volume of issues, despite having received copies of nearly all of the firm's new publications, the editor received a note which began 'We trust you will pardon us for drawing your attention to the following', explained the position, and went on to urge greater consideration for Clark issues.[49] Similarly, the editor of the *Methodist Times* had his attention drawn to the fact that, despite his having been sent a copy of the first volume of the *Dictionary of the Bible,* a work, it was pointed out, of recognised importance, he had not published a review of it.[50] Such careful handling of editors — not harrying them, but monitoring their performance and gently intervening when necessary — was essential if the kind of relationship with the press which was conducive to favourable reviewing was to be maintained.

The distribution of review copies, if wisely done, could be a most effective means of promotion. There was an element of unpredictability which was absent from say, the distribution of catalogues and brochures, but in general, if the work were competent, a judicious scattering of review copies would yield a pleasing crop of notices, and these in turn, both directly and indirectly through being quoted in advertisements (another example of the interplay between two elements of the promotion strategy) would lead to further sales.

Once again, the cost-effectiveness of this means of promotion is unquantifiable. The following Table itemises the total cost to the Clarks (calculated on the unit production cost) of review copies distributed in the case of some of the titles published in the financial year 1895–96.[51] No record appears to have been kept of the postal costs of distributing review copies.

Table 23

Cost of review copies distributed of some 1895–96 titles		
Title	No. of review copies*	Cost of review copies*
S. R. Driver – *Deuteronomy*	80	£21 11*s.* 0*d.*
G. F. Moore – *Judges*	60	£17 14*s.* 6*d.*
E. P. Gould – *St. Mark*	70	£12 6*s.* 10*d.*
W. Sanday – *Romans*	100	£22 5*s.* 0*d.*
G. P. Fisher – *History of Christian Doctrine*	60	£15 10*s.* 0*d.*
P. J. Gloag – *Synoptic Gospels*	75	£8 14*s.* 0*d.*
J. Crawford – *Brotherhood of Man*	75	£7 12*s.* 0*d.*
S. D. F. Salmond – *Immortality*	105	£21 1*s.* 0*d.*
C. J. Hefele – *Councils of the Church* (*Vol. 5*)	50	£7 16*s.* 0*d.*
J. S. Candlish – *Ephesians* (*B.C.H.*)	120	£3 15*s.* 10*d.*

Table 23 (*continued*)

* Both these figures are approximations. The number of presentation copies listed in the *Stock and Sales Book* includes those given to the author: an arbitrary figure has been deducted from these totals to arrive at the number quoted above. The total cost price of the review copies is based on a rough estimate of the unit production cost of the work in question.

The comparatively expensive nature of this means of promotion underlines the fact that considerable wisdom was called for in its execution if it were to be both successful and cost-effective.

Other means of promotion

There were a number of other minor elements in the overall promotion strategy.

In the case of magazines, readers could be asked to encourage their friends and colleagues to take out a subscription. This strategy was followed (with, however, no appreciable results) in the case of the *Presbyterian Review*.[52] Again, copies of a periodical could be distributed gratis in an attempt to induce more people to subscribe. This was done in the cases of the *Monthly Interpreter*,[53] and of the *Critical Review*, several thousand copies of which were given away for this purpose. This free distribution was, the firm felt, 'the most effectual way' of promoting a periodical;[54] even more effective, it is implied, than the circulation of prospectuses.

In the case of books, the theological and trade press would often carry announcements of forthcoming titles (as opposed to advertisements for them) at no charge to the publisher. Thus the Clarks wrote to J. Hamlyn Hill, author of a work on St Ephraem's *Commentary* (1896): 'We sent the Announcement you kindly drew up to several papers of literary standing.'[55] Again, reviews of Clark publications could feature prominently in the *Expository Times* and the *Critical Review*. As we noted earlier, the firm were not enthusiastic about the appearance in their journals of reviews which extensively criticised their publications; they were more than happy, however, to give house-room to warm appreciations. Thus John M. Clark wrote to Hastings

> I am hopeful that even already some good has result from your kind references to our books in the E.T., and when the 'Enlargement' becomes a fact, I quite believe that additional impetus will be given.[56]

A review of Hamlyn Hill's forthcoming edition of Tatian's *Diatessaron* (1894) appeared in the *Expository Times*, and was used for promotional purposes; gratis copies of the issue containing the review were sent to some potential customers, and the notice was kept in type, so that additional copies could be run off and circulated to announce the work.[57] A final additional means of promoting books was the insertion of advertising material at the back of other publications, where it would catch the reader's attention at a time when, having just completed one book, he would be most susceptible to the blandishment of another. The *Bible Class Handbook* series was open also to advertising material from other publishers,[58] but, for the most part, these end-of-book advertising opportunities were used by the Clarks themselves. Most of their titles, it would appear, contained some advertising, and only one author, J. Hamlyn Hill, seems ever to have objected to this. Hamlyn Hill, who had been raising trouble at every turn over the issue of his edition of the *Diatessaron,* clearly felt that the Clarks had no right to defile his book with advertisements, even although it was being issued at their risk. He was promptly told 'We were certainly quite entitled to insert them'[59] and equally promptly responded by seeking payment for the inclusion of this advertising matter at the end of his book. He was thereupon put in his place once more: 'Such a thing is unheard of in publishing.'[60] The Clarks, of course, continued to use this valuable means of advertising, which was targeted at their existing audience.

These additional arrows in the quiver of promotional strategy were cheap in financial terms, but valuable indeed in terms of the impact they could have.

The success and cost-effectiveness of the three chief methods of promoting books — by advertising, brochures and review copies — varied considerably, but these three strategies were each inter-related, and each indispensable. While it is impossible to quantify their effectiveness or exact impact on the profitability of the firm's publishing programme, it is certain that they were essential to the continuing vitality of T. & T. Clark.[61] Table 24 gathers together the financial data on these three main elements of the firm's promotional strategy in respect of those titles issued in the financial year 1895–96.

Table 24

Promotional expenditure on certain titles issued 1895–96						
Title	Total outlay 1895–96 borne by the Clarks	Advertising budget + % of outlay represented by this figure	Expenditure on prospectus etc + % of outlay represented by this figure	Expenditure on review copies + % of outlay represented by this figure	Total promotional expenditure + % of outlay represented by this figure	'Proportion of lists' contribution 1895–96
S. R. Driver *Deuteronomy*	£436 7*s*. 3*d*.	£25 2*s*. 1*d*. 5.75%	£6 0*s*. 5*d*. 1.37%	£21 11*s*. 0*d*. 4.93%	£52 13*s*. 6*d*. 12.07%	£3
G. F. Moore *Judges*	£295 6*s*. 9*d*.	£24 14*s*. 11*d*. 8.37%	No prospectus	£17 14*s*. 6*d*. 6.00%	£42 9*s*. 5*d*. 14.38%	£3
E. P. Gould *St. Mark*	£190 5*s*. 5*d*.	£24 14*s*. 11*d*. 13.00%	No prospectus	£12 6*s*. 10*d*. 6.48%	£37 1*s*. 9*d*. 19.49%	£3
W. Sanday *Romans*	£574 3*s*. 3*d*.	£27 14*s*. 11*d*. 4.83%	No prospectus	£22 5*s*. 0*d*. 3.87%	£49 19*s*. 11*d*. 8.7%	£3
G. P. Fisher *History of Christian Doctrine*	£208 9*s*. 5*d*.	£4 2*s*. 4*d*. 1.97%	£1 14*s*. 9*d*. 0.83%	£15 10*s*. 0*d*. 7.43%	£21 7*s*. 1*d*. 10.24%	£3
P. J. Gloag *Synoptic Gospels*	£93 8*s*. 4*d*.	£8 4*s*. 4*d*. 8.79%	8*s*. 7*d*. 0.45%	£8 14*s*. 0*d*. 9.31%	£17 6*s*. 11*d*. 18.56%	10*s*.
J. Crawford *Brotherhood of Mankind*	£81 14*s*. 11*d*. (shared by author)	£9 2*s*. 6*d*. 11.16%	15*s*. 0*d*. 0.91%	£7 12*s*. 0*d*. 9.29%	£17 9*s*. 6*d*. 21.37%	10*s*.
S. D. Salmond *Immortality*	£432 5*s*. 0*d*.	£14 11*s*. 2*d*. 3.36%	£1 19*s*. 2*d*. 0.45%	£21 1*s*. 0*d*. 4.86%	£37 11*s*. 4*d*. 8.69%	£3
C. J. Hefele *Councils of the Church (Vol 5)*	£168 19*s*. 6*d*.	£1 17*s*. 6*d*. 1.1%	£1 11*s*. 3*d*. 0.92%	£7 16*s*. 0*d*. 4.61%	£11 4*s*. 9*d*. 6.65%	£3
J. S. Candlish *Ephesians (Bible Class Handbooks)*	£68 2*s*. 7*d*.	3*s*. 7*d*. 0.25%	No prospectus	£3 15*s*. 10*d*. 5.56%	£3 19*s*. 5*d*. 5.82%	5*s*.
Thus, up to 21% of the total outlay in the first year of issue could be devoted to promotional expenditure. (This percentage excludes the 'Proportion of Lists' contribution.)						

Chapter 11
Distribution

If the firm were to benefit from the interest in their publications which the promotional strategy had created, it was essential that their distribution network be both efficient and cost-effective. Although in very special circumstances as we will see the Clarks sold direct to individuals, in general they distributed their publications through the trade, selling to British retail and wholesale outlets, and to foreign booksellers.

Sales to the trade

The Clarks would seem to have had no regular system of representation to the UK trade, most shops being informed of new Clark titles through the catalogue. From time to time however, the London trade and some of the Scottish booksellers were visited by a member of the firm. John M. Clark attempted to subscribe Newman Hall's *The Lord's Prayer* to booksellers in London in 1883, for example.[62] And the first part of S.D.F. Salmond's *Bible Class Primer* on *The Shorter Catechism* (1887) was 'shown round the trade in Edinburgh and Glasgow.'[63] Sales to retail outlets were usually considered 'firm'; there is no evidence that works were supplied on sale-or-return to any shops. In general, relationships with the retail outlets were good, and there seem to have been few serious problems with bankrupt or recalcitrant booksellers. When payment was long delayed, the Clarks did not hesitate to take action through the appropriate channels; R. Lindsay of Glasgow, for example, was, in 1879 threatened with action through the Trade Protection Society if he did not immediately remit the sum he owed.[64]

The Clarks, as well as supplying direct to English firms, also used the services of two London wholesalers, Simpkin, Marshall, and Hamilton, Adams. These firms both kept in stock a very full selection of Clark publications — in December 1895, for example, Hamilton, Adams had goods on hand to the value of £332 0*s.* 4*d.*, while Simpkin, Marshall's stock of Clark titles was valued at £291 6*s.* 5½*d.*[65] — this stock, it would seem, was still the Edinburgh firm's property.[66] The wholesalers were informed of new publications well in advance: the firm were in touch with Simpkin, Marshall about the forthcoming *Dictionary of the Bible* as early as January 1896, at the same time as the very first public announcement of the work was being sent to periodical editors.[67] The connection with the wholesalers was a very valuable one for the Clarks at least in terms of volume distribution. The following Table lists the value of sales, presumably after deduction of the wholesaler's discount, to the two London firms between 1881 and 1900.[68]

Table 25

Sales to the London wholesalers, 1881–1900		
Calendar Year	Sales to Simpkin Marshall	Sales to Hamilton Adams
1881 (June–Dec)	£699 5*s*. 0*d*.	£612 6*s*. 4*d*.
1882	£1,423 8*s*. 4*d*.	£1,179 11*s*. 7*d*.
1883	£1,429 16*s*. 10*d*.	£1,444 4*s*. 1*d*.
1884	£1,453 7*s*. 3*d*.	£1,431 16*s*. 9*d*.
1885	£1,447 7*s*. 2*d*.	£1,413 0*s*. 2½*d*.
1886	£1,483 12*s*. 6*d*.	£1,532 17*s*. 11*d*.
1887	£1,471 9*s*. 0½*d*.	£1,467 10*s*. 1½*d*.
1888	£1,416 11*s*. 8*d*.	£1,350 13*s*. 8*d*.
1889	£1,366 3*s*. 4*d*.	£1,515 11*s*. 11*d*.
1890	£1,720 8*s*. 10½*d*.	£1,489 0*s*. 7½*d*.
1891	£2,034 1*s*. 6½*d*.	£1,667 7*s*. 3½*d*.
1892	£2,266 10*s*. 3*d*.	£2,107 2*s*. 4½*d*.
1893	£1,946 0*s*. 5*d*.	£1,803 15*s*. 11*d*.
1894	£1,802 2*s*. 8½*d*.	£2,034 12*s*. 4½*d*.
1895	£2,124 0*s*. 3½*d*.	£2,248 1*s*. 6½*d*.
1896	£2,135 3*s*. 8*d*.	£2,414 5*s*. 10*d*.
1897	£2,539 6*s*. 9*d*.	£2,662 15*s*. 7½*d*.
1898	£2,822 19*s*. 9½*d*.	£2,922 5*s*. 1*d*.
1899	£3,090 14*s*. 8*d*.	£3,751 12*s*. 4*d*.
1900	£3,344 14*s*. 3*d*.	£3,418 3*s*. 10*d*.

These are important figures, showing as they do that, after a static period in the 1880s, the firm's sales through the wholesale outlets increased fairly consistently. This increase reflected the growth pattern of their total sales, which expanded in step with the development of publishing policy under John M. Clark over the last decade of the century.

Another wholesale firm was used by the Clarks on one occasion. The English distribution of the *Monthly Interpreter* was, as we have seen, entrusted to the firm of Kegan Paul, who also procured advertising for that journal.[69] There was some friction between the two firms on the question of territories. The Clarks had been willing to concede that Scottish customers who normally dealt with Kegan Paul should obtain their supplies of the *Monthly Interpreter* from them also; they expected that the English firm would reciprocate by permitting them to supply the journal to such English accounts as they were in the habit of servicing. Kegan Paul took issue with this, whereupon the Clarks retorted that such a reciprocal agreement was the only way forward. 'To act otherwise would surely be altogether one-sided especially as regards us who have all the risk.'[70] This somewhat unhappy partnership terminated after the demise of the *Monthly Interpreter*.

We have discussed fully in Chapter 6 the distribution of Clark titles through foreign publishers, who agreed to market an edition of a work in their country. The Clarks also sold to foreign booksellers, chiefly in Europe, North America, and the Colonies. Such sales could only be made, of course, if the bookseller were outwith the territory covered by a foreign publisher with whom the Clarks had an agreement in respect of the work in question. They had a good working relationship with many of these foreign booksellers, feeling free, for example, to send one of them some new titles which had not been requested, accompanied by the following note:

> Although we have no order from you for [the enclosed] we think you will readily dispose of them as they are both good works and suitable to your class of customers, and we hope to be favoured with a repeat at an early date.[71]

The general impression received, therefore, is of a reasonably effective distribution system handling Clark titles in increasing volume as the century drew to a close.

The terms on offer to UK retail booksellers were listed in the firm's trade catalogues, which itemised retail and trade prices for each title: in 1889, there was a discount of 25% on general publications, and 10% on subscription titles. By 1900, a 33⅓% discount seems to have been offered on general publications, subscription titles still carried a discount of 10%, and the limited number of net books were sold to the trade at a discount of 25%. A further 2½% discount was allowable on general publications, provided the account were settled within the six-month period in which the sale took place.[72] (Accounts were due to be paid half-yearly, by 1 February and 1 August.) Given that many booksellers sold to their customers at a discount of 25%, their profit must have been extremely meagre. Booksellers could elect to pay by bill accounts relating to general publications. (Bills could be dated at three months if the sum involved were between ten and thirty pounds, at four months if it were between thirty and fifty pounds, and at six months if it were over fifty pounds.) In addition, the 'odd book' system operated, twenty-five books being supplied for the price of twenty-four, or thirteen for the price of twelve and a half. The Clarks undertook to pay for the carriage of consignments of books as far as London.

They were opposed to any further special discounts, which they felt adversely affected both the title in question, and their trade in general. Consequently, as we have seen, they were not in favour of pre-publication special offers, considering that these caused 'trouble and unpleasantness' with those who claimed not to have heard of a work before publication.[73] Consequently, also, they were not in favour of remaindering. If in part this was because they felt that to sell off a poor-selling title at a reduced price was rather unfair to the author,[74] it was chiefly because they considered that remaindering had a detrimental effect on their reputation as successful publishers. Thus Thomas Clark wrote to George Matheson: 'I have a strong feeling against any work of my publishing being offered at a reduced price through the booksellers as it affects my other publications.'[75]

The firm was almost equally lacking in enthusiasm about net books. It has been noted that the *Dictionary of the Bible* was not issued under a net pricing arrangement, and very few nineteenth century Clark titles (only nine in 1901) were net books since, in their experience, 'Most of the Booksellers refuse [d] to stock [such books].'[76]

Whereas on general publications retailers were offered a discount of 25% or 33⅓% on the nominal retail price, plus an additional 2½% discount, presumably on the discounted price, if their accounts were settled within the six-month period in which the purchase was made, the wholesalers Hamilton, Adams and Simpkin, Marshall were supplied at a discount of 25% or 33⅓% plus an additional discount of 10%, again presumably on the discounted price. And whereas on subscription titles retailers were offered a flat rate 10% discount on the retail price, the wholesalers were supplied at a discount of 10% plus an additional 5%. In a very limited number of cases, the wholesalers seem to have been supplied at the same rate as the retailers; possibly these cases involved US publications, or certain works issued on commission. Presumably, the wholesalers supplied to the retail trade on the same terms as the Clarks did, and they would therefore have been left with a very small margin: in the case of general publications it would have been 7½% of 75% or 7½% of 66⅔% of the nominal retail price; in the case of subscription works it would have been 5% of 90% of the retail price.[77] The terms agreed with Kegan Paul for the distribution of the *Monthly Interpreter* departed from this norm. The magazine had a retail price of 1*s.* 0*d.* and a trade price of 8½*d.*, and on this the distributors claimed an additional 10% discount.[78] They were authorised to supply to 'bona fide exporters to Foreign countries, or the colonies', and to W.H. Smith at 8½*d.* plus 10% discount; in respect of copies supplied to these customers, Kegan Paul no doubt claimed an additional 10% discount for themselves.[79] On entering this agreement, the Clarks, while commenting that Kegan Paul's terms 'allow[ed] very little to the publisher' nevertheless considered that 'their name [might] be of service.'[80] In the long term, as we have seen, the agreement was profitable to neither party.

In general, the Clarks supplied colonial booksellers on the same terms as their UK customers. When a bookseller from elsewhere in the world wished to open an account, however, terms were usually laid down by the firm on an *ad hoc* basis, according to their estimate of the credit-worthiness of the customer, and of the volume of orders he seemed likely to send to Edinburgh. In assessing this second factor, the Clarks based their judgement largely on the degree of enthusiasm for their publications which was evinced by the bookseller. It is not clear which party paid for the shipping of goods: the bookseller had to cover the cost of the Consul's export certificate, where appropriate, plus the cost of packing cases.[81] Some examples of terms follow, listed in ascending order of generosity. C.F. Roper of New York was offered 10% on such subscription titles as the Clarks could supply him with (Scribners holding the franchise on the *Ante-Nicene Library* and the *St Augustine* series); on general publications he was promised 30% discount plus an additional 2½% for cash with order, a method of payment upon which the Edinburgh firm insisted in his case.[82] Wise, Coffin and Co. of Dunedin were offered 10% on subscription titles, and on general works 25% or 30% plus an additional 5% discount on settlement. The 'odd book' arrangement was to apply, and there was no pre-payment clause.[83] Rowsell and Hutchison of Toronto were offered identical terms, with the exception that the additional discount on general works was to be 10%.[84] On condition that they undertook to order more than one hundred pounds worth of books per year, more generous terms still were offered to the Toronto Willard Tract Depository. On subscription titles, they were to be allowed 10% discount plus a further 5%. On the firm's general titles, they were to be given a straight discount of 45% on the nominal retail price. It was to be understood that all outstanding sums had to be paid by 1 February and 1 August each year.[85] Very similar, although not quite so generous, terms were concluded with W.J. Gage of Toronto; again these were dependent upon a reasonable level of sales being maintained. Gage was to be allowed 10% plus a further 5% discount on subscription titles. On the firm's general titles, he was to be allowed a discount of 30% plus a further 10%, plus an additional 5% on the amount of his invoice if the remittance were sent immediately upon receipt of the goods. Gage was in fact receiving a discount of 30% plus 10% of 70% plus 5% (70% – 10% of 70%), the equivalent of a straight discount of 40.15%, somewhat less than the 45% discount allowed to the Willard Depository.[86]

A wide range of terms were therefore offered by the Clarks in their dealings with UK retails and wholesalers, and with foreign booksellers. The discounts offered and the margins remaining were presumably carefully calculated so that profits, albeit modest ones, would accrue.

Direct selling

It must have been a great temptation to the Clarks, servicing as they were a clearly-defined target audience with whom they had regular contact by means of direct-mail advertising, to eliminate the role of the middleman, and sell directly to their customers using parcel post. The threat from the booksellers of retaliation and boycott must have seemed less intimidating to highly-specialised publishers such as T. & T. Clark, who had very close links with the market they were serving, than to general publishers, whose success depended on maximising sales to a diffuse audience. It was a temptation which the Clarks managed to resist, out of a sense of loyalty to the trade, as well as from a realisation that such a course was, after all, in their own best interests. These two elements — loyalty to the trade and the firm's own interests — feature in a letter to B. Broomhall, who had asked for special concessions on Clark titles for Wesleyan local preachers:

> We have great difficulty in complying with your request — not because we are unwilling to assist Wesleyan Local Preachers in the way you indicate, but on account of the *Booksellers* through which we deal. They make their living by selling books, & the question arises, is it right to pass them over in this way. In almost every case where we have responded to similar requests, complications with the trade have followed.[87]

The Clarks no doubt realised that, if they sold direct, not only would they incur the wrath of the booksellers, but also they would be incessantly importuned by allegedly penniless students, priests and clergy all laying claim to greater discounts than were given to the trade.[88] And so direct selling remained the exception rather than the rule. The Clarks were never involved in door-to-door canvassing operations;[89] they claimed that they had 'very few private Accounts, & in nearly every case refer[red] private correspondents to local booksellers';[90] they were even reluctant to supply books at special rates to their authors, having found from experience that 'it [was] a most dangerous thing to give *special* terms even to the author of a book . . . as it [led] to endless complications with the Booksellers.'[91]

There were however, some exceptions to this rule. It is almost certain that the firm's subscription series would have been sold direct to the public as well as routed through the booksellers. And the Clarks were at least prepared to consider publishing an individual work on subscription in order to ensure that there was a sufficiently large market for it before going to press. When the viability of a translation of a work by Nebe was being discussed, they commented 'if it were published at all it must be by subscription ensuring a large number of purchasers beforehand';[92] this work would certainly have been sold direct to the subscribers.

There were, moreover, certain categories of purchaser to whom the Clarks were prepared to consider supplying direct at a discount. In the first place, works which were suitable for use as student texts were from time to time sold in bulk to college principals, because the Clarks considered that 'It [was] absolutely necessary with [their] class of books to give every consideration to Divinity Students (many of them being simply unable to give the regular price)'.[93] Divinity students would, after all, help to form the backbone of the firm's regular market once they had qualified; it was both wise and politic to encourage them in the habit of purchasing Clark books in their student years. Hence, provided stated quantities were ordered, individual volumes from the subscription series were supplied to college principals at the subscription prices, whereas the non-subscription price normally obtained in the case of such selective purchases.[94] Hence, too, general works were supplied direct to colleges, sometimes at considerable discounts and hence, as we noted earlier, the *Critical Review* was supplied to students for an annual subscription of 4*s*. 0*d*. as opposed to 6*s*. 0*d*.[95]

In the second place, certain libraries were supplied direct at a discount by the firm. Volumes of the *Ante-Nicene Library* were available on special terms to missionary libraries.[96] And another library, which had clearly requested a free grant of books, was told that if works were ordered from the catalogue (on the terms which would have been given by retail booksellers), the firm would 'add to [the order] as much as [they could] as a presentation to your library'; this was, in effect, another way of giving a discount.[97]

In the third place, works were sometimes supplied direct at a discount to denominational organisations. It was clearly the Clarks' practice to listen sympathetically to requests such as those from the Wesleyan local preachers, and to agree to meet them where possible.

Complications with booksellers could arise in such cases, sometimes because of indiscretions on the part of those receiving special terms; it has already been noted that, having been supplied with copies of the first volume of the *Dictionary of the Bible* at a reduced rate for the express purpose of selling it cheaply to Primitive Methodist ministers, T. Mitchell of the Primitive Methodist Book Room in London put the cat among the pigeons by circulating an advertisement to some Congregational and Baptist ministers offering the volume to them at the low price of 19*s.* 6*d.* Not surprisingly, the booksellers were up in arms.[98] A very complicated correspondence took place with Mitchell over the following two years regarding the supply of Clark publications to the Primitive Methodist Denomination at special terms. Mitchell had asked to be supplied with books for lay preacher's libraries at a discount of 50%. The Clarks explained that, because of the costings of their titles, this would be impossible. Instead, they proposed an elaborate scheme by which they would in effect be giving the Primitive Methodists a sizable discount without bringing the wrath of the Trade upon them. They promised to give Mitchell a donation which would vary in size according to the extent of his purchases. On orders worth up to fifty pounds, they would give a donation of 5% of the cost of the order. For purchases worth between fifty and one hundred pounds, the donation would amount to 7½%, while it would reach 10% in the case of more costly orders.[99] A year later, different, and even more complex terms were in operation, the Clarks giving discounts, plus a 10% donation in return for all orders. Clearly Mitchell had been buying extensively, for the 1900 letter begins 'We thank you most cordially for the kind interest you take in promoting the circulation of our publications,' and continues by stating that the Clarks were 'anxious to meet [his] wishes as far as it [was] in [their] power.' The discounts which were agreed were as follows: 10% + 5% on subscription titles, 30% + 10% on general publications, with 'odd books' at the increased rate of twenty-six for the price of twenty-four or thirteen for the price of twelve, and 21% discount on net books. All this was in addition to the 10% donation. Although in a sense such terms could be justified by the fact that the Primitive Methodist Bookroom was a retail outlet, it is clear that they could have caused considerable resentment among booksellers, especially since the discount was being passed on to the final purchasers in at least some cases, and it is small wonder that the Clarks concluded by stating 'We trust in the assurance contained in your letter that the terms will be kept strictly private.'[100]

In the fourth place, presumably where the firm felt there was a genuine need, and took pity on a correspondent, works were supplied direct to individual customers at a discount. We have seen for example that W.E. Adam was supplied with a copy of the first volume of the *Dictionary of the Bible* at a greatly reduced rate.

This direct selling involved the Clarks in much additional work, led to disputes with the Trade, and, since discounts frequently equalled those given to booksellers, produced little additional profit. Hence the firm's motivation for selling direct must have been based on their desire to be of service to the theological community, and to engender goodwill among the theological colleges and their students.

All publishers, but especially those who are known to be committed to a cause, find themselves inundated with requests for free grants of their publications. The Clarks were no exception, and very often they seem to have complied with requests which they considered reasonable. Apart from a desire to promote goodwill, the only possible motive for agreeing to supply publications free was a commitment to assist the spread of scholarship. And goodwill must be seen as a commodity of questionable value in those content to beg for, rather than to buy, one's publications. One example: a set of the *Ante-Nicene Library* was supplied, apparently at no cost, to the library of the London Tract Society in 1886.[101]

The Clarks' distribution system, though complicated, and made more so by their willingness to assist where possible those who requested free grants or books at reduced rates, seems to have operated with reasonable efficiency. Between 1895 and 1901, for example, the firm serviced accounts in 167 towns (40 in Scotland, 92 elsewhere in the UK, and 35 overseas), the number of accounts totalling 448 (139 in Scotland, 238 elsewhere in the UK, including 73 in London, and 71 overseas). Of these 448 accounts, 272 did less than £10 worth of business over the six years in question, but such small accounts were offset by some very large ones including those with Simpkin, Marshall and Hamilton, Adams.[102]

Part IV

Chapter 12
Overall profitability

There were those who assumed that T. & T. Clark was an immensely profitable concern. For example, George Adam Smith wrote with some bitterness to the Edinburgh map-publishers Bartholomew around the turn of the century that the Clarks were 'a rich firm' who had 'too long fattened upon poor ministers and scholars.'[1] There is no indication of what gave rise to this jaundiced comment. Clearly, however, T. & T. Clark's operation appeared to be a lucrative one. How accurate was this impression?

It is true that throughout their theological publishing programme the Clarks aimed with varying degrees of consistency at the higher point of success, but their business sense was too acute to permit neglect of financial imperatives. The *Stock and Sales Book — Individual Titles*[2] contains sufficient financial data for the four financial years beginning 1895–96 to enable an assessment of the profitability of individual categories of publication, and of the firm as a whole to be made.

The accounts for each financial year (which ran from July to June) contain two main sections. The first deals with the performance of the Clark list on a title-by-title basis, while the second presents a summary of income and outlay over the year in question. In this second section, on the credit side is detailed the sums realised by those titles which yielded a profit, and any other income the firm may have had. Set against this are the losses made by those titles which failed to break even, together with the firm's operational overheads. The total number of titles on the Clark list was 660 in 1895–96, 685 in 1896–97, 706 in 1897–98, and 720 in 1898–99.

The profitability of individual categories of publication

Appendix B contains a detailed analysis of the figures for 1896–97, broken down into the different categories of publication issued by the Clarks.[3] A comparison of the profitability of different categories can be made by applying a number of measures to each: in Appendix B, these measures are described and applied in the case of the figures for 1896–97. In fact, there was considerable variation in the comparative profitability of many of the categories from year to year. This, of course, is only to be expected; within a given year, several titles which were expensive but slow-selling, and therefore slow to break even might be issued in a given category; the same year might see a higher proportion than usual of steady, but not spectacularly selling back-list titles in the same category requiring reprinting. Given such conditions, the category in question was unlikely to perform well over that year.

The categories can, however, be very roughly ranked in descending order of profitability over the four years. These categories varied greatly in size; the fact that legal publications (39 titles in print in 1895–96) head the list does not imply that they contributed the largest sum to the firm's profits, simply that, given their size proportionate to the other categories, they performed best. The next most profitable works are the co-editions produced with Scribner, which were already reasonably profitable as a group despite the amount of investment required in the production of new titles. Next come the series containing works of British origin, and translations of Patristic work, and these are followed by, jointly, translations and miscellaneous theological works; the Clark's more overt financial cautiousness in the case of the latter category clearly did not pay off in terms of increasing profitability. Major reference works are next in descending order of profitability. This category includes a handful of titles, including the *Dictionary of the Bible*, which called for on-going, large-scale investment. Next come works of transatlantic origin, excluding co-editions, and last of all periodicals.

Despite the middle-ranking position of categories containing British, Patristic and European series, there is evidence that, taken as a whole the maturer series performed significantly better than the average. These included John Owen's *Works,* the *Bible Class Primers,* the *Ante-Nicene Library,* the *Library* of works by St Augustine, Calvin's *Works,* Meyer's *Commentaries,* the *Foreign Theological Library,* and Lange's *Commentaries.* An outlay on these series of £715 9*s.* 4*d.* in 1895–96 produced a profit of £1,092 19*s.* 11*d.*, a return of 152.76%. The following year, over which the general percentage return fell, saw an increase in this figure in respect of these series to 184%, while in 1896–97 they showed a return of 178%, and 165% in 1898–99.

Irrespective of category, the publishing of such series would therefore seem to have been more profitable than the rest of the Clarks' operation. It must be remembered, however, that these series were not only mature, having active back-lists, but also (with the exception of the *Bible Class Primers*) closed, requiring no investment on new titles: the high return is explained by these factors. These series, therefore, were the legacy of the past, which enabled the firm to lay the foundations of future prosperity by launching the titles which would ensure that business remained buoyant in the coming decades.

In assessing the profitability of works on the firm's lists, it is perhaps in the last analysis most satisfactory to cut across the categories, and conclude that, the inevitable and not infrequent exceptions apart, the profitability of works depended on the point in their life-cycle which they had reached. Some items on the Clark list were old and moribund. They had performed well over the years, but they reflected the thinking of a previous generation, and they were becoming increasingly unprofitable. At the other end of the spectrum, there were very new items, individual titles and series, which were demanding large investment to get them under way, but which had not yet established themselves in the market-place. It was the Clarks' hope that such works would become increasingly profitable. In the centre of the spectrum were the completed and well-established series, and thriving back-list titles from which the bulk of the profit was produced, profit which was used both to support the older titles towards a gracious demise, and to fund new investment. A publishing house is a vibrant organism: if it is well-managed, new shoots will develop into mature, self-supporting branches; inevitably, in time, these will become dead wood. The management challenge lies in anticipating what kind of publications must be undertaken if the list is still to be thriving in ten years' time.

Overall profitability of the firm

The accounts for the four financial years beginning 1895–96 also allow an assessment to be made of T. & T. Clark's overall profitability. Table 26 lists the total outlay, turnover, gross profit and percentage return on the firm's publishing over the four financial years beginning 1895–96. There was a decline in profitability between 1895–96 and 1897–98, and an upturn in 1898–99. Outlay mounted steadily throughout the first three years of the period, and fell back only slightly in 1898–99. Turnover did not increase in proportion to the outlay, while the gross profit fell steadily, until the spiral of decline was arrested in 1898–99. When the publishing strategy of the firm is taken into account, it is clear that the downward spiral is to be explained in terms of growing pains rather than terminal decline. 1896–97 and 1897–98 saw major investment in new titles, investment which, by 1898–99 had begun to bear fruit. Table 27 highlights the Clarks' commitment to new titles, listing outlay, turnover and profit/loss on new publications issued over the four financial years beginning 1895–96.

It is also possible to take overheads into account, and to assess the Clarks' return on their capital investment for the three financial years beginning 1896–97. (In the case of 1895–96, the value of stock-in-hand cannot be estimated, and the level of return yielded that year cannot therefore be accurately calculated.) The calculations are set out in Table 28. (The data on which the figures for total annual overheads, and total prior outlay on stock-in-hand are based are itemised in Appendix C.)

The Clarks' return on their investment over the three years was therefore 4.94%, 2.83% and 4.98%. This series of figures confirms that the downward spiral had been arrested. The investment which was to lay the foundation of the firm's future prosperity, investment which seriously affected profitability over 1896–97 and 1897–98, was beginning to pay off. And in a decade which saw the bank rate rise from 2.5% to 5%, and the return on government consols, nominally fixed at 2.75%, vary between 2.8% and 2.5%,[5] this level of return may be said to have been reasonable, if certainly not spectacular.

Table 26

Profitability of T. & T. Clark's entire programme, excluding overheads 1895–96 — 1898–99				
	1895–96	1896–97	1897–98	1898–99
Total outlay	£6,800 13*s*. 6*d*.	£7,145 10*s*. 4*d*.	£9,968 16*s*. 3*d*.	£9,903 7*s*. 9*d*.
Total turnover	£11,042 3*s*. 7*d*.	£10,036 8*s*. 4*d*.	£12,152 4*s*. 0*d*.	£13,104 16*s*. 9*d*.
Total profit (excluding overheads)	£4,241 10*s*. 1*d*.	£2,890 18*s*. 0*d*.	£2,183 7*s*. 9*d*.	£3,201 9*s*. 0*d*.
% return	62.36%	40.45%	21.9%	32.32%

Table 27

Investment in new titles 1895–96 — 1898–99				
	1895–96	1896–97	1897–98	1898–99
Number of new titles	12	24	23	18
Investment in new titles	£3,148 1*s*. 5*d*.	£2,995 11*s*. 7*d*.	£5,526 8*s*. 6*d*.	£4,885 6*s*. 11*d*.
Turnover of new titles	£3,571 16*s*. 5*d*.	£2,376 16*s*. 8*d*.	£4,241 6*s*. 3*d*.	£4,022 13*s*. 5*d*.
Profit/deficit on new titles	+£423 15*s*. 0*d*.	−£618 14*s*. 11*d*.	−£1,285 2*s*. 3*d*.	−£862 13*s*. 6*d*.

Table 28

Overall Profitability of T. & T. Clark			
	1896–97	1897–98	1898–99
(a) Total Annual Overheads	£1,286 3*s*. 8*d*.	£1,175 17*s*. 7*d*.	£1,323 13*s*. 1*d*.
(b) Total Annual Outlay on Publications	£7,145 10*s*. 4*d*.	£9,968 16*s*. 3*d*.	£9,903 7*s*. 9*d*.
(c) Total Annual Income from Sales	£10,036 8*s*. 4*d*.	£12,152 4*s*. 0*d*.	£13,104 16*s*. 9*d*.
(d) Total Prior Outlay on Stock in hand at start of year	£24,021 15*s*. 7*d*.	£24,393 4*s*. 2*d*.	£26,451 0*s*. 10*d*.
(e) Gross Profit (c−[a+b])	£1,604 14*s*. 4*d*.	£1,007 10*s*. 2*d*.	£1,877 15*s*. 11*d*.
(f) Total Capital Committed (a+b+d)*	£32,453 9*s*. 7*d*.	£35,537 18*s*. 0*d*.	£37,678 1*s*. 8*d*.
Return on capital $\frac{c \times 100}{f}$%	4.94%	2.83%	4.98%

* The premises at 38 George Street were owned personally by Sir Thomas Clark;[4] an annual rental features among the firm's overheads, this rental being paid to Sir Thomas. Consequently the capital invested in the building is not taken into account in these calculations.

We noted that, if a publishing house is to continue thriving, its principals must accurately anticipate future demand. The Clarks' foresight was indeed accurate. The moderately progressive works in which they invested guaranteed the continuing development of the firm, even if the overall returns were not spectacular. But aiming as they did so often at the higher point of success, they trod that path directed as much by a sense of mission as by business imperatives. Had you put it to John Maurice Clark that his firm seemed to be a living denial of Christ's assertion that one cannot serve both God and mammon, he would probably have retorted that he was serving God and God alone, and that any financial success which accrued was to be interpreted as being a reward for faithful service.

Epilogue

The New Century

1901–1923

The Influence of James Hastings

The firm continued to thrive during the first few years of the new century. New volumes appeared in both the *International* series, new series were begun, and general theological publishing continued. But without question, the Clarks' major pre-occupation was the stream of publications expertly edited by James Hastings. The *Dictionary of the Bible* was followed by the *Dictionary of Christ and the Gospels* (2 vols, 1906 and 1908), a completely new one-volume *Dictionary of the Bible* (1909), *The Great Texts of the Bible* (20 vols plus index volume, 1910–19), *The Greater Men and Women of the Bible* (6 vols, 1913–16) and the *Dictionary of the Apostolic Church* (2 vols, 1915 and 1918). Three works appeared in the *Great Christian Doctrines* series, on *Prayer* (1915), *Faith* (1919), and *Peace* (1922), while six volumes of children's sermons extracted from the *Expository Times* were issued as *The Children's Great Texts of the Bible* in 1920 and 1921. And the *Expository Times* itself continued to appear.

But Hastings' major undertaking was the *Encyclopaedia of Religion and Ethics,* to which an international team of 886 scholars contributed. Work began on the *Encyclopaedia* in 1902: six years later the first volume was published, and by 1916 eight more had appeared. After delays caused by the War, the remaining three volumes were issued in 1918, 1920 and 1921, and an index volume, drawn up to Hastings' own design, appeared posthumously in 1926.

This was the crowning achievement of the Hastings/Clark partnership. 'It has been an arduous undertaking for us,' wrote John Maurice Clark immediately before the publication of the final volume, 'but I am very proud of it, and am thankful that I have been spared to see its completion.'[1]

The scale of the Clarks' commitment to Hastings' projects, and conversely, the central role which those projects played in T. & T. Clark's development can be illustrated statistically by examining the firm's trading and royalty accounts and sales figures. For example, in the financial year 1915–16, literary outlay totalled £8,323 17*s*. 11½*d*., of which more than half, £4,592 5*s*. 0*d*. was accounted for by Hastings' titles.[2] Again, in financial year 1922–23, for which particularly detailed figures are available, out of a total trading income of £18,521 17*s*. 8¾*d*., sales of the following Hastings titles contributed £7,115 5*s*. 0¼*d*.:

Expository Times	£1,734 5*s*. 6*d*.
Encyclopaedia of Religion and Ethics	£2,372 9*s*. 0¼*d*.
Dictionary of the Apostolic Church	£1,260 4*s*. 6*d*.
Dictionary of Christ and the Gospels	£210 12*s*. 7*d*.
Dictionary of the Bible	£11 13*s*. 7*d*.
Children's Great Texts of the Bible	£533 18*s*. 7*d*.
Great Texts of the Bible	£271 12*s*. 11*d*.
Greater Men and Women of the Bible	£720 8*s*. 4*d*.

Most of these titles were reprinted and continued to sell for many decades, some into the third quarter of the twentieth century. The *Encyclopaedia of Religion and Ethics,* for example, was still selling in batches of fifty to the Standard Literature Company of India in the 1980s.

The royalty accounts also emphasise the centrality of the Hastings canon to the Clarks. He seems to have received 7½% on all the works he edited, although during his lifetime this was frequently augmented by ex-gratia payments. In the financial year 1922–23, when royalties paid in respect of sales of all other Clark titles totalled just £550 1*s*. 6½*d*., Hastings' executors received £1,366 17*s*. 4*d*. Even in 1928–29, six years after his death, they received £949 9*s*. 5¼*d*. whereas total royalties to all other authors amounted to £1,045 8*s*. 3*d*. At least until the 1940s, his works contributed several hundred pounds each year to his estate.[3]

Sales figures of Hastings' works, where they have been preserved, are also impressive. Table 29 lists total sales in the UK and American markets of the *Dictionary of the Bible* up to 1910, and up to 1920.[4]

Table 29

Dictionary of the Bible – Sales				
	Sales to June 1910		Sales July 1910–June 1920	
	UK	US	UK	US
Volume 1	15,677	18,582	3,525	5,129
Volume 2	16,573	17,838	2,383	5,340
Volume 3	16,177	17,077	2,440	5,651
Volume 4	15,907	16,232	2,511	5,866
Extra vol.	12,362	7,882	2,658	6,349
Total	76,696	77,611	13,517	28,335

Possibly Hastings' most enduring contribution, albeit that its longevity is the result of successive editors maintaining the high standards he set, is the

Expository Times. Hastings was succeeded by his son and daughter Edward and Ann; C. Leslie Mitton became editor in 1964, and held the office until 1976, when the present editor, Cyril S. Rodd took over. Under these editors, the *Expository Times* has kept the name of T. & T. Clark regularly before the eyes of potential customers in a context of academic excellence. And more than this, it has been the backbone of the firm's theology list, ensuring a regular flow of income even through the most difficult years, when total income declined significantly. Table 30 lists the proportion of total income contributed by the journal in eleven representative financial years. Full costings for the *Expository Times* have been preserved from 1950–51 — 1954–55, and these appear in Table 31. The return on investment generated by the journal, at least in these years in the 1950s, was not so large as the return yielded by the firm as a whole. But the *Expository Times* was a steady and reliable source of income.

Table 30

Contribution of the Expository Times to total trading income.			
Year	Total trading income	Income generated by *Expository Times* (including advertising revenue)	% of income generated by *Expository Times*
1921–1922	£22,611 14*s.* 1*d.*	£2,120 17*s.* 9½*d.*	9.37%
1926–1927	£18,065 0*s.* 5½*d.*	£2,175 19*s.* 5*d.*	12.04%
1931–1932	£10,375 1*s.* 6½*d.*	£2,435 6*s.* 1*d.*	23.47%
1936–1937	£9,957 12*s.* 1¾*d.*	£2,463 8*s.* 9*d.*	24.73%
1941–1942	£9,524 11*s.* 5¼*d.*	£2,730 5*s.* 0½*d.*	28.66%
1946–1947	£17,675 3*s.* 11½*d.*	£3,942 13*s.* 1½*d.*	22.3%
1951–1952	£28,148 3*s.* 10*d.*	£5,054 19*s.* 3*d.*	17.95%
1956–1957	£38,742 3*s.* 6*d.*	£6,660 17*s.* 9*d.*	17.19%
1961–1962	£59,133 6*s.* 7*d.*	£10,200 7*s.* 8*d.*	17.24%
1966–1967	£77,414 13*s.* 7*d.*	£14,148 12*s.* 10*d.*	18.27%
1971–1972	£85,979.70	£17,662.30	20.54%

Hastings' contribution to the financial success of T. & T. Clark in the early twentieth century can thus be demonstrated statistically. But his greatest contribution to the firm, and one as enduring as it is inestimable, was the influence of his work on the prestige of the imprint.

This is not to say that every project Hastings suggested was taken up enthusiastically by John Maurice Clark. From Hastings' restless mind there flowed a constant stream of proposals for new dictionaries and series. One reason for his superlative editorial achievement was an almost obsessive perfectionism; this same obsessiveness seems to have driven him to classify and categorise the whole corpus of theological and biblical knowledge. All of his proposals were doubtless of theological value, but only some were commercially

Table 31

Expository Times: Return on investment 1950–51 — 1954–55*					
	1950–51	1951–52	1952–53	1953–54	1954–55
Outlay on *Expository Times*					
Production expenses	£2,107	£2,571	£2,638	£2,770	£2,792
Literary expenses	£672	£764	£772	£772	£772
Share of overheads†	£781	£933	£920	£977	£975
Total	£3,560	£4,268	£4,330	£4,519	£4,539
Receipts from *Expository Times*, including advertising income	£4,226	£5,055	£5,199	£5,398	£5,629
% Return on investment	18.7%	18.4%	20.06%	19.45%	24.01%

* Based on calculations done by T.G.R.D. Clark in 1956
† 18% of the fixed overheads were assigned to the *Expository Times* on a fixed time basis.

viable, and it must have called for all John Maurice's reserves of tact to decline those which were not without offending Hastings. All his proposals were discussed in detail before being accepted or declined, and in some cases, the opinion of Scribners was also sought before a final decision was reached.

In the spring of 1910, Thomas George Clark visited the United States to visit Clark authors and customers, and to negotiate with Scribners. He reported back to John Maurice on the American firm's reaction to some of Hastings' ideas:

> In regard to Hastings' schemes, I find all of them more than doubtful of their success. The only ones which appeal to them at all are *The Names and Places of the Bible, The Lord's Prayer, & Sermon on the Mount.* He [presumably Charles Scribner II] looks (and all agree), on the *Lesser Texts* as hopeless. *The Ten Commandments & Seven Words* equally so.
>
> *God's Great Gifts* series they greatly hesitate about, and the *Pastor* Series equally: but they were most emphatic about the *Lesser Texts.*[5]

John Maurice Clark's last years in the firm

Keeping this large publishing programme on course was no small challenge for the principals of such a small firm, and after the turn of the century, John Maurice Clark found himself under increasing strain owing to the weight of his civic and business commitments. His health broke down the spring of 1909, and to recuperate he travelled to Ceylon, where he was a director of the Labugama Rubber and Tea Company. His son Thomas Clark joined the firm, becoming a Partner in 1911, but the pressures were increased by the Great War, which had a devastating effect upon the publishing industry. Staff and paper were in short supply, and the economy in crisis. Both Thomas Clark and Thomas George Clark were away from George Street for the duration of the War, the latter working for a government ministry.

A further blow came in the autumn of 1918, when Thomas George announced his intention of resigning from the firm. Writing to John Maurice on 9 November 1918, he began 'I don't know that you will be surprised to receive this letter, somehow I believe not.' The War had brought many changes, affecting both himself and his family, and now that his ministry job was coming to an end a decision about the future had to be taken. One of his sons had opted for a career in the Marines, the other, young Thomas George, who had been injured at the 1915 Gretna rail disaster and who was later to join the firm, preferred the prospect of outdoor life to office routine, and of himself he claimed 'I . . . know quite well that I could never settle down to office life and its monotony after the interesting and varied work of the last four years.' Consequently he had decided to move south with the family, and study agriculture.

> This of course means that I must give up my partnership at 38 and this I regret both for sentimental reasons, believe me although you have often twitted me of having no strong feelings of that kind, but I can assure you they are there strongly. Also because it breaks connection with George Street where I have had so many happy days.

He added, it would seem in anticipation of criticism from John Maurice, 'I am not afraid of hard work provided it is congenial.'

This was a great blow to John Maurice. A pencil draft of his deeply moving response has been preserved, dated 15 November 1918. It is an understanding and sympathetic letter; the last phrase of the first sentence: 'I was hoping you would have looked in at "38" so that we might talk over things' was changed to the more gentle (but possibly slightly patronising) 'so that we might have a little talk over things.' The letter reveals both the pressure that John Maurice had been labouring under, and the sense of betrayal that he felt at being abandoned by his brother.

He began, not by going to the heart of the matter, but by describing the intense difficulties he was facing. The post-War influenza epidemic was raging, and all but two of the staff were off sick. 'Tom does admirably, but of course he is new to much of the work.' As for himself, he spoke of 'this awful strain' which would only be relieved by 'the return of the invalids.' Then he addressed the matter in hand:

> Many thanks for your kind letter. Your decision is a great shock to me, even if I sometimes feared from things you said that it might come to this. Of course, I cannot but agree that if, as you say, you find work at 38 "monotonous" and not congenial then there is nothing more to be said, especially as it is clear that we must all work far harder now than we did before the War . . .
>
> Nevertheless, I feel heartbroken at the prospect of your not only leaving the business, but leaving Edinburgh. It seems such a collapse from the happy times of old when we were all together. But I must not say more, as I don't want to hurt you too.

The withdrawal of Thomas George's capital at that point would be a 'serious matter', but he hoped that the solicitors would be able to 'straighten things out'. And then one final sentence:

> No-one will ever know what the strain of those four & a half years has meant to me, but whatever happens my conscience is clear that in the interests of all concerned I never spared myself in any [illegible] to save the business.

Thomas George thanked John Maurice for this letter 'which I am sure you meant to be kindly', and continued

> I can assure you that in many ways the thought of severing with 38 hurts deep when I think of it, but I am convinced that my decision is right. One cannot help their nature, and I am sure you will get on pleasantly and successfully with the help of Tom who I am glad to know is settling down so well to civil life once more.[6]

The financial arrangements for Thomas George's withdrawal from the partnership were completed by the spring of 1919.

Despite having the help of the young Thomas Clark, John Maurice did not experience much easing of the pressures he was facing. Two years later, in February 1921 his health broke down again, and suffering according to his doctors from 'nervous exhaustion through overwork' he was despatched to Mentone in the south of France to recuperate.[7] In a moving comment, William Robertson Nicoll, whose health was also precarious, described himself and Clark as victims of the War, suffering because of their tireless commitment to their work and to the national interest.[8]

The firm's accounts reflect the very difficult trading conditions which were experienced in the years surrounding the Great War. (Appendix D contains a Table which summarises these accounts from 1911–12 until 1989.) Income from sales climbed to a peak of £26,631 7*s.* 7½*d.* in 1912–13; each of the subsequent five financial years saw an ever-increasing decline in the level of sales, which had fallen to £11,889 17*s.* 0½*d.* by 1917–18. Thereafter sales rose over the next three financial years, reaching £26,674 2*s.* 7*d.* by 1920–21, but a serious decline followed, and not until 1951–52 did sales again top £25,000. The level of investment also dropped in the years up to 1917–18, from a peak of £22,475 17*s.* 11¾*d.* in 1913–14 to £9,433 2*s.* 7½*d.* The annual percentage return on investment including overheads actually increased over that period, from 14.94% in 1913–14 to 26.04% in 1917–18, but of course in the later years the percentage was of a much smaller sum. 1918–19 saw a return of only 2.31%; income from sales was £18,765 1*s.* 3½*d.* while outlay was £18,340 9*s.* 4½*d.* But in that year James Hastings received royalty payments for both 1917–18 and 1918–19, a total of £2,242 19*s.* 6*d.* Between then and 1921–22, the return on investment was less than 7%.

In June 1921, the year in which the firm celebrated its centenary, John Maurice described to Nicoll the economic difficulties against which the firm was contending, hoping that he might be prepared to discuss the issue in the *British Weekly*. 'The continual high cost of production', he wrote, 'especially for books of a technical nature like most of what we publish, and with much Hebrew or Greek typography, is very disconcerting.' There had been complaints about the high prices of certain Clark titles, and indeed, some people who had standing orders for the *International Critical Commentary* had refused to accept the recently-published volumes on *Job* and *Galatians* because they considered them to be over-priced. But according to Clark, the two books between them cost almost four thousand pounds to produce. And the price of the *Galatians* title, thirty-five shillings, was 'really far below the cost of production per copy.' 'This is not "business",' Clark continued, 'but we feared that a higher price would simply kill the book, and so we decided to face a substantial loss, in the interests of the Series as a whole.' Commenting on the state of the theological market in general he acknowledged 'how hard it must be for many ministers to buy books at present, even at moderate prices', but he asserted 'the fact remains that it is now impossible to issue scholarly Works at anything like the prices ruling in pre-war times, and in the interests of scholarship that is greatly be regretted.' He urged that, just as substantial fees were paid for medical or legal advice, so 'a fair price should not be grudged for expert literary advice in Theology or Philosophy and other sciences.'[9]

Nicoll, although he did not raise the matter in the *British Weekly,* was in full agreement. 'The problems presented to publishers just now are more difficult than they have ever been in my time, which runs back over forty years.'[10] He was, however, sanguine about the future prospects for the industry, and continued 'I think, however, there will be a reaction in this also, and I take rather a hopeful view.' But it must have been with great sadness that John Maurice Clark spent the last days of his working life wrestling with such apparently intractable economic problems.

Neither Nicoll nor Clark were to live to see any upturn in business. John Maurice retired from the firm in 1923, and died on 27 May 1924 at his home at 17 Rothesay Terrace, Edinburgh. The death certificate gives the cause of death as 'carcinoma of stomach and liver'. His movable estate in the UK and overseas totalled £139,270 9*s.* 11*d.*, which was widely invested.

1923–1930

Sir Thomas Clark as sole Partner

In 1921 John Maurice Clark had written: 'I am very thankful that I have my eldest son as my Partner and successor',[11] and on his retirement that son, Thomas Clark, who upon his father's death the following year was to inherit his knighthood, took over as head of the firm and sole partner. His brother, John Maurice junior, was briefly involved in the business.

The difficult trading conditions did not immediately improve, and the firm passed through a period of stagnation in the 1920s and 30s. The high wave of achievement initiated jointly by John Maurice Clark and James Hastings was not sustained following the death of the former. The vision of forward growth had faltered, and only the legacy of the past maintained the firm's solvency.

Sir Thomas had an interest in theological matters, and was involved in Lady Glenorchy's Church of which he was a member, but he lacked both his father's passionate commitment to the advance of theology and, it must be said, his shrewd business acumen. Sir Thomas was not short of capital, theologians and churchmen on both sides of the Atlantic held the firm in the highest esteem, and theological publishing has often proved buoyant during economic recession, as more people have been prompted to ask metaphysical questions. The momentum could have been regained much earlier than it was had the young Thomas Clark shared his father's vision and adventurousness.

The accounts illustrate the problems which the firm faced in the 1920s and 30s. From 1920–21 onwards, with the exception of a couple of years when there was a modest temporary upturn, sales declined year by year, reaching a low of £8,943 16*s*. 5*d*. in 1932–33, and thereafter remaining virtually static for the next decade. For the most part, investment fell in tandem with declining sales. At the end of one financial year in the 1920s, 1927–28, the Trading Account showed a loss. Outlay exceeded income by £513 16*s*. 4¼*d*. During the 1930s, a Trading Account loss was shown at the end of seven financial years: the greatest loss was one of £2,574 5*s*. 2½*d*. in 1934–35. It may well be the case that this outlay reflected necessary investment in such major works as Karl Barth's *Church Dogmatics,* works which were to restore the fortunes of the firm in later years. (The levels of loss on the Trading Account were exacerbated by the fact that between 1930–31 and 1944–45 Thomas George Clark's salary was included there rather than in the Profit and Loss Account, where Partners' salaries normally feature. Initially, Thomas George received £600 per annum. This was increased to £750 from 1936–37.) From 1928–29 onwards, the value of book-stock in hand is shown in the Trading Account as noted at the beginning of Appendix D. Stock valuation (an annual depreciation factor of 25% was built-in) fluctuated between five and eight thousand pounds from 1928–29 — 1937–38. Thereafter the basis of stock valuation agreed with the Inland Revenue was adjusted, and the value of stock fell to much healthier levels, reaching £1,930 0*s*. 0*d*. in 1941–42.

In 1930, Sir Thomas Clark had been joined in partnership by his cousin Thomas George Clark, son of John M. Clark's brother Thomas George, and grandson of the first Sir Thomas Clark.[12] This was the Thomas George Clark who, having suffered a thigh injury at Gretna and having been advised by his doctors that a sedentary life was not for him, had accompanied his father to agricultural college, feeling unable to 'face the life of an office'.[13] However, by 1927 the slump in farming had forced him to change his mind; he began work at 38 George Street that year, and found it sufficiently fufilling to enter into partnership three years later. He remained in the firm until his retirement in 1983; Sir Thomas had retired eighteen years previously. What agriculture had lost had, to theological publishing, been pure gain.

1930–1956

Two Thomas Clarks at the helm

The young Thomas George Clark's first love was farming; unlike many of the earlier partners he did not have a deep personal interest in theology, although according to his son Ramsay Clark, 'while not a "religious" religious man he had a quiet faith in religion and indeed in himself.' However, he held a great respect for the integrity of the firm and its past history, and wanted to carry it on in adherence to the basic ethics of its founders. To achieve this goal, he brought to bear his considerable practical business acumen, coupled with total commitment.

It is Ramsay Clark's perception that when his father joined the firm 'it was in quite a parlous condition', and that 'quietly over the years he brought it up.' And from the early 1940s, this perception is borne out by the accounts: sales rose slowly but steadily year by year from £9,524 11*s*. 5¼*d*. in 1941–42 to £44,439 18*s*. 5*d*. in 1955–56. Only in 1952–53 and 1954–55 were there temporary downturns in sales. Investment also rose from £9,132 5*s*. 9*d*. in 1941–42 to £31,037 13*s*. 0½*d*. in 1955–56. Return on investment averaged 30.5%. However, the value of bookstock in hand as a percentage of outlay also increased.

In retrospect, the turning point was reached in 1936, although there was no immediate impact upon the Trading Account. For it was in that year that the first volume of Karl Barth's massive *Church Dogmatics* was published. This major work by arguably the most significant theologian of the twentieth century was to appear in translation in fourteen volumes between 1936 and 1969, an index volume following eight years later. The team of translators was led by G.W. Bromiley and T.F. Torrance. This project marked a return to the visionary publishing of the 1890s, and it was to pay great dividends both economically and in increasing the prestige of the imprint. It is difficult to exaggerate the importance to the firm of the *Church Dogmatics,* yet there was a time in the early 1930s when it seemed that the Clarks would not secure the rights to it. It would appear that only Thomas George's perseverance brought it safely into the Clark fold.

In 1956, the two Thomases were joined by Thomas George's son, T.G. Ramsay D. Clark, who was completing training in Edinburgh as a Chartered Accountant; his presence was to benefit the firm's accountancy as much as his father's was benefitting its organisational efficiency.

1956–1973

Two decades of growth

Over these decades, the firm's theological publishing prospered. Further volumes of Barth's *Dogmatics* were issued, the *Expository Times* increased its readership, and a revision of some volumes in the *International Critical Commentary* series was launched.

The Trading Accounts demonstrate that the general tendency throughout the years 1956–1973 was towards growth. There were a few erratic results, however. After rising steadily from £38,742 3*s*. 6*d*. in 1956–57 to £45,023 9*s*. 10*d*. in 1959–60, sales leaped to £60,719 13*s*. 9*d*. in 1960–61. Over the next five financial years sales levels lay between £59,000 and £66,000, before 1966–67 saw another leap to £77,414 13*s*. 7*d*. This level was sustained the following year; there were two leaner years, and then sales rose again to £78,853.27 in 1970–71 and £85,979.70 in 1972–73, the last full year of the

Partnership. Investment levels remained high, and there was a tendency towards overstocking in the late fifties and early sixties. Nevertheless, the return on investment on the Trading Account averaged 32.5% over the sixteen years 1956–57 – 1971–72.

Table 32

Estimated costings of three volumes of Barth's Dogmatics*			
	Vol III pt 2 (1960) 55/-	Vol III pt 3 (1961) 50/-	Vol III, pt 4 (1961) 55/-
Length of run	4000	4000	4000
Production costs Composition		£910 10*s*. 0*d*.	£1,237 17*s*. 6*d*.
Author's corrections	£140 0*s*. 0*d*.	£120 0*s*. 0*d*.	£150 0*s*. 0*d*.
Machining	£363 6*s*. 3*d*.	£296 9*s*. 3*d*.	£408 4*s*. 9*d*.
Paper	£556 8*s*. 0*d*.	£454 15*s*. 0*d*.	£585 0*s*. 0*d*.
Binding	£524 0*s*. 0*d*.	£496 0*s*. 0*d*.	£544 0*s*. 0*d*.
Dust wrapper	£26 0*s*. 0*d*.	£26 0*s*. 0*d*.	£27 0*s*. 0*d*.
Binders' brasses	£10 0*s*. 0*d*.	£10 0*s*. 0*d*.	£10 0*s*. 0*d*.
Miscellaneous	£25 0*s*. 0*d*.	£25 0*s*. 0*d*.	£25 0*s*. 0*d*.
Advertising	£80 0*s*. 0*d*.	£80 0*s*. 0*d*.	£80 0*s*. 0*d*.
Sub-Total (A)	£2,843 9*s*. 3*d*.	£2,418 14*s*. 3*d*.	£3,067 2*s*. 3*d*.
Clarks overheads (25%)	£710 17*s*. 4*d*.	£604 13*s*. 7*d*.	£766 15*s*. 7*d*.
Literary expenses Translator's fee	£432 0*s*. 0*d*.	£351 0*s*. 0*d*.	£485 0*s*. 0*d*.
Editor's fee	£216 0*s*. 0*d*.	£176 0*s*. 0*d*.	£242 0*s*. 0*d*.
Royalty of 7½% of published price	£825 0*s*. 0*d*.	£750 0*s*. 0*d*.	£825 0*s*. 0*d*.
Sub-Total (B)	£2,183 17*s*. 4*d*.	£1,881 13*s*. 7*d*.	£2,318 15*s*. 7*d*.
Total: A+B	£5,027 6*s*. 7*d*.	£4,300 7*s*. 10*d*.	£5,385 17*s*. 10*d*.
Unit cost	£1 5*s*. 2*d*.	£1 1*s*. 6*d*.	£1 6*s*. 11*d*.
Income per copy sold after 33.3% trade discount	£1 16*s*. 8*d*.	£1 13*s*. 4*d*.	£1 16*s*. 8*d*.
% return	45.69%	55.03%	36.22%
* Based on the Estimates and Costs Book 27 May 1957 – February 1961			

Table 33

Cost of reprinting Thayer's Greek-English Lexicon of the New Testament (1958) 55/-	
Length of run	2000
Production costs	
Alterations to plates	£1 14*s*. 6*d*.
Machining	£527 18*s*. 11*d*.
Paper	£500 15*s*. 4*d*.
Binding	£550 0*s*. 0*d*.
Advertising	£20 0*s*. 0*d*.
Sub-Total A	£1,600 8*s*. 9*d*.
Clark's overheads 25%	£400 2*s*. 2*d*.
Literary expenses:	
Royalty (apparently 9%)	£990 0*s*. 0*d*.
Sub-Total B	£1,390 2*s*. 2*d*.
Total: A+B	£2,990 10*s*. 11*d*.
Unit cost	£1 9*s*. 1*d*.
Income per copy sold after 33.3% trade discount	£1 16*s*. 8*d*.
% return	26.07

Table 32, based on an *Estimates and Costs Book* from the late 1950s, shows estimated costings for three volumes of Barth's *Dogmatics*. These costings apparently include all overheads, but later costings of other works include a charge of 10% of the production costs in respect of 'management overheads', in addition to the 25% added to costs here in respect of general overheads. The level of return expected from these volumes is reasonable — 45. 69%, 55.03% and 36.22% — but it would no doubt be several years before the entire printings sold out. Table 33 shows the costs of reprinting Thayer's *Greek/English Lexicon* in 1958. Surprisingly, given that no composition costs were involved, the retail price at which the Clarks felt they could sell the work would give a return of only 26.07%.

38 George Street in 1959

The current T. & T. Clark office manageress, Mrs Jacqueline Milne, Ramsay Clark's PA for many years, and office manageress for Geoffrey Green, remembers the Dickensian quality of life at 38 George Street in 1959, when she joined the firm as a teenager. The office fittings were very old; all the staff with one exception shared an enormous table. The exception was the manager, the white-haired Douglas Clunie, who ruled over his domain from a tall desk in the corner, at which he would run his finger up and down ledger columns, mentally computing with an incredible rapidity. It was Clunie who interviewed Jacqueline Milne, taking the nervous sixteen-year-old into a back room, and subjecting her to standard arithmetic and geography tests. She was to find herself in a male-dominated environment, sharing the downstairs office with Clunie and two other long-serving members of staff, David Swanson and George Randle. There were only two other women in the office: the partners' secretary, Mrs Frances Walker who had served the firm for many years and Ms Violet Hanley.

Although in 1959 the office was open in the evenings and on Saturdays, work in those days before computers and photocopiers and fax machines proceeded at a gentler rate than it does today. Book-keeping procedures were time-consuming; distribution was handled in-house, endless packages of *Expository Times* being despatched each month; Edinburgh mail was delivered by hand; yet according to Jacqueline Milne's recollections there was always time to complete the day's work before the working day drew to its close. New titles were few and far between: it was a major event when finished copies of a completely new work were received.

There was a family atmosphere in '38', a mutual commitment between partners and staff. If you had personal problems of any kind you could go to them, and they would try to help. Apparently at one point attempts were made from outside to unionise the firm's staff. It was allegedly the most socialistically-minded member of staff who declared to a visiting union official: 'What do we need with a union here? If we've any difficulties we just go to Ramsay and he sorts them out!' These warm staff relationships did not stop at the office door; there were, for example marvellous annual Christmas staff dinners at the Roxburgh Hotel.

By 1959, Sir Thomas did not have much active involvement in the business, but he visited the office periodically. When this imposing figure strode in the front door you had to stand up, and intone 'Good morning, Sir Thomas!' The upstairs offices could be entered from a side door; occasionally you would hear footsteps on the staircase as some old wartime comrade of Sir Thomas's, down on his luck, came in hope of receiving a subvention. Sir Thomas's son, John Douglas, also worked in the office at this time. Jacqueline Milne recalls Thomas George as 'a marvellous old man': a meticulous bookkeeper, he had boundless enthusiasm for the business, and for his own personal interests in ornithology and botany. Ramsay Clark had joined the firm three years before, and was bringing his particular skills to bear. One perhaps unanticipated task which he was assigned was the setting-up and maintenance of the three first-floor window boxes. The frontispiece, taken probably in the late 1950s, shows these in full bloom.

'38' was therefore something of a time capsule by 1959. But already there had been changes, and these were to accelerate.

Continuity and change

Looking back over the history of the firm, Ramsay Clark is conscious that the policies and practices implemented in 38 George Street when he was there in the 1950s and 60s were in many respects a continuation of those implemented in the 1890s by John Maurice Clark.

There had, however, been some significant changes. In the first place, whereas the first Sir Thomas and John Maurice had had at least a working knowledge of theology, Ramsay Clark and his father never attempted to give the impression that they were to any great extent theologically inclined; rather, they were both motivated by a desire to keep the business going, and to preserve the ethical approach to publishing which had characterised the founders. However, although they were thus more guided by business imperatives than by a direct desire to further theology, the end result was the same: they sought to publish solid, first-rate academic volumes which would give a fair return on the capital employed. This meant, of course, that they were even more dependent on guidance from their theologically-trained authors and editors. But although these men had no formal contracts with the firm, they were always ready with advice and guidance, and helped sift the 'tremendous number' of unsolicited manuscripts received by the firm. From amongst the many brilliant scholars and fine Christians he worked with, Ramsay Clark speaks especially highly of Charles Cranfield, editor of the New Testament works in the I.C.C. revision. 'I think of all the men I have met during my publishing career he stands out in my memory as a remarkable Christian and scholar, a truly great and kindly man in his own quiet and unassuming fashion.' Another gifted scholar who stands out in Ramsay Clark's memory is J. A. Emerton, Old Testament editor of the I.C.C. revision. Combining their own training and experience with specialist advice from this loose team, Thomas George and Ramsay were able to keep the firm on course.

Secondly, the firm's publishing had become truly interdenominational. Clark authors had, of course, always come from a wide range of church backgrounds, but this policy was broadened still further. Works by Roman Catholic authors were published, and the Catholic magazine *Concilium,* founded in 1965, was issued from 38 George Street.

A third change was the great increase in importance of the overseas market. By the mid-1970s, exports accounted for 74.8% of book sales, and 48.66% of *Expository Times* subscriptions. Overall, exports accounted for 61.75% of turnover. By 1990, although the firm remained aware of the potential of the global market, exports generated a much lower percentage of turnover owing to the increasing strength of British sales.

The United States remained a major customer. When Scribners stopped handling Clark works, they were sold through Zondervan, Kregel, Eerdmans, and various other American firms, no one of them being responsible for the whole range of Clark titles. The Clarks sold direct to these firms in editions of 50–100 copies, or even in sheets. Owing to pressure of work, Thomas George and Ramsay found little time to visit theological publishers in America to market their titles; however, because of the reputation of the imprint, representatives of these companies visited them in George Street seeking American rights in new works. These bulk orders, dependent very much upon the enthusiasms of individuals within the American firms, had fallen off by the end of the 1970s and to counter this decline, The Seabury Press of New York was appointed in 1983 as T. & T. Clark's main US agent. In 1985, this firm was succeeded by Fortress Press, which represented Clark titles in the States for two years until it was merged with the Augsburg Press, at which point the Edinburgh firm withdrew its agency status. There had been constant friction between these agents and other American firms who wish to sell Clark titles at cut prices. From 1987, T. & T. Clark has done its own marketing and distribution in the United States, working through Books International Incorporated.

Besides America, in Ramsay Clark's time the firm had extensive markets in the Continent of Europe, Australia, India and Japan. Many of these markets too were secured not in response to initiatives from George Street, but as a result of theological publishers from these countries visiting Edinburgh. There were frequent visitors from India and Japan, for example. Ramsay Clark recalls the horror he felt when, on leaving 36 George Street, two Japanese publishers turned to bow to him while unconsciously edging backwards towards the steep staircase. Having visions of two valued customers losing their dignity if not their lives in a painfully rapid descent to the pavement beneath, he felt compelled to interrupt their solemn *sayonaras*. The international market has remained important to T. & T. Clark, and the firm has representation throughout most of Europe.

But there are many more similarities in policy and practice between the 1890s and the 1950s and 60s than there are differences.

As we have seen, the emphasis remained on academic theology. From the mid-twentieth century onwards, there has been a resurgence of religious and theological publishing in the United Kingdom, and several firms such as Inter-Varsity Press and Banner of Truth Trust have published evangelical theological titles aimed at a general readership. It might have been expected that, with their firm's evangelical tradition, this is a path which the Clarks would have followed. However, they made it a matter of policy to limit their output to academic works for a specialist audience. Their promotion and distribution system was tailored to the exigencies of this market. Further, their limited capital as a partnership did not permit a rapid diversification. Capital had to be earmarked for reprints of old works, some of which could be very costly because, since the plates had become worn from printing many impressions, the type had to be reset. The Clarks therefore proceeded with great caution in the fifties and sixties: sometimes only a couple of new titles were published in any one year, and certainly no more than ten.

However, despite the emphasis on business imperatives, the Clarks remained willing, as their predecessors had been, to publish some manifestly uneconomic works. Ramsay Clark explains their policy: 'We accepted that some titles we were asked to publish hadn't a hope of succeeding, but we were prepared to take a loss on them if they were of particular interest, or met a specific need, or if, indeed we were asked by one of our favourite editors (and by favourite I probably also mean most lucrative!) to do a work for a friend, or because he thought it should be done. But we were only prepared to take a modest loss. And the work had to be of exceptional intrinsic value.' This policy is identical to that followed by John Maurice.

Since very few titles were published each year, the firm depended, as it always had done, on the strength of the backlist. Older titles for which there was still a demand were reprinted, or issued in revised editions. The *Encyclopaedia of Religion and Ethics* for example, was reprinted in the fifties and again in the seventies. Ramsay Clark admits that at one point, the firm was getting the name of being a reprint house, but considers that those levelling this criticism were not fully aware of the major importance of the works in question. Nevertheless, having such a reputation did not augur well for the future prosperity of the firm.

The problems faced in the fifties and sixties were also remarkably similar to those encountered in the 1890s. There were arguments with booksellers over discounts. And occasional difficulties with authors: there is a delightful story of a group of over-committed scholars being virtually imprisoned by Ramsay Clark, his patience exhausted, to ensure that the arguments over a certain long-delayed project were settled and agreement reached between them; only then were they released. Also, authors occasionally complained about levels of remuneration. Clark's royalties have always been adequate, and high-selling authors were frequently given ex-gratia payments in addition. But Ramsay Clark has noticed a change of emphasis since the 1950s, when the Clark imprint was perhaps less vulnerable to competition. In the 1950s scholars were delighted to be asked to write for the firm; the honour was reward in itself, and the royalty almost an incidental extra. Now the emphasis is much more on the royalty, and much less on the honour. There were problems also with piracy in the United States. The Clarks spent a great deal of time arguing with American firms over rights in their books. The original editions of volumes in the *International Critical Commentary* series were going out of copyright in America, and American versions were produced by, among others, Zondervan. It was partly to overcome this problem that the revision of the I.C.C. was undertaken.

The firm's marketing and distribution strategies had changed little in sixty years. Works were promoted by advertising, and by circularising catalogues and brochures, while sales were made through academic and stockholding booksellers, and by direct mail to personal customers and university and college departments. The Clarks used the same firms for printing and binding their works: for printing chiefly Morrison and Gibb, but also Oxford University Press, Aberdeen University Press and, until their demise, R. & R. Clark (no relation), and for binding Hunter and Foulis.

The Clarks' involvement in trade affairs continued. Between 1908 and 1911, John Maurice Clark was President of the Edinburgh Booksellers Society Ltd. (which had been founded as The Society of Booksellers and Stationers of Edinburgh, Leith and Suburbs on 17 December 1792; it assumed its present designation in 1879.) Sir Thomas Clark presided over the same body between 1940 and 1943, and since that year the Treasurership of the Society has been in the hands of Clarks – Thomas George's until 1973, and subsequently Ramsay's.

T. & T. Clark was, in Ramsay's time as in John Maurice's, a small operation. When Ramsay joined the firm, there were, besides the partners, only five members of staff including the packer. Ramsay acknowledges that the firm 'always relied enormously on the members of its staff, and we had I suppose you could call it a family relationship with them, which thank goodness continued all my working life, and I still go in and see them, and it's very pleasant.' By the early 1970s, the staff had increased to fifteen.

Very possibly, after the Second World War, there should have been less continuity, more changes to prepare the firm for future growth. It is easy to sympathise with the partners' cautious approach to investment, but without investment there can be no growth. It is impossible to avoid the conclusion that, by the late 1960s, the firm was placing over-much reliance on a backlist which could not indefinitely sustain its existence. New titles were appearing, but not in sufficient number to sustain the firm's reputation as a prestigious and vibrant concern, and to lay down the backlist of the future. Had it not been for the two Clarks' decision in 1973 to join with John Bartholomew and Son, a merger which, with the advantage of the subsequent taxation relief, allowed much greater investment, the future of T. & T. Clark would have been less buoyant. It survived, but by all accounts it was a close-run thing.

By the late 1960s, Thomas George and Ramsay Clark had become concerned about the firm's future, on economic grounds, and especially since there seemed to be no likely candidate to succeed them in Partnership. They had had close links with the Edinburgh map-publishing firm John Bartholomew and Son, which had been founded in 1826, just five years after the first Thomas Clark set up shop. Bartholomews was in 1970 still a family firm, with John, Robert and Peter Bartholomew the sixth generation in active management,[14] along with David Ross Stewart as Managing Director. The Clarks approached the Bartholomews who agreed to take over T. & T. Clark with effect from 1 April 1973, the goodwill element being fixed at £40,000. The property at 36 and 38 George Street was not included in the deal. It had been owned personally by Sir Thomas Clark, who had inherited it from John Maurice, and before the takeover he sold it to Thomas George and Ramsay, who thereafter rented it to the firm. (Sir Thomas, who had retired in 1965, had no financial interest in the future of the firm, but he backed the takeover arrangements wholeheartedly.) The tax implications made the continuance of the Partnership impossible after the takeover: on 15 June 1973 T. & T. Clark became a Private Limited Company, with Ramsay Clark as Managing Director. Thereafter, the Bartholomews were represented on the Clark Board by Peter Bartholomew and David Ross Stewart. The former, on his death, was succeeded on the Board by David Cunningham. Following the subsequent takeovers, there was also a token representative from the respective parent companies. Apropos of the takeover, a long-standing friend of Ramsay Clark, Douglas Foulis of Hunter and Foulis the Edinburgh book binders, wrote the following wryly humorous note to him on 16 March 1973:

> Dear Ramsay,
> Just to say that I'm delighted that you have decided to combine with Bartholomews. It must be right and it is a courageous step to take — altho' the alternatives were not many. But it strengthens the home-based Scottish publishing of you both, & that couldn't be healthier!
> Good luck — and I'm sure it will be more enjoyable for more of the time than before — altho' very annoying for a bit of the time!

1973 onwards

Management regimes

Since 1973 there have been five distinct management regimes in the history of T. & T. Clark, each to date briefer than the preceding one.

Until 1980, the Bartholomew Group was independent, and the Clarks were given complete freedom in the way they ran the business.

A significant event took place on 3 March 1975. Geoffrey Green, who now owns the firm, joined T. & T. Clark. Green, having graduated from Edinburgh University in 1970, had gone to the United States to undertake doctoral research in New York and Boston on the history of American theatre. He married in America, and returned to Edinburgh with his wife late in 1974 to see his thesis through its final stages, and sit his oral examination. He fully intended returning to the States, where there were several possible openings for him in teaching, but seeking a temporary job in Edinburgh, he contacted various firms, not all of which were involved in publishing. However the Bartholomews, with whom he was in touch, knew that the Clarks were seeking to appoint an academic to the firm. In fact, they had anticipated appointing someone with theological training, but when Geoffrey Green met Ramsay Clark, he was offered a job, and joined the firm some weeks later.

Like Ramsay Clark before him, Geoffrey Green learned publishing from the bottom up. He began by packing books and addressing envelopes, all the time learning his trade from Ramsay Clark and from the lectures at Napier College which he attended for two and a half days each week, lectures covering everything from editing to ink technology. Gradually he became involved in all aspects of editing, marketing and production. He brought his own vision and enthusiasm to bear, and so successful was he that when Ramsay Clark retired in 1987, Geoffrey Green became Managing Director, having been Publishing Director since 1977.

For all that he entered the trade almost by chance, he is easy both with the creative and with the management aspects of publishing and has his own clearly-focused ideas of where the firm should be going, and the determination to see these ideas become reality. He and the Clarks managed to keep the business afloat in the turbulent waters of the mid-70s economic slump; Ramsay Clark feels that it survived the recession 'better than most firms'. Its survival was due to the undoubted strength of the backlist, to the additional investment which being part of the Bartholomew Group made possible, and also to the impact which the arrival of Geoffrey Green had on publishing development. Because the stock had been moved to Bartholomew's warehouse, less space was required and the Clarks sold 38 George Street, and moved the firm into 36.

In 1980, the Group was the target of a successful £2 million takeover bid by Reader's Digest. Prior to this, Reader's Digest, although it had many international branches issuing the magazine, had no subsidiaries involved in publishing of a different nature. A new chief executive, Jack O'Hara, who was, in fact, a Scot from Dundee, launched the firm into a programme of acquisition, taking over companies involved in different aspects of publishing. A high level of organisation enabled Reader's Digest to run their own operation with great efficiency, but they were simply not equipped to own a conglomerate. Geared to sell magazines, and fast-selling books and records, they did not understand the publishing scene from the point of view of a small, specialist firm. For executives to whom a short print-run was 25,000, and a title which remained in print after six months virtually a failure, the approach to publishing at 36 George Street seemed positively Dickensian. Although the Clarks and Geoffrey Green found these executives charming to work with, their management style was highly bureaucratic, demanding the completion of endless forms, standardised to deal with international periodical publishing, but hardly with the issue of specialist academic theology. During this time, Ramsay Clark had to devote three or four evenings per week to doing nothing other than wrestling with this torrent of paperwork. The link with Reader's Digest was, however, financially a fruitful one for T. & T. Clark. The Edinburgh firm was asked to produce two popular titles on behalf of Reader's Digest: *You and your rights in Scotland,* and *The Family Guide to the Bible.* Between them, these works generated £90,000 of income.

Thomas George Clark retired in 1983; two years later, as business was improving, and more space was required, T. & T. Clark moved across George Street to number 59.

Also around that time, Jack O'Hara fell out of favour with the Trustees of Reader's Digest, and resigned. Several of the subsidiaries purchased under O'Hara's regime were disposed of, and David Ross Stewart, Managing Director of the Bartholomew Group, was instructed to find a buyer for the Group. Times Books, publishers of the *Times Atlas,* were Bartholomew's biggest customer. It seemed that a merger between the Group and Times Books, which was owned by News International, was appropriate, and negotiations were entered into. As from 1 February 1985 the Bartholomew Group became part of News International, itself a subsidiary of NewsCorp, the Australian holding company.

And so began the third management regime since 1973. For four years, Bartholomew and T. & T. Clark were left largely to manage their own affairs by the parent company, since their activities were so different from those in the News International mainstream. Ramsay Clark retired in 1987.

By 1988, News International owned 40% of the voting shares of the Scottish publishers Collins, founded in 1819. Later in 1989 they launched a successful bid to acquire the firm. At this time, they already owned the American publishers Harper and Row. The two firms were combined as HarperCollins, which is wholly owned by the Australian parent company. HarperCollins was given control of all the book publishing interests of NewsCorp. These moves had serious implications for the Bartholomew firm since both Collins and Bartholomews had important map publishing interests: thereafter all cartographic staff were centred in Edinburgh. T. & T. Clark was left in comparative freedom. Its specialist output required approaches quite different from those used by Collins in mass-distributing to the popular market.

This fourth management regime was to last only two years. By 1991, due to financial constraints, NewsCorp was eager to sell a limited number of its subsidiaries. Attempts had been made to integrate T. & T. Clark with HarperCollins in London (a Scottish office was to have been retained), but it became clear that there was little in common between the style of publishing which Geoffrey Green wished to develop and that favoured by HarperCollins executives, even for their Academic Division. When this integration failed to materialise, T. & T. Clark, because of its geographical remoteness from London became a prime candidate for sale, and a management buy-out, led by Geoffrey Green, was successfully floated.

Throughout the period from 1973 until 1990 annual outlay has increased steadily with one or two fluctuations from £83,254 in 1973–74 to £647,246 in 1988–89. Turnover has also increased steadily, from £123,189 in 1973–74 to £745,364 in 1988–89. Both these increases are much greater than the rate of inflation. The relationship between outlay and turnover has not remained constant, however, and there has therefore been considerable variation in the annual rate of return. A loss was shown at the end of three financial years. In one case, 1981–82, the loss was a significant 22.33% of investment, due both to a large increase in outlay, and a modest decrease in income over the previous year. The volatility of these figures is, however, more apparent than actual, since it arises from changes in accounting and stock valuation policies. The average percentage return generated in the years for which we have figures for the full twelve months was 15.33%.

New developments

There have been a number of significant developments since 1973 in the structure of T. & T. Clark's operations. Prior to that time, ultimate responsibility for editing, promotion, marketing and book-keeping lay with the partners, who were assisted by a non-professional staff. By the mid-1980s, the firm had been transformed into a more conventional publishing company.

There are now four small, but discrete departments operating within the firm, each professionally manned: a sales department, a production department, a publishing department, subdivided into theology and legal publishing, and a book-keeping department. There are no in-house editors. A substantial amount of editing is done by Geoffrey Green; other editorial work is contracted out to freelancers. Whereas in the 1970s the firm had its own warehouse, Clark titles are now distributed by Edinburgh University Press. In 1991, there were twelve staff based at 59 George Street.

Following the takeover by Bartholomew, a sales representative had been assigned to T. & T. Clark in an attempt to increase sales through retail outlets. This development, however, proved to be relatively ineffective: the specialist market at which the firm's books were targeted was, as ever, best reached through circularising catalogues, brochures and prospectuses direct to customers, to theological colleges, and to stock-holding and academic booksellers, who were already almost as familiar with Clark titles as the Clarks themselves. However, competition increased throughout the seventies, and it became clear that the prestige of the imprint alone was no longer sufficient to sustain the firm through recession to the next period of growth. It was in response to this situation that a sales department with a staff initially of one, later of two, was established at George Street. The main emphasis remains on circularising catalogues and brochures, but there is now a much more sophisticated approach to the production and distribution of these. Members of the sales department also visit key accounts every six months, and organise publicity and launching ceremonies for significant new titles.

Running alongside the developments in structure were developments in strategy as Ramsay Clark and Geoffrey Green laid down the firm's future course.

The first stage was to revitalise the firm's theology publishing. The Directors recognised that T. & T. Clark could not survive indefinitely on its backlist, and that restoring an active publishing programme would involve considerable risks, especially as none of them were theologically trained. A start was made by accelerating the publication of works which were in progress, but which, for one reason or another, had been delayed. The index volume to Barth's *Dogmatics* had been in the Edinburgh office for some years awaiting publication. Geoffrey Green was responsible for activating this project, and the volume appeared in 1977. He also encouraged progress on the remaining volumes of the new English edition of Emil Schürer's *History of the Jewish People in the Age of Jesus Christ,* which was being revised and edited by Geza Vermes, Fergus Millar, and Matthew Black. The three volumes appeared in four parts in 1973, 1979, 1986 and 1987. Later, he was deeply involved in the multi-volume work *The Glory of the Lord* by Hans Urs von Balthasar, which appeared between 1982 and 1991. Another major project in the 1980s was the appearance of the first volumes of *The Aramaic Bible,* edited by Martin McNamara, the first translation into English of all the extant Targums. There was also a major initiative to produce a new seven-volume *Encyclopaedia* to replace the *Encyclopaedia of Religion and Ethics.* This had been discussed at length by Ramsay Clark with Macmillan in London in the early 1970s; and the idea was again mooted by Geoffrey Green before being eventually abandoned when a similar American work began to appear.

By the early 1980s, therefore, ten or twelve new theology works were appearing each year. In addition, T. & T. Clark's turnover was increased by carrying more titles of American origin, purchased in small British editions.

Year by year more titles were added. Geoffrey Green seeks to maintain balance in each season's list, balance in terms of theological viewpoint, so that no one perspective is represented to the exclusion of others, and a balance in terms of the origin of the works on the list: roughly one-third in any list will be of British origin, one-third will be translations, and one-third imports from the United States.

A major project which arose from the Reader's Digest connection was the *Family Guide to the Bible,* a work aimed at a popular market which T. & T. Clark produced for Reader's Digest in New York. This appeared in the early 1980s, and generated £40,000, a massive cash injection which helped finance other projects such as the von Balthasar series, which required an investment of more than £100,000.

The second stage in re-thinking the firm's strategy involved deciding whether T. & T. Clark should diversify, or go all-out to become market leaders in theology publishing. There is no doubt that T. & T. Clark could have reached this position. The market is a global one, and whereas popular religious publishing firms multiplied in the two decades after 1970, the number of houses in Britain and the UK which were prepared to issue serious academic works actually declined. The fact that T. & T. Clark is inundated each year with 250 unsolicited manuscripts, many of a high quality, is perhaps indicative of the small number of outlets available for work of this kind. To join the market leaders like S.C.M. Press and Cambridge University Press and similar American publishers, the firm's output would have had to increase to between sixty and one hundred titles per year. This could have been done. But T. & T. Clark had, in Geoffrey Green's opinion, reached a plateau in the development of its theology publishing; if the firm were to continue expanding in that direction, it would have to break through into a bigger league, doubling staff, doubling investment, doubling risk. It was decided not to pursue that goal.

Instead, with Ramsay Clark's and David Ross Stewart's wholehearted encouragement, Geoffrey Green turned his attention to legal publishing. There was a time when the firm's law publishing had dwindled almost to nothing. Since the nineteenth century, the *Session Cases* had been issued by the Clarks; for a period the publication of this series was taken over by Douglas Grant of Oliver and Boyd, but on the demise of that firm, T. & T. Clark again assumed responsibility for it.

In the early 1980s, the firm was asked to develop for Reader's Digest a popular legal work, *You and Your Rights in Scotland.* This project took two years to complete. What was in effect a separate company was established to handle the work, and twenty people were employed on short-term contracts to undertake it. The project was valuable in several respects. It generated £50,000 for the firm. It brought Geoffrey Green, who headed up the operation, into contact with many Scottish lawyers and legal academics, and thus helped him in his development of the legal side of the firm's business. A law publishing department was set up at 59 George Street with Elizabeth Thompson as publisher, and in the winter of 1988–89, T. & T. Clark acquired William Hodge, a Glasgow law publishing firm, and took over all of Hodge's active titles, including the *Scottish Law Directory*.

In 1990 the Law Department began to issue the monthly *Times Law Reports,* an indexed collection of the reports of legal cases which have appeared in *The Times* newspaper. Previous publication of these in collected form had ceased in the 1950s. The rights to issue the *Law Reports* was obtained for the firm by virtue of its connection with Times Books, but these rights were retained after the management buy-out.

Towards the future

Looking ahead, Geoffrey Green has two goals. Firstly, he aims to establish T. & T. Clark's legal publishing on a sound basis. Whereas the market for the firm's theological output is international in scope, the market for works on Scots law is geographically limited. And the competition is intense. Clark's chief competitors are Butterworth (part of the Reid Group) and Green (linked to Sweet and Maxwell, and ultimately part of International Thompson). But Geoffrey Green feels that T. & T. Clark can find a niche for itself producing books aimed at the Scottish legal community, and leavening this local output with some national and international law publishing.

Secondly, when the firm's legal publishing has been established, he would like to develop some other area of academic publishing, perhaps in a field closely related to theology and law, such as philosophy, or medieval history. His aim, however, is not to turn T. & T. Clark into yet another monolithic academic publishing house, but rather to create within the firm what he calls 'a constellation' of specialist businesses, linked more by the character of these — by the way in which they publish and sell their books — than by the subjects they specialise in.

The staff at 59 George Street are very much behind the new regime, revelling in the freedom from the multinationals which T. & T. Clark has won. The certainty that he had their support was a crucial factor in persuading Geoffrey Green to proceed with the buy-out.

Looking back over the history of the firm, and over his own experiences in it, Ramsay Clark accepts (and Geoffrey Green agrees) that the Clark form of publishing will never make anyone rich. He has found working for the firm abundantly satisfying, if thoroughly aggravating at times; for him the greatest reward has been the realisation 'that you've probably left a great deal of worth which will no doubt be looked at and thought about and quoted from for many years to come.'

For the future, he feels that if T. & T. Clark is 'given half a chance in this day and age of take-overs and skulduggery and general mayhem, then it's got a future. And a very good future too.'

Appendices

Appendix A

MacNiven and Wallace, Edinburgh

MacNiven and Wallace, an Edinburgh bookselling firm which ventured briefly into publishing, was established in 1878. The *Bookseller* records that following the dissolution of the partnership of MacLaren and MacNiven, John MacNiven had taken into partnership one Alexander D.L. Wallace, who like MacNiven himself, had been an old apprentice of John MacLaren.[1] The new business had its address at 144 Princes Street, and traded as MacNiven and Wallace.

Beginning in 1879, the young firm, 'ambitious to overstep the old borders, did a little tentative publishing.'[2] In fact, a fairly wide range of works was issued, chiefly in the following series:

Bible Class Primers
Cabinet of Biography
Evangelical Classics
Evangelical Succession Lectures
Household Library of Exposition
Jewel Poets
St Giles Lectures

The firm had the good fortune to appoint as literary adviser the rising William Robertson Nicoll, who at that stage was still Free Church Minister in Kelso.[3] In 1881, the *Bookseller* paid quiet tribute to their output: 'They have published very few books at present, but those which they have issued are not only marked by the soundness of their literary judgement, but by the taste displayed in the selection of paper, print and binding.[4]

In 1882, the expanding firm took over John MacLaren and Son, the partnership established by MacLaren in 1878 upon the dissolution of his previous one with MacNiven, and moved to 132 Princes Street.[5] Although the firm continued its bookselling operation, the publishing experiment seems to have virtually come to an end in 1884. The reason for this is not clear, although *The Publishers' Circular* claimed it was simply because the partners found 'that the retail trade and the library required all their energies and attention.'[6] When the firm's publishing activities ceased two of the successful series were transferred to other publishers, the *Bible Class Primers* to T. & T. Clark,[7] and the *Household Library of Exposition* to Hodder and Stoughton.[8] Some individual titles also migrated to other houses; for example Louisa Gray's *Mine*

Own People went to Nelson, and a *Life of Carlyle* by Robertson Nicoll's brother Henry went to Ward Lock, who issued it in 1885.

MacNiven and Wallace did continue to publish some works. 'They say they have now given up publishing, except on "commission".'[9] As well as publishing on commission they acted as Hodder's Scottish agents, certainly for the *British Weekly*; they issued *The Theological Review and Free Church College Quarterly* (which also bore Hodder's imprint: T. & T. Clark were later to take over this work as *The Critical Review*);[10] and they published the annual *Scottish Church and University Almanac.*[11]

Appendix B

The profitability of each category of publication, 1896–97

Clark publications fall into eight main categories which, for the most part, correspond to those discussed in Part II. These are:

Category A	Series of completely British origin, and translations Patristic works
Category B	Translations, including series such as the *Foreign Theological Library*
Category C	Works of transatlantic origin, excluding co-editions
Category D	Co-editions produced with Scribner
Category E	Periodicals
Category F	Major reference works requiring large investment
Category G	Miscellaneous theological works
Category H	Legal publications

The profitability of each of these categories is analysed in Table 34 which is based on the *Stock and Sales Book — Individual Titles*.[1,2]

The compilation of the Table was somewhat complicated by the fact that the *Stock and Sales Book* deals with most of the Clark series for accounting purposes as individual items. It was therefore impossible to calculate a separate profit or loss figure for each title in the series. Where a given category contained both individual titles, and series listed as individual items, it was necessary, in order to reach meaningful conclusions, to itemise data for individual titles and series separately. This process adds considerably to the complexity of the Table which, for each category, contains the following sections:

(Profit)

(a) The total number of profit-making items, excluding series counted as one item. The limited number of works which exactly broke even making neither profit or loss, including those on which there was no sale and no expenditure over the year in question are included here.

(b) The total number of profit-making series counted as one item.

(c) The total number of profit-making lines, including series counted as one item (a + b).

(d) The total outlay on profit-making items, excluding series counted as one item.

(e) The turnover on profit-making items, excluding series counted as one item (d + f).

(f) The total profit on profit-making items, excluding series counted as one item.

(g) The average profit per profit-making item, excluding series counted as one item (f/a).

(h) The outlay on profit-making series counted as one item.

(i) The turnover on profit-making series counted as one item (h + j).

(j) The profit on profit-making series counted as one item.

(k) The total outlay on all profit-making lines (d + h).

(l) The total profit on all profit-making lines (f + j).

(m) The total turnover on all profit-making lines (e + i).

(Loss)

(n) The total number of loss-making items, excluding series counted as one item.

(o) The total number of loss-making series counted as one item.

(p) The total number of loss-making lines, including series counted as one item (n + o).

(q) The total outlay on loss-making items, excluding series counted as one item.

(r) The turnover on loss-making items, excluding series counted as one item (q - s).

(s) The total loss on loss-making items, excluding series counted as one item.

(t) The average loss per loss-making item, excluding series counted as one item (s/n).

(u) The outlay on loss-making series counted as one item.

(v) The turnover on loss-making series counted as one item (u - w).

(w) The loss on loss-making series counted as one item.

(x) The total outlay on all loss-making lines (q + u).

(y) The total loss on all loss-making lines (s + w).

(z) The total turnover on all loss-making lines (r + v).

(Synthesis)

(aa) Total number of items in the category, excluding series counted as one item (a + n).

(ab) The total number of items in the category (excluding series counted as one item) expressed as a percentage of the grand total of items (excluding series counted as one item).

(ac) The total number of lines in each category, including series counted as one item (c + p).

(ad) The number of items (excluding series counted as one item) in the category to make a profit expressed as a percentage of the total number of items (excluding series counted as one item) in the category ($\frac{a \times 100}{aa}$).

(ae) The average outlay per item in the category (excluding series counted as one item) ($\frac{d + q}{aa}$).

(af) The average turnover per item in the category (excluding series counted as one item) ($\frac{e + r}{aa}$).

(ag) The total outlay on the category (k + x).

(ah) The total profit on the category (l−y). This figure is arrived at by subtracting the total loss on loss-making items from the total profit on profit-making items. As the notes accompanying the Table indicate, the firm's profit on trading before deduction of overheads was slightly greater than the sum total of the profits realised by the different categories. This is because of various other sources of income such as incoming royalties and, notably, the commission earned on sales of the annual volumes of *Session Cases* which the Clarks published. Since they appear to have borne no risk in respect of these volumes, merely receiving a commission of 7½%, the *Session Cases* are not included in Category H.[3]

(ai) The profit realised by the category expressed as a percentage of the total profit.

(aj) The percentage return on investment on the category over the year in question ($\frac{ah \times 100}{ag}$).

(ak) The average profit per item in the category (excluding series counted as one item) ($\frac{f - s}{aa}$).

Based on the data in Table 34, the profitability of each category can be assessed according to six criteria:

I) The average profit per profit-making item: as a rule of thumb it can be said that the higher this is the more profitable the category.

II) The average loss per loss-making item: here, although something of a simplification, it can be said that the lowest figure will indicate the most profitable category.

III) The percentage of items in the category to make a profit: the higher this figure is, the more profitable the category is likely to be.

IV) The difference between the size of a category (excluding series counted as one item) expressed as a percentage of the total issue (ab), and the contribution made by that category expressed as a percentage of the total net profit realised by all items on the list (excluding series counted as one). A category which has say 12% of the total number of items yet produces 15% of the total profit is more lucrative than one containing say 20% of the total number of items which produce only 19% of the total profit.

V) The average profit per item in the category: the higher this figure is, the more profitable the category.

VI) The percentage return on investment: once again, the higher this figure is the better.

The categories are tested against these criteria, and then, according to their performance when measured by each criterion, are ranked in order from one to eight, the results being entered on a grid. In the case of 1896–97 the following results are obtained:

Placing	1	2	3	4	5	6	7	8
Criterion								
I	F	D	G	H	A	B	E	C
II	F[1]	A	H	G	B	C	E	D
III	F[1]	D	B	H	G	C	A	E
IV[2]	D	F	H	E	G	B	A	C
V	F	D	H	G	B	A	C	E
VI	B	H	D	G	A	F	E	C

(1) F is, of course, an exceptional category, containing no loss-making items.

(2) It can be calculated from (f) and (s) that the profit from items excluding series counted as one was contributed by the categories as follows:

A	3.76%
B	13.21%
C	−7.67%
D	35.55%
E	−2.40%
F	10.28%
G	32.07%
H	15.18%

The difference between the sizes of the categories expressed as a percentage of the total issue and their yield expressed as a percentage of the total net profit realised by all items excluding series counted as one was therefore as follows:

A	−9.9	B	−8.83	C	−17.91	D	+32.45
E	−3.02	F	+9.97	G	−4.88	H	+2.14

Letting positions 1–8 in the Table above be valued at 8 to 1 respectively:

$$A = 4 + 7 + 2 + 2 + 3 + 4 = 22$$
$$B = 3 + 4 + 6 + 3 + 4 + 8 = 28$$
$$C = 1 + 3 + 3 + 1 + 2 + 1 = 11$$
$$D = 7 + 1 + 7 + 8 + 7 + 6 = 36$$
$$E = 2 + 2 + 1 + 5 + 1 + 2 = 13$$
$$F = 8 + 8 + 8 + 7 + 8 + 3 = 42$$
$$G = 6 + 5 + 4 + 4 + 5 + 5 = 29$$
$$H = 5 + 6 + 5 + 6 + 6 + 7 = 35$$

The order of profitability according to the above tests is therefore as follows:

1	2	3	4	5	6	7	8
F	D	H	G	B	A	E	C

Category F owes its position to the exceptional nature of the case. Category H, which over the four financial years proved to be the most profitable category, here ranks in third place.

Table 34

Annual performance 1896–97							
Category	(a) Total profit-making items (Excl. series counted as one item)	(b) Total profit-making series counted as one item	(c) Total profit-making lines (Incl. series counted as one item) (a+b)	(d) Total outlay on profit-making items (Excl. series counted as one item)	(e) Turnover on profit-making items (Excl. series counted as one item) (d+f)	(f) Total profit on profit-making items (Excl. series counted as one item)	(g) Average profit per profit-making item (f/a)
A	25	3[1]	28	£515 1*s.* 7*d.*	£698 5*s.* 2*d.*	£183 3*s.* 7*d.*	£7 6*s.* 6*d.*
B	63	3[2]	66	£134 11*s.* 3*d.*	£529 2*s.* 4*d.*	£394 11*s.* 1*d.*	£6 5*s.* 3*d.*
C	24	0	24	£43 15*s.* 7*d.*	£137 2*s.* 10*d.*	£93 7*s.* 3*d.*	£3 17*s.* 10*d.*
D	9	0	9	£303 11*s.* 9*d.*	£999 19*s.* 2*d.*	£696 7*s.* 5*d.*	£77 7*s.* 6*d.*
E	1	0	1	£295 9*s.* 4*d.*	£299 19*s.* 9*d.*	£4 10*s.* 5*d.*	£4 10*s.* 5*d.*
F	1[3]	0	1	£868 3*s.* 6*d.*	£1,044 0*s.* 4*d.*	£175 16*s.* 10*d.*	£175 16*s.* 10*d.*
G	100	0	100	£613 4*s.* 3*d.*	£1,471 19*s.* 7*d.*	£858 15*s.* 4*d.*	£8 11*s.* 9*d.*
H	37	0	37	£122 16*s.* 7*d.*	£435 5*s.* 1*d.*	£312 8*s.* 6*d.*	£8 8*s.* 11*d.*
All publications	260	6	266	£2,896 13*s.* 10*d.*	£5,615 14*s.* 3*d.*	£2,719 0*s.* 5*d.*	£10 9*s.* 0*d.*

(1) The three series are the collection of works by John Owen, the *Bible Class Primers* and the *Ante-Nicene Library*.
(2) The works of Calvin, the *Foreign Theological Library*, and the series of commentaries by Meyer.
(3) Moulton and Geden's *Concordance*. £325 8*s.* 6*d.* had been credited towards the cost of the work in the 1895–96 accounts, and this allowed the Clarks to show a notional profit of £175 16*s.* 6*d.* on the title by mid-1897.

Table 34 (*continued*)

	Annual performance 1896–97					
Category	(h) Outlay on profit-making series counted as one item	(i) Turnover on profit-making series counted as one item (h+j)	(j) Profit on profit-making series counted as one item	(k) Total outlay on all profit-making lines (d+h)	(l) Total profit on all profit-making lines (f+j)	(m) Total turnover on all profit-making lines (e+i)
A	£347 14*s*. 7*d*.	£610 4*s*. 11*d*.	£262 10*s*. 4*d*.	£862 16*s*. 2*d*.	£445 13*s*. 11*d*.	£1,308 10*s*. 1*d*.
B	£227 16*s*. 8*d*.	£1,176 0*s*. 3*d*.	£948 3*s*. 7*d*.	£362 7*s*. 11*d*.	£1,342 14*s*. 8*d*.	£1,705 2*s*. 7*d*.
C	–	–	–	£43 15*s*. 7*d*.	£93 7*s*. 3*d*.	£137 2*s*. 10*d*.
D	–	–	–	£303 11*s*. 9*d*.	£696 7*s*. 5*d*.	£999 19*s*. 2*d*.
E	–	–	–	£295 9*s*. 4*d*.	£4 10*s*. 5*d*.	£299 19*s*. 9*d*.
F	–	–	–	£868 3*s*. 6*d*.	£175 16*s*. 10*d*.	£1,044 0*s*. 4*d*.
G	–	–	–	£613 4*s*. 3*d*.	£858 15*s*. 4*d*.	£1,471 19*s*. 7*d*.
H	–	–	–	£122 16*s*. 7*d*.	£312 8*s*. 6*d*.	£435 5*s*. 1*d*.
All publications	£575 11*s*. 3*d*.	£1,786 5*s*. 2*d*.	£1,210 13*s*. 11*d*.	£3,472 5*s*. 1*d*.	£3,929 14*s*. 4*d*.	£7,401 19*s*. 5*d*.

Table 34 (*continued*)

	Annual performance 1896–97					
Category	(n) Total loss-making items (Excl. series counted as one item)	(o) Total loss-making series counted as one item	(p) Total loss-making items (Incl. series counted as one item (n+o)	(q) Total outlay on loss-making items (Excl. series counted as one item)	(r) Turnover on loss-making items (Excl. series counted as one item) (q−s)	(s) Total loss on loss-making items (Excl. series counted as one item)
A	19	1[4]	20	£348 6*s*. 1*d*.	£229 9*s*. 1*d*.	£118 17*s*. 0*d*.
B	8	0	8	£376 12*s*. 7*d*.	£208 0*s*. 6*d*.	£168 12*s*. 1*d*.
C	9	1[5]	10	£459 15*s*. 1*d*.	£235 3*s*. 8*d*.	£224 11*s*. 5*d*.
D	1	0	1	£636 16*s*. 9*d*.	£548 7*s*. 3*d*.	£88 9*s*. 6*d*.
E	1	0	1	£965 6*s*. 1*d*.	£919 12*s*. 2*d*.	£45 13*s*. 11*d*.
F	0	0	0	–	–	–
G	19	0	19	£744 1*s*. 2*d*.	£433 10*s*. 11*d*.	£310 10*s*. 3*d*.
H	5	0	5	£76 6*s*. 5*d*.	£23 10*s*. 10*d*.	£52 15*s*. 7*d*.
All publications	62	2	64	£3,607 4*s*. 2*d*.	£2,597 14*s*. 5*d*.	£1,009 9*s*. 9*d*.

(4)The *St Augustine Library*.
(5)Lange's Commentaries.

Table 34 (*continued*)

Category	Annual performance 1896–97						
	(t) Average loss per loss-making item (Excl. series counted as one item) (s/n)	(u) Outlay on loss-making series counted as one item	(v) Turnover on loss-making series counted as one item (u−w)	(w) Loss on loss-making series counted as one item	(x) Total outlay on all loss-making lines (q+u)	(y) Total loss on all loss-making lines (s+w)	(z) Total turnover on all loss-making lines (r+v)
A	£6 5*s.* 0*d.*	£47 3*s.* 9*d.*	£21 2*s.* 6*d.*	£26 1*s.* 3*d.*	£395 9*s.* 10*d.*	£144 18*s.* 3*d.*	£250 11*s.* 7*d.*
B	£21 1*s.* 6*d.*	—	—	—	£376 12*s.* 7*d.*	£168 12*s.* 1*d.*	£208 0*s.* 6*d.*
C	£24 19*s.* 0*d.*	£18 17*s.* 4*d.*	£15 12*s.* 0*d.*	£3 5*s.* 4*d.*	£478 12*s.* 5*d.*	£227 16*s.* 9*d.*	£250 15*s.* 8*d.*
D	£88 9*s.* 6*d.*	—	—	—	£636 16*s.* 9*d.*	£88 9*s.* 6*d.*	£548 7*s.* 3*d.*
E	£45 13*s.* 11*d.*	—	—	—	£965 6*s.* 1*d.*	£45 13*s.* 11*d.*	£919 12*s.* 2*d.*
F	—	—	—	—	—	—	—
G	£16 6*s.* 10*d.*	—	—	—	£744 1*s.* 2*d.*	£310 10*s.* 3*d.*	£433 10*s.* 11*d.*
H	£10 11*s.* 0*d.*	—	—	—	£76 6*s.* 5*d.*	£52 15*s.* 7*d.*	£23 10*s.* 10*d.*
All publications	£16 5*s.* 8*d.*	£66 1*s.* 1*d.*	£36 14*s.* 6*d.*	£29 6*s.* 7*d.*	£3,673 5*s.* 3*d.*	£1,038 16*s.* 4*d.*	£2,634 8*s.* 11*d.*

Table 34 (*continued*)

Annual performance 1896–97						
Category	(aa) Total no. of items in category (Excl. series counted as one) (a+n)	(ab) Category total as % of grand total of items (Excl. series counted as one item)	(ac) Total no. of lines (Incl. series) (c+p)	(ad) % of total items in category (Excl. series counted as one) to make a profit $\frac{a}{aa} \times 100$	(ae) Average outlay per item in category (Excl. series) $\frac{d+q}{aa}$	(af) Average turnover per item (Excl. series) $\frac{e+r}{aa}$
A	44	13.66%	48	56.81%	£19 12*s.* 5*d.*	£21 1*s.* 9*d.*
B	71	22.04%	74	88.73%	£7 4*s.* 0*d.*	£10 7*s.* 8*d.*
C	33	10.24%	34	72.72%	£15 5*s.* 0*d.*	£11 5*s.* 8*d.*
D	10	3.10%	10	90.00%	£94 0*s.* 10*d.*	£154 16*s.* 8*d.*
E	2	0.62%	2	50.00%	£580 7*s.* 9*d.*	£609 15*s.* 11*d.*
F	1	0.31%	1	100.00%	£868 3*s.* 6*d.*	£1,044 0*s.* 4*d.*
G	119	36.95%	119	84.03%	£11 8*s.* 0*d.*	£16 0*s.* 0*d.*
H	42	13.04%	42	88.09%	£4 14*s.* 10*d.*	£10 18*s.* 6*d.*
All publications	322		330	80.74%	£20 4*s.* 0*d.*	£25 10*s.* 0*d.*

Table 34 (*continued*)

Category	Annual performance 1896–97				
	(ag) Total outlay (k+x)	(ah) Total profit on category (l−y)	(ai) Category profit (ah) as a % of total profit	(aj) % return on category $\frac{ah \times 100}{ag}$	(ak) Average profit per item in category (Excl. series) $\frac{f-s}{aa}$
A	£1,258 6*s*. 0*d*.	£300 15*s*. 8*d*.	10.40%	23.90%	£1 9*s*. 3*d*.
B	£739 0*s*. 6*d*.	£1,174 2*s*. 7*d*.	40.61%	158.87%	£3 3*s*. 8*d*.
C	£522 8*s*. 0*d*.	Loss £134 9*s*. 6*d*.	− 4.65%	−25.74%	Loss £3 19*s*. 6*d*.
D	£940 8*s*. 6*d*.	£607 17*s*. 11*d*.	21.02%	64.64%	£60 15*s*. 7*d*.
E	£1,260 15*s*. 5*d*.	Loss £41 3*s*. 6*d*.	− 1.42%	− 3.26%	Loss £20 11*s*. 9*d*.
F	£868 3*s*. 6*d*.	£175 16*s*. 10*d*.	6.08%	20.25%	£175 16*s*. 10*d*.
G	£1,357 5*s*. 5*d*.	£548 5*s*. 1*d*.	18.96%	40.39%	£4 12*s*. 0*d*.
H	£199 3*s*. 0*d*.	£259 12*s*. 11*d*.	8.98%	130.37%	£6 3*s*. 8*d*.
All publications	£7,145 10*s*. 4*d*.	£2,890 18*s*. 0*d*.[6]		40.45%	£5 6*s*. 0*d*.

(6)The actual profit figure before deduction of overheads was somewhat higher than this, totalling £4,281 14*s*. 4*d*., the difference being made up by commission on the sales of *Session Cases*, which at 7½% realised £223 0*s*. 11*d*., and by various incoming royalties.

Appendix C

Total annual overheads/Total prior outlay on stock in hand[1]

The total annual overhead figures used in Chapter 12, are based on the data in Table 35.

When we come to estimate the firm's total prior outlay on stock-in-hand at the start of the three financial years 1896–97, 1897–98 and 1898–99, some degree of guesswork is inevitably involved. There are two principal reasons why our final figures can only be notional ones.

In the first place the *Stock and Sales Book* does not include stock figures for four of the major series issued by the Clarks: the *Foreign Theological Library*, the *Ante-Nicene Library* and the series of works by St Augustine and H.A.W. Meyer. The firm presumably kept its stock records for these series elsewhere. For the present calculations, the stock-in-hand was estimated for the three financial years as follows, on the basis of reprint and binding figures:

> *Foreign Theological Library* 3,460 vols bound, 22,490 in sheets. (On the basis of an average of 20 bound copies and 130 in sheets for each of 173 volumes.)
> *Ante-Nicene Library* 320 vols bound, 1,280 in sheets. (On the basis of an average of 20 bound copies and 80 in sheets for each of 16 volumes.)
> *St Augustine's Works* 160 vols bound, 320 in sheets. (On the basis of an average of 10 bound copies and 20 in sheets for each of 16 volumes.)
> H.A.W. Meyer's *Commentary* 200 volumes bound, 800 in sheets. (On the basis of 10 bound copies, 40 in sheets for each of 20 volumes.)

The second cause of uncertainty in making the present calculations is even more extensive in its implications. Our method of procedure is to establish the value at trade prices of the stock in hand, and then to work back from that figure in an attempt to calculate the Clarks' initial outlay. This would be straightforward if the firm's percentage return on its investment were constant. In fact, of course, it was not; it varied from title to title, and the average varied from year to year. We assume here a return of 40% on bound stock; that is, we take the value of stock at trade prices as being 140% of the Clarks' initial outlay on the residual stock from the print run. A further problem arises when it comes to the unbound stock. The binding costs per unit did not comprise a standard proportion of the total unit production cost in the case of every title, rather varying according to the cost of the book. In some cases, binding costs amounted to 25% of the unit production cost; in others, they were as low as 8%. Here we assume for all titles that binding costs would amount to 15% of the unit production cost. In the case of unbound stock, still assuming a return of 40%, we take the value of stock at trade price as being 164.7% of the Clarks' initial outlay.[2] Although somewhat artificial, these calculations allow for a reasonably accurate estimate of the prior outlay on stock in hand.

At the start of financial year 1896–97, the firm had in hand 177,384 units of stock at a total catalogue trade value of £45,614.41.[3] This comprised 27,945 units of bound stock with a catalogue trade value of £5,278.92, and 149,439 units of unbound stock with a catalogue value of £40,335.49. In fact, however, when additional discounts were taken into account, the Clarks received only 85% of the catalogue trade price. The stock value can therefore be said to have been as follows:

Bound stock	£5,278.92 × 85% = £4,487.08
Unbound stock	£40,335.49 × 85% = £34,285.16

Using the procedures outlined above, the outlay on this stock can be calculated as follows:

Bound stock $\text{Outlay} = \frac{\pounds 4{,}487.08}{140} \times 100 = \pounds 3{,}205.05$

Unbound stock $\text{Outlay} = \frac{\pounds 34{,}285.16}{164.7} \times 100 = \pounds 20{,}816.73$

The firm's total outlay on stock in hand can therefore be estimated at £24,021.78.

At the start of financial year 1897–98, the firm had in hand 178,050 units of stock at a total catalogue trade value of £46,286.56. This comprised 29,153 units of bound stock with a catalogue trade value of £5,548.40, and 148,897 units of unbound stock with a catalogue trade value of £40,738.16. Taking into account additional discounts, the stock value can therefore be said to have been as follows:

Bound stock	£5,548.40 × 85% = £4,716.14
Unbound stock	£40,738.16 × 85% = £34,627.43

Again using the procedures outlined above, the outlay on this stock can be calculated as follows:

Bound stock $\text{Outlay} = \frac{\pounds 4{,}716.14}{140} \times 100 = \pounds 3{,}368.67$

Unbound stock $\text{Outlay} = \frac{\pounds 34{,}627.43}{164.7} \times 100 = \pounds 21{,}024.54$

The firm's total outlay on stock in hand can therefore be estimated at £24,393.21.

At the start of financial year 1898–99, the firm had in hand 181,693 units of stock at a total catalogue trade value of £50,074.72. This comprised 31,882 units of bound stock with a catalogue trade value of £6,677.33, and 149,811 units of unbound stock with a catalogue trade value of £43,397.39. Taking into account additional discounts, the stock value can therefore be said to have been as follows:

Bound stock	£6,677.33 × 85% = £5,675.73
Unbound stock	£43,397.39 × 85% = £36,887.78

Once again using the procedures outlined above, the outlay on this stock can be calculated as follows:

Bound stock Outlay = $\frac{\text{£}5{,}675.73}{140} \times 100 = \text{£}4{,}054.09$

Unbound stock Outlay = $\frac{\text{£}36{,}887.78}{164.7} \times 100 = \text{£}22{,}396.95$

The firm's total outlay on stock in hand can therefore be estimated at £26,451.04.

Table 35

Overheads 1896–97, 1897–98 and 1898–99						
Category of expenditure	1896–97	% of total[1]	1897–98	% of total[1]	1898–99	% of total[1]
Property (rent/rates/gas)	£190 6*s.* 6*d.*[2]	12.49%	£195 13*s.* 10*d.*[2]	14.31%	£196 2*s.* 10*d.*[2]	12.78%
Salaries	£599 3*s.* 6*d.*[3]	39.32%	£627 13*s.* 0*d.*[3]	45.90%	£651 4*s.* 0*d.*[3]	42.44%
Travelling expenses	£32 12*s.* 3*d.*[4]	2.14%	£44 11*s.* 4*d.*[4]	3.25%	£29 1*s.* 1*d.*[4]	1.89%
London and Edinburgh Shipping Co.	£31 3*s.* 5*d.*	2.04%	£33 2*s.* 11*d.*	2.42%	£35 4*s.* 0*d.*	2.29%
Insurance	£56 8*s.* 4*d.*[5]	3.70%	£31 17*s.* 6*d.*[5]	2.33%	£20 5*s.* 0*d.*[5]	1.31%
Catalogues etc.	£120 12*s.* 11*d.*[6]	7.91%	£103 1*s.* 8*d.*[6]	7.53%	£130 14*s.* 5*d.*[6]	8.52%
Cost of early stages of *Dictionary of the Bible*	£131 8*s.* 3*d.*	8.62%	—	—	—	—
Bad debt contingency	£20 0*s.* 0*d.*	1.31%	£30 0*s.* 0*d.*	2.19%	£75 0*s.* 0*d.*	4.88%
To Scribner for US advertising	£50 0*s.* 0*d.*[7]	3.28%	£50 0*s.* 0*d.*[7]	3.65%	£50 0*s.* 0*d.*[7]	3.25%
⅓ cost of alterations to type	£49 8*s.* 8*d.*	3.24%	—	—	—	—
Miscellaneous	£242 7*s.* 7*d.*[8]	15.90%	£251 7*s.* 4*d.*[8]	18.38%	£346 11*s.* 9*d.*[8]	22.59%
	£1,523 11*s.* 5*d.*		£1,367 7*s.* 7*d.*		£1,534 3*s.* 1*d.*	
Deduct contribution charged to books to cover cost of promotional material, the 'proportion of lists'	£192 15*s.* 0*d.*		£191 10*s.* 0*d.*		£210 10*s.* 0*d.*	
	£1,330 16*s.* 5*d.*		£1,175 17*s.* 7*d.*		£1,323 13*s.* 1*d.*	
Further deductions	£44 12*s.* 9*d.*[9]		—		—	
	£1,286 3*s.* 8*d.*		£1,175 17*s.* 7*d.*		£1,323 13*s.* 1*d.*	

Table 35 *(Notes)*

(1) These figures are expressed as a percentage of the total before deductions were made.

(2) These figures break down as follows:

	1896–97	1897–98	1898–99
Rent (George St. and Greenside premises)	£171 17*s*. 7*d*.	£171 17*s*. 7*d*.	£171 18*s*. 3*d*.
Rates	£15 17*s*. 1*d*.	£21 15*s*. 6*d*.	£21 17*s*. 6*d*.
Gas	£2 11*s*. 10*d*.	£2 0*s*. 9*d*.	£2 7*s*. 1*d*.
	£190 6*s*. 6*d*.	£195 13*s*. 10*d*.	£196 2*s*. 10*d*.

(3) The salaries were paid as follows:

	1896–97	1897–98	1898–99
Davidson	£273 0*s*. 0*d*.	£279 0*s*. 0*d*.	£290 0*s*. 0*d*.
Elder	£57 4*s*. 0*d*.	£57 4*s*. 0*d*.	£57 4*s*. 0*d*.
Corrigal	£127 0*s*. 0*d*.	£131 0*s*. 0*d*.	£135 0*s*. 0*d*.
Ryan	£44 0*s*. 6*d*.	£49 6*s*. 0*d*.	£54 10*s*. 0*d*.
Banks	£32 15*s*. 0*d*.	£42 15*s*. 0*d*.	£45 6*s*. 0*d*.*
Stoddart	£53 14*s*. 0*d*.	£56 8*s*. 0*d*.	£57 4*s*. 0*d*.
Christmas gifts	£11 10*s*. 0*d*.	£12 0*s*. 0*d*.	£12 0*s*. 0*d*.
	£599 3*s*. 6*d*.	£627 13*s*. 0*d*.	£651 4*s*. 0*d*.

* The accounts err by £3 16*s*. 0*d*. in calculating the total sum paid to Banks in 1898–99

(4) These travelling expenses were largely paid in respect of journeys made by John Maurice Clark and his brother Thomas. Occasionally, payment was made in respect of journeys made by Matthew Davidson, one of their staff, and by Professor S.D.F. Salmond. The cost of travelling to Glasgow amounted to between 7*s*. 0*d*. and 9*s*. 0*d*; a trip to Aberdeen cost £2 4*s*. 0*d*., and one to London £8 12*s*. 0*d*.

(5) Except for the 1898–99 figure, these sums include the premiums for insurance on James Hastings' life.

Table 35 (*Notes continued*)

(6) This figure was more than cancelled out by the amount raised by debiting a small sum, the 'proportion of the lists', from most of the firm's titles. The total raised in this manner is deducted at the foot of the table.

(7) This represented half of the Scribner firm's advertising outlay on Clark titles.

(8) These miscellaneous sums cover a large number of payments to trade societies, and other firms. They also include petty cash payments, which totalled £169 6*s*. 9*d*. in 1896–97, £133 12*s*. 8*d*. in 1897–98, and £287 3*s*. 2*d*. in 1898–99. The petty cash books have not been preserved, but these sizeable sums may have included outlay on postages. Some examples of the miscellaneous payments in 1897–98:

Trade Protection Society	£1 1*s*. 0*d*.
Burn and Baillie (Plumbers)	4*s*. 6*d*.
Desk and chair	£7 17*s*. 2*d*.
Publishers' Association	£5 5*s*. 0*d*.
Milne and Barclay (Painters)	£6 18*s*. 0*d*.
Addressing 625 envelopes	4*s*. 6*d*.
Packing paper	£13 8*s*. 9*d*.
Stationery	£2 13*s*. 4*d*.
New College Book Scheme	£1 1*s*. 0*d*.
Mahood Testimonial	10*s*. 0*d*.
Advertising not charged to individual titles	£39 13*s*. 3*d*.

(9) This sum in part represents other income received by the Clarks, generated for example by sales of other publishers' works. Almost three-quarters of the £44 12*s*. 9*d*., however, was accounted for in terms of discounts granted by Duncan, Hunter, Rosenbluth and Sinclair. It is not clear what transactions these would be in respect of.

Appendix D

Financial data from 1911–12 — 1989

Tables 36 and 37 present Trading Account data from 1911–12 until 1989.

For each year, Table 36 lists total income from sales, total outlay including overheads, and the trading profit, and records the percentage return on investment over the year. Figures from 1896–97 — 1898–99, calculated on a similar basis, are included for comparison.

After the end of the partnership, a 'Management Charge' was paid to Bartholomews each year until 1982. The Bartholomews were thus recovering their outlay in purchasing the firm. This charge was, however, something in the nature of an inter-company loan, and as such still appeared in T. & T. Clark's balance sheet. It has not been included in calculating pre-tax profits which appear in the Table.

Similarly, during the Reader's Digest period, that firm levied a company tax amounting to 4% of T. & T. Clark's turnover.

During the Partnership, the partners' salaries were normally included in the Profit and Loss Account, and not in the Trading Account, and hence have not been taken into the reckoning in calculating trading profit for this Table. However, Thomas George Clark's salary is included in the Trading Account between 1930–31 and 1944–45. Until 1935–36 he received £600 per annum, and thereafter £750. Following 1973, the Director's salaries have been included in assessing the pre-tax profits.

Bookstock levels are included in the Trading Accounts for the first time in 1928–29. Before that date, all production outlay within a given financial year is charged; from 1928–29 onwards, the annual production outlay is added to the total value of bookstock-in-hand at the start of the year; then, from this total, the value of bookstock-in-hand at the end of the year is subtracted, and the resulting figure entered as outlay. In other words, from 1928–29 onwards only the production cost of books actually sold during a given year is charged to the Trading Account. The value of bookstock was calculated on a 25% annual depreciation basis.

Table 36 lists the value of bookstock-in-hand at the end of the financial year from 1928–29 until the end of the partnership in 1973, and records this figure as a percentage of annual outlay.

Table 37 lists in respect of five sample years the allocation of outlay between Production Expenses, Literary Expenses, and Overheads.

Table 36

Trading Account Data 1911–12 – 1989 with comparative data 1896–97 – 1898–99

	1896–97	1897–98	1898–99	1911-12	1912–13
Trading income	£10,036 8*s.* 4*d.*	£12,152 4*s.* 0*d.*	£13,104 16*s.* 9*d.*	£25,713 0*s.* 7*d.*	£26,631 7*s.* 7½*d.*
Trading outlay	£8,431 14*s.* 0*d.*	£11,144 13*s.* 10*d.*	£11,227 0*s.* 10*d.*	£21,865 0*s.* 4*d.*	£21,155 11*s.* 0½*d.*
Profit on trading	£1,604 14*s.* 4*d.*	£1,007 10*s.* 2*d.*	£1,877 15*s.* 11*d.*	£3,848 0*s.* 3*d.*	£5,475 16*s.* 7*d.*
% return	19.03%	9.04%	16.72%	17.59%	25.88%

1913–14	1914–15	1915–16	1916–17	1917–18	1918–19
£25,834 3*s.* 4¼*d.*	£24,363 7*s.* 11½*d.*	£20,380 13*s.* 4½*d.*	£13,219 14*s.* 4½*d.*	£11,889 17*s.* 0½*d.*	£18,765 1*s.* 3½*d.*
£22,475 17*s.* 11¾*d.*	£21,434 9*s.* 7*d.*	£16,630 10*s.* 2½*d.*	£10,171 15*s.* 6¾*d.*	£9,433 2*s.* 7½*d.*	£18,340 9*s.* 4½*d.*
£3,358 5*s.* 4½*d.*	£2,928 18*s.* 4½*d.*	£3,750 3*s.* 2*d.*	£3,047 18*s.* 9¾*d.*	£2,456 14*s.* 5*d.*	£424 11*s.* 11*d.*
14.94%	13.66%	22.54%	29.96%	26.04%	2.31%

1919–20	1920–21	1921–22	1922–23	1923–24	1924–25
£19,347 16*s.* 7¾*d.*	£26,674 2*s.* 7*d.*	£22,611 14*s.* 1*d.*	£18,521 17*s.* 8¾*d.*	£18,205 17*s.* 2*d.*	£17,192 16*s.* 0*d.*
£17,966 11*s.* 4½*d.*	£25,298 12*s.* 8¾*d.*	£21,286 2*s.* 7*d.*	£15,517 1*s.* 0*d.*	£15,710 10*s.* 0¾*d.*	£15,224 11*s.* 7¼*d.*
£1,381 5*s.* 3¼*d.*	£1,375 9*s.* 10¼*d.*	£1,325 11*s.* 6*d.*	£3,004 16*s.* 8¾*d.*	£2,495 7*s.* 1¼*d.*	£1,968 4*s.* 4¾*d.*
7.68%	5.43%	6.22%	19.36%	15.88%	12.92%

Table 36 (*continued*)

Trading Account Data 1911–12 – 1989 with comparative data 1896–97 – 1898–99						
	1925–26	1926–27	1927–28	1928–29	1929–30	1930–31
Trading income	£15,805 1*s.* 6½*d.*	£18,065 0*s.* 5½*d.*	£15,219 6*s.* 6¼*d.*	£16,481 10*s.* 2½*d.*	£13,577 13*s.* 6¾*d.*	£11,802 1*s.* 10*d.*
Trading outlay	£13,284 8*s.* 7¾*d.*	£16,789 19*s.* 6½*d.*	£15,733 2*s.* 10½*d.*	£14,378 11*s.* 5½*d.*	£12,477 15*s.* 8¼*d.*	£9,418 16*s.* 8½*d.*
Profit on trading	£2,520 12*s.* 10¾*d.*	£1,275 0*s.* 11*d.*	(£513 16*s.* 4¼*d.*)	£2,102 18*s.* 9*d.*	£1,099 17*s.* 10½*d.*	£2,383 5*s.* 1½*d.*
% return	18.97%	7.59%	−3.26%	14.62%	8.81%	25.30%
			Book stock at year end	£6,181 7*s.* 7*d.*	£5,027 19*s.* 2*d.*	£7,698 18*s.* 1*d.*
			Stock as % of outlay	42.99%	40.29%	81.73%

1931–32	1932–33	1933–34	1934–35	1935–36	1936–37
£10,375 1*s.* 6½*d.*	£8,943 16*s.* 5*d.*	£9,046 3*s.* 3*d.*	£9,995 9*s.* 11*d.*	£9,916 11*s.* 8½*d.*	£9,957 12*s.* 1¾*d.*
£9,456 18*s.* 9¾*d.*	£9,536 3*s.* 0½*d.*	£7,822 19*s.* 2¼*d.*	£12,569 15*s.* 1½*d.*	£10,647 15*s.* 10¾*d.*	£9,984 17*s.* 4¾*d.*
£918 2*s.* 8¾*d.*	(£592 6*s.* 7½*d.*)	£1,223 4*s.* 0¾*d.*	(£2,574 5*s.* 2½*d.*)	(£731 4*s.* 2¼*d.*)	(£27 5*s.* 3*d.*)
9.7%	−6.21%	15.63%	−20.47%	−6.86%	0.27%
£7,802 15*s.* 9*d.*	£7,241 18*s.* 6*d.*	£8,395 18*s.* 6*d.*	£6,264 19*s.* 4*d.*	£5,221 0*s.* 0*d.*	£7,217 0*s.* 0*d.*
82.5%	75.94%	107.32%	49.84%	49.03%	72.27%

1937–38	1938–39	1939–40	1940–41	1941–42	1942–43
£10,924 12*s.* 10*d.*	£10,797 14*s.* 1*d.*	£9,147 3*s.* 4*d.*	£8,819 4*s.* 8*d.*	£9,524 11*s.* 5¼*d.*	£11,242 4*s.* 6½*d.*
£11,735 2*s.* 6½*d.*	£12,821 19*s.* 2½*d.*	£10,688 6*s.* 8¾*d.*	£8,724 9*s.* 6¾*d.*	£9,132 5*s.* 9*d.*	£8,530 2*s.* 6*d.*
(£810 9*s.* 8½*d.*)	(£2,024 5*s.* 1½*d.*)	(£1,541 3*s.* 4¾*d.*)	£94 15*s.* 1¼*d.*	£392 5*s.* 8¼*d.*	£2,712 2*s.* 0½*d.*
−6.90%	−15.78%	−14.41%	1.08%	4.29%	31.79%
£5,897 0*s.* 0*d.*	£4,108 0*s.* 0*d.*	£2,940 0*s.* 0*d.*	£2,229 0*s.* 0*d.*	£1,930 0*s.* 0*d.*	£2,640 0*s.* 0*d.*
50.25%	32.03%	27.50%	25.54%	21.13%	30.94%

Table 36 (*continued*)

Trading Account Data 1911–12 – 1989 with comparative data 1896–97 – 1898–99						
	1943–44	1944–45	1945–46	1946–47	1947–48	1948–49
Trading income	£11,889 3*s.* 8*d.*	£12,296 10*s.* 1¾*d.*	£13,650 15*s.* 6*d.*	£17,675 3*s.* 11½*d.*	£18,220 13*s.* 7¼*d.*	£18,397 2*s.* 6*d.*
Trading outlay	£9,318 14*s.* 9¼*d.*	£10,439 6*s.* 8*d.*	£9,865 17*s.* 8*d.*	£11,440 12*s.* 7*d.*	£11,609 2*s.* 9¾*d.*	£14,150 15*s.* 8½*d.*
Profit on trading	£2,570 8*s.* 10¾*d.*	£1,857 3*s.* 5¾*d.*	£3,784 17*s.* 10*d.*	£6,234 11*s.* 4½*d.*	£6,611 10*s.* 9½*d.*	£4,246 6*s.* 9½*d.*
% return	27.58%	17.79%	38.36%	54.49%	56.95%	30%
Book stock at year end	£2,541 0*s.* 0*d.*	£2,208 0*s.* 0*d.*	£2,510 0*s.* 0*d.*	£4,731 0*s.* 0*d.*	£7,863 3*s.* 7*d.*	£8,682 0*s.* 0*d.*
Stock as % of outlay	27.26%	21.15%	25.44%	41.35%	67.73%	61.35%

1949–50	1950–51	1951–52	1952–53	1953–54	1954–55
£21,354 18*s.* 7½*d.*	£22,456 2*s.* 10*d.*	£28,148 3*s.* 10*d.*	£27,387 17*s.* 2*d.*	£28,805 19*s.* 0*d.*	£28,725 6*s.* 6*d.*
£17,988 17*s.* 11*d.*	£16,995 15*s.* 6½*d.*	£22,256 8*s.* 1¾*d.*	£20,923 6*s.* 0*d.*	£23,401 8*s.* 8*d.*	£23,033 6*s.* 5¼*d.*
£3,366 0*s.* 8½*d.*	£5,460 7*s.* 3½*d.*	£5,891 15*s.* 8¼*d.*	£6,464 11*s.* 2*d.*	£5,404 10*s.* 4*d.*	£5,692 0*s.* 0¾*d.*
18.71%	32.12%	26.47%	30.89%	23.09%	24.71%
£9,020 0*s.* 0*d.*	£10,964 0*s.* 0*d.*	£12,159 0*s.* 0*d.*	£12,437 0*s.* 0*d.*	£14,364 0*s.* 0*d.*	£16,130 0*s.* 0*d.*
50.14%	64.51%	54.63%	59.44%	61.38%	70.02%

1955–56	1956–57	1957–58	1958–59	1959–60	1960–61
£44,439 18*s.* 5*d.*	£38,742 3*s.* 6*d.*	£39,373 8*s.* 0*d.*	£44,139 17*s.* 11*d.*	£45,023 9*s.* 10*d.*	£60,719 13*s.* 9*d.*
£31,037 13*s.* 0½*d.*	£30,359 5*s.* 9¾*d.*	£33,880 6*s.* 3½*d.*	£31,162 5*s.* 5*d.*	£32,589 18*s.* 1*d.*	£48,245 19*s.* 9*d.*
£13,402 5*s.* 4½*d.*	£8,382 17*s.* 8¼*d.*	£5,493 1*s.* 8½*d.*	£12,977 12*s.* 6*d.*	£12,433 11*s.* 9*d.*	£12,473 14*s.* 0*d.*
43%	27.61%	16.21%	41.64%	38.15%	25.85%
£20,344 0*s.* 0*d.*	£26,279 0*s.* 0*d.*	£30,171 0*s.* 0*d.*	£28,281 0*s.* 0*d.*	£33,417 0*s.* 0*d.*	£28,159 0*s.* 0*d.*
65.54%	86.56%	89.05%	90.75%	102.53%	58.36%

Table 36 (*continued*)

Trading Account Data 1911–12 – 1989 with comparative data 1896–97 – 1898–99						
	1961–62	1962–63	1963–64	1964–65	1965–66	1966–67
Trading income	£59,133 6*s.* 7*d.*	£59,393 4*s.* 2*d.*	£63,220 14*s.* 3*d.*	£61,163 2*s.* 11*d.*	£66,343 7*s.* 1*d.*	£77,414 13*s.* 7*d.*
Trading outlay	£43,056 14*s.* 9*d.*	£42,464 8*s.* 9*d.*	£46,083 1*s.* 7*d.*	£50,727 10*s.* 4*d.*	£49,695 13*s.* 5*d.*	£49,873 9*s.* 10*d.*
Profit on trading	£16,076 11*s.* 10*d.*	£16,928 15*s.* 5*d.*	£17,137 12*s.* 8*d.*	£10,435 12*s.* 7*d.*	£16,647 13*s.* 8*d.*	£27,541 3*s.* 9*d.*
% return	37.33%	39.86%	37.18%	20.57%	33.49%	55.22%
Book stock at year end	£34,271 0*s.* 0*d.*	£39,557 0*s.* 0*d.*	£45,852 0*s.* 0*d.*	£34,976 0*s.* 0*d.*	£26,900 0*s.* 0*d.*	£21,671 0*s.* 0*d.*
Stock as % of outlay	79.59%	93.15%	99.49%	68.94%	54.12%	43.45%

1967–68	1968–69	1969–70	1970–71	1971–72	July 1972 – March 1973
£77,481 8*s.* 4*d.*	£66,686 1*s.* 5*d.*	£68,548 2*s.* 8*d.*	£78,853.27	£85,979.70	£72,641.42
£53,769 0*s.* 2*d.*	£51,906 7*s.* 0*d.*	£53,131 17*s.* 6*d.*	£63,167.01	£70,235.53	£48,676.09
£23,712 8*s.* 2*d.*	£14,779 14*s.* 5*d.*	£15,416 5*s.* 2*d.*	£15,686.26	£15,744.17	£23,965.33
44.1%	28.51%	29.01%	24.83%	22.41%	49.23%
£31,283 0*s.* 0*d.*	£33,160 0*s.* 0*d.*	£25,398 0*s.* 0*d.*	£33,178.00	£23,554.00	£18,574.00
58.18%	63.88%	47.8%	52.52%	33.53%	35.15%

April–Sept 30 1973	1973–74	1974–75	1975–76	1976–77	1977–78
£35,334.15	£123,189.20	£148,441.03	£194,617	£193,452	£190,114
£29,317.81	£83,254.16	£132,841.09	£141,789	£147,995	£147,999
£6,016.34	£39,935.04	£15,599.94	£52,828	£45,457	£42,115
20.52%	47.96%	11.74%	37.25%	30.71%	28.45%

Table 36 (*continued*)

Trading Account Data 1911–12 – 1989 with comparative data 1896–97 – 1898–99						
	1978–79	1979–80	Oct 1980–30 June 1981	1981–82	1982–83	1983–84
Trading income	£247,059	£296,925	£224,702	£273,168	£444,332	£395,425
Trading outlay	£191,039	£268,671	£209,947	£351,738	£427,311	£404,198
Profit on trading	£56,020	£28,254	£14,755	(£78,570)	£17,021	(£8,773)
% return	29.32%	16.75%	7.02%	−22.33%	3.98%	−2.17%

1984–85	1985–86	1986–87	1987–88	1988–89
£419,547	£518,463	£490,231	£557,788	£745,364
£423,198	£449,810	£449,633	£505,537	£647,246
(£3,651)	£68,653	£40,598	£52,251	£98,118
−0.86%	15.26%	9.02%	10.33%	15.15%

Table 37

Allocation of total outlay in five sample years										
	1930–31		1940–41		1950–51		1960–61		1970–71	
	Outlay	% of total	Outlay	% of total	Outlay	% of total	Outlay	% of total	Outlay	% of total
Production expenses	£2,693 0*s.* 11½*d.*	28.59	£2,848 8*s.* 9½*d.*	32.64	£9,234 3*s.* 9½*d.*	54.33	£30,980 16*s.* 3*d.*	64.21	£35,858.75	56.76
Literary expenses	£3,008 17*s.* 8*d.*	31.94	£2,379 1*s.* 7¾*d.*	27.26	£2,647 4*s.* 3*d.*	15.57	£6,259 16*s.* 11*d.*	12.97	£5,494.57	8.69
Overheads	£3,716 18*s.* 1*d.*	39.46	£3,496 19*s.* 1½*d.*	40.08	£5,114 7*s.* 6*d.*	30.09	£11,005 6*s.* 7*d.*	22.81	£21,813.69	34.5
Total	£9,418 16*s.* 8½*d.*		£8,724 9*s.* 6¾*d.*		£16,995 15*s.* 6½*d.*		£48,245 19*s.* 9*d.*		£63,167.01	

Appendix E

Advertising platforms regularly used by T. & T. Clark 1886–96[1]

Aberdeen Free Press
Academy
Agora
Athenaeum
Baptist Magazine
Barmouth Advertiser
Belfast Witness
Bible Difficulties
Blackwood's Magazine
Bookman
Bookseller
British Quarterly Review
British Weekly
Brook and Chrystal's List
Cambridge University Calendar
Century Magazine
Christian Commonwealth
Christian Leader
Christian Pictorial
Christian Progress
Christian World
Christian World Pulpit
Chrystal's Guide
Church Bells
Church Family Newspaper
Church Quarterly Review
Church Times
Churchman
Congregational Review
Contemporary Review
Critical Review
Daily Chronicle
Daily News

Daily Review
Dumfries Standard
Dundee Advertiser
Dundee Courier
Durham University Calendar
Ecclesiastical Gazette
Edinburgh Review
Edinburgh University Calendar
Eisteddfod Programme
English Independent
Expositor
Expository Times
Free Church Exhibition Catalogue
Free Church Monthly
Freeman
Glasgow Herald
Glasgow Mail
Glasgow University Calendar
Goleaud
Guardian
Heywood's Catalogue
Illustrated Missionary News
Independent
Inverness Courier
Irish Christian Advocate
Irish Church News
Jewish Quarterly Review
John Bull
King's Own
Languages
Leeds Mercury
The Liberal
Life and Work
Literary Churchman
Literary Opinion
Literary World
Living Waters
Luzac's Oriental List
Macmillan's Magazine
Manchester Examiner
Methodist Recorder
Methodist Times
Modern Church
Monthly Tidings
Nature
Newbery House Magazine
Nonconformist

North British Daily Mail
Northern Daily News
Oxford University Calendar
Perthshire Advertiser
Pray and Trust
Preacher's Analyst
Presbyterian
Presbyterian Church Official Handbook
Presbyterian Messenger
Presbyterian Official Calendar
Publishers' Circular
Quarterly Review
Record
Religious Review of Reviews
Review of the Churches
Ruabon S.S. Programme
S.V.M.U. Magazine (Smith's Missions)
St Andrews University Calendar
Scots Observer
Scotsman
Scottish Church
Scottish Church Almanac
Scottish Congregational Magazine
Scottish Congregational Year Book
Scottish Guardian
Scottish Leader
Scottish News
Scottish Weekly
Speaker
Spectator
Stirling Observer
Sunday School
Sunday School Chronicle
Sword and Trowel
Tablet
Theological Monthly
Theological Review
Thinker
Welsh S.S. Union 'Lesson Book'
Wesleyan Methodist Magazine
Witherow's Catechism
Young Man
Young Woman
Youth

(The extent of the firm's advertising in each of the above varied considerably.)

Notes

Notes

Introduction

1 See John A.H. Dempster, 'Aspects of Brethren Publishing Enterprise in late nineteenth-century Scotland,' *Publishing History,* XX (1986), pp. 61–101.

2 For a discussion of this issue see John A.H. Dempster, *Certain Aspects of Some Nineteenth Century Scottish Religious Book Publishers: Blackie and Son and Thomas Nelson and Sons – a Study in Motivation,* (MA thesis, University of Strathclyde, 1983).

Part I

1 *The Publishing House of T. & T. Clark, Edinburgh* (1882), p. 3. (Reprinted from *The Bookseller,* July 1882.)

2 Obituary, *Bookseller,* 30 December 1865, p. 1132.

3 *The Publishing House,* p. 4.

4 And, indeed, until 1985 when T. & T. Clark crossed the road to 59 George Street.

5 *The Publishing House,* p. 4.

6 Ibid. The obituary in *The Bookseller* gives the date at which the young Thomas Clark became a partner as 1848. This seems unlikely, firstly because *The Publishing House* was issued by the younger Thomas Clark himself, and therefore may be presumed to be accurate, and secondly, because that publication links as cause and effect the opening of young Thomas Clark's partnership and the commencement of the *Foreign Theological Library* which dates from 1846. It is worth noting, however, that for all it bears the imprimatur of the firm, *The Publishing House* places the death of the founder in 1868 (p. 7), when in fact he died in 1865. (Obituary, *Bookseller,* 30 December 1865, p. 1132.)

7 Obituary, *Bookseller,* 30 December 1865, p. 1132.

8 *Reminiscences of Booksellers and Bookselling in Edinburgh in the Time of William IV* (Edinburgh, 1905) p. 27.

9 An edition by Negris and Duncan of a work by Professor Robinson.

10 Humphrey Carpenter and Mari Pritchard, *The Oxford Companion to Children's Literature* (Oxford, 1984).

11 C.A. Malcolm, 'Scottish Legal Periodicals: Past and Present', *Scottish Law Review,* 45 (1929) pp. 155–159 (p. 155).

12 *Bookseller,* 30 December 1865, p. 1132.
13 Scottish Record Office, SC49/31/81, fols 533–582.
14 Obituary, *Scotsman,* 25 December 1900, p. 4.
15 James Harvey, *In Memoriam Sir Thomas Clark* (Edinburgh, n.d.), p. 3.
16 'Publishers of Today: Messrs. T. & T. Clark', *Publishers' Circular,* 1302, 13 June 1891, pp. 634–35,
17 Ibid.
18 Ibid.
19 Roger Burlingame, *Of Making Many Books: A Hundred Years of Reading, Writing and Publishing* (1946), pp. 162–63. Burlingame records that the 'stern Thomas Clark . . . is said to have relaxed one night to the point of going with C.S. to Drury Lane to meet a famous actress in her green room after the play.'
20 Harvey, op. cit. pp. 22–23. The congregation initially worshipped in Lady Glenorchy's Chapel; after the Disruption in 1843, which led to the founding of the Free Church of Scotland, a new building was erected for what had become Lady Glenorchy's Free Church; and in 1900 the congregation joined in the union of Free and United Free Presbyterian Churches. Clark's father was an elder at Lady Glenorchy's from 1830 to 1860.
21 Harvey, pp. 9, 25.
22 Harvey, p. 25.
23 Thomas Clark—S.D.F. Salmond, 4 July 1883. (In a letter book recently deposited in the N.L.S.)
24 Obituary, *Scotsman,* 25 December 1900, p. 4.
25 Harvey, pp. 25–26.
26 *Scotsman,* 25 December 1900, p. 4 (supports 1883): *Bookseller,* 4 September 1886, p. 847 (supports 1884).
27 *Who Was Who 1897–1915* (1920).
28 *Bookseller,* 4 September 1886, p. 847.
29 *Scotsman,* 25 December 1900, p. 4, where it was noted that 'Sir Thomas was a Liberal in politics, and belonged to the Unionist wing of the party; but he did not take any prominent part in political affairs.'
30 *Scottish Leader,* quoted in *Publishers' Circular,* 1302, 13 June 1891, pp. 634–35.
31 *Publishers' Circular,* 1302, 13 June 1891, pp. 634–35,
32 James Harvey, 'The Publishing House of Messrs, T. & T. Clark, Edinburgh', *Expository Times,* 51, October 1939, pp. 10–11 (p. 11).
33 *Bookseller,* 7 March 1894, p. 204.
34 *Publishers' Circular,* 1612, 22 May 1897, p. 616.
35 *Scotsman,* 25 December 1900, p. 4.
36 His eldest daughter had died shortly before his own death. (Harvey, *In Memoriam Sir Thomas Clark,* p. 9.)
37 Testamentary material relating to Sir Thomas Clark is to be found in the Scottish Record Office, SC70/1/416, fols 863–868; SC70/4/327, fols. 343–358; SC70/1/398, fols 361–401.
38 *Publishers' Circular,* p. 170.
39 *Bookseller,* p. 957.
40 This Society, for 'Original Translations of John Calvin's Writings', had been founded in Edinburgh in 1843. (Arthur Giles, *Across Western Waves and Home in a Royal Capital* (1898), p. 288.
41 *Bookseller,* p. 584.
42 Clark had earlier, in 1870, published Schaff's three-volume *History of the Christian Church.*
43 *Paper and Impression Book 1878–1890,* N.L.S., Dep. 247/144.
44 C.A. Malcolm, 'Scottish Legal Periodicals: Past and Present', *Scottish Law Review,* 534 (1929), pp. 155–159 (pp. 157–58).
45 *The Publishing House,* p. 3.
46 Thomas Clark — Philip Schaff, 28 February 1882. (This letter is in a Letter Book

recently deposited in the N.L.S.) Clark was negotiating terms for UK publication of Schaff's *Encyclopaedia of Living Divines* which appeared in 1887.

47 Information from the Archivist of Edinburgh Academy; 'Edinburgh Academy Chronicle', 71, p. 152.

48 Information from the Archivist of Edinburgh University.

49 James Harvey, *In Memoriam Sir Thomas Clark*, pp. 5–6.

50 *Scotsman*, 28 May 1924, p. 8.

51 *Glasgow Herald*, 28 May 1924, p. 6.

52 James Harvey, 'The Publishing House of Messrs. T. & T. Clark, Edinburgh', *Expository Times*, 51 (1939), pp. 10–13 (p. 12).

53 [Obituary of Thomas Clark the younger], *Scotsman*, 25 December 1900, p. 4.

54 *Scotsman*, 28 May 1924, p. 8. Clark's obituary in the *Expository Times* (July 1924, pp. 477–78) adds nothing substantial to our knowledge about him.

55 *Bookseller*, 7 March 1894, p. 204.

56 *Expository Times*, 12, p. 240.

57 'Publishers of Today: Messrs. T. & T. Clark', *Publishers' Circular*, 13 June 1891, pp. 634–36 (p. 635).

58 *Expository Times*, 12, p. 240.

59 J.M. Clark— W.R. Clark of Toronto, 5 September 1894, N.L.S., Dep. 247/37. fol. 1006.

60 'Publishers of Today: Messrs. T. & T. Clark', *Publishers' Circular*, 13 June 1891, pp. 634–36.

61 J.M. Clark— W.R. Clark, 19 March 1896, N.L.S., Dep. 247/38, fol. 875.

62 For a brief biography of Hastings see John A.H. Dempster, ' "Incomparable Encyclopaedist": The life and work of Dr James Hastings', *Expository Times*, 100, (1988–89), pp. 4–8.

63 W. Robertson Nicoll, 'The Rev. James Hastings', *British Weekly*, 19 October 1922, p. 50.

64 J.M. Clark-J. Hastings, 11 February 1904, N.L.S., Dep. 247/40c, fol. 82.

65 J. M. Clark— William Robertson Nicoll, 23 December 1921, N.L.S., Dep. 247/18.

66 *Scottish Notes and Queries*, 13 (3rd series) September 1935, pp. 137–38.

67 Advertisement, *Bookseller*, 6 November 1890, p. 1275.

68 T. & T. Clark— J.S. Smiles, 17 November 1890. (In a letter book recently deposited in the N.L.S.)

69 N.L.S., Dep. 247/39.

70 'Nisi dominus frustra' is, in fact, the motto on the arms of the City of Edinburgh.

71 A draft of this letter has recently been deposited in the N.L.S.

72 A.J. Gossip, 'Reverend James Hastings, D.D.', *Expository Times*, 51 (1939–40), pp. 7–9 (p. 7).

73 T. & T. Clark— S.D.F. Salmond, N.L.S., Dep. 247/40a, fol. 510. The outlay on MacPhail's book was, the letter went on to say, small compared with that on many other works whose risk was borne by the Clarks.

74 N.L.S., Dep. 247/4. (12 April 1882) Thomas Clark also wrote seeking advice from Frederick Godet in very similar terms to those he must have used to Marcus Dods:

> I have no doubt of the great ability of the work and of its value in many respects; neither have I of the devoutness of its author, or of his desire for the promotion of truth. I feel also that his *theological* conclusions are not so far from orthodox views as to make one hesitate about publishing them.
>
> But what I would like your judgement upon more particularly is his view of the sources of the Gospels, especially as regards the Gospel of St John.
>
> I fear to publish what would weaken our Christian defences or injure the minds of the young. Undoubtedly at the present day there must be a large amount of freedom of discussion. In your opinion does Weiss pass over the limits with which you think I would be justified in publishing his work?
>
> Pray excuse my troubling you, but I know no-one on whom I can so much

depend as you, for you hold all christian essentials combined with christian freedom.

(Thomas Clark–Frederick Godet, 11 April 1882. This letter is in a Letter Book recently deposited in the N.L.S.)

75 Newspaper cutting dated 6 February 1922. Source unknown.

76 *Bookseller,* 1860, p. 440.

77 Op. cit., p. 13.

78 Ibid., p. 19.

79 12 December 1890, N.L.S., Dep. 247/36, fol. 149.

80 The Clarks made one more point to Mead, that small books were uneconomic. But, in fact *Romans Dissected* was published in 1891, after Mead (See T. & T. Clark— C.M. Mead, 22 December 1890, N.L.S., Dep. 247/36, fol. 156.) agreed to add some pages at the end of the book explaining its satirical intent, and to put an appropriate motto on the title page.

81 J.M. Clark— Charles Scribner, 14 October 1897, N.L.S., Dep. 247/39, fol. 923.

82 J.M. Clark— C.A. Briggs, 1 November 1897, N.L.S., Dep. 247–39, fol. 954.

83 14 October 1897 (see note 81).

84 1 November 1897 (see note 82).

85 J.M. Clark— Charles Scribner, 2 July 1898, N.L.S., Dep. 247/40, fol. 403.

86 T. & T. Clark— Scribners, 14 September 1899, N.L.S., Dep. 247/40a, fol. 195.

87 'Publishers of Today: Messrs. T. & T. Clark', 13 June 1891, pp. 634–36.

88 In *The Publishing House.*

89 Ibid., pp. 14–15.

90 Ibid., p. 9.

91 Ibid.

92 Ibid., pp. 10–11.

93 Ibid., pp. 11–12.

94 Ibid., pp. 15–16.

95 Ibid., pp. 8–9.

96 See T. & T. Clark—Scribners, 9 April 1885, N.L.S., Dep. 247/33, fol. 936.

97 Advertisement, *Bookseller,* 7 October 1884, p. 1069.

98 N.L.S., Dep. 247/34, fol. 838. This draft of the instructions to I.T.L. authors appears to have been prepared by C.A. Briggs of New York, but it was certainly approved by John M. Clark, as well as by Scribner.

99 A new translation of the New Testament in which the books were arranged in the order in which they were supposed to have been written.

100 It is not clear who this Macintosh was. It could hardly have been the Hugh Macintosh whose *Is Christ infallible and the Bible true?* was published by the Clarks in 1901. (This work attacks the more extreme higher critics, rejecting both rationalism and a traditionalism which sees the Bible as absolutely inerrant. It upholds a middle way, maintaining that the Bible is true, trustworthy and of Divine authority in its teaching.) John M. Clark manifestly disagreed with the work mentioned in Nicoll's letter, and would scarcely have published it himself. And Hugh Macintosh's work was favourably reviewed in several quarters, including the *Critical Review* which noted 'It is not criticism but criticism gone mad that he objects to.'

101 William Robertson Nicoll— John M. Clark, 12 February 1901. N.L.S., Dep. 247/18.

102 *In Memoriam Sir Thomas Clark,* p. 27.

103 Ibid., p. 5.

104 W.R. Nicoll, 'The Completion of a Great Encyclopaedia', *British Weekly,* 2 February 1922.

105 'Entre Nous', *Expository Times,* 12 (1900–01), p. 240. A fascinating glimpse of that 'steady, evangelical, yet never intolerant hand' at work is provided by a draft of a letter written by Sir Thomas on 25 June 1895, to Samuel Davidson, formerly Professor at the Royal Academical Institute in Belfast. Davidson had been known

to the Clarks for many years: as far back as 1839 they had published the first volume of his *Lectures on Biblical Criticism.* Now he had written his autobiography, and submitted it to Sir Thomas for comment. After reading the work, he found it difficult to respond:

> I am sure you will believe me when I say that I desire to give an impartial opinion, keeping back any difficulties which I may have from my personally seeing many things from a different standpoint, and looking at the subject simply from what I think would be best for your interest and reputation.

In the course of the work, Davidson had referred somewhat scathingly to other scholars. Clark attempted gently to persuade him not to go into print with comments which he might later regret:

> There are many things in all our lives which we would desire to forget and especially I think would be sorry to perpetuate in print perhaps to be read by unsympathising eyes, and you will pardon me for saying that there are words in your MS with regard to some who are gone, and even to some who still remain, who, however mistaken in what they said or did, were yet Godfearing men who acted as their consciences dictated: I would intreat [sic] you to expunge or to modify much that you have written in this direction. Some of those whom you thus strongly characterize were personal friends of my own.

The work, presumably changed in line with these suggestions, finally appeared in 1899. Sir Thomas' letter is among a collection recently deposited in the N.L.S.

106 *Bookseller,* 7 October 1884, p. 1069.

107 James Harvey, 'The Publishing House of Messrs. T. & T. Clark, Edinburgh', *Expository Times,* 51 (1939–40), pp. 10–13 (p. 11).

108 Which the Clarks had initially published in two volumes in 1858 and 1859.

109 T. & T. Clark— J.H. Moulton, 30 October 1896, N.L.S., Dep. 247/39, fol. 273.

110 Ibid.

111 T. & T. Clark— A. Plummer, 23 December 1899, N.L.S., Dep. 247/40a, fol. 406.

112 *The Publishing House of T. & T. Clark, Edinburgh,* p. 19.

113 T. & T. Clark— Charles Welford, Scribner's UK agent, 7 June 1884, N.L.S., Dep. 247/33, fol. 595. The work in question was Arnold H. Guyot's *Creation, Or, the Biblical Cosmogony in the Light of Modern Science.* It is worth noting that the Clarks were possibly depreciating the book in an attempt to get it at a lower price, for they comment immediately after the passage quoted above that they 'could not venture on more than 1*s.* 6*d.*'

114 Stade's *History of Israel,* offered to the Clarks by Houghton, Mifflin of Boston, USA. T. & T. Clark — Houghton, Mifflin, 10 November 1885, N.L.S., Dep. 247/34, fol. 179.

115 The work was George T. Ladd's *The Doctrine of Sacred Scripture* (1883). T. & T. Clark—Scribners, 12 February 1884, N.L.S., Dep. 247/33, fol. 464. The damage to which the letter refers was probably chiefly financial.

116 J.M. Clark—C.M. Mead, 22 December 1890, N.L.S., Dep. 247/36, fol. 156.

117 J.M. Clark—Scribners, 2 July 1898, N.L.S., Dep. 247/40, fol. 403.

118 J.M. Clark—W.P. Dickson, 14 July 1898, N.L.S., Dep. 247/40, fol. 419.

119 T. & T. Clark—Samuel Driver, 17 January 1893, N.L.S., Dep. 247/37, fol. 57. 'Perhaps little harm could be done in a Commentary on *Proverbs,* but it might be prejudicial to the *Series* if it were supposed to be in any way connected with Unitarians.' In fact, Toy's volume *did* appear in the I.C.C. series in 1899.

120 Op. cit., p. 15.

121 'The Publishing House of Messrs. T. & T. Clark, Edinburgh', *Expository Times,* 51 (1939–40), pp. 10–13 (p. 12).

122 *Expository Times,* 12 (1900–01), p. 240.

123 T. & T. Clark—Edward Hull, 14 November 1896, N.L.S., Dep. 247/39, fol. 304.

124 T. & T. Clark—David Kerr, 29 March 1887, N.L.S., Dep. 247/34, fol. 671.

125 T. & T. Clark—J.F. Spriggs, 25 November 1897, N.L.S., Dep. 247/40, fol. 7.

126 T. & T. Clark—W.F. Lofthouse, 8 January 1896, N.L.S., Dep. 247/38, fol. 756.
127 T. & T. Clark—J. Hamlyn Hill, 13 January 1896, N.L.S., Dep. 247/38, fol. 764.
128 *Bookseller*, 7 October 1884, p. 1069.
129 Draft of advice to I.T.L. authors, N.L.S., Dep. 247/34, fol. 838.
130 T. & T. Clark—C.A. Briggs, 21 January 1888, N.L.S., Dep. 247/34, fol. 930. The name of the author in question is illegible.
131 Edited by Philip Schaff, and published in 1879.
132 T. & T. Clark—Alfred Plummer, 5 June 1900, N.L.S., Dep. 247/40a, fol. 687.
133 T. & T. Clark—James Stalker, 12 October 1886, N.L.S., Dep. 247/34, fol. 510.
134 J.M. Clark—Scribners, 9 October 1900, N.L.S., Dep. 247/40a, fol. 897.
135 T. & T. Clark—J.A. Selbie, 31 December 1898, N.L.S., Dep. 247/40, fol. 782. Selbie assisted Hastings in editing the *Dictionary of the Bible*. The König work was published by the firm in 1899 as *The Exiles' Book of Consolation*.
136 T. & T. Clark—J.A. Selbie, 10 January 1899, N.L.S., Dep. 247/40, fol. 803.
137 T. & T. Clark—Bishop Martensen, 7 June 1879, N.L.S., Dep. 247/32, fol. 83. The two volumes in question, *Christian Ethics–Individual,* and *Christian Ethics–Social* were published in, respectively, 1881 and 1882.
138 T. & T. Clark—T. Adamson, 11 December 1896, N.L.S., Dep. 247/39, fol. 384.
139 J.M. Clark—James Hastings, 28 July 1899, N.L.S., Dep. 247/40a, fol. 130.
140 T. & T. Clark—James Hill, 1 August 1882, N.L.S., Dep. 247/33, fol. 11.
141 T. & T. Clark—Mrs Candlish, 17 July 1899, N.L.S., Dep. 247/40a, fol. 98.
142 T. & T. Clark—R.J. Jeffrey, 5 May 1882. (In a letter book recently deposited in the N.L.S.)
143 J.M. Clark—Charles Scribner, 14 October 1897, N.L.S., Dep. 247/39, fol. 923.
144 T. & T. Clark—Mrs Candlish, 17 July 1899, N.L.S., Dep. 247/40a, fol. 98.
145 J.M. Clark—J.F. Spriggs, 25 November 1897, N.L.S., Dep. 247/40, fol. 7.
146 13 June 1891, p. 635. For John M. Clark's view of the theological market in Scotland, and of English publishers' misconceptions of it, see his anonymous contribution to *The Academy* (1282, 28 November 1896) Book Market column, where he wrote as follows:

> I am glad to notice that you do not intend, in 'the Book Market', to overlook the claims of *Theology*. North of the Tweed, theological works are always in demand. A strange impression seems to exist in the South (I have heard it stated more than once in London) that Scotchmen do not read the works of Anglican theologians, but confine themselves to books by their own countrymen, with perhaps the addition of the Puritan divines! There could be no greater mistake, for it is a well-known fact here that our Scotch clergymen — and many laymen too — keep themselves abreast of the times in respect to Biblical Criticism; and in nearly every Scotch manse may be found the works of such theologians as Driver, Sanday, Ellicott, Gore, Cheyne, etc.

It is clear from the letter which Clark sent to *The Academy* with this contribution that the piece had been requested by the editor, and that it was Clark who wished it to appear anonymously. In this letter (J.M. Clark—The Editor, *The Academy,* 24 November 1896, N.L.S., Dep. 247/39, fol. 337.) Clark, after disarmingly commenting that the editor might, if he so wished, dispose of his piece in the waste paper basket, went on to reveal something of the frustration he felt in the face of English publishers' lack of appreciation of the depth of the Scottish market for theology:

It is very hard for the Publisher of Canon Driver's & Canon Sanday's most important books to be told as I was told in a London Publisher's establishment, that Scotch Clergymen read mainly such books as *The Bonnie Briar Bush* & not books by Prof. Sanday!

147 *The Publishing House of T. & T. Clark, Edinburgh,* p. 13.
148 T. Clark—M. Banks, 20 March 1879, N.L.S., Dep. 247/32, fol. 26.
149 T. Clark—Dabney Hampden, 3 March 1880, N.L.S., Dep. 247/32, fol. 268.

150 The firm's initial reaction was that 'It would be impossible for our Firm to publish criticism upon one of our own publications . . .' (T. & T. Clark—W.P. Dickson, 14 July 1898, N.L.S., Dep. 247/40, fol. 419.) They were, however, glad to have had the criticism from 'as able a hand as yours' (Ibid.), and began to consider whether it *might* be possible to publish the work if McGiffert would consent to read it, and possibly write a reply to be published conjointly with it. (T. & T. Clark—A.C. McGiffert, 21 September 1898, N.L.S., Dep. 247/40, fol. 532.) However, this plan fell through.

151 T. Clark—M. Banks, 20 March 1879, N.L.S., Dep. 247/32, fol. 26. This decision may have been influenced in part by a desire to keep Godet on the firm's list. Certainly, several more volumes by him were issued by the Clarks before the author's death in 1900.

152 See, e.g. T. & T. Clark—R.M. Edgar, 19 June 1893, N.L.S., Dep. 247/37, fol. 301.

153 T. & T. Clark—J. McDonald Inglis, 18 February 1887, N.L.S., Dep. 247/34, fol. 632.

154 T. & T. Clark—Robert Watts, 1 September 1887, N.L. S., Dep. 247/34, fol. 796. Admittedly, the work in question was extremely abstruse — *The Reign of Causality: A Vindication of the Scientific Principle of Telic Causal Efficiency.*

155 Robert Watts, whose work appeared later in 1887.

156 T. & T. Clark—C.H.H. Wright, 9 April 1884, N.L.S., Dep. 247/33, fol. 536. The work under consideration was by Friedrich E. König, probably his *Religious History of Israel*, 1885.

157 T. & T. Clark—Dr Stock, 24 March 1879, N.L.S. , Dep. 247/32, fol. 32.

158 T. & T. Clark—Thomas Adamson, 11 December 1896, N. L.S., Dep. 247/39, fol. 384. The work in question was his *Spirit of Power.*

159 T. & T. Clark—James Hill, 1 August 1882, N.L.S., Dep. 247/33, fol. 11.

160 Of a work by Jellinghaus: T. & T. Clark—Walter Sloan, China Inland Mission, 13 May 1899, N.L.S., Dep. 247/40, fol. 955.

161 J.M. Clark—W.F. Moulton, 11 February 1897, N.L.S., Dep. 247/39, fol. 477.

162 T. & T. Clark—Miss E. Wright, 24 July 1885, N. L.S., Dep. 247/34, fol. 39.

163 T. & T. Clark—James Hastings, 28 July 1899, N.L.S., Dep. 247/40a, fol. 130.

164 T. & T. Clark—Frank Ballard, 8 March 1900, N.L.S., Dep. 247/40a, fol. 525.

165 T. Clark—M. Cave, 22 June 1885, N.L.S., Dep. 247/34, fol. 18.

166 T. & T. Clark—James Aitchison, 2 July 1900, N.L.S. , Dep. 247/40a, fol. 738.

167 T. & T. Clark—D.W. Simon, 16 May 1900, N.L.S., Dep. 247/40a, fol. 663.

168 Quoted in James Harvey, *In Memoriam Sir Thomas Clark* (Edinburgh, n.d.), p. 6.

169 The Clarks' relationships with publishers on the other side of the Atlantic will be dealt with in Chapter 6.

170 T. & T. Clark—Miss E. Wright, 24 July 1885, N.L.S., Dep. 247/34, fol. 39.

171 T. & T. Clark—David Kerr, 29 March 1887, N.L.S., Dep. 247/34, fol. 671.

172 It could be argued, of course, that the firm was merely attempting to add some sweetness to its rejection letters.

173 T. & T. Clark—Scribners, 22 June 1898, N.L.S., Dep. 247/40, fol. 387.

174 T. & T. Clark—Hodder and Stoughton, 6 October 1886, N.L.S., Dep. 247/34, fol. 499.

175 See J.M. Clark—Franz Delitzsch, 7 October 1886, N.L.S., Dep. 247/34, fol. 501; T. & T. Clark—Hodder and Stoughton, 7 October 1886, N.L.S., Dep. 247/34, fol. 503; T. & T. Clark—W.R. Nicoll, 13 October 1886, N.L.S., Dep. 247/34, fol. 513; J.M. Clark—Franz Delitzsch, 15 October 1886, N.L.S., Dep. 247/34, fol. 518.

176 J.M. Clark—Franz Delitzsch, 15 October 1886, N.L.S., Dep. 247/34, fol. 518.

177 The Clarks' reaction to Hodder in this matter was particularly pointed because, of the first five books issued by the London firm in its *Foreign Biblical Library,* no fewer than three had been issued in previous editions by T. & T. Clark. Apart from the work by Delitzsch, there was *A Manual of Introduction to the New*

Testament by Bernard Weiss, and a *Church History*, by Johann H. Kurtz. (See T. H. Darlow, *William Robertson Nicoll* (London, 1925), p. 461.) Interestingly, according to the list in Darlow's work, there were no further issues in the *Foreign Biblical Library* beyond the five titles initially announced. This may well indicate that Hodder accepted the Clarks' criticism, a criticism surely justified, for the London firm was carrying competition to the point of discourtesy.

178 T. & T. Clark—Hodder and Stoughton, 5 December 1879, N.L.S. , Dep. 247/32, fol. 210.

179 Hodder was as closely connected with the Congregational Union as was Clark with the Free Church of Scotland. It would seem likely that Hodder apologised in this instance, for Clark wrote some years later (T. & T. Clark—William Robertson Nicoll, 13 October 1886, N.L.S., Dep. 247/34, fol. 513) 'We have always looked upon Mr. Hodder as a personal friend, and upon one or two occasions, when we came a little into collision, *he* honourably apologised.'

180 The work in question was Paton J. Gloag's *The Messianic Prophecies.*

181 T. & T. Clark—W.R. Nicoll, 13 October 1886, N.L.S., Dep. 247/34, fol. 513.

182 See T. & T. Clark—S.D.F. Salmond, 24 April 1900, N.L.S., Dep. 247/40a, fol. 616.

183 T. & T. Clark—Hodder and Stoughton, 5 December 1879, N.L.S. , Dep. 247/32, fol. 210.

184 This quotation is from the earliest letter regarding the Hodder re-issue of *Psalms.* (T. & T. Clark—Hodder and Stoughton, 6 October 1886, N.L.S., Dep. 247/34, fol. 499.)

185 T. & T. Clark—James Cooper, 5 February 1900, N.L.S., Dep. 247/40a, fol. 458.

186 *The Publishing House*, p. 7. The specific 'imitators and rivals' referred to were those who were competing with the *Foreign Theological Library*, aiming (not very successfully, according to the author) to 'introduce to English readers specimens of a free type of continental divinity'.

187 John Attenborough, *A Living Memory: Hodder and Stoughton Publishers 1868–1975* (London, 1975), pp. 15–17.

188 Norman L. Walker—George M. Brown of Nelson, 13 October 1894, Edinburgh University Library, Nelson Archive, G. M. Brown–Letters, 1893.

189 See Norman L. Walker—George M. Brown, 25 October 1894, Edinburgh University Library, Nelson Archive, G.M. Brown–Letters, 1893.

190 T. & T. Clark—W.R. Nicoll, 13 October 1886, N.L.S., Dep. 247/34, fol. 513.

191 Ibid.

192 T.H. Darlow, *William Robertson Nicoll* (London, 1925), p. 45.

193 T. & T. Clark—W.R. Nicoll, 13 October 1886, N.L.S., Dep. 247/34, fol. 513.

194 The work initially appeared in three volumes between 1860 and 1863; Volume 1 was revised and issued in two parts in 1893. (Alasdair I. MacLeod, 'James Hastings and the Encyclopaedia of Religion and Ethics' (unpublished MS, n.d.) p. 4.

195 T. & T. Clark—the Editor of the *Daily News*, 10 November 1899, N.L.S., Dep. 247/40a, fol. 325.

196 T. & T. Clark—Scribners, 27 January 1896, N.L.S., Dep. 247/38, fol. 788a.

197 Clark did not think it wise for Scribners to handle both the *Dictionary of the Bible* and the *Encyclopaedia Biblica* — See T. & T. Clark—Scribners, 27 January 1896, N.L.S., Dep. 247/38, fol. 788a.

198 T. & T. Clark—D.D. Ormond, Free Church Editorial Committee, 18 November 1898, N.L.S., Dep. 247/40, fol. 679.

199 *Free Church of Scotland Assembly Proceedings*, 1899.

200 In the case of more popular religious works there would be competition on two levels: on one level, competition with similar religious titles issued by other houses; on another level, competition with such general titles as might allure the casual purchaser. As the century drew to a close, while the total number of titles published in the UK increased (from 4,570 in 1869 to 7,570 in 1899), the number of

religious works included in that total declined (from 1,047 in 1869 to 693 in 1899). (Patrick Scott, 'The Business of Belief: The Emergence of "Religious" Publishing', *Studies in Church History* (1973), pp. 213–224 (p. 224).) Clearly, while the market for general works was increasing, that for religious works was on the decline. Such popular religious titles as were published faced increasing competition from general books. Serious theological works such as the Clarks published were not, of course, in direct competition with general titles.

201 T. & T. Clark—Alexander Whyte, 28 June 1887, N.L.S., Dep. 247/34, fol. 743.

202 T. & T. Clark—Hodder and Stoughton, 5 December 1879, N.L.S. , Dep. 247/32, fol. 210.

203 T. & T. Clark—William Robertson Nicoll, 13 October 1886, N.L.S., Dep. 247/34, fol. 513.

Part II

1 The financial year ran from July to June. This information is contained in N.L.S., Dep. 247/138, which, in the N.L.S. repertory of the Deposit, is given the mistakenly narrow title 'Stock and sales book, individual titles 1896–97'.

2 A reasonably complete list of series issued by the Clarks in the nineteenth century follows:

St Augustine's Works
The Ante-Nicene Library
The Biblical Cabinet
Bible Class Handbooks
Bible Class Primers
Cabinet Library of Scarce and Celebrated Tracts
Calvin's Works
Eras of the Christian Church
Foreign Theological Library
Foreign Devotional Library
History of the Christian Church
International Critical Commentary
International Theological Library
Lange's Commentaries
Meyer's Critical and Exegetical Commentary on the New Testament
World's Epoch Makers

3 T. & T. Clark — James B. Johnston, 12 August 1896, N.L.S., Dep. 247/39.

4 T. & T. Clark — Charles Scribner, 14 October 1897, N.L.S., Dep. 247/39, fol. 923.

5 T. & T. Clark — Scribners, 30 May 1898, N.L.S., Dep. 247/40, fol. 344.

6 *Bookseller*, 30 September 1865, p. 584.

7 *Catalogue, c.*1875.

8 T. & T. Clark — R. A. Macfie, 17 November 1887, N.L.S., Dep. 247/34, fol. 873.

9 *Dictionary of National Biography*. The punctuality with which the Clark series was issued was often contrasted favourably with the extreme slowness which characterised the appearance of its Oxford counterpart. For example, the *Bookseller* commented (1 June 1869, p. 470)

> the regularity with which the publishers issue the four annual volumes of this series, according to promise, affords a favourable contrast with the dilatory manner in which the Oxford amateurs issued their 'Library of the Fathers', the incompleteness of which is discreditable to its managers. Would it not be well for Dr. Pusey and his associates to make some arrangement with Messrs, Clark for amalgamation with the 'Ante-Nicene Library'?

10 *Bookseller*, 31 December 1866, p. 1341.

11 'The Literature of Tractarianism', *Bookseller,* 3 February 1880, pp. 106a-106c (p. 106c).
12 *Ibid.*
13 *Ibid.*
14 T. & T. Clark — the Bishop of New York, 25 September 1884, N.L.S., Dep. 247/33, fol. 684.
15 The *Ante-Nicene Library* was initially issued in the United States through the agency of Scribners; the subsequent threatened piracy of the Series by the Christian Literature Publishing Company, with which the Clarks were compelled through force of circumstances to conclude an agreement, is discussed in Chapter 6.
16 *Bookseller,* 29 June 1867, p. 433.
17 N.L.S., Dep. 247/138.
18 T. & T. Clark, *Trade List,* November 1872; *Catalogue, c.*1875.
19 T. & T. Clark, *Colonial Catalogue,* 1902 (issued 1901).
20 N.L.S., Dep. 247/138, fols. 83–84, etc.
21 It would appear from the *Stock and Sales Book* (N.L.S., Dep. 247/138) that all the non-subscription sales were channelled through the wholesalers.
22 Announcement in the *Bookseller,* 3 October 1871, p. 843.
23 Patrick C. Simpson, *The Life of Principal Rainy* (London, n.d.), I, p. 135.
24 T. & T. Clark, *Trade List,* November 1872; *Catalogue, c.*1875.
25 T. & T. Clark, *Catalogue, c.*1894.
26 N.L.S., Dep. 247/138.
27 Again it would appear from the *Stock and Sales Book* that all the non-subscription sales were channelled through the wholesaler.
28 Thomas Clark — Alexander Whyte, 29 September 1879, N.L.S., Dep. 247/32, fol. 155.
29 T. & T. Clark — James Nisbet and Co., 18 October 1879, N.L.S., Dep. 247/32, fol. 176.
30 *Stock and Sales Book, Individual Titles,* N.L.S., Dep. 247/138, fol. 69.
31 See T. & T. Clark — Alexander Whyte, 28 June 1887, N.L.S., Dep. 247/34, fol. 743.
32 See T. & T. Clark — J. Parry, 28 April 1885 and 1 May 1885, N.L.S., Dep. 247/33, fols 955, 959.
33 T. & T. Clark — The Presbyterian News Co., Toronto, 24 May 1893, N.L.S., Dep. 247/37, fol. 260. See John Tebbel, *A History of Book Publishing in the United States: The Expansion of an Industry 1865–1919,* II (1975), pp. 331–334, 359–360 for details of the Revell firm.
34 T. & T. Clark — The Presbyterian News Co., Toronto, 24 May 1893, N.L.S., Dep. 247/37, fol. 260.
35 For example, *Life of Christ,* first issued in 1879, had sold 12,000 copies by March 1883, as opposed to Marcus Dods' *Haggai,* issued the same year, which had sold only 500 copies, and the same author's *Genesis* (1882), which had sold a more satisfactory 2,000. (T. & T. Clark — Marcus Dods, 8 March 1883, N.L.S., Dep. 247/33, fol. 217.
36 Thomas Clark–Alexander Whyte, 29 September 1879, N.L.S., Dep. 247/32, fol. 155.
37 See T. & T. Clark — James Nisbet & Co., 18 October 1879, N.L.S., Dep. 247/32, fol. 176.
38 T. & T. Clark — Macniven and Wallace, 4 March 1884, N.L.S., Dep. 247/33, fol. 493.
39 For Nicoll's move to Hodder and Stoughton and for details of the *Library* see T.H. Darlow, *William Robertson Nicoll* (1925), pp. 45–46, 460.
40 T. & T. Clark — Macniven and Wallace, N.L.S., Dep. 247/33, fol. 514.
41 T. & T. Clark — S. D. F. Salmond, 19 February 1898, N.L.S., Dep. 247/40, fol. 154a.

42 T. & T. Clark – S. D. F. Salmond, 17 February 1887, N.L.S., Dep. 247/34, fol. 626.

43 T. & T. Clark – D. D. Ormond (of the Free Church Editorial Committee), 18 November 1898, N.L.S., Dep. 247/40, fol. 679. For a discussion of the view held in certain quarters in the Free Church in 1895 that Thomas Nelson and Sons were profiteering at the expense of the Church in issuing the *Free Church Monthly* see John A. H. Dempster, 'Thomas Nelson and Sons in the late Nineteenth Century: A Study in Motivation' Part 2, *Publishing History,* XIV (1983), pp. 5–63 (pp. 33–40).

44 The Clarks were quick to point out Spurgeon's approbation to a correspondent, the editor of a periodical to which they had sent an advertisement for the *Primers,* who felt that the Series had a less than orthodox view of the historicity of the Genesis record, and claimed that Spurgeon 'abhorred' the teaching of the Primers. (T. & T. Clark – J. Urquhart (Editor of *King's Own*), 28 November 1893, N.L.S., Dep. 247/37, fol. 548.)

45 T. & T. Clark – S. D. F. Salmond, 19 February 1898, N.L.S., Dep. 247/40, fol. 154a.

46 *Stock and Sales Book, Individual Titles,* N.L.S., Dep. 247/138, fol. 58.

47 N.L.S., Dep. 247/138.

48 This is the implication of T. & T. Clark – S. D. F. Salmond, 12 August 1887, N.L.S., Dep. 247/34, fol. 773.

49 T. & T. Clark – Scribners, 10 September 1896, N.L.S., Dep. 247/39, fol. 172.

50 T. & T. Clark – S. D. F. Salmond, 12 August 1887, N.L.S., Dep. 247/34, fol. 773; T. & T. Clark – Hugh Callan, 3 January 1899, N.L.S., Dep. 247/40, fol. 784; T. & T. Clark – R.? Rester, N.L.S., Dep. 247/40, fol. 848.

51 T. & T. Clark – Scribners, 13 May 1899, N.L.S., Dep. 247/40, fol. 980.

52 Ibid.

53 T. & T. Clark – Oliphant Smeaton, 16 November 1898, N.L.S., Dep. 247/40, fol. 672. It is not clear whether the 12½% royalty was an alternative to a lower royalty, or (more likely from the wording) to a down payment.

54 T. & T. Clark – the Editor of the *Bookseller,* 12 June 1900, N.L.S., Dep. 247/40a, fol. 699.

55 See T. & T. Clark – Oliphant Smeaton, 8 December 1900, N.L.S., Dep. 247/40b, fol. 22. This letter is interesting for what it reveals of the firm's close relationship with the editor, and appreciative attitude towards him:

> Before Sunday comes we wish you to receive a note from us just to say that (referring especially to [Arthur] Lillie's 'Buddha') we know the best of Editors may make a mistake – or rather, let us say, that the best Author he selects may make a mistake – & we do not wish you to feel disheartened or depressed. We are very sensible that you have done & are doing all you can for the Series, and we have no doubt that some of the future Volumes will make up for the one or two inferior ones which have already appeared – such as 'Buddha', & perhaps 'Wesley' too, for we hear [F.J.] Snell also severely criticised. [T.M.] Lindsay's 'Luther', however, is splendid, there is no doubt of that, & we know it is impossible to get all the Vols. equally good . . . You will, we know, exercise every care & vigilance, & we should never dream of suggesting a change of Editor.

56 It was, indeed, one of the conditions imposed upon the incumbent of the Cunningham Lectureship that his lectures be published at his own risk in an edition of not fewer than 750 copies. (*Extract Declaration of Trust,* printed at the front of James Walker's Cunningham Lectures on the *Theology and Theologians of Scotland,* which T. & T. Clark published.)

57 The details of the constitution of this Lectureship are given in the *Extract Declaration of Trust,* dated 1 March 1862, printed at the front of James Walker's Cunningham series. (See note 56.) One William Webster, wishing to further the cause of theological literature in Scotland, and to commemorate William

Cunningham, a New College Professor, put in Trust the sum of £2,000 to finance 'the Cunningham Lectureship', as it was to be known. The *Declaration of Trust* defines those who were eligible to be considered for the Lectureship (Free Church ministers and professors, and occasionally ministers and professors from other denominations), and stipulates that they could be appointed for either two or three years, at the end of which they would be expected to deliver, within the New College term time, a series of at least six lectures, which they would afterwards be required to publish at their own risk. Other conditions were also laid down.

58 Thomas Clark — T. W. Stoughton, 5 December 1879, N.L.S., Dep. 247/32, fol. 210.

59 T. & T. Clark — W. G. Blaikie, 28 February 1888, N.L.S., Dep. 247/34, fol. 985. The implication is that, contrary to the conditions in the *Extract Declaration of Trust,* the Clarks, rather than the author had been bearing the risk. In Blaikie's case they were prepared to accept the work because they agreed with the lecturer's assessment that his material might be more popular in book form than had been some of the recent Cunningham Lectures.

60 T. & T. Clark — Herr Hertz, Berlin, 21 September 1886, N.L.S., Dep. 247/34, fol. 480.

61 T. & T. Clark — Walter Sloan of the China Inland Mission, 13 May 1899, N.L.S., Dep. 247/40, fol. 985.

62 T. & T. Clark — H. MacDonald Scott, Leipzig, 27 March 1880, N.L.S., Dep. 247/32, fol. 287.

63 T. & T. Clark — J. Beveridge, 5 October 1895, N.L.S., Dep. 247/38, fol. 622. The reasons given for the Clarks' attitude were, firstly, that Dahle was himself eager to see the work translated, and, secondly, that Beveridge had already expended considerable efforts on the translation. The work was published later in 1895.

64 John M. Clark — Professor Godet, 30 January 1897, N.L.S., Dep. 247/39, fol. 450.

65 The un-named Wesleyan Methodist contributor to *The Publishing House,* pp. 17–18.

66 T. & T. Clark — Edward Lummis, 15 June 1900, N.L.S., Dep. 247/40a, fol. 705.

67 Ibid.

68 T. & T. Clark — Edward E. Whitfield, 7 September 1896, N.L.S., Dep. 247/39, fol. 157.

69 T. & T. Clark — Edward Lummis, 15 June 1900, N.L.S., Dep. 247/40a, fol. 705.

70 Published in Tubingen in five volumes between 1909 and 1913.

71 Volume 4, col. 649. Quoted in Alasdair I. MacLeod, *James Hastings and the Encyclopaedia of Religion and Ethics* (unpublished paper, n.d.), p. 17.

72 T. & T. Clark — Moulton, 14 June 1897, N.L.S., Dep. 247/39, fol. 722.

73 See T. & T. Clark — Bishop Martensen, 7 June 1879, N.L.S., Dep. 247/32, fol. 83; T. & T. Clark — Dr Simon, 7 August 1879, N.L.S., Dep. 247/32, fol. 100; T. & T. Clark — Messrs Vandenhoeck and Ruprecht, 21 May 1880, N.L.S., Dep. 247/32, fol. 314.

74 T. & T. Clark — R. T. Cunningham, 17 November 1885, N.L.S., Dep. 247/34, fol. 187.

75 T. & T. Clark — F. E. König, 30 May 1899, N.L.S., Dep. 247/40a, fol. 16.

76 T. & T. Clark — H. Martensen, 7 June 1879, N.L.S., Dep. 247/32, fol. 83. The Clarks were conscious that this was a small honorarium, but the first volume of the work had not been hugely successful, and since over a year had elapsed since their initial publication, the firm could not secure sole rights in the succeeding volumes. Further payments would be made to Martensen if the work's sales merited these.

77 T. & T. Clark — Emil Schürer of Keil, 18 November 1884, N.L.S., Dep. 247/33, fol. 741.

78 Ibid.

79 T. & T. Clark — Emil Schürer, 29 November 1884, N.L.S., Dep. 247/33, fol. 754.

80 T. & T. Clark — G. Dalman, 22 February 1900, N.L.S., Dep. 247/40a, fol. 496.

81 Thomas Clark-Hertz, Berlin, 24 July 1879, N.L.S., Dep. 247/32, fol. 115. The work in question was Professor Isaac A. Dorner's *Dogmatik*.
82 T. & T. Clark – Samuel R. Driver, Oxford, 17 January 1893, N.L.S., Dep. 247/37, fol. 57.
83 T. & T. Clark – Hertz, 3 November 1885, N.L.S., Dep. 247/34, fol. 173. This was presumably the work published by the Clarks in 1887 at 14*s*. 0*d*. as *A System of Christian Ethics*.
84 T. & T. Clark – Hertz, 29 September 1879, N.L.S., Dep. 247/32, fol. 158; T. & T. Clark – Hertz, 7 October 1879, N.L.S., Dep. 247/32, fol. 163.
85 T. & T. Clark – C. H. H. Wright, Belfast (the translator), 9 April 1884, N.L.S., Dep. 247/33, fol. 536; T. & T. Clark – C. H. H. Wright, 21 April 1884, N.L.S., Dep. 247/33, fol. 545; T. & T. Clark – F. E. König, 28 April 1884, N.L.S., Dep. 247/33, fol. 554.
86 T. & T. Clark – Hertz, Berlin, 21 September 1886, N.L.S., Dep. 247/35, fol. 480. The work in question was by Professor Bernhard Weiss, one of whose earlier books, a *Life of Christ,* had been published in translation by the Clarks only after much agonising, as we have seen. The work had, they claimed 'been very far from a success with us'.
87 T. & T. Clark – Vandenhoeck and Ruprecht, 21 May 1880, N.L.S., Dep. 247/32, fol. 314.
88 T. & T. Clark – Hertz, 24 July 1879, N.L.S., Dep. 247/32, fol. 115.
89 T. & T. Clark – Edward Lummis, 15 June 1900, N.L.S., Dep. 247/40a, fol. 705.
90 T. & T. Clark – ?Walde, 16 January 1893, N.L.S., Dep. 247/37, fol. 52.
91 John M. Clark – S. R. Driver, 17 January 1893, N.L.S., Dep. 247/37, fol. 57.
92 T. & T. Clark – F. E. König, 26 November 1900, N.L.S., Dep. 247/40b, fol. 5.
93 T. & T. Clark – Neil Buchanan, 2 May 1893, N.L.S., Dep. 247/37, fol. 228. Buchanan was the translator of the *New Testament Theology* of J. H. C. W. Beyschlag of Hallé, which was issued in two volumes at 18*s*. 0*d*. (1894).
94 T. & T. Clark – Dr Simon, 8 July 1879, N.L.S., Dep. 247/32, fol. 100.
95 T. & T. Clark – Dr Simon, 8 July 1879, N.L.S., Dep. 247/32, fol. 100. The work in question was I. A. Dorner's *System of Christian Doctrine* which eventually ran to four volumes in the F.T.L., selling at £2 2*s*. 0*d*.
96 T. & T. Clark – J. A. Selbie, 10 January 1899, N.L.S., Dep. 247/40, fol. 803.
97 T. & T. Clark – F. Crombie, 17 November 1887, N.L.S., Dep. 247/34, fol. 872.
98 *Stock and Sales Book, Individual Titles,* N.L.S., Dep. 247/138; T. & T. Clark – Neil Buchanan, 2 May 1893, N.L.S., Dep. 247/37, fol. 228.
99 T. & T. Clark – F. Crombie, 17 November 1887, N.L.S., Dep. 247/34, fol. 872.
100 T. & T. Clark – J. Campbell, 25 June 1885, N.L.S., Dep. 247/34, fol. 14. It is not clear at which point translators were normally paid for their work. In this case, it was obviously some time *after* publication.
101 John M. Clark – Neil Buchanan, 2 May 1893, N.L.S., Dep. 247/37, fol. 228.
102 T. & T. Clark – Scribners, 30 March 1885, N.L.S., Dep. 247/33, fol. 916.
103 T. & T. Clark – J. Beveridge, 5 November 1896, N.L.S., Dep. 247/39, fol. 284. Clearly, the Clarks had written previously to Beveridge, complaining about the cost of corrections at proof stage, to which Beveridge had replied by reminding the firm that many of the changes had been made at their instigation. The letter quoted is their response to this point. The work in question is Dahle's *Life after Death*.
104 T. & T. Clark – Scribners, 30 March 1885, N.L.S., Dep. 247/33, fol. 916. The Clarks were also prepared, if Scribners wished, to supply them with the 250 copies in sheets at 7*s*. 6*d*. per volume.
105 T. & T. Clark – Scribners, 9 April 1885, N.L.S., Dep. 247/33, fol. 936. The Clarks would also be prepared to supply Scribners with the 250 copies in sheets at 7*s*. 6*d*. per set.
106 T. & T. Clark, *Trade List,* November 1889.
107 The sources for this study are T. & T. Clark – James M. MacDonald, 24 May

1886, 2 June 1886, 7 June 1886, 10 June 1886, 25 June 1886, N.L.S., Dep. 247/34, fols. 382, 395, 398, 403, 420; T. & T. Clark — Professor Nöldeke, Strasburg, 24 May 1886, N.L.S., Dep. 247/34, fol. 384; a copy of a note from the United States journal *Hebraica*, N.L.S., Dep. 247/34, fol. 404.

108 T. & T. Clark — James M. MacDonald, 24 May 1886.

109 The balance of MacDonald's honorarium was also to be paid upon the sale of the first four hundred copies. It was also stipulated that the payment to Nöldeke must include any claim of the publisher, Herr Weigel.

110 T. & T. Clark — James M. MacDonald, 2 June 1886, N.L.S., Dep. 247/34, fol. 395.

111 T. & T. Clark — James M. MacDonald, 7 June 1886, N.L.S., Dep. 247/34, fol. 398.

112 T. & T. Clark — James M. MacDonald, 10 June 1886, N.L.S., Dep. 247/34, fol. 403.

113 Copy in N.L.S., Dep. 247/34, fol. 404.

114 T. & T. Clark — W. Done, 25 January 1894, N.L.S., Dep. 247/37, fol. 629.

115 John M. Clark — S. R. Driver, 18 August 1894, N.L.S., Dep. 247/37, fol. 991.

116 T. & T. Clark — John MacPherson, 7 September 1894, N.L.S., Dep. 247/37, fol. 1009.

117 Sir Thomas Clark — John MacPherson, 25 March 1895, N.L.S., Dep. 247/38, fol. 343.

118 T. & T. Clark — John MacPherson, 4 April 1895, N.L.S., Dep. 247/38, fol. 359.

119 T. & T. Clark — John MacPherson, 19 July 1895, N.L.S., Dep. 247/38, fol. 516.

120 *Stock and Sales Book, Individual Titles,* N.L.S., Dep. 247/138, fol. 321.

121 See T. & T. Clark — Alex. Grieve, 24 May 1899, N.L.S., Dep. 247/40a, fol. 8.

122 T. & T. Clark — Adolf Diessmann, 8 August 1898, N.L.S., Dep. 247/40, fol. 461.

123 The sources for this study are T. & T. Clark — Alexander Grieve, 24 May 1899, 26 May 1899, 16 June 1899, 4 July 1899, 16 July 1899, 21 August 1899, 9 September 1899, 25 September 1899, 27 September 1899, 27 November 1899, 15 December 1899, 15 February 1900, 20 June 1900, 2 July 1900, 20 October 1900, 23 March 1901, N.L.S., Dep. 247/40a, fols 8, 11, 44, 81, 108, 154, 179, 223, 230, 356, 389, 482, 714, 740, 928, Dep. 247/40b, fol. 179; T. & T. Clark — W. M. Ramsay, 9 June 1899, 22 September 1899, 25 September 1899, N.L.S., Dep. 247/40a, fols 28, 213, 221; T. & T. Clark — A. King and Co., 23 June 1899, 29 June 1899, 21 July 1899, 1 June 1900, 21 July 1900, N.L.S., Dep. 247/40a, fols 57, 71, 111, 684, 787; Copy of letter from W. M. Ramsay — T. & T. Clark, 23 September 1899. N.L.S., Dep. 247/40, fol. 219.

124 John M. Clark — Alex. Grieve, 27 November 1899, N.L.S., Dep. 247/40a, fol. 356.

125 Copy of W. M. Ramsay — T. & T. Clark, 23 September 1899, N.L.S., Dep. 247/40a, fol. 21.

126 John M. Clark — Alex. Grieve, 20 June 1900, N.L.S., Dep. 247/40a, fol. 714.

127 John M. Clark — Alex. Grieve, 20 October 1900, N.L.S., Dep. 247/40, fol. 928.

128 John M. Clark — Alex. Grieve, 23 March 1901, N.L.S., Dep. 247/40b, fol. 179.

129 T. & T. Clark — Mrs Lyttleton, 4 March 1885, N.L.S., Dep. 247/33, fol. 884. In fact the firm proceeded with publication of the translation outwith the Series.

130 T. & T. Clark — J. Beveridge, 5 October 1895, N.L.S., Dep. 247/38, fol. 622. In this case too, the Clarks agreed in the end to publish the work.

131 T. & T. Clark — Dr Simon, 1 July 1879, N.L.S., 247/32, fol. 94.

132 T. & T. Clark — J. Bosworth, 27 February 1883, N.L.S., Dep. 247/33, fol. 201. The work was apparently popular in the Apostolic Church with which Bosworth was involved.

133 T. & T. Clark — Thomas Desprès, 16 July 1885, N.L.S., Dep. 247/34, fol. 33.

134 T. & T. Clark — Thomas Desprès, 1 September 1887, N.L.S., Dep. 247/34, fol. 794. The Clarks commented 'We can assure you we are doing what we can, but of course we cannot *make* books sell'.

135 N.L.S., Dep. 247/138.
136 *The Publishing House,* p. 8.
137 *Publishers' Circular,* 1846, p. 42.
138 *T. & T. Clark's Publications* (*c.*1891).
139 *Colonial Catalogue* (issued 1901), pp. 44–45.
140 *The Publishing House of T. & T. Clark, Edinburgh* (1882), p. 13.
141 *Catalogue*, *c.*1891, p. 28.
142 T. & T. Clark – Professor F. Crombie, 17 November 1887, N.L.S., Dep. 247/34, fol. 872.
143 *The Publishing House,* p. 17.
144 Ibid., p. 16.
145 Ibid., p. 17.
146 Which was co-published with the American firm of Houghton, Mifflin & Co.
147 T. & T. Clark – Houghton, Mifflin & Co., Boston, 7 August 1882, N.L.S., Dep. 247/33, fol. 18.
148 His *System of Christian Doctrine.*
149 *The Publishing House,* p. 18.
150 T. & T. Clark – James Hill, 1 August 1882, N.L.S., Dep. 247/33, fol. 11.
151 N.L.S., Dep. 247/138.
152 This information is drawn from the firm's *Trade List* (November 1872); catalogues for *c.*1878 and *c.*1891; and the *Colonial Catalogue* (November 1901).
153 These prices were in force for most of the century, although in 1846 at least the Series would seem to have been issued at an annual subscription rate of £1 0*s.* 0*d.* (Note in *Publishers' Circular,* 1846, p. 42.)
154 *Stock and Sales Book, Individual Titles,* N.L.S., Dep. 247/138, fols 75–82, etc.
155 Quotations from, respectively, the *Guardian* magazine, and the American theologian Philip Schaff, as quoted in *T. & T. Clark's Publications* (*c.*1875).
156 F. L. Cross, *Oxford Dictionary of the Christian Church,* second edition, (1974), p. 912.
157 T. & T. Clark – Vandenhoeck and Ruprecht, 21 May 1880, N.L.S., Dep. 247/32, fol. 314.
158 *T. & T. Clark's Publications* (*c.*1891).
159 *Stock and Sales Book, Individual Titles,* N.L.S., Dep. 247/138.
160 F. L. Cross, *Oxford Dictionary of the Christian Church,* second edition, (1974), p. 912.
161 This is the implication of a sentence in T. & T. Clark – Vandenhoeck and Ruprecht, 21 May 1880, N.L.S., Dep. 247/32, fol. 314.
162 T. & T. Clark – Scribners, 27 October 1883, N.L.S., Dep. 247/33, fol. 381; T. & T. Clark – Funk and Wagnalls, 16 January 1884, N.L.S., Dep. 247/33, fol. 438.
163 Thomas Clark – Dabney Hampden, 3 March 1880, N.L.S., Dep. 247/32, fol. 268.
164 T. & T. Clark – Scribners, 20 February 1883, N.L.S., Dep. 247/33, fol. 189.
165 T. & T. Clark – Charles Welford, 2 October 1883, N.L.S., Dep. 247/33, fol. 356.
166 T. & T. Clark – The University Press, Chicago, 16 June 1898, N.L.S., Dep. 247/40, fol. 375.
167 T. & T. Clark – Scribners, 14 April 1885, N.L.S., Dep. 247/33, fol. 940.
168 *American Presbyterianism,* however, was not a success in the UK market, and their experience with it caused the Clarks to decline a similar work by Philip Schaff, another American author with whom they had a close relationship and who had supplied them with valuable work. The firm very much regretted having to decline his *Church and State,* but added 'Our experience with . . . *American Presbyterianism* has been by no means encouraging, & we fear that Dr Schaff's book also will not have a remunerative sale outside of the States.' (T. & T. Clark – Scribners, 25 February 1888, N.L.S., Dep. 247/34, fol. 983.) Clearly, the Clarks did not invariably accept works because of the relationship they had with the author.
169 T. & T. Clark – L. W. Bangs, 18 February 1887, N.L.S., Dep. 247/34, fol. 629.

170 T. & T. Clark – Christian Literature Publishing Company, 9 June 1887, N.L.S., Dep. 247/34, fol. 725.
171 See Ibid.
172 T. & T. Clark – Scribners, 1 March 1887, N.L.S., Dep. 247/34, fol. 646.
173 T. & T. Clark – Funk and Wagnalls, 7 December 1882, N.L.S., Dep. 247/33, fol. 110.
174 T. & T. Clark – Funk and Wagnalls, 6 February 1883, N.L.S., Dep. 247/33, fol. 167.
175 T. & T. Clark – Funk and Wagnalls, 3 March 1883, N.L.S., Dep. 247/33, fol. 209.
176 T. & T. Clark – Funk and Wagnalls, 25 March 1884, N.L.S., Dep. 247/33, fol. 517.
177 T. & T. Clark – Funk and Wagnalls, 7 December 1882, N.L.S., Dep. 247/33, fol. 110.
178 T. & T. Clark – Copyright Department, British Museum, 19 May 1880, N.L.S., Dep. 247/32, fol. 312. The Act in question was the 1842 Copyright Act (5 & 6 Vict. cap. 45). Sections six and seven dealt with the supply of deposit copies of works to the British Museum. Section eight ordered the deposit of four further copies at Stationers' Hall for distribution to the Bodleian Library, to Cambridge University Library, to the Advocates' Library, Edinburgh, and to the Library of Trinity College, Dublin.
179 Thomas Clark – Dabney Hampden, 3 March 1880, N.L.S., Dep. 247/32, fol. 268.
180 T. & T. Clark – C. A. Briggs, 31 March 1885, N.L.S., Dep. 247/33, fol. 918.
181 T. & T. Clark – Scribners, 23 February 1886, N.L.S., Dep. 247/33, fol. 293.
182 T. & T. Clark – Scribners, 12 February 1884, N.L.S., Dep. 247/33, fol. 464.
183 Ibid.
184 T. & T. Clark – Houghton, Mifflin, 10 November 1885, N.L.S., Dep. 247/34, fol. 179. The work in question was Stades' *History of Israel.*
185 T. & T. Clark – C. Welford (Scribner's London Agent), 7 June 1884, N.L.S., Dep. 247/33, fol. 595. The letter continued 'We could not venture on more than 1*s.* 6*d.* for an Edition [illegible]'. The work had a retail price of 5*s.* 6*d.*
186 T. & T. Clark – Christian Literature Publishing Company, 16 March 1897, N.L.S., Dep. 247/39, fol. 559.
187 T. & T. Clark – Philip Schaff, 12 December 1882, N.L.S., Dep. 247/33, fol. 113.
188 T. & T. Clark – Christian Literature Publishing Company, 16 March 1897, N.L.S., Dep. 247/39, fol. 559.
189 T. & T. Clark – Scribners, 12 February 1884, N.L.S., Dep. 247/33, fol. 464.
190 Ibid.
191 Published in 1885.
192 T. & T. Clark – Scribners, 14 April 1885, N.L.S., Dep. 247/33, fol. 940
193 T. & T. Clark – Scribners, 25 February 1888, N.L.S., Dep. 247/34, fol. 983.
194 Due to an error, the Clarks note the loss as being £4 13*s.* 0*d.*
195 T. & T. Clark – C. A. Briggs, 20 February 1885, N.L.S., Dep. 247/33, fol. 874.
196 Ibid.
197 T. & T. Clark – C. A. Briggs, 31 March 1885, N.L.S., Dep. 247/33, fol. 918.
198 T. & T. Clark – C. A. Briggs, 20 February 1885, N.L.S., Dep. 247/33, fol. 874.
199 T. & T. Clark – Scribners, 8 December 1885, N.L.S., Dep. 247/34, fol. 213. 450 copies of the January 1885 number had been sent. (T. & T. Clark – C. A. Briggs, 20 February 1885, N.L.S., Dep. 247/33, fol. 874)
200 T. & T. Clark – Scribners, 23 February 1886, N.L.S., Dep. 247/34, fol. 293.
201 T. & T. Clark – Scribners, 10 January 1888, N.L.S., Dep. 247/34, fol. 922.
202 T. & T. Clark – S. D. F. Samond, 15 July 1886, N.L.S., Dep. 247/34, fol. 440.
203 T. & T. Clark – C. A. Briggs, 24 February 1886, N.L.S., Dep. 247/34, fol. 296.
204 T. & T. Clark – Scribners, 18 January 1887, N.L.S., Dep. 247/34, fol. 589.
205 T. & T. Clark – C. A. Briggs, 20 February 1885, N.L.S., Dep. 247/33, fol. 874.
206 T. & T. Clark – Scribners, 23 February 1886, N.L.S., Dep. 247/34, fol. 293.
207 T. & T. Clark – Scribners, 10 January 1888, N.L.S., Dep. 247/34, fol. 922.

208 T. & T. Clark – Scribners, 18 January 1887, N.L.S., Dep. 247/34, fol. 589.
209 T. & T. Clark – Scribners, 10 January 1888, N.L.S., Dep. 247/34, fol. 922.
210 Where the prices are noted as follows: per issue-trade, 3*s.* 2*d.*; retail, 3*s.* 6*d.* net: per annum (four issues) – trade 11*s.* 3*d.*; retail 12*s.* 6*d.* net.
211 T. & T. Clark, *Catalogue*, (*c.* 1894).
212 *Trade Catalogue.*
213 *Stock and Sales Book, Individual Titles,* N.L.S., Dep. 247/138.
214 T. & T. Clark, *Catalogue* (*c.* 1894), p. 22.
215 N.L.S., Dep. 247/138.
216 No copies were bought of the volumes on the *Swiss Reformation* so it is impossible to be certain what the Clarks' buying price was in the case of that title.
217 In 1896–97, £1 was charged to each title as its contribution to the promotion budget. On average, twenty-four copies were sold of each title in the Series. Each copy sold therefore contributed 10*d.* to the 'Proportion of Lists'. The Series was not separately advertised. Over 1897–98, each title contributed only 10*s.* 0*d.* to the 'Proportion of Lists', but specific advertising of the Series cost 2*s.* 3*d.* per title in addition to this. Sales averaged twenty-one per title. Each copy sold therefore contributed 7*d.* to the promotion budget.
218 T. & T. Clark – Christian Literature Publishing Company, 31 August 1896, N.L.S., Dep. 247/39, fol. 142a.
219 T. & T. Clark – Christian Literature Publishing Company, 15 December 1896, N.L.S., Dep. 247/39, fol. 392.
220 Ibid.
221 T. & T. Clark – Christian Literature Publishing Company, 31 August 1896, N.L.S., Dep. 247/39, fol. 142a.
222 Ibid.
223 *Stock and Sales Book, Individual Titles,* N.L.S., Dep. 247/138.
224 T. & T. Clark – Christian Literature Publishing Company, 15 December 1896, N.L.S., Dep. 247/39, fol. 392.
225 T. & T. Clark – Christian Literature Publishing Company, 5 February 1897, N.L.S., Dep. 247/39, fol. 467.
226 T. & T. Clark – Christian Literature Publishing Company, 16 March 1897, N.L.S., Dep. 247/39, fol. 559.
227 Quoted in T. & T. Clark – Henry Gee, 19 March 1897, N.L.S., Dep. 247/39, fol. 572.
228 Ibid.
229 For the letters to Bartlet see T. & T. Clark – Vernon Bartlet, 6 April 1897 and 22 April 1897, N.L.S., Dep. 247/39, fols. 611 and 641.
230 T. & T. Clark, *Colonial Catalogue,* (1902), p. 9.
231 T. & T. Clark – Christian Literature Publishing Company, 20 October 1887, N.L.S., Dep. 247/34, fol. 845.
232 See T. & T. Clark – Christian Literature Publishing Company, 10 November 1893, N.L.S., Dep. 247/37, fol. 516.
233 T. & T. Clark – Funk and Wagnalls, 16 January 1884, N.L.S., Dep. 247/33, fol. 438.
234 *Encyclopaedia Britannica,* fifteenth edition (1985), *Micropaedia,* vol. 10, pp. 570–71.
235 Roger Burlingame, *Of Making Many Books: A Hundred Years of Reading, Writing and Publishing* (New York, 1946), pp. 162–64.
236 Ibid.
237 John Tebbel, *A History of Book Publishing in the United States,* 4 vols, II (1975), pp. 222–26.
238 Ibid., p. 224.
239 See Tebbel, op. cit., p. 222.
240 John M. Clark – James Hastings, 11 February 1904, N.L.S., Dep. 247/40c, fol. 82.

241 T. & T. Clark – Scribners, 12 February 1884, N.L.S., Dep. 247/33, fol. 464.
242 T. & T. Clark – Scribners, 24 February 1885, N.L.S., Dep. 247/33, fol. 876.
243 N.L.S., Dep. 247/33, fol. 787.
244 It no doubt suited Scribners also to be able to decline works which they felt were unlikely to have a satisfactory sale.
245 T. & T. Clark – Scribners, 27 August 1897, N.L.S., Dep. 247/39, fol. 825.
246 T. & T. Clark – ?, 4 July 1883, N.L.S., Dep. 247/33, fol. 296.
247 T. & T. Clark – J. D. Kirkpatrick, 3 March 1885, N.L.S., Dep. 247/33, fol. 882.
248 T. & T. Clark – Scribners, 19 December 1882, N.L.S., Dep. 247/33, fol. 120.
249 T. & T. Clark – Putnam, 11 October 1893, N.L.S., Dep. 247/37, fol. 441.
250 T. & T. Clark – Scribners, 8 September 1884, N.L.S., Dep. 247/33, fol. 663. Clark enclosed with the letter three other letters addressed to the houses of Funk and Wagnalls, Randolph, and Bartlett in which similar proposals were made about the *Monthly Intepreter*, and asked Scribners to post these if they were declining the offer 'as there [was] no time to lose'.
251 T. & T. Clark – Scribners, 4 July 1894, N.L.S., Dep. 247/37, fol. 894.
252 It may well have been the case that little money in fact changed hands, the sums owed by each firm merely being set against one another. This principle certainly operated in the two firms' co-editions programme.
253 The data in the Table is from Trade Ledgers 1881–1890, 1890–1895, 1895–1901, N.L.S., Dep. 247/99a, 100, 100a.
254 N.L.S., Dep. 247/100a.
255 *A History of Book Publishing in the United States*, 4 vols, II (1975), p. 332. See pp. 331–334 and pp. 359–60 for material on Revell and the company he founded.
256 Ibid., p. 332.
257 T. & T. Clark – Fleming H. Revell, 25 April 1883, N.L.S., Dep. 247/33, fol. 259.
258 T. & T. Clark – Presbyterian News Company, 22 June 1893, N.L.S., Dep. 247/37, fol. 303.
259 T. & T. Clark – A. E. Whatham, Michigan, 5 November [sic-actually December] 1893, N.L.S., Dep. 247/37, fol. 561.
260 See John Tebbel, *A History of Book Publishing in the United States*, 4 vols, II (1975), pp. 373–74 for data on the firm.
261 Ibid., p. 373.
262 Ibid., p. 558.
263 Ibid.
264 Ibid., p. 559.
265 N.L.S., Dep. 247/100a.
266 The *Ledger* does record the Clarks' royalty income from Fleming H. Revell on his sales of Stalker's *Life of Christ* and *Life of St Paul* at 5c. per copy. This income was received annually in February: in the five years commencing February 1897 it amounted to 19*s*. 8*d*., £3 19*s*. 3*d*., £1 10*s*. 2*d*., £2 10*s*. 0*d*.
267 *International Copyright Law and the Publishers in the Reign of Queen Victoria* (1968), p. 16.
268 Ibid., pp. 64–65.
269 It seems unlikely, incidentally, that US piracies of Clark titles were ever imported into the UK.
270 T. & T. Clark – Philip Schaff, 12 December 1882, N.L.S., Dep. 247/33, fol. 113.
271 T. & T. Clark – Scribners, 24 February 1885, N.L.S., Dep. 247/33, fol. 876. The Clarks may have been slightly exaggerating here, for the aim of the letter was, in part, to persuade the US firm to take the risk of importing editions from Edinburgh.
272 See T. & T. Clark – Christian Literature Publishing Company, 10 November 1893, N.L.S., Dep. 247/37, fol. 516.
273 See T. & T. Clark – Funk and Wagnalls, 7 December 1882, N.L.S., Dep. 247/33, fol. 110, and T. & T. Clark – Scribners, 8 September 1884, N.L.S., Dep. 247/33, fol. 663.

274 A US pirate need not, of course, notify the Clarks of the existence of an unauthorised reprint, but the Edinburgh firm was very quickly apprised of such piracies by their official US agents.

275 T. & T. Clark – The Bishop of New York, 25 September 1884, N.L.S., Dep. 247/33, fol. 684.

276 T. & T. Clark – Christian Literature Publishing Company, 13 October 1884, N.L.S., Dep. 247/33, fol. 709.

277 T. & T. Clark – Scribners, 20 January 1885, N.L.S., Dep. 247/33, fol. 820.

278 T. & T. Clark – Christian Literature Publishing Company, 22 November 1884, 20 December 1884, N.L.S., Dep. 247/33, fols 745, 787. The Company also had Canadian rights in the Series, certainly by 1887. (T. & T. Clark – Christian Literature Publishing Company, 20 October 1887, N.L.S., Dep. 247/34, fol. 845.)

279 See T. & T. Clark – Scribners, 20 December 1884, N.L.S., Dep. 247/33, fol. 786.

280 T. & T. Clark – Scribners, 30 March 1885, N.L.S., Dep. 247/33, fol. 916.

281 T. & T. Clark – Christian Literature Publishing Company, 1 May 1885, N.L.S., Dep. 247/33, fol. 960.

282 T. & T. Clark – Philip Schaff, 27 January 1885, N.L.S., Dep. 247/33, fol. 833.

283 T. & T. Clark – Christian Literature Publishing Company, 1 May 1885, N.L.S., Dep. 247/33, fol. 960.

284 T. & T. Clark – Christian Literature Publishing Company, 9 May 1885, N.L.S., Dep. 247/33, fol. 975. It is interesting that Scribners' stocks should have been so low. Is this in fact an indication that they had been selling very few copies of the Series, or was it merely that the Clarks had not been supplying them while negotiations with the Company were under way? If the former were the case, it would indicate that the Clarks' income from American sales of their own edition had been modest; given that the Company was hoping to sell at least one thousand copies of each volume of its edition, the Clarks' income from this reluctantly authorised reprint might well have outstripped their former income from sales through Scribners.

285 Ibid.

286 T. & T. Clark – Christian Literature Publishing Company, 9 May 1885 and 6 June 1885, N.L.S., Dep. 247/33, fols 960, 975.

287 T. & T. Clark – Christian Literature Publishing Company, 30 June 1885 and 6 August 1885, N.L.S., Dep. 247/34, fols 19, 52.

288 T. & T. Clark – Christian Literature Publishing Company, 6 August and 15 September 1885, N.L.S., Dep. 247/34, fols 52, 95.

289 T. & T. Clark – Christian Literature Publishing Company, 13 November 1885, N.L.S., Dep. 247/34, fol. 183.

290 T. & T. Clark – Christian Literature Publishing Company, 2 November 1886, N.L.S., Dep. 247/34, fol. 534.

291 T. & T. Clark – Christian Literature Publishing Company, 9 June 1887, N.L.S., Dep. 247/34, fol. 725. There is no record of whether or not the Clarks' experiment with this series proved to be successful.

292 T. & T. Clark – Christian Literature Publishing Company, 17 August 1893, N.L.S., Dep. 247/37, fol. 367.

293 T. & T. Clark – The Bishop of New York, 25 September 1884, N.L.S., Dep. 247/33, fol. 684.

294 T. & T. Clark – Funk and Wagnalls, 16 January 1884, N.L.S., Dep. 247/33, fol. 438.

295 T. & T. Clark – Scribners, 8 September 1884, N.L.S., Dep. 247/33, fol. 663.

296 See, for example, T. & T. Clark – Scribners, 1 December 1890, N.L.S., Dep. 247/36, fol. 130.

297 T. & T. Clark – Scribners, 30 March 1885, N.L.S., Dep. 247/33, fol. 916.

298 T. & T. Clark – Scribners, 24 February 1885, N.L.S., Dep. 247/33, fol. 876.

299 T. & T. Clark – Christian Literature Publishing Company, 17 August 1893, N.L.S., Dep. 247/37, fol. 367.

300 Ibid.
301 There would appear to be no record of the number of copies being sold by Scribners at this point.
302 T. & T. Clark – Christian Literature Publishing Company, 17 August 1893, N.L.S., Dep. 247/37, fol. 367.
303 T. & T. Clark – Christian Literature Publishing Company, 10 November 1893, N.L.S., Dep. 247/37, fol. 516.
304 T. & T. Clark – Scribners, 27 August 1897, N.L.S., Dep. 247/39, fol. 825.
305 T. & T. Clark – Christian Literature Publishing Company, 2 September 1897, N.L.S., Dep. 247/39, fol. 833.
306 T. & T. Clark – Christian Literature Publishing Company, 27 September 1897, N.L.S., Dep. 247/39, fol. 900.
307 T. & T. Clark – Scribners, 27 August 1897, N.L.S., Dep. 247/39, fol. 825.
308 *Stock and Sales Book, Individual Titles,* N.L.S., Dep. 247/138, fol. 310.
309 See *Stock and Sales Book, Individual Titles,* N.L.S., Dep. 247/138 for the data on which this figure is based.
310 T. & T. Clark – Professor Laidlaw, 21 July 1891, N.L.S., Dep. 247/36, fol. 408.
311 T. & T. Clark – Scribners, 8 March 1894, N.L.S., Dep. 247/37, fol. 708.
312 See T. & T. Clark – Scribners, 5 November 1898, N.L.S., Dep. 247/40, fol. 651.
313 *Stock and Sales Book, Individual Titles,* N.L.S., Dep. 247/138, fol. 51.
314 Figures from *Stock Sales Notebook 1896–97,* N.L.S., Dep. 247/71.
315 See T. & T. Clark – Houghton, Mifflin and Co., 7 August 1882, N.L.S., Dep. 247/33, fol. 18, where the Clarks were at pains to point out the need for the translation to be as accurate and elegant as possible.
316 T. & T. Clark – Philip Schaff, 2 September 1879, N.L.S., Dep. 247/32, fol. 139.
317 T. & T. Clark – Philip Schaff, 22 September 1879, N.L.S., Dep. 247/32, fol. 150.
318 *British Library Catalogue.*
319 T. & T. Clark – Philip Schaff, 3 January 1885, N.L.S., Dep. 247/33, fol. 799.
320 See T. & T. Clark – Philip Schaff, 3 January 1885, N.L.S., Dep. 247/33, fol. 799.
321 See, for example, T. & T. Clark – Principal Douglas, 2 August 1879, N.L.S., Dep. 247/32, fol. 129.
322 T. & T. Clark – Scribners, 16 February 1880, N.L.S., Dep. 247/32, fol. 252. In fact, Scribners, who produced the first volume, had violated the agreement by sending the Clarks an invoice for the plates, and then by including the sum in their statement despite protests from Thomas Clark, who pointed out that 'Had our vol. been first we should never have dreamt of making any such charge in advance.' There is no record of whether or not Scribners withdrew their invoice.
323 T. & T. Clark – Scribners, 2 August 1883, N.L.S., Dep. 247/33, fol. 319.
324 T. & T. Clark – Dr Plumptre, 2 August 1879, N.L.S., Dep. 247/32, fol. 128. It was in 1879 that Charles Scribner II became head of the firm.
325 T. & T. Clark – Principal Douglas, 2 August 1879, N.L.S., Dep. 247/32, fol. 129.
326 Ibid. See also T. & T. Clark – Philip Schaff, 2 September 1879, N.L.S., Dep. 247/32, fol. 139.
327 Thomas Clark – Philip Schaff, 2 September 1879, N.L.S., Dep. 247/32, fol. 139.
328 The *Revised New Testament* was published on 17 May 1881, on which day one million copies were distributed. Peter Sutcliffe, *The Oxford University Press: An Informal History* (Oxford, 1978) p. 51.
329 T. & T. Clark – Messrs Price and Clay, 16 December 1879, N.L.S., Dep. 247/32, fol. 217.
330 Thomas Clark – Messrs Price and Clay, 29 January 1880, N.L.S., Dep. 247/32, fol. 240.
331 See Thomas Clark – Messrs Price and Clay, 29 January 1880, N.L.S., Dep. 247/32, fol. 240; and T. & T. Clark – Philip Schaff, 12 February 1880, N.L.S., Dep. 247/32, fol. 248.
332 Thomas Clark – Messrs Price and Clay, 29 January 1880, N.L.S., Dep. 247/32, fol. 240.

333 T. & T. Clark – Philip Schaff, 17 February 1880, N.L.S., Dep. 247/32, fol. 253.
334 T. & T. Clark – Scribners, 18 December 1879, N.L.S., Dep. 247/32, fol. 221.
335 T. & T. Clark – Scribners, 12 February 1884, N.L.S., Dep. 247/33, fol. 464.
336 T. & T. Clark – Philip Schaff, 3 January 1885, N.L.S., Dep. 247/33, fol. 799.
337 T. & T. Clark – S. D. F. Salmond, 11 February 1887, N.L.S., Dep. 247/34, fol. 617.
338 T. & T. Clark – C. A. Briggs, 6 September 1887, N.L.S., Dep. 247/34, fol. 800.
339 'Draft of Advice to I.T.L. Authors', N.L.S., Dep. 247/34, fol. 838. This document was approved by the Clarks, by Scribners, and by C. A. Briggs, the American editor. The copy in the Clark letter book carries minor alterations which had been inserted in the original by Scribners.
340 See, for example, T. & T. Clark – S. D. F. Salmond, 24 April 1900, N.L.S., Dep. 247/40a, fol. 616.
341 T. & T. Clark – C. A. Briggs, 13 August 1887, N.L.S., Dep. 247/34, fol. 774.
342 Ibid.
343 T. & T. Clark – C. A. Briggs, 24 August 1887, N.L.S., Dep. 247/34, fol. 787.
344 C. A. Briggs, who was American editor of both series, had sent the Clarks a letter of resignation, presumably from the *Library*, for them to submit to Scribners if the crisis could not be averted. (T. & T. Clark – C. A. Briggs, 13 August 1887, N.L.S., Dep. 247/34, fol. 774).
345 See *The New Cambridge Modern History*, Volume XI, *Material Progress and World-Wide Problems 1879–1898*, edited by F. H. Hinsley, (1970), pp. 671–73.
346 John M. Clark – C. A. Briggs, 7 January 1896, N.L.S., Dep. 247/38, fol. 750.
347 T. & T. Clark – C. A. Briggs, 6 September 1887, N.L.S., Dep. 247/34, fol. 800.
348 T. & T. Clark – Scribners, 9 April 1887, N.L.S., Dep. 247/34, fol. 680.
349 C. A. Briggs – T. & T. Clark, 8 April 1895, N.L.S., Dep. 247/2.
350 'Draft of Advice to I.T.L. Authors', N.L.S., Dep. 247/34, fol. 838.
351 T. & T. Clark – C. A. Briggs, 6 September 1887, N.L.S., Dep. 247/34, fol. 800.
352 T. & T. Clark – S. D. F. Salmond, 17 June 1897, N.L.S., Dep. 247/39, fol. 728.
353 'Draft of Advice to I.T.L. Authors', N.L.S., Dep. 247/34, fol. 838.
354 T. & T. Clark – S. D. F. Salmond, 17 June 1897, N.L.S., Dep. 247/39, fol. 728. The author in question, Principal Whitehouse, was presumably Owen Charles Whitehouse, Principal of Cheshunt College (Countess of Huntingdon's College) 1895–1905. (*Who Was Who, 1916–28*) He contributed to many of James Hastings' reference works, and to the *Expository Times* and *Critical Review*.
355 T. & T. Clark – C. A. Briggs, 6 February 1888, N.L.S., Dep. 247/34, fol. 958; T. & T. Clark – Principal Fairbairn, 7 April 1896, N.L.S., Dep. 247/38, fol. 913.
356 T. & T. Clark – Scribners, 9 April 1887, N.L.S., Dep. 247/34, fol. 680.
357 From a note appended by Scribners to the 'Draft of Advice to I.T.L. Authors', N.L.S., Dep. 247/34, fol. 838.
358 Ibid. On the subject of remuneration to authors, it is interesting to note the Clarks' deliberations when they were considering commissioning a work from Dr John Watson who was accustomed to receiving a much greater return for his fictional works written as 'Ian MacLaren' than the Clarks could offer for works of theological scholarship. It is instructive to notice the Clarks' awareness of the difference in remuneration to be expected from popular works as opposed to works of academic theology. 'I fear', wrote John Clark to S.D.F. Salmond with regard to Watson

> you would have difficulty in getting him to accept the terms, as he must naturally get much larger return out of what, to him, must be vastly easier work. The type in Novels etc. can now be set up by Linotype (type-setting) Machines, & the cost of production is as nothing compared with those Volumes. [The I.T.L.] The sales, too, are enormous, & quite permit of handsome royalties.

'But', he continued,

> most people will understand that at once, & in the interests of scholarship

Dr Watson *might* be induced to accept.
(John M. Clark — S. D. F. Salmond, 17 June 1897, N.L.S., Dep. 247/39, fol. 728.)
In fact, the plan to commission a work from Watson came to nothing.

359 T. & T. Clark — Scribners, 9 April 1887, N.L.S., Dep. 247/34, fol. 680.
360 T. & T. Clark — Scribners, 22 June 1898, N.L.S., Dep. 247/40, fol. 387. It is noted there that Longman were paying one hundred pounds for each two-hundred page volume in their *Epochs of Church History* series.
361 T. & T. Clark — C. A. Briggs, 6 February 1888, N.L.S., Dep. 247/34, fol. 958.
362 T. & T. Clark — Scribners, 22 June 1898, N.L.S., Dep. 247/40, fol. 387.
363 If the same principle operated with the I.T.L. as with the I.C.C., the editors would each receive a royalty of 2½% on each copy sold on their side of the Atlantic. (T. & T. Clark — A. Plummer, 1 March 1888, N.L.S., Dep. 247/34, fol. 988.)
364 'Draft of Advice to I.T.L. Authors', N.L.S., Dep. 247/34, fol. 838.
365 T. & T. Clark — C. A. Briggs, 6 September 1887, N.L.S., Dep. 247/34, fol. 800.
366 T. & T. Clark — Scribners, 3 December 1887, N.L.S., Dep. 247/34, fol. 895.
367 Quoted in T. & T. Clark — C. A. Briggs, 3 December 1887, N.L.S., Dep. 247/34, fol. 897.
368 T. & T. Clark — Scribners, 9 April 1887, N.L.S., Dep. 247/34, fol. 680.
369 T. & T. Clark — S. D. F. Salmond, 30 November 1897, N.L.S., Dep. 247/40, fol. 18.
370 T. & T. Clark — Scribners, 30 May 1898, N.L.S., Dep. 247/40, fol. 344.
371 T. & T. Clark — C. A. Briggs, 30 December 1887, N.L.S., Dep. 247/34, fol. 917.
372 *Colonial Catalogue,* (1902).
373 'Draft of Advice to I.T.L. Authors', N.L.S., Dep. 247/34, fol. 838.
374 See T. & T. Clark — Scribners, 14 October 1897, N.L.S., Dep. 247/39, fol. 923.
375 T. & T. Clark — Scribners, 11 January 1898, N.L.S., Dep. 247/40, fol. 78.
376 T. & T. Clark — Scribners, 2 July 1898, N.L.S., Dep. 247/40, fol. 403.
377 T. & T. Clark — Scribners, 2 December 1897, N.L.S., Dep. 247/40, fol. 22.
378 T. & T. Clark — A. Plummer, 30 November 1897, N.L.S., Dep. 247/40, fol. 19.
379 'Draft of Advice to I.T.L. Authors', N.L.S., Dep. 247/34, fol. 838.
380 See T. & T. Clark — Scribners, 3 August 1891, N.L.S., Dep. 247/36, fol. 422, a letter accompanying the account to Scribner in respect of a work which the Clarks had originated, Driver's *Introduction to the Literature of the Old Testament.*
381 T. & T. Clark — Scribners, 9 April 1887, N.L.S., Dep. 247/34, fol. 680.
382 *Colonial Catalogue,* (1902).
383 C. A. Briggs — T. & T. Clark, 8 April 1895, N.L.S., Dep. 247/2.
384 T. & T. Clark — S. D. F. Salmond, 23 March 1896, N.L.S., Dep. 247/38, fol. 882.
385 T. & T. Clark — Scribners, 30 May 1898, N.L.S., Dep. 247/40, fol. 344.
386 It bears the publication date '1902', but was probably issued in late 1901.
387 'Draft of Advice to I.T.L. Authors', N.L.S., Dep. 247/34, fol. 838.
388 T. & T. Clark — A. Plummer, 1 March 1888, N.L.S., Dep. 247/34, fol. 988.
389 T. & T. Clark — Scribners, 9 April 1887, N.L.S., Dep. 247/34, fol. 680.
390 Data on this title is from the *Stock and Sales Book, Individual Titles,* N.L.S., Dep. 247/138, fol. 49.
391 Ibid.
392 Ibid.
393 *Colonial Catalogue,* (1902).
394 N.L.S., Dep. 247/138.
395 T. & T. Clark — Edward Lummis, 15 June 1900, N.L.S., Dep. 247/40a, fol. 705.
396 T. & T. Clark — S. R. Driver, 6 December 1887, N.L.S., Dep. 247/34, fol. 898; T. & T. Clark — A. Plummer, 20 January 1888, N.L.S., Dep. 247/34, fol. 928.
397 T. & T. Clark — C A Briggs, 13 August 1887, N.L.S., Dep. 247/34, fol. 774.
398 T. & T. Clark — Scribners, 9 June 1887, N.L.S., Dep. 247/34, fol. 722.
399 T. & T. Clark — Scribners, 2 July 1887, N.L.S., Dep. 247/34, fol. 745.
400 T. & T. Clark — C. A. Briggs, 13 August 1887, N.L.S., Dep. 247/34, fol. 774;

T. & T. Clark — Scribners, 15 March 1888, N.L.S., Dep. 247/35, fol. 13.
401 T. & T. Clark — C. A. Briggs, N.L.S., Dep. 247/34, fol. 787.
402 'We have no difficulty in going on alone were it not for the risk of pirating in America'. (T. & T. Clark — C. A. Briggs, 13 August 1887, N.L.S., Dep. 247/34, fol. 774).
403 T. & T. Clark — A. Plummer, 20 January 1888, N.L.S., Dep. 247/34, fol. 928.
404 Ibid.
405 T. & T. Clark — C. A. Briggs, 29 August 1887, N.L.S., Dep. 247/34, fol. 791.
406 T. & T. Clark — C. A. Briggs, 21 January 1888, N.L.S., Dep. 247/34, fol. 930.
407 T. & T. Clark — S. R. Driver, 17 January 1893, N.L.S., Dep. 247/37, fol. 57.
408 T. & T. Clark — C. A. Briggs, 6 September 1887, N.L.S., Dep. 247/34, fol. 800.
409 T. & T. Clark — C. A. Briggs, 29 August 1887, N.L.S., Dep. 247/34, fol. 791.
410 T. & T. Clark — A. Plummer, 20 January 1888, N.L.S., Dep. 247/34, fol. 928.
411 T. & T. Clark — A. Plummer, 23 December 1899, N.L.S., Dep. 247/40a, fol. 406. The Clarks suggested that Eaton and Fairweather, whose names had been put forward as possible contributors to the Series by James Hastings, were in fact unsuitable, because they were not sufficiently well-known outwith their own Church. Similarly, the Clarks, suggested that a Mr Milligan, who was being considered as a possible author of the volume on *Hebrews,* was unsuitable because 'he would scarcely carry sufficient weight'. (T. & T. Clark — A. Plummer, 5 June 1900, N.L.S., Dep. 247/40a, fol. 687.)
412 T. & T. Clark — S. R. Driver, 6 February 1888, N.L.S., Dep. 247/34, fol. 959.
413 T. & T. Clark — S. R. Driver, 13 September 1887, N.L.S., Dep. 247/34, fol. 812.
414 *Colonial Catalogue,* (1902).
415 T. & T. Clark — S. R. Driver, 31 December 1895, N.L.S., Dep. 247/38, fol. 743. When Driver passed this comment on to Briggs, he reacted angrily, ignoring the fact that the Ryle review had been for the most part favourable. Briggs pronounced himself 'utterly disgusted', 'deeply offended' and 'outraged', accusing Ryle of being critical because the author had not been born in Britain! As so often, the Clarks poured oil on troubled waters, sending a full text of Ryle's review, and generally placating the over-reacting editor. The tact of the Clark firm played no small part from time to time in keeping the Series appearing regularly by preserving the unanimity of the team. (T. & T. Clark — C. A. Briggs, 3 February 1896, N.L.S., Dep. 247/38, fol. 798.
416 T. & T. Clark — A. Plummer, 14 September 1896, N.L.S., Dep. 247/39, fol. 177.
417 T. & T. Clark — C. J. Dinmont, who had lodged a complaint, 10 September 1896, N.L.S., Dep. 247/39, fol. 174.
418 T. & T. Clark — Scribners, December 1895, N.L.S., Dep. 247/38, fol. 690.
419 *Colonial Catalogue,* (1902).
420 *Stock and Sales Book, Individual Titles,* N.L.S., Dep. 247/138.
421 Ibid.
422 Ibid.
423 Dep. 247/138.
424 T. & T. Clark — S. D. F. Samond, 16 July 1886, N.L.S., Dep. 247/34, fol. 440.
425 C. A. Malcolm, 'Scottish Legal Periodicals: Past and Present', *Scottish Law Review,* 45 (1929), pp. 154–159.
426 T. & T. Clark — A. S. Geden, 26 April 1895, N.L.S., Dep. 247/38, fol. 415a. The work under discussion was W. F. Moulton and A. S. Geden's *Concordance to the Greek New Testament,* which the publishers who were initially to be responsible for the project, Bell, had planned to issue in parts.
427 T. & T. Clark's *Colonial Catalogue,* 1902. The arrangements covering the joint issue of this Latin/Syriac work are to be found in T. & T. Clark — Reuther and Reichard, Berlin, 27 October 1893, N.L.S., Dep. 247/37, fol. 494. There was also a plan to issue each volume of the *Dictionary of the Bible* in six parts which would have appeared concurrently with the volume, but this proposal would seem to have been dropped. It was discussed in T. & T. Clark — James Hastings, 16 July

1897, N.L.S., Dep. 247/39, fol. 774, and in T. & T. Clark – Scribners, 20 November 1897, N.L.S., Dep. 247/39, fol. 987. The rationale of issuing in parts was presumably that such a form of publication would appeal to impecunious theology students, who could ill afford to purchase the work in volume form.

428 *Stock and Sales Book, Individual Titles,* N.L.S., Dep. 247/138, fol. 54. It is unclear what the Clarks' normal returns policy was.

429 *Stock Sales Notebook 1896–97,* N.L.S., Dep. 247/71.

430 T. & T. Clark – William Cruickshank, 8 September 1896, N.L.S., Dep. 247/39, fol. 161.

431 J. M. Clark – S. D. F. Salmond, 3 July 1896, N.L.S., Dep. 247/39, fol. 51.

432 J. M. Clark – S. D. F. Salmond, 28 January 1897, N.L.S., Dep. 247/39, fol. 443.

433 Ibid. It is always conceivable, of course, that Clark advertisements were simply inserted to fill space not taken up by other, outside advertisers. Were this the case, it might well have been economically more attractive to the Clarks to *sell* more advertising space than to use that space to promote their own titles.

434 J. M. Clark – James Hastings, 8 December 1890, N.L.S., Dep. 247/36, fol. 139.

435 T. & T. Clark – J. S. Exell, 19 December 1884, N.L.S., Dep. 247/33, fol. 782.

436 T. & T. Clark – J. S. Exell, 5 December 1884, N.L.S., Dep. 247/33, fol. 762.

437 T. & T. Clark – J. S. Exell, 24 September 1884, N.L.S., Dep. 247/33, fol. 682. The Clarks themselves, of course, as we noted earlier, were none too happy about the Ladd work, which was an American purchase.

438 T. & T. Clark – J. S. Exell, 5 December 1884, N.L.S., Dep. 247/33, fol. 762.

439 Possibly he was John MacPherson of Findhorn whose works appeared in the Clark list.

440 T. & T. Clark – S. D. F. Salmond, 17 December 1898, N.L.S., Dep. 247/40, insert.

441 T. & T. Clark – J. S. Exell, 24 September 1884, N.L.S., Dep. 247/33, fol. 682.

442 T. & T. Clark – Scribners, 15 February 1891, N.L.S., Dep. 247/36, fol. 220.

443 T. & T. Clark – S. D. F. Salmond, 12 December 1889, N.L.S., Dep. 247/35, fol. 70.

444 T. & T. Clark – J. S. Exell, 18 August 1884, N.L.S., Dep. 247/33, fol. 638.

445 T. & T. Clark – J. S. Exell, 22 December 1884, N.L.S., Dep. 247/33, fol. 789.

446 T. & T. Clark – S. D. F. Salmond, 15 July 1886, N.L.S., Dep. 247/34, fol. 440.

447 J. M. Clark – S. D. F. Salmond, 25 January 1897, N.L.S., Dep. 247/39, fol. 439.

448 T. & T. Clark – S. D. F. Salmond, 15 July 1886, N.L.S., Dep. 247/34, fol. 440.

449 T. & T. Clark – J. S. Exell, 18 August 1884, N.L.S., Dep. 247/33, fol. 638.

450 T. & T. Clark – J. S. Exell, 28 August 1884, N.L.S., Dep. 247/33, fol. 652.

451 J. M. Clark – S. D. F. Salmond, 25 January 1897, N.L.S., Dep. 247/39, fol. 439.

452 T. & T. Clark – Scribners, 8 September 1884, N.L.S., Dep. 247/33, fol. 663.

453 T. & T. Clark – J. S. Exell, 9 October 1885, N.L.S., Dep. 247/34, fol. 135.

454 See T. & T. Clark – J. Knox Mitchell, New York, 14 August 1891, N.L.S., Dep. 247/36, fol. 432. Mitchell had, in fact, been seeking the role of American editor of the *Review;* Salmond's arrangements had, he was told, rendered such a post unnecessary for the present at least.

455 J. M. Clark – S. D. F. Salmond, 3 July 1896, N.L.S., Dep. 247/39, fol. 51.

456 See T. & T. Clark – R. M. Wenley, 30 June 1896, N.L.S., Dep. 247/39, fol. 46.

457 W. G. Blaikie, *An Autobiography: 'Recollections of a Busy Life'* (London, 1901), pp. 139–147.

458 T. & T. Clark – J. S. Exell, 18 August 1884, N.L.S., Dep. 247/33, fol. 638.

459 J. M. Clark – W. E. Gladstone, 17 December 1895, N.L.S., Dep. 247/38, fol. 727. 'Of course such space as you might desire would be allotted to you.'

460 T. & T. Clark – S. D. F. Salmond, 15 July 1886, N.L.S., Dep. 247/34, fol. 440.

461 J. M. Clark – S. D. F. Salmond, 12 December 1889, N.L.S., Dep. 247/35, fol. 704.

462 T. & T. Clark – J. S. Exell, 19 March 1885, N.L.S., Dep. 247/33, fol. 901.

463 J. M. Clark – S. D. F. Salmond, 12 December 1889, N.L.S., Dep. 247/35, fol.

704.
464 T. & T. Clark — J. S. Exell, 19 March 1885, N.L.S., Dep. 247/33, fol. 901.
465 T. & T. Clark — J. S. Exell, 19 December 1884, N.L.S., Dep. 247/33, fol. 782.
466 T. & T. Clark — J. S. Exell, 22 December 1884, N.L.S., Dep. 247/33, fol. 789.
467 T. & T. Clark — W. Cruickshank, 8 August 1891, N.L.S., Dep. 247/36, fol. 428.
468 J. M. Clark — S. D. F. Salmond, 11 July 1896, N.L.S., Dep. 247/39, fol. 69.
469 Ibid.
470 T. & T. Clark — C. N. Johnstone and John Chisholm, 6 October 1890, N.L.S., Dep. 247/36, fol. 44.
471 J. M. Clark — S. D. F. Salmond, 11 July 1896, N.L.S., Dep. 247/39, fol. 68.
472 T. & T. Clark — Principal Cave (Hackney College), 14 November 1890, N.L.S., Dep. 247/36, fol. 107.
473 J. M. Clark — S. D. F. Salmond, 25 January 1897, N.L.S., Dep. 247/39, fol. 443.
474 T. & T. Clark — ?, 8 May 1893, N.L.S., Dep. 247/37, fol. 240.
475 T. & T. Clark — William Cruickshank, 8 September 1896, N.L.S., Dep. 247/39, fol. 161.
476 T. & T. Clark — C. H. H. Wright, 25 January 1897, N.L.S., Dep. 247/39, fol. 438.
477 T. & T. Clark — Scribners, 15 February 1891, N.L.S., Dep. 247/36, fol. 220.
478 T. & T. Clark — J. S. Exell, 19 December 1884, N.L.S., Dep. 247/33, fol. 782.
479 T. & T. Clark — William Cruickshank, 26 October 1897, N.L.S., Dep. 247/39, fol. 946. The letter is interesting in showing how important to the Clarks was the maintenance of their reputation. It would appear that they had had their attention drawn to Cruickshank's misdemeanours by some of their customers, who clearly felt it was inappropriate that the firm should continue their association with him.
480 T. & T. Clark — Spriggs, 1 November 1897, N.L.S., Dep. 247/39, fol. 956.
481 T. & T. Clark — S. D. F. Salmond, 28 January 1897, N.L.S., Dep. 247/39, fol. 443.
482 William G. Blaikie, *An Autobiography: 'Recollections of a Busy Life'* (London, 1901), p. 137.
483 *Bookseller,* 1860, p. 440.
484 See, for example, William G. Blaikie, *An Autobiography: 'Recollections of a Busy Life'* (London, 1901), pp. 136–147; 'The Story of the "North British Review"', *Scottish Review,* 3 January 1907, p. 20; *Scottish Notes and Queries,* August 1901, pp. 24–25; *Scottish Notes and Queries,* March 1933, pp. 37–39; Joanne Shattock, 'Editorial Policy and the Quarterlies: The Case of *The North British Review', Victorian Periodicals Newsletter,* 10 (1977), pp. 130–139; Joanne Shattock, 'Problems of Parentage: the *North British Review* and the Free Church of Scotland', in *The Victorian Periodical Press: Samplings and Soundings,* edited by Joanne Shattock and Michael Wolff (Leicester, 1982), pp. 145–166. With the exception of Blaikie's book, all this material majors on the early life of the *North British,* and pays scant attention to the Clarks' brief proprietorship, which occurred at a time when the *Review* is generally considered to have become a spent force.
485 See previous note.
486 'The Story of the "North British Review"', *Scottish Review,* 3 January 1907, p. 20.
487 'Problems of Parentage: the *North British Review* and the Free Church of Scotland,' in *The Victorian Periodical Press: Samplings and Soundings,* edited by Joanne Shattock and Michael Wolff (Leicester, 1982), pp. 145–166 (p. 164).
488 Ibid., p. 163.
489 William Garden Blaikie, *An Autobiography: 'Recollections of a Busy Life'* (London, 1901).
490 Ibid., p. 138.
491 Ibid., p. 147.
492 Ibid., p. 139.
493 'The Readership of the Periodical Press in Mid-Victorian Britain,' *Victorian Periodicals Newsletter,* 13 (1971) pp. 3–22, (p. 13).

494 *Bookseller*, 7 October 1884, p. 1069.

495 T. & T. Clark — J. S. Exell, 18 August 1884, N.L.S., Dep. 247/33, fol. 638.

496 T. & T. Clark — J. S. Exell, 28 August 1884, N.L.S., Dep. 247/33, fol. 652. The text of the agreement with Exell is included, along with a copy of a letter to him dated 21 August 1884, in a letter book which has recently been deposited in the N.L.S.

497 T. & T. Clark — Scribners, 8 September 1884, N.L.S., Dep. 247/33, fol. 663.

498 T. & T. Clark — J. S. Exell, 23 September 1884, N.L.S., Dep. 247/33, fol. 680.

499 T. & T. Clark — J. S. Exell, 24 September 1884, N.L.S., Dep. 247/33, fol. 682.

500 T. & T. Clark — J. S. Exell, 19 December 1884, N.L.S., Dep. 247/33, fol. 782.

501 T. & T. Clark — J. S. Exell, 9 October 1885, N.L.S., Dep. 247/34, fol. 135.

502 T. & T. Clark — J. S. Exell, 12 May 1886, N.L.S., Dep. 247/34, fol. 369.

503 T. & T. Clark — J. S. Exell, 1 October 1886, N.L.S., Dep. 247/34, fol. 493.

504 T. & T. Clark — J. S. Exell, 4 October 1884, N.L.S., Dep. 247/33, fol. 699.

505 T. & T. Clark — J. S. Exell, 19 December 1884, N.L.S., Dep. 247/33, fol. 782.

506 T. & T. Clark — Kegan Paul, 23 September 1884, N.L.S., Dep. 247/33, fol. 679.

507 T. & T. Clark — Kegan Paul, Trench & Co., 18 July 1885, N.L.S., Dep. 247/34, fol. 34.

508 If £27=90%, 100%=£30. £30÷8½*d*.=847.

509 T. & T. Clark — J. S. Exell, 28 August 1884, N.L.S., Dep. 247/33, fol. 652.

510 T. & T. Clark — J. S. Exell, 5 November 1884, N.L.S., Dep. 247/33, fol. 735.

511 T. & T. Clark — J. S. Exell, 23 October 1885, N.L.S., Dep. 247/34, fol. 158.

512 T. & T. Clark — J. S. Exell, 1 October 1886, N.L.S., Dep. 247/34, fol. 493.

513 T. & T. Clark — J. S. Exell, 19 March 1885, N.L.S., Dep. 247/33, fol. 901.

514 T. & T. Clark — J. S. Exell, 9 October 1885, N.L.S., Dep. 247/34, fol. 135. The contributor in question was C. A. Briggs.

515 T. & T. Clark — J. S. Exell, 4 October 1884, N.L.S., Dep. 247/33, fol. 699.

516 T. & T. Clark — J. S. Exell, 24 May 1886, N.L.S., Dep. 247/34, fol. 381.

517 T. & T. Clark — J. S. Exell, 12 May 1886 and 24 May 1886, N.L.S., Dep. 247/34, fols 369 and 381.

518 T. & T. Clark — J. S. Exell, 1 October 1886, N.L.S., Dep. 247/34, fol. 493.

519 T. & T. Clark — S. R. Driver, 23 October 1886, N.L.S., Dep. 247/34, fol. 528. Exell edited volumes 36 and 37 of the *British and Foreign Evangelical Review* (1887 and 1888). Thereafter, the journal became the *Theological Monthly* (1889–1891); no editor's name is mentioned in the issues of the new title, and it is not clear whether Exell was involved with it.

Interestingly, in view of the extent of their outlay in attempting to establish the *Monthly Interpreter*, and in the light of S. D. F. Salmond's opinion that 'there was still room for such a periodical', the Clarks had been prepared in June 1886 to continue issuing it if Marcus Dods were willing to take over the editorship, either himself or in collaboration with Salmond:

> We would not hesitate to try it again if it were possible for you to see your way to undertake the editorship. Kindly consider this. We do not think that after a selection of contributors had been made the labour would be great and we are sure that many of the best of the present contributors would willingly continue.

(T. & T. Clark — Marcus Dods, 8 June 1886. In a letter book recently deposited in the N.L.S.) It is interesting to contrast the lack of enthusiasm towards this suggestion on the part of Dods, and presumably of Salmond also, with the latter's concurrent enthusiasm for establishing a theological *quarterly* about which the Clarks were not sanguine. (See T. &. T. Clark–S. D. F. Salmond, 15 July 1886, N.L.S. Dep. 247/34, fol. 440.) Why did Salmond not regard assuming responsibility for the *Interpreter* as an acceptable compromise? Was it because in a quarterly 'heavier' material could be published than would be appropriate in a monthly? Or was it rather that he considered the *Monthly Interpreter* to have been so blighted by Exell's stewardship as to be beyond redemption?

520 T. & T. Clark – S. D. F. Salmond, 28 January 1890, N.L.S., Dep. 247/35, fol. 762.
521 'Sudden Death of the Rev. Dr. James Hastings', *Aberdeen Daily Journal*, 16 October 1922.
522 *Bookseller*, 9 October 1889, p. 986.
523 See W. R. Nicoll, 'The Rev. Dr. James Hastings', *British Weekly*, 19 October 1922, p. 50.
524 T. & T. Clark – James Hastings, 20 January 1890, N.L.S., Dep. 247/35, fol. 751.
525 See T. & T. Clark – James Hastings, 17 December 1889, 30 December 1889, N.L.S., Dep. 247/35, fols 709, 733.
526 Although previous discussions had clearly taken place, the Clarks' earliest letter to Hastings would appear to be that dated 17 December 1889 (N.L.S., Dep. 247/35, fol. 709). It discusses the contents of the January number, and the promotional strategy for the journal. It requests that Hastings supply a detailed statement from Aberdeen University Press of the printing costs in respect of the first three issues: it was the Clarks' intention to meet these costs. It raises the matter of William Diack's desire to retain the franchise for Aberdeen. The Clarks wanted wholesalers John Menzies to handle the journal; they would only accept if they could have the entire wholesale agency, including Aberdeen. Despite the fact that the Menzies firm had agreed to offer Diack 'the most advantageous terms they possibly [could]', he was reluctant to accept, and was causing difficulties by retaining the list of current subscribers.
527 It continued to be printed in Aberdeen by the Aberdeen University Press until the sixth issue, that for March 1890. Thereafter it was printed by Morrison and Gibb in Edinburgh. (*Scottish Notes and Queries*, September 1935, pp. 137–38 (p. 137).)
528 Op. cit., p. 5.
529 However, each page of the *Expository Times* contained two columns of text, while each page of the *Monthly Interpreter* had contained only one column.
530 T. & T. Clark – James Hastings, 20 January 1890, N.L.S., Dep. 247/35, fol. 751.
531 T. & T. Clark – W. Cruickshank, N.L.S., Dep. 247/39, fol. 161.
532 T. & T. Clark – C. H. H. Wright, 25 January 1897, N.L.S., Dep. 247/39, fol. 438.
533 T. & T. Clark – James Hastings, 8 December 1890, N.L.S., Dep. 247/36, fol. 139.
534 *Stock and Sales Book, Individual Titles*, N.L.S., Dep. 247/138.
535 It is most surprising that there is no record of sales to Scribners in the accounts for the previous years. All the sales listed there are at 4*s*. 2*d*. per dozen, and it is inconceivable that a US firm would be supplied at the UK trade price. One can only assume that, for some inexplicable reason, US sales were omitted from the accounts.
536 J. M. Clark – S. D. F. Salmond, 12 December 1889, Dep. 247/35, fol. 704.
537 T. & T. Clark – S. D. F. Salmond, 15 July 1886, N.L.S., Dep. 247/34, fol. 440.
538 J. M. Clark – S. D. F. Salmond, 12 December 1889, N.L.S., Dep. 247/35, fol. 704.
539 They pointed out that 'The Publishers would be at very considerable expense for providing new books and Magazines not sent in by the respective Publishers', and reminded Salmond that, in addition to payment, the reviewers would also be permitted to keep the books. (T. & T. Clark – S. D. F. Salmond, 31 December 1889, N.L.S., Dep. 247/35, fol. 735. See also T. & T. Clark – S. D. F. Salmond, 17 January 1890, N.L.S., Dep. 247/35, fol. 747.)
540 T. & T. Clark – S. D. F. Salmond, 26 April 1890, N.L.S., Dep. 247/35, fol. 881.
541 T. & T. Clark – Scribners, 1 December 1890 and 15 February 1891, N.L.S., Dep. 247/36, fols 130, 220.
542 *Publishers' Circular*, 7 March 1891, p. 242.
543 T. & T. Clark – R. M. Wenley, 30 June 1896, N.L.S., Dep. 247/39, fol. 46.
544 T. & T. Clark – S. D. F. Salmond, 28 January 1897, N.L.S., Dep. 247/39, fol. 443.

545 In *Stock and Sales Book, Individual Titles*, N.L.S., Dep. 247/138.
546 T. & T. Clark – S. D. F. Salmond, 11 July 1896, N.L.S., Dep. 247/39, fol. 68.
547 Williams and Norgate issued the *Critical Review* from 1900 until its demise in November 1904, with Salmond as editor. The frequency of the journal was increased by them to six issues per year. (See *Scottish Notes and Queries*, October 1935, p. 156.)
548 T. Clark – C. K. Mead, 25 September 1879, N.L.S., Dep. 247/32, fol. 153. Clark must have been sorely tried, for the work was not to see the light of day for another seven years, and already in 1879 he was pointing out with the mildest irritation 'I may mention that had it not been that I knew Professor Thayer was engaged on it and I did not wish to interfere I would have had Grimm published long ago as it is now eight or ten years since I talked with him about it and mentioned that I had it in contemplation.'
549 T. & T. Clark – J. H. Thayer, 8 March 1888, N.L.S., Dep. 247/34, fol. 997. A phrase in this letter would seem to suggest that there was some element of commission publishing in the final agreement with Thayer, but the details are unclear.
550 *Stock and Sales Book, Individual Titles*, N.L.S., Dep. 247/138.
551 J. M. Clark–W. F. Moulton, 11 February 1897, N.L.S., Dep. 247/39, fol. 477.
552 T. & T. Clark – Scribners, 23 February 1897, N.L.S., Dep. 247/39, fol. 500.
553 T. & T. Clark – Scribners, 2 February 1897, N.L.S., Dep. 247/39, fol. 457.
554 *Bookseller*, 8 April 1897, p. 377.
555 T. & T. Clark – A. S. Geden, 2 April 1895, N.L.S., Dep. 247/38, fol. 353.
556 T. & T. Clark – A. S. Geden, 26 April 1895, N.L.S., Dep. 247/38, fol. 415a.
557 See T. & T. Clark – A. S. Geden, and T. & T. Clark – Joseph Thornton and Son, 12 March 1897 and 15 March 1897, N. L.S., Dep. 247/39, fols 553 and 557.
558 T. & T. Clark – A. S. Geden, 26 April 1895, N.L.S., Dep. 247/38, fol. 415.
559 T. & T. Clark – A. S. Geden, 1 October 1895, N.L.S., Dep. 247/38, fol. 615.
560 T. & T. Clark – A. S. Geden, 11 February 1897, N.L.S., Dep. 247/39, fol. 475.
561 The Clarks' anxiety was magnified by several technical problems which arose in the course of production. The printers were slow, and some of the types fell out, necessitating the printing of cancels. (T. & T. Clark – W. F. Moulton, 11 February 1897, N.L.S., Dep. 247/39, fol. 477.) Apparently certain Greek types could only be bought from a given type-founder who held the monopoly, and his type had a slightly different size of body compared with other types, causing it to become dislodged when used in conjunction with them.
562 T. & T. Clark – Scribners, 9 July 1897, N.L.S., Dep. 247/39, fol. 755.
563 T. & T. Clark – Scribners, 2 February 1897, N.L.S., Dep. 247/39, fol. 457.
564 T. & T. Clark – Scribners, 9 July 1897, N.L.S., Dep. 247/39, fol. 755.
565 T. & T. Clark – A. S. Geden, 24 September 1895, N.L.S., Dep. 247/38, fol. 596.
566 T. & T. Clark – A. S. Geden, 24 November 1896, N.L.S., Dep. 247/39, fol. 338.
567 T. & T. Clark – Scribners, 2 February 1897, N.L.S., Dep. 247/39, fol. 457.
568 T. & T. Clark – A. S. Geden, 26 April 1895 and 5 October 1895, N.L.S., Dep. 247/38, fols 415a, 624.
569 T. & T. Clark – Scribners, 31 March 1897, N.L.S., Dep. 247/39, fol. 601. It is not clear whether the orders secured under the Bell contract are included, but presumably they are. It would seem that Bell had been planning to issue the work in parts, and to offer special pre-publication terms, for the Clarks found it necessary to explain to Geden that they eschewed both courses. Part-publication they held to be unprofitable, as is noted earlier in the main text. As for pre-publication offers, they felt that such a strategy only served to cause 'trouble & unpleasantness' due to post-publication complaints from those who claimed not to have heard of the work in question before publication. (T. & T. Clark – A. S. Geden, 26 April 1895, N.L.S., Dep. 247/38, fol. 415a)
570 T. & T. Clark – Scribners, 23 February 1897, N.L.S., Dep. 247/39, fol. 500.
571 *Stock and Sales Book, Individual Titles*, N.L.S., Dep. 247/138, fols 159, 274, 382.

572 J. M. Clark – J. MacPherson, 5 September 1893, N.L.S., Dep. 247/37, fol. 386.
573 Ibid.
574 Obituary of James Hastings, *Aberdeen University Review,* 10 (1922-23) pp. 85-86 (p. 85).
575 *Annals of the Free Church of Scotland 1843-1900,* edited by William Ewing (1914). By 1922, Selbie had become a Professor at the Aberdeen United Free Church College, having in 1906 resigned his charge in order to devote himself to his editorial work. (Obituary of James Hastings, *Aberdeen University Review,* 10 (1922-23) pp. 85-86 (p. 85); R. Bruce Taylor, 'John Alexander Selbie', *Expository Times,* 18 (1906-07) p. 202.)
576 T. & T. Clark – Simpkin, Marshall, 23 January 1896, N.L.S., Dep. 247/38, fol. 782.
577 T. & T. Clark – Scribners, 15 February 1897, N.L.S., Dep. 247/39, fol. 480.
578 T. & T. Clark – James Hastings, 16 July 1897, N.L.S., Dep. 247/39, fol. 774.
579 T. & T. Clark – James Hastings, 7 June 1898, N.L.S., Dep. 247/40, fol. 361.
580 'Entre Nous', *Expository Times,* 10 (1898-99) p. 96. The volumes of the *Dictionary* were widely reviewed as they appeared. There follows a list of abbreviated references to selected reviews. *Volume One – Publishers' Circular,* 19 March 1898, p. 329; *Bookman,* May 1898, p. 42; *Athenaeum,* 16 April 1898, pp. 494-95; *Jewish Quarterly Review,* January 1899, pp. 349-54; *Church Quarterly Review,* July 1898, pp. 392-408; *Critical Review*, April 1898, pp. 178-184. *Volume Two – Athenaeum,* 9 September 1899, pp. 343-44; *Church Quarterly Review,* July 1899, pp. 295-308; *Critical Review,* July 1899, 259-266. *Volume Three – Critical Review,* November 1900, pp. 483-501; *Athenaeum,* 15 September 1900, pp. 341-42; *Church Quarterly Review,* October 1900, pp. 120-137. *Volume Four – Bookman,* August 1902, pp. 172-175; *Athenaeum,* 21 June 1902, pp. 773-74. *Extra Volume – Athenaeum,* 17 September 1904, pp. 375-76; *Bookman,* December 1904, pp. 129-131.
581 In 1909 there was issued a completely new one-volume *Dictionary of the Bible,* produced for the benefit of those whose financial or intellectual resources precluded their using the five-volume work. (Preface) In the preparation of this volume, Hastings was assisted by J. A. Selbie and J. C. Lambert, together with Shailer Mathews, Professor of Theology and Dean of the Divinity School at the University of Chicago. This work was translated into Chinese (D. MacGillivray, 'The Chinese Hastings' "Dictionary of the Bible"', *Expository Times,* 28 (1916-17) pp. 12-14.) and sold at least 4,000 copies in that language.
582 See S. D. F. Salmond [Review of Volume One of the *Dictionary of the Bible*], Critical Review, 8 (1898), pp. 178-184 (p. 180).
583 T. & T. Clark – Scribners, 8 March 1894, N.L.S., Dep. 247/37, fol. 70.
584 T. & T. Clark – Simpkin Marshall, 7 December 1897, N.L.S., Dep. 247/40, fol. 28.
585 H. A. A. Kennedy [Review of Volume Three of the *Dictionary of the Bible*], *Critical Review,* 10 (1900), pp. 483-501 (p. 495).
586 T. & T. Clark – Marcus Dods, 31 October 1898, N.L.S., Dep. 247/40, fol. 626.
587 T. & T. Clark – Scribners, 27 January 1896, N.L.S., Dep. 247/38, fol. 788a. Admittedly, the firm were attempting in this letter to persuade Scribners to handle their work in the US rather than the Black work (Scribners were already agents for Black's *Encyclopaedia Britannica*) and this may have influenced their comments.
588 William Fulton, 'James Hastings The Dictionarian', *Expository Times,* 63 (1951-52), pp. 162-64 (p. 163).
589 T. & T. Clark – Scribners, 15 February 1897, N.L.S., Dep. 247/39, fol. 480.
590 T. & T. Clark – James Hastings, 16 July 1897, N.L.S., Dep. 247/39, fol. 774.
591 T. & T. Clark – Scribners, 15 September 1897, N.L.S., Dep. 247/39, fol. 861.
592 T. & T. Clark – the Editor, *Daily News,* 10 November 1899, N.L.S., Dep. 247/40a, fol. 325.

593 T. & T. Clark – S. D. F. Salmond, 24 April 1900, N.L.S., Dep. 247/40a, fol. 616.
594 Frederick Macmillan, *The Net Book Agreement 1899 and The Book War, 1906-1908* (Glasgow, 1924).
595 Ibid., p. 4.
596 Ibid., p. 29. Authors' royalties were to remain constant despite these changes.
597 T. & T. Clark – James Hastings, 16 July 1897, N.L.S., Dep. 247/39, fol. 774.
598 T. & T. Clark – A. & R. Milne, Aberdeen, 4 February 1898, N.L.S., Dep. 247/40, fol. 132.
599 T. & T. Clark – James Hastings, 16 July 1897, N.L.S., Dep. 247/39, fol. 774.
600 T. & T. Clark – Simpkin, Marshall, 7 December 1897, N.L.S., Dep. 247/40, fol. 28.
601 T. & T. Clark – Scribners, 27 December 1897, N.L.S., Dep. 247/40, fol. 56.
602 T. & T. Clark – A. and R. Milne, Aberdeen, 4 February 1898, N.L.S., Dep. 247/40, fol. 132. Milne had been unhappy about the fact that the *Dictionary* was to be non-net.
603 T. & T. Clark – Scribners, 8 March 1894, N.L.S., Dep. 247/37, fol. 708.
604 T. & T. Clark – Scribners, 12 December 1895, N.L.S., Dep. 247/38, fol. 718a.
605 T. & T. Clark – Scribners, 27 January 1896, N.L. S., Dep. 247/38, fol. 788a.
606 T. & T. Clark – Scribners, 12 December 1895, N.L.S., Dep. 247/38, fol. 718a.
607 T. & T. Clark – James Hastings, 12 May 1896, N.L.S., Dep. 247/38, fol. 962.
608 T. & T. Clark – Scribners, 15 February 1897, N.L.S., Dep. 247/39, fol. 480.
609 *Stock and Sales Book, Individual Titles,* N.L.S., Dep. 247/138, fol. 293.
610 *Trade Ledger 1895-1901*, N.L.S., Dep. 247/100a, fol. 732.
611 *Stock and Sales Book, Individual Titles,* N.L.S., Dep. 247/138, fol. 291.
612 T. & T. Clark – Scribners, 8 June 1896, N.L.S., Dep. 247/39, fol. 5.
613 T. & T. Clark – Scribners, 22 January 1898, N.L.S., Dep. 247/40, fol. 105.
614 T. & T. Clark – James Hastings, 7 June 1898, N.L.S., Dep. 247/40, fol. 361.
615 T. & T. Clark – Scribners, 29 December 1897, N.L.S., Dep. 247/40, fol. 62.
616 T. & T. Clark – W. E. Adam, 28 May 1898, N.L.S., Dep. 247/40, fol. 341.
617 T. & T. Clark – J. Mitchell, Primitive Methodist Book Room, 5 December 1898, N.L.S., Dep. 247/40, fol. 716.
618 T. & T. Clark – James Hastings, 7 June 1898, N.L.S., Dep. 247/40, fol. 361.
619 In *Stock and Sales Book, Individual Titles,* N.L.S., Dep. 247/138, fols 290–293.
620 In fact, some of it, totalling £250 0*s*. 6*d*., had been included in the firm's overheads in the previous financial year as expenditure on the project had gathered momentum.
621 £1,045 15*s*. 10*d*. ÷ 17*s*. 2*d*. = 1,218. Each of these copies would cost the firm 10*d*. to bind; hence the divisor is 17*s*. 2*d*. rather than 18*s*. 0*d*.
622 1,218+84=1,302. 2,160−1,302=858.
623 858×17*s*. 2*d*.
624 When the income from Scribners is taken into account, the profit totals £1,113 18*s*. 6*d*., a return on the initial investment of 33.26%.
625

Printing	£75 9*s*. 9*d*.
Paper	£121 9*s*. 9*d*.
Maps	£32 15*s*. 0*d*.
Binding	£143 9*s*. 0*d*.
	£373 3*s*. 5*d*.

626 One of the most important miscellaneous works was James Moffatt's *The Historical New Testament* which, at the end of the century, was being prepared for publication in 1901.
627 T. & T. Clark – James Hastings, 28 July 1899, N.L.S., Dep. 247/40a, fol. 130.
628 T. & T. Clark – Mrs Candlish, 17 July 1899, N.L.S., Dep. 247/40a, fol. 98.
629 J. M. Clark – Robert Watts, 1 September 1887, N.L.S., Dep. 247/34, fol. 796.
630 T. & T. Clark – J. Hutcheson Stirling, 27 July 1893, N.L.S., Dep. 247/37, fol. 342. Admittedly the work under discussion, Stirling's *Darwinianism* was likely to sell well, and was therefore likely to be viewed by the Clarks as a good investment.

633 T. & T. Clark — E. J. Nurse, 3 November 1898, N.L.S., Dep. 247/40, fol. 646. Nurse responded by asking whether the Clarks' readers could revise the work for him, a proposal which the firm did not entertain. 'Strict accuracy on the part of the Author himself would be absolutely necessary in such a work.'

634 T. & T. Clark — W. S. Bruce, 10 March 1899, N.L.S., Dep. 247/40, fol. 911. Bruce's *Ethics of the Old Testament* (published in 1895) had sold only eleven copies over the past year, and the firm was beginning to lose hope about it. Sixty-six copies had been sold over 1896-97.

635 T. & T. Clark — G. Elmslie Troup, 22 February 1893, N.L.S. , Dep. 247/37, fol. 112.

636 T. & T. Clark — A. H. Moncur Sime, 22 August 1899, N.L.S., Dep. 247/40a, fol. 155. It was in fact proposed that Sime's work, *The Epic of God,* should be published under a risk-sharing agreement, but it was ultimately rejected.

637 T. & T. Clark — D. W. Simon, Bradford, 20 June 1899, N.L.S., Dep. 247/40a, fol. 54. The work in question was Simon's *Reconciliation by Incarnation* (1898).

638 T. & T. Clark — D. W. Simon, 16 May 1900, N.L.S., Dep. 247/40a, fol. 663.

639 T. & T. Clark — J. J. Halcombe, 29 May 1893, N.L.S., Dep. 247/37, fol. 264. The work appeared as *What Think Ye of the Gospels?* (1893).

640 T. & T. Clark — J. Hutchinson Stirling, 10 August 1899, N.L.S., Dep. 247/40a, fol. 431. The work appeared in 1900 with the *is* still in italics.

641 T. & T. Clark — Robert Watts, Belfast, 1 September 1887, N.L.S., Dep. 247/34, fol. 796.

642 T. & T. Clark — J. MacDonald Inglis, 18 February 1887, N.L.S., Dep. 247/34, fol. 632. The work was not published by the firm, although risk-sharing terms were discussed.

643 T. & T. Clark — R. M. Edgar, 19 June 1893, N.L.S., Dep. 247/37, fol. 301.

644 T. & T. Clark — Mrs Candlish, 17 July 1899, N.L.S., Dep. 247/40a, fol. 98. Under discussion was a proposal to publish posthumously a collection of sermons by J. S. Candlish. The Clarks agreed to this proposal only after Dr Denney consented to write a preface to the work. (See T. & T. Clark — Mrs Candlish, 27 July 1899, N.L.S., Dep. 247/40a, fol. 126.)

645 T. & T. Clark — James Aitchison, 2 July 1900, N.L.S., Dep. 247/40a, fol. 738.

646 T. & T. Clark — Dr Killen, 26 June 1886, N.L.S., Dep. 247/34, fol. 419.

647 T. & T. Clark — the Revd Dr Stock, 24 March 1879, N.L.S., Dep. 247/32, fol. 32.

648 T. & T. Clark — Thomas Adamson, 11 December 1896, N.L.S., Dep. 247/39, fol. 384.

649 See, for example, the discussion over the issue of the posthumous work by Candlish. Denney suggested that a biographical sketch of Candlish, to be written by a Dr Wells, should be included. This idea was not accepted by the Clarks, who felt that such a biographical study would give the work a denominational slant. (T. & T. Clark — Mrs Candlish, 27 July 1899, N.L.S., Dep. 247/40a, fol. 126.)

650 T. & T. Clark — V. H. Stanton, 17 October 1885, N.L.S., Dep. 247/34, fol. 151.

651 T. & T. Clark — A. H. Moncur Sime, 22 August 1899, N.L.S., Dep. 247/40a, fol. 155.

652 See, for example, the seventh clause of the *Agreement Between Messrs. T. & T. Clark, Publishers, Edinburgh, and the Rev. James Hamlyn Hill,* N.L.S., Dep. 247/37, fol. 211.

653 T. & T. Clark — Alfred Cave, 25 June 1885, N.L.S., Dep. 247/34, fol. 15.

654 T. & T. Clark — Alfred Cave, 22 June 1885, N.L.S., Dep. 247/34, fol. 8.

655 T. & T. Clark — Paton J. Gloag, 9 November 1886, N.L.S., Dep. 247/34, fol. 540.

656 T. & T. Clark — J. Hamlyn Hill, 28 March 1893, N.L.S., Dep. 247/37, fol. 173.

657 T. & T. Clark — R. Johnstone, 21 November 1887, N.L.S., Dep. 247/34, fol. 877. The work was published in 1888.

658 T. & T. Clark — A. B. Bruce, 25 May 1884, N.L.S., Dep. 247/37, fol. 835.

657 T. & T. Clark – R. Johnstone, 21 November 1887, N.L.S., Dep. 247/34, fol. 877. The work was published in 1888.
658 T. & T. Clark – A. B. Bruce, 25 May 1884, N.L.S., Dep. 247/37, fol. 835.
659 Matheson's response to this was to offer to buy the remaining 380 copies of his work (*The Growth of the Spirit of Christianity* (1877)) from the firm in sheets at a reduced price. The Clarks agreed to sell him these at 7*s*. 6*d*. per copy. See T. & T. Clark – G. Matheson, 19 February 1880 and 15 April 1880, N.L.S., Dep. 247/32, fols 257, 292.
660 T. & T. Clark – A. B. Bruce, 25 May 1894, N.L.S., Dep. 247/37, fol. 835. Bruce, in fact, was initially less than satisfied with a 12½% royalty. The firm outlined the costs of printing, binding and distributing a new work, pointed out that 12½% was 'conceived a liberal royalty', indicated that it would be difficult to promise more than that on the first three or four impressions of a book, and offered the incentive of an extra honorarium on the author's previous successful work on *The Kingdom of God* (1889), and the prospect of a similar extra honorarium on the new book if it proved to be successful also. Bruce accepted their terms.
661 T. & T. Clark – A. E. Garvie, 13 June 1899, N.L.S., Dep. 247/40a, fol. 31.
662 Ibid.
663 T. & T. Clark – G. Elmslie Troup, 21 April 1893, N.L.S., Dep. 247/37, fol. 214.
664 T. & T. Clark – Scribners, 27 June 1888, N.L.S., Dep. 247/35, fol. 116.
665 T. & T. Clark – Robert Rainy, 23 May 1894, N.L.S., Dep. 247/37, fol. 833.
666 See T. & T. Clark – D. W. Simon, 8 June 1898, N.L.S., Dep. 247/40, fol. 365.
667 T. & T. Clark – J. E. H. Thomson, 12 May 1893, N.L.S., Dep. 247/37, fol. 247.
668 T. & T. Clark – W. F. Skene, 18 July 1891, N.L.S., Dep. 247/36, fol. 403. The work in question was his *The Lord's Supper and the Passover Ritual*; he in fact shared the risk of the work with the Clarks.
669 *Agreement Between Messrs. T. & T. Clark, Publishers . . . and the Rev. James Hamlyn Hill*, 20 April 1893, N.L.S., Dep. 247/37, fol. 211.
670 See, for example, T. & T. Clark – A. E. Jarvie, 13 June 1899, N.L.S., Dep. 247/40a, fol. 31, and T. & T. Clark – R. J. Drummond, 26 February 1900, N.L.S., Dep. 247/40a, fol. 504.
671 T. & T. Clark – J. Hamlyn Hill, 4 November 1893, N.L.S., Dep. 247/37, fol. 508.
672 Denis Judd, *The Boer War* (London 1977), pp. 131–32.
673 T. & T. Clark – J. Hutchison Stirling, 18 January 1900, N.L.S., Dep. 247/40a, fol. 431.
674 T. & T. Clark – John Cole, 11 December 1879, N.L.S., Dep. 247/32, fol. 214.
675 T. & T. Clark – George Matheson, 19 February 1880, N.L.S., Dep. 247/32, fol. 257. Matheson responded as we noted by agreeing to purchase the Clarks' remaining stocks of the work at a special price.
676 T. & T. Clark – Charles A. Salmond, 14 December 1893, N.L.S., Dep. 247/37, fol. 575.
677 T. & T. Clark – W. S. Bruce, 10 March 1899, N.L.S., Dep. 247/40, fol. 911. The work did, however, sell 298 copies over 1895–96.
678 The financial details are from *Stock and Sales Book, Individual Titles,* N.L.S., Dep. 247/138.
679 Over 1895–96, 125 were sold at 4*s*. 6*d*., 18 at 5*s*. 6*d*., 7 at 4*s*. 0*d*. and 133 at 4*s*. 10*d*.
680 Over 1895–96, 175 copies were sold at 8*s*. 0*d*., 17 at 17*s*. 9*d*., and 1035 at 9*s*. 0*d*.
681 Or slightly fewer than twenty-eight if some of them had bought copies in multiples of two dozen.
682 T. & T. Clark – T. Adamson, 11 December 1896, N.L.S., Dep. 247/39, fol. 384.
683 Over 1896–97, 355 copies were sold at 8*d*. (75 to Scribners and 280 to the author) and 473 at 7.75*d*.
684 T. & T. Clark – Thornley Smith, 6 February 1884, N.L.S., Dep. 247/33, fol. 460.
685 T. & T. Clark – J. Hamlyn Hill, 9 March 1896, N.L.S., Dep. 247/38, fol. 651. The work in question, an essay on St Ephraem's Gospel Commentary, was in fact published at Hill's insistence (1896).

686 T. & T. Clark — J. Hutchison Stirling, 27 July 1893, N.L.S., Dep. 247/37, fol. 342. Stirling's *Darwinianism* was published later that year at the Clarks' risk. It is uncertain whether the use of the word 'entire' in the sentence quoted indicates a willingness to consider a risk-*sharing* agreement.
687 T. & T. Clark — the Revd Dr Stock, 24 March 1879, N.L.S., Dep. 247/32, fol. 32.
688 T. & T. Clark — H. E. Ryle, 3 June 1896, N.L.S., Dep. 247/38, fol. 994.
689 T. & T. Clark — A. H. Moncur Sime, 22 August 1899, N.L.S., Dep. 247/40a, fol. 155.
690 T. & T. Clark — J. Hutchison Stirling, 24 July 1899, N.L.S., Dep. 247/40a, fol. 118. The work in question was *What* is *Thought*?
691 Although it was a gross exaggeration for the Clarks to claim that 'many of [their books were] author's books.' (T. & T. Clark — W. Mortimer Servis, 29 December 1818 (sic-actually 1879), N.L.S., Dep. 247/32, fol. 227.) This statement is as much a distortion of the truth as that quoted earlier in which the Clarks commented that they almost totally avoided commission publishing. These statements were both exaggerations, tailored to suit the circumstances in which they were made; that quoted earlier was addressed to an author with whose work the Clarks wished to have nothing to do; while that made to Mortimer Servis was intended as an explanation of why the firm could not give a grant of books to Servis' library either freely or at a greatly reduced price; 'many of them are author's books which we cannot give away.'
692 T. & T. Clark — Richard Chandler, London, 4 December 1886, N.L.S., Dep. 247/34, fol. 562. The work would seem to have been published anonymously — see T. & T. Clark — Richard Chandler, 21 February 1887, N.L.S., Dep. 247/34, fol. 634.
693 Another, quite different reason for publishing on commission emerges in the correspondence in 1893 with J. Hamlyn Hill over his translation of Tatian's *Diatessaron* (1894). Hill had consistently bombarded the Clarks with letters which were critical of almost every aspect of the production of his work, which was being published at their expense. At length, their patience wore out:

> You seem to be suspicious of our every action, and you make it exceedingly difficult for us to take a thorough interest in the book. While it was passing through the press you were constantly giving us unnecessary trouble about it, but this [a complaint about the Clarks advertising their own titles at the end of the book] surely is the climax.

In frustration, the Clarks offered to let Hill take over financial responsibility for the book: it would be distributed by them or by 'some other Publisher in whom you have confidence.' The firm was in effect calling Hill's bluff, and in fact he left the work in their hands. (T. & T. Clark — J. Hamlyn Hill, 19 December 1893, N.L.S., Dep. 247/37, fol. 581.)
694 T. & T. Clark — Frank Ballard, 8 March 1900, N.L.S., Dep. 247/40a, fol. 525.
695 T. & T. Clark — R. Watts, 8 September 1887, N.L.S., Dep. 247/34, fol. 802.
696 T. & T. Clark — W. F. Skene, 18 July 1891, N.L.S., Dep. 247/36, fol. 403.
697 T. & T. Clark — J. E. H. Thomson, 12 May 1893, N.L.S., Dep. 247/37, fol. 247. Owing in part to expensive corrections made by the author at proof stage, the Clarks saw little hope of realising much profit from the work.
698 T. & T. Clark — A. H. Moncur Sime, 22 August 1899, N.L.S., Dep. 247/40a, fol. 155. In fact, the firm rejected the work when they had had the opportunity of inspecting the completed MS. (T. & T. Clark — A. H. Moncur Sime, 18 October 1899, N.L.S., Dep. 247/40a, fol. 269.
699 T. & T. Clark — W. F. Skene, 18 July 1891, N.L.S., Dep. 247/36, fol. 403.
700 T. & T. Clark — J. McDonald Inglis, 18 February 1887, N.L.S., Dep. 247/34, fol. 632.
701 T. & T. Clark — W. D. Killen, 26 June 1886, N.L.S., Dep. 247/34, fol. 419.
702 J. M. Clark — Robert Watts, 1 September 1887, N.L.S., Dep. 247/34, fol. 796.
703 T. & T. Clark — C. M. Mead, 22 December 1890, N.L.S., Dep. 247/36, fol. 149.

704 T. & T. Clark – Richard Chandler, 4 December 1886, N.L.S., Dep. 247/34, fol. 562.
705 T. & T. Clark – Prof. Laidlaw, 21 July 1891, N.L.S., Dep. 247/36, fol. 408.
706 T. & T. Clark – C. Salmond, 23 January 1894, N.L.S., Dep. 247/37, fol. 623.
707 T. & T. Clark – S. Stuart Allen, Melville, Muller and Slade, London, 2 December 1896, N.L.S., Dep. 247/39, fol. 365.
708 N.L.S., Dep. 247/138.
709 75 were sold at 3*s*. 0*d*., and 184 at 3*s*. 3*d*.
710 12 were sold at 4*s*. 0*d*., 24 at 5*s*. 4*d*., and 14 at 4*s*. 10*d*.

Part III

1 The most detailed information on advertising expenditure is contained in the *Advertisement Book 1886–96*, N.L.S., Dep. 247/127. The *Stock and Sales Book – Individual Titles* gives details of the total spent on advertising each title on the Clark list during the financial years which it covers, 1895–96, 1896–97, 1897–98, 1898–99. (N.L.S., Dep. 247/138.)
2 T. & T. Clark – J. F. Spriggs, 25 November 1897, N.L.S., Dep. 247/40, fol. 7.
3 T. & T. Clark – Scribners, 4 July 1894, N.L.S., Dep. 247/37, fol. 894.
4 T. & T. Clark – S. R. Driver, 28 January 1897, N.L.S., Dep. 247/39, fol. 445.
5 T. & T. Clark – W. S. Bruce, 10 March 1899, N.L.S., Dep. 247/40, fol. 911.
6 T. & T. Clark – J. S. Exell, 22 December 1884, N.L.S., Dep. 247/33, fol. 789; T & T. Clark – S. D. F. Salmond, 11 July 1896, N.L.S., Dep. 247/39. fol. 68.
7 T. & T. Clark – C. A. Briggs, 20 February 1885, N.L.S., Dep. 247/33, fol. 874.
8 T. & T. Clark – Scribners, 10 January 1888, N.L.S., Dep. 247/34, fol. 922.
9 T. & T. Clark – G. T. Ladd, 31 March 1884, N.L.S., Dep. 247/33, fol. 522.
10 Stanley Unwin, *The Truth About Publishing* (London, 1926), p. 263.
11 T. & T. Clark – D. W. Simon, 20 June 1899, N.L.S., Dep. 247/40a, fol. 54.
12 T. & T. Clark – J. F. Spriggs, 24 January 1899, N.L.S., Dep. 247/40, fol. 841.
13 T. & T. Clark – Henry L. Smith, Charles Scribners Sons, 26 November 1897, N.L.S., Dep. 247/40, fol. 9. On the other hand, of course, the Clarks occasionally faced criticism of their advertising and their publications from the editors of periodicals which took a *more* orthodox position than they did. Thus, when an advertisement for the *Bible Class Primer* series was inserted in *King's Own*, its editor protested, holding that the Primers undermined the historicity of the biblical accounts of the Patriarchs, and alleging that C. H. Spurgeon 'abhorred' the teaching of the Primers. Both charges were vigorously refuted by the Clarks, who drew attention to Spurgeon's favourable notices of the Series in the *Sword and Trowel*, and pointed out 'If you will look at the Primer on Abraham, you will see how entirely the old orthodox view is maintained.' (T. & T. Clark – the Revd J. Urquhart, 28 November and 4 December 1893, N.L.S., Dep. 247/37, fols 548, 558.
14 T. & T. Clark – J. F. Spriggs, 25 November 1897, N.L.S., Dep. 247/40, fol. 7.
15 The following letter is probably referring to the information on the verso of the title page rather than to details given in advertisements, but it does illustrate the conscientious honesty with which John M. Clark approached his work. He is here writing to S. R. Driver regarding a further printing of his *Introduction to the Literature of the Old Testament:*

> After I wrote to you last night, it occurred to me that, after all, it would hardly be right to call the *second* 500 of the proposed 5th edn of 1000 copies *Eighth* Thousand, as, although our sales would by that time have *passed* 7000, still we would not have printed 8000 (only 7500) and I am anxious to avoid doing anything not strictly honourable.

A week later, he concluded 'as we shall have passed 7000 it is perhaps quite fair to put *Eighth* thousand on the last 500.' Although such cavilling over a minor detail may perhaps seem to be obsessive, it does encourage one to put great confidence in Clark's honesty and business integrity on the principle that he who is faithful over little will be faithful also over much. (John M. Clark – S. R. Driver, 21 December 1893 and 28 December 1893, N.L.S., Dep. 247/37, fols 587 and 591.)

16 T. & T. Clark – J. M. Hodgson, 12 September 1898, N.L.S., Dep. 247/40, fol. 507.

17 T. & T. Clark – James Nisbet, 18 October 1879, N.L.S., Dep. 247/32, fol. 176.

18 T. & T. Clark – E. Stock, 14 December 1885, N.L.S., Dep. 247/34, fol. 219.

19 Based on the data in the *Stock and Sales Book, Individual Titles*, N.L.S., Dep. 247/138.

20 T. & T. Clark – Henry L. Smith, Charles Scribners Sons, 31 January 1898, N.L.S., Dep. 247/40, fol. 123.

21 T. & T. Clark – J. F. Spriggs, 25 November 1897, N.L.S., Dep. 247/40, fol. 7.

22 T. & T. Clark – Philip Schaff, 27 October 1885, N.L.S., Dep. 247/34, fol. 164.

23 T. & T. Clark – S. D. F. Salmond, 17 February 1887, N.L.S., Dep. 247/34, fol. 626.

24 T. & T. Clark – J. Hamlyn Hill, 13 January 1896, N.L.S., Dep. 247/38, fol. 764.

25 T. & T. Clark – Macmillan and Bowes, 7 April 1883, N.L.S., Dep. 247/33, fol. 239.

26 *Stock and Sales Book, Individual Titles*, N.L.S., Dep. 247/138, fol. [99].

27 T. & T. Clark – Samuel Green, 8 May 1897, N.L.S., Dep. 247/39, fol. 672.

28 T. & T. Clark – C. Newman Hall, 24 October 1883, N.L.S., Dep. 247/33, fol. 372.

29 T. & T. Clark – J. S. Exell, 22 December 1884, N.L.S., Dep. 247/33, fol. 789.

30 T. & T. Clark – C. A. Briggs, 20 February 1885, N.L.S., Dep. 247/33, fol. 874.

31 T. & T. Clark – Scribners, 23 February 1886, N.L.S., Dep. 247/34, fol. 293.

32 T. & T. Clark – J. H. Thayer, 8 March 1888, N.L.S., Dep. 247/34, fol. 997.

33 T. & T. Clark – Scribners, 22 January 1898, N.L.S., Dep. 247/40, fol. 105.

34 T. & T. Clark – Scribners, 23 February 1886, N.L.S., Dep. 247/34, fol. 293.

35 *Stock and Sales Book, Individual Titles*, N.L.S., Dep. 247/138.

36 T. & T. Clark – Scribners, 24 October 1883, N.L.S., Dep. 247/33, fol. 373.

37 T. & T. Clark – Christian Literature Publishing Company, 31 August 1896, N.L.S., Dep. 247/39, fol. 142a.

38 T. & T. Clark – J. Campbell (the unfortunate translator), 25 June 1885, N.L.S., Dep. 247/34, fol. 14.

39 Other copies, five in 1900, had to be sent to the copyright libraries (T. & T. Clark – W. Clark, 22 March 1900, N.L.S., Dep. 247/40a, fol. 544.)

40 See, for example, T. & T. Clark – Scribners, 14 April 1885, N.L.S., Dep. 247/33, fol. 940, where the subject is *American Presbyterianism* by C. A. Briggs; and T. & T. Clark – L. W. Bangs (Scribners' London agent), 18 February 1887, N.L.S., Dep. 247/34, fol. 629, where the subject is a work by Samuel Harris on *The Self Revelation of God*.

41 T. & T. Clark – The University Press, Chicago, 16 June 1898, N.L.S., Dep. 247/40, fol. 375.

42 T. & T. Clark – C. H. H. Wright, 26 April, 1886, N.L.S., Dep. 247/34, fol. 350.

43 T. & T. Clark – J. Vernon Bartlett, 14 February 1900, N.L.S., Dep. 247/40a, fol. 479.

44 T. & T. Clark – D. W. Simon, 6 October 1898, N.L.S., Dep. 247/40, fol. 564.

45 T. & T. Clark – S. D. F. Salmond, 7 November 1895 N.L.S., Dep. 247/38, fol. 663.

46 T. & T. Clark – D. W. Simon, 6 October 1898, N.L.S., Dep. 247/40, fol. 564.

47 T. & T. Clark – W. Clark, 22 March 1900, N.L.S., Dep. 247/40a, fol. 544: 'we always get numerous applications from other Editors.'

48 T. & T. Clark – J. Beveridge, 5 November 1896, N.L.S., Dep. 247/39, fol. 284.

Beveridge had translated a work for the Clarks.

49 T. & T. Clark — the Editor, *The Guardian*, 4 January 1886, N.L.S., Dep. 247/34, fol. 234.

50 T. & T. Clark — the Editor, *The Methodist Times*, 1 June 1898, N.L.S., Dep. 247/40, fol. 348.

51 *Stock and Sales Book, Individual Titles*, N.L.S., Dep. 247/138.

52 T. & T. Clark — Scribners, 10 January 1888, N.L.S., Dep. 247/34, fol. 922.

53 T. & T. Clark — J. S. Exell, 22 December 1884, N.L.S., Dep. 247/33, fol. 789.

54 T. & T. Clark — S. D. F. Salmond, 11 July 1896, N.L.S., Dep. 247/39, fol. 68.

55 T. & T. Clark — J. Hamlyn Hill, 30 May 1896, N.L.S., Dep. 247/38, fol. 985.

56 J. M. Clark — James Hastings, 8 December 1890, N.L.S., Dep. 247/36, fol. 139.

57 T. & T. Clark — J. Hamlyn Hill, 7 August 1893, N.L.S., Dep. 247/37, fol. 352.

58 T. & T. Clark — James Nisbet and Co., 18 October 1879, N.L.S., Dep. 247/32, fol. 176.

59 T. & T. Clark — J. Hamlyn Hill, 19 December 1893, N.L.S., Dep. 247/37, fol. 581.

60 T. & T. Clark — J. Hamlyn Hill, 5 January 1894, N.L.S., Dep. 247/37, fol. 603.

61 One problem which did arise was that successful advertising could encourage the demand for Clark titles through libraries rather than actually promoting further sales. This was particularly true of periodicals: because the *Presbyterian Review* was to be seen in most, if not all the College Libraries, 'the students [would not] buy it.' (T. & T. Clark — C. A. Briggs, 24 February 1886, N.L.S., Dep. 247/34, fol. 296.); when the *Journal of Jurisprudence* was wound up, the Clarks commented

> If members of the Legal profession had really taken an interest in the Magazine it might have survived, but the majority appeared to be satisfied with reading it in the Libraries. (T. & T. Clark — C. N. Johnstone and John Chisholm, 6 October 1890, N.L.S., Dep. 247/36, fol. 44.)

This was the case in America too. John M. Clark saw well-worn copies of the *Critical Review* in most of the leading US Colleges; individuals, however enthusiastic they might be about it, tended to be content with the library copy. (T. & T. Clark — S. D. F. Salmond, 11 July 1896, N.L.S., Dep. 247/39, fol. 68.) The principle applied to book advertising too, however. Having agreed to supply volumes from the *Ante-Nicene Library* to missionary libraries on special terms, the Clarks clearly had received from a public library a request to be supplied on the same terms. This request was promptly turned down: 'the only chance we have of sales would be gone if copies were given away to Public Libraries.' The implication of this is not that Public Libraries were the only source of sales, rather that if the libraries were given copies cheaply, potential readers who might otherwise have bought the books would have borrowed them instead. (T. & T. Clark — R. A. Macfie, 17 November 1887, N.L.S., Dep. 247/34, fol. 873.) Although sales to libraries could impede the Clarks' sales to the public, however, it was not always easy for them to persuade even the libraries to buy copies of their works. Mudie's, for example, would only order a certain work once they had had enquiries for it from their subscribers. A Clark author was urged to ask any of his friends who belonged to Mudie's Library to request his book. (T. & T. Clark — J. Hamlyn Hill, 7 February 1894, N.L.S., Dep. 247/37, fol. 659. The work in question was Hill's edition of Tatian's *Diatessaron*.

62 T. Clark — C. Newman Hall, 24 October 1883, N.L.S., Dep. 247/33, fol. 372.

63 T. & T. Clark — S. D. F. Salmond, 12 August 1887 N.L.S., Dep. 247/34, fol. 773.

64 T. & T. Clark — R. Lindsay, 7 November 1879, N.L.S., Dep. 247/32, fol. 191.

65 *Trade Ledger 1895–1901*, N.L.S., Dep. 247/100a.

66 The *Stock and Sales Book, Individual Titles* (N.L.S., Dep. 247/138) lists numbers of most titles on hand at 'S' and 'H'-presumably the two wholesalers.

67 T. & T. Clark — Simpkin, Marshall, 23 January 1896, N.L.S., Dep. 247/38, fol. 782.

68 Drawn from *Trade Ledger 1881–1890, Trade Ledger 1890–1895, Trade Ledger 1895–1901*, N.L.S., Dep. 247/99a, 100, 100a.

69 T. & T. Clark – J. S. Exell, 4 October 1884, N.L.S., Dep. 247/33, fol. 699; T. & T. Clark – Kegan Paul, 30 October 1884 and 18 July 1885, N.L.S., Dep. 247/33, fol. 727, and Dep. 247/34, fol. 34.

70 T. & T. Clark – Kegan Paul, 30 October 1884, N.L.S., Dep. 247/33, fol. 727.

71 T. & T. Clark – M. L. Hutchison, Melbourne, 21 September 1883, N.L.S., Dep. 247/33, fol. 345.

72 There is some evidence which might suggest that, in fact, discounts were larger. One author was reminded in 1886 that 'Most booksellers now (at least in large towns) give their private customers 3*d*. off the 1/- so that they expect a larger discount than formerly, which takes at least 40% off the selling price.' (T. & T. Clark – Thomas Whitelaw, 24 November 1886, N.L.S., Dep. 247/34, fol. 559.) Eight years later, A. B. Bruce was told that the average trade discount was 42%. (T. & T. Clark – A. B. Bruce, 25 May 1894, N.L.S., Dep. 247/37, fol. 835.) These figures may well have been the average pertaining on books sold through the wholesalers. It is extremely unlikely that they were, in fact, overall average discount levels. It is worth noting that the figures were quoted in both cases to authors who had been asking for higher percentage royalties, as a reason for not granting their requests.

73 T. & T. Clark – A. S. Geden, 26 April 1895, N.L.S., Dep. 247/38, fol. 415a.

74 So W. S. Bruce, author of the slow-selling *Ethics of the Old Testament* (1895) was told. (T. & T. Clark – W. S. Bruce, 10 March 1899, N.L.S., Dep. 247/40, fol. 911.)

75 T. Clark – George Matheson, 15 April 1880, N.L.S., Dep. 247/32, fol. 292.

76 T. & T. Clark – Alfred Cave, 15 February 1896, N.L.S., Dep. 247/38, fol. 815a.

77 The levels of discount to wholesalers noted in this paragraph are calculated from the data in the *Trade Ledger, 1895–1901*, N.L.S., Dep. 247/100a.

78 T. & T. Clark – Kegan Paul, 23 September 1884, N.L.S., Dep. 247/33, fol. 679.

79 T. & T. Clark – Kegan Paul, 30 September 1884 and 3 October 1884, N.L.S., Dep. 247/33, fols 693, 697.

80 T. & T. Clark – J. S. Exell, 4 October 1884, N.L.S., Dep. 247/33, fol. 699.

81 The Clarks pointed out to Messrs Ferree and Co., of Philadelphia, for example, that the Consul's certificate would cost around 15*s*. 4*d*., and that the charge for packing cases was 7*s*. 6*d*. per box, each box being large enough to contain two hundred demy volumes. (T. & T. Clark-Messrs Ferree and Co., 22 October 1879, N.L.S., Dep. 247/32, fol. 180.)

82 T. & T. Clark – C. F. Roper, 27 February 1880, N.L.S., Dep. 247/32, fol. 264.

83 T. & T. Clark – Wise, Coffin and Co., 29 August 1887, N.L.S., Dep. 247/34, fol. 790.

84 T. & T. Clark – Rowsell and Hutchison, 5 March 1887, N.L.S., Dep. 247/34, fol. 650.

85 T. & T. Clark – S. R. Briggs, Willard Tract Depository, 23 February 1887 and 22 August 1887, N.L.S., Dep. 247/34, fols 641 and 785.

86 T. & T. Clark – W. J. Gage, 10 September 1887, N.L.S., Dep. 247/34, fol. 805.

87 T. & T. Clark – B. Broomhall, London, 6 November 1896, N.L.S., Dep. 247/39, fol. 287. Broomhall had claimed that the Religious Tract Society and other leading London publishers were supplying him at reduced rates. While the Clarks recognised that the RTS might, because of its constitution, have been acting in this way, they very gently implied that they doubted whether any other London houses would be co-operating: 'we shall be obliged if you will kindly tell us which of the other leading London Publishers have agreed to supply their books at reduced rates.'

88 An exactly parallel quotation to this, dating from four years later, is contained in a letter to J. C. Eamer of the Primitive Methodist Publishing House (T. & T. Clark – J. C. Eamer, 6 November 1900, N.L.S., Dep. 247/40a, fol. 963.) Eamer had

clearly proposed some direct-sale scheme, and the firm made the following response:

> While we greatly appreciate your kindness — & were we to agree to your proposal it would no doubt be greatly to our advantage from a commercial point of view — still we feel we cannot conscientiously support a scheme which we are sure you will admit must have the effect of enticing away from the Booksellers many of their regular customers. [The scheme might be workable within the Primitive Methodist Denomination, but if it goes outside it] trouble is sure to arise with the Trade, &, as we say, we cannot help feeling that they would have a legitimate grievance.

89 T. & T. Clark — Scribners, 29 December 1897, N.L.S., Dep. 247/40, fol. 62.
90 T. & T. Clark — Simpkin, Marshall, Hamilton, Kent and Co., 28 January 1898, N.L.S., Dep. 247/40, fol. 120.
91 T. & T. Clark — Hugh Callan, 3 January 1899, N.L.S., Dep. 247/40, fol. 784.
92 T. & T. Clark — James Hill, 1 August 1882, N.L.S., Dep. 247/33, fol. 11. In fact the work was not proceeded with.
93 T. & T. Clark — Hamilton Adams, 23 November 1893, N.L.S., Dep. 247/37, fol. 541.
94 Ibid.
95 T. & T. Clark — Alfred Cave, 14 November 1890, N.L.S., Dep. 247/36, fol. 107.
96 T. & T. Clark — R. A. Macfie, 17 November 1887, N.L.S., Dep. 247/34, fol. 873.
97 T. & T. Clark — W. Mortimer Servis, 29 December 1818 (sic — actually 1879), N.L.S., Dep. 247/32, fol. 227.
98 T. & T. Clark — T. Mitchell, 5 December 1898, N.L.S., Dep. 247/40, fol. 716. Mitchell had apparently received a donation from another source to reduce further the price that Primitive Methodist ministers would have to pay for the book.
99 T. & T. Clark — T. Mitchell, 2 October 1899 and 4 October 1899, N.L.S., Dep. 247/40a, fols 240, 243.
100 T. & T. Clark — Primitive Methodist Book Depot, 3 October 1900, N.L.S., Dep. 247/40a, fol. 880.
101 T. & T. Clark — R. A. Macfie, 30 March 1886, N.L.S., Dep. 247/34, fol. 314.
102 Figures from *Trade Ledger 1895–1901*, N.L.S., Dep. 247/100a.

Part IV

1 George Adam Smith — Bartholomew, 3 May[?] A copy of this letter in the T. & T. Clark archive has recently been deposited in the N.L.S.
2 N.L.S. Deposit 247/138.
3 A similarly full analysis of the figures for the three subsequent financial years is included in the thesis on which this present work is based. John A. H. Dempster, *The Profitability of Progressive Theology Publishing in Late Nineteenth Century Scotland as illustrated by the experience of T. & T. Clark of Edinburgh in the 1880s and 1890s*, PhD thesis, University of Strathclyde, 1987.
4 See the Valuation Rolls in the Scottish Record Office.
5 B. R. Mitchell, *Abstract of British Historical Statistics* (1962), pp. 455, 458.

Epilogue

Much of the data in this Epilogue is drawn from sources only recently deposited in the National Library of Scotland by Mr T. G. Ramsay D. Clark. Where no location or repertory number is given in the following references it may be assumed that the document in question has yet to be catalogued by the Library. This epilogue also draws upon personal information given to the author by Mr Ramsay Clark, by Dr Green of T.

& T. Clark, by Mr David Ross Stewart, formally Managing Director of the Bartholomew Group and by Mrs Jacqueline Milne, currently Office Manager at T. & T. Clark. The author recorded a long interview with Mr Clark at Ford, Midlothian, on 11 March 1991; interviewed Mr Ross Stewart by telephone on 2 April 1991; interviewed Dr Geoffrey Green at 59 George St, Edinburgh on 4 April 1991; and interviewed Mrs Milne at 59 George St, Edinburgh on 24 May 1991.

1 John M. Clark — William Robertson Nicoll, 23 December 1921, N.L.S., Dep. 247/18.

2 *Balance Sheet and Related Accounts, 1915–16.*

3 *Balance Sheets and Related Accounts, 1922–23* and *1928–29.*

4 *Dictionary of the Bible Editor's Statement Book.*

5 Thomas George Clark — John Maurice Clark, 25 April [1910]. On this same transatlantic trip, Thomas George Clark encountered in Toronto a Dr Law, who voiced the only criticism of James Hastings' methods which the present writer has come across. Of this Dr Law, Clark noted that he was 'fairly pleasant, the only man I met who did not invite me to lunch or dinner!' before recording that 'he [was] furious at Hastings as being the most unbusiness like man he ever met — some misunderstanding about articles for D[ictionary of the] A[postolic] C[hurch].'

6 Thomas George Clark — John Maurice Clark, 25 November 1918.

7 John M. Clark — William Robertson Nicoll, 13 June 1921, N.L.S., Dep. 247/18.

8 William Robertson Nicoll — John M. Clark, 28 June 1921, N.L.S., Dep. 247/18.

9 John M. Clark — William Robertson Nicoll, 13 June 1921, N.L.S., Dep. 247/18.

10 William Robertson Nicoll — John M. Clark 28 June 1921, N.L.S., Dep. 247/18.

11 John M. Clark — William Robertson Nicoll, 13 June 1921, N.L.S., Dep. 247/18.

12\. James Harvey, 'The Publishing House of Messrs. T. & T. Clark, Edinburgh'. *Expository Times*, 51 (1939) pp. 10–13 (pp. 11–12); A. J. Gossip, 'James Hastings', *Expository Times*, 76 (1964–65) pp. 3–5 (p.4).

13 Thomas George Clark — John Maurice Clark, 9 November 1918.

14 F. A. Mumby and Ian Norrie, *Publishing and Bookselling*, (1974), p. 517.

Appendices

Appendix A

1 2 December 1878, p. 1210. See also 'Booksellers of Today: Messrs. MacNiven & Wallace, Edinburgh', *Publishers' Circular*, 1310, 8 August 1891, p. 131. John MacLaren, a former Oliphant employee (Obituary, *Publishers' Circular*, 1433, 16 December 1893, p. 704.) had, in around 1849 purchased the firm of John Elder (formerly Elder and Ogilvy) at 138 Princes Street. ('Booksellers of Today: Messrs. MacNiven & Wallace, Edinburgh', *Publishers' Circular*, 1310, 8 August 1891, p. 131. See also Arthur Giles, *Across Western Waves and Home in a Royal Capital* (n.d. but 1898), pp. 317–18.)

2 *Publishers' Circular*, 1310, 8 August 1891, p. 131.

3 T. H. Darlow, *William Robertson Nicoll* (1925), pp. 43–4.

4 *Bookseller*, 6 January 1881, p. 4.

5 *Bookseller*, 5 July 1882, p. 593.

6 *Publisher's Circular*, 1310, 8 August 1891, p. 13.

7 *Bookseller*, 5 April 1884, p. 357.

8 Darlow, op. cit., p. 460.

9 T. & T. Clark — David Kerr, Greenock, 13 April 1887, N.L.S., Dep. 247/34, fol. 685.

10 See *Scottish Notes and Queries*, 2nd Series, 13, May 1935, p. 75.

11 *Bookseller*, 2 February 1884, p. 99 records details of a legal action by MacNiven and Wallace against Messrs J. A. Cameron and Co. on the grounds of the latter's alleged infringement of copyright on statistics and information in the 1883 edition.

Appendix B

1 N.L.S. Deposit 247/138.

2 Figures have not been rounded up or down, although halfpennies have been ignored. Several errors in the accounts have been corrected.

3 The sales of *Session Cases*, and an earlier series, the *Digest of Cases* (1867–1877), which was still in print, are itemised for the years covered by Part IV in N.L.S., Dep. 247/56. (Dep. 247/56 to Dep. 247/66 inclusive are *Statement Books* listing the sales of *Session Cases*, etc. between 1859 and 1947.) The figures for sales of *Session Cases* between 1895 and 1899 are as follows:

	Value of Sales
July–Dec. 1895	£727 2*s*. 6*d*.
Jan.–June 1896	£740 9*s*. 0*d*.
July–Dec. 1896	£879 18*s*. 1*d*.
Jan.–June 1897	£1,324 19*s*. 0*d*.
July–Dec. 1897	£851 11*s*. 9*d*.
Jan.–June 1898	£1,060 16*s*. 6*d*.
July–Dec. 1898	£862 1*s*. 7*d*.
Jan.–June 1899	£1,093 15*s*. 8*d*.

On these, the firm received a 7½% commission. Their commission income from sales of *Session Cases* and *Digest of Cases* during the four years beginning July 1895 was as follows:

1895–96	£122 14*s*. 9*d*.
1896–97	£223 0*s*. 11*d*.
1897–98	£228 16*s*. 2*d*.
1898–99	£130 0*s*. 9*d*.

(This data is from the *Stock and Sales Book, Individual Titles*, N.L.S., Dep. 247/138.)

Appendix C

1 The data is from the *Stock and Sales Book, Individual Titles*, N.L.S., Dep. 247/138.

2 This is arrived at as follows. A work with a trade value of £1.05 would cost the firm £0.75 including binding. (£1.05 = 140% of £0.75) If the work were unbound, however, it would, in sheets, have cost the Clarks £0.75 – 15% = £0.63. The trade value would therefore be 164.7% of the firm's outlay, a percentage which holds good for all prices.

3 This included 40,418 units in the *Bible Class Primer* series.

Appendix E

1 The data is from *The Advertisement Book*, 1886–96, N.L.S., Dep. 247/127.

List of Sources

List of Sources

A. Primary Sources

1. Manuscript Sources

The main manuscript source is the extensive T. & T. Clark archive, housed in the National Library of Scotland (Deposit 247). The portion of this archive relating to the nineteenth century contains letter books, statement books, stock and sales records, trade ledgers, a 'Paper and impression book 1878–1890', and an 'Advertisements book 1886–96'.

The Edinburgh City Valuation Rolls (Scottish Record Office).

Testamentory material relating to Thomas Clark, Sir Thomas Clark and Sir John M. Clark, Scottish Record Office SC49/3/81, fols 533–582; SC70/1/398, fols 361–401; SC70/1/416, fols 863–868; SC70/4/327, fols 343–358; SC70/1/716, fol. 313; ODV/4956–36.

2. Printed Sources

The files of:

The Bookseller

The Critical Review of Theological and Philosophical Literature

The Expository Times

The Publishers' Circular

The Theological Review and Free Church Quarterly

Such of T. & T. Clark's nineteenth-century catalogues as have been preserved:

'T. & T. Clark's Publications', *c.*1875, *c.*1878, *c.*1891, *c.*1894.

Colonial Catalogue 1902 (Issued November 1901).

'Trade List', November 1872, 1889.

Anderson, Robert, 'Booksellers' Assistants', *Publishers' Circular*, 1612, 22 May 1897, p. 616. (A letter to the editor)

'The Ante-Nicene Library', *Bookseller*, 31 December 1866, p. 1341, 29 June 1867, p. 433.

Blaikie, W. G., *An Autobiography: 'Recollections of a Busy Life'* (London, 1901).

'Booksellers of Today: Messrs. MacNiven & Wallace, Edinburgh', *Publishers' Circular*, 1310, 8 August 1891, p. 131.

Dictionary of National Biography.

Giles, Arthur, *Across Western Waves and Home in a Royal Capital* (1898).

Harvey, James, *In Memoriam Sir Thomas Clark* (Edinburgh, n.d.).
Harvey, James, 'The Publishing House of Messrs T. & T. Clark, Edinburgh', *Expository Times*, 51 (1939–40), pp. 10–13.
'The Literature of Tractarianism', *Bookseller*, 3 February 1880, pp. 106a–106c.
MacMillan, Frederick, *The Net Book Agreement 1899 and The Book War, 1906–08* (Glasgow, 1924).
'A New "Library of the Fathers"', *Bookseller*, 30 September 1865, p. 584.
[Obituary of John MacLaren], *Publishers' Circular*, 1433, 16 December 1893, p. 704.
[Obituary of John Maurice Clark], *Expository Times*, 35 (1923–24), pp. 477–78.
[Obituary of John Maurice Clark], *Glasgow Herald*, 28 May 1924, p. 6.
[Obituary of John Maurice Clark], *Scotsman*, 28 May 1924, p. 8.
[Obituary of Thomas Clark (founder)], *Bookseller*, 30 December 1865, p. 1132.
[Obituary of the first Sir Thomas Clark], 'Entre Nous', *Expository Times* 12 (1900–01), 240.
[Obituary of the first Sir Thomas Clark], *Scotsman*, 25 December 1900, p.4.
'Publishers of Today: Messrs T. & T. Clark', *Publishers' Circular*, 1302, 13 June 1891, pp. 634–35.
The Publishing House of T. & T. Clark, Edinburgh (1882) (Reprinted from 'The Bookseller', July 1882).
Simpson, Patrick C. *The Life of Principal Rainy*, 2 vols (London, n.d.).
Taylor, R. Bruce, 'John Alexander Selbie', *Expository Times*, 18 (1906–07), p. 202.
Thin, James, *Reminiscences of Booksellers and Bookselling in Edinburgh in the Time of William IV* (Edinburgh, 1905).
'Trade and Literary Gossip', *Bookseller*, 4 September 1886, p. 847.
Who Was Who 1897–1915 (1920).

B. Secondary Sources

Annals of the Free Church of Scotland 1843–1900, edited by William Ewing (1914).
Attenborough, John, *A Living Memory: Hodder and Stoughton Publishers 1868–1975* (London, 1975).
Burlingame, Roger, *Of Making Many Books: A Hundred Years of Reading, Writing and Publishing* (1946).
Carpenter, Humphrey and Pritchard, Mari, *The Oxford Companion to Children's Literature* (Oxford, 1984).
Cheyne, A. C., *The Transforming of the Kirk* (Edinburgh, 1983).
[Critical Review], *Scottish Notes and Queries*, October 1935, p. 156.
Cross, F. L., *The Oxford Dictionary of the Christian Church*, second edition (1974).
Davis, L. E., and Hughes, J. R. T., 'A Dollar–Sterling Exchange 1803–1895', *Economic History Review* (1960), pp. 52–78.
Dempster, John A. H., 'Certain Aspects of some Nineteenth Century Scottish religious book publishers: Blackie and Son and Thomas Nelson and Sons — A Study in Motivation' (MA dissertation, University of Strathclyde, 1983). (The material on Thomas Nelson and Sons has appeared in *Publishing History*, XIII (1983), pp. 41–87, XIV (1983) pp. 5–63.)
Dempster, John, A. H., '"Incomparable Encyclopaedist": The life and work of Dr James Hastings', *Expository Times*, 100 (1988–89), pp. 4–8.
Dempster, John A. H., *T. & T. Clark of Edinburgh: A Draft Register of Issues 1832–1901* (unpublished MS).
Drummond, Andrew, and Bulloch, James, *The Church in Late Victorian Scotland 1874–1900* (Edinburgh, 1978).
Ellegård, Alvar, 'The Readership of the Periodical Press in Mid-Victorian Britain', *Victorian Periodicals Newsletter*, 13 (1971) pp. 3–22.
[The Expository Times], *Scottish Notes and Queries*, September 1935, pp. 137–38.
The Fasti of the United Free Church of Scotland 1900–1929, edited by John Alexander Lamb (Edinburgh, 1956).

Fulton, William, 'James Hastings the Dictionarian', *Expository Times*, 63 (1951–52), pp. 162–64.
Malcolm, C. A., 'Scottish Legal Periodicals: Past and Present', *Scottish Law Review*, 45 (1929) pp. 155–159.
Mitchell, B. R., *Abstract of British Historical Statistics* (1962).
Mumby, F. A. and Norrie, Ian, *Publishing and Bookselling* (1974)
The New Cambridge Modern History, Volume XI, *Material Progress and World-Wide Problems 1879–1898*, edited by F. H. Hinsley (1970).
[The North British Review], *Scottish Notes and Queries*, March 1933, pp. 37–39.
Nowell-Smith, Simon, *International Copyright Law and the Publisher in the Reign of Queen Victoria* (1968).
Scott, Patrick, 'The Business of Belief: The Emergence of "Religious" Publishing', *Studies in Church History* (1973), pp. 213–224.
Sharpe, Eric J., *Comparative Religion: A History* (London, 1975).
Shattock, Joanne, 'Editorial Policy and the Quarterlies: The Case of *The North British Review*', *Victorian Periodicals Newsletter*, 10 (1977) pp. 130–139.
Shattock, Joanne, 'Problems of Parentage: the *North British Reeview* and the Free Church of Scotland', in *The Victorian Periodical Press: Samplings And Soundings*, edited by Joanne Shattock and Michael Wolff (Leicester, 1982), pp. 145–166.
'The Story of the "North British Review"', *Scottish Review*, 3 January 1907, p. 20.
Strahan, James, *Andrew Bruce Davidson* (1917).
Sutcliffe, Peter, *The Oxford University Press: An Informal History* (Oxford, 1978).
Tebbel, John, *A History of Book Publishing in the United States*, 4 vols (1972, 1975, 1978, 1981).
Unwin, Stanley, *The Truth About Publishing* (London, 1926).

Index

INDEX

Scope of the index

The Introduction, the whole of the main text, the Epilogue and Appendices have been indexed, but not the Foreword and Preface. The list of periodicals included in Appendix D has not been indexed. The Notes have been selectively indexed: references have been created for significant material not included in the main text.

The thinking of successive generations of Clarks permeated all the firm's activities discussed in this book. I have indexed significant personal references to the various members of the family, but in a very real sense the whole volume is the story of their work, and those seeking to understand them should not limit themselves to the passages referred to in the index.

Where a title referred to is a serial, this is denoted. The nature of each business featuring in the index has been included where possible.

Each time the economics of a particular title are discuss, I have included where they are available the following data:

advertising costs; binding costs; breakeven point; cost of paper; edition size; income from US sales; percentage return on investment; printing costs; rate of sale; retail price; typesetting costs; payment to author; sales figures; stereotyping costs.

The many examples of these data have not been individually indexed.

Abbreviations

The following abbreviations have been used throughout the index:

A.N.L.	*Ante-Nicene Library*
B.C.H.	*Bible Class Handbooks*
B.C.P.	*Bible Class Primers*
C.	Clark
C.R.	*Critical Review*

D.B.	*Dictionary of the Bible*
E.C.C.	*Eras of the Christian Church*
E.R.E.	*Encyclopaedia of Religion and Ethics*
E.T.	*Expository Times*
F.C.	Free Church of Scotland
I.C.C.	*International Critical Commentary*
I.P.C.	*Illustrated Popular Commentary*
I.T.L.	*International Theological Library*
M.G.	Moulton and Geden's *Concordance*
M.I.	*Monthly Interpreter*
N.B.R.	*North British Review*
N.T.	New Testament
P.R.	*Presbyterian Review*
Sir J.M.C.	the first Sir John Maurice Clark
Sir T.C.	the first Sir Thomas Clark
T.C.	Thomas Clark (founder of the firm)
T. & T.C.	T. & T. Clark
UK	United Kingdom
US	United States

Special usages

bis or *ter*, immediately following a page reference, indicate that there are two, or three separate references to the subject on that page.

Where the reference is to a note or a table, the page number is immediately followed by the letter 'n' or the letters 'tab', which in turn are followed by the number of the note or table.

References within square brackets ([ ]) denote that the individual or work is referred to on the page noted, while not being mentioned by name there.

A. & C. Black (publishing house), 37–8, 182–3, 183
A. & R. Milne (Aberdeen booksellers), 328n598
Abbot, Thomas Kingsmill (Trinity College, Dublin)
work, *Ephesians and Colossians* 141, 146 tab 5
Aberdeen University Press, 73, 74, 257, 325nn526, 527
Academy (periodical), 304n146
acceptance of manuscripts, *see* assessment of manuscripts
accounts, T. & T. C's
described, 235, 269
handled by new book-keeping department, 261
slow procedures, 254
accounts with T. & T. C.
numbers of, 232
Acton, Lord, 160
Adam, W.E. 187–8, 231
Adamson, Thomas
work, *The Spirit of Power* 25, 194, 195, 202–3, 305n158
advertising (*see also* announcements of forthcoming works), 213–7, 257
of C. titles in C. journals, 149, 158, 168 *bis*, 171, 172, 322n433
by editor of his own work, 163
effects of cost on profitability of small books, 28, 194
honesty of, 332n15
Kegan Paul secures for *M.I.*, 226
by other firms in C. journals, 157–8, 161
outlay not charged to specific titles, 285 tab 35n8
of periodicals, 156 *bis*
periodicals regularly used for, 293–5
Presbyterian Review, 94
prompts demand through libraries, 334n61
protest from editor over orthodoxy of work advertised, 332n13
at rear of book, 223
revenue from in *C.R.*, 171 *bis*, 172 *ter*
revenue from in *E.T.*, 167 tab 16, 168 *ter*
series, 43
space sold in *B.C.H.* series, 51 tab 5n6
in US 106, 283 tab 35, 285 tab 35n7
in US edition of *E.T.*, 118 *ter*
of US-originated titles, 106
value of *E.T.* as 'shop window' for T. & T. C., 119, 149
aims of T. & T. C. (*see also* motivation of T. & T. C.), 16
accused of profiteering, 235
academic excellence, 23–6, 170, 255, 256
adhering to Christian fundamentals, 22–3, 23, 131–2, 147–8, 301n74, 302n100
avoiding denominational bias, 21–2, 128, 154–5, 170, 194, 255, 329n649
of *D.B.*, 182–3
of *E.T.*, 165
God-centredness, 23, 30–1
of *I.T.L.*, 126, 130–2 *passim*
international marketing, *see* exports
of *M.I.*, 161
meeting a need, 176, 181–2
mid–20th century, 250–1, 254–5, 256
preserving reputation, 227
profit-making, 235
publishing moderately progressive works, 19–21, 183
selecting appropriate authors, 24–5 (*see also under* authors)
serving theological community, 231
Aitchison, James (Falkirk), 193–4, 305n166
A. King (printers), *see* Aberdeen University Press
Alexander Gardner (publishing house), xviii
Alexander, W. Lindsay (Principal, Congregational Theological Hall, Scotland), 148
Allen, S. Stuart (of Melville, Muller and Slade, London), 332n707
Allen, A.V.G.
work, *Christian Institutions*, 131, 138
American market, *see* USA; exports to USA; imports from USA
announcements of forthcoming works, 36, 222
anonymous work, 331n692
The Ante-Nicene Library 7, 36, 44–47, 79, 81, 83, 102, 106, 109, 112–115, 115–6, 228, 230, 232, 236, 274 tab 34, 280, [317n284], 334–5n61
Armstrong, A.C. (US publishing house), 110, 112
Arnobius
works (in *A.N.L.*), 46 tab 1
assessment of manuscripts
acceptance conditional on editorial support being obtained, 25, 193, 195
an autobiography assessed by Sir T.C., 302–3n105

(assessment of manuscripts *cont.*)
experts consulted, 25, 255
for *F.T.L.*, 77
recommended by others, 25, 68–9, 72, 194–5, 256
reasons for rejection, 23, 25, 25–6, 26, 27–30 *passim*, 33, 43, 58, 61, 191, 192–4 *passim*, 204, 205, 313n168, 329n633
selection policy, 192–5
an unwise acceptance, 68–9
of works to buy from US, 86–7, 89, 313n168
Associated Booksellers of Great Britain and Ireland, 184 *bis*
Association for Booksellers' Assistants (Edinburgh), 7
Augsburg Press (US publishing house), 255
Augustine, Saint
works, 8, 47–9, 102, 109, 114, 115, 228, 236, 276 tab 34, 280
Australia, 256
authors (*see also* relationships with authors; remuneration of authors)
ablest sought, 24–5, 57, 127, 128, 192, 321n411
attitudes of to Net Book Agreement, 184 *bis*
calibre of periodical contributors, 154–6, 161
competition with other houses over, 33–6
cultivating a popular a., 24, 128
known beyond their own denominations sought, 321n411
selection of for *I.C.C.*, 139–40, 321n411
selection of for *I.T.L.*, 127–8
Authorised Version of the Bible *see* Bible, King James Version

backlist (*see also* reprints), 236–7, 256–7, 258
bad debt contingency, 283 tab 35
Bagley, Mr (of Christian Literature Publishing Company), 118
Baird Lectures, 35, 58
Baker, Isaac D. (partner of Charles Scribner I), 103
Ballard, Frank
work, *The Miracle of Unbelief*, 65, 205
Balthasar, Hans Urs von
work, *The Glory of the Lord*, 262, 263
Bangs, Lemuel W. (Scribners' London agent), 104
Banks, M., 304n148
Banner of Truth Trust (publishing house), 256
Baptist Churches
ministers offered *D.B.* cheaply, 187, 231
work advertised to ministers of, 218
Barth, Karl
work, *Church Dogmatics*, 250, 251 *bis*, 252, 262
Bartholomew, John, 258
Bartholomew, John & Son (map-publishing house) *see* John Bartholomew & Son
Bartholomew, Peter, 258
Bartholomew, Robert, 258 *bis*
Bartholomew Group, 258, 259 *bis*, 260 *bis*, 261, 286
Bartlet, J. Vernon (Oxford University)
work, *The Apostolic Age*, 99, 220
Bartlett (US publishing house), 316n250
The Basket of Flowers, 4
Bath and Wells, Bishop of, 25
Bayne, Dr Peter
work, *The Free Church of Scotland*, 198
Bell (George) & Sons (publishing house) *see* George Bell and Sons
Bengel, J.A.
work, *Gnomon of the New Testament*, 9
Beside the Bonny Briar Bush, 128
Beveridge, J., 67, 220, 310n63, 311n103, 333n48
Beyschlag, J.H.C.W.
work, *New Testament Theology*, 66, 76, 311n93
Bible, King James Version, 123
Bible, Revised Version, 124–5, 318n328
Bible Class Handbooks, 8, 12, 39, 49–52, 215, 222–3
promotion of *Ephesians* vol., 216 tab 21, 219 tab 22, 221 tab 23, 224 tab 24
Bible Class Primers, 8, 12, 38, 53–57, 225, 236 *bis*, 267 *bis*, 274 tab 34, 338n3 (App. C)
new series of *Primers* launched under closer F.C. control, 38
Bible dictionaries, *see* dictionaries of the Bible
The Biblical Cabinet , 4, 7, 43, 61
Bigg, Charles
work, *Peter and Jude*, 141, 146 tab 15
binding
affect of cost on profitability of small books, 28, 194
costs as % of production costs, 281
firm used by T. & T. C., 257

(binding, *cont.*)
problems caused due to differing UK/ US practices, 88, 99
binding cases for periodicals, sale of, 168
Bishop of Bath and Wells, *see* Bath and Wells, Bishop of
Bishop of Gloucester, *see* Gloucester, Bishop of
Black, A. & C. (publishing house), *see* A. & C. Black
Black, J. Sutherland, 37
Black, Matthew, 262
Blackie & Son (publishing house), 39
Blackwood (publishing house), 35
Blaikie, W.G. (*see also* North British Review)
Cunningham Lectures published, 58, 310n59
Boer War, affect of on book trade, 30, 198–9
Books International Incorporated (US distributors), 255
The Bookseller (periodical)
announcement of Clark titles, 44, 45
booksellers, (*see also* trade terms)
attitudes to Net Book Agreement, 184–5
Clarks preside over trade body, 257
danger of antagonising through direct selling, 39, 187, 229–31
number having accounts with T. & T. C., 232
relationships with, 225, 257, 261
relationships with foreign, 227
and part-publications, 148
and subscription sales, 78
supplied with overprinted copies of C. catalogue, 218
Booksellers' Assistants, Association for (Edinburgh), *see* Association for Booksellers' Assistants
Booksellers' Association (pre–1852), 184
Bosworth, J., 75
bound copies held in stock, *see* stock in hand
bound volumes, sales of periodicals in, 167 tab 16n6, 171 tab 17n6
Boyd, R.M., 188 tab 20n8
breadth of output
interdenominational emphasis, 255
moderately-progressive works, 19–21
patristic theology, 45
breakeven point, normal, 198
Briggs, C.A. (of Union Seminary, New York), 11, 18, 35, 150, 153, 302n98, 324n514
edits *Presbyterian Review*, 93
US editor of *I.C.C.*, 137–40 *passim*, 321n415
US editor of *I.T.L.*, 127–33 *passim*, 319nn339, 344
work, *American Presbyterianism*, 86, 90 *bis*, 313n168, 333n40
British and Foreign Evangelical Review (periodical), 148, 164
British Guiana, 127
British Quarterly Review (periodical), 152, 155
British Weekly (periodical), 99, 152, 220, 248, 249
effectiveness as advertising medium, 208
influence of, 98, 165
Scottish distribution of, 268
Broadus, John Albert
proposed work, *Pastoral Theology*, 131
Brockelmann, Carolo
work, *Lexicon Syriacum*, 148
Bromiley, G.W., 251
Brooks, Phillips (Bishop, Protestant Episcopal Church, Massachusetts) (1835–93)
proposed work, *Homiletics*, 131
Broomhall, B., 229
Brown, Francis (President, Union Seminary, New York)
proposed work *Contemporary History of the Old Testament*, 131
Brown, John (Professor of Exegetical Theology in the United Secession Church), 148
Brown, Dr John
work, *Philological Tracts*, 4
Bruce, A.B. (of Free Church College, Glasgow), 128, 195
praises James Moffatt, 24
works, *Apologetics*, 131 *bis*, 133, 137, 138 tab 14; *The Humiliation of Christ*, 110, 112; *The Kingdom of God*, 330n660; *The Pauline Conception of Christianity*, 196, 330n660; *The Training of the Twelve Apostles*, 110, 112
Bruce, W.S.
work, *Ethics of the Old Testament*, 199, 214, 329n634, 330n677, 335n74
Bruder, C.H. (author of a Greek N.T. Concordance), 176
Buchanan, Neil, 67, 311n93
Burton, Ernest De W. (Chicago University)

(Burton, *cont.*)
work *Syntax of the Moods and Tenses in New Testament Greek*, 86, 220
Butterworth (publishing house), 264

C.F. Roper (New York booksellers), 228
Cabinet of Biography (issued by MacNiven and Wallace), 267
The Cabinet Library of Scarce and Celebrated Tracts, 4
Calvin, John
Works, 7, 44, 236, 274 tab 34
Calvin Translation Society, 44, 300n40
Cambridge University Press (publishing house), [124], 263
Cameron, J.A. & Coy (publishing house), *see* J.A. Cameron & Coy
Cameron, Andrew, 148
Canada, exports to, 102, 118
Candlish, James S. (of Free Church College, Glasgow)
widow seeks posthumous publication of sermons, 25, 330nn644, 649
work, *Ephesians*, 49, 48 tab 5n7, 216 tab 21, 219 tab 22, 221 tab 23, 224 tab 24
canvassers, 187, 230
carriage charges (*see also* transit), 227
annual outlay on to London, 283 tab 35
to colonies, 228
transatlantic, 87, 186
cases for binding periodicals, *see* binding cases for periodicals
catalogues of C. publications, 217–9, 225, 257
annual outlay on, 283 tab 35
the best method of promotion, 213, 261, 262
Catholic Presbyterian (periodical), 215
Cave, Alfred (Hackney College), 155
work, *Introduction to Theology*, 195, 329n632
Cave, M., 305n165
Chalmers, Thomas (leader of the Free Church of Scotland), 160
Chandler, Richard
work, *Hebrews*, 204, 206
charges for carriage, *see* carriage charges
Charles Scribners' Sons (US publishing house) (*see also* co-editions; profitability of co-editions), 85, 103, 103–7, 111, 176, 219, 228
advertising C. titles 213, 214–5, 283 tab 35, 285 tab 35n7
C. catalogue distributed in US, 217
Charles Scribner II becomes head of firm, 318n324
and Christian Literature Publishing Coy edition of the *A.N.L.*, 113, 115
and *D.B.*, 38, 185–6
dispute over C. commissioning *I.T.L.* authors to write for *D.B.*, 35, 126
distribute *E.T.* in US, 166
distribute *M.I.* in US, 153, 161
extent of their agency in C. titles, 102
and the *I.P.C.*, 123–5
and *International* series 103, 125–46 *passim*
London agent, 86
offended if critical review of one of their books appeared in C. journal, 151
opinion sought before proceeding with Hastings' works, 246
purchase Christian Literature Publishing Company, 109
purchase editions of C. works 68, 81, 116–21 *passim*
sell editions to T. & T. C., 87, 90–8 *passim*, 175
stop handling C. works, 255
Ceylon, 246
Cheyne, T.K., 37
Chicago University Press, 333n41
Children's Great Texts of the Bible, 243, 244
China Inland Mission, 305n160
Chisholm, John, 8
Christian Literature Club (Scribner's), 120
Christian Literature Publishing Company, 85, 105, 109
and *A.N.L.*, 102, 112–115
and *E.C.C.*, 98–101, 219
and *E.T.*, 118–9, 166
offer *Nicene and Post-Nicene Fathers* to T. & T.C., 115
and *St. Augustine* series, 102, 114, 115
Christian World (periodical), 220
Christie, Mr, 66
Christlieb
work, *Homiletic*, 76
Christmas
gifts to staff, 284 tab 35n3
staff dinners, 254
theology in the Christmas marketplace, 198, 202, 215
Churchman (periodical), 215
Church of England
clergymen seen as major market for *M.I.*, 161
Church of England Association, 156

Church of Scotland, publishing by, xviii
circulation figures of periodicals
and advertisers, 157
of *C.R.*, 171 tab 17, 171 *bis*, 172 *bis*
of *E.T.*, 166, 167 tab 16, 167, 168
of *N.B.R.*, 159, 160
sales necessary for success of a Quarterly, 169
Clark, R. & R. (printers), *see* R. & R. Clark
Clark, T. & T. (publishing house), *see* T. & T. Clark
Clark, John (brother of founder), 5, [300n 20]
Clark, Sir John Maurice (1859–1923)
'an alarming undertaking' – the Moulton/Geden *Concordance*, 29, 176
on Anglo-American relations during Venezuela dispute, 127
'an arduous undertaking' – the *E.R.E.*, 243
attitude to his son Thomas Clark, 249
becomes sole partner, 10
and Charles Scribner II, 104–5
church activities, 10
civic affairs, 10
complains about US scholar's theological position, 18
contribution to the firm, 11, 104
contributes to *The Academy*, 304n146
death of, 249
education, 9, 30–1
enthusiasm for publishing, 9
estate, 249
father's expectations of him, 31
honesty of, example, 332–3n15
joins the firm, 6, 9
knowledge of the market, 26
last years in the firm, 246–9
military activities, 9–10
owns 38 George Street, 258
owns shares in Canadian company; loses thereby, 108
perseveres through Boer War, 30
policies continued in late 20th century, 254
president of the Edinburgh Booksellers Society, 257
pressures of publishing progressive works, 20
relationship with James Hastings, 11, 245–6
sense of mission, 16
subscribes new titles to booksellers, 225
visits US (1896), 10, 185
and W.E. Gladstone, 154
Clark, John Maurice (son of Sir John Maurice C., 1859–1923), 249
Clark, Sir John Douglas (son of Sir Thomas C., partner 1911–65), 254
Clark, Thomas (founder)
establishes and develops the firm, 3, 249
knowledge of European book market, 3
last years, 3, 5
and *Law Chronicle*, 147
proposes theological periodical, 147
Clark, Sir Thomas (1823–1900)
and Charles Scribner I and Charles Welford, 6, 104, 300n19
church activities, 6
civic responsibilities, 6
commended for his knowledge of the market, 5
cultivates US market, 6
death of eldest daughter, 300n36
early life, 5
early trade experience, 3
friendship with theologians, 5
and an incompetent editor, 164
influence on Scottish theology, 21
influence on Sir John M. Clark (1859–1923), 10, 30–1
joins the firm, 3, 299n6
last years, 7, 10
and [Matthew] Hodder, 306n179
owns 38 George Street personally, 239 tab 28
political views, 300n29
relationship with unwise autobiographer, 302–3n105
spiritual commitment, 6
view of the role of publisher, 16, 30–1
and W.G. Blaikie, 160
Clark, Sir Thomas (partner 1911–65), 246 *bis*, 247, 249–51 *passim*, 254, 257, 258
Clark, Thomas George (partner 1930–83), 247, 250–60 *passim*, 286
Clark, Thomas George R.D. (partner 1894–1919), 10, 246–8 *passim*, 250, 337n5 (Epilogue)
Clark, Thomas George Ramsay D. (partner 1956–87), 246 tab 31, 251 *bis*, 253, 254–64 *passim*, 336n (Epilogue)
Clark, W.R., 11, 301nn59, 61

Clark's Biblical Magazine and Review (projected periodical), 147–8
Clarke, Dr W.N.
  work, *Outline of Christian Theology*, 150–1, 193, 214
Clay (University Press Secretary), *see* Price and Clay
Clerical World (periodical), 152
Cleveland (US President), 127
Clunie, Douglas (T.&.T.C. manager), 253
Clyde, James (Edinburgh schoolmaster), 9
co-editions (*see also* profitability of co-editions), 121–46
Cole, John
  work, *Life of St Augustine*, 199
Collins (publishing house), *see* William Collins
Colonial sales, *see* exports
commission publishing (*see also* risk-sharing), 28, 204–210 *passim*, 331n693
  Clarks' attitude to, 29, 192, 331n 691
  Primers published for F.C., 38
  wholesale terms in respect of some works published on, 228
commissioning of authors, *see* authors
comparative religion
  growing interest in reflected in the list, 57–8
competition
  alleged between US publishers to distribute *D.B.*, 185
competition with other publishers (*see also* 'piracy' in North America), 33–9 *passim*, 98–9, 306–7n200
  M.I. v. *Expositor*, 37, 163
  over periodical market, 93–4, 151–2
  with Scribner over commissioning of authors, 126
Concilium (periodical), 255
Concordance to the Greek Testament (Moulton and Geden), 21, 29, 175, 176–80, 184, 274 tab 34n3, 321n426
Congregational Union
  attracting readership from for new Quarterly, 155
  and Hodder and Stoughton, 36, 306n179
  ministers offered *D.B.* cheaply, 187, 231
  work advertised to ministers, 218
Consular Certificate (for exports), 188 tab 20n9, 228, 335n81
contributors to periodicals, *see under* authors; remuneration of authors
Cooper, James, 36, 306n185
copyright (*see also* 'piracy' in North America)
  deposit, 88, 314n178, 333n39
  in *I.C.C.*, 139
  in *I.T.L.*, 129
  in Revised Edition of Bible: T. & T. C. allegedly infringe, 124–5
  international, 110, 112–3, 129
  strategy required to get US copyright in *D.B.*, 186, 188 tab 20n9
  and translations, 63 *bis*
cost of production, *see* production costs
cost-sharing (with authors), *see* risk-sharing
covers, periodicals, *see* design
Cox, Samuel, 35, 37
Coxe, A.C. (Bishop of New York), 109, 112, 114
Cranfield, Charles, 255
Crawford, J.H.
  work, *The Brotherhood of Man*, 207–8, 210 tab 21, 211, 213 tab 22, 221 tab 23, 224 tab 24
credit control, 225
Cremer, Hermann (University of Greifswald)
  work, *Biblico-Theological Lexicon of New Testament Greek*, 175
The Critical Review of Theological and Philosophical Literature (periodical) (*see also Theological Review*), 12–3, 93, 148, 169–72, 326n547
  adverse reviews of C. works, 99, 141, 150–1
  circulation, 157, 166, 334n61
  distinctiveness of content praised, 151–2
  doubled in size to boost sales, 153
  importance to advertisers, 158
  marketed in US, 116, 117, 154
  profitability of, 149 *bis*, 154, 158
  promotion of, 156 *bis*, 157, 214, 222
  review solicited from W.E. Gladstone, 154
  sold direct to students, 157, 230
  unprofitable due to being a Quarterly, 152
  used to advertise C. titles, 158, 215
  used to review C. titles, 222
Crombie, Frederick (St Mary's College, St Andrews), 66, 77
Cruickshank, William (London advertising agent), 158

cultural orientation
chance of success in UK market of certain US works damaged due to their, 89–90, 130
Cunningham, William, 148, 309–10n57
Cunningham Lectures, 12, 35, 58, 309–10nn56, 57
Cunningham [not traced in B.L. Catalogue]
work, *Commentary on Romans*, 27
Cunningham, David (of Bartholomews), 258
customer loyalty to C. imprint, maintaining, 43
customs officials, accused of damaging a consignment, 87–8

Dahle, Lars Nielsen
work, *Life after Death*, 61, 75, 76 *bis*, 310n63, 311n103
Daily News, 37
Dalman, G.
work, *Die Morte Jesu*, 64
Davidson, Professor A.B. (New College, Edinburgh),
on *D.B.* editorial team, 181
work, *Theology of the Old Testament*, 128 *bis*, 129, 131
Davidson, Matthew (C. staff member), 284 tab 35n3
Davidson, Samuel (Royal Academical Institute, Belfast, 302–3n105
work, *Lectures on Biblical Criticism*, 302–3n105
debts owed to T. & T. C., *see* bad debt contingency
Delitzsch, Franz
works, *Commentary on Job*, 62; *Commentary on the Psalms*, 34–5, 80 tab 7; *A System of Biblical Psychology*, 79
Denney, Professor
compared with James Moffatt, 24, 192
and posthumous Candlish work, 25, 329nn644, 649
design
high standard of d. in *M.G.*, 177
in *D.B.*, 183
of periodical covers, distinctiveness sought, 151
reputation for high class, 207
Desprès, Thomas, 75
Diack, William (Aberdeen bookseller), 164, 165, 166, 325n 526
Dickinson's Quarterly (periodical), 152
Dickson, W.P. (University of Glasgow), 27, 82, 303n118
dictionaries of the Bible, available prior to *D.B.*, 182
Dictionary of the Apostolic Church, 243, 244
Dictionary of the Bible (multi-vol. edn), 165, 175, 181–90
competition from *Encyclopaedia Biblica*, 37–8, 182–3, 185
income from (1922–3), 244
issued non-net, 228
profitability of, 236
promoted, 218, 221, 226
proposed issue in parts, 321–22n427
reviews of, list of some, 327n580
sales figures, 244
scale of investment, 11, 29, 195, 283 tab 35
selection of authors, 35, 126, 140
special terms offered, 231
theological moderation, 20
Dictionary of the Bible (one-vol. edn), 243, 327n581
Dictionary of Christ and the Gospels, 243, 244
Die Religion in Geschichte und Gegenwart, 62
Diessmann, Adolf
work, *Bible Studies*, 72–4
Dillmann, C.F.A.
work, *Genesis*, 71–2, 76
diplomacy in negotiations, 82, 104–5, 112–5, 117
direct-mail promotion, 217–9
direct selling, 39, 105–6, 229–32, 257, 335–6nn87, 88
of *D.B.*, 187
of *M.G.*, 176–7
of periodicals to students, 157
discounts, *see* trade terms
distribution, 225–32, 257
C. asked to handle d. of work originated elsewhere, 207
currently through Edinburgh University Press, 261
effectiveness of d. of *C.R.* questioned, 172
handled in-house, 254
international d. in the 20th century, 255–6
of *M.I.*, 161–2
diversification, considered, 263, 264
Dods, Marcus
and *B.C.H.*, 49
and higher criticism, 16–7
and plan to save *M.I.*, 324n519
and St Augustine's works, 8, 47

(Dods, Marcus, *cont.*)
works, *Haggai*, 51 tab 5n 4, 308n35; *Genesis*, 308n35
Donaldson, James, 7, 44–5
Dorner, Isaac A., 78
works, *History of Protestant Theology*, 75; *System of Christian Doctrine* ([*Dogmatik*]), 64, 80 tab 7, 311nn81, 95, 313n148; *System of Christian Ethics* ([*Christliche Gittenlehre*]), 63, 64, 311n83
Douglas, George C.M., 123
Douglas, Henry (Kirkcaldy minister), 10
Driver, Professor S.R. (Oxford)
advises on complexity of proposed translation, 71
assesses MSS, 25
on *D.B.* editorial team, 181
UK editor of *I.C.C.*, 137–40 *passim*
works, *Deuteronomy*, 141, 142–3, 143, 146 tab 15, 216 tab 21, 219 tab 22, 221 tab 23, 224 tab 24; *Introduction to the Literature of the New Testament*, 65; *Introduction to the Literature of the Old Testament*, 131, 133, 137 *bis*, 138 tab 14, 213–4, 320n380, 332–3n15
Du Bose, W.P.
work, *The Ecumenical Councils*, 98 *ter*, 99
Duns, John, 160 *bis*
Dusterdieck, F.H.C.
work, *Commentary on Revelation*, 83

Eamer, J.C. (Primitive Methodist Publishing House), 335–6n88
Edinburgh Academy, 9
Edinburgh Booksellers Society Ltd, 257
Edinburgh Merchant Company, 10
Edinburgh Review (periodical), 159
Edinburgh University, 9
Edinburgh University Press, 261
editing
late 20th century, no in-house e., 261
Edgar, R.M., 305n152
editors (*see also* relationships with editors; remuneration of editors)
constraints placed upon by quarterly publication, 152
failures of *I.T.L.* e., 131–2, 132
qualities sought in periodical e., 154
Edmonston and Douglas (Edinburgh publishing house), 160
Eerdmans (US publishing house), 255
Elder, John (Edinburgh bookseller), *see* John Elder
Elder and Ogilvy (Edinburgh booksellers), 337n1 (App. A)
Ellegård, Alvar
on the *N.B.R.*, 161
Ellicott, Bishop Charles J., 123
Elliot (?Andrew) (publishing house), 33
Elliot Stock (publishing house), 33, 215
Emerton, Professor J. A., 255
Encyclopaedia Biblica (issued by A. & C. Black), 37, 182–3, 185
Encyclopaedia Britannica, 38
Encyclopaedia of Religion and Ethics, 165, 243
assessment of its achievement, 17, 62
attracting contributors, 145
continuing sales, 244
effect of WW1, 30
income from, 244
last vol. dedicated to Sir J.M.C., 11
project to replace, 262
reprinted, 256
scale of investment, 11
Epochs of Church History series (issued by Longman), 34, [98–9], 320n360
Eras of the Christian Church, 12, 89, 90, 98–101, 109, 219
Ernesti, J.A.
work, *Principles of Biblical Interpretation of the New Testament*, 4
Europe, 3, 256
Evangelical Classics (issued by MacNiven and Wallace), 267
evangelical revival
early 19th century, effect on publishing, xviii
in US, post-Civil War, 107–8
Evangelical Succession Lectures (issued by MacNiven and Wallace), 267
evangelical theology
20th century resurgence in publishing, 256
Everybody's Paper (US periodical), 107
exchange rate, effect on international trading, 85
Exell, J.S. (*see also Monthly Interpreter*), 155
edits *British and Foreign Evangelical Review*, 164, 324n519
'well-known' in the US, 153
work, *Thirty Thousand Thoughts*, 163
exports
Colonial catalogue, 217
number of overseas accounts, 232
through foreign and Colonial booksellers, 227, 228–9
20th century markets, 244, 255–6

(exports, *cont.*)
worldwide market for *F.T.L.*, 77; for *E.T.* and *C.R.*, 166
exports to USA (*see also* co-editions; profitability of co-editions; profitability of exports; USA), 115–21 *passim*
B.C.P., 54
D.B., 185–6
exchange rate, effect of on, 85
effect on work's profitability, 86, 101
market cultivated by Sir T.C., 6
periodicals, 153–4
sales of editions, 68
through booksellers, 227
in 20th century, 255
works published on commission 207
Expositor (periodical issued by Hodder), 35, 37, 152 *bis*, 163
Expository Times, 12, 37, 99, 154, 164–8, 243, 251, 254, 255, 325n526
achievement of, 148, 149
advertisers, importance of to, 158
advertises C. titles, 215
editors of, 245
importance to T. & T. C. in 20th century, 244–5
income from, 244, 245
North American distribution of, 105, 106, 111, 117–9
promotion of, 156 *bis*
reviews C. titles, 149, 222

Fairbairn, Andrew Martin
proposed *I.T.L.* Vol., *Religion of the World*, 131
Fairbairn, Patrick (Free Church College, Glasgow), 155
Work, *Imperial Bible Dictionary*, 182
The Family Guide to the Bible, 260, 262
Fergusson, A.W., 17
financial year, 235, 307n1
Fisher, G.P. (Yale University)
work, *History of Christian Doctrine*, 131 *bis*, 133, 134–5, 136, 138 tab 14, 216 tab 21, 219 tab 22, 221 tab 23, 224 tab 24
Flint, Robert
proposed work, *Religious Philosophy*, 131
Foreign Biblical Library (issued by Hodder), 36, 305n177
Foreign Devotional Library, 307n2
Foreign Evangelical Review, see British and Foreign Evangelical Review
The Foreign Theological Library, 17, 42, 43, 77–81, 274 tab 34
influence, 19
initiated, 7, 299n6
orthodoxy commended, 23
profitability, 121, 236
rivals, 36, 306n186
stock in hand, 280
wound up, 62, 75
Forrest, David W.
work, *The Christ of History and Experience*, 58
Fortress Press (US publishing house), 255
Foulis, Douglas, 258
France, 248
Fraser, Alexander Campbell, 159–60
Free Church of Scotland
Hodder issues works by F.C. authors, 36
and *N.B.R.*, 159–60
relationship with T. & T. C., 9, 21, 35, 38, 39, 49, 53–4, 128
and *Theological Review*, [93], 169–70
free grants of books, 230, 231, 232
frequency of issue of periodicals, factors determining the optimum, 152–3
Fulton, John, 98
Funk, Isaac K., 108
Funk and Wagnalls (US publishing house), 84, 87, 103, 108–9, 109–12 *passim*, 122, 316n250
Funke, Otto, 33

Gage, W.J. (Toronto bookseller), *see* W.J. Gage
Gardner, Alexander (publishing house), *see* Alexander Gardner
Garvie, A.E.
work, *The Ritschlian Theology*, 196, 197
Geden, A.S.
work, *see Concordance to the Greek Testament*
Gee, Henry (Highbury Training College), 99
Gemmell (publishing house), 33
General Assemblies of the Scottish Churches, 215
George Bell and Sons (publishing house), 176, 321n426, 326n569
German language, difficulties in translating, 71–2, 78
Gifford Lectures, 12, 58
Gladden, Washington
work, *The Christian Pastor*, 130, 131, 132, 135–6, 138 tab 14
Gladstone, W.E., 154, 160

Gloag, Paton J.
works, *Introduction to the Catholic Epistles*, 196; *Introduction to the Synoptic Gospels*, 199–200, 216 tab 21, 219 tab 22, 221 tab 23, 224 tab 24; *Life of St John*, 56; *The Messianic Prophecies*, 306n180
Gloucester, Bishop of, 25
Godet, Friedrich, 301–2n74
works, *Commentary on Romans*, 28; *Epistles of St Paul*, 76; *John's Gospel*, 80 tab 7
gold standard, 85
Gossip, A.J., 16
Gould, E.P.
work, *St Mark*, 132, 141, 143–4, 146 tab 15, 216 tab 21, 219 tab 22, 221 tab 23, 224 tab 24
Grant, Douglas, 263
Gray, Louisa
work, *Mine own People* (issued by Macniven and Wallace), 267–8
Great Christian Doctrines series, 243
Great Texts of the Bible, 243, 244
Great War
effect on book trade, 30, 246, 248
effect on *E.R.E.*, 243
effect on Sir J.M.C., 247–8
and W.R. Nicoll, 248
Greater Men and Women of the Bible, 243, 244
Greek type, monopoly in, 326n561
Greek and English Lexicon of the New Testament, 4
Green (publishing house), 264
Green, Dr Geoffrey (proprietor, T. & T. C.), 253, 259, 261, 262–64 *passim*, 336n (Epilogue)
Green, Samuel
work, *The Ancient Faith*, 218
Gretna rail disaster (1915), 247, 250
Grieve, Alexander, 72–4
Grimm, C.L.W.
work, edition of Wilke's *Clavis Novi Testamenti*, 175
'guarantee', borne by author, 205
Guardian (periodical), 221
Guyot, Arnold
work, *Creation*, 89, 303n113

Halcombe, J.J.
work, *What think ye of the Gospels?*, [193], 329n639
Hall, C. Newman
work, *The Lord's Prayer*, 218, 225
Hamilton, Adams and Co. (wholesalers), 3, 81, 162, 225, 226, 228, 232
Hampden, Dabney, 304n149
Hanley, Violet (on T. & T. C's staff), 252
Harnack and Schürer
work, *Theologische Literaturzeitung*, 170
Harper, W.R. (Chicago University), 77
Harper and Row (US publishing house), 260
HarperCollins, 260, 261
Harris, Samuel (Yale College)
works, *God the Creator and Lord of All*, 91, 91–2; *The Self-Revelation of God*, 87, 333n40
Harvey, James, 20, 23
Hastings, Ann, 245
Hastings, Edward, 245
Hastings, James (*see also The Children's Great Texts of the Bible; Dictionary of the Apostolic Church; Dictionary of the Bible* (multi-vol. edn); *Dictionary of the Bible* (1–vol. edn); *Dictionary of Christ and the Gospels; Encyclopaedia of Religion and Ethics; Expository Times; Great Christian Doctrines* series; *Great Texts of the Bible; Greater Men and Women of the Bible*)
accused of being unbusinesslike, 337n5 (Epilogue)
assesses MSS, 25, 72
assessment of the Cs' theocentric approach, 23
comments used to promote work to Scribners, 116
importance to T. & T. C., 11, 16, 165, 243–6
life insured while working on *D.B.*, 188 tab 20, 284 tab 35n5
list of his works, 243
obsessive perfectionism of, 245
projects not all accepted, 245–6
recommends MSS for publication, 25, 28–9, 194, 195, 202
recommendations not all followed, 25, 29
relationship with Scribners, 104
relationship with T. & T. C., 11
view of James Moffatt, 24–5
Hatch Edwin
proposed work, *Contemporary History of the New Testament*, 131
Headlam, *see* Sanday, William
Hebraica (US periodical), 70 *bis*

Hefele, C.J.
work, *Councils of the Church*, 216 tab 21, 219 tab 22, 221 tab 23, 224 tab 24
Hertz (Berlin publishing house), 64 *bis*, 65, 310n60
Herzog, Johan J.
work, *Religious Encyclopaedia*, 87–8, 111, 122–3
higher criticism
conservative serial proposed to counter, 147–8
D.B.'s moderate approach, [38], 183
development in 19th century, 15
dilemmas h.c. posed T. & T. C., [17 *bis*], 17–18, [18], 22, 301–2n74, 302n100
rationalism damages a book's sales, 89
Hill, James, 304n140, 305n159
Hill, J. Hamlyn, 204, 304n127, 329n652
works, *A Dissertation on the Gospel Commentary of St Ephraem the Syrian*, 208–10, 222, 223, 330n685; edition of Tatian's *Diatessaron*, 196, 198 *bis*, 222, 331n693, 334n61
Hodder, [Matthew], 36, 306n179
Hodder and Stoughton (publishing house), 33, 34 *bis*, 35 *ter*, 36–7, 39, 53, 152, 169, 267, 268
Hodge, Charles
work, *Commentary on Romans*, 27
Hodge, William (Glasgow legal publishing house), 263
Hodgson, J.M. (Principal, Congregational Theological Hall, Scotland)
work, *Theologia Pectoris*, 215
Homiletical Quarterly (US periodical), 163
Homiletic Review (US periodical), 109
Houghton, Mr (of Houghton, Mifflin and Co.), 122
Houghton, Mifflin and Co. (Boston, US publishing house), 122, 303n114, 313n147
Household Library of Exposition series (founded by MacNiven and Wallace), 49, 267 *bis*
Hull, Edward, 303n123
Hulsean Lectures, 12, 58
Hunter, M. (Edinburgh schoolmaster), 9
Hunter and Foulis (bookbinders) 257, 258

Imperial Bible Dictionary (Fairbairn), 182
import duty, 87
imports from USA (*see also* profitability of imports)
as many review copies as possible sought, 219–20
late 20th century, 262
wholesale terms on some, 228
index
to the *L.R.E.*, 243
to be supplied by authors for *I.T.L.* vols, 132
India, exports to, 244, 256
Inglis, J. McDonald, 206, 305n153, 329n642
Inland Revenue, 250
in-print life of titles, *see* longevity of titles
insurance, annual outlay on, 283 tab 35
International Critical Commentary series
aims, 21
complaints about cost of some later vols, 248–9
and F.T.L., 62–3
history of, 12, 137–46, 243
and I.T.L., 126–7
N.T. editor in mid-20th century, 255
O.T. edition in mid-20th century, 255
payment to authors, 34
promotion of, 219 tab 22n
reflects 'genuine' UK scholarship, 62
rejection of sub-standard scholars, 22, 24
revision of in 1950s, 251, 257
Unitarian author contributes title, 22
International Theological Library series
aims, 21
damaged by McGiffert work, 26, 43–4
history of, 12, 125–37, 243, 302n98
only most able scholars invited to contribute, 24
payment to authors, 34
reflects 'genuine' UK scholarship, 62, 121
T. & T. C. charged with diverting energies of *I.T.L.* authors, 35, 126
International Thompson (conglomorate), 264
Inter-Varsity Press (publishing house), 256
investment
1896–1989, 287–91 tab 36
1911–22, 248
1923–30, 250
1930–56, 251
1956–73, 251–2
analysis of outlay, 292 tab 37
in *A.N.L.*, 45
in *C.R.*, 169

(investment, *cont.*)
in *I.T.L.*, 133–4
in *M.G.*, 176, 177 *bis*
lack of capital delays diversification, 256
over-cautious approach to, 257–8
scale of under Sir J.M.C., 11, 238 tab 27
slow to yield return, 78, 81, 82, 84 *bis*
Irish Presbyterian Church (Bible Class Handbook), 51 tab 5n4

J.A. Cameron and Co. (publishing house), 338n 11
Jackson, Welford and Hodder (publishing house), 36
James Nisbet (publishing house), 215, 334n58
James Parker and Co. (publishing house), 109
Japan, 256 *bis*
Jeffrey, R.J., 304n 142
Jellinghaus, H.F.B., 61, 305n 160
Jewel Poets series (issued by MacNiven and Wallace), 267
John Bartholomew and Son (map-publishing house) (*see also* Bartholomew Group), 235, 258 *bis*
John Elder (Edinburgh booksellers), 337n1 (App. A)
John MacLaren and Son (Edinburgh booksellers), 267
John Menzies (distributors), 166, 325n526
Johnston, James B., 307n3
Johnstone, Robert (President, United Presbyterian College) work, *1st Peter*, 196
Johnstone and Hunter (Edinburgh publishing house), 148
Journal of Jurisprudence (periodical), 8, 147, 156, 334n61
journal publishing, *see* periodical publishing

Kegan Paul (London distributors), 162, 226–7, 228
Keil, C.F.
works, *Bible Archaeology*, 66, 78 *Commentary on the Pentateuch*, 80 tab 7, 81
Kennedy, W.P., 160
Kerr, David, 23, 305n171
Kerr Lectures, 12, 58
Kidd Lectures, 58
Killen, W.B.
work, *The Ignatian Epistles Entirely Spurious*, 206
Kilpatrick, T.B.
work, *Christian Character*, 55–6 tab 6n8
King, A. (printers), *see* Aberdeen University Press
King James Version of the Bible, *see*, Bible, King James Version
King's Own (periodical), 309n44, 332n13
Koegel, Rudolf, 27
König, F.E., (Leipzig, later Rostock University), 65
works, *Deutero-Isaiah*, 25; *Exiles Book of Consolation*, 63, 66; *Religious History of Israel*, 64, 67, 219, 305n156
Kregel (US publishing house), 255
Kurtz, Johann H.
work, *Church History*, 305–6n177

Labugama Rubber and Tea Co. (Ceylon), 246
Lady Glenorchy's Church, Edinburgh, 6, 249, 300n20
Ladd, George T. (Yale College), 85
work, *The Doctrine of Sacred Scripture*, 89, [90], [117], 150, 214, 219, 303n115
Laidlaw, Professor John, 207
Lambert, J.C., 327n581
Lange, J.P.
work, *Commentaries*, 7, 88, 94–7, 106, 236, 276 tab 34n5
Law, Dr (Toronto), 337n 5 (Epilogue)
Law Chronicle (periodical), 5, 147
lecture series, 12, 35, 58–9
lectures, in general sell poorly, 28, 58, 193, 310n59
Lee, Professor Robert (Edinburgh University), 148
legal publishing, *see* publishing, legal
length of books
discussion over length of *D.B.*, 183
how to make books seem longer than they actually are, 183
lengthy books not acceptable to English readers, 29, 89, 193–4
payment to authors by length, 128–9
small books not economically viable, 28, 194
small books viable if issued as part of series, 43
small vols in series yield larger returns than do large, 136–7, 144
Liberal Party, 300n29

libraries
advertising prompts demand through, 334n61
difficulty in selling to, 334n61
free grant to library, 232, 331n691
library subscriptions to periodicals obviate need for personal subscriptions, 93, 156
supplied at special discount, 230, 334n61
life of titles in print, *see* longevity of titles
Lilley, J.P.
work, *Principles of Protestantism*, 52 tab 5n8
Lillie, Arthur
work, *Buddha*, 309n55
Lindsay, R. (Glasgow bookseller), 225
Lindsay, T.M.
works, *Luther*, 309n55; *St Luke's Gospel*, 39
Linotype typesetting machines, 319n358
Lipsius
work, *Theologischer Jahresbericht*, 170
list, T. & T. C's
balance in the late 20th century, 262
no. of titles in print, 42, 235
literary style, *see* style, literary
Locke, Clinton
work, *The Great Western Schism*, 89–90, 99
Lofthouse, W.F., 304n126
London Tract Society, library of, 232
longevity of titles, 77, 81, 90–1, 236–7
Reader's Digest approach, 260
Longman (publishing house), 34, 98, 320n360
Lotze, R.H.
work, *Microcosmus*, 67, 68, 117
Luthardt, C.E., 61
work, *Commentary on St John*, 61

MacDonald, James, 68–70
McGiffert, Arthur C.
assures Sir T. C. of adherence to Christian fundamentals, 22, 132 *bis*
work, *A History of Christianity in the Apostolic Age*, 18, 26, [27], 43–4, 131 *bis*, 136, 138 tab 14
MacGregor, James (New Zealand)
works, *Apology of the Christian Religion*, 199; *Studies in the History of New Testament Apologetics*, 207
Macintosh (ultra-conservative theological writer), 20
Macintosh, Hugh
work, *Is Christ Infallible and the Bible True?*, 302n100
MacIntyre, Ronald George
work, *Elijah and Elisha*, 56
'MacLaren, Ian', *see* Watson, Dr John
MacLaren, John (Edinburgh bookseller), 267 *bis*, 337n1 (App. A)
MacLaren and MacNiven (Edinburgh booksellers), 267
Macmillan (publishing house), 184, 262
Macmillan, Frederick, 183–4
Macmillan and Bowes (Cambridge booksellers), 218
McNamara, Martin
work, *The Aramaic Bible*, 262
MacNiven, John (Edinburgh bookseller), 267
MacNiven and Wallace (Edinburgh publishing house) (*see also Bible Class Primers*), 33, 169 *bis*, 267–8
MacPherson (book reviewer), 151
MacPherson, John, 71–2, 76, 322n439
'McRealsham, E.D.' (Charles M. Mead)
work, *Romans Dissected*, 17–8, [22], 206, 302n80
Mahood Testimonial, 285 tab 35n 8
Mair, Dr (*M.I.* contributor), 155
management structure, 261
manuscripts
assessment of, *see* assessment of manuscripts
need to be complete before typesetting to avoid corrections at proof stage, 128, 132
unsolicited, *see* unsolicited manuscripts
market for Clark titles
audience for *E.T.* and *C.R.*, 149
English as well as Scottish aimed at, 194
fluctuation of, 30
in 20th century, 255–6
known intimately by Sir J.M.C., 26, 304n146
market aimed at by *I.T.L.*, 126
market for religious works declining, 306–7n200
not the 'popular' market, 213
for periodicals, 151–6 *passim*
response to *D.B.*, 181
marketing (*see also* direct selling), 213–224, 257
limits of marketing, 312n134
possible selling of title to booksellers in units of two dozen, 203
representation, 261
sales department established, 261, 262

Martensen, Hans (Bishop of Zealand)
work, *Christian Ethics*, 25, 63, 80 tab 7, 304n137
Matheson, George
work, *The Growth of the Spirit of Christianity*, [196], 199, 227, 330n 659
Mathews, Shailer (University of Chicago), 327n581
Mead, Charles M., *see* 'McRealsham, E.D.'
Melville, Muller and Slade (London business), 332n707
Mentone (France), 248
Menzies, John (distributors), *see* John Menzies
merger with Bartholomews, 258
Methodist Churches
Primitive Methodist Bookroom and T. & T. C., 187, 231
Primitive Methodist Publishing House and T. & T. C., 335–6n88
relationships with T. & T. C., 21
special terms sought for Wesleyan preachers, 229
Methodist Times (periodical), 221
The Metropolitan Pulpit (US periodical), 109
Meyer, H.A.W., 64
work, *Critical and Exegetical Commentary on the New Testament*, 8, 81–4, 110, 111, 112, 236, 274 tab 34n2, 280
Millar, Fergus, 262
Milne, A. & R. (Aberdeen booksellers), *see* A. & R. Milne
Milne, Jacqueline (office manageress), 253, 254, 336n (Epilogue)
missionary libraries, 230
Mitchell, J. Knox, 322n454
Mitchell, T. (Primitive Methodist Bookroom), 231
Mitton, C. Leslie, 245
Moffatt, James
assessment of his motives, 20
the epitome of a C. author, 24–25
work, *The Historical New Testament*, 20, 24–5, 192, 328n626
Monthly Interpreter (periodical), 7, 153, 195
accused of competing with *Expositor*, 37
advertised, 214, 218, 222
advertisers, difficulty in attracting, 158, 215, 226
aims, 20, 21
cover design, 151
editor attempts to hijack Hodder author, 35
editor's lackadaisical approach, 150
history, 161–4, 164, 168, 226, 228
marketed in US, 106, 111, 116, 117, 153–4
plan to rescue it, 324n519
poor remuneration for contributors, [155]
promotion, 156 *bis*
reasons for failure, 154
and rival journals, 152*bis*
size of each issue discussed, [153]
weekly journal initially proposed, 153
wide range of contributors promised, 154
Moody, Dwight L., 108
Moore, G.F.
work, *Judges*, 141 *bis*, 143, 146 tab 15, 216 tab 21, 219 tab 22, 221 tab 23, 224 tab 24
Morrison and Gibb (Edinburgh printers), 87, 257, 325n527
motivation of T. & T. C. (*see also* aims of T. & T. C.)
decisions made on grounds other than purely economic, 26–30 *passim*, 47, 61, 66, 77, 81, 84, 101, 119, 149, 172–3, 181–2, 248–9, 256, 310n63
decisions made on purely economic grounds, 26–30 *passim*, 65, 195
for importing works from US, 86, 89, 116–7
minimising risk, 192, 195–7, 204–5, 205, 206, 207, 210
of God and mammon, 238
pragmatism, 111, 115, 119, [121], 184
moulds, from which to cast stereoplates, 200, 202
Moulton, W.F.
work (*see also Concordance to the Greek Testament*), edition of G.B. Winer's *Grammar of New Testament Greek*, 21
Mudie's Library, 334n61
Murphy, J.G., 123

nails
damage caused by, 87–8
provenance of, hotly disputed, 88
Napier College (Edinburgh), 259
Naville, Ernest
work, *The Christ*, 75 *bis*
Nebe, August, 25, 29, 230
negotiations, *see* diplomacy in negotiations
Negris and Duncan, 299n9

Nelson, Thomas (1822–92), 36
Nelson, Thomas (publishing house), *see* Thomas Nelson and Sons
Net Book Agreement, 183–5
M.G. issued as a net book, 177, 179 tab 18n5
net books, T. & T. C. feel they perform badly, 185, 228
New College Book Scheme, 285 tab 35n8
new titles, a rarity in 1959, 254, 256
New World (US periodical), 215, 220
New Zealand, 207
NewsCorp, 260 *bis*, 261
News International, 260
Nicene and Post-Nicene Fathers series, 115
Nicoll, Henry
work, *Life of Christ*, 268
Nicoll, William Robertson, 268
affect on of WW1, 248
assesses Sir T. C's achievement, 21
complains about competition, 35, 36–7
discusses book trade post-WW1, 249
E.T., view of, 165
and *Household Library of Exposition*, 53
joins Hodder, 53
MacNiven and Wallace, N. on staff of, 267
quarterlies, profitability of, N's view, 152
T. & T. C's commitment to progressive theology, N's view of, 20 *bis*
Nisbet, James (publishing house), *see* James Nisbet
Nöldeke
work, *Syriac Grammar*, 68–70
North British Review, 8, 148, 154, 159–61
novels
cost of typesetting, 319n358
one published by the firm, 4–5
Nowell-Smith, Simon, 110
Nurse, E.J., 192, 329n633

obersetzungerecht, *see* translation right
'odd book system', *see under* trade terms
office routine at 38 George Street, 253–4
O'Hara, Jack (Chief Executive, Readers' Digest), 259, 260
Oliphant (publishing house), 337n1 (App. A)
Oliphant, Anderson and Ferrier (publishing house), 57, 108
Oliver and Boyd (publishing house), 263
Olney, Richard (US Secretary of State), 127
Origen, works, in *A.N.L.*, 46 tab 1
output of British publishing trade, increasing, 306–7n200
output of T. & T. Clark
annual output, 1950s, 256
level necessary for T. & T. C. to become market leaders, 263
no. of titles on list, 42, 235
overheads, 239 tab 28, 283–5 tab 35, 292 tab 37
amount charged for to a vol. of Barth's *Dogmatics*, 252 tab 32
Owen, John
Works, 7, 236, 274 tab 34n1
Oxford Library of Fathers, 45, [307n9]
Oxford University Press (printers and publishers), [124], 142, 257

packing cases for exports
paid for by importing booksellers, 228
size and cost of, 335n81
pagination, numbering columns rather than pages gives illusion of greater length, 37, 183
paper
high-quality for *M.G.*, 177
shortage during WW1, 246
thicker p. gives illusion of greater length, 37, 183
Parker, James and Co. (publishing house), *see* James Parker and Co.
Parry, J., 308n32
'part-publication'
of *D.B.* contemplated, 183, 321–2n427
opposition to, 148
periodical publishing (*see also Clark's Biblical Magazine and Review; Concilium; Critical Review; Expository Times; Journal of Jurisprudence; Law Chronicle; Monthly Interpreter; North British Review*; 'part-publication'; *Presbyterian Review*; profitability of periodical publishing), 8, 147–73
British market flooded, 93
promotion by free distribution, 222
readers encouraged to promote among friends, 222
value of *E.T.* as 'shop window' for T. & T. C., 119
petty cash payments, 285 tab 35n8
'piracy' in North America, 105, 121
case for US reprint of *A.N.L.* refuted, 109, 112–3
defined, 102, 110

('piracy' in North America, *cont.*)
implications of, 110–11
many C. works pirate-proof, 111, 117
of specific works, 49, 110
in 20th century, 257
vulnerability of T. & T. C. to, 113
plates, printing
amended, 140
British p, criticised by US printers, 141–2
exported to US to print edition there, 102, 116, 132–3, 141–2, 179 tab 18n6, 186
imported from US to print UK edition, 87
Plummer, Alfred (University College, Durham)
suggestion of authors for *I.C.C.* rejected, 22, 24
UK editor of *I.C.C.*, 137–41 *passim*
work, *St Luke*, 141, 146 tab 15
Plymouth Brethren, publishing by, xviii
Police News (periodical), 158
'popular' theological works
Family Guide to the Bible, 262
Funk and Wagnalls specialise in US, [109]
T. & T. C. consider enlisting 'Ian MacLaren', 128
T. & T. C's attitude to, 24, 111, 193–4
post, the
Edinburgh mail hand-delivered, 254
postal charges, 218, 221
posthumous works
example, 207
rarely profitable, 25–6, 193, 194
Preachers' Monthly (periodical), 152
premises at 36/38 George Street
description, 1959, 253–4
move to 59 George Street, 260, 299n4
owned personally by individual Clarks, 239 tab 28n, 258
rental, 1890s, 283 tab 35, 284 tab 35n2
38 George Street sold, 259
pre-publication offers, 227, 326n569
Presbyterian News Company (Toronto), 108
Presbyterian Review (periodical), 8, 87, 93–4, 152, 214, 218 *bis*, 222, 334n61
presentation copies
free grants to libraries, 230, 232
to Primitive Methodist Bookroom, 231
press, the, relationships with, *see* relationships with editors of non-C. publications
Price and Clay (Secretaries to the University Presses), 124 *bis*, 125
Primitive Methodist Book Room, 187, 231 *bis*
Primitive Methodist Publishing House, 335–6n88
printers (*see also* relationships with printers)
US ways of 'making ready' criticised, 142
printing plates, *see* plates, printing
print runs
normal C. length, 198
Readers' Digest approach, 260
production department established, 261
profit-sharing, *see* remuneration of authors
profitability of co-editions (*see also* co-editions), 121–46, 236, 269–79
profitability of exports, 101–21 *passim*
profitability of imports, 85–101 *passim*, 236, 269–79
of Grimm/Thayer, 175–6
profitability of individual titles, 236, 269–79
examples, 169–90 *passim*, 197–210 *passim*
factors affecting, 197–9
size of work, 28–9
time of year when published, 28–9
sale of US edition essential, 86, 110–1, 115–6
profitability of legal publishing, 236, 269–79
profitability of periodical publishing, 236, 269–79
affected by library subscriptions obviating need for personal subscriptions, 93, 156
of *C.R.*, 170–2
exports to US, 117–9
of *E.T.*, 166–8
factors affecting, 151–8
intangible benefits of publishing prestigious titles, 147, 149
of *M.I.*, 161, 163–4
of *N.B.R.*, [159], [160]
profitability of series (*see also* series publishing), 43–59 *passim*, 94–101, 236 *ter*, 269–79
of *I.C.C.*, 142–6, 248–9
of *I.T.L.*, 133–38
profitability of T. & T. Clark
1821–46, 5
1886–89, 13
1890s, 235–9, 269–79
1896–1989, 287–91
1911–22, 248
1922–30, 250

(profitabiity of T. & T. Clark, *cont.*)
1930–56, 251
1956–73, 251
1973–90, 261
cash injection from Bible Guide, 262–3
cash injection from legal guide, 263
contribution of Hastings' titles, 243–4
strategy for keeping in profit, 26–30 *passim*
profitability of translations, 61–8 *passim*, 75–84 *passim*, 236, 269–70
promotion (*see also* publicity)
A. & C. Black make a work appear to be a bargain by printing it on thick paper, 183
launch ceremonies, 262
of forthcoming works to wholesalers, 225–6
of new works to Scribners, 116, 117
supplying new works unsolicited to overseas booksellers, 227
proofs
editor's slowness in correcting, 163
numerous revisions of *M.G.*, 177
ruinous cost of alterations at proof stage, 67–8, 128, 198
'proportion of lists', 217, 283 tab 35
prospectuses, distribution of, 156, 186, [213], 217–9, 221, [257], 261, 262
pseudonymous book, *see* 'McRealsham, E.D.'
publication date, effect on sales of, 198–9
publicity (*see also* advertising; announcements of forthcoming works; promotion), 213–23
cross-fertilisation between different kinds of advertising, 218–9, 221
for *D.B.*, 186
funded by 'proportion of lists' charge to each title, 217
of *M.G.*, 178 tab 18n3
of periodicals, 94, 156–7
Publishers' Association, 184, 285 tab 35n8
Publishers' Circular, 26
publishing, the Readers' Digest approach, 260
publishing, legal (*see also* profitability of legal publishing), 2, 4, 5, 8, 147, 263, 264
publishing, religious
adaptation necessary for survival, xix, 15
assumes greater importance to the firm, 4
by churches, xviii
evangelical publishing, 20th century resurgence, 256
factors affecting the market in the 19th century, 15, 62
ignorance of London publishers of strength of Scottish r.p., 157–8, 304n146
impervious to depression, 108, 249–50
increasing importance of English-language theology, 62, 121, 175
late 20th century development of the C. list, 262–3
over-publishing by some houses, 191
market-leader, possibility of becoming, 263
the theological periodical market-place, 151–4 *passim*
in USA, 103–9 *passim*
in Victorian Scotland, xviii
publishing department established, 261
Pusey, E.B., 45
Putnam (US publishing house), 106

Quarterly (*Dickinson's*) (periodical), *see Dickinson's Quarterly*
Quarterly Review (periodical), 159
quarterly *Reviews*
days of successful q. rs past, 152
most English q. rs subsidised, 172
sales of *P.R.* damaged by its appearing later than other q. rs, 93–4

R. & R. Clark (printers), 257
Rainy, Robert (Principal, New College, Edinburgh), 47, 97
work, *The Ancient Catholic Church*, 131, 133
Ramsay, W.M. (Aberdeen University), 72–4
Randle, George (on C. staff), 253
Randolph (US publishing house), 163, 316n250
rationalism, damages book sales, 89
readers, publishers'
T. & T. C's external referees, 25, 255
Readers' Digest, 259, 260 *bis*, 262, 263, 286
reference books, major, 175–90 *passim*
Reid Group, 264
rejection of manuscripts, *see* assessment of manuscripts
relationships with authors (*see also* remuneration of authors)
acquaintance with biblical scholars, 140
authors charged for corrections on proof, 198

(relationships with authors, *cont.*)
consulted on promotion, 218
delays in completion of MSS, 128, 257
disagreement over advertising at rear of book, 223, 331n693
eagerness to please an author, 310n63
limits of this policy, 313n168
receive no special terms, 230
remaindering, would offend authors, 227
reminded of the need for accuracy, 329n633
review copies, extra circulated at author's expense, 220
Sir T. C. and an unwise autobiographer, 302–3n105
T. & T. C. anxious for author's sake that works sell well, 198
of works issued on commission, 204–7
relationships with editors
advice taken on titles to publish, 256
with James Hastings, 11, 118–9, 181–90 *passim*
with *I.C.C.* editors, 139–40, 321n415
with *I.T.L.* editors, 127
with Moulton and Geden, 177
with Oliphant Smeaton, 309n55
with periodical editors, 149–51, 160, 161–4 *passim*, 165, 170
supreme indulgence shown, 45
relationships with editors of non-Clark publications, 220–1
relationships with printers, 257
Aberdeen University Press, 73
extra discounts given on *M.G.* due to production difficulties, 177, 178 tab 18n1
Oxford University Press, 142
relationships with translators, 68–70, 310n63
religious publishing, *see* publishing, religious
religious revival, *see* evangelical revival
Religious Tract Society, London, 33, 335n87
remaindering, 227
example of, 75
remuneration of authors (*see also* royalties), 123, 195–7, 319n358, 320n360
complaints over, 257
contributors to *D.B.*, 187
contributors to periodicals, 155, 162, 163, 169, 170
honoraria, 129, 330n660
by length, 128–9, 137
literary expenses for five sample years, 292 tab 37
payment sought in respect of advertising at rear of book, 223
in respect of editions pirated in US, 49
in respect of translations, 63–4, 69, 310n76
in respect of *I.C.C.* and *I.T.L.*, 34, 128–9, 133, 140
under risk-sharing agreements, 205–6
remuneration of editors
of *D.B.*, 188 tab 20n8
of Hastings, 244
of *I.C.C.*, 140, 320n363
of *I.T.L.*, 129, 320n363
Moulton and Geden, 177, 180
of periodicals, 162, 165–6, 167 tab 16n3, 169, 170
remuneration of translators, 66–7, 69, 311n100, 312n109
representation to the trade, 225, 261, [262]
reprints
annual totals, 8
capital-intensive in 1950s–60s, 256
T. & T. C. gets name of being reprint house, 256
retail prices (*see also* Net Book Agreement)
direct sales at low prices, 187, 230–2
discount expected by ultimate purchasers, 184, 335n72
factors affecting setting of, 77, 91, 197–8, 249
pre-publication offers, 326n569
returns of unsold works, 322n428
part-publications, 148
Reusch, Franz H.
work, *Nature and the Bible*, 20, 68, 75
Reuss, E.W.E.
work, *History of the Sacred Scriptures of the New Testament*, 78, 122
Reuther and Reichard (Berlin publishing house), 148
Revell, Fleming H. (US publishing house), 49, 107–8, 109, 110, 111, 118, 316n266
review copies (*see also* presentation copies), 219–22
examples of no. distributed, 87, 92n3, 201, 220
of periodicals, 94, 156
requested by editors, 333n47
retained by reviewers in addition to fee, 325n539
reviews of Clark titles, 37, 93–4, 98, 99, 170, 219, 220, 327n580

(reviews of Clark titles, *cont.*)
in C. journals, 141, 149, 150–1, 168, 222
good reviews don't always generate sales, 186
quoted in advertisements, 215
Revised Version of the Bible, *see* Bible, Revised Version
Revisers, of the English Bible, 176
revival, religious, *see* evangelical revival
reward book, published by the firm, 4
rights in works (*see also* translation right)
no one US Company has sole agency in C. works, 105–6
T. & T.C. buy British rights in US works, 87
T. & T.C. sell rights in their works, 102, 113, 114–5, 116
risk-sharing, with author, 192, 204–10 *passim*
author underwrites loss, 200
element of r.s. in case of *M.G.*, 177–8
Rivington (publishing house), 45
Roberts, Alexander, 7, 44
Robinson, Professor, 299n 9
Rodd, Cyril S., 245
Roman Catholic authors, works by, 20, 255
Roper, C.F. (New York bookseller), *see* C.F. Roper
Rowsell and Hutchison (Toronto booksellers), 229
Roxburgh Hotel (Edinburgh), 254
Royal Scots (Leith Battalion), 10
royalties (*see also* remuneration of authors), 328n596
examples, 51 tab 5n6, 57, 129, 196–7, 200, 201, 206, 330n660
total paid in two years in the 1920s, 244
paid to Hastings, 244
royalties received by T. & T. C.
on *D.B.*, 186
on *M.G.*, 179 tab 18n7
on Revell's editions of Stalker works, 316n266
Ruskin, John, 160
Ryle, Professor Herbert E. 141, 204, 321n415

S.C.M. Press (publishing house), 263
St Andrew (periodical), 214
Saint Augustine, *see* Augustine, Saint
St Giles Lectures (issued by MacNiven and Wallace), 267
salaries, 250, 283 tab 35, 284 tab 35, 286
'sale or return basis', supply of books on, 225
sales department, 261, 262
sales figures, total through wholesalers, 226 tab 25
Salmond, S.D.F. (Free Church College, Aberdeen), 16, 93, 217, 306n182
consulted over assessment of MSS, 25
edits *B.C.P.*, 53
and *I.T.L.*, 12, 125–33 *passim*
and plan to rescue *M.I.*, 324n519
proposes quarterly journal, 152 *bis*, 153, 169
travelling expenses, 284 tab 35n4
works (*see also Critical Review*)
The Christian Doctrine of Immortality, 120, 154, 200–2, 216 tab 21, 219 tab 22, 221 tab 23, 224 tab 24; *The Shorter Catechism*, 225
Sanday, Professor William, Oxford, 167 tab 16n4
and the I.C.C., 137
involved with *D.B.*, 181
works, *Literature of the New Testament*, 131; *Romans* (with Headlam), 141, 146 tab 15, 216 tab 21, 219 tab 22, 221 tab 23, 224 tab 24
Schaff, Philip (Union Theological Seminary, New York), 110, 114, 217
deficient performance of *I.P.C.* contributor, 24, 140
edits the *Illustrated Popular Commentary*, 123–5
and Herzog's *Religious Encyclopaedia*, 122
and Lange's *Commentaries*, 94
works, *Apostolic Christianity*, 97–8; *Ante-Nicene Christianity*, 97–8; *Church and State*, declined by T. & T. C., 313n168; *Encyclopaedia of Living Divines*, 301n46; *The German Reformation*, 97–8; *History of the Christian Church*, 8, 97–8; *Nicene and Post-Nicene Christianity*, 97–8; *Medieval Christianity*, 97–8; *The Swiss Reformation*, 97–8; *Symbolics* (proposed), 131
Schmidt, Christophe von
work, *The Basket of Flowers*, 4
Schürer, Emil (University of Kiel)
work, *History of the Jewish People in the Time of Christ*, 63, 80 tab 7, 81, 262
Scott, C.A.
work, *The Making of Israel*, 55 tab 6n7

Scottish Church and University Almanac (issued by MacNiven and Wallace), 268
Scottish Law Directory, 263
Scottish Law Magazine (periodical), 8, 147
Scottish Law Review (periodical), 8, 147
Scottish Life Assurance Company, 10
Scribner, Arthur Hawley, 104
Scribner, Charles I, 6, 103, 300n19
Scribner, Charles II, 18, 26, 104, 104–5, 318n324
Scribner, John Blair, 104
Scribner and Welford (US publishing house), 103–4
Scribner, Armstrong and Co. (US publishing house), 104
Scribners (US publishing house), *see* Charles Scribner's Sons
Seabury Press (New York), appointed T. & T. C's main US agent, 255
Selbie, John A., 25, 66, 181, 327nn575, 581
serial publishing, *see* periodical publishing
series publishing (*see also* Augustine, Saint, *Works; The Ante-Nicene Library; The Biblical Cabinet; Bible Class Handbooks; Bible Class Primers; The Cabinet Library of Scarce and Celebrated Tracts;* Calvin, John *Works; Eras of the Christian Church; Foreign Devotional Library; Foreign Theological Library; International Critical Commentary; International Theological Library;* Lange, J.P., *Commentaries*; Meyer, H.A.W., *Critical and Exegetical Commentary on the New Testament*; profitability of series; *The Student's Cabinet Library of Useful Tracts; World's Epoch Makers)*
  benefits of series publishing, 43–4, 59, 75, 77
  competition between *I.T.L.* and *I.C.C.*?, 126
  drawback of commitment to issue series on subscription, 82–3
  history and profitability of series of British origin and of Patristic works, 44–59
  need to reprint even slow-selling titles to maintain series, 52
  reluctant permission to reprint series in US, 112–5
  series imported from US, 94–101
  series requires extensive US sale to break even, 112, 115–16
  whole series affected by a few sub-standard titles, 26, 43–4, 57, 99
sermons, in general sell poorly, 28, 193
Session Cases, 263, 271ah, 338n3 (App. B)
settlement dates, 227
Shattock, Joanne, on the *N.B.R.*, 159, 160
sheets, printed
  how not to pack for export, 87, 88
  without signature cause problems for binders, 88, 99
  works supplied to US in, 102
shipping charges, *see* carriage charges
signatures (on printed sheets), absence of causes problems for binders, 88, 99
Sime, A.H. Moncur
  work, *The Epic of God*, 195, 206, 329n636
Simon, David W. (Principal, United College, Bradford), 155, 305n 167
  work, *Reconciliation by Incarnation*, 214, 220, 329n 637
Simpkin, Marshall (wholesalers), 225, 226, 226 tab 25, 228, 232
size of each issue of a periodical
  effect on sales, 153
  C.R. increased in size, 171
  E.T. increased in size, 166
Skene, W.F.
  work, *The Lord's Supper*, [198], 205, 330n668
Skinner, Professor
  consulted over MSS, 25
Sloan, Walter (China Inland Mission), 305n160
small books, *see* length of books
Smeaton, Oliphant
  edits *W.E.M.*, 12, 57, 309n55
  work, *The Medici and the Italian Renaissance*, 57
Smith, George Adam, 235
Smith, Henry P.
  work, *The Books of Samuel*, 141, 146 tab 15
Smith, W.H. (booksellers), *see* W.H. Smith
Smith, Dr William (author of a Bible dictionary), 37, 182
Smith, William Robertson, 37
Smyth, S. P. Newman
  work, *Christian Ethics*, 131, 133, 137, 138 tab 14

Snell, F.J.
work, *Wesley*, 309n55
The Society of Authors, 184
The Society of Booksellers and Stationers of Edinburgh, Leith and Suburbs, 257
Somerville, David
work, *St Paul's Conception of Christ*, 58
Spriggs, J.F. (London advertising agent), 158, 213
Spurgeon, Charles H., 54, 215, 309n44, 332n13
Sri Lanka, *see* Ceylon
Stade, Bernhard
work, *History of Israel*, 303n114, 314n184
staff (*see also* salaries)
commitment to the new regime, 264
extra s. for special project, 263
and 1918 influenza epidemic, 247
in 1959, 253–4
number of, 257, 261
relationships with, 253–4, 257
shortage during WW1, 246
Stalker, James
T. & T. C. urge him to complete *The Mind of Christ*, 24
works, *The Life of Christ*, 24, 49, [51], 110, [111], 308n35, 316n266; *The Life of St Paul*, 24, 49, [51], 51, 110, [111], 316n266
Standard Literature Company (India), 244
Stanton, V.H. (Trinity College, Cambridge)
work, *The Jewish and the Christian Messiah*, 195
Stead, F.H.
work, *The Kingdom of God*, 54
stereoplates, *see* plates, printing
Stevens, G.B. (Yale University)
work, *The Theology of the New Testament*, 131, 138 tab 14
Stewart, David Ross (M.D. of John Bartholomew and Son), 258 *bis*, 260, 263, 336n (Epilogue)
Stewart, William (Glasgow University), 82
Stirling, J. Hutchison, 204 *bis*
works, *Darwinianism*, 328n630; *What is Thought*, 193, 199
Stirling Tract Enterprise, xviii
Stock, the Revd Dr, 204, 305n157
stock in hand, 280–2
examples of quantities of bound copies held in stock, 95, 96 tab 9, 178 tab 18n2, 200, 202, 209
stock valuation
1896–99, 239 tab 28(d), 280–2
1923–30, 250
1927–73, 288–90 tab 36
1930–56, 251
1956–73, 252
depreciation, 285
students
colleges supplied cheaply for resale to, 230
direct selling of periodicals to, 157
work aimed at students assigned 'affordable' retail price, 198
Student's Cabinet Library of Useful Tracts, 4
style, literary
directions to *I.T.L.* authors, 131
effective style a condition of acceptance, 192–3
problems caused by US expressions used in books published in UK, 89–90, 132, 141
subscription sales
benefits of, 78, 230
drawback of, 82–3
M.G. originally to be issued on subscription, 176, 177
series issued on subscription, 46, 47–8, 77, 78, 79, 81, 82, 95
trade discount on subscription titles, 227, 228
survival of religious publishing houses, adaption necessary to ensure, xix, 15
Swanson, David (on C. staff), 253
Sweet and Maxwell (publishing group), 264
Swete, Professor H.B. (Cambridge University) on *D.B.* editorial team, 181
Sword and Trowel (periodical), 54

T. & T. Clark
aims, *see* aims of T. & T. C.
breadth of publications, *see* breadth of output
and British denominations, *see* Free Church of Scotland; Church of Scotland; Methodist Churches; Unitarian Churches)
history
1821–46, 3–5
1846–86, 5–9
1886–1900, 9–13
1901–23, 243–9
1923–30, 249–50
1930–56, 250–1

(T. & T. Clark, *cont.*)
1956–73, 251–8
1973–91, 259–64
influence on Scottish theology, 20–1
management structure (late 20th century), 261
motivation, *see* motivation of T. & T. C.
profitability, *see* profitability of T. & T. C.
reputation for orthodoxy, 17–19, 22–3
Targums, 262
Tatian
work, *Diatessaron, see under* Hill, J. Hamlyn
Tebbell, John, 104, 109
Ten Epochs of Church History (US series), *see Eras of the Christian Church* series, the title under which it appeared in the UK
trade terms, *see* terms, trade
Territorial Force Association, 10
territories, dispute with wholesalers over, 226
Terrot, Bishop C.H., 148
Tertullian
Works (in *A.N.L.*), 46 tab 1
Testamentum Domini Nostri Jesu Christi, 36
Textus Receptus, 176
Thayer, Joseph (Harvard University)
work, *A Greek-English Lexicon of the New Testament*, 9, 175, 218, 253, 253 tab 33, 326n548
Theological Monthly (periodical), 152, 324n519
theological publishing, *see* publishing, religious
Theological Review and Free Church [later *New College*] *Quarterly* (forerunner of *The Critical Review*, q.v.), 152, 155 *bis*, 169–70, 268
Theologische Literaturzeitung (German periodical), 170
Theologischer Jahresbericht, 170
Thiersch, H.W.J.
work, *On Christian Commonwealth*, 75
Thomas Nelson and Sons (publishing house), 33, 36, 268, 309n43
Thompson, Elizabeth (law publisher with T. & T. C.), 263
Thomson, E.A.
posthumous work, *Memorials of a Ministry*, 207 *bis*
Thomson, J.E.H.
work, *Books which Influenced our Lord*, 198, 205
Times Books, 260, 263
The Times Atlas, 260
The Times Law Reports, 263
Tischendorf, L.F.C., 176
titles of publications
appropriate title important to success of work, 193
series title changed to avoid clashing with competitor, 98–9
Tophel, Gustave (Geneva)
work, *The Work of the Holy Spirit in Man*, 75
Torrance, T.F., 251
Toy, Crawford, H. (Harvard), 22, [140]
work, *Proverbs*, 140, 141, 303n119
Tractarian Movement, 45
trade, the, *see* booksellers
trade conditions (*see also* Christmas; Great War), 30, 89, 93, 127
best time of year for advertising, 215
conditions pertaining at time of publication affect sales, 198–9
difficulty of predicting strong sellers, 192
increasing number of titles published, 306–7n200
in 1920s and 30s, 249
in US, 106, 127
over-production, 191, 205
post-WW1, 248–9
problems facing booksellers prior to Net Book Agreement, 184
Trade Protection Society, 225, 285 tab 35n8
trade terms (*see also* trade prices), 144, 196, 227–9
discounts on *D.B.*, 189 tab 20nn 11, 12
discounts on *M.G.*, 177, 179 tab 18n5
disputes over, 257
on *E.T.*, 167 tab 16n5
offered on sales to Scribner, 120
on periodicals sold direct, 157
to distributor on *M.I.*, 162
'25 copies for 24' ('odd book system'), 91, 144, 167, 168, 189, 200, 202, 203, 208, 210, 227, 231
trade unions, and T. & T. C. staff, 254
transit
damage in, 87–8
delay in, 93–4, 98
translations (*see also* profitability of translations; translators), 61–84
C. works translated, 49, 65, 137
competent t. vital, 78, 219

(translations, *cont.*)
competition with other house to issue specific work, 34–5
a good translation an improvement on original, 78
improvement in quality of, 78
influence of, 19
issued by T. & T. C. in the late 20th century, 262
issued by T.C. (founder), 3
made viable by being part of series, 75
quality of Clark translation, 41, 78
works re-translated, 78
translators (*see also* relationships with translators; remuneration of translators; translations) difficulty of securing competent t., 71–2
a rogue translator, 68–70
translation right, 63–6, 68–9, 82
travelling expenses, 283 tab 35, 284 tab 35n4
Troup, G. Elmslie
work, *Words to Young Christians*, 192, 197
Trumbull, Henry Clay
work, *The Threshold Covenant*, 91
turnover
1895–96, 237, 238 tab 26
1896–1989, 287–91
1911–22, 248
1923–30, 250
1930–56, 251
1956–73, 251
1973–90, 261
percentage from exports, 255
typesetting
cheaper for popular works, 319n358
cost of alterations to type, 283 tab 35
cost of t. post-WW1, 248
cost of specialist t. makes works pirate-proof, 111
fount, new cut for *M.G.*, 177
of *I.T.L.*, 132–3
often-reprinted works require re-setting, 256
type falls out of forme, 326n561
typesize, in periodicals, affect on sales, 153

unbound stock in hand, *see* stock in hand
Unitarian Churches, 22, 140
The University Press, Chicago, 333n41
unsolicited manuscripts, 23, 25, 191, 255, 263
Unwin, Stanley, 214
Urquhart, J. (periodical editor), 309n44, 332n13
USA (*see also* co-editions; exports to USA; imports from USA; profitability of exports; profitability of imports)
development of publishing links with, 11, 85–146
marketing books of US origin in UK: some problems due to cultural orientation, 89–90, 130, 132
Venezuela dispute, 127

Vandenhoek and Ruprecht (German publishing house), 64, 82
vanity publishing, anathema to the Clarks, 204–5
Venezuela dispute, 127
Vermes, Geza, 262
Vincent, M.R.
works, *The Age of Hildebrand*, 98
Philippians and Philemon, 141, 146 tab 15
von Schmidt, Christophe, *see* Schmidt, Christophe von

W.H. Smith (booksellers), 228
W.J. Gage (bookseller, Toronto), 229
wages, *see* salaries
Wagnalls (of Funk and Wagnalls, q.v.), 108
Walker, Frances (Partners' secretary), 254
Walker, Norman L., 36
Walker, William L.
work, *The Spirit and the Incarnation*, 19
Wallace, Alexander D.L. (Edinburgh bookseller), 267
warehousing
now distribute through Edinburgh University Press, 261
stock moved to Bartholomew's warehouse, 259
Watson, Dr John, 128, 320n358
work, *Beside the Bonny Briar Bush*, 128, 304n146
Watts, Robert, 206, 215
work, *The Reign of Causality*, 205, 305nn154, 155
Webster, William, 309–10n57
Weiss, Bernhard, 61, 311n86
works, *A Life of Christ*, 16, 63, 150, [301–2n 74], 311n86; *A Manual of Introduction to the New Testament*, 305–6n177
Welford, Charles, 103
Wells, Dr, 329n649

Welsh language, C. works translated into, 49
Wenley, R.M. (US theologian), 154
Wesleyan preachers, 229, 230
Westcott, Canon Brooke Foss, 195
Westcott and Hort (editors of the Greek Testament), 176
Wetheral, Mr (last editor of *N.B.R.*), 160
Whitehouse, Owen Charles, 319n354
wholesalers
  discounts offered to, 228, 335n72
  T. & T. C. uses services of, 225–7
Whyte, Alexander, 39, 49
Wilke, C.G.
  work, *Clavis Novi Testamenti*, 175
Willard Tract Depository (Toronto), 102, 108, 111, 118, 229 *bis*
William Collins (publishing house) (*see also* HarperCollins), 260 *bis*
Williams and Norgate (London publishing house), 160, 172, 326n547
Winer, G.B.
  work, *Grammar of New Testament Greek*, 21
Wise, Coffin and Co. (booksellers, Dunedin), 228
Witherow, Thomas
  work, *The Reformation*, 56 tab 6n10
Wittenberg College (Springfield, Ohio), 108
Workman, G.C.
  work, *The Text of Jeremiah*, 198
World's Epoch Makers series, 12, 30, 57–8
World War 1, *see* Great War
Wright, C.H.H. (Trinity College, Dublin), 305n156
  work, *Biblical Essays*, 220
Wright, Miss E., 33, 305n162

Xmas, *see* Christmas

You and your rights in Scotland, 260, 263

Zondervan (US publishing house), 255, 257